ADO.NET Programming

T0130693

ADO.NET
Programming

ARLEN S. FELDMAN

MANNING

Greenwich
(74° w. long.)

For online information and ordering of this and other Manning books,
go to www.manning.com. The publisher offers discounts on this book
when ordered in quantity. For more information, please contact:

Special Sales Department
Manning Publications Co.
209 Bruce Park Avenue   Fax: (203) 661-9018
Greenwich, CT 06830   email: orders@manning.com

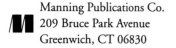
Manning Publications Co.   Copyeditor: Tiffany Taylor
209 Bruce Park Avenue   Typesetter: Martine Maguire-Weltecke
Greenwich, CT 06830   Cover designer: Leslie Haimes

ISBN 1-930110-29-4
Printed in the United States of America
1 2 3 4 5 6 7 8 9 10 – VHG – 06 05 04 03 02

To Jeff Feldman

contents

Part 6   *Useful extras 413*

preface

When Microsoft first announced the new .NET (pronounced "dot net") platform, one of my first questions was what support the company would provide for database access—not an unreasonable question, considering that I make my living writing client/server and three-tier database applications.

The answer was originally ADO+, renamed ADO.NET, which implied a newer version of Microsoft's ADO technology built on top of OLE DB. Both of these technologies are familiar to many developers. I was wrong, however: ADO.NET is an entirely new technology, built from the ground up. It does share some features with ADO and OLE DB, but it has a different philosophy and some new approaches.

One purpose of this book is to show users of these other technologies where ADO.NET fits in, and what it does and does not do. The other, more important purpose, is to provide a practical guide to using the features of ADO.NET. For this reason, most chapters are based around using specific classes and capabilities; follow-up chapters go into detail about options and variations.

I never thought of myself as a database expert. Over the years, as projects came up, I simply did whatever development was required, including writing a great deal of data-access code. Although books about the particulars of different database engines abounded, few sources of information were available on the best ways to address problems or to avoid pitfalls. I discovered them in the usual way—I was bitten by problems and eventually figured my way around them. In self-defense, I ended up studying databases and access mechanisms.

Because of this background, I do more with this book than just introduce and explain ADO.NET: I attempt to point out issues and coding practices that I have picked up over the years. I focus on the practical versus the purely "correct" approaches, although I don't think these two types are always in conflict. I will say, though, that my suggestions cannot possibly cover every circumstance, and should be considered in that light—only you can understand the needs of your applications.

As for my background, I have been developing for almost 20 years; for much of that time, the type of work I did could be classified as "database application work." I currently work for FrontRange Solutions and am the chief architect for a new product line based entirely on .NET (and extensively using ADO.NET). Prior to this, I worked on HEAT, one of the major help desk/support applications on the market. I also wrote the generic data access code used by HEAT, which allows it to talk to 13 different database engines.

I apologize in advance for my sense of humor. I tend to be a tad sarcastic, and, as some of the reviewers have noted, it is not always obvious when I am trying to be humorous and when I am genuinely complaining about something. By default, assume I am being "funny," unless you completely agree with the statement—in which case it was completely serious!

Thank you for purchasing this book. I hope it will be useful to you, whether you are a database application pro just moving over to .NET, or a developer with relatively little experience with database access.

acknowledgments

This book could not have been written without the help of a huge number of people. First, I must thank Sandy Pham for reading numerous drafts and providing OLE DB (and other) code, as well as being a sounding board for concepts. Maxx Daymon allowed me to steal some of his remoting code, and also provided technical feedback on a number of topics. Anton Swanevelder reviewed and assisted with XPath and XSLT. Sagiri Fukaya provided me the Japanese text that appears in the book, and Nancy Markley assisted with Oracle issues. Eric Hybner kindly built the installer for the samples. Chu Xu did the technical review and made numerous suggestions and corrections that substantially improved the text.

At Microsoft, I must thank Kent Sharkey for all his assistance, particularly in helping to find the right people to answer my silly questions. Also, Prashant Sridharan took time out of a *very* busy schedule to help me find reviewers at Microsoft. I must also thank David Schleifer and the entire ADO.NET team, both for building something for me to write about, and for fielding the occasional question.

At Manning, I must thank my publisher, Marjan Brace; my editor, Lianna Wlasiuk; Ted Kennedy for handling all the reviews; Mary Piergies, the project editor; Tiffany Taylor, the copy editor; Martine Maguire-Weltecke, the typesetter; Syd Brown, the design editor; Leslie Haimes for designing the cover; Elizabeth Martin, the proofreader; and, of course, Susan Capparelle for getting me involved with the project in the first place.

Finally, thanks to the many reviewers whose comments have dramatically improved the contents of this book. All the mistakes are my own, but much of what is good comes from the suggestions of the reviewers: Malcolm Ah Kun, Robert Booth, Shaykat Chaudhuri, Mary Chipman, James Dooley, Eric Kinateder, Sandy Pham, Patrick Steele, Chu Xu, and Michael Xu.

about this book

This book is written with the assumption that you are already somewhat familiar with .NET and know how to create new projects, compile them, and so forth. Most of the code samples are written in C#, so it will be helpful if you are familiar with that language; but converting to VB.NET or Managed C++ should be fairly easy, because the ADO.NET classes are the same. If you are just stepping into the .NET world, a number of books provide a good introduction. One I would recommend is Manning's *Microsoft .NET for Programmers* by Fergal Grimes.

Another assumption is that you have at least a basic understanding of database concepts and SQL, although you should be able to glean quite a lot from the samples. I talk about configuring your system to work with the code samples in the book in chapter 4.

Many of the samples are written to work with Microsoft SQL Server, because much of ADO.NET is specific to that engine. If you do not have SQL Server, you can use MSDE (Microsoft Data Engine—the desktop edition of SQL Server), which is free. It is shipped with many Microsoft products, including certain versions of Office and Visual Studio, and can also be downloaded from the Microsoft web site.

One downside of MSDE is that it doesn't have an interface for doing things like creating databases; so, you must use another tool, such as Microsoft Access.

Several Oracle samples appear in the book, and readers who intend to work with Oracle may want to set up an Oracle server or use Oracle Personal Edition. Just for variety, there are also a couple of examples using Access.

This book will be useful to a wide range of developers:

- Developers who are familiar with a previous technology and who are just switching to ADO.NET
- Developers who are relatively new to database programming and who are using ADO.NET as their first data access mechanism
- Developers writing to a single, specific database, such as SQL Server or Oracle
- Developers attempting to write code that will work with multiple different databases

ORGANIZATION

The book is broken into seven distinct parts:

- Part 1 is a high-level overview of several topics. The first chapter talks about the history of Microsoft's data access technologies and their goals. The second chapter is a high-level overview of ADO.NET. The third chapter is an introduction to XML. Chapter 4 explains how to get the sample code, and how to set up and run the various examples.

- Part 2 provides the nuts and bolts of ADO.NET—how to connect to a database, how to read data, that sort of thing. There are chapters specifically on using SQL Server, using OLE DB, and genericizing code so that it will work with multiple different engines. Other chapters explore topics such as parameters, stored procedures, and transactions.

- Part 3 is all about the DataSet. The DataSet lets you retrieve data from the database, manipulate it, and then send your data back to the database. It is very sophisticated and allows for the handling of relationships, queries, and constraints, which are all discussed. The last chapter in part 3 shows how to send a DataSet over a network to other computers.

- Part 4 shows how you can use the DataSet with some of the .NET controls that are data-aware, such as the DataGrid. There are chapters on rich client applications and also on web applications.

- Part 5 talks about XML, which is used throughout .NET. There is some general discussion of XML and ways to work with DataSets and XML. I also discuss using XPath for querying XML and XSLT for transforming XML from one form to another, and talk about the XML features built into SQL Server.

- Part 6 is a grab-bag of topics, covering such things as connection pooling, distributed transactions, using ADO Recordsets from ADO.NET, and reading schema information from the database.

- Part 7 contains the appendices. The first talks about using ODBC from ADO.NET. The remaining appendices provide in-depth reference material about some of the more important ADO.NET classes. In some ways, this information is similar to that provided by the .NET help, but the methods and properties are grouped in a more logical fashion, and I provide more germane examples and explanations than the help does.

Depending on your personal experience, you may find yourself skipping some of the introductory material. I have attempted to make the chapters stand alone, although in some places I could not do that, because it would have required the duplication of a large amount of information. I do, however, reference the prerequisite information as appropriate.

SOURCE CODE

Source code for all the programming examples in this book, including the examples in the tutorials, is available for download from the publisher's web site, www.manning.com/feldman.

Code conventions

All code samples appear in the following fixed-width font:

```
public void MyFunction()
{
    DoSomething();
}
```

When references to code appear in the text, I leave class names and interface names in the same font as the rest of the document. Functions, properties, methods, and other code items appear in the code font.

Code annotations accompany many segments of code. Certain annotations are marked with chronologically ordered bullets, such as ❶. These annotations have further explanations that follow the code.

AUTHOR ONLINE

Purchase of *ADO.NET Programming* includes free access to a private web forum run by Manning Publications where you can make comments about the book, ask technical questions, and receive help from the author and from other users. To access the forum and subscribe to it, point your web browser to www.manning.com/feldman. This page provides information on how to get on the forum once you are registered, what kind of help is available, and the rules of conduct on the forum.

Manning's commitment to our readers is to provide a venue where a meaningful dialog between individual readers and between readers and the author can take place. It is not a commitment to any specific amount of participation on the part of the author, whose contribution to the AO remains voluntary (and unpaid). We suggest you try asking the author some challenging questions lest his interest stray!

The Author Online forum and the archives of previous discussions will be accessible from the publisher's web site as long as the book is in print.

about the cover illustration

The figure on the cover of *ADO.NET Programming* is a "Gonagues Cazando," a huntsman from a region of Sri Lanka. The island in the Indian Ocean was famous for its spices and a destination on the busy trading routes between Europe and Asia. The country was formerly known as Ceylon, and even earlier was named "Serendip" by traders, the root of the word serendipity. The illustration is taken from a Spanish compendium of regional dress customs first published in Madrid in 1799. The book's title page states:

> *Coleccion general de los Trages que usan actualmente todas las Nacionas del Mundo desubierto, dibujados y grabados con la mayor exactitud por R.M.V.A.R. Obra muy util y en special para los que tienen la del viajero universal*

which we translate, as literally as possible, thus:

> *General collection of costumes currently used in the nations of the known world, designed and printed with great exactitude by R.M.V.A.R. This work is very useful especially for those who hold themselves to be universal travelers*

Although nothing is known of the designers, engravers, and workers who colored this illustration by hand, the "exactitude" of their execution is evident in this drawing. The "Gonagues Cazando" is of course just one of many figures in this colorful collection. Their diversity speaks vividly of the uniqueness and individuality of the world's villages, towns, and regions just 200 years ago. This was a time when the dress codes of two towns or tribes, separated by a few dozen miles, identified people uniquely as belonging to one or the other. The collection brings to life a sense of isolation and distance of that period and of every other historic period except our own hyperkinetic present.

Dress codes have changed since then and the diversity by region, so rich at the time, has faded away. It is now often hard to tell the inhabitant of one continent from another. Perhaps, trying to view it optimistically, we have traded a cultural and visual richness for a more varied personal life. Or a more varied and interesting intellectual and technical life.

We at Manning celebrate the inventiveness, the initiative, and the fun of the computer business with book covers based on the colorful tapestry of regional life of two centuries ago brought back to life by the pictures from this collection.

ADO.NET overview

Part 1 of this book provides a high-level overview of ADO.NET. It begins with a history of previous data access technologies, talks about the pieces that make up ADO.NET, and also explains how ADO.NET works with XML.

Chapter 4, "Setup for samples," explains how to set up your machine so you can run the examples shown in the later chapters. The instructions include where to find the sample code and sample databases online.

C H A P T E R   1

Microsoft technologies past and present

For many years, talking to databases was a highly proprietary capability—every different system had its own type of database and its own communications mechanisms. Over time, though, the movement toward open standards and common interfaces has taken hold. In fact, SQL can be thought of as one of the first major catalysts in this movement.

Microsoft became seriously involved with database access in the early 1990s and has gone through a number of approaches over the years to make it easier to talk to databases. Some of the technologies described in this chapter were developed by different groups at Microsoft at more or less the same time. Others were built to solve some specific problem in the area of performance, flexibility, or ease of use.

Each iteration has gained something from the older mechanisms, and ADO.NET is no exception—it has some major benefits over previous mechanisms. At the same time, it does *not* deal with everything addressed by each of the older technologies. Sometimes this is the case because the capabilities became obsolete, and sometimes because of the time pressure to get .NET out the door. One of the most important reasons, though, is that ADO.NET's goals are not identical to those of the previous technologies. (Chapter 2, "ADO.NET from 3,048 Meters," talks about the goals of ADO.NET and how the technology is divided.)

This chapter provides a brief summary of the major database access technologies that Microsoft has developed. It will provide you with some perspective and help relate how ADO.NET fits into the data-access picture. Throughout the book, I refer to various capabilities of these older technologies, and it help if you at least know the terminology.

I expect that a number of readers have used one or more of these technologies in the past, and I hope this book will ease your transition to ADO.NET. On the other hand, in case this is your first data-access technology, I have tried to avoid making the book too dependent on knowledge of other technologies. In either case, this chapter provides a review and guide to the older technologies.

1.1 ALPHABET SOUP

It's no surprise that Microsoft's past technologies are a jumble of acronyms, considering that this company first brought us COM, and now .NET, perhaps the two hardest things to search for on the Internet![1] Table 1.1 shows the technologies we'll talk about in this chapter. Not all of them are access technologies—some are just wrappers, but they are worth mentioning so the terms won't catch you off guard.

Table 1.1   Microsoft database access technology acronyms—alphabet soup

Acronym	Meaning
ADO	ActiveX Data Objects
DAO	Data Access Objects
Jet	Short for the Jet engine for accessing data
MDAC	Microsoft Data Access Components
ODBC	Open DataBase Connectivity
OLE DB	OLE DataBase
RDO	Remote Data Objects

Some of these technologies stand alone; others sit on top of another technology. Figure 1.1 shows how the different technologies get access to the database.

---

[1]   Okay—C, C++, and C# are also pretty tough to find!

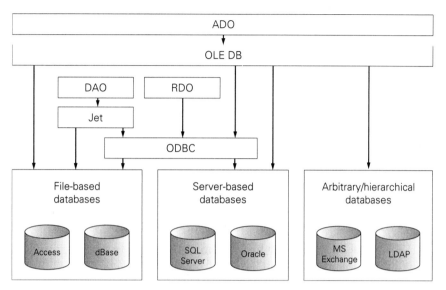

Figure 1.1   Pre-ADO.NET database access technologies, and how they relate

The next sections go into detail about each of these different technologies.

1.2   ODBC: OPEN DATABASE CONNECTIVITY

ODBC was designed by a consortium of companies, including Microsoft, Lotus, Oracle, and IBM, and a number of standards bodies, including X/Open, SQL Access Group, ANSI, and ISO. ODBC was one of the first major attempts to create a generic way of talking to different database engines. It's accessed via a straight-C API.

The promise of ODBC was that you could virtually swap in a new database engine without changing any code. It accomplished this in a couple of ways:

- A generic form of SQL that each ODBC driver converted into its native form. Although SQL is a standard, it provides quite a lot of room for ambiguity; many database vendors considered their proprietary modifications to be value-added benefits. For example, the format for outer joins is different in almost every engine.

- A functionality query paradigm by which the programmer could ask the ODBC driver what it could or could not do, and then act appropriately.

How close did ODBC's creators get to this utopian concept of seamless database support? Well, fairly close. It is quite straightforward to build a *simple* ODBC application that generically talks to virtually any driver. However, for more complex applications, you almost always need to tweak things a little.

One of the major applications I worked on can talk to 13 different database engines via ODBC. For nine of those engines, we had to make changes—sometimes very

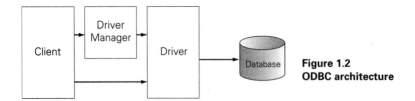

Figure 1.2
ODBC architecture

minor, sometimes quite extreme. Part of the reason is that ODBC did not (perhaps wisely) attempt to address certain advanced functionality, such as stored procedures and DDL (Data Definition Language; used to manipulate database structures).

ODBC is far from being a dead technology:

- Virtually all major database vendors now ship ODBC drivers for their engines.

- OLE DB provides a data provider for ODBC, which is extensively used.

- Because Microsoft will be providing an ODBC data provider for ADO.NET, it is possible to use ODBC drivers from .NET!

The architecture of ODBC is fairly straightforward, as shown in figure 1.2.

An application uses the Driver Manager to locate the appropriate ODBC driver. The manager then more or less gets out of the way. Most requests from that point go straight to the ODBC driver, unless the driver is not capable of providing a particular service; in that case the manager can attempt to fake the capability.

1.2.1 What type of data was ODBC designed to access?

ODBC was specifically built to access relational data from a relational database. Although it can talk to text files, Excel spreadsheets, and other types of data, it must present them as it would present tables in a database.

1.3 MICROSOFT JET AND DAO: DATA ACCESS OBJECTS

When Microsoft released its desktop database application, Access, it used a technology called *Jet* and the *Jet engine* to access its own database files (mdb files) and also to access other data, such as dBase, Paradox, and relational databases via ODBC.

Sitting on top of Jet are Data Access Objects (DAO), a set of COM objects that let programmers use Visual Basic and other languages to access Jet (see figure 1.3).

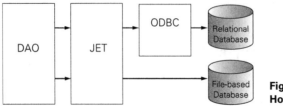

Figure 1.3
How DAO talks to databases

DAO provides a simple object model in which a database contains TableDefs, which contain Fields, and so forth. Although DAO was a step in the right direction, it has some flaws:

- Because Jet was used to provide access to ODBC and was also the implementation of the ODBC driver for Access, dBase, Paradox, and so on, some people had strange problems with circular references.
- It was not terribly fast—especially when talking to fully fledged server engines. In fact, in the early days, it was not uncommon to hear the Jet engine referred to as the *prop plane*.

ODBCDirect We should mention a technology that was developed to address some of the performance issues involved with Jet talking to ODBC: ODBCDirect. Basically, it had the same object model as DAO, but didn't load Jet.

1.3.1 What type of data were Jet and DAO designed to access?

Jet and DAO were primarily built to support file-based databases, meaning that a lot of support exists for operations dealing with positioning within a table (move to the next row, the previous row, and so forth). Although they can be used to access relational databases, doing so tends to be slow.

1.4 *RDO: REMOTE DATA OBJECTS*

RDO attempted to address some of the problems that DAO had when accessing relational databases. RDO is basically an object model on top of ODBC, so it does not have to go through nearly as many layers. Like DAO, it provides a fairly sensible object model (Table contains Columns, and so forth); but because it is closer to ODBC and designed for performance, it exposes more complex objects, such as connections, which DAO developers never have to worry about.

Because RDO is a thin layer on top of ODBC (see figure 1.4), it is virtually as fast as the ODBC driver. However, when talking to desktop databases (Access, dBase), it goes through the Jet ODBC driver; so, it can be slightly *slower* than DAO. Overall, though, it is a much more robust engine, and it's still used by many applications.

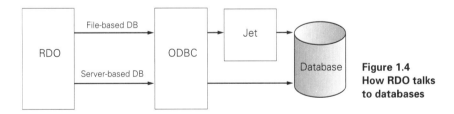

**Figure 1.4
How RDO talks
to databases**

1.4.1 What type of data was RDO designed to access?

RDO was specifically created to allow higher speed access, via ODBC, to relational database engines, such as SQL Server and Oracle. Although it can be used to access desktop databases, it is not terribly fast in those scenarios.

1.5 OLE DB

OLE DB was designed from the ground up to be a replacement for ODBC, based on Microsoft's COM technology. Microsoft went one better, though—instead of limiting OLE DB to relational data, the company designed it to provide access to almost any type of data, no matter how it was stored. For example, OLE DB could be used to access email in Microsoft Exchange, or OLAP (On Line Analytical Processing) services for data mining.

Another key goal of OLE DB was that it had to be fast. This speed, coupled with its flexibility and its use of COM, made it fairly complex and difficult to use. There are many dozens of interfaces, which may or may not be supported by the various data providers.

Data providers are the equivalent of ODBC drivers. In theory, a data provider would exist for SQL Server, Oracle, Exchange, and any other source of data. In practice, though, Microsoft knew that it would take time to get vendors to support OLE DB; so, one of the first data providers it shipped was a wrapper for ODBC.

1.5.1 What type of data was OLE DB designed to access?

OLE DB was designed to access virtually any kind of data, whether it is stored relationally in tables, in directories (such as with email), or free-form. This mammoth task was achieved, but at the cost of making OLE DB very large and complicated.

1.6 ADO: ACTIVEX DATA OBJECTS

Although OLE DB provided the ultimate in flexibility, it was difficult to use—and virtually impossible to use from a late-bound language like Visual Basic. For those reasons, Microsoft wisely shipped ADO to provide a much-simplified interface. Where OLE DB has dozens of interfaces, ADO has about 10.

Although ADO.NET is somewhat different than ADO, enough similarities exist to merit showing the ADO object model (figure 1.5).

Because ADO sits on top of OLE DB, which doesn't necessarily require its data providers to all have the same functionality, some functionality in ADO may not be present. For example, the ADO Command object, which is used to pass SQL, has little meaning if the data provider does not support SQL.

ADO is not as flexible as OLE DB, but it does provide a fairly good compromise between power and ease of use. It is a little slower than OLE DB, but still performs fairly well.

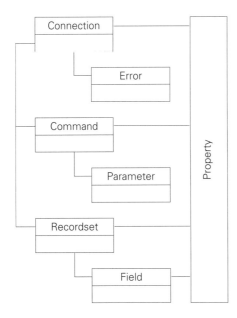

Figure 1.5
ADO Object model

ADO (and OLE DB) also provides support for the idea of *disconnected data*, which is key for many stateless applications.

STATELESS   In order to make web applications (or for that matter, multi-tier applications in general) efficient, many server applications do not store anything about their users. Instead, every time a user makes a request, the server builds all the objects it needs to fulfill the request, does any work it needs to do, sends back results, and then throws everything away.

This approach is referred to as *stateless* because the server does not store any state information about its clients. It is more scalable[2] because the server is not loaded down with information about clients that may not reconnect for a long time.

DISCONNECTED   Because the server must retrieve data and then forget about it in a
DATA   stateless world, it is up to the client to keep track of the data and what needs to change in that data. For example, if a client asks for a number of rows of data, then deletes three rows, adds two rows, and changes two more, it cannot depend on the database to make the changes automatically. Rather, it must pass the information about the changes back to the server, so the server can update the database.

ADO provides this functionality via the use of a *disconnected Recordset*. ADO.NET has a similar, but more powerful feature, called a *DataSet*.

---

[2]   It is important to remember that *scalable* does not necessarily mean fast. Scalable applications are generally built so that the Nth user has the same performance as the first user. A high-performance application is likely to be faster until a lot of users have been added to the system.

1.6.1 What type of data was ADO designed to access?

As a wrapper to OLE DB, ADO does have some of the abilities to access arbitrary data; but, in reality, ADO is quite focused on relational data. ADO also provides support for multi-tier architectures via the use of disconnected Recordsets.

1.7 MDAC: MICROSOFT DATA ACCESS COMPONENTS

MDAC is not an access mechanism. Rather, it is Microsoft's delivery mechanism for its data access components. I mention it here just to prevent confusion when the term is used. MDAC includes ODBC, OLE DB, and ADO. It also includes drivers for SQL Server, Access (Jet), and Oracle, along with a number of other database-related components.

Prior to MDAC, the wrong version of one data-access component often caused all sorts of strange problems to occur. Now, once a version of MDAC is installed, everything should match. Of course, the trick is to get the *right* version of MDAC! ADO.NET does not rely on MDAC; instead, it takes advantage of the versioning capabilities of .NET to distribute new versions. However, because you can access OLE DB and ODBC via ADO.NET, you are not necessarily free from worrying about MDAC.

1.8 SUMMARY

Each of the technologies discussed in this chapter has a different focus and was developed to address a specific need. Table 1.2 shows some of the differences among them.

Table 1.2 Comparing data access technologies

Technology	Speed	Ease of use	Primarily supported data	Supports disconnected data
ADO	Fairly fast	Simple	Relational	Yes
Jet/DAO	Slow	Very simple	File databases	No
ODBC	Very fast	Difficult	Relational	No
OLE DB	Very fast	Difficult	Relational File databases Hierarchical Arbitrary	Yes
RDO	Fairly fast for relational data	Simple	Relational	No

Some of these ratings are somewhat arbitrary. For example, for a COM developer, OLE DB is fairly straightforward and easy to use. Similarly, depending on the type of data being accessed and the location of the database, the speed of Jet may be perfectly adequate.

The "Primarily supported data" and "Supports disconnected data" columns can also be misleading. There *are* ways to make Jet talk to a relational database, or to make ODBC talk to hierarchical data or work in a disconnected manner. Likewise, I can dig a hole with my shoe, but I'd rather use a shovel. This table simply indicates the primary purpose of the technology.

If table 1.2 included another row for ADO.NET, this is how I would rate it:

Technology	Speed	Ease of use	Primarily supported data	Supports disconnected data
ADO.NET	Fast	Simple	Relational	Yes

I am not rating it like this simply because I am writing a book on the subject. Rather, I think Microsoft has done a good job of balancing performance, capabilities, and speed. Note that the primary data support for ADO.NET is relational—ADO.NET is really built for accessing relational data. However, as you will see in later chapters, it is possible to retrieve hierarchical data and access file databases.

Knowing the history of the Microsoft data-access technologies may be interesting, but this really is a book on ADO.NET. Chapter 2 presents a high-level overview of ADO.NET and explains how it differs from these other technologies. It also provides an outline for how the rest of the book is laid out.

C H A P T E R   2

ADO.NET from 3,048 meters

It is a rare opportunity to get to build something from scratch. When Microsoft chose the approach for data access from .NET, the company could have gone a number of different directions. One possibility would have been to wrap OLE DB, or provide a slightly updated version of ADO (which, of course, many people believe ADO.NET to be). However, the world has changed since these older technologies were developed, and they didn't necessarily have the same goals as .NET. This chapter talks about the goals of ADO.NET, and then provides a high-level overview of its major pieces. For those not familiar with the metric system, 3,048 meters is the 10,000-foot view. Much of the rest of the book is dedicated to exploring these pieces in great detail.

2.1   THE GOALS OF ADO.NET

Rather than just putting a new face on an older technology, Microsoft took the opportunity to develop a new access mechanism that learned from previous technologies, but was a better fit for the .NET world.

The new access technology had a number of goals:

- *Multi-tier*—Although you can use most previous Microsoft data access technologies in a multi-tier environment, it is usually quite difficult to move code from, for example, a 2-tier client/server application to a true 3-tier application. ADO.NET was built from the ground up to allow code to be used on different tiers easily without having to be significantly modified.

- *Disconnected*—Part of this multi-tier support is based on the fact that ADO.NET assumes a temporary connection to the database. Data is read from the database and then can be transported and changed without touching the database. Only when the system needs to commit the changes to the database must the system touch the database again.

- *XML-based*—It is probably no surprise that, like much of the technology coming from Microsoft today, ADO.NET is steeped in XML. XML is used to transport data between tiers; it is also very easy to convert data back and forth between relational data and XML data.

- *Scalable*—ADO.NET, coupled with other features of .NET, makes it easy to build stateless applications, which are generally far more scalable than applications that remember information on the server about each user. You can also build applications that maintain state fairly efficiently, which, although not quite as scalable, *can* provide better performance.

- *Fast*—It is exceedingly important to Microsoft that applications written using ADO.NET (and .NET in general) perform well, in order for the technology to become accepted. For this reason, a lot of effort has gone into performance tuning. It is especially advantageous when used with SQL Server, because the SQL Server data provider can talk natively to the engine. In fact, the SQL Server ADO.NET provider has shown itself to be 10 to 15 percent faster than the native OLE DB provider in some of Microsoft's early tests.

One thing is something of a departure from some of the previous technologies. Although you can use ADO.NET to talk to a variety of different back-end databases (SQL Server, Oracle, and so forth), ADO.NET has not focused to the same extent on allowing movement between different engines without changing code.

That doesn't mean you can't write code that is *fairly* generic, but it is not the highest priority of ADO.NET. I would say there are several reasons behind Microsoft's direction here:

- Providing a thinner layer between the caller and the database engine provides performance advantages, and the caller is free to take advantage of the special features offered by the engine.

- Most development is done against a single engine, and providing overly generic functionality can easily complicate what would otherwise be simple. OLE DB is an excellent example of this problem.

- Microsoft was working against an aggressive schedule to make the first release of .NET. Presumably, later versions of ADO.NET will provide more functionality for gathering information about the engine, and so forth.

That all being said, you may notice that a number of sections within this book talk about building generic code that can be swapped between engines fairly easily. I do this for two reasons:

- I assume that a fair number of developers want to support different engines easily. I know that the current project on which I am working, written using .NET and ADO.NET, is designed to work with a large number of different back ends.
- It is not uncommon for a decision to be made to switch to a different database without necessarily considering the impact on existing code. By remaining fairly generic, that impact can be significantly reduced.

2.2 ZOOMING IN ON ADO.NET

Although a number of different classes make up ADO.NET, the pieces can be broken down into several fairly distinct components, as shown in figure 2.1.

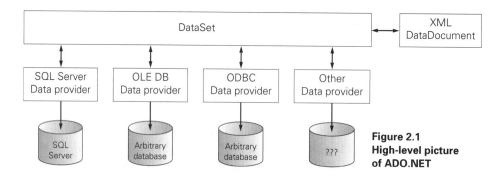

**Figure 2.1
High-level picture
of ADO.NET**

2.2.1 .NET data providers

Just as with OLE DB, ADO.NET has data providers for each targeted engine. A data provider wraps all the functionality required to talk to a particular database engine or data access technology. Version 1 of .NET includes two data providers:

- *SQL Server data provider*—As the name implies, this data provider is specific to the SQL Server engine (version 7.0 or higher). It also works with MSDE, the lower-end version of SQL Server.
- *OLE DB data provider*[1]—Just as OLE DB provided a wrapper for ODBC to ease transitioning, so ADO.NET provides a wrapper for OLE DB. This provider is used to talk to engines that have OLE DB drivers.

A third data provider has also been created, which wraps ODBC. It did not ship with the first release of .NET, but is available for download from the Microsoft web site. This data provider gives you access to hundreds of existing ODBC drivers. In addition, it is assumed that other engines such as Oracle, DB2, and Sybase will have native .NET data providers over time. These data providers will most likely be built by the vendors of those engines, rather than by Microsoft.

Each data provider contains a number of objects to provide various capabilities, such as connections and commands. Like OLE DB, these objects derive from specific interfaces; but unlike OLE DB, the objects can be used directly, and different data providers can have substantially different functionality.

Figure 2.2 shows the major objects in each data provider.

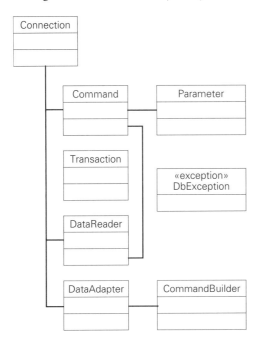

**Figure 2.2
Principal objects
within a data provider**

No classes in ADO.NET have the *exact* names shown in figure 2.2. Usually, though, an interface presents the general functionality and a class that implements that interface within each separate data provider. For example:

- *IDbCommand*—The interface that provides the functionality for a database command, such as an `Update` or a `Select`. It exists in the `System.Data` namespace. An interface defines a series of properties and methods that must exist in any object that *implements* the interface. If an object implements an interface, it is derived from that interface, and can be cast to that interface.

---

[1] Quite some confusion will probably exist between OLE DB *data providers* and the ADO.NET OLE DB *data provider*.

- *SqlCommand*—The SQL Server–specific object for commands, which implements the IDbCommand interface. It exists in the `System.Data.SqlClient` namespace.
- *OleDbCommand*—The OLE DB–specific object for commands, which implements the IDbCommand interface. It exists in the `System.Data.OleDb` namespace.

The objects in figure 2.2 are all discussed in detail in chapters 5 through 14. The following is a brief description of the purpose of each object:

- *Connection*—A connection, as the name implies, wraps the concept of a connection with a database. You must have a connection before you can execute commands and read data from the database.
- *Command*—A command represents an instruction being sent to the database, usually in SQL, such as an `Insert`, `Update`, `Delete`, `Select`, or the name of a stored procedure. Commands can either return data (such as from a `Select` command) or just a changed row-count for operations like an `Update`.
- *Parameter*—You can specify parameters to a command that need to be "inserted" appropriately by the database engine. This functionality is provided by the Parameter class. In addition, a ParameterCollection object holds a collection of parameters.
- *Transaction*—Rather than just tying transactions to a connection, as with earlier data access technologies, ADO.NET separates out the concept of a transaction and allows it to be associated with some number of commands. This provides much finer control.
- *DataReader*—The DataReader is like a forward-only cursor into a result set. For example, if a command is used to select a number of rows, it is possible to move through each row, one at a time, and retrieve the data from that row. The DataReader is a fast access mechanism for retrieving data.
- *DataAdapters*—DataAdapters are primarily designed to provide a liaison between a data provider and a DataSet. DataSets are discussed in more detail in the next section, but they are basically independent collections of data. To maintain that independence, they cannot know anything specific about how they get their data. A DataAdapter allows for a DataSet to be filled from a database query.
- *CommandBuilder*—When a DataSet needs to write its changes back to a database, it does so using the DataAdapter. The DataAdapter must know how to do `Deletes`, `Updates`, and `Inserts`, and this functionality can be customized. However, for *simple* applications, you can use the CommandBuilder to provide default commands for these operations. The commands that are generated, though, are not high-performance and can have other problems.
- *DbException*—As with most of .NET, when an error occurs, an exception is thrown that must be caught. This includes data errors (for example, if a `Select` references a nonexistent column).

2.2.2 The DataSet

At the most fundamental level, a DataSet is simply a container for data. However, it is a very elaborate container that provides a large amount of functionality for working with the data it holds. It is conceptually similar to an ADO Recordset, but with several key differences:

- A DataSet can contain more than one table. A DataSet contains a collection of DataTables (discussed later), each of which represents a single table.

- A DataSet is not tied in any way to a database or data table. Although it is possible (and quite likely) that a DataSet will be filled by the results of database queries, the DataSet itself is just the container for the data. You certainly can fill a DataSet manually. This ability is quite important, because it allows DataSets to operate in a completely disconnected manner.

- When the data within a DataSet is changed, those changes are not automatically made to the underlying database. Rather, the DataSet keeps track of the changes—Inserts, Updates, and Deletes. Only when a DataSet is given to a DataAdapter to update the database are the changes actually written. This behavior is not unlike a disconnected ADO Recordset.

- You can query against a DataSet in a number of ways, including having it execute simple SQL statements without touching the database at all.

- DataSets can be responsible for data integrity, preventing illegal data from being put in place, again without touching the underlying database.

- DataSets can very easily be converted back and forth to XML. This feature is especially useful because .NET uses this mechanism to transport DataSets between tiers. A client can request a DataSet object from a server, and the server will just return that DataSet object. .NET will automatically convert it to XML, and then convert it back into a DataSet on the client.

This process is more efficient than disconnected ADO Recordsets. The main reason is that, because ADO uses COM, every element in the Recordset (every field in every row) must be marshaled into a COM type, and later marshaled back. With a DataSet, only a string is being sent. There is some overhead in converting to and from XML, but that code is highly optimized.

DataSets have quite a lot of functionality. Figure 2.3 shows the main classes that make up a DataSet.

Although these classes are discussed in detail in chapters 15 through 20, here is a brief explanation of each of the objects:

- *DataSet*—This is the principal class; but, perhaps surprisingly, it's little more than a container for the other objects. It does, however, have some properties that control how the other objects operate.

- *DataTable*—A DataTable represents a single table's results or, more accurately, represents the results of a single query. The distinction is that `Selects` that cross table boundaries (for example, by using a join), will still end up in a single DataTable. Think of a DataTable as the result set from a single `Select` statement.

- *DataColumn*—The DataColumn contains information about the column of results, which—at least if the DataSet is filled from a database—is synonymous with a field. Information in a DataColumn includes a name, data type, and length. You can also calculate a DataColumn's value using an expression.

- *DataRow*—There is a DataRow for each row of data in the DataTable. You can ask the DataRow for the value in a particular column. To add data to a DataTable, a new DataRow is created and added. A DataRow can also be changed or deleted.

- *DataRelation*—A DataRelation relates two different DataTables to one another. For example, consider a `Teacher` DataTable and a `Classes` DataTable. Both tables have a `TeacherID` field, so the two tables can be related via that field.

- *Constraint*—Constraints are used to prevent certain types of changes to the data in a DataSet. There are currently two different types of constraints: the ForeignKeyConstraint enforces that a value entered into a field in one table *must* exist in a column in another table, and the UniqueConstraint enforces that a value entered into a field is unique within that field for all records in the DataSet.

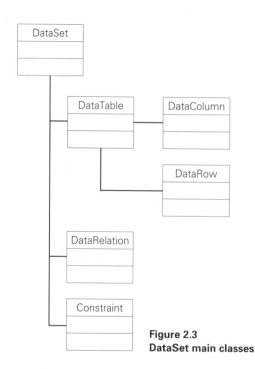

Figure 2.3
DataSet main classes

A DataSet must have all this functionality (which somewhat duplicates the database) because it must be self-sufficient. All the work is done on a DataSet without any connection to the data source.

As changes are made to the data, the DataSet keeps track. The fact that it does this means you can roll back changes, as well. At some point, all the changes will be written to the database (or somewhere), at which time the DataSet can be told to incorporate all the changes (or roll them all back).

How much data in a DataSet?

You may have noticed that much of the functionality of a DataSet relies on it containing *all* the appropriate data. For example, a UniqueConstraint would not be very useful if it was being compared to only half the data in the actual table.

Because the DataSet has no connection to the database, it has no way of looking at data it does not contain. This simplifies things, especially in a multi-tier model, because it means the client has all the information it needs. But it can also cause problems when you have a lot of data. Imagine a customer list containing a million customers (or even 100,000 customers). It would be impractical to read them in to a DataSet, let alone to transmit that DataSet across the wire to a client, even if that client had a fairly good connection and was not dialed in at modem speeds.

Of course, the data that fills the DataSet can easily be limited based on a criterion (an SQL where clause), so that only an appropriate amount of data will be sent. The problem is that then the client is only dealing with a subset of the data and cannot rely on the built-in functionality (or any client-based functionality) to enforce constraints such as the UniqueConstraint.

There are ways around these problems, but they largely come down to design decisions in your application.

2.3   SUMMARY

I am one of those people who really wants to understand the reason behind the way things work, as well as understand how to *make* them work. There are a couple of reasons—first of all, I am naturally nosy; and second, it has saved me a lot of pain trying to use something in a way other than intended (the mental equivalent of trying to use a can opener as a hammer)!

It is not that I am adverse to stretching technologies and using them in ways never dreamt of by their designers;[2] but all things being equal, I generally try to begin by seeing if the technology I plan to use is really designed to work the way I intend to use it. If nothing else, I have a better chance of finding useful documentation.

---

[2]   I once spent an hour on the phone with an ODBC engineer explaining how our (shipping) application worked, only to be told that ODBC couldn't be used that way!

That is the reason why I spent so much time in this chapter discussing the philosophies behind ADO.NET. Understanding the disconnected model might, I hope, prevent you from trying to use a DataSet as a front-end to a live database cursor (or at least make you realize that making it happen will hurt a lot). The other goals of ADO.NET are important, but assuming the disconnected data model from the start requires a fundamental design shift from older technologies.

That is not to say the breakdown of the technology is not important, although the decisions for that breakdown make more sense when you understand the underlying philosophy. For example, the fact that the DataSet is completely disconnected from the data providers is a good coding practice, but it's critical to the disconnected model.

Like OLE DB and COM, ADO.NET is interface based, and interfaces exist for all the important pieces of a data provider—IDbConnection, IDbCommand, and so forth. One of the great things about .NET versus COM is that you can get beyond these interfaces to provide additional functionality. This ability is cool for two reasons—first, the interfaces do not have to be loaded with all sorts of arbitrary functionality that is specific to one or two implementers; and second, data provider *providers* don't have to jump through all sorts of hoops to provide extra functionality.

If you don't fight the disconnected model, and instead choose to embrace it, then ADO.NET gives you a great tool for simplifying your life—the DataSet, which is actually a collection of classes working together to provide database-like functionality without the database. That is not to say the DataSet is a panacea—there are always trade-offs you must understand, such as knowing how much data it's practical to send over the wire. However, it is a great tool in a lot of situations.

Chapter 3 will talk about working with data and XML; although not strictly part of ADO.NET, XML is still very much related to working with data. As you will see, ADO.NET has a lot of tools for interacting with XML.

C H A P T E R   3

XML and ADO.NET

If there can be said to be one unifying concept behind .NET, it would have to be XML. Not only does the system use XML to transfer data and communicate between components, but all the .NET servers and services use XML as a way to expose their capabilities and data.

I do not intend to provide an entire XML reference in this book, and this chapter is primarily about the ways in which ADO.NET can exploit XML; but I begin this chapter by providing a brief history and explanation of XML and related concepts, in case you have not yet had the opportunity to look into XML in any depth. I first attempt to give a context for the creation of XML and its goals. Next I talk about the nature of XML and its surrounding technologies, such as schemas, transforms, and XPath queries. Finally, I talk about XML in .NET and specifically in ADO.NET.

This chapter is fairly high-level; but part 5, beginning with chapter 26 ("DataSets and XML") goes into much more detail about ADO.NET and XML, and demonstrates many of the technologies described here.

3.1 XML

As you probably already know, XML stands for eXtensible Markup Language, and is a way of representing data. In the early days of computing, data was usually manipulated via highly proprietary structures that rarely could be passed between different applications. Eventually, some generic formats appeared, including the very popular comma-delimited file (CSV[1] file), in which each "record" of data is represented as a line within a file, and each value is separated by a comma or some other character.

This approach is fine as it goes, but it has some serious limitations:

- Both the creator and the consumer of the file must understand what each piece of data means. For example, if you open a file and the third value is the number 7, you have no way of knowing what that 7 means—is it a credit rating, the user's favorite number, or the number of times that the user complained? Either the creator and consumer must have explicit knowledge of the structure of the file *or* there needs to be some sort of manual mapping process.

- Every row must contain a slot for every *possible* piece of data, even if that particular record doesn't have a value for that data. This requirement can make the file especially complex if the data from row to row is not exactly the same type of data.

- The CSV format cannot readily represent complex or hierarchical data. For example, if a record contains other records that may optionally represent other records, there is no convenient way to deal with the relationships.

- No way exists to determine whether the data in the file is garbage or meaningful, or if any particular values are appropriate.

- When you're transferring data between different systems, if each has a different set of rules for the way a CSV file should be set up, the process of converting between the formats is laborious.

The first really comprehensive attempt to address these issues was the creation of Standard Generalized Markup Language (SGML). The concept behind SGML (and XML, for that matter) was to come up with a standard way of not only representing data, but representing the *semantics* of the data—what should be in the data and where. The terminology tends to get a little confusing, because both SGML and XML are used to refer to two different things:

- The definition of a particular *markup language* to represent a type of data
- The data or *document* based on that definition

SGML is very powerful—and very complicated. Although it certainly was popular in certain niches,[2] its complexity kept it out of the mainstream. XML was created to provide the most important subset of SGML functionality, but in a simple enough manner that it could be used by the great unwashed masses (us!). To be fair, it was less a matter of making it easy for people, and more a matter of making it useable by tools.

---

[1] Comma separated values.

[2] Particularly the government and defense industries

Interestingly, the best-known markup language is not defined in either SGML or XML: Hypertext Markup Language (HTML), which is used to create web pages. As with XML, though, you can think of HTML as the language that defines what is legal (what tags can be put onto a web page) and also the data (the HTML *pages* that use HTML). HTML is an abstract language[3] for defining web pages—it doesn't say "put this text in this font at this point on the screen"; instead it says, "here is some text that I consider to be a header." For example:

```
<H1>My Title</H1>
```

H1 is an HTML tag indicating a first-level header. As you might assume or know, there are also H2 and H3 tags and so on to indicate increasingly less important headers. The point, though, is that the semantics of the tag are important—"The text between the tags represents an important header." One browser might display that text in a large font, and another might bold it or show it as red. In addition, because the text is marked as a header, the tool can do things like build a table of contents showing the headers—the tag provides the *meaning* of the data, not just the data.

HTML is a well-known and very specific markup language understood by browsers, designed to represent hypertext documents. The idea behind XML is that you can define other markup languages to represent virtually any kind of data you would like. To use a common example, this book has a number of characteristics that are the same for many books, such as:

- A title
- An author
- Chapters

So it would be possible to define the book as XML, which might look something like this:

```
<Book>
    <Title>ADO.NET Programming</Title>
    <Author>Arlen Feldman</Author>
    <ChapterList>
        <Chapter Number="1">
            <Name>Microsoft technologies past and present</Name>
        </Chapter>
        <Chapter Number="2">
            <Name>ADO.NET from 3,048 meters</Name>
        </Chapter>
        .
        .
        .
    </ChapterList>
</Book>
```

---

[3] At least it started out that way—it has become more and more cluttered as web designers have demanded more control over the way their data is presented.

If I wanted to, I could represent the entire book, including this text, in this manner. This ability is useful for a number of reasons:

- This format is far easier to read than a comma-delimited file; you can read the XML and understand its content.

- Because XML follows a very consistent format, you can build tools that can read the XML, search the XML for particular items, and otherwise work with the data.

- As long as some basic agreement can be made about the way in which the XML for representing a book should be laid out, various different tools can work directly with the data with no mapping.

- Once you have figured out what things should be included in your definition, and in what order, you can make sure the definition is legal. For example, maybe specifying a title is required, but specifying an author is optional (depending on how well this book does, for example, I may want to remove my name).

3.1.1　XML terminology

Throughout this book, you will see a number of XML terms in use. This section briefly explains the most common and important.

XML document

An XML document is a complete set of *well-formed* XML (see figure 3.1). A document contains a number of other things, such as elements, and can also contain references to things like schemas or DTDs (explained later). An XML document must have one and only one *root element*.

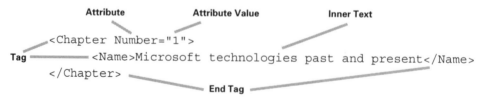

Figure 3.1　Parts of an XML document

Tag

A tag is an item within an XML document that contains data. Tags are also referred to as *elements*. A tag starts with a less-than symbol (<) and ends with a greater-than symbol (>). At a minimum, the tag contains the tag name. Whenever a tag appears, there must be a matching end tag, which has the same name but is preceded by a forward slash (/). Here is an example:

```
<Name>Microsoft technologies past and present</Name>
```

This example shows a tag called `Name`, containing the text "Microsoft technologies past and present". The tag *contains* everything that appears between the start and end tags—including other tags. For example, in figure 3.1, The `Chapter` tag contains a `Name` tag.

Tags do not have to contain anything; this can be the case either to indicate that there is no data, or if the tag contains values just using *attributes*. If the tag doesn't contain anything, then the notation changes slightly. The following shows a `Name` tag with no data:

```
<Name/>
```

Notice the forward slash ending the tag. Although in some instances you might end up temporarily with start and end tags (`<Name></Name>`), this is technically not legal or *well-formed*.

Root element

The root element is the first tag in an XML document. It must be the only tag at the particular level. So, for example:

```
<Book>
   <Title>ADO.NET Programming</Title>
   <Author>Arlen Feldman</Author>
</Book>
```

In this example, `Book` is the root element. It would not be legal to have any other tags at that level. For example, the following XML is *not* legal:

```
<Book>
   <Title>ADO.NET Programming</Title>
   <Author>Arlen Feldman</Author>
</Book>
<Book>
   <Title>Microsoft .NET for Programmers</Title>
   <Author>Fergal Grimes</Author>
<Book>
```

If you wanted to keep more than one book in a single XML document, you would have to add a different root element. For example:

```
<BookList>
   <Book>
      <Title>ADO.NET Programming</Title>
      <Author>Arlen Feldman</Author>
   </Book>
   <Book>
      <Title>Microsoft .NET for Programmers</Title>
      <Author>Fergal Grimes</Author>
   <Book>
</BookList>
```

Now, `BookList` is the root element, and the document is once again well-formed.

Attribute

You can put data inside an element, as in the previous examples, or you can put data into a declaration within the tag itself. This is referred to as an *attribute* and looks like this:

```
<Chapter Number="1">
```

The attribute here is called `Number`, and the value it contains is the number 1. The value for an attribute is always contained in quotes.

Some basic rules will help you decide whether you should keep data in an attribute or an element. For example, you don't want attributes that contain complex data—such as XML, carriage returns, or quotes—because these things can mess up the XML parser. Beyond that, it is a matter of deciding how to represent your data in the most effective manner for your goals.

Given that one of the goals of XML is readability, I generally split data between attributes and elements based on how readable the results are. Often, the attribute describes something about the contained data. In the following example, the attribute specifies the type of the data:

```
<Value DataType="Number">12345</Value>
```

Inner text

This is the text contained within a tag.

Inner XML

This is everything contained within a tag, including text and XML. To clarify the difference between this and the inner text, look at the following example:

```
<Book>
    <Title>ADO.NET Programming</Title>
    <Author>Arlen Feldman</Author>
</Book>
```

The inner XML of the `Book` tag is

```
<Title>ADO.NET Programming</Title>
<Author>Arlen Feldman</Author>
```

However, the inner text is

```
ADO.NET ProgrammingArlen Feldman
```

This is one of those things that can trip you up quite easily. In the simple case, such as with the `Title` or `Author` tag, the inner text is clear. When the tag contains other tags, though, the inner text gets more complicated.

Well-formed

I have used the term *well-formed* several times. A well-formed XML document obeys all the basic rules of XML. For example, all tags have matching end tags, only one root tag, and so forth. A well-formed XML document also starts with a special pseudo-tag indicating that the contents of the file contain XML and specifying the version of XML in use:

```
<?xml version="1.0"?>
```

This is not really a tag, and so is not closed. However, it should appear at the top of all your XML documents.

Other things can be contained in XML documents, some of which will be touched on in part 5 of this book. XML documents can also contain references to items such as Schemas, the focus of the next section.

3.2 SCHEMAS

Making sure that an XML document is well-formed guarantees only that it obeys XML's rules. What about the rules of the data you are storing? For example, most books have only one title, so XML representing a book should have only one `title` tag. If you want to make sure the XML is not merely well-formed, but also correct based on the type of contained data, you must have some way of specifying the rules for the XML—that is, the *schema* for the XML. You can use several different mechanisms to do this:

- *Document Type Definition (DTD)*—DTDs were the first mechanism for defining the schema of an XML document and are still used extensively. DTDs are *relatively* straightforward—each tag knows what tags it can legally contain, and so on. The format for a DTD is very much like a language grammar.[2]

- *XML Schema Definition (XSD)*—While DTDs are standard, they have several issues. First, there is a limit to how specific you can get with the definition for the XML. Second, DTDs look nothing like XML—meaning you have to learn an entirely different language in order to create DTDs. An XSD is legal XML, so you can confirm that a schema is legal by applying the appropriate XSD schema to it.

- *XML Data Reduced (XDR)*—XDRs fall between DTDs and XSDs. While the XSD standards were being hammered out, XDR was a simplified version used primarily by Microsoft's XML parser. Although .NET is primarily XSD focused, support still exists for XDR and for converting XDRs to XSDs. SQL Server 2000 was released before the schema standard was finalized, so it currently supports only XDRs.

All of these mechanisms let you do basically the same thing—specify which tags are allowed where, what attributes are legal, and what values are allowed in each attribute. Inside an XML document, you can reference a schema or DTD, thereby allowing the parser reading your XML to make sure it is well-formed XML and that it complies with your schema. For example, the following XML references a schema called `TeacherSchema`:

```
<?xml version="1.0"?>
<Class xmlns:xsi="http://www.w3.org/2001/XMLSchema-instance"
          xsi:noNamespaceSchemaLocation="TeacherSchema.XSD">
   <Teacher>Mr. Biddick</Teacher>
   <Classroom>A1</Classroom>
   <Period>2</Period>
</Class>
```

Here is the same XML, but using a DTD instead of a schema:

```
<?xml version="1.0"?>
<!DOCTYPE Teacher SYSTEM "Teacher.DTD">
<Class>
   <Teacher>Mr. Biddick</Teacher>
   <Classroom>A1</Classroom>
   <Period>2</Period>
</Class>
```

Going into a great deal of detail on any of these mechanisms is beyond the scope of this book. .NET primarily concentrates on the use of XSDs, but it supports DTDs and XDRs. Chapter 27, "DataSets and Schemas," talks quite a bit about schemas and their use with ADO.NET.

The great thing about defining a schema is that it provides a consistent way of talking about a particular kind of data. So, for example, all booksellers could agree to use a particular schema for representing book information; then any program that needed to read in book information would work with any bookseller's data. Some publishers might *extend* the schema to add additional data, but the basic information would remain compatible. If the program was written to read the extra information, it would pick it up—otherwise it would be ignored.

The downside is that an *agreement* must be made within each industry that wants to trade information in a consistent manner. This turns out to be the biggest problem—many companies believe that their way of representing data should remain proprietary, or should contain completely different structures than others' data. The base of the problem lies with the fact that an agreement requires *competing* companies to work together, with a final goal of making products and services able to integrate with other companies arbitrarily. The bigger companies generally want someone to integrate *only* with them, and the smaller companies frequently don't have the infrastructure to support the effort.

Nonetheless, progress is being made. For example, a generally accepted standard exists for defining books—in fact, two of them![4] Many other industries are also working toward standards. For more information on schemas, you can go the World Wide

---

[4] DocBook and Open eBook.

Web Consortium (W3C) web site at http://www.w3.org. The W3C is the organization primarily responsible for maintaining web-based standards.

In the meantime, even if you need to handle different schemas, there is a mechanism for translating between schemas.

3.3   TRANSFORMS AND XSLT

You might want to translate an XML document from one schema to another for a couple of reasons:

- The scenario discussed in the last section, where there is no common format. You can write one piece of code to read in the data based on a particular schema, but provide a transform to turn other schemas into the expected format.

- To transform data to a new medium, such as a web page. For example, you might build the general information for a web page in XML, and then transform it to HTML just before displaying it. You could specify, for example, that headers should be blue and regular text should be black.

The XML standard for transforming documents is called XSL (XML Style Language), or just *stylesheets*. The process of transforming the document is referred to as an XSL Transform, or XSLT for short. In fact, stylesheets were popular before XML, for separating some of the details of an HTML document's style from the content. The same stylesheet could be used on a number of pages, which could then all be modified by just modifying the stylesheet. (Whole books have been written on XSLT, so I haven't tried to do anything here but introduce the terminology and briefly explain the concept behind XSLT; chapter 28, "XPath queries and XSL transforms," provides a simple example.)

XSL works by basically providing a list of instructions that indicate what should be found in the original document and what should appear in the new document. For this process to work, we need a way to identify items in the original document—a way to search an XML document.

3.4   XPATH AND SEARCHING XML

One of the key parts of XSL is the ability to find nodes within an XML document so they can be transformed and placed in the new document. The mechanism for doing this is called XPath, and it was originally just part of the XSL spec. People quickly realized, however, that being able to search for items in an XML document was useful, so XPath has become a standard on its own.

XPath is *very* different from SQL. This makes sense, considering that it is designed to search the hierarchical structure of an XML document rather than the relational data of a database. A big part of XPath is the ability to do searches like "find all nodes in the document that are named X and whose parent nodes are named Y." I cover the basic syntax of XPath in chapter 28.

3.4.1 The DOM and other ways of searching

XPath is one way of searching a document, but it is not the only one. The most basic mechanism for searching is to manually navigate the *DOM*—the Document Object Model. If you think of an XML document as a series of nodes representing the various tags, with child nodes representing the nested tags, and so forth, you don't have to go far to consider each node an object. You could ask each object for its value, its attributes, or its children.

When you are working with XML, you will frequently work with something called an *XML parser*, whose primary job is to expose the content of an XML document as a series of objects. Prior to .NET, the most commonly used XML parser in the Microsoft world was the MSXML parser. .NET provides its own parser, which I will talk about in the next section.

You can also search XML some other ways. For example, you can use the Simple API for XML (SAX) standard. Using SAX is kind of the reverse of using the DOM—instead of searching for something specific, SAX tells *you* when it has found particular things. SAX is not yet an official standard, and .NET does not currently have built-in support, but several samples exist that show how to implement SAX in .NET.

Another way of searching XML in .NET uses the DataSet/XML capabilities of ADO.NET; I will discuss this method in section 3.6.

3.5 .NET AND XML

.NET uses XML extensively—it is the core of the remoting and serialization mechanisms, and it is the format for most of the definition files within the system. Naturally, .NET also provides the capability to work directly with XML—the same mechanisms that are used internally by .NET.

The most common mechanism for working with XML is to use the DOM. Once you load a string or file containing the XML into an XmlDocument, you can access the various elements of the document as a series of objects. You can maneuver through the objects by asking them for their attributes and values, and also by asking for their children, or even by asking for various children's children by specifying which tag you want. You can also execute XPath queries directly against the XmlDocument or any of its children. You'll find many examples of using the XmlDocument and XPath in part 5 of this book.

One issue with the DOM is that it is somewhat heavy—if you think about creating an object for each node in a large XML tree, that could be a *lot* of objects. Frequently that situation is unavoidable, if you need to work with the document in a flexible manner; but if you *know* you need to work through a document quickly—either you are writing it out or reading it in, and you know you are starting at the top and working your way down to the bottom (without passing go, without collecting $200)—then you can use one of two classes or their derivations:

- *The XmlReader*—Once you load a string or XML file into the XmlReader, you can step through the document element by element. You cannot back up, but if you know you want to work through the whole document from start to finish, then that is not a major problem.
- *The XmlWriter*—The obvious opposite to the XmlReader. The writer lets you write out XML, in order, to a stream. Again, you cannot back up.

The obvious advantage of these classes is that they are considerably faster than using an XmlDocument. That is not to say that an XmlDocument is slow—it has been the focus of massive amounts of optimization work by the Microsoft team. However, there is no way the flexibility of the object model could be as fast as reading or writing a stream. Still, the speed of an XmlDocument is unlikely to be a problem until your XML documents become large.

3.6 ADO.NET AND XML

One of the cool things about ADO.NET, and the reason I've included an introductory chapter on XML in this book, is that the ADO.NET DataSets understand and can work with XML. For example, you can create a DataSet from XML, and a DataSet can also write out its contents to XML.

A DataSet represents some number of tables and the relationships between those tables. That is the *schema* for the DataSet. Conveniently, XML is all about schemas, so it is a very natural fit—you can provide a DataSet with a schema that specifies the tables and relationships that it should contain, and then load an XML document based on that schema. Alternatively, if you don't have a schema, the DataSet can *infer* one from the data—basically, it can figure out the most appropriate schema.

Defining the schema of a DataSet based on an XML schema is not just something you can do at runtime. When you work with a regular DataSet, it is fairly generic—you access the elements via methods and properties. For example, you might say

```
MyDataTable.Tables["Teachers"].Rows[0]["TeacherName"].ToString()
```

in order to access a particular table and field. If you mistyped something, you would not know it until the code was run; there is no way to know at compile-time if a Teachers table or a TeacherName field exists in the DataSet.

However, .NET provides tools that can create a very specialized DataSet, called a *strongly typed* DataSet, which is mapped directly to your planned structure. These strongly typed DataSets are based on a schema definition, which is then converted, via various tools, into actual code. So, you could rewrite the previous statement as follows:

```
MyDataTable.Teachers.Rows[0].TeacherName
```

Not only is this more readable, but the compiler will not let you compile the code if the table or field does not exist. You will see examples of strongly typed DataSets in part 4, as part of the discussion on data-bound controls; you'll also find a more involved discussion in chapter 27.

Going back and forth between the relational DataSet and XML is pretty cool—you can do an SQL-like query against the DataSet, and then convert to XML and do an XPath query. ADO.NET goes one step further, though—instead of just converting back and forth between a DataSet and XML, you can link an XML document to a DataSet so that changes made in the DataSet automatically show up in the XML document and vice versa. This technique is demonstrated in chapter 26.

When you are working with databases, you traditionally get back relational data. However, SQL Server has a number of XML-based features that, for example, allow data to be retrieved directly as XML. ADO.NET provides direct support for some of these features via the SQL Server data provider, as you will see in chapter 29, "SQL Server XML features."

3.7   SUMMARY

I usually dislike it when books provide introductory chapters on topics other than the subject of the book. For example, you will note that there is no "introduction to C#" or "introduction to SQL" here. My feeling is that I can't provide enough information to be of use to a novice, and the information would be irrelevant and annoying for an expert. I am making the assumption that you are already familiar with C# before reading this book, or you have at least looked through one of the many C# books that have been written. Likewise, if you are interested in working with databases via .NET, you probably have a passing familiarity with SQL. However, XML is a key technology of .NET that you could easily know very little about.

This chapter and the later chapters in part 5 dedicated to XML and ADO.NET will provide you with a basic familiarity with XML, if you are not already familiar with it. If you intend to do any serious work with XML, I recommend picking up a reference book on the topic.

This chapter has introduced and (I hope) explained a number of terms. It is yet another alphabet soup, with a heavy emphasis on the letter X. You can get quite far just knowing the basics of XML—elements and attributes. Schemas (or DTDs) are useful if you are transferring data between different systems; but, frankly, one of their more common uses is to make it easier to manually edit your XML—if you have an editor that enforces schemas, you are less likely to mess up!

This chapter has been a high-level overview. Part 5 of this book is dedicated to the use of XML with ADO.NET. It is impossible to talk about this subject without seeing quite a bit of XML in action.

C H A P T E R   4

Setup for samples

Throughout the book, a number of code samples demonstrate various facets of ADO.NET. Depending on your personal learning style, you may want to type the samples in yourself, or you may want to download the source code from the Manning web site. In either case, because this is a database book, you also need to have a couple of databases configured. In addition to the sample code, the web site provides a configuration tool that will configure a database for you—although you will still have to do setup work.

This brief chapter discusses downloading the example code and setting up a SQL Server database, and provides instructions for configuring an Oracle database if required. Finally, I talk a little about the coding style in the samples.

This is the last introductory chapter. After this, we will begin doing something useful!

4.1 SETTING UP YOUR MACHINE

There are only a couple of prerequisites for working with the examples in the book:

- *Operating system*—All of the test code was written and tested on a Windows 2000 machine, and all of the screen shots were captured under Windows 2000. However, Windows XP should work with no problems.

- *Visual Studio.NET*—Obviously, you must have Visual Studio.NET installed. The code in the book was tested against an almost-final release version. If there are any changes for the final release of .NET, they will be documented on the web site.

- *Microsoft SQL Server 2000*—Many of the examples in the book assume that you have SQL Server 2000 installed. If you do not have SQL Server 2000, you can use MSDE instead (the Microsoft Desktop Edition of SQL Server, which can be downloaded from Microsoft's web site), provided you own a qualifying product, such as Visual Studio.
- *IIS*—If you want to do any of the web examples, you will need to have Microsoft Internet Information Server (IIS) installed. It comes with Windows 2000, but it is not installed by default with the Professional version.

4.2 DOWNLOADING THE SAMPLE CODE

You can access the sample code from the Manning web site at http://www.manning.com/feldman.

One of the options on the page is to download samples; this option will download an installer. By default, when you run the installer, the samples will be put on your hard drive in the following directory:

```
C:\ADONETProgramming
```

You can choose a different directory if you like, but some samples will then not work correctly—for example, any examples that reference the included Access database or any of the XML files. Under the main directory, you will find the following directories:

- *Data*—Contains an Access database and some XML files used in various examples
- *Utility*—Contains utilities (primarily tools for populating the sample databases)
- *Chapter 6 through Chapter 33*—Separate directories containing the sample code used in each of the chapters

To locate the sample code in the chapters, just browse to the appropriate directory and open the solution file for the project.

4.3 SETTING UP DATABASES

The majority of the examples throughout the book are written against a SQL Server 2000 database, although some examples are written against Oracle and Access databases. The following sections describe setting up each of them in turn.

4.3.1 SQL Server

You must follow two steps to set up the SQL Server database to use with the samples. First, the database itself must be created; and second, the SQLServerCreate utility must be run.

Creating the database

To create the database, run the SQL Server Enterprise Manager and expand the tree to the Databases node (figure 4.1).

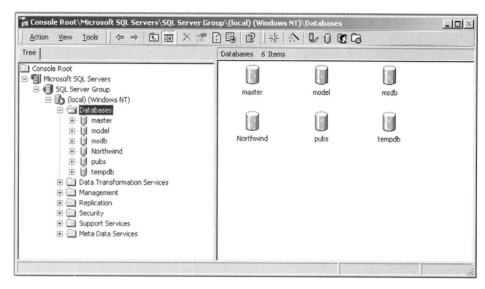

Figure 4.1   SQL Server 2000 Enterprise Manager

Right-click on Databases and select New Database. In the dialog, enter the name ADONETSamples (figure 4.2).

That is about it (other than clicking OK)—the database now exists. All that is left is to load some data.

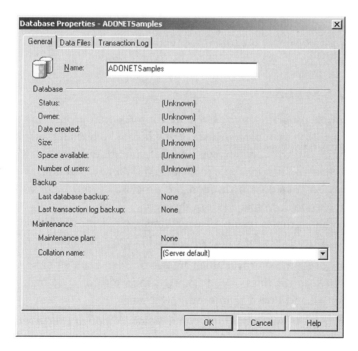

**Figure 4.2
Creating the new
database**

Loading data into the SQL Server

I have created a utility program called LoadSQLServer, which can be found in this directory:

```
C:\ADONETProgramming\Utility
```

Just run this utility. By default, it will load data into the ADONETSamples database you just created. You can also select a different database, but be aware that the sample code references ADONETSamples by name, so you will have to change the code.

4.3.2 Access

The Access database used in examples is downloaded with the samples. By default it will be installed as:

```
C:\ADONETProgramming\Data\ADONetSamplesAccess.MDB
```

You can change the install location if you like; but, again, you will then also have to change the path in some of the samples.

4.3.3 Oracle

If you want to follow along with the Oracle examples, I have created a utility called LoadOracle that will set up the samples tables in the default Oracle instance. It prompts for a User ID and Password. The Oracle examples in the book use *Scott* and *tiger* for these values, so if you have disabled that default account, you will need to modify the code. My testing has been against Oracle version 8.1, but the code should also work with later (and probably earlier) versions. You can use either the Microsoft or Oracle OLE DB driver with the sample code (if these terms don't mean anything to you, don't worry—providers are discussed with connection strings in chapter 9, "Connections").

4.4 CODE AND STYLES

Most of the example programs in the book are console applications. Any place where this is not the case (for example, with the DataGrid or web examples), instructions are given for setting up the code appropriately. If you are not familiar with creating console applications, the first example in chapter 6 ("Basic Operations with the SQL Server Data Provider") steps you through the process. If you're still confused, just look at the sample code downloaded from the web.

The code in the examples uses my own coding style. I mostly follow the coding style that Microsoft proposes for using with .NET, except for a couple of things:

- I frequently use some short variable names—ds for a DataSet, for example. I do so largely to keep the lines of code shorter; the width of code that will fit on a page is limited, and I tried to minimize wrapping.

- I use a very minimal subset of Hungarian notation. Although I agree with Microsoft that Hungarian notation is verbose, confusing, and hard to read, I do feel that, for some circumstances, putting a prefix on the front of a variable is helpful. So, for example, you will often see things like

```
string strConnect = "some data here";
```

where Microsoft would just have:

```
string connect = "some data here";
```

This is largely a personal preference.[1] In examples of this length, it is unlikely to make a difference either way, but I find it helpful in larger projects. Because I was working on a production application at the same time I was writing this book, I didn't want to try to switch styles back and forth (to maintain my own sanity). My apologies to those of you who have trouble with the different style.

One more thing—I have tried to keep all the examples short and to the point. That means I often exclude error-handling code or arrange code in a manner that might not be the most "correct," but that helps you see the underlying concept. Keep this in mind if you copy the code directly from the book—you will still need to add and rearrange appropriately for your applications.

4.5   SUMMARY

Some people just read a book and never try the examples. Others work through all or some of the examples in great detail, and perhaps experiment and expand on them. I have tried to make the examples in this book useful for both groups—if you just want to glance through the code, you should get the basic idea; but the code is complete enough to be run, tested, and modified.

I have run every single piece of code in this book, whether it is a single line or several pages. However, I have not necessarily done it in the order the code appears in the book, so your output might not match exactly. For example, if I demonstrated deleting data after I demonstrated retrieving data, but I tested them in the reverse order, then the final output might have fewer rows!

Although .NET will have shipped by the time you read this, I worked on the book with various prereleases. I *think* I have kept the book up to date as .NET has changed, but it is possible that there are a few discrepancies. These will be noted on the Manning web site as found, and I guarantee that all the sample code on the web site will be tested against the final release (the deadline for the sample code is later than the deadline for the written material).

Setting up the databases for testing should be fairly straightforward for SQL Server or Oracle (assuming Oracle is already installed); and, the code I wrote for installing the tables may be useful to you as well. Setting up Access doesn't really require any steps.

Now that the introductory and housekeeping tasks are over, it's time to get into the details of ADO.NET. Chapters 5 through 14, which make up part 2, are all about the low-level use of ADO.NET.

---

[1]   Or, for some, a religious issue.

ADO.NET basics

Part 2 of this book goes into detail about the low-level data access pieces of ADO.NET, such as connections and commands. By the end of part 2, you should feel comfortable doing any basic SQL task via ADO.NET.

Chapter 5 discusses the classes that make up a data provider. Chapters 6 through 8 show how to use the SQL Server and OLE DB providers to access data, and also how to abstract the code to make it work generically with either provider.

The next three chapters after that talk about and demonstrate some of the capabilities of the Connection, Command, and DataReader classes. Chapters 12 and 13 talk about using parameters and working with stored procedures, and chapter 14 talks about transactions.

C H A P T E R   5

.NET data providers

The first part of this book provided a *very* high-level overview of the big pieces of ADO.NET. Starting with this chapter, part 2 will get closer to the details of the classes and show how to make this stuff work.

A lot of the more exciting aspects of ADO.NET relate to the use of the DataSet, which is the only topic of part 3. However, before getting to that, you need to understand how to do all the relatively boring, straightforward database stuff we all know and love.

This chapter explains the reasons for the existence of data providers and gives you a summary of the main classes in each provider.[1] In chapters 6 through 14 you will see these objects being used in real-world examples.

5.1   WHAT IS A DATA PROVIDER?

Quite simply, a *data provider* is the liaison between your code and the database. Rather than providing a single set of generic handlers for talking to databases, there is a data provider to talk to each different type of database/data-source (see figure 5.1).

---

[1]   If you were using the first beta of .NET, data providers were called managed providers.

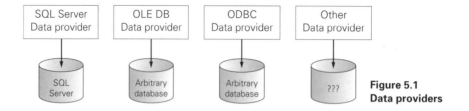

Figure 5.1
Data providers

I just told you that a custom data provider exists for each flavor of database—you may have noticed, however, that figure 5.1 shows a fairly slim set of data providers. Chalk this down to the fact that .NET is extremely new—the only data providers available today are those that Microsoft has built. The assumption is that each major database vendor will write its own custom data provider (strangely, Microsoft seems reticent about building its own high-performance Oracle or DB/2 data provider[2]).

Does this mean that you are stuck with using only SQL Server? Not at all. One of the data providers is a wrapper for OLE DB, Microsoft's previous major database access technology. Many companies have already written OLE DB providers, and using the ADO.NET OLE DB data provider gives you access to all of these legacy providers.

Microsoft has also released an ODBC data provider, although it doesn't ship with .NET. It allows access to the huge number of ODBC drivers that are out there. (ODBC is the previous, *previous* data access mechanism from Microsoft.)

I'll say a few words about each of the different providers.

5.1.1 SQL Server data provider

The SQL Server data provider is optimized for talking to Microsoft SQL Server and MSDE, the Desktop Edition of SQL Server. Because it is so specific, and it talks directly to SQL Server, it is considerably faster than the OLE DB data provider when talking to SQL Server.

The SQL Server data provider works with SQL Server version 7.0 or greater, although some functionality requires at least SQL Server 2000.

5.1.2 OLE DB data provider

The OLE DB data provider literally sits on top of OLE DB, and can be used to talk to virtually any data source that OLE DB can talk to. The advantage of this data provider is that it lets you use a large number of legacy drivers. The disadvantage is that it is generic, so it does not perform quite as well as a provider written specifically to a database engine.

The OLE DB data provider will not talk to all OLE DB data providers, because OLE DB is designed to talk to a large range of data (relational databases, OLAP,

---

[2] It has come to my attention that my sense of humor isn't always obvious to everyone. Just in case: yes, I am being ironic here!

LDAP, and so forth), whereas ADO.NET is much more focused on talking to relational data. You also cannot use the OLE DB provider that wraps ODBC, but you can use the ODBC data provider.

5.1.3   ODBC data provider

Although it didn't ship with the first version of .NET, the ODBC data provider gives you access to the myriad existing ODBC drivers available. There are many more ODBC drivers than OLE DB data providers, and frequently multiple different drivers are available for the same data source.

Appendix A discusses the installation and use of the ODBC data provider.

5.1.4   Other data providers

It is expected that other database vendors will produce data providers that talk specifically to their engines. In the next year or so, expect to see data providers for Oracle, DB/2, Sybase, and many other databases.

5.2   HOW ARE DATA PROVIDERS ORGANIZED?

Each data provider is in its own namespace and provides a full collection of objects that can be used directly. Most of the objects, though, are derived from a set of common interfaces.

5.2.1   Interfaces and namespaces

The approach of providing a set of common interfaces gives a lot of flexibility to the writers of data providers:

- Because most objects are derived from common interfaces, they can be used quite interchangeably and consistently. For example, if you mostly stick to using the interfaces in your code, you can *fairly* easily switch your code from using SQL Server to using Oracle (once an Oracle data provider is written).

- If a data provider needs to provide special functionality unique to it, it can just provide those specialized classes and methods. For example, SQL Server has a lot of native XML capabilities, so Microsoft has added methods to its versions of the objects to access these capabilities.

Each data provider is stored in its own namespace, which must be referenced to be used.

NAMESPACE   A namespace is a logical grouping of classes and other supporting things like interfaces, enums, and so forth. .NET is broken into a large number of different namespaces, based on the functionality they contain. For example, the SQL Server data provider's code is contained in a namespace called `System.Data.SqlClient`.

Table 5.1 shows the namespaces that are important to ADO.NET.

Table 5.1   ADO.NET namespaces

Data provider	Namespace
Data provider interfaces	`System.Data`
SQL Server data provider	`System.Data.SqlClient`
OLE DB data provider	`System.Data.OleDb`
Common objects and utilities	`System.Data.Common`

When a company creates a new data provider, it is free to add its own classes and methods that are specific to the data source. However, all data providers are expected to have a certain set of objects that behave in a certain way. Of course, each new data provider will be in its own unique namespace.

5.3   STANDARD OBJECTS

Microsoft has created a set of interfaces that defines this basic set of objects, and each existing data provider implements these interfaces. For example, an interface called IDbConnection defines functionality for connecting to a database. For SQL Server, this interface is implemented by a class called SqlConnection, and for OLE DB, the interface is implemented by a class called OleDbConnection.

INTERFACE   An interface is a definition for a set of properties and methods with no implementation. A class is said to *implement* an interface if it is derived from that interface. For this to happen, the class must contain all the methods and properties that the interface defines.

Although an object in C# can be derived from only one other object, it can be derived from, or *implement*, any number of interfaces.

Figure 5.2 shows the classes that should exist in every data provider. The diagram is generic in that it doesn't show the specific names of either the interfaces or the classes that implement those interfaces for each provider.

The following sections talk about the standard data provider classes. Among other things, for each object, we'll examine the interface and the specific classes that implement the interface. Each subsection will also explain, at a high level, the purpose for each class.

In chapters 6, 7, and 8, you will see these classes in use; the remaining chapters of part 2 will delve into the intricacies of the more important classes.

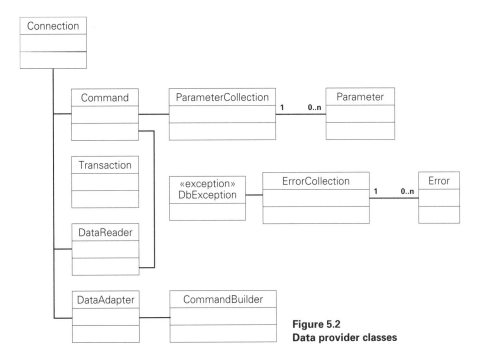

Figure 5.2
Data provider classes

5.3.1   The Connection interface and classes

Table 5.2 shows the classes that implement the connection for each of the providers, as well as the interface these classes implement. If you are working with just one type of data provider, you will rarely care about the interfaces; but if you want to write more generic code, they become more critical. (Chapter 8 talks in depth about writing generic code.)

Table 5.2   Connection implementations

Class	Provider	Interface
SqlConnection	SQL Server	IDbConnection
OleDbConnection	OLE DB	IDbConnection

A connection object represents a connection to the associated data source (SQL Server or any OLE DB data source). As you might assume, you need to have a connection before you can do anything useful with a data source.

The primary property on a connection is the connection string that tells it how to connect to the data source. An SQL Server connection string example might be as follows:

```
"server=ArF733;database=Test;user id=sa"
```

The arguments in this example specify that the SQL Server engine is running on a server called ArF733, the data is stored in a database called Test, and the user ID to log in with is *sa*—the system administrator's account. (As is all too common, this example doesn't include a password for the system administrator's account. Of course, you wouldn't do that on your server, would you?)

Probably the most important methods on a connection are

- Open()—Opens the connection
- Close()—Closes the connection

In addition, a number of properties provide information about the connection once it has been opened and about handling for transactions. (The next couple of chapters will show connection objects in use, and chapter 9 discusses the connection object and connection strings.)

Just about every example in this book relies on a connection object. You will see a direct example in chapter 6.

5.3.2 The Command interface and classes

Table 5.3 shows the classes and interface for the command object.

Table 5.3 Command implementations

Class	Provider	Interface
SqlCommand	SQL Server	IDbCommand
OleDbCommand	OLE DB	IDbCommand

If you want to do something with a data source—read data, change data, or just about anything else—you will almost always need to use a command object. The command object is used to send instructions to a data source.

A command has a couple of important properties:

- Connection—The connection object against which the command will be executed
- CommandText—The SQL command to be sent

There are several different methods for executing the SQL command, depending on the expected result. The two you will use most are:

- ExecuteReader()—Used for Select statements or any command expected to return a result set. This method returns a DataReader that can be used to move through the data in a forward-only, read-only manner.
- ExecuteNonQuery()—Used for statements that are not expected to return a result set, such as Inserts, Updates, and Deletes. This method returns the number of rows affected by the command.

Commands will be shown in use in the next couple of chapters, and chapter 10 goes into many of the gory details of the command object.

5.3.3 The ParameterCollection and Parameter interfaces and classes

For each provider, there is both a parameter implementation and a "collection of parameters" implementation (table 5.4).

Table 5.4 ParameterCollection and Parameter implementations

Class	Provider	Interface
SqlParameterCollection	SQL Server	IDataParameterCollection
SqlParameter		IDataParameter
OleDbParameterCollection	OLE DB	IDataParameterCollection
OleDbParameter		IDataParameter

A ParameterCollection holds the parameters that are associated with a particular command. Parameters are used to provide additional information to the database about SQL that is being executed.

There are two major reasons to use Parameters with SQL. The first and most common reason is to send arguments to stored procedures; second, parameters are also useful for certain types of efficiency issues.

Parameters and stored procedures

Stored procedures are basically little functions that exist inside the database server. Like regular functions, they can take parameters as arguments. You can pass these arguments as you would pass arguments to a regular function:

```
"MyStoredProcedure 'C2','Mr. Roberts'";
```

You can also bind values to the parameters directly:

```
Parameters["@Classroom"].Value = "C2";
Parameters["@Teacher"].Value = "Mr. Roberts";
```

This approach offers several advantages:

- It can be more efficient (although not always, depending on how often the procedure will be called).
- The data is passed as the native data type, rather than converted to text to be embedded in the SQL and then converted back to the original type by the database engine.
- Parameters can be used to retrieve data from the stored procedure as well as to send it.
- It is easy to specify some parameters and not others, without worrying about the order of the parameters.
- Because the name of the parameter is shown, it makes the code more readable.

Efficiency issues

Most commonly in SQL, when a statement is written, it contains all the information required to execute:

```
UPDATE Teachers SET Classroom='A1' WHERE Name='Mr. Biddick'
```

This statement will work fine for the specific teacher and classroom (Mr. Biddick, A1), but what happens if a number of classrooms need to be changed for a number of teachers? Of course, it would be possible to build a new string for each case and execute it separately, but that approach has a couple of problems:

- It is inefficient to build strings (especially with more complex examples), reset all the objects, and execute everything from scratch.
- Many databases are smart enough to remember how to do specific tasks so that they are faster the next time. This is usually referred to as an *execution plan*, and you can think of it as a compiled version of a query.

The problem with an execution plan is that it is generally based on the exact text of the SQL. Therefore, the following two strings would be considered completely different statements:

```
UPDATE Teachers SET Classroom='A1' WHERE Name='Mr. Biddick'
UPDATE Teachers SET Classroom='B2' WHERE Name='Ms. Fortune'
```

By using parameters, you can put in *placeholders* for the data that will change, and then specify the appropriate values:

```
UPDATE Teachers SET Classroom=? WHERE Name=?
```

Each ? will be replaced with a value at runtime when binding takes place.[3] The following code can be used to specify the values for each parameter from the previous example:

```
Parameters[0].Value = "A1";
Parameters[1].Value = "Mr. Biddick";
```

The same update can then be executed over and over, just changing the values for the parameters.

Chapter 12 goes into depth about using parameters, and chapter 13 talks about using parameters with stored procedures.

---

[3] The format for parameters is different for SQL Server and OLE DB. The question mark (?) is used for OLE DB. SQL Server uses named parameters.

5.3.4 The Transaction interface and classes

Unlike many previous data-access technologies, ADO.NET has objects to represent transactions (table 5.5).

Table 5.5 Transaction implementations

Class	Provider	Interface
SqlTransaction	SQL Server	IDbTransaction
OleDbTransaction	OLE DB	IDbTransaction

Normally, when an SQL command is executed through ADO.NET, the effects of the command take place immediately. Sometimes, though, it is highly desirable to tie together several different commands and have them all succeed or fail as a unit. Consider the following example:

```
UPDATE Inventory SET Quantity=Quantity-1 WHERE Item='Wdgt'
INSERT INTO Orders (Item,Quantity) VALUES ('Wdgt',1)
```

If the first command completes but the second one does not, then the inventory will show an incorrect count, because the order will not have gone through.

By wrapping these commands in a transaction, they can be treated as a single, atomic event. The transaction can then be *committed*, in which case the results of both commands will be made permanent; or the transaction can be *rolled back*, in which case neither of the commands will appear to have happened.

There is a class to represent a transaction, rather than just some methods on the connection class, because it allows multiple transactions to be handled simultaneously. In theory, you could have one transaction that handles one set of operations while another unrelated transaction runs independently. Unfortunately, though, that approach is not really supported by the underlying databases—the databases cannot handle independent transactions on the same connection. However, in the future, the databases will support this capability, and .NET already has a design that can support it when it appears.

Chapter 14 discusses transactions. Chapter 33 talks about transactions that involve more than one data source or other objects (distributed transactions).

5.3.5 The DataReader interfaces and classes

A DataReader is used for reading results from an SQL statement. The DataReader objects implement more than one interface (table 5.6).

Table 5.6 DataReader implementations

Class	Provider	Interface
SqlDataReader	SQL Server	IDataReader, IDataRecord
OleDbDataReader	OLE DB	IDataReader, IDataRecord

SQL queries can be broken roughly into two general categories—those that return a result set and those that do not (profound, eh?). For commands that do not return a result set (Insert, Update, Delete, and so forth) the most you can expect back is whether the command succeeded, and maybe a count of the number of records affected.

For commands that *do* return a result set (Select and certain stored procedures), there needs to be a way of looking at the results. The DataReader is the ADO.NET mechanism for quickly stepping through a result set.

A DataReader has the ability to step through the result set in a *forward-only* manner. That means it can't go backward or jump arbitrarily around in the data. For each record, methods are available to return the data in each column.

DataReaders are designed to be fast—ask for data, read the data, close the connection. Although the methods on a DataReader only allow for a single record to be read at a time, it is highly likely that the underlying implementation reads much bigger blocks of data at a time for efficiency. DataReaders are also read-only, so they don't need to keep track of where data came from or how to put it back.

DataReaders will be used in the next several chapters to look at returned data, and will be discussed in detail in chapter 11.

5.3.6 The DataAdapter interface and classes

Those of you who have read a little about ADO.NET and have heard of the DataSet might be surprised that the DataSet so far has not featured in any of the discussions about data providers. That is the case because the DataSet is specifically designed to be "data source agnostic." Once you have data in a DataSet, you can move it to other tiers of your application (via remoting), tie it to user interface objects (such as data tables), and generally work with your data in any way you need.

As useful as this capability sounds, the DataSet is designed to work with relational data that comes from a database. It would be very annoying if you had to manually transfer data from the DataSet to the database code just to achieve this functionality.

That is where the DataAdapter classes come in. Table 5.7 shows the DataAdapter classes and interface.

Table 5.7   DataAdapter implementations

Class	Provider	Interface
SqlDataAdapter	SQL Server	IDbDataAdapter
OleDbDataAdapter	OLE DB	IDbDataAdapter

In most previous data access technologies, the way data was accessed was tied tightly to the way the data was manipulated. For example, in ADO, a Recordset holds data and can directly send changes to the database when the user changes data within the Recordset.

That sounds very object-oriented—you tell the object to do something, and it does it. The problem is that this approach is very *tightly coupled.* It assumes that the data connection is always available and, for that matter, that the data is coming from a database.

Separating the part of the code responsible for talking to the database from the part of the code used for manipulating data offers a number of advantages:

- It is no longer necessary to maintain a connection while the data manipulation is taking place, which means the connection can be used elsewhere.

- The data manipulation can take place on a different tier of your application (possibly a physically different computer) than the connection to the database, by transferring the information to be manipulated (as with a classic three-tier application).

- The data manipulation code is no longer tied to just database access—it becomes a generic mechanism for manipulating data.

- You can use one set of data access mechanisms for reading the data and a different mechanism for writing it later. You can, for example, read the data from one database and write it to a different database.

- Because the data manipulation code does not have data access code, and the data access code does not have data manipulation code, both sets of code become simpler.

ADO started to address this capability with Disconnected Recordsets. ADO.NET takes the concept further. The two different objects are

- *The DataAdapter*—Responsible for obtaining the data and, later, for writing changes to the database.

- *The DataSet*—The object that allows for manipulation of the data. Not only does it have capabilities for adding, removing, and changing data, but it is also designed to be easily transportable to a different tier via remoting mechanisms.

The DataAdapter contains four important properties, each of which is really nothing more than a command object. These four properties are:

- `SelectCommand`—Used to select the data to use
- `InsertCommand`—Used to insert new data
- `UpdateCommand`—Used to update existing data
- `DeleteCommand`—Used to remove data

Most of these command objects can be automatically generated by ADO.NET via the use of a CommandBuilder (discussed next), or can be custom provided to handle special cases, use stored procedures, and so forth.

You can load data into a DataSet via the `Fill()` method on a DataAdapter. The `Update()` method takes the changes in a DataSet and, using the appropriate `Insert`, `Update`, and `Delete` commands, writes the data back to the data source.

The DataSet and the DataAdapter are the topic of the chapters in part 3 of this book.

5.3.7   CommandBuilder classes

In the previous section, I talked about the fact that you can manually specify the commands to use for Inserts, Updates, and Deletes for a DataAdapter. That is all well and good, but what if you just want the system to handle the simple cases for you? That is where the CommandBuilders come in (table 5.8).

Table 5.8   CommandBuilder implementations

Class	Provider	Interface
SqlCommandBuilder	SQL Server	n.a.
OleDbCommandBuilder	OLE DB	n.a.

You may notice that, unlike the other classes discussed so far, the CommandBuilders do not implement an interface. That is because they are really just utility objects that may or may not be provided by any particular data provider, or may be implemented in a substantially different way.

The CommandBuilders are utility objects especially designed to work with a Data-Adapter. The previous section explained that most of the command objects for a Data-Adapter can be automatically created; this is done using the CommandBuilder.

Because the DataAdapter is designed to be flexible, it does not have built-in mechanisms for any of the commands. But Microsoft knows that a great many DataAdapters will use fairly straightforward Selects, and fairly straightforward Insert, Update, and Delete commands; so, the company provided the CommandBuilder to avoid developers' having to generate this common code.

The CommandBuilder cannot do several tasks:

- It cannot generate a Select statement automatically—there is no way for the CommandBuilder to know what data is desired.

- It cannot generate Insert, Update, or Delete statements for overly complex queries. For example, if the query contains a join, then the CommandBuilder cannot be used.

- It cannot take advantage of special knowledge about the data, or use stored procedures and so forth. Any special behavior must be implemented by the developer.

What it can do, though, is speed up the use of DataAdapters for the most common cases. It is important to know, though, that the commands generated by the CommandBuilders are not necessarily efficient. CommandBuilders are discussed in part 3, which focuses on the use of the DataSet.

5.3.8   The DbException, ErrorCollection, and Error classes

The exception-handling and error-handling in ADO.NET is specific to the data provider (table 5.9).

Table 5.9 Exception and error implementations

Class	Provider	Interface
SqlException	SQL Server	n.a.
SqlErrorCollection		
SqlError		
OleDbException	OLE DB	n.a.
OleDbErrorCollection		
OleDbError		

Once again, you will notice that there are no general interfaces here. Although I understand the reason—the error information returned by the different providers is quite different—I still wish Microsoft had created even a simple base class for these objects. At least a couple of properties are basically the same from any provider, and a base class would have made coding generically somewhat simpler.

.NET generally uses exceptions to indicate errors, and ADO.NET follows this standard. When a database error occurs, the appropriate exception is thrown. Issues that can throw an exception include:

- *Incorrect use of a database object*—For example, attempting to execute a command before a connection has been made to the database
- *Invalid SQL*—SQL that is either illegal or references missing tables or columns
- *Missing parameters*—SQL that references parameters that are not specified
- *Permission problems*—SQL that attempts an operation the client does not have rights to perform

Once an exception has been caught, you can step through the error collection and look at each error in turn. The error objects differ from SQL Server to OLE DB, but information they generally contain includes:

- *Message*—A short description of the error
- *Number/state*—A unique identifier for the type of error

Although no specific chapter discusses error handling in detail, you'll see error handling in several examples throughout the rest of the book.

5.4 SUMMARY

This chapter has presented something of a whirlwind tour of the major classes within a data provider. It should be enough to make you comfortable with the objects you will encounter in the next couple of chapters, which provide a hands-on look at using these classes.

Those of you who have a lot of experience using previous data access mechanisms, such as ADO, probably feel that not a lot is new here, beyond some terminology changes. Especially at this level, that is fairly true; much of what you read in this chapter and will see in the next two chapters will be little more than a chance to pick up the ADO.NET syntax.

One good thing is that the various classes are nicely segmented and simple. In particular, because each data provider has its own set of classes for everything, you don't have to wade through irrelevant methods or work with mechanisms made complicated by having to support a weird case. At the same time, there *are* interfaces that allow for code to be written generically.

You will learn many other useful things about ADO.NET throughout the rest of the book. Also, Microsoft claims that ADO.NET is faster than ADO. For example, the .NET SQL Server data provider has shown itself to be 10 to 20 percent faster than using ADO to access SQL Server via OLE DB!

So much for the theory. In the next chapter, we will finally get around to using ADO.NET to do something.

C H A P T E R   6

Basic operations with the SQL Server data provider

Chapter 5 spent a lot of time discussing the classes in a data provider and their general purpose. This chapter is much more practical—it shows you how to do useful things with ADO.NET!

By the time you are done with this chapter, you should feel confident about jumping into your C# compiler and spitting out some code for doing straightforward SQL—reading and updating data.

The code in this chapter does compile and run (really, I tested it). For space reasons, though, the methods around the code are excluded; you will have to put them in yourself. I do, however, go through the entire exercise of setting up the first code sample. Alternately, the code is available for download from the Manning web site at http://www.manning.com/feldman.

The sample code in this chapter assumes the existence of a SQL Server database called ADONetSamples, containing the various tables referenced. For instructions on setting up this database, please refer to chapter 4.

This chapter deals specifically with accessing data with SQL Server, and chapter 7 concentrates on using OLE DB. Chapter 8 shows how to make the code generic, such that the same code can be used to talk to either data provider (and any new data providers, as well).

At one point I considered combining these into a single chapter, because they cover more or less the same material. However, I felt it was clearer to separate the topics. If you know you will be working with OLE DB, you can probably skip chapter 6. Likewise, if you intend to work only with SQL Server, then you can skip chapter 7.

6.1 REFERENCING THE APPROPRIATE NAMESPACE

First, a bit of housekeeping. Before you can access the classes in the SQL Server data provider, you must reference the appropriate namespace at the top of the file containing the code. In C#, you do so with the `using` statement:

```
using System;
using System.Data.SqlClient;

namespace MyApplication
{

   .
   .
   .

```

It will be obvious if you have forgotten to do this, because the compiler will complain that none of the SqlClient classes exist!

6.2 EXECUTING SIMPLE SQL

No matter how complex your applications become, at some point it is highly likely that you will want to throw some simple SQL at the database engine—to insert a row, update a value, or whatever. In ADO.NET, these types of operations are all done in a similar way.

The example in listing 6.1 shows how to add some data to a table containing information about teachers. The code connects to a database, inserts a row of data into a table, and then disconnects.

Listing 6.1   C# example: simple Insert

```
string strConnect = "server=localhost; "
           + "Initial Catalog=ADONetSamples; "
           + " UID=sa;PWD=";
SqlConnection conn = null;
try
{
   conn = new SqlConnection(strConnect);
   conn.Open();
```

❶ Connect to database

```
        string strSQL =   "INSERT INTO Teachers "
                        + "(TeacherName,Classroom,Subject) "
                        + "VALUES ('Mr. Kriefels','7A','Physics')";

        SqlCommand comm = new SqlCommand(strSQL,conn);    ❷ Create command object

        int Return = comm.ExecuteNonQuery();    ❸ Execute command

        Console.WriteLine("Insert returned {0}",Return);

    }
    catch(SqlException ex)     ❹ Catch database exceptions
    {
        Console.WriteLine("Failed: {0}",ex.ToString());
    }
    finally
    {
        if(conn != null)
            conn.Close();     ❺ Close connection
    }
```

❶ Before you can do anything, you must connect to the database. The connection string (`strConnect`) defines the parameters for how the connection should be made (table 6.1).

Table 6.1   Connection string parameters from listing 6.1

Parameter	Description
server=localhost	Tells SQL Server to connect to a database on the local system. Could also reference a specific server by name.
Initial Catalog=ADONetSamples	Specifies the name of the database to which you wish to connect.
UID=sa	The SQL Server user ID to use.
PWD=	The password for the user ID (in this case, it is blank).

You can specify a number of other parameters in the connection string, with a semi-colon (;) between them. (Chapter 9 talks about connection string options.)

The next line creates a new connection object variable, and the first lines in the try block create and open the connection:

```
conn = new SqlConnection(strConnect);
conn.Open();
```

If something went wrong—for example, if the database was not found or the password and user ID were not legal, the `Open()` command would throw an exception.

❷ A new SQL command object is created, and two arguments are passed to the constructor:

- strSQL—The string containing the SQL to execute
- conn—The connection object to use to execute the command

The SqlCommand object can be created and initialized a number of different ways. The important thing is that the command contains the SQL to execute and the connection object to use. (Chapter 10 goes into more detail on this topic.)

❸ There are several different execute methods on the command object. The ExecuteNonQuery() method is specifically for executing SQL commands that do not return a result set. The return value from ExecuteNonQuery() will be the number of rows affected by the command. If something went wrong (for example, if the SQL was not legal), then the code would have thrown an exception.

❹ If anything goes wrong at any stage within the try block, then an SQL exception will be thrown. The catch block currently does not do much with the error except display it as text, but the code here could easily step through the collection of errors and display a better error message, or try to fix the problem.

Note that this particular catch block will *only* catch SqlExceptions. It will not catch any other sort of error. Other errors would need to be caught in an additional catch block or at a higher level.

❺ It is important that the database connection be explicitly closed when the code is done with it, which is why the Close() command is inside a finally block—putting code in a finally block guarantees that it will be called whether or not an exception is thrown. The code checks for null because it is *possible* (although unlikely) that an exception might be thrown on or before the line that creates the connection.

The obvious reason the connection must be closed is so that the resources associated with it are released. The reason it must be closed *explicitly* comes down to the nature of .NET and the idea of garbage-collected code.

In many other object-oriented database libraries, the code would be written so that when the connection object goes out of scope, the object is deleted and the resources are released automatically. In fact, even with ADO.NET, resources will be released when the object is deleted.

The problem is knowing when the object will be deleted. In a garbage-collected environment, such as .NET, memory is not released automatically when leaving an execution block (such as a function). Instead, the garbage collector deletes an object when it feels the need to free memory. That could be a long time after the code executed! Even if you have no intention of using the resources again any time soon, it is still a good practice to always close connections and release other resources explicitly.

We could use an alternate notation here. C# has a `using` statement, which automatically handles the freeing of resources:

```
using( SqlConnection conn = new SqlConnection(strConnect) )
{
    // Various commands that use the connection
}
```

This code is resolved into a try/finally block. It is equivalent to

```
SqlConnection conn = new SqlConnection(strConnect);
try
{
    // Various commands that use the connection
}
finally
{
    if(conn != null)
        conn.Dispose();
}
```

`Dispose()` is sort of a generic version of `Close()` that is implemented on classes that have some sort of final operation, such as releasing a resource.

I don't generally like the `using` statement, because it hides what is going on behind the scenes and because it doesn't provide a mechanism for catching and handling exceptions. Of course, I could put a `try/catch` block inside the `using` statement, but then things are even less clear. However, `using` offers a couple of advantages—it does make sure the resource is released, and it is space-efficient if you are not catching an exception.

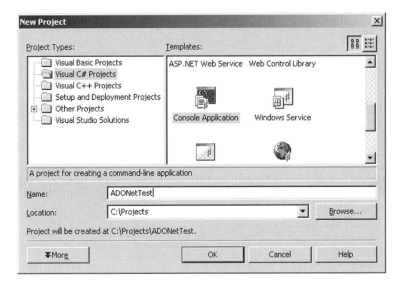

Figure 6.1
Creating a
new console
application

6.2.1 Example summary

The basic code used in this example is appropriate for most simple SQL commands that don't return results. It can be used for standard `Inserts`, `Updates`, and `Deletes`, calling stored procedures, setting security rights, and so forth.

6.2.2 Running the example code

If you are relatively new to C# and Visual Studio.NET, this section goes over the steps required to run this code. The process is straightforward. The first step is to create a new project, which we can do from the menu, under File → New → Project, or by clicking the New Project button on the startup page.

The type of project we want to create is a C# Console Application (see figure 6.1). In this case, we're creating a console application called ADONetTest. When we click the OK button, the project will be created with a default startup class called Class1; this class should be opened automatically, with just a small shell of code:

```
using System;

namespace ADONetTest
{
   /// <summary>
   /// Summary description for Class1.
   /// </summary>
   class Class1
   {
       static void Main(string[] args)
       {
         //
         // TODO: Add code to start application here
         //
       }
   }
}
```

The static `Main` function is the method that will be called when the application is first run. We could just stick code in this method, but it can become annoying if we want to call other functions; so, I generally create an instance of the class and call a method on that instance that has code in it. I also put the various `using` statements at the top, to provide access to the classes that are needed. Listing 6.2 shows the entire code for the Insert data example from listing 6.1.

Listing 6.2   The entire code for the example

```
using System;
using System.Data.SqlClient;

namespace ADONetTest
{
```

```
/// <summary>
/// Summary description for Class1.
/// </summary>
class Class1
{
    static void Main(string[] args)
    {
        Class1 oClass = new Class1();
        oClass.DoStuff();
    }

    /// <summary>Method that executes test code</summary>
    public void DoStuff()
    {
    string strConnect =   "server=localhost;"
                        + "Initial Catalog=ADONetSamples;"
                        + "UID=sa;PWD=";

    SqlConnection conn = null;
    try
    {
        conn = new SqlConnection(strConnect);
        conn.Open();

        string strSQL =    "INSERT INTO Teachers "
                         + "(TeacherName,Classroom,Subject) "
                         + "VALUES ('Mr. Kriefels','7A','Physics')";

        SqlCommand comm = new SqlCommand(strSQL,conn);

        int Return = comm.ExecuteNonQuery();

        Console.WriteLine("Insert returned {0}",Return);
    }
    catch(SqlException ex)
    {
        Console.WriteLine("Failed: {0}",ex.ToString());
    }
    finally
    {
        if(conn != null)
            conn.Close();
    }
    }
}
}
```

For most of the rest of the samples, I won't list all the code, but you should be able to easily set up the examples by following the pattern presented here.

6.3 EXECUTING SQL WITH RESULTS

Having data in a database is not particularly useful unless there is a convenient way to retrieve that data. In chapter 16, you will see how to read data directly into a DataSet in order to manipulate it and store the results. First, though, the example in listing 6.3 shows how to retrieve specific information from the example Teachers table. The code executes a query and steps through the results.

Listing 6.3   C# example: simple Select

```csharp
string strConnect = "server=localhost;
                Initial Catalog=ADONetSamples;
                UID=sa;PWD=";

SqlConnection conn = null;
SqlDataReader reader = null;
try
{
   conn = new SqlConnection(strConnect);
   conn.Open();

   string strSQL =   "SELECT TeacherName,Classroom,Subject"
                    + " FROM Teachers";              ❶ Select statement

   SqlCommand comm = new SqlCommand(strSQL,conn);

   reader = comm.ExecuteReader();          ❷ Execute commad

   // Always call Read before accessing data.
   while (reader.Read())            ❸ Step through data
   {
      Console.WriteLine(reader.GetString(0) + ", " +
      reader.GetString(1) + ", " +
      reader.GetString(2));
   }
}
catch(SqlException ex)
{
   Console.WriteLine("Failed: {0}",ex.ToString());
}
finally
{
   // Always call Close when done reading.
   if(reader != null)
      reader.Close();              ❹ Close reader

   conn.Close();
}
```

❶ It is probably obvious, but the SQL we pass here can be any `Select` statement that is legal for SQL Server—it can include joins, subqueries, functions, and so forth.

❷ Unlike the first example, we are expecting back a result set from the query, so we use the `ExecuteReader()` method instead of `ExecuteNonQuery()`. The `ExecuteReader()` method executes the statement and returns a DataReader that allows access to the results. The DataReader does not contain the results, but retrieves the results as the user asks for them. This is an important point: until the data has all been read or the DataReader has been closed, the DataReader is still using the connection and the data is, at least partially, still on the database server.

The DataReader acts as though it reads only a single row of data at a time, but it is reasonable to assume that the implementation is rather more efficient and reads a block of records at a time.

Note that we declare the `SqlDataReader` variable outside of the `try` block—we do this so we can make sure it is closed in the `finally` block later.

❸ The `Read()` command tells the DataReader to step to the next row of data. Note the way in which the logic is written: `Read()` is called before the first row is read. That first call to `Read()` positions the DataReader on the first row, as shown in figure 6.2.

	Top			
	Row 1	Mr. Biddick	A1	Math
	Row 2	Ms. Fortune	B2	English
	Row 3	Mr. Kriefels	C3	Physics

Figure 6.2   Position of the cursor before the first `Read()`

Each call to `Read()` moves the cursor to the next row of data. As you may have noticed, there is no way to move the cursor backward—the DataReader only allows movement to the next record, one at a time. Also, there is no way to update any of the data—it can only be read. The official-sounding term calls this a *forward-only, read-only* cursor.

The `Read()` function will return `true` as long as it can position the cursor on a legal row of data. As soon as it runs out of rows, it will return `false`.

In this example, all the columns are strings, so the `GetString()` method is used. The indexer (the official name for positional access via the brackets `[]`) refers to the zero-based column. Additional methods on the DataReader read other types of data. For example, if the second column (index 1 starting from 0) had a number, then a different method would be used:

```
reader.GetInt32(1)
```

Overrides exist for many different data types; these are explored in more depth in chapter 11.

It is also possible to access a column's data by name:

```
reader["TeacherName"].ToString()
```

This technique is a bit slower, because the column name must be looked up. When we use the indexer, the return value is an object, rather than a specific data type. That is the reason `ToString()` is called on the result.

❹ As with the connection, it is a good idea to explicitly close the reader, rather than waiting for the garbage collector to do so at its convenience. The reader is closed in the `finally` block to make sure the code is called even if something goes wrong. We have to check to make sure the reader is not `null`, though, in case an exception was thrown before the `ExecuteReader()` call.

6.3.1 Example summary

This fairly simple pattern for reading data will work in a large number of situations. The DataReader is both convenient and fast, providing you want to quickly read through a result set in a forward-only manner or are copying the data to a more convenient place. In fact, the DataAdapter uses a DataReader in order to populate a DataSet. (The DataReader is discussed in chapter 11.)

6.4 SUMMARY

Perhaps surprisingly, the two code examples in this chapter give you an enormous amount of power. You can do more advanced things, of course, but just using the code shown here, modified appropriately, you can execute any sort of standard SQL and get back results. I know developers who have managed to go an entire career without using anything more advanced than what was shown in this chapter!

Chapter 7 shows how to do virtually the same things, but using OLE DB against a database other than SQL Server.

C H A P T E R   7

Basic operations with the OLE DB data provider

Chapter 6 showed how to access a SQL Server database to read and modify data. As much as it saddens Microsoft, though, not everyone in the world uses SQL Server. At the moment, the main way to talk to any other database from ADO.NET is via the OLE DB data provider, which goes through OLE DB to talk to a database.

In the next year or so, you can expect to see custom data providers written for all the major database engines, just as previously the database vendors created OLE DB providers and ODBC drivers. In the meantime, OLE DB is a fairly robust technology with enough acceptance that the likelihood of finding an OLE DB provider for your particular engine is quite high. Microsoft has also created an ODBC data provider that shipped soon after .NET; it opens access to the hundreds of ODBC drivers that have already been written. (Appendix A shows how to install and use the ODBC data provider.)

I admit that I do not stray far from the Microsoft path in this chapter. All the examples use a Microsoft Access database, because it is simple to acquire and set up. (Chapter 4 runs through the procedure for acquiring and setting up the test Access database.)

The same basic code will work against Oracle or other engines, and you are welcome to do your testing against the engine of your choice. However, if you've chosen to set up Oracle, I am unwilling to spend the several chapters necessary to explain the installation procedures![1]

You may notice a marked similarity between the code samples in this chapter and the previous chapter. Microsoft has done a good job of making the data providers operate the same way. In fact, chapter 8 shows that, apart from connecting and some database-specific handling, you can write code that will generically work with any provider.

7.1 THE OLE DB DATA PROVIDER NAMESPACE

Before you can use the classes in the OLE DB data provider, the appropriate namespace must be referenced at the top of the file containing the code. This reference will look like the following:

```
using System;
using System.Data.OleDb;

namespace MyApplication
{

    .
    .
    .

```

This namespace contains all the classes associated with the OLE DB data provider.

7.2 EXECUTING SIMPLE SQL

The first example (listing 7.1) connects to a Microsoft Access database, inserts a row of data into a table that contains a list of teachers, and then disconnects. As I mentioned earlier, this code is virtually identical to the SQL Server version. The code in this example can be used with only minimal changes to execute most simple SQL commands that don't return results, such as Inserts, Updates, Deletes, calling stored procedures, and so forth. This code will also work with most different database engines. The important thing to remember is that the SQL for more advanced commands (such as outer joins or working with stored procedures) can vary from engine to engine.

---

[1] Yes, I am being a bit sarcastic here—Oracle is a good engine, but the installation frequently is a nightmare.

Listing 7.1   C# example: Simple Insert with OLE DB

```
string strConnect = "Provider=Microsoft.Jet.OLEDB.4.0;" +
                  + "Data Source=c:\\ADOSample\\ADONetSamplesAccess.MDB;"
                  + "User ID=;Password=";
```
❶ Connect to database

```
OleDbConnection conn = new OleDbConnection(strConnect);
try
{
   conn.Open();

   string strSQL =   "INSERT INTO Teachers "
                  + " (TeacherName,Classroom,Subject) "
                  + " VALUES ('Mr. Kriefels','7A','Physics')";

   OleDbCommand comm = new OleDbCommand(strSQL,conn);
```
❷ Create command

```
   int iReturn = comm.ExecuteNonQuery();
```
❸ Execute command

```
   Console.WriteLine("Insert returned {0}",iReturn);
}
catch(OleDbException ex)
```
❹ Catch database exceptions

```
{
   Console.WriteLine("Failed: {0}",ex.ToString());
}
finally
{
   conn.Close();
```
❺ Close connection

```
}
```

❶ Before you can do anything, you must connect to the database. Although the procedure is basically the same as for SQL Server, the parameters (specified in `strConnect`) are slightly different (table 7.1).

Table 7.1   Connection string parameters from listing 7.1

Parameter	Description
`Provider= Microsoft.Jet.OLEDB.4.0`	This rather daunting-looking string is how Microsoft chose to expose the OLE DB provider for the current version of Access. Microsoft has a naming convention for Jet (the engine behind Access and Microsoft's other file-based drivers) that is quite elaborate and includes the version number of the data provider. Because OLE DB makes extensive use of COM, the version number is important because it allows for multiple versions of the Jet driver to be used on the same machine. Chapter 9 explains how to specify a different provider, such as Oracle.

continued on next page

Table 7.1   Connection string parameters from listing 7.1 (continued)

Parameter	Description
`Data Source= c:\\ADOSample\\ ADONetSamplesAccess.MDB`	This specifies the full path and name of the database to which you wish to connect. Strictly speaking, the path does not need to be provided—you can just put ADONetSamplesAccess.MDB, as long as the MDB file is in the path and can be found.
	The double backslashes (\\) are used because of the C# syntax. A backslash in a string indicates that the following character is an escape character (for example, \t is a tab). A double backslash means to use the special character backslash. Be careful—I cannot tell you how many times I have corrected nonworking code by pointing out this simple but common mistake.
`User ID=`	The sample access database does not require a user ID; but if it did, it would be specified here. It is also acceptable to omit this parameter.
`Password=`	There is also no password on this database, and this argument can also be omitted.

You can specify a number of other parameters in an OLE DB connection string, separated by semicolons (`;`). (Chapter 9 talks about connection objects and options for connection strings.)

The other connection lines create a new connection object and then open the connection:

```
OleDbConnection conn = new OleDbConnection(strConnect);
conn.Open();
```

If something went wrong—for example, if the data source was not found, or the user ID and password were not legal, then the `Open()` command would throw an exception.

❷ The pattern for creating the command object is virtually the same as for SQL Server, except that the object created is an OleDbCommand rather than an SqlCommand:

```
OleDbCommand comm = new OleDbCommand(strSQL,conn);
```

A new OLE DB command object is created, and two arguments are passed to the constructor:

- `strSQL`—The string containing the SQL to execute
- `conn`—The connection object to use to execute the command

The OleDbCommand object can be created and initialized a number of different ways. The important thing is that the command contains the SQL to execute and the connection object to use. (Chapter 10 talks about command objects and how they can be created and used.)

❸ Executing a command with no return result is identical for the SQL Server data provider and for the OLE DB data provider:

```
int iReturn = comm.ExecuteNonQuery();
```

The `ExecuteNonQuery()` method is specifically designed to efficiently execute SQL that does not return a result set. The return result will usually be the number of rows affected by the command, although some back ends will just return –1, indicating success. There are a number of other execute methods for different purposes, although OLE DB does not have all the methods SQL Server provides.

If the SQL was not legal, then this statement would throw an exception.

❹ If anything goes wrong at any stage within the `try` block, then an OLE DB exception will be thrown. The `catch` block in the example just displays the text of the message, but it could easily do more.

Unfortunately there is no single base class for the database exceptions. It would be nice to have a generic `catch` block that would catch any sort of database error:

Not legal:

```
catch(DbException ex)
```

However, the SQL Server exception and the attached errors contain considerably more information about the problem than the more generic OLE DB exception and errors. In this example, you write out the exception as a string to the console. In a real application, of course, you would do something more useful—such as prompt the user to correct the problem, or rethrow the exception with additional information.

❺ I will keep saying this, because it is so important: You must explicitly close the connection when you are done with it, in order to release the associated resources. Yes, the garbage collector will eventually do it, but you never know when.

With SQL Server, you could probably go a long time without realizing you forgot to do this—SQL Server is efficient enough that it can handle a large number of open connections (as long as you don't run out of licenses). Access will begin reacting much more quickly—the Access engine can only handle up to four connections from each client application[2] and will do very strange things when that number is exceeded. Unfortunately, it does not necessarily throw an exception, thus creating an exceedingly troublesome bug to troubleshoot.

The `Close()` method is put inside a `finally` block to guarantee that it will be called whether or not an exception is thrown, even if the `catch` block throws another exception itself.

---

[2] Note that this limitation is *per client application*, not per database, or even per machine. Many more users can access the same database from different clients. The documentation is particularly obscure, and I will admit that I spent days troubleshooting this problem the first time I ran into it.

7.3 EXECUTING *SQL* WITH RESULTS

Now that you have gone to such an effort to put data into the database, it would be nice to be able to get it out again in a useful manner. The example in listing 7.2 shows how to execute a query and step through the results. As with the first example, more similarities than differences exist between the SQL Server–specific version and the OLE DB version.

Listing 7.2   C# example: simple Select using OLE DB

```csharp
string strConnect = "Provider=Microsoft.Jet.OLEDB.4.0;" +
                + "Data Source=c:\\ADOSample\\ADONetSamplesAccess.MDB;"
                + "UID=;PWD=";

OleDbConnection conn = new OleDbConnection(strConnect);
OleDbDataReader reader = null;
try
{
   conn.Open();

   string strSQL =   "SELECT TeacherName,Classroom,Subject "
                 + "FROM Teachers";

   OleDbCommand comm = new OleDbCommand(strSQL,conn);

   reader = comm.ExecuteReader();        ❶ Execute command

   // Always call Read before accessing data.
   while ( reader.Read() )               ❷ Step through data
   {
      Console.WriteLine( reader.GetString(0) + ", " +
                         reader.GetString(1) + ", " +
                         reader.GetString(2));
   }

}
catch(OleDbException ex)
{
   Console.WriteLine("Failed: {0}",ex.ToString());
}
finally
{
   // Always call Close when done reading.
   if(reader != null)
      reader.Close();        ❸ Close reader

   conn.Close();
}
```

❶ Connecting to the database and creating the command object are the same as in the previous example, as is the code for handling an exception. The first major difference is the way in which the command is executed.

The `ExecuteReader()` method is specifically designed to handle queries that are expected to return a result set. As with the SQL Server DataReader, the OLE DB DataReader doesn't contain all the results, but acts as a forward-only, read-only cursor into the data.

This approach may seem inefficient, but it really isn't—the reader only *acts* as though it reads a single row at a time. In reality, we can assume that the provider is moving data around in a much more efficient manner.

❷ This code is the same for SQL Server and for OLE DB. The `Read()` command tells the DataReader to step to the next row of data (see figure 7.1).

⇨	Top			
	Row 1	Mr. Biddick	A1	Math
	Row 2	Ms. Fortune	B2	English
	Row 3	Mr. Kriefels	C3	Physics

Figure 7.1   Position of the cursor before the first Read()

Note that the cursor is initially positioned *before* the first row of data. The first call to `Read()` positions the cursor on the first row. The `Read()` method will return `true` as long as it has successfully positioned itself at a row of data. As soon as it passes the last row, it will return `false`.

On each row, we can access data from individual columns. `GetString()` is used in the example because all the columns are text, but other methods retrieve data for other data types (`GetInt32()` and so forth).

The DataReader is discussed in much more detail in chapter 11.

❸ As with the connection, it is a good idea to explicitly close the reader, rather than waiting for the garbage collector to get around to doing it. In theory, closing the connection should close the reader as well, but it is not wise to rely on this—if the connection is being pooled, for example, you can get some strange results, such as exceptions being thrown because of a reader left open on the connection.

The close is done in the `finally` block in case an exception is thrown. We must check to make sure that the reader is not `null`, because it is possible that an exception was thrown before the call to `ExecuteReader()`.

7.3.1 Example summary

At least for simple operations, the way the SQL Server data provider and the OLE DB data provider work is very similar. This example will work for many situations for reading data.

The DataReader is a very efficient mechanism for reading through data quickly. If you want to manipulate the data, then the DataReader can be used to read the data into a different set of objects. For example, the DataAdapter uses the DataReader to populate a DataSet.

7.4 SUMMARY

By adding the OLE DB data provider to ADO.NET, Microsoft has opened up a whole world of different engines. This includes not only traditional relational database engines, but also specialized data sources, such as OLAP or spreadsheets. Of course, ADO.NET is focused on relational data and so will have some trouble with hierarchical or arbitrary data (although there is some support in the DataReader for handling this type of data; see the example in chapter 11).

Even though the examples in this chapter were very simple, you should have seen enough to be able to handle all the basic SQL you will need for your applications. Of course, there is a lot more to ADO.NET, in terms of both low-level concepts and the DataSet.

Comparing this chapter with the last, you should notice that the SQL Server and OLE DB data providers work virtually identically, at least for the simple cases. These patterns should be the same for any new providers that are written. In chapter 8, you will see how to use these similarities by writing code that will work against *any* data provider.

C H A P T E R   8

Writing database-independent code

One of the first questions you might be asking about this chapter is why there is value in writing database-independent code. After all, most development is done against a single database engine, and you have probably spent a considerable amount of time learning the nuances of that engine. There are a couple of reasons:

- You might be attempting to build an application that can be used against multiple different databases.
- You might work for a company that changes to a different database vendor—not an uncommon occurrence.[1]

I have to admit that I have a tendency to write code in the most generic manner possible; although doing so costs extra time up front, it has saved me more times than I can count when requirements have changed.

ADO.NET does not provide the same level of support for writing generic code that, for example, ODBC does, but it is still possible to go quite far generically, as you will see in this chapter.

---

[1] Not that management would ever consider making such a dramatic change without talking to their highly skilled developers first!

8.1 CONNECTING TO A DATABASE

Currently, you must write very specific code to connect to a database. Doing so is not a huge problem right now, when there are only two or three different providers, but imagine what a nuisance it will be when there are dozens or hundreds.

Microsoft is planning to provide a mechanism for handling this situation more easily in a future version of .NET. This mechanism will work like a factory, where you specify the provider you want and get back an appropriate connection object. There will also need to be a mechanism for providers to register themselves with the factory, so they can be found. .NET has a no-registration philosophy, so this may be a sticky problem for Microsoft to solve.

In the meantime, you must do all the work of connecting yourself (see listing 8.1). Once the connection has been made, though, it can be used generically (note that the exception-handling code has been removed to save space).

Listing 8.1   C# example: connecting and calling the same function

```csharp
using System.Data;
using System.Data.OleDb;               ❶ Namespaces
using System.Data.SqlClient;

class ADONetTest
{

   public void ReadSqlServerData()
   {
      string strConnect =    "server=localhost;"
                          + "Initial Catalog=ADONetSamples;"
                          + "UID=sa;PWD=";

      SqlConnection conn = new SqlConnection(strConnect);
      conn.Open();
      ReadSomeData(conn);      ❷ Generically read data
   }

   public void ReadOleDbData()
   {
      string strConnect = "Provider=Microsoft.Jet.OLEDB.4.0;" +
              + "Data Source=c:\\ADOSample\\ADONetSamplesAccess.MDB;"
              + "User ID=;Password=";

      OleDbConnection conn = new OleDbConnection(strConnect);
      conn.Open();
      ReadSomeData(conn);      ❷ Generically read data
   }
      .
      .
      .
```

❶ In the previous chapters, we had to include one namespace for the specific data provider we were using. Now that we are talking to two different databases, we have to include the two namespaces; but we also have to include a third namespace for the generic handling:

- `System.Data`—This namespace holds the generic data access functionality, including all of the data interfaces that are implemented by the DataAdapters.
- `System.Data.OleDb`—This namespace holds the OLE DB DataAdapter-specific code.
- `System.Data.SqlClient`—This namespace holds the SQL Server Data-Adapter-specific code.

We only need the `OleDb` and the `SqlClient` namespaces for this little bit of connection code. If the connection code were done in a separate file, we would only need the generic interfaces from the `System.Data` namespace.

❷ The code for creating and opening a connection to either a SQL Server data source or an OLE DB data source (in this case, Access) is quite specific. However, both functions call the same member function to read data. The next section shows this function.

8.2   EXECUTING A COMMAND

The purpose of the method in this example is to do a simple select from the Teachers table. However, this code is written so that it will work against any data source (as long as that data source contains a table named Teachers):

```
public void ReadSomeData(IDbConnection conn)        ❶ Pass connection
{
   string strSQL =   "SELECT TeacherName,Classroom,Subject "
                   + "FROM Teachers";          ❷ Generic SQL

   IDbCommand comm = conn.CreateCommand();      ❸ Create and configure
   comm.CommandText = strSQL;                      command
   comm.CommandType = CommandType.Text;

   IDataReader reader = comm.ExecuteReader();    ❹ Execute and
   DisplayResults(reader);                          read results

   reader.Close();
}
```

❶ Rather than defining the connection parameter as an `OleDbConnection` or an `SqlConnection`, the function takes an `IDbConnection`, which is an interface implemented by both the connection objects. The great advantage is that the code will work with any data provider connection object. If, at a later date, you decide to switch your code to a new data provider, this code can remain unchanged.

INTERFACE An interface is a named definition of a set of methods and properties. In order to use an object, you must use the various methods and properties exposed by that object. The combination of those methods and properties is said to be that object's interface.

Frequently, it is desirable for multiple objects to have the same interface, so that the methods and properties in the objects can be called without regard to the actual nature of the object. In order to do this, an object must implement all the methods and properties of the desired interface *and* must derive from that interface, so that the compiler knows the object is contractually obligated to implement all the methods and properties of the interface.

Although a class in C# can only be derived from one class, it can be derived from, or *implement*, any number of interfaces.

❷ Obviously, the SQL here is written assuming that the same table structures exist in both data sources. It is important to remember, though, that SQL is not identical from engine to engine. Although simple constructs are usually the same, things like outer joins and stored procedures can be handled differently. There are also capabilities in some engines that are not available in others.

If you truly intend to support multiple engines, you might consider building an object for generating specialized SQL. For example, this method might have a method for generating outer join code:

```
SqlBuilder² builder = SqlBuilder.CreateForConnection(conn);
strWhere += builder.OuterJoinClause("table1","table2",
                                    "Field1","Field2");
```

Obviously this is a fairly simplistic example, and building such an object will be quite time-consuming; but, if you intend to build completely generic code, the benefits are great. Imagine the `CreateForConnection()` method being a static method that returns an appropriate derivation of SqlBuilder:

```
public static SqlBuilder CreateForConnection(IDbConnection conn)
{
   if(conn.GetType() == typeof(SqlConnection))
      return new SQLServerSqlBuilder();
   else if(conn.GetType() == typeof(OleDbConnection))
      return new OleDbSqlBuilder();
   .
   .
   .
```

❸ In chapters 6 and 7, we created and initialized a specific type of command object with the connection and the SQL to execute. This approach is not possible here, because we don't know what type of command object is needed.

---

² Note that this is not an ADO.NET class—it is a possible name for a utility class you would build yourself.

Fortunately, connection objects can create a new command object and, because a connection object knows the data provider with which it is associated, can produce the appropriate command object. Because both data providers implement the IDbCommand interface, we don't really care which one we get—we can treat it generically.

Because the connection is providing the command object, the command object already knows about the connection. However, it does not know about the SQL to execute. That is what the next two lines provide:

```
comm.CommandText = strSQL;
comm.CommandType = CommandType.Text;
```

The CommandText property contains the string of SQL to execute, and the Command-Type property specifies how to interpret the CommandText. Actually, CommandType.Text is the default, so this line is technically not necessary. CommandType.Text just means that the CommandText contains SQL text to execute. The other values that can be used here are discussed in chapter 10.

❹ This line is basically identical to chapter 7's examples, except that we expect to get back an interface, rather than a known object (SqlDataReader or OleDbDataReader). Because both DataReaders implement this interface, we don't care which we get back.

The code for reading the results from the DataReader has been moved into its own function. All that function needs is an interface to a generic IDataReader. The code for the DisplayResults() function is shown in the next section.

8.3   READING RESULTS

The code in this example is designed to write out the results of the query from the previous example. In fact, this code is written generically enough that it will write out the results from any single query against any data provider:

```
public void DisplayResults(IDataReader reader)      ❶ Pass data reader
{
    IDataRecord record = reader as IDataRecord;      ❷ Reader interfaces

    int iCount = record.FieldCount;      ❸ Get field count
    while(reader.Read())      ❹ Step through rows
    {
        for(int i = 0;i < iCount;i++)
        {
            if(i > 0)
                Console.Write(", ");                              Get
                                                                  data
            Console.Write(record.GetValue(i).ToString().Trim()); ❺
        }

        Console.WriteLine("");
    }
}
```

❶ This function does not care which DataReader is being passed—it only cares that it is a DataReader. Because both DataReaders (OleDbDataReader and SqlDataReader) implement the IDataReader interface, an IDataReader is the parameter to the function.

❷ Unlike most of the other data provider classes, each DataReader implements two different interfaces:

- *IDataReader*—Responsible for stepping through data. The Read() method is on this interface, as well as methods for dealing with additional result sets that might have been returned.
- *IDataRecord*—Responsible for accessing the data in a particular record. This interface has methods such as GetString() and GetInt32() that will return data for specific columns.

To make it clear that methods are being called on these two different interfaces, the example code explicitly converts the IDataReader interface to an IDataRecord interface. In fact, it is not necessary to do this cast, because the IDataReader interface is derived from the IDataRecord interface. That means any class that implements IDataReader must also implement all the methods and properties of IDataRecord.

If one interface is derived from the other, then what is the value of having two interfaces? The IDataRecord interface can still be used on other objects that need to expose data but that don't provide navigation methods in the same manner as a DataReader. It also clarifies which methods are related to navigation, versus the methods related to reading data from a particular record.

❸ This method returns the number of fields in each row. Although we know that in this example we are working with exactly three fields, this function is more general—it will display however many columns are present. This call is made prior to stepping through data because the value should not change from row to row.

❹ Just as with any DataReader, this method moves to the next row and will return true until there is no more data. The first call to Read() moves to the first row.

❺ When we know exactly what data to expect, we can specifically ask the data record for data in the appropriate format. For example, we can call GetDateTime() or Get-Float(), which will return data as the appropriate data type. When we know the data types, these calls tend to be more efficient because there is no need to *box* the data.

Although boxing is useful, overhead is involved; so, you should avoid it if possible. However, in the DisplayResults() method, we don't know the data type of each column, so we need to treat each column as an object:

```
record.GetValue(i)
```

BOXING   Boxing is the process of taking a simple value type (such as an integer or a bool) and wrapping it up in an object so that it can behave like an object. Boxing allows all data types to be accessed efficiently, and yet still be used interchangeably with objects. When you are adding numbers, for example, it is much more efficient to work with a real integer data type; but when you want to put a bunch of numbers into a generic collection, you need the numbers to act as an object.

C# has real integers that are handled efficiently, but when an integer needs to act as an object, it will be wrapped or boxed into an object that represents an integer. Later it can be pulled out, or *unboxed* back into a regular integer.

This method returns the value as an object, boxing it if required. Of course, we want to print out the value, so we need to convert it to a string; and we want to get rid of extra white space at the end, so that the printout will look better:

```
record.GetValue(i).ToString().Trim()
```

8.3.1 Example summary

A couple of lines in this example make the output a little prettier, such as putting a comma between each value and putting each record on its own line. When we run this code, the output looks like figure 8.1.

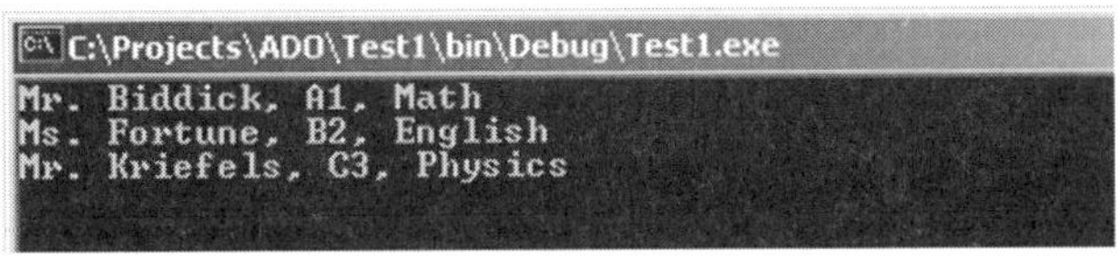

**Figure 8.1
Output from the
DisplayResults()
method**

8.4 DATE/TIME FIELDS

One issue with writing generic code is dealing with the different ways the data providers handle date/time information. The following is the format used by the SQL Server data provider with SQL Server 2000 (if you are using SQL Server 7, use the OLE DB format):

```
YYYY-MM-DDTHH:MI:SS
```

The date and time are separated by a *T*, and the time is specified using a 24-hour clock. For example:

```
UPDATE MyTable SET MyDateTime='2001-05-29T16:30:00'
```

OLE DB, however, does not accept this format. If the underlying engine supports a specific type of format, that format will generally work. But for *most* drivers, you can use this format:

```
YYYY-MM-DD HH:MI:SS
```

The major difference is the absence of the *T* between the fields. For example:

```
UPDATE MyTable SET MyDateTime='2001-05-29 16:30:00'
```

You can also use binding to avoid the problem altogether, as discussed in chapter 12.

8.5   VB.NET

Because this chapter is all about generic code, the following example shows how to accomplish the previous example using VB.NET instead of C#. One of the key benefits of .NET in general is that the same class library is used in all managed languages. That means it is easy to convert a sample from one language to another, with just a little understanding of the original language.

You may have noticed that most of the examples in this book are written in C#. I did this because C# is a language that was created explicitly to work with .NET, and it is also the language in which most of the underlying class library is written. Microsoft claims that all languages can be equal players under .NET, and from a compiled and speed perspective that is true. However, it certainly feels less awkward to code in C# for .NET than, say, Managed C++.

If you are a VB.NET programmer, you should easily be able to see how to convert the C# examples. Listing 8.2 shows the code just shown in C#, converted to VB.NET. Although I don't go into the same level of detail for the code in this example, you will see an almost line-by-line similarity.

Listing 8.2   VB.NET example: connecting, executing, and reading

```vbnet
Imports System.Data
Imports System.Data.SqlClient          ❶ Imports
Imports System.Data.OleDb

Module Module1

    Sub Main()

        Try

            ReadSqlServerData()
            ReadOleDbData()

        Catch ex As Exception

            Console.WriteLine(ex.ToString())

        End Try

    End Sub

    'Reads data using SQL Server
    Sub ReadSqlServerData()                ❷ Read SQL Server data

        Dim strConnect As String = "server=localhost;" _
                & "Initial Catalog=ADONetSamples ;UID=sa;PWD="

        Dim Conn As New SqlConnection()
        Conn.ConnectionString = strConnect
```

```vbnet
    Conn.Open()

    ReadSomeData(Conn)

    Conn.Close()

End Sub

'Reads data using OLE DB
Sub ReadOleDbData()
```

3 **Read OLE DB data**

```vbnet
    Dim strConnect As String = _
        "Provider=Microsoft.Jet.OLEDB.4.0;" _
      & "Data Source=c:\ADOSample\ADONetSamplesAccess.MDB; " _
      & "User ID=;Password="

    Dim Conn As New OleDbConnection()
    Conn.ConnectionString = strConnect

    Conn.Open()

    ReadSomeData(Conn)

    Conn.Close()

End Sub

'Executes a select against the data source
Sub ReadSomeData(ByVal Conn As IDbConnection)
```

4 **Read data**

```vbnet
    Dim strSQL As String = "SELECT TeacherName,Classroom," _
      & "Subject FROM Teachers"

    Dim Comm As IDbCommand = Conn.CreateCommand()
    Comm.CommandText = strSQL
    Comm.CommandType = CommandType.Text

    Dim Reader As IDataReader = Comm.ExecuteReader()

    DisplayResults(Reader)

    Reader.Close()

End Sub

'Displays the results contained within the reader
Sub DisplayResults(ByVal Reader As IDataReader)
```

5 **Display results**

```vbnet
    Dim Record As IDataRecord = Reader

    Dim Count As Integer = Reader.FieldCount
    Dim I As Integer
    While Reader.Read()
```

```
            For I = 0 To (Count - 1)

                If (I > 0) Then
                    Console.Write(", ")
                End If

                Console.Write(Record.GetValue(I).ToString().Trim())

            Next
            Console.WriteLine("")

        End While

    End Sub

End Module
```

❶ The imports statement is the VB.NET equivalent of the C# using statement. The three namespaces must be included:

- System.Data—Contains general data access functionality and all of the common interfaces
- System.Data.SqlClient—Contains the SQL Server–specific code necessary for the SQL Server connection function
- System.Data.OleDb—Contains the OLE DB–specific code necessary for the SQL Server connection function

❷ This subroutine connects to the SQL Server database and then calls the generic ReadSomeData subroutine.

❸ This subroutine connects to the Access database and then calls the generic Read-SomeData subroutine. The connection string does *not* have to use the double back-slash notation (\\) that C# uses, because VB.NET does not do escape sequences in the same way.

❹ This subroutine requests a list of teachers from the Teachers table. Because the code here uses interfaces instead of explicit classes, it will work with either data provider.

❺ Again, this method is generic, using only the interfaces. As with the C# example, the IDataReader interface is passed to the routine and is converted for clarity to an IDataRecord interface for certain calls.

8.6   SUMMARY

For many people, this chapter will only be of intellectual interest. It is certainly not common for applications to expend the extra effort required to arbitrarily support multiple engines. However, ADO.NET makes it possible to at least partially accomplish multiprovider support fairly easily. It's worth doing if you think there *may* be a chance it will be useful.

At the same time, ADO.NET does not solve all the problems of multiengine support. A number of aspects are missing:

- The ability to create connections generically (a connection factory of some kind).
- The ability to query the database engine to determine what is or is not supported, what type of data types are legal, and so forth. It is possible to do these things, but the process is not very straightforward. Chapter 32 explores this topic in detail.
- A "generic" SQL syntax that works across all engines (via a translation mechanism), such as is provided by ODBC.

You can work around these problems, and it is hoped that Microsoft will address most of these issues directly in future releases of .NET. It seems unlikely, though, that the generic SQL syntax will ever become part of ADO.NET—for that, at least, you are probably on your own. Still, even with these limitations, writing to interfaces and using other techniques from this chapter will certainly speed up porting to or supporting different engines.

Chapters 5 through 8 have provided a high-level overview of ADO.NET data providers and shown how to accomplish simple tasks. Chapters 9 through 14 dive much deeper into the specific classes and show some more advanced capabilities, starting with an in-depth look at the connection classes.

C H A P T E R   9

Connections

The connection classes have been key components of all the examples shown so far. In many ways, the connection is a simple class to understand and use—you provide some connection parameters and then tell the connection to connect. However, figuring out those parameters can be quite troublesome.

The connection classes have a fair number of interesting properties, methods, and events, and these are explored in exhaustive detail in appendix B. Although this chapter talks about some of the methods and properties, it is more concerned with ways in which connection strings can be built for connecting to various different database engines.

9.1   CONNECTION PROPERTIES

Most of the properties on the connection classes are read-only. The reason is that most of the values are set as part of the connection string or are read from the database engine once the connection has been made. Some of the things you can do within a connection string include:

- Specifying the location of the database
- Providing security information, including the user name, password, and use of special security capabilities, such as integrated security (using Windows authentication information to connect to SQL Server)
- Setting up connection pooling, so that connections can be reused efficiently

You can also do a number of other things, like controlling the timeout or packet size of a connection. The actual format and capabilities available differ depending on which data provider you are using, and, in the case of the OLE DB data provider, also differ based on the underlying engine to which you are connecting.

However, some common properties of a connection are defined on the base IDb-Connection interface, from which SqlConnection and OleDbConnection are derived. The following example shows a method that takes any type of connection object and writes out this common information:

```
public void WriteConnectionInfo(IDbConnection conn)
{
    Console.WriteLine("ConnectionString = {0}",conn.ConnectionString);
    Console.WriteLine("ConnectionTimeout = {0}",conn.ConnectionTimeout);
    Console.WriteLine("Database = {0}",conn.Database);
    Console.WriteLine("State = {0}",
                Enum.Format(typeof(ConnectionState),conn.State,"g"));
}
```

This code is straightforward, except for the State property—all that code simply converts the enumerated value to a string. The output from this code appears in figure 9.1.

Figure 9.1 Output from IDbConnection properties

As you can see from the connection string (which I hope is now familiar), this connection object is connected to the ADONetSamples database on the local machine. The other properties provide some other information about the connection:

- ConnectionTimeout—The number of seconds of inactivity to wait before automatically shutting down the connection. If this value were 0, then there would be no timeout. The default is 15 seconds.

- Database—The database to which the connection is connected. For SQL Server, it is easy to figure this out from the connection string, but some engines are not quite so forthcoming; you connect to a server or a port, rather than a specific database.

- State—The current condition of the connection. This value will be either Open or Closed, although Microsoft has defined some other values for future use, such as Connecting and Executing.

You can specify a number of other aspects about a connection, although most of them don't have properties for reading back the information. The next several sections talk about connecting to various different data sources.

9.2 SQL SERVER DATA PROVIDER CONNECTION STRINGS

Because the SQL Server data provider only has to worry about a single database engine, it is easy to talk about all the legal values that can appear in a connection string. With OLE DB, doing so is quite a bit harder. This section first talks a little about the formatting rules for connection strings, and then breaks down the various legal parameters. Not all the parameters are covered here—only the most commonly used. You can refer to appendix B for a more complete list.

9.2.1 SQL Server connection string format

The SQL Server connection string is made up of a series of name/value pairs separated by semicolons:

```
Data Source=localhost;Initial Catalog=ADONetSamples;UID=sa;PWD=
```

In this example, not all of the parameters have values. For example, PWD= specifies no password, which is the same as excluding the argument from the string altogether. However, you should never have a blank password in any production system.

It is also legal to put quotes around the values, which is necessary if the argument contains a quote:

```
Data Source="Arlen's Server"
```

or

```
Data Source='my "favorite" server'
```

You can use either single or double quotes, as long as the string does not include the same type of quote. The name of the parameter is not case sensitive, and, except in the actual name or value of the parameter, all white space is ignored. So,

```
Data Source = localhost
```

is the same as

```
Data Source=localhost
```

but

```
Data Source=local host
```

would not be legal.

9.2.2 Common SQL Server connection parameters

Table 9.1 shows the primary set of legal connection string parameters. These are the parameters you are apt to use all the time, and that have appeared in most of the examples to this point. Many of the parameters have multiple aliases to accommodate formats that have gathered over the years. There is no behavioral difference between the parameter and its aliases.

Table 9.1 Basic SQL Server connection parameters

Parameter	Meaning
Data Source	Specifies the name of the server where the SQL Server is located. If SQL Server is running on the local machine, then the special value `localhost` can be used.
	Aliases: `Server`, `Address`, `Addr`, `Network Address`

	Examples: `Data Source = localhost`
	         `Data Source=MyServer`
	         `Address = 127.0.0.1`

Initial Catalog	Specifies the name of the database.
	Alias: `Database`
	Example: `Initial Catalog=ADOTestDB`
User ID	Specifies the user login account to use.
	Alias: `UID`
	Examples: `User ID = Bob` `UID=Fred`
Password	Specifies the password for the user login account to use.
	Alias: `PWD`
	Examples: `Password=secret` `PWD=hello`
Connect Timeout	Specifies how much time the connection should spend attempting to connect before giving up and generating an error. The units are seconds. The connection timeout defaults to 15 seconds if it is not set. If the value is set to `0`, then the connection will attempt to connect forever (it will never timeout).
	Alias: `Connection Timeout`
	Example: `Connect Timeout=60`

Here is an example using all of these values:

```
SqlConnection conn = new SqlConnection("data source=localhost;" +
  "Initial Catalog=ADONetSamples; UID=sa;PWD=secret;" +
  "Connect Timeout=20");
conn.Open();
```

There are a whole host of other connection properties, including properties for connection pooling, security, and a number of oddball situations, such as specifying a different language to be used for error messages. Appendix B covers all of them, and chapter 31 goes into connection pooling in detail.

9.2.3 The Open and Close methods

The `Open()` method is the critical step in using a connection. You can put any garbage you like into the connection string. It is not until you call `Open()` that the connection string will be used to connect and set parameters. If any of the parameters are not legal, or the connection cannot be made, then the `Open()` command will throw an exception.

The obvious partner to the `Open()` command is the `Close()` command, which disconnects from the database, or at least indicates that you are no longer planning to use the connection—if you are using connection pooling, it just returns the connection to the pool. It is very important that you call `Close()` when you are done with the connection, to free up the resources—garbage collection will eventually clean up for you, but you have no idea when this will happen, and leaving unused connections open can cause some very strange and unpleasant side-effects.

9.3 OLE DB CONNECTION STRINGS

Connecting to an OLE DB provider can be quite challenging. As with SQL Server, a number of parameters can be passed, but the parameters to pass are different for different providers; and, because providers can be used to talk to multiple data sources, it is possible that the parameters for the data sources can be different as well.

The most important parameter on an OLE DB connection string is the provider, which specifies *which* OLE DB data provider needs to be used. Table 9.2 shows some common providers and the value of the provider parameter, which is not always obvious.

Table 9.2   Commonly used OLE DB providers

Type of data	Provider string
Microsoft Access (MDB)	Provider=Microsoft.Jet.OLEDB.4.0
Microsoft SQL Server	Provider=SQLOLEDB
Microsoft provider for Oracle	Provider=MSDAORA
Oracle provider for Oracle	Provider=OraOLEDB.Oracle
Data Shaping provider (a utility provider that allows access to other relational data sources in a hierarchical manner)	Provider=MSDataShape

There are, of course, many other OLE DB providers, including many with very specific syntax. The ADO.NET OLE DB provider will not talk to all drivers—it is smart enough to know, to some extent, which drivers are compatible. So, for example, you cannot use the OLE DB provider for ODBC.

The format for specifying a connection string is much the same as for SQL Server, except for the use of the different provider. The following example shows how to connect to an Oracle database using the OLE DB data provider:

```
strConnect = "Provider= MSDAORA;Data Source=ADONETOR;" +
                "User ID=scott;Password=tiger";
OleDbConnection conn = new OleDbConnection(strConnect);
conn.Open();
```

The following sections show how to connect to the various providers listed in table 9.2. Although I cannot cover all the existing OLE DB providers, the format will be fairly similar.

9.3.1   Microsoft Access

The primary parameter that must be provided is the data source, which identifies the name and location of the MDB file. Optional parameters include a user name and password:

```
strConnect = @"Provider=Microsoft.Jet.OLEDB.4.0;" +
             @"Data Source=c:\ADOSample\ADONetSamplesAccess.MDB;User ID=;Password=";
```

The data source is the path and filename. If the Access file were located in the current directory, then the path could be omitted. Note that single slashes instead of double slashes appear in the path, unlike previous examples. That is the case because we put an at sign (@) in front of the string, which tells C# to treat the entire string literally and ignore any escape sequences.

In this example the user ID and password are blank, so those parameters could have been omitted. If we needed to specify any Access-specific parameters, we could add them to the end of the string, separated by semicolons (;).

9.3.2   Microsoft SQL Server

It is relatively unnecessary to connect to SQL Server via OLE DB when an ADO.NET data provider is specifically written to SQL Server. However, doing so might be useful in a couple of situations:

- Talking to a version of SQL Server prior to 7.0
- Using OLE DB generic functionality to talk to arbitrary data sources

The connection arguments, except for the provider, are basically the same as for the ADO.NET SQL Server data provider:

```
strConnect = "Provider=SQLOLEDB;Data Source=localhost;" +
             "Initial Catalog=ADONetSamples;UID=sa;PWD=";
```

This will create a connection to the same database we have been using via the ADO.NET SQL Server data provider.

9.3.3   Oracle

You may notice that two different Oracle data providers are listed in table 9.2: one provided by Microsoft, and one provided by Oracle. Each has pluses and minuses. The Microsoft data provider has support for more features and behaves more like the SQL Server data provider. The Oracle data provider supports Oracle-specific capabilities better and *theoretically* performs better. To be honest, I haven't seen a huge difference in performance between the two.

Whichever provider you choose, the notation is quite similar, aside from the provider. Here is the format for the Microsoft provider:

```
strConnect = "Provider= MSDAORA;Data Source=ADONETOR;" +
             "User ID=scott;Password=tiger";
```

And here is the format for the Oracle provider:

```
strConnect = "Provider= OraOLEDB.Oracle;Data Source=ADONETOR;" +
             "User ID=scott;Password=tiger";
```

The `Data Source` in both cases refers either to the name of a server or to a value in a text file called tnsnames.ora. This file specifies how the data source maps to a particular database. Here is the entry for ADONETOR in the tnsnames.ora file on my machine (Oracle is installed locally):

```
ADONETOR =
  (DESCRIPTION =
    (ADDRESS_LIST =
      (ADDRESS = (PROTOCOL = TCP)(HOST = arf733)(PORT = 1521))
    )
    (CONNECT_DATA =
      (SERVICE_NAME = ADONETOR)
    )
  )
```

The user ID and password shown (scott and tiger) are one of the default accounts for an Oracle sample database. As with the user ID *sa* on SQL Server with no password, no one has bothered to remove the default scott/tiger values for a huge number of Oracle databases out in the world. (It's a good thing to know if you feel like hacking into some web sites.) Seriously, though, if you are planning to expose your database to the outside world, don't forget to remove those defaults!

9.3.4   Data Shaping

Data Shaping is a Microsoft concept that allows data to be retrieved from a relational database but be returned as a hierarchy (like a tree). For example, if a teacher teaches a number of classes, the list of classes might be represented as a single item for each teacher that contains multiple items:

Teacher	Classes
Ms. Fortune	Basket Weaving
	Chemistry
Mr. Kriefels	Physics
	Geometry

Notice how there are multiple rows in the Classes column for each row in the Teacher column. Of course, you can get this information using a join, but you end up with repeated information. You can also pull back the data using multiple queries and combine the results in memory, or do a query as you move to each new row. In fact, that is all the Data Shaping provider does, but it saves your having to do all of the work yourself.

The connection string for the Data Shaping provider is interesting, in that you have to specify an additional provider for the actual location of the data:

```
string strConnect = "Provider=MSDataShape;Data Provider=SQLOLEDB;" +
    "Data Source=localhost;Initial Catalog=ADONetSamples;user id=sa";
```

The provider being specified is for the Data Shaping service. It then uses the value specified in the `Data Provider` parameter to connect to the source of the data—in this case, the SQL Server OLE DB provider. The rest of the information should look familiar; it is the information required to connect to SQL Server.

Data Shaping is somewhat complicated and beyond the scope of this book. However, an example of reading hierarchical data with the Data Shaping provider appears in chapter 11.

9.3.5   ODBC

Most anyone who has worked with OLE DB is aware that there is an OLE DB provider that allows you to talk to ODBC. You might think you could just specify the appropriate provider (MSDASQL) and connect to the huge number of existing ODBC drivers.

However, this is not the case. ADO.NET will throw an exception if you attempt to use this driver. Because of the way ODBC works, there were problems with allowing access to ODBC via OLE DB from ADO.NET.[1] Although Microsoft could have fixed these problems, it decided to provide an ODBC data provider.

This is a much better solution. ODBC is extremely fast (one reason you might choose to use it), but adding the OLE DB provider layer slows it down and adds unnecessary complexity. Unfortunately, Microsoft did not have time to include the ODBC data provider in the first version of .NET. It did, however, ship the data provider separately very soon after .NET shipped. Appendix A talks about the installation and use of this data provider.

9.4   SUMMARY

For a relatively small class, there is a lot to know about connections and connection strings. Much of the time you can get by knowing just the basics about connections, but determining how to get connected can frequently be time consuming.

There is much more to the connection classes, as you will discover if you are brave enough to read appendix B; it provides details about all the properties and methods of the classes, as well as examples of using the various events they expose.

It is usually fairly easy to connect to SQL Server once you know where the database is located and how to connect. OLE DB, however, can get quite complicated, because every provider has a different approach to defining connection information. If you were already talking to OLE DB before moving to .NET, though, then you should be able to use the same connection information.

Chapter 10 talks about the command classes and shows some of the various different ways of executing commands.

---

[1] Aren't acronyms wonderful?

C H A P T E R   1 0

Command classes

Chapter 9 spent a lot of time talking about connecting to a data source. Although that is certainly a critical step, it isn't very useful by itself—unless you can do something with that connection. That is where the command classes come in. Virtually all work you do with a data source is done directly or indirectly via the use of a command object.

You have already seen several examples of the use of a command object in previous chapters. This chapter will extend these examples to show some other ways you can use command objects. If you want even more detail, appendix C provides in-depth coverage of all the methods and properties of the command classes.

Several aspects of the command classes will *not* be covered in detail in this chapter because they are large enough topics to justify being broken out into their own chapters. These topics are parameters, which are covered in chapters 12 and 13, and transactions, which are discussed in chapter 14. Technically, they are their own classes and should be covered separately anyway; but they are very much tied to the command objects.

10.1 COMMAND INTERFACES AND IMPLEMENTATIONS

The command object, as the name implies, is the way commands are sent to the database. When you are trying to do basic database operations, execute stored procedures, retrieve data, fill DataSets, and so forth, you will end up using a command object, either directly or indirectly.

As with most of the database objects, a base interface defines common functionality, and there's an implementation within each data provider (table 10.1).

Table 10.1   Command implementations

Class	Provider	Interface
SqlCommand	SQL Server	IDbCommand
OleDbCommand	OLE DB	IDbCommand

The functionality between the two different classes is very similar, although there are differences in the SQL that each can handle—in fact, with the OLE DB data provider, the legal SQL can differ from engine to engine.

10.2 COMMANDTEXT AND COMMANDTYPE

The CommandText property on the command objects is by far their most important property, literally specifying what a command is supposed to do. By default it contains a string (usually SQL) to execute. However, it can also do a couple of other things, controlled by the CommandType property. The CommandType has three legal values, each with its own meaning:

- Text—When the CommandType is set to Text (the default), it indicates that the CommandText contains some commands to be executed. The next section talks about legal command text, but the following example shows a simple use:

```
SqlCommand comm = new SqlCommand(conn);
comm.CommandType = CommandType.Text;
comm.CommandText = "Update Teachers Set ClassRoom='G2' " +
                   " WHERE TeacherID=2";
```

- StoredProcedure—If the CommandType is set to StoredProcedure, then the CommandText contains the name of a stored procedure to execute. Not all engines support this syntax. Using stored procedures is discussed in chapter 13, but the following simple example shows the usage:

```
SqlCommand comm = new SqlCommand(conn);
comm.CommandType = CommandType.StoredProcedure;
comm.CommandText = "GetTeacher";
```

- `TableDirect`—This special mode is supported only by the OLE DB data provider. It requests all data from a particular table, where the `CommandText` specifies the name of the table. It is the equivalent of leaving the `CommandType` set to `Text` and doing a `SELECT * FROM sometable`. The following code shows an example:

```
OleDbCommand comm = new OleDbCommand(conn);
comm.CommandType = CommandType.TableDirect;
comm.CommandText = "Teachers";
```

Unless you work extensively with stored procedures, most of the time the default value of `Text` will be appropriate. The next section talks about options for command text.

10.2.1 Command text

When the command type is set to `Text`, the command text can be set to any legal command string for the underlying data source. Usually this string will be SQL, although it might be something special for very specialized data sources. If it is SQL, then it could be one of the standard DML (Data Manipulation Language) commands, such as:

```
SELECT * FROM MyTable
INSERT INTO MyTable (Field1,Field2) VALUES ('Bob',1)
UPDATE MyTable SET Field1='Fred' WHERE Field2=1
DELETE FROM MyTable WHERE Field1='Bob'
```

These commands are similar from database to database, based on the SQL standards. There are, however, some minor differences. For example, the format for an outer join differs from engine to engine. The format for SQL Server is as follows:

```
SELECT Field1,Field2 FROM MyTable1,MyTable2 WHERE
MyTable1.Field3 *= MyTable2.Field3
```

And here's the format for Oracle:

```
SELECT Field1,Field2 FROM MyTable1,MyTable2 WHERE
MyTable1.Field3 = MyTable2.Field3 (+)
```

OUTER JOIN A type of join where one side of the join always appears, even if no records meet the join expression.

When two tables are joined together through a normal join statement, the result is *multiplicative*—that is, all matching columns are joined in all combinations:

Student	
Name	**StudentID**
Bob	1
Fred	2

Languages	
Language	**StudentID**
English	1
French	1

The results of a standard join would be:

StudentID	Name	Language
1	Bob	English
1	Bob	French

There are two interesting things about the result. First, the first record of student Bob is repeated twice, because the Student ID 1 appears twice in the join; the second record (Fred) never appears, because there is no match in the second table. If, however, an outer join is used, then all the values will appear from either the first table specified (a left outer join) or the second table specified (a right outer join):

StudentID	Name	Language
1	Bob	English
1	Bob	French
2	Fred	(null)

We still get the two rows for each combination of the first row, but now we also get an instance of the second row from the first table. Of course, the Language field is null for that row because there is no matching row in the second table.

For the specific details of the appropriate syntax for your database engine, you will need to refer to the appropriate documentation. This is just a warning that the same SQL will not always transparently transfer.

Commands can also send DDL (Data Definition Language) to the database:

```
CREATE TABLE MyTable (Field1 VARCHAR(15), Field2 INTEGER)
DROP TABLE MyTable
ALTER TABLE MyTable ADD Field3 VARCHAR(20)
```

These types of statements are usually quite different from engine to engine, if they are even present.

You can also call stored procedures. When you do this, you can specify the command type to be StoredProcedure. This tells the provider that the CommandText contains nothing more than the name of a stored procedure. You can also use the data provider–specific syntax for calling a stored procedure, and leave the CommandType set to Text. For example, using the Oracle provider, you could send the following text:

```
BEGIN someprocedure(42); END;
```

This technique is important, because the Oracle OLE DB provider does not support calling stored procedures directly using the StoredProcedure value for CommandText, although the Microsoft provider does.

10.3 EXECUTE METHODS ON COMMANDS

By far the most important methods on the command objects are the methods for executing the command. There are a number of different execute methods, although not all of them are available in both data providers. You have already seen `ExecuteNonQuery()` and `ExecuteReader()` in previous examples. Table 10.2 shows all the available execute methods.

Table 10.2 Execute methods

Execute method	Purpose
ExecuteNonQuery	This execute method is used for executing statements that are not expected to return results, such as an Insert or an Update. This method usually returns the number of rows that were changed by the statement, but in some circumstances will only return a nonzero result (usually −1), indicating success.
ExecuteReader	This method is used when a result set is expected back, usually from a Select or a stored procedure. The return value is a DataReader that can be used to step through results.
ExecuteScalar	This method is used when a result is expected—but only a single value (for example, when a Count was selected).
ExecuteXmlReader	(SQL Server only.) SQL Server has the ability to return results as XML. Using the `ExecuteXmlReader` method, the returned results can be put directly into an XML reader that allows easy navigation through the XML.

The following sections provide examples for each of the execute methods.

10.3.1 ExecuteNonQuery example

Any time you want to execute SQL that does *not* return a result set, you can use the `ExecuteNonQuery()` method. It is specifically designed for this purpose. Generally it will return the number of rows affected by executing the SQL, although for some commands it will return a −1 to indicate that something was done.[1]

The following code does a simple insert into the Teachers table using `ExecuteNonQuery()`:

```
public void TestExecuteNonQuery(SqlConnection conn)
{
    string strSQL = "INSERT INTO Teachers"
        + " (TeacherName,Classroom) VALUES ('Mr. Dewitt','D4')";

    SqlCommand comm = new SqlCommand(strSQL,conn);

    int iReturn = comm.ExecuteNonQuery();

    Console.WriteLine("ExecuteNonQuery returned {0}",iReturn);
}
```

---

[1] Specifically, `Insert`, `Update`, and `Delete` will return a row count, whereas all other commands will return −1. Some older engines will also return −1 even for `Inserts`, `Updates`, and `Deletes`.

The output looks like figure 10.1.

**Figure 10.1
Output from the
`ExecuteNonQuery()`
example**

10.3.2   ExecuteReader example

When you want to execute SQL that returns results, you will most often use the
`ExecuteReader()` method, which returns a DataReader for stepping through
results. (The DataReader is a fairly powerful class, and is covered in chapter 11.) The
following rather simple example just selects data from the Teachers table and writes it
out to the console:

```
public void TestExecuteReader(SqlConnection conn)

    string strSQL = "SELECT TeacherName,Classroom,Subject"
                    + " FROM Teachers";

    SqlCommand comm = new SqlCommand(strSQL,conn);

    SqlDataReader reader = comm.ExecuteReader();

    while ( reader.Read() )
    {
       Console.WriteLine( reader.GetString(0) + ", " +
               reader.GetString(1) + ", " +
               reader.GetString(2));
    }

    reader.Close();
```

The output looks like figure 10.2.

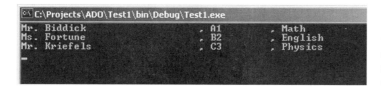

**Figure 10.2
Output from the
`ExecuteReader`
example**

10.3.3   ExecuteScalar example

Sometimes you want to execute SQL that returns a single value. You can use the
`ExecuteReader()` method, but it is a little heavy if you are expecting a single
result. The `ExecuteScalar()` method is specifically provided to handle the situation where you either are expecting one simple result, or don't really care about the
results that are returned as long as *something* is returned.

The following example gets a count of records in the Teachers table and returns a single integer value:

```
public void TestExecuteScalar(SqlConnection conn)
{
    string strSQL = "SELECT COUNT(*) FROM Teachers";
    SqlCommand comm = new SqlCommand(strSQL,conn);

    int iCount = (int)comm.ExecuteScalar();

    Console.WriteLine("ExecuteScalar returned {0}",iCount);
}
```

The out put looks like figure 10.3.

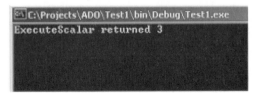

Figure 10.3
Output from the
ExecuteScalar
example

You may have noticed that the result from `ExecuteScalar()` is being typecast to an integer in the example. The actual return type from `ExecuteScalar()` is an object. However, we know that the SQL we are passing will return an integer, because we asked for a count. If we executed SQL that we expected to return, for example, a `DateTime` value (for example, the maximum `DateTime` value from a particular table), then we would typecast the object to a `DateTime`.

If we had no way of knowing the return type, we could always rely on the basic behavior of any object, which always lets us turn a result into a string via the `ToString()` method. Alternatively, we could look at the object's type to determine how to use the value.

10.3.4   ExecuteXmlReader example

The `ExecuteXmlReader()` method only exists on the SQL Server data provider's version of command (SqlCommand) and relies on XML functionality built into SQL Server 2000. Microsoft has gone to considerable lengths to support XML in its products. In fact, with SQL Server, you can read and write data, change schemas, and do a number of other things via XML. (Chapter 30 talks about SQL Server's support for XML.) The following example reads data from SQL Server as XML and then outputs it:

```
using System.Xml;

public void TestExecuteXmlReader(SqlConnection conn)
{
    string strSQL = "SELECT * FROM Teachers FOR XML AUTO";
    SqlCommand comm = new SqlCommand(strSQL,conn);

    XmlReader reader = comm.ExecuteXmlReader();
```

```
        reader.Read();
        while(!reader.EOF)
            Console.WriteLine(reader.ReadOuterXml());

        reader.Close();
    }
```

The using System.Xml directive should really appear above the class, but is shown here to indicate that it must be included to access the XmlReader class.

The output looks like figure 10.4.

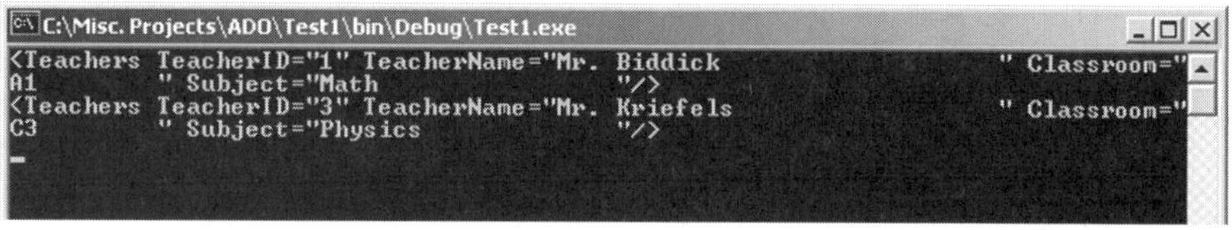

Figure 10.4 Output from the `ExecuteXmlReader` example

In its simplest format, SQL Server returns each field as an XML attribute; but there are other ways in which the data can be returned, which are shown in chapter 30.

10.4 SUMMARY

We have just scratched the surface of the command classes with this chapter; appendix C goes into a lot more depth about the command's methods and properties. Commands are also reliant on some other classes, such as the DataReader (discussed in the next chapter), which allow results to be processed, and Parameters (discussed in chapter 12), which allow for different values to be passed to and from the command.

One thing that is nice about the command classes is the way in which they split up the execution of different types of SQL. For example, you don't have to mess around with a DataReader if you are just executing an Update statement, or go through similar overhead when you are reading XML directly from SQL Server. This not only makes your code significantly cleaner, but allows the writer of the data provider to make the code considerably more efficient.

You will see command objects used in ever-more-complex examples as the book progresses; part 3 shows how they are used in conjunction with the DataSet. Chapter 11 explores the DataReader, which is returned from a call to the command's ExecuteReader() method.

CHAPTER 11

Reading data with the DataReader

ADO.NET has two distinct mechanisms for dealing with result sets of data: the DataSet and the DataReader. A DataSet (discussed in detail in part 3) is a highly flexible class, or rather set of classes, that allows data to be viewed and manipulated in complex ways and later stored back to its source. In comparison, the DataReader is fairly simplistic—it allows data to be read, with no ability for manipulation. In fact, when reading, the data must be read in a forward-only manner—you start at the beginning of the data and move forward one record at a time until you are done.

11.1 WHY USE A DATAREADER?

Why would you use the much simpler DataReader, when you have access to the apparently more functional DataSet? There are a couple of reasons. First, a DataSet doesn't really have the ability to read data—it must be filled with data. You can do so using a DataAdapter, which uses the DataReader to access the data to fill the DataSet. (You will see more on this topic in part 3.)

The second reason is that the DataReader is a much lighter object than a DataSet—a cost is associated with all the added functionality of a DataSet, which may be an issue depending on the type of application you are building. In any case, because of the added costs, the DataReader can be significantly faster than a DataSet; in fact, if you consider that all the work the DataReader might potentially do *must* take place to fill a DataSet, in addition to the work and storage that take place for the DataSet, the DataSet is guaranteed to be slower.

That is not to say you should avoid using the DataSet. If you need to manipulate data or transmit it to another tier of your system, the DataSet is an excellent mechanism. However, if you just need to step through a result set of data, the DataReader is definitely the way to go.

Most of the time, you will get a DataReader by calling `ExecuteReader()` on a command object (discussed in the previous chapter). This chapter will concentrate on the different things you can do with a DataReader. For a complete guide to all the properties and methods of the DataReader classes, you can look in appendix D.

11.2   DATAREADER CLASSES AND INTERFACES

Unlike most of the other ADO.NET objects, two interfaces are associated with each DataReader:

- *IDataReader*—This interface is responsible for stepping from record to record and from result set to result set.

- *IDataRecord*—This interface is responsible for accessing the data in the current row.

You usually don't need to worry about which interface contains which methods or properties. Even if you are writing generic code that passes the interface around, you do not need to worry about casting back and forth between the interfaces. The IDataReader interface is derived from the IDataRecord interface, so you can call any IDataRecord methods on an IDataReader reference. Of course, if you pass an IDataRecord interface reference, you will have to typecast it to an IDataReader interface if you need to call any IDataReader methods.

Table 11.1 shows the DataReader classes and interfaces.

Table 11.1   DataReader implementations and interfaces

Class	Provider	Interface
SqlDataReader	SQL Server	IDataReader, IDataRecord
OleDbDataReader	OLE DB	IDataReader, IDataRecord

11.3 EFFICIENCY

The methods on a DataReader make it appear as though one row at a time is read from the database and transferred to the client. In practice, though, that process would be inefficient. The DataReaders bring over data in efficient lumps, based on the network packet size and other factors. However, the DataReader makes it appear as though only one row is sent at a time. The nice thing about this approach is that the underlying code is efficient, but the DataReader is still very easy to use (see figure 11.1).

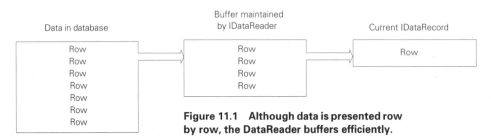

Figure 11.1   Although data is presented row by row, the DataReader buffers efficiently.

It is also possible that less than an entire row might be brought over at a time. For example, imagine a situation where a column contains a very large picture as binary data. Although you can have the DataReader read it in its entirety, there are methods that allow for the image to be read in pieces—doing so would allow the image to begin to be displayed before the whole image was retrieved from the server.

11.4 GETTING DATA FROM A READER

Many different methods let you access data from a reader. If you already know the structure, the Get methods are probably the best choice, because they automatically return the data as the appropriate data type:

```
public void DisplayReaderResults(IDataReader reader)
{
    while(reader.Read())
    {
        Console.WriteLine("Text field: {0}",reader.GetString(0));
        Console.WriteLine("Number field: {1}",reader.GetInt32(1));
        Console.WriteLine("DateTime fields: {2}",reader.GetDateTime(2));
    }
}
```

There are a large number of Get methods, providing support for virtually every data type. A complete list of all the Get methods is shown in appendix D.

You can also access the data from a reader somewhat more generically, or reference fields by name. An *indexer* property on the DataReader allows you to access the fields as though the reader was an array:

```
reader[1]   // Second column (0-based)
```

or

```
reader["TeacherName"]
```

One downside to this approach is that the data is returned as an object, so you will need to typecast if you want to use the data as a native type:

```
int iPeriod = (int)reader["Period"];
```

Of course, if you are just planning to output the data as a string anyway, then an object is fine—you can use the ToString() method.

The named indexer is very handy; but it is also a fraction slower than the numeric access method, because a lookup is required. In most cases this difference will not matter, but if performance is very important, you can determine the ordinal position of the column once and then use the position from that point forward:

```
int iTeacherPos = reader.GetOrdinal("TeacherName");
string strTeacherName = reader[iTeacherPos].ToString();
```

You can also get the name of a field from its position—and, while you are at it, the underlying .NET data type of the field and the data type being used by the database:

```
string strFieldName = reader.GetName(1);
Type typeField = reader.GetFieldType(1);
string strDatabaseType = reader.GetDataTypeName(1);
```

This information may or may not be useful, depending on your application. The example in listing 11.1 retrieves the data from the Teachers table using indexers, and displays some extra info about each row.

Listing 11.1 Retrieving data and information about the data

```
public void TestDataReaderAccess(IDbConnection conn)
{
    // Select some data
    string strSQL = "SELECT * FROM Teachers";
    IDbCommand comm = conn.CreateCommand();
    comm.CommandText = strSQL;
    comm.CommandType = CommandType.Text;

    // Get the reader
    IDataReader reader = comm.ExecuteReader();          ❶ Retrieve reader

    // Output the column info
    int iColumnCount = reader.FieldCount;
    Console.WriteLine("Field name\t.NET type\tDatabase type");
    Console.WriteLine("----------\t---------\t-------------");
    for(int i = 0;i < iColumnCount;i++)
    {
        Console.WriteLine("{0}\t{1}\t{2}",
                    reader.GetName(i).PadRight(10),          ❷ Write out info
                    reader.GetFieldType(i).ToString(),         about column
                    reader.GetDataTypeName(i));
    }
```

```
          Console.WriteLine("");

          // Output the data
          Console.WriteLine("Data");
          Console.WriteLine("----");
          while (reader.Read())
          {
             for(int i = 0;i < iColumnCount;i++)
             {
                if(i > 0)
                   Console.Write(", ");
                Console.Write(reader[i].ToString().Trim());       ❸ Retrieve data
             }                                                       from column
             Console.WriteLine("");
          }
          Console.WriteLine("");

          //always call Close when done reading.
          reader.Close();
       }
```

❶ Notice that this example uses the generic version of the reader. This code will work no matter what type of connection we pass (assuming there is a table called Teachers!).

   This code returns a pointer to an `IDataReader`. However, we can call any methods on `IDataRecord` as well, because `IDataReader` is derived from `IData-Record`.

❷ Aside from some fancy formatting (wow, tabs—I feel like I'm back in the 70s. Groovy!), this code uses the methods just described to access the data about the columns. It also uses the `FieldCount` property to determine how many columns are in the result set.

❸ Previous examples used the `GetValue()` method to retrieve the data from a column as an object. There is little difference here, except that we use the indexer, which also returns an object. Because all objects implement `ToString()`, we can always convert to a string and then call `Trim()` to get rid of spaces to improve the output.

   The output is in figure 11.2. Isn't it pretty? I always thought that GUIs were overrated!

```
C:\Projects\ADO\Test1\bin\Debug\Test1.exe

Field name        .NET type           Database type
----------        ---------           -------------
TeacherID         System.Int32        int
TeacherName       System.String       char
Classroom         System.String       char
Subject           System.String       char

Data
----
1, Mr. Biddick, G9, Math
2, Ms. Fortune, A1, English
3, Mr. Kriefels, C3, Physics
```

Figure 11.2
Output from
listing 11.1

CHAPTER 11   READING DATA WITH THE DATAREADER

11.5 READING MULTIPLE RESULT SETS

In all the examples you have seen so far, only a single result set has been returned from any given command. Ninety-nine percent of the time, this is what you would expect. However, in some cases you might get multiple return result sets from a single command:

- *Batch SQL*—Some engines allow you to combine multiple statements as a single command.

- *Stored procedures*—A stored procedure can return any number of sets of results.

Why would you want to return multiple result sets? Doing so can be more efficient in many cases. First, you are sending only one command to the engine; and second, the results can be combined when returned, which can also be more efficient (especially if the result sets are small). Remember that in multi-tier programming, minimizing round trips is one of the keys to efficiency.[1]

The example in listing 11.2 uses a stored procedure to retrieve multiple data sets. The `GetClassesAndTeachers` stored procedure does two selects.

Listing 11.2   Using a reader with multiple result sets

```
public void DoubleSelect(SqlConnection conn)
{
    string strSQL = "GetClassesAndTeachers";
    SqlCommand comm = new SqlCommand(strSQL,conn);
    comm.CommandType = CommandType.StoredProcedure;      ❶ Execute stored
                                                            procedure

    SqlDataReader reader = comm.ExecuteReader();

    do
    {
        int iCount = reader.FieldCount;          ❷ Data reading loop
        while(reader.Read())
        {
            for(int i = 0;i < iCount;i++)
            {
                if(i > 0)       Console.Write(", ");
                Console.Write(reader.GetValue(i).ToString().Trim());
            }
            Console.WriteLine("");
        }
        Console.WriteLine("-----");
    } while (reader.NextResult());               ❸ NextResult

    reader.Close();
}
```

---

[1] This is also the biggest reason why it is so hard to convert client/server applications to three-tier applications. Although this rule applies to client/server coding, it is seldom applied!

1 Note that the command type has been set to `StoredProcedure`, because we are executing a stored procedure. In fact, this value does not matter with SQL Server—the command would be executed even if the type were set to `Text`, but there are advantages to letting the provider know that a stored procedure is being executed (as discussed in chapter 13).

2 As with all the previous DataReader examples, this loop steps through each row and writes out data. There is also a little formatting code to make the output more readable.

3 This is the special handling for multiple results. Calling `NextResult()` moves the reader onto the next result set if there is one. Note that this call is done inside a `do` loop, rather than a `while` loop, as with the `Read()` command. We do so because `NextResult()` works slightly differently than `Read()`. The first call to `Read()` moves the reader to the first row of data, whereas the reader is automatically positioned on the first result set.

Although this behavior is slightly inconsistent, it is very convenient. It is rare for multiple result sets to be returned. If the reader started life before the first result set, every piece of code using a reader would end up having to call `NextResult()` at least once, even though few would care about the call. However, we can conveniently use the reader within a `while` loop. If it started on the first row, additional logic would have to be put in place every time to see if the result set was empty before starting a loop.

11.5.1 Example output

The stored procedure does two selects—one from the Classes table and one from the Teachers table. Figure 11.3 shows the output from the code.

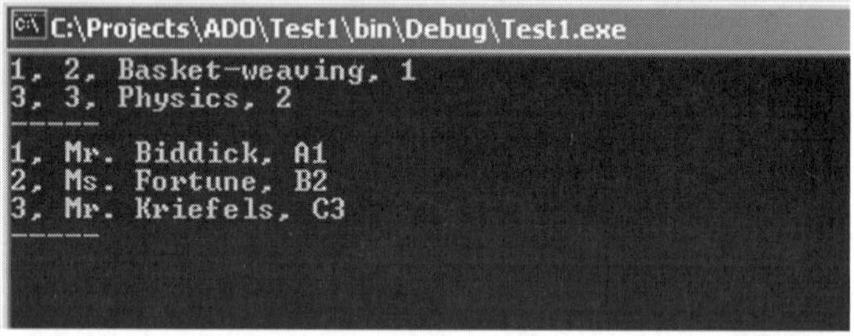

**Figure 11.3
Output from
listing 11.2**

11.6 *READING LARGE DATA*

One of the earlier sections of this chapter talked about the fact that the DataReader can buffer data to make it more efficient, by reading in more data than was requested. What happens, though, when you need to read in a *lot* of data? For example, imagine reading in a picture or a very large description that contains megabytes of data. In such cases, you don't want to read in more data—you want to read in less, perhaps to display part of the data, or perhaps to provide a mechanism for canceling.

The data record provides a couple of methods for doing just that—one for reading in large string data, GetChars(), and one for reading in large binary data, Get-Bytes() (not to be confused with the GetByte() and GetChar() methods that return a single byte or a single character, respectively).

The example in listing 11.3 shows the use of the GetChars() method to read in the data from a large text field in 8K chunks, allowing them to be written out in pieces. The Description field in the example just contains the numbers from 1 to 100,000 as a string. The GetBytes() method works more or less the same way. I won't show the output from this method, because it would take up a lot of pages.[2]

Listing 11.3 Reading large data in pieces

```
public void TestReadPieces(SqlConnection conn)
{
    string strSQL = "SELECT Name,Phone,Description FROM LargeDataTest";

    SqlCommand comm = new SqlCommand(strSQL,conn);

    SqlDataReader reader = comm.ExecuteReader();

    while(reader.Read())
    {
        Console.WriteLine("Name = {0}",reader.GetString(0));
        Console.WriteLine("Phone = {0}",reader.GetString(1));
        Console.Write("Description = ");

        // Read the description in 8K chunks
        int iChunk = 8192;
        char[] buffer = new char[iChunk];       ❶ Set up buffer
        long lPos = 0;
        long lRead = 0;
        while(true)
        {
            lRead = reader.GetChars(2,lPos,buffer,0,iChunk);   ❷ Get part
            if(lRead > 0)       // we read some data                of data
            {
                Console.Write(buffer);
                lPos += lRead;
            }

            if(lRead < iChunk) // No more data to read    ❸ Exit loop
                break;
        }
        Console.WriteLine("");
    }
}
```

❶ This code sets up an 8K character buffer, which will be used to hold each chunk of data. We created the buffer inside the while loop because doing so makes the example easier to read, and because we know there is only one row in the result set. Obviously, in a real-world case, you would create the buffer outside the loop.

_____

[2] Hmm—a bigger book might make the publisher happy . . .

❷ This call to GetChars() specifies the next chunk of the data to read. The arguments passed here include the position in the data that is desired and the location in the buffer where the data should be placed, as well as the maximum amount of data to read.

We could do several different things here. We could create a huge buffer capable of holding all the data, and just fill it in pieces; or we could skip over the beginning of the buffer and read a chunk from the end. For the purpose of the example, though, the code just reads a chunk at a time and writes it to the console.

You may wonder how the information is brought over from the server when this method is used. That is purely at the discretion of the data provider—it could be reading significantly larger chunks at a time, or it could wait until you ask for data before retrieving it. In the worst case, the entire contents of the column would be read over before filling the first request; this approach would negate the benefits of the call.

❸ Each time the GetChars() method is called, it returns the number of characters that were read. This should always be the same number as the quantity you requested (8,192), until the end of the data is reached. At this point, however many characters are left will be read, and the number of characters left will be less than requested. We use this fact to know when to jump out of our loop.

11.7 WRITING LARGE DATA

The previous example showed how to read large amounts of data, but it would also be nice to know how to *write* large data back to the database. This topic has little to do with the DataReader, but because we are talking about large data, it seems like a reasonable detour.

You can use a couple of different approaches to insert large data. You *can* build an SQL statement that includes the data, even if that data is several megabytes. That technique will work, although it is painful, because you have to create a string large enough to hold all of the data.

A more efficient approach is to use parameters, which are the topic of chapter 12. You can create a single parameter and store the data to that parameter, or you can do some simple SQL to write the data in a number of chunks:

```
UPDATE LargeDataTest SET Description=Description+@Chunk
     WHERE Name=@Name
```

This method has a lot of drawbacks, including the amount of work that needs to be done by the server and its inappropriateness for use with binary data (you can't just add strings of bytes). If you are using SQL Server, you can use the UPDATETEXT method, which is specifically designed for setting large text.

To use UPDATETEXT, you must first have a row into which the data can be inserted, and you must retrieve a reference to the text or data to update. The code in listing 11.4 shows how to accomplish this; but I should warn you that it is quite complex and relies heavily on the use of parameters, which will not be discussed until the next chapter.

Listing 11.4 Inserting large data into SQL Server

```
public void TestMemoPiecesInsertSQL(SqlConnection conn)
{
    // First insert the record                                    ❶ Insert data
    string strInsert = "INSERT INTO LargeDataTest"
               + " (Name,Phone,Description) "
               + " Values ('Fred','(123) 456-7890','A')";
    SqlCommand comm1 = new SqlCommand(strInsert,conn);
    comm1.ExecuteNonQuery();


    // Now get the reference to the text                          ❷ Get
    // The value will be stored in the paramPointer parameter        pointer
                                                                     to text
    string strRetrieve = "SELECT @Pointer = TEXTPTR(Description)"
                  + "FROM LargeDataTest WHERE Name='Fred'";
    SqlCommand comm2 = new SqlCommand(strRetrieve,conn);
    SqlParameter paramPointer =
       comm2.Parameters.Add("@Pointer",SqlDbType.Binary,16);
    paramPointer.Direction = ParameterDirection.Output;
    comm2.ExecuteNonQuery();

    // Create statement for doing the update
    // that actually puts in the data
    string strUpdate =
       "UPDATETEXT LargeDataTest.Description @Pointer @Offset 0 @Data";
    SqlCommand comm3 = new SqlCommand(strUpdate,conn);
    SqlParameter paramUpdatePointer =
       comm3.Parameters.Add("@Pointer",SqlDbType.Binary, 16);
    SqlParameter paramOffset =
       comm3.Parameters.Add("@Offset",SqlDbType.Int);        Build update ❸
    SqlParameter paramData =                                   statement
       comm3.Parameters.Add("@Data",SqlDbType.Text,1000);

    // Point the text pointer param to the retrieved pointer
    paramUpdatePointer.Value = paramPointer.Value;
                                                   ❹ Set pointer data

    // Put the data into the record in chunks
    int iOffset = 0;                                           ❺ Set data
    string strText;
    for(int i = 1;i < 26;i++)
    {
        strText = new String(Convert.ToChar(i+64),1000);
        paramOffset.Value = iOffset;
        paramData.Value = strText;
        comm3.ExecuteNonQuery();
        iOffset += 1000;
    }
}
```

❶ Nothing unusual here—this code inserts the data. We're using Name as a unique identifier, which simplifies the example but is not really reliable (we should probably use the identity column or other unique identifier approach). One thing is special, though—some data (the letter *A*) goes into the large text field; something must be there before UPDATETEXT will work.

❷ In order for UPDATETEXT to work, we need SQL Server to give us a pointer to the text on the server. This is done using the TEXTPTR function, which will return a 16-byte pointer. We are using an out parameter to retrieve the value; don't worry about it—I discuss out parameters in chapter 12.

It is important, though, that the where clause limit the return to a single value, or we will not get a valid value for the update. If we need to retrieve multiple values, then we cannot use the parameter approach, but must do a query and retrieve the separate values.

❸ The update statement uses the special UPDATETEXT command. The command requires us to provide a number of arguments:

- The table and field to update, separated by a dot (.).
- The pointer we retrieved using TEXTPTR, which we are passing using the @Pointer parameter.
- The point, or offset, within the field where the new data should be placed. We provide this via the use of the @Offset parameter.
- The amount of data at the offset point to be replaced with the new text. In this case, we want to add the data to the end and don't want to overwrite anything, so we pass 0.
- The block of data itself, which we pass with the @Data parameter.

The parameters here are just placeholders. When we set the parameters' values and then execute the command, imagine the parameter in the command being replaced with the value to which we set the parameter. So, suppose we had something that looked like this:

```
SET Value = @SomeParameter
```

We are saying something like @SomeParameter = 3, which at runtime makes the statement become

```
SET Value = 3
```

This is a simplification that I will rectify in the next chapter, but is reasonable for this example.

❹ This code sets the parameter to use in the UPDATETEXT statement, using the value retrieved from the TEXTPTR function.

5 After all that, we can finally add the data. This code steps through all the letters of the alphabet and adds 1,000 of each (1,000 *A*s, 1,000 *B*s, and so forth). The code updates the offset, moving it forward 1,000 characters at a time; sets the data to your string; and then re-executes the UPDATETEXT statement.

11.7.1 Example summary

This is a specialized mechanism, but it can be quite handy if you need it—especially if you are working with binary data rather than text. If you use the code from section 11.5 to read the data, you will see that there is now a record with the Name field set to Fred and about 26K of data.

11.8 READING HIERARCHICAL DATA

Most of the time, the data being retrieved by ADO.NET will be relational—tables that relate to other tables. Sometimes, though, you might want to work with data that is hierarchical (in a tree-type structure). Some specialized databases, such as Raima, are explicitly designed to work in a hierarchical manner. Microsoft also has a special OLE DB provider called Data Shaping that lets data be retrieved from a relational database and then treated as hierarchical.

A more thorough (although still brief) explanation of Data Shaping appears in chapter 9. It allows the results of a query to be returned as a single data column of another query. You can then drill down into that data column and step through the results it contains.

The example in listing 11.5 uses the Microsoft Data Shaping provider to read the list of teachers, along with their classes. The classes are returned as a single data item, which is then read separately. This example demonstrates the use of the Depth property of IDataRecord, as well as the GetData() method. This example is fairly complex, and so it's broken into a number of pieces.

> **Listing 11.5 Reading hierarchical data**

```
public void DoShapeRead()
{
  string strConnect = "Provider=MSDataShape; "        ❶ Connect via
    + "Data Provider=SQLOLEDB;Data Source=localhost;"    Data Shaping
    + "Initial Catalog=ADONetSamples;user id=sa";        provider

  OleDbConnection conn = new OleDbConnection(strConnect);
  conn.Open();
  string strSQL=@"SHAPE
    {SELECT TeacherID,TeacherName,Classroom FROM Teachers}    ❷ Request
    APPEND ({SELECT TeacherID,ClassName,Period FROM Classes}    data
    AS ClassInfo
    RELATE TeacherID TO TeacherID)";

  OleDbCommand comm = new OleDbCommand(strSQL,conn);

  OleDbDataReader reader = comm.ExecuteReader();
  Console.WriteLine("Depth = {0}",reader.Depth);    ❸ Initial depth
```

```
IDataReader reader2 = null;
while(reader.Read())
{
  Console.WriteLine("{0}, {1}",reader.GetString(1).Trim(),        ❹  Basic
                               reader.GetString(2).Trim());           info

  reader2 = reader.GetData(3);    ❺  Access nested data
  while(reader2.Read())
  {
    Console.WriteLine("Depth ({0})-->{1}, {2}",
                      reader2.Depth,
                      reader2.GetString(1).Trim(),        ❻  Nested depth
                      reader2.GetInt32(2));
  }
  reader2.Close();              ❼  Close inner reader
  Console.WriteLine("-----");
}
reader.Close();
}
```

❶ This connection string specifies the Microsoft Data Shaper as the provider and tells the Data Shaper provider how to connect to a different provider (the SQL Server OLE DB provider) to read data. Although this example uses the OLE DB provider to connect to SQL Server, all of the parameters should look familiar from the SQL Server data provider.

❷ Understanding the details of the Microsoft Data Shaper is far beyond the scope of this book. Although the statement does contain some SQL, the format of the command is unique to the data provider. Suffice to say that this command says to read information from all the rows of the Teachers table and to create an additional Class-Info column in each row that contains the associated rows from the Classes table.

One thing you may have noticed is the way in which the string has been specified. Rather than joining together a number of separate strings, the code uses the @ notation, which indicates that all text up to the closing quote should be considered part of the same string, even if it crosses multiple lines.

❸ The reader that is returned from ExecuteReader() is a standard reader, just as in the other examples. Just to prove this, this line prints out the Depth of the reader, which will return 0.

❹ Again, like most other examples, this code prints out a couple of elements from the reader—nothing special.

❺ This line uses the specialized GetData() method on IDataRecord. Instead of returning a simple value, as with most of the Get() methods, it returns a new DataReader that can be used to step through the associated data.

The DataReader could also have been accessed a couple of other ways, such as by referencing the column using the indexer:

```
reader2 = (IDataReader)reader["ClassInfo"];
```

However, the `GetData()` method is built specifically to return a column that contains nested data. Once the reader has been returned, it can be used like our other reader to step through rows and access data.

6 This line prints out the individual rows in our special column. Just to show that this data is nested, it also prints out the `Depth` property, which will be `1`, indicating that this is an additional level deep (the first level is level 0). The Data Shaper allows multiple levels of nesting, so it would be possible for one of the columns in the nested DataReader to contain nested data, and so on.

7 It is very important to close the inner reader before attempting to continue stepping through the data in the outer reader. In fact, if we do not do this, the next time the code attempts to move to a new row in the outer reader, an exception will be thrown.

11.8.1 Example output

All that work seems extreme, but using the Data Shaper can have some significant benefits if it is appropriate. Figure 11.4 shows the output of the code.

```
C:\Projects\ADO\Test1\bin\Debug\Test1.exe
Depth = 0
Mr. Biddick, A1

Ms. Fortune, B2
Depth (1)-->Basket-weaving, 1
Depth (1)-->Chemistry, 3

Mr. Kriefels, C3
Depth (1)-->Physics, 2
Depth (1)-->Geometry, 4
```

Figure 11.4
Output from Listing 11.5: nested data

11.9 SUMMARY

This has been a fairly diverse chapter. A big part of the reason is not the complexity of the DataReader, per se, but the large number of special cases that it must handle. In fact, considering how useful the DataReader is, its interfaces are surprisingly simple to use. In my opinion, this is the hallmark of a good design and good separation of functionality. Although there are more advanced ways of dealing with results (specifically, the DataSet), there are many cases in which the lightweight DataReader is exactly what is needed.

More information about the DataReader didn't make it into this chapter. However, appendix D spends a lot of time with the DataReader, going into every method and property in depth. If you want to learn more, you should read that appendix. However, this chapter has given you enough information to be able to read data in virtually all circumstances. Later, in part 3, you will start working with the DataSet, which indirectly uses the DataReader to load data.

C H A P T E R   1 2

Parameters and binding data

Although chapter 10 went into detail about the command classes, two topics were largely skipped over: transactions (discussed in chapter 14) and parameters, which are the main topic of this and the next chapter.

The term *binding data* is a holdover from ODBC days, and most references just talk about "using parameters." However, the term still has some validity—instead of passing all the information as part of a command, certain parameters are *bound* to variables, which can then be set and changed through multiple calls to the command.

Parameters are also useful when you're working with stored procedures, both to send data to the stored procedure and to retrieve data from a stored procedure. That, in fact, is the major topic of chapter 13. This chapter shows the benefits of using parameters to bind data.

12.1   WHY BIND DATA?

Imagine that we wanted to insert a number of new rows into a table:

	TeacherName	Classroom	Subject
New Row 1	Mrs. Martell	G1	Math
New Row 2	Mrs. Stokesbury	G2	English
New Row 3	Mr. Dewitt	G3	Social Studies

We could build a method that takes an array of Teachers (an object that represents a teacher and their information), and does each insert in turn:

```
public void SaveTeachers(Teacher[] aTeachers, SqlConnection conn)
{
   // Step through each teacher in turn
   foreach(Teacher t in aTeachers)
   {
      string strSQL = "INSERT INTO Teachers "
                 + "(TeacherName,Classroom,Subject) VALUES ('";
      strSQL += t.TeacherName;
      strSQL += "','";
      strSQL += t.Classroom;
      strSQL += "','";
      strSQL += t.Subject;
      strSQL += "')";

      SqlCommand comm = new SqlCommand(strSQL,conn);
      comm.ExecuteNonQuery();
   }
}
```

This technique will work, of course, but it has several obvious problems and one less obvious problem. The obvious ones first:

- Building the string this way is not only inefficient, it is quite ungainly.

- A new command object is created every time you insert a row.

- If any of the properties of the Teacher object contain single quotes, the statement won't be legal SQL.

This next version deals with these issues better:

```
using System.Text;

public void SaveTeachers(Teacher[] aTeachers, SqlConnection conn)
{
   SqlCommand comm = new SqlCommand();
   comm.Connection = conn;

   // Step through each teacher in turn
   foreach(Teacher t in aTeachers)
   {
```

```
StringBuilder sb = new StringBuilder();
sb.AppendFormat("INSERT INTO Teachers"
    + " (TeacherName,Classroom,Subject)"
    + "  VALUES ('{0}','{1}','{2}')",
            t.TeacherName,t.Classroom,t.Subject);

comm.CommandText = sb.ToString();
comm.ExecuteNonQuery();
    }
}
```

(The using System.Text directive should really be at the top of the file, and is there to provide access to the string builder.)

This seems like a much better solution. First, by using a string builder, a single line builds the insert statement in a much more efficient manner. Second, the command object is created outside of the loop and is reused. However, there are still some problems.

We still have the issue with illegal characters in the text. This could be resolved by searching each property for single quotes and escaping the single quotes (putting two single quotes (' ') every place a single quote appeared. Doing so is something of a pain, but a workable solution.

The other problem comes down to the manner in which the database engine executes the statement. The explanation here is based on SQL Server, but most full-blown database engines work in a similar way:

- *Prepare an execution plan*—This step is the equivalent of compiling the SQL statement—taking it from a string and turning it into something the database can execute. Although massive resources at Microsoft and other companies go into making this process as efficient as possible, it still takes time.

- *Execute the execution plan*—This is the equivalent of running the compiled SQL statement.

SQL Server is slightly smarter here—it keeps track of old execution plans for a while, so if the same SQL comes through, it uses the previous execution plan rather than creating a new one. The problem, though, is that the text must be *exactly* the same. So:

```
INSERT INTO MyTable (Field1) VALUES ('Value1')
```

and

```
INSERT INTO MyTable (Field1) VALUES ('Value2')
```

are considered to be completely different statements and must, therefore, have their own execution plans.

It would be nice if there were a way to prepare an execution plan once that could be used multiple times with different arguments, just like a function:

```
DoInsert(string TeacherName,string Classroom,string Subject)
```

You could do this using a stored procedure, but that is a heavy solution if you are planning to use this code only occasionally. You need a way to create such a function on-the-fly. In fact, although the syntax is different, you can do exactly that. The arguments are called *parameters*, and they are used with the command objects.

12.2 USING PARAMETERS

By using parameters, you can pass the identical command text to the database and just change the arguments from call to call, as if you were calling a function. The syntax for doing this, though, differs between the SQL Server and OLE DB data providers.

12.2.1 Parameters with SQL Server

SQL Server parameters must be given names. Unless you are calling stored procedures, though, it does not matter what names you use. The code in listing 12.1 repeats the previous example, but with the use of parameters.

Listing 12.1 Inserting data with parameters

```
public void SaveTeachers(Teacher[] aTeachers, SqlConnection conn)
{
    string strSQL = "INSERT INTO Teachers "
                  + "(TeacherName, Classroom, Subject) VALUES "
                  + " (@TeacherName, @Classroom, @Subject)";      ❶ Insert state-
                                                                      ment with
    SqlCommand comm = new SqlCommand(strSQL, conn);                  parameters

    // Create parameters
    comm.Parameters.Add("@TeacherName", SqlDbType.Char, 30);     ❷ Create
    comm.Parameters.Add("@Classroom", SqlDbType.Char, 10);          parameters
    comm.Parameters.Add("@Subject", SqlDbType.Char, 20);

    // Step through each teacher in turn
    comm.Prepare();                          ❸ Prepare statement
    foreach(Teacher t in aTeachers)
    {
        comm.Parameters["@TeacherName"].Value = t.TeacherName;    ❹ Set values
        comm.Parameters["@Classroom"].Value = t.Classroom;           for para-
        comm.Parameters["@Subject"].Value = t.Subject;               meters

        comm.ExecuteNonQuery();    ❺ Execute statement
    }
}
```

❶ You may have noticed that the code is slightly longer than the previous code. However, it is more efficient. Obviously the benefits are greater when inserting more than three rows!

The only difference between this and any other insert statement is that, instead of values, there are placeholders for the values—@TeacherName, @Classroom, and @Subject. These placeholders will be replaced by the values in the respective parameters by the database. Note that this is done by the database, and not by the data provider. If the data provider replaced the values in the string before sending it to the database, we would be back to square one.

The major advantage of this statement is that it does not change when the values change. Thus an execution plan created for the first row will work for all subsequent rows.

② The command object has a collection of parameters that are associated with the statement. The `Add()` method adds a new parameter to that collection:

- *Parameter name*—The first argument is the name of the parameter, which must match the name of the placeholder in the SQL string.

- *Data type*—The second parameter identifies the data type of the parameter, and can be one of the values from the `SqlDbType` enumeration, which is shown later in this chapter.

- *Length*—The maximum length to be used for any parameter value. This argument only needs to be specified for data types that can have different lengths, such as strings—an integer is always the same size. The maximum length must be specified because the parameter sets up a buffer for the data. If a value comes along that is longer than the length, it will simply be truncated. If no length is specified, then the length of the first value is used, with potentially bad results if the first value is not the longest.

A parameter is created for each of the placeholders in the SQL, and has the same name as the placeholder. This is how SQL Server knows how to associate the values.

③ Calling `Prepare()` tells SQL Server to create an execution plan that will be used multiple times in the future. Although the command will work without calling `Prepare`, it is not as efficient, because the database will see each call to execute as a new command every time.

④ This code simply puts the data into the parameter. The `Parameters` collection can either be indexed by name as in the example

```
comm.Parameters["@TeacherName"].Value = t.TeacherName;
```

or can be indexed by position, which is slightly faster but not quite as readable:

```
comm.Parameters[0].Value = t.TeacherName;
```

We must set a value for every parameter in the string, or the code will throw an exception, indicating that it has a parameter without a value. If we want the value to be `null`, we must use a special notation, described in section 12.3.

⑤ This could be any of the execute statements on the command object, such as `ExecuteReader()`. Parameters can be used with any SQL statement, which may or may not return result sets.

SQL data types

When you create a parameter, one of the pieces of information you must provide is the data type of the data, so the database can set up an appropriate buffer to hold the value. The data type of the parameter must be specified as an SQL Server data type. These values are available in the `SqlDbType` enumeration, which is shown in table 12.1.

This table is included for reference, and makes for fairly boring reading. The information included in the table is the value from the `SqlDbType` enum, the type of associated data, and the .NET data type with which the value is associated.

Table 12.1 `SqlDbType` enumeration

Value	.NET Data Type	Meaning
BigInt	Int64	A 64-bit integer.
Binary	byte[] (byte array)	Fixed length binary data up to 8,000 bytes.
Bit	bool	0 or 1.
Char	string	Fixed-length string up to 8,000 characters. The name of this type is slightly confusing—it does not represent a single character.
DateTime	DateTime	A date/time value.
Decimal	Decimal	A highly accurate number with a decimal component.
Float	double	A floating-point value. Note that this type maps to the `double` data type in C#, not the `float` data type.
Image	byte[] (byte array)	Variable-length binary data up to 2 GB.
Int	Int32 or int	A 32-bit integer.
Money	Decimal	A decimal value that is precise to four decimal places.
NChar	string	Fixed-length Unicode string up to 4,000 characters.
NText	string	Variable-length Unicode string up to 1 GB.
NVarChar	string	Variable length Unicode string up to 4,000 characters.
Real	Single	A floating-point value, smaller than the `Float` type.
SmallDateTime	DateTime	A date/time value limited to a much smaller range of values and less accurate than the `DateTime` type.
SmallInt	Int16	A 16-bit integer.
SmallMoney	Decimal	A monetary amount equally as accurate as `Money`, but with a much smaller range of legal values.
Text	string	A variable-length string up to 2 GB.
Timestamp	DateTime	Another way of storing date/time information, basically as a string—*yyyymmddhhmmss*.
TinyInt	byte	An 8-bit unsigned integer.
UniqueIdentifier	Guid	A GUID value (globally unique identifer).
VarBinary	byte[] (byte array)	Variable-length binary data, up to 8,000 characters.
VarChar	string	Variable-length character data, up to 8,000 characters.
Variant	object	A data type that contain different types of data, including text, numbers, binary data, or a date/time.

A number of these data types might seem redundant, or at least somewhat picky. However, if you think about a database storing a couple of million rows, using a `TinyInt` versus a standard `Int` can make a difference. The following sections explain the reasoning behind some of the different types.

Var types

You may have noticed that there is a `Var` version of many of the data types:

Fixed length	Variable length
Char	VarChar
Binary	VarBinary
NChar	NVarChar

When you use the fixed types on the left, you are guaranteed that the data will take up the same amount of space for each record. If a `Char` field has a length of 100, then storing "Now is the winter of our discontent" and storing "A" will both take up 100 characters.

The `Var` versions, however, take up only as much space as they need to hold the data. There is a little overhead, because the variable-length fields store a pointer to another location where the actual data is stored. This indirection also means that the variable-length versions are a tiny bit slower to retrieve. The trade-off of which data type to use must be based on the type of data to be stored.

Decimal and float types

It might seem that when you store a number in a database, that number will be stored and retrieved. However, this assumption does not take into account the way binary computers store numbers and, specifically, limitations in the way floating-point numbers are stored. The limitations of a floating-point system vary based on the amount of precision to store and special guards that work to deal with problems.

For example, the value 0.1 cannot be directly stored as a floating-point value, and some database engines will take the value 0.1 and return the value 0.09999999999. How big a deal is this? That depends on the data—if you are storing financial information, rounding problems can cause serious consternation. So, SQL Server and .NET have data types that are specifically designed to deal with highly precise numbers. There are two different approaches:

- Store the whole part of the number and the decimal part of the number separately (the approach taken by the `decimal` type)
- Multiply the number by a specific amount, such as 10,000, so that it is a whole number (the approach taken by the `money` data type)

Both of these approaches take up more space than floating-point numbers, but they are more reliable, if that reliability is required.

Extremely large types

SQL Server has support for several data types capable of holding about 2 GB of data per record:

- `Image`
- `NText`
- `Text`

Obviously the database does not set aside 2 GB for each record, whether or not it is used. Instead, these data types store a reference to a variable storage container. SQL Server also has variable-length data fields that can hold up to 8,000 bytes. Given that they are both variable, why are there two sets of data types? Two reasons:

- The shorter data types can be used in indexes, which speed up performance.
- Because the larger data types are assumed to hold more data, they deal with much larger pages of data at a time. A large data type might retrieve 32K of data at a time, which would be quite wasteful if the data is never greater than 8,000 characters.

Unicode data types

SQL Server has three data types specifically made to hold Unicode data:

- `NChar`
- `NText`
- `NVarChar`

Unicode is a text encoding style specifically designed to store data from every language and every alphabet. Over time, three different flavors of Unicode have developed.[1] SQL Server uses a form of Unicode called UCS-2, which uses 2 bytes to store every character. This might explain why the Unicode data types store exactly half the amount of the standard data types.

Windows 2000 & XP, and .NET, use a format of Unicode called UTC-16, which *usually* uses 2 bytes per character, but sometimes uses additional bytes to handle a larger range of characters.

Normally, you don't need to worry about the overhead of storing Unicode characters. But if you are working in Japanese, Vietnamese, Kanji, or several other Asian languages, you may need to use these data types.

12.2.2   Parameters with the OLE DB data provider

Although the concepts for using parameters are basically the same for SQL Server and OLE DB, there are a couple of important differences. The code in listing 12.2 does exactly the same thing as the SQL Server example, but it uses the OLE DB notation.

---

[1] Other formats are UTC-8, which uses between 1 and 4 bytes for each character, and UTC-32, which uses 4 bytes for every character.

Listing 12.2   OLE DB Parameter binding example

```
public void SaveTeachersOleDb(Teacher[] aTeachers,
                             OleDbConnection conn)
{
    string strSQL = "INSERT INTO Teachers "
            + "(TeacherName,Classroom,Subject) VALUES (?,?,?)";

    OleDbCommand comm = new OleDbCommand(strSQL,conn);

    // Create parameters
    comm.Parameters.Add("TeacherName",OleDbType.Char,30);
    comm.Parameters.Add("Classroom",OleDbType.Char,10);
    comm.Parameters.Add("Subject",OleDbType.Char,20);

    // Step through each teacher in turn
    comm.Prepare();
    foreach(Teacher t in aTeachers)
    {
        comm.Parameters[0].Value = t.TeacherName;
        comm.Parameters[1].Value = t.Classroom;
        comm.Parameters[2].Value = t.Subject;

        comm.ExecuteNonQuery();
    }
}
```

1 Place-holders

2 Create parameters

1 This example is almost exactly the same as for SQL Server, so I am only highlighting the differences. Unlike the SQL Server placeholders, OLE DB placeholders are not named. Instead, a question mark is used to indicate the placement of the argument. When the engine needs to match values to parameters, it does so positionally—the first parameter goes to the first question mark, and so on.

2 Even though the placeholders do not have names, the parameter collection requires a name to be specified for each parameter—this is done to make the ParametersCollection interface consistent between the providers. There is some value to using logical names, because you can refer to the parameter by that name. In the example, though, the actual values are set using the parameter's position in the collection.

OleDbType values

The data types for parameters are also different from SQL Server, although they are quite similar. The legal values are stored in an enumeration called OleDbType. The values are shown in table 12.2, along with a description and the .NET data type to which the OleDbType can be associated. Again, you should just skim this chart—it is here for reference.

Table 12.2   OleDbType enumeration

Value	.NET Data Type	Meaning
BigInt	Int64	A 64-bit integer.
Binary	byte[] (byte array)	A sequence of bytes.
Boolean	bool	A Boolean true/false value.
BSTR	string	A Unicode string.
Char	string	A string. Note that Char refers to a string and not a single character.
Currency	Decimal	A monetary amount accurate to 4 decimal places.
Date	DateTime	A date/time value.
DBDate	DateTime	A date only.
DBTime	TimeSpan	A time only.
DBTimeStamp	DateTime	A date and time stored as a string.
Decimal	Decimal	An accurate decimal value.
Double	double	A floating-point number.
Empty	n.a.	A null value.
Error	Exception	An error code.
Filetime	DateTime	Another date/time value, which is very accurate but has a smaller range than Date.
Guid	Guid	A GUID value.
IDispatch	object	A pointer to an OLE Automation object. ADO.NET does not currently support this type, but it is included in the enum for completeness.
Integer	Int32 or int	A 32-bit integer.
IUnknown	object	A pointer to a COM object. ADO.NET does not currently support this type, but it is included in the enum for completeness.
LongVarBinary	byte[] (byte array)	A large, variable-length sequence of bytes.
LongVarChar	string	A large, variable-length sequence of characters.
LongVarWChar	string	A large, variable-length sequence of Unicode characters.
Numeric	Decimal	An accurate decimal value type.
PropVariant	object	An arbitrary type. In theory, any object could be stored here, but in practice it is limited to a set of basic types.
Single	Single	A floating-point value, smaller than a double.
SmallInt	Int16	A 16-bit integer.
TinyInt	SByte	An 8-bit integer.
UnsignedBigInt	UInt64	A 64-bit integer that only allows positive values.
UnsignedInt	UInt32	A 32-bit integer that only allows positive values.
UnsignedSmallInt	UInt16	A 16-bit integer that only allows positive values.
UnsignedTinyInt	byte	An 8-bit integer that only allows positive values.

continued on next page

Table 12.2   OleDbType enumeration *(continued)*

Value	.NET Data Type	Meaning
VarBinary	byte[] (byte array)	A variable-length sequence of bytes, limited in size based on the provider.
VarChar	string	A variable-length sequence of characters, limited in size based on the provider.
Variant	object	A special type that can hold a string, number, date/time, or binary data.
VarNumeric	Decimal	A variable-length numeric value.
VarWChar	string	A variable-length sequence of Unicode characters.
WChar	string	A fixed-length sequence of Unicode characters.

The first thing you may notice is that there are quite a few more data types here than for SQL Server—that is the case because the SQL Server list only has to worry about types used by SQL Server, whereas the OLE DB list must take into account any possible types used by *any* OLE DB data provider.

Another difference is that there is no guaranteed one-to-one mapping between types. Because the OLE DB types must cover so many types, they are somewhat more generic. So, for example, the LongVarChar type might map to Text.

Finally, the allowed size for each data type with SQL Server is well known. With OLE DB, it can vary depending on the underlying provider. You will need to look in the documentation for your database vendor in order to determine the most appropriate data types to use.

12.3   *WORKING WITH NULL VALUES*

A null value in a field indicates that no value has been set for that field—this is different from an empty string or a numeric field containing 0. It means there is no value at all. Nulls are something of a nuisance to work with, because they can cause problems with indexes and queries, but sometimes they are necessary.

In SQL Server (and some other engines), you can specify a null value directly in SQL:

```
UPDATE MyTable SET Field1=NULL WHERE Field2='Value'
```

The special value NULL is used here. When binding data, though, a null must be handled a little differently. The example in listing 12.3 is more or less the same SQL Server binding example used earlier, except that a null value is now handled for the Subject.

Listing 12.3   Binding null values

```
public void SaveTeachers(Teacher[] aTeachers,SqlConnection conn)
{
    string strSQL = @"INSERT INTO Teachers
                    (TeacherName,Classroom,Subject) VALUES
                        (@TeacherName,@Classroom,@Subject)";

    SqlCommand comm = new SqlCommand(strSQL,conn);
```

```
// Create parameters
comm.Parameters.Add("@TeacherName",SqlDbType.Char,30);
comm.Parameters.Add("@Classroom",SqlDbType.Char,10);
comm.Parameters.Add("@Subject",SqlDbType.Char,20);
comm.Parameters["@Subject"].IsNullable = true;         ❶ Specify that
                                                          column
                                                          allows null
// Step through each teacher in turn
comm.Prepare();
foreach(Teacher t in aTeachers)
{
   comm.Parameters["@TeacherName"].Value = t.TeacherName;
   comm.Parameters["@Classroom"].Value = t.Classroom;
   if(t.Subject == null)                               ❷ Use DBNull.Value
comm.Parameters["@Subject"].Value = DBNull.Value;
   else
      comm.Parameters["@Subject"].Value = t.Subject;

   comm.ExecuteNonQuery();
}
}
```

❶ It is a good idea to make sure the parameter knows to accept null values, although this is not, strictly speaking, required with SQL Server. Other data providers might be more fussy.

❷ This is a special value specifically provided to specify a null value for a field. We cannot simply set the `Value` property to `null`, or we will receive an error stating that the parameter has not been set.

This same approach will work with OLE DB (for once there is no special value); `DBNull.Value` can be used with both SQL Server and OLE DB.

12.4   WORKING WITH UNICODE TYPES

Because .NET uses Unicode all the way through, it is very easy to work with Unicode data types. The string object can hold Unicode characters without any special handling on your part. All you have to do is set the value appropriately. Note the use of the `NChar` data type in this code:

```
strText = "私の本を買って頂き、ありがとうございました。";
comm.Parameters.Add("Japanese",SqlDbType.NChar,30);
comm.Parameters[@"Japanese"] .Value = strText;
```

12.5   BINDING DATES AND TIMES

Another advantage of using binding versus building strings is that issues such as date/time formats simply go away. All that is required is for the parameter to be set to the appropriate type. The engine deals with the issue appropriately:

```
comm.Parameters.Add("MyDateTimeField",OleDbType.Date);
comm.Parameters[1].Value = DateTime.Now;
```

12.6 SUMMARY

For some people, this chapter will have given a review and an explanation of how to do a well-known task using ADO.NET instead of a previous technology. Surprisingly, though, many people are unfamiliar with the concept of binding parameters and its associated advantages. In either case, this chapter has provided the basic information and showed how to deal with several of the special cases that frequently trip people up.

The use of parameters is fairly similar from SQL Server to OLE DB, with the exception of the use of named parameters versus the question-mark placeholder. The ODBC data provider, discussed in appendix A, also uses question marks for parameters.

We are not yet done with parameters. Chapter 13 concentrates on using parameters with stored procedures, both to pass data into a stored procedure and to retrieve data.

C H A P T E R   1 3

Working with stored procedures

The previous chapter spent some time talking about the use of parameters, but it did not go into the details of using parameters with stored procedures. This chapter talks about stored procedures in general, and also about the use of parameters with stored procedures.

13.1   USING STORED PROCEDURES

There is a lot of passion about the use or nonuse of stored procedures. Some developers feel that stored procedures are the only way to get reasonable performance. Others believe that putting stored procedures into a server is a violation of layer separation, tying the business logic tightly to the database engine.

I have never believed in absolutes, but in general I prefer to avoid using stored procedures (especially in three-tier applications) because I feel the logic should be in the application server and not in the database. I also find that many applications that rely on stored procedures are difficult to install. However, using them offers some advantages, including performance[1] and atomicity for certain operations, and there are definitely times when they are the appropriate choice.

That said, when I write an application that uses stored procedures, I usually make the application create the stored procedures itself via SQL, along with the tables, indexes, and so forth, rather than relying on a separate installation. If you are concerned about giving your application too much access to the database, then you can make this a separate setup utility, or require an administrator to log in when allowing the application to do administrative work. Just relying on stored procedures and other database artifacts being present because an administrator set them up leads to very fragile applications.

Whatever the merits of stored procedures, this chapter covers some of the issues with creating, calling, and passing data back and forth from stored procedures. However, this book does not pretend to be an SQL primer, so there is no explanation about the details of stored procedures or their capabilities on different engines.

13.2 SIMPLE STORED PROCEDURES

Calling a stored procedure that does not take arguments is simple—basically, doing so just requires specifying the name of the stored procedure:

```
public void ReadStoredProc(SqlConnection conn)
{
    string strSQL = "GetClasses";
    SqlCommand comm = new SqlCommand(strSQL,conn);
    comm.CommandType = CommandType.StoredProcedure;

    SqlDataReader reader = comm.ExecuteReader();

    DisplayResults(reader);

    reader.Close();
}
```

All this example does is set the `CommandText` to the name of the stored procedure and the `CommandType` to `StoredProcedure`. The execute could be any of the legal execute commands—it depends on what the stored procedure is designed to do.

In this code, the `CommandType` is explicitly set to `StoredProcedure`, which allows the data provider to do special handling. You can always pass any legal SQL to a command (leaving the `CommandType` as `Text`), including SQL that executes a stored procedure:

```
string strSQL = "Exec GetClasses";
```

However, this approach limits what you can do with parameters, as shown later in this chapter.

---

[1] With the current version of SQL Server, there is no speed benefit between using a stored procedure versus passing SQL, once an execution plan has been created the first time.

13.3 PASSING ARGUMENTS TO A STORED PROCEDURE

Stored procedures can take arguments, just like functions, although the notation is different. In fact, just about every database engine has its own format. You can take a couple of different approaches, depending on how tied you are to a particular engine.

13.3.1 Using the database's notation

This first approach is very database specific—you pass the parameter to the stored procedure using that database engine's notation. The following example uses SQL Server, but could just have easily been done in Oracle (with a different syntax for the stored procedure and a different way of executing the command).

The code in this and the next section use the following stored procedure, which does nothing more than select information about a particular teacher whose name must be provided:

```
GetTeacher(@TeacherName varchar(30)) AS
SELECT TeacherName,Classroom,Subject FROM Teachers
WHERE TeacherName=@TeacherName
```

The following code calls the stored procedure, using SQL Server's notation:

```
public void DisplayTeacher(SqlConnection conn)
{
    string strSQL = "GetTeacher 'Mr. Biddick'";        ❶ Specify argument

    SqlCommand comm = new SqlCommand(strSQL,conn);
    comm.CommandType = CommandType.Text;               ❷ CommandType

    SqlDataReader reader = comm.ExecuteReader();
    DisplayReaderResults(reader);
    reader.Close();
}
```

❶ This is the SQL Server–specific notation for specifying arguments to stored procedures. Had there been more than one argument, they would be separated by commas. SQL Server is quite flexible when calling stored procedures—it would be legal, for example, to more explicitly put the Exec keyword before the procedure, but the engine is smart enough to recognize the intent of the command without it.

❷ Notice that the command type here is Text and not StoredProcedure, because you want the command text to be treated as straight SQL to be interpreted by the engine. This code assumes a knowledge of the database's specific syntax.

Oracle version

Just so users of OLE DB don't feel left out, here is the syntax for calling an Oracle stored procedure natively:

```
strSQL = "BEGIN  CALL GetTeacher('Mr. Biddick');  END;";
```

I would have provided an Access version as well, but because Access doesn't support stored procedures, doing so would have been a difficult task!

13.3.2 Using parameters

This next example has the same result as the previous one, but it uses ADO.NET to call the stored procedure. This approach offers several advantages. First, it means you can use parameters, which, as explained in chapter 12, is more efficient when making multiple calls. Second, the format of the command becomes database neutral—it should work with most engines that support stored procedures.

One warning for Oracle users—the Oracle OLE DB data provider does not currently support this notation, although the Microsoft OLE DB data provider for Oracle does.

Here's the code:

```
public void DisplayTeacher(SqlConnection conn)
{
    string strSQL = "GetTeacher";                    ❶ Command text

    SqlCommand comm = new SqlCommand(strSQL,conn);
    comm.CommandType = CommandType.StoredProcedure;  ❷ CommandType
    comm.Parameters.Add("@TeacherName","Mr. Biddick"); ❸
    SqlDataReader reader = comm.ExecuteReader();      Bind parameter
    DisplayReaderResults(reader);
    reader.Close();
}
```

❶ The command text is the name of the stored procedure to run. In fact, it would have been illegal to specify any other information in this string, because the next line specifies that the text contains a stored procedure's name.

❷ This time the command type *is* StoredProcedure. The only thing in the command text is the name of the stored procedure, and you want the data provider to handle the parameters and syntax issues for you.

❸ This statement is a shortcut notation for creating a parameter and assigning a value to it. Notice that, unlike the examples in chapter 12, the parameter name does not appear anywhere in the command text. However, there is a parameter of that name on the stored procedure.

This approach offers a couple of advantages versus specifying the text:

- It is more efficient. The reasons are explored in chapter 12.
- Optional parameters can be skipped. When you use the text approach, parameters must be listed in order.
- The engine's specific syntax is not required.

Of course, this procedure would work for any number of parameters; you would just need to add more parameters to the parameters collection. Likewise, you could execute the stored procedure multiple times with multiple different values by using the prepare mechanism explained in chapter 12, and by changing the values.

13.4 READING DATA FROM A STORED PROCEDURE

There are a number of different ways to get data out of a stored procedure, but each method is dependent on the way the stored procedure is designed to be used. The first method should be very familiar.

13.4.1 Using a DataReader

One of the things a stored procedure can do is return one or more result sets, just by doing a `Select`. In fact, the `DisplayTeacher` example given earlier does exactly that, and the code creates a DataReader and steps through the data. I will not repeat the code here, but you can look at either version of `DisplayTeacher` to see how this technique works.

13.4.2 Out parameters

As well as having parameters designed to be passed into a stored procedure, a stored procedure can have parameters designed to return values to the calling code. An out parameter can either be purely outward-bound, or can be an in-out parameter that passes a value into the procedure and also returns a value.

My stored procedure example is not very useful, because I do not want to get hung up on the syntax and complexities of stored procedures. What this stored procedure does, however, is set the value in two out parameters:

```
CREATE PROCEDURE GetDataOut
(@OutputString varchar(30) Output,@OutputNumber int Output) AS
Set @OutputString = 'Hello'
Set @OutputNumber = 37
```

Imagine that these values are being set based on some highly complex business logic, rather than being completely bogus! The following code can be used to read the values:

```
public void TestGetDataOut(SqlConnection conn)
{
    SqlCommand comm = new SqlCommand("GetDataOut",conn);
    comm.CommandType = CommandType.StoredProcedure;

    comm.Parameters.Add("@OutputString",SqlDbType.VarChar,30);
    comm.Parameters["@OutputString"].Direction =
                        ParameterDirection.Output;              ❶ Specify
                                                                  parameter
                                                                  type
    comm.Parameters.Add("@OutputNumber",SqlDbType.Int);
    comm.Parameters["@OutputNumber"].Direction =
                        ParameterDirection.Output;

    comm.ExecuteNonQuery();

    Console.WriteLine("Output string = {0}",
                comm.Parameters["@OutputString"].Value);        ❷ Retrieve
    Console.WriteLine("Output number = {0}",                      parameters'
                comm.Parameters["@OutputNumber"].Value);          value
}
```

❶ Much of this example should be familiar, such as specifying the name of the stored procedure and using ExecuteNonQuery() to execute the command. I'll just delve a little deeper into the parts that are new.

The previous examples using parameters have been content to leave the Direction parameter with its default value (ParameterDirection.Input), implying that the value is being passed *into* the database. In this example, though, we want to get data out, and so we must specify that the parameter is to be used for Output.

It is legal to create a parameter that both passes a value into the procedure and expects to have its value set. In that case, the Direction would be set to ParameterDirection.InputOutput.

Everything else about the parameter is normal, specifying the data type and, for the string parameter, the maximum length of the value.

❷ Instead of setting the value before executing, this code retrieves the value from the Value property, which was set by the database when the Execute() command was called. The type of the Value property will depend on the data type, but in the example it is treated as an object.

Output

Just to show that everything acts as expected, figure 13.1 shows the output from the example.

```
C:\Projects\ADO\Test1\bin\Debug\Test1.exe
Output string = Hello
Output number = 37
```

Figure 13.1
Example output

13.4.3 Returning a single result

A stored procedure can have a return result, just like a function. The following incredibly silly example is a stored procedure that returns a single numeric value:

```
CREATE PROCEDURE GetANumber AS
Return(42)
```

Again, you must use your imagination to assume that this code does something useful.

ADO.NET provides a special parameter for reading the return result from a stored procedure, which is demonstrated in the following example:

```
public void TestGetANumber(SqlConnection conn)
{
    SqlCommand comm = new SqlCommand("GetANumber",conn);
    comm.CommandType = CommandType.StoredProcedure;

    comm.Parameters.Add("RETURN",SqlDbType.Int);
    comm.Parameters["RETURN"].Direction
                          = ParameterDirection.ReturnValue;

    comm.ExecuteNonQuery();
```

```
Console.WriteLine(
    "Return value = {0}",comm.Parameters["RETURN"].Value);
}
```

There is only one special item in this example—the use of the special parameter `Direction ReturnValue`. By using this value, the provider knows to put the return result from the procedure into that parameter. Note that the name of the parameter (RETURN in this case) is meaningless—only the value in `Direction` is important.

Getting the `ReturnValue` does not in any way preclude the use of out parameters as well. For that matter, the stored procedure could have some in, out, and in/out parameters, and a return value, and also do a select that returns a result set.

The output from this example is exactly as expected (see figure 13.2).

`C:\Projects\ADO\Test1\bin\Debug\Test1.exe`
`Return value = 42`

Figure 13.2
Example results

13.5   DETERMINING THE PARAMETERS FOR A STORED PROCEDURE

So far, we have always specified the parameters used by the stored procedure up front. If you know what parameters a stored procedure requires, this is the most efficient way of calling a stored procedure with parameters. If you *don't* know what the parameters are, however, then it would be nice if .NET could figure it out for you. In fact, there is a way to read the list of parameters that a stored procedure uses.

The methods are exposed on the CommandBuilders and work more or less the same way for SQL Server and for OLE DB, although not all OLE DB providers support the mechanism. CommandBuilders are support classes for DataSets, and you will see a lot more of them in part 3; but we will use the `DeriveParameters` method to get the parameter data.

One caveat with using `DeriveParameters` is that it requires an additional round-trip to the database, so you probably don't want to do things this way every time you call a stored procedure—maybe just the first time you make the call.

The following code calls the earlier `GetTeacher` stored procedure, but uses the CommandBuilder to fill the parameters collection instead of adding it manually. For convenience, I am assuming that the appropriate parameter has been found, but you would most likely need a mechanism for asking the user how to set the parameter:

```
public void DisplayTeacherReadParams(SqlConnection conn)
{
    string strSQL = "GetTeacher";

    SqlCommand comm = new SqlCommand(strSQL,conn);
    comm.CommandType = CommandType.StoredProcedure;

    // Determine the parameters
    SqlCommandBuilder.DeriveParameters(comm);          ❶ Read parameters

    // Write out the parameters - set the TeacherName if found
```

```
    foreach(SqlParameter param in comm.Parameters)          ❷ Step through/
    {                                                           set parameters

        Console.WriteLine("Parameter: {0}",param.ParameterName);
        if(param.ParameterName == "@TeacherName")
            param.Value = "Mr. Biddick";
    }
    Console.WriteLine();

    SqlDataReader reader = comm.ExecuteReader();
    DisplayReaderResults(reader);
    reader.Close();
}
```

❶ This code is similar to the code where you manually set the parameters. The first real difference is that we are using the static method on the SqlCommandBuilder to automatically fill the parameters collection. Notice that the `DeriveParameters` method takes the command as an argument. The command type must be set to `StoredProcedure`, and the name of the stored procedure must be set as the command text before the method is called—otherwise, the CommandBuilder has no way to know which stored procedure to check.

If we are using OLE DB, the call is virtually identical, except the method to call will be

```
OleDbCommandBuilder.DeriveParameters(comm);
```

❷ This code steps through all the parameters and writes out their names. If the parameter happens to be `@TeacherName`, then we set the value. You will see in the results that the `@TeacherName` parameter is there even though it was not manually added. In fact, there will be at least one other parameter as well.

13.5.1 Example results

Figure 13.3 shows the results from the example, which includes the list of parameters as well as the data returned by the stored procedure.

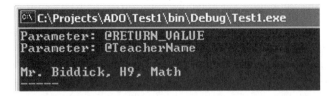

Figure 13.3
Example output

The `@TeacherName` parameter is there, as expected, along with another parameter—`@RETURN_VALUE`. This name was automatically generated, but if you look at the `Direction` property of the parameter, you will see it is set to `ParameterDirection.ReturnValue`. This is the return value from the stored procedure discussed in the last section. It happens that the `GetTeacher` stored procedure has no return value, but the parameter is generated automatically—just in case.

13.6 CREATING STORED PROCEDURES USING CODE

In the introduction to this chapter, I mentioned that if I use a stored procedure in a program, I always make sure the program is capable of creating that stored procedure. This code is not run every time the program runs—it is usually executed the first time the program is run, or after a check that determines if the stored procedure is present. Alternately, it is in an administrative program that is only run as part of installation or for maintenance.

The following example shows a mechanism for creating a stored procedure on the fly. The example is SQL Server specific, but the same basic concept will work for just about any engine—after adjusting the SQL. In the example, the details are hard-coded. In real life, though, I would suggest you do this as a method that takes arguments of the name of the stored procedure and the creation string. This information could be read from a resource, or from a file that ships with the product.

The example creates the `GetANumber` stored procedure used in the previous example. In fact, I created most of the stored procedures in this chapter using this approach so that I could easily move my test code between machines. Here's the code:

```
public void CreateStoredProc(SqlConnection conn)
{
    // First, drop the procedure if it exists
    string strSQL;
    SqlCommand comm = null;
    try
    {
        strSQL = "DROP PROCEDURE GetANumber";            ❶ Drop procedure
        comm = new SqlCommand(strSQL,conn);
        comm.ExecuteNonQuery();
    }
    catch {}

    // Now create the procedure
    strSQL = "CREATE PROCEDURE GetANumber AS Return(42)";   ❷ Create
    comm = new SqlCommand(strSQL,conn);                         procedure
    comm.ExecuteNonQuery();
}
```

❶ We cannot always guarantee that this is the first time the procedure will be created—it is possible that the code is changing an existing stored procedure, or that this is part of a batch repair process because some number of procedures are missing.

For these reasons, it is a good idea to first get rid of any existing procedure before doing a create. We do so using the `Drop` command. Although we can check to see if the procedure exists, and not create the procedure under that circumstance, we can't easily guarantee that a different version of the same procedure might be present.

At the same time, it is possible that this *is* the first time the procedure is being created, and that it doesn't exist. Under that situation, the `Drop` command will throw an exception. Thus the drop operation is done within a `try`/`catch` block.

In this example, we don't care why the command failed, but just assume that the problem was the nonexistence of the stored procedure. A more elegant function would make sure the error returned was as expected, instead of, say, a security problem.

In fact, whenever you're writing data-access code that can fail, it is always a good idea to wrap that code into a `try/catch` block. I have omitted that code from most samples simply to conserve space.

❷ Now that we are guaranteed the procedure does not exist, we can go ahead and create the procedure. We do so simply by using the engine-specific SQL for a create. To confirm that the create succeeded, we could test calling the procedure, or just look inside SQL Server's Enterprise Manager (figure 13.4).

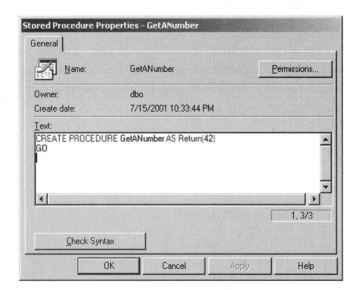

Figure 13.4
SQL Server Enterprise Manager: looking at a stored procedure

13.7 READING IDENTITY COLUMNS

One of the questions I hear quite often is how to retrieve the value from an identity column when doing inserts. Although the answer does not necessarily require the use of a stored procedure, it does use output parameters and can be done using a stored procedure.

IDENTITY COLUMN — A column within a database table used as a primary key that is automatically generated by the database, usually as an ever-increasing number. The advantage is that the value is guaranteed to be unique. The disadvantage is that, because the value is generated by the database, the client doesn't necessarily have access to the value if it needs it for another reference.

I'll show several approaches in the following sections. I should warn you, though, that except for the GUID approach, the others are all SQL Server specific.

13.7.1 The GUID approach

One common solution to the problem of having a unique identifier is to use a GUID. Because a GUID is guaranteed to be unique, you can create the identifier on the client and then pass it to the database, meaning that both the client and the database have the value. However using GUIDs has some disadvantages. First, a GUID is huge—even trimmed down, it is still 32 characters. Second, there is no guarantee of order—just because one GUID is created before another GUID doesn't in any way guarantee that it has a lower value.

Nonetheless, creating a GUID is very easy, and might be the best solution. Here is one way of creating a GUID in .NET:

```
Guid MyGuid = Guid.NewGuid();
string strGuid = MyGuid.ToString();
```

GUID   A globally unique identifier made up of 128 bits. A GUID is a Microsoft version of a universal unique identifier (UUID). For once, Microsoft was feeling modest about its claims for an identifier.

GUIDs are generated using an algorithm that is based on the identifier of the computer's network card ID, which is guaranteed unique. If no network card is available, then the algorithm is complex enough that the value will still be unique. Supposedly, it will take 10,000 years of constant generation to cause a duplicate to be generated.

The GUID format is made up of several hexadecimal numbers. Here is a GUID that I just generated on my machine:

```
552ec4be-4ae3-434d-ad7b-9f70b0f139b1
```

When using a GUID as an identifier, it is usual to remove the dashes and capitalize the value:

```
B6469647EF3E4424BB42295DFB39F836
```

SQL Server also has a special data type specifically for storing GUIDs.

13.7.2 The stored procedure approach

You can use a stored procedure to access the identity value, because the identity value is stored in a special variable available within a stored procedure. The following SQL Server stored procedure takes three input parameters for the new data and one output parameter to retrieve the identity value:

```
CREATE PROCEDURE InsertTeacher(
    @TeacherName varchar(30),
    @Classroom varchar(10),
    @Subject varchar(20),
    @TeacherID int OUT) AS

INSERT INTO Teachers (TeacherName,Classroom,Subject) VALUES
     (@TeacherName,@Classroom,@Subject)
SET @TeacherID = @@Identity
```

I have bolded the important items in this statement. First, an outbound parameter called @TeacherID stores the identity value. The other important statement is SET, which stores a value in the @TeacherID parameter.

The @@Identity variable is a special value that SQL Server uses to store the identity value whenever an insert takes place. All we are doing is storing the value from the @@Identity variable in the @TeacherID parameter.

Reading the value in the @TeacherID parameter is no different than reading any other out parameter. Here is the code:

```
public void TestIdentityStoredProcedure(SqlConnection conn)
{
    SqlCommand comm = new SqlCommand("InsertTeacher",conn);
    comm.CommandType = CommandType.StoredProcedure;

    // Input parameters
    comm.Parameters.Add("@TeacherName","Mr. Underwood");
    comm.Parameters.Add("@Classroom","G7");
    comm.Parameters.Add("@Subject","Science");

    // Output parameter - for the identity
    comm.Parameters.Add("@TeacherID",SqlDbType.Int);
    comm.Parameters["@TeacherID"].Direction =
                                ParameterDirection.Output;

    comm.ExecuteNonQuery();

    Console.WriteLine("New Teacher ID= {0}",
                        comm.Parameters["@TeacherID"].Value);
}
```

The output is shown in figure 13.5.

Figure 13.5
Stored procedure example output

13.7.3 The batch SQL approach

Using the stored procedure works well, but you don't always want to create a stored procedure. Fortunately, SQL Server can provide the same functionality without your having to do a stored procedure. The approach is similar—you are more or less writing a stored procedure in-line, by putting together a couple of different statements. Except for the creation of the command, the code is identical:

```
public void TestIdentityValue(SqlConnection conn)
{
    string strSQL = @"INSERT INTO Teachers
                    (TeacherName,Classroom,Subject) VALUES
                    (@TeacherName,@Classroom,@Subject);
                    SET @TeacherID = @@Identity";

    SqlCommand comm = new SqlCommand(strSQL,conn);
```

```
        comm.Parameters.Add("@TeacherName","Mr. Underwood");
        comm.Parameters.Add("@Classroom","G7");
        comm.Parameters.Add("@Subject","Science");

        comm.Parameters.Add("@TeacherID",SqlDbType.Int);
        comm.Parameters["@TeacherID"].Direction =
                                    ParameterDirection.Output;

        comm.ExecuteNonQuery();

        Console.WriteLine("New Teacher ID = {0}",
                        comm.Parameters["@TeacherID"].Value);
}
```

The important code here is bolded, and we are using the @ notation to allow multiple lines without doing a bunch of string adds.

The first part of the SQL is just an insert statement with parameters. However, the semicolon (;) indicates that another statement follows—we are doing more than one thing with a single command. The SET command is the same as in the stored procedure, and the @@Identity variable is still available, even though we are not in a stored procedure.

I have to say that I think this is a pretty cool technique!

13.8   SUMMARY

The last two chapters have spent considerable time talking about the use of parameters. For many instances, you can avoid using them altogether, although a performance cost is associated with such a decision. When you're talking to stored procedures, however, it is hard to avoid using parameters.

Whether or not you are a fan of stored procedures, they are around to stay. In fact, a future release of SQL Server will make it possible to write highly complex stored procedures in any .NET language, rather than just T-SQL. These procedures will be compiled, and will allow for a whole variety of interesting applications to be written almost exclusively within the database engine.

This is a cool idea, not taking into account the merits of putting your logic directly inside the database engine. It will be interesting to see how well it works and how popular it is.

Chapters 12 and 13 have delved into the Parameter classes in some depth, a topic mostly skipped by the chapter on the Command classes. Chapter 14 looks at the other class we glossed over when talking about commands: Transactions.

CHAPTER 14

Transactions

Virtually all of the examples in the previous chapters have done a single thing at a time—insert a single row of data, do a single update statement, and so forth. It might seem straightforward to assume that doing more than one thing is simply an extension of this process—do an insert, do another insert, and so on. In fact, some examples did exactly that.

What happens, though, when multiple operations are dependent on each other? For example, imagine that you do one update to remove $100.00 from a user's account, and then you do an update to add that $100.00 to another user's account. It is certainly important that either both transactions take place, or neither of them takes place. But what if the power goes out between the two statements?

That is where transactions come in. A transaction is simply a way of linking several different commands together such that they are either all successful or they are all canceled. In fact, although it wasn't obvious, transactions were being used in the previous examples—except that each transaction consisted of a single command. This chapter explains how to use ADO.NET to extend a transaction over multiple commands.

Of course, our example assumes that both accounts are stored in the same database, and that assumption is used throughout this chapter—any number of operations *on the same database* can be easily linked together inside a single transaction. You can have a transaction that crosses databases, and even involves arbitrary objects that are not databases, but you must complete some amount of work as part of the transaction. This process is referred to as a *distributed transaction*, and is the topic of chapter 33.

This chapter is relatively short, and is the end of our detailed discussion of the classes within each data provider.

14.1 WRAPPING MULTIPLE COMMANDS INTO A TRANSACTION

The easiest way to understand how transactions are done in ADO.NET is via an example. It is straightforward to use a transaction in ADO.NET, although perhaps not quite as straightforward as in some previous data access technologies. (I will discuss some of the reasons later.)

The following example swaps two teachers' classrooms in the Teachers table. If only one of the statements succeeded, then there would be two teachers operating in the same classroom, which could be awkward. This first example is written against SQL Server. The semantics are identical for OLE DB, however, if you replace *Sql* with *OleDb* in the names of the objects (SqlTransaction becomes OleDbTransaction, and so forth):

```
public void TestTransaction(SqlConnection conn)
{
    SqlTransaction tran = conn.BeginTransaction();        ❶ Create transaction

    SqlCommand comm = new SqlCommand();
    comm.Connection = conn;
    comm.Transaction = tran;        ❷ Associate command
                                        with transaction
    // Statement 1
    comm.CommandText = "UPDATE Teachers SET Classroom='B2' "
                        +"WHERE TeacherName='Mr. Biddick'";
    bool bOkay1 = (comm.ExecuteNonQuery() == 1);

    // Statement 2                                          ❸ Determine
    comm.CommandText = "UPDATE Teachers SET Classroom='A1' "   success
                        +"WHERE TeacherName='Ms. Fortune'";
    bool bOkay2 = (comm.ExecuteNonQuery() == 1);

    if(bOkay1 && bOkay2)
        tran.Commit();        ❹ Committing changes
    else
        tran.Rollback();      ❺ Rolling back changes
}
```

❶ Calling `BeginTransaction()` on the connection object creates a Transaction object that is responsible for the transaction operations. Transactions are always associated with a connection, which is why the connection object has the responsibility for creating the transaction.

Once a transaction has begun, *every command* that takes place with that connection is part of the transaction, regardless of whether the command is associated directly with the transaction. This concept is explained later, in section 14.2, on multiple simultaneous transactions.

❷ In order for a command to be associated with a particular transaction, the command should be told about the transaction. As I implied earlier, the command will be part of the transaction whether or not this is done, but this limitation of the data provider will eventually be corrected. If we do not make this association, then our code will break when the data provider becomes more capable.

❸ Although one worry for the transaction is a possible interruption (such as the power going out) in the middle of an operation, another worry is something going wrong with one or more of the individual operations; this situation would mean that all the operations should be canceled. This line of code checks to make sure one and only one record was affected by the SQL. If that is not true, then we want to cancel everything.

You might think that we could use our check, and we don't need the transaction at all here—if the first operation fails, then simply don't do the second operation. But what happens if the first operation succeeds and the second one fails? Then we would be half complete. This result would get worse if there were more than two operations.

❹ Once the code has determined that both statements succeeded, we need to tell the database we are satisfied with the results and want to make them permanent. This step is referred to as *committing* the changes.

❺ If something goes wrong, then we want to cancel both statements and act as though we never sent the commands. Doing so is called *rolling back* changes. The database will return the data back to its original state.

If the operation was interrupted, such as by a power outage, and neither `Commit` nor `Rollback` was called, then the database would eventually (when it came back up, or when it realized the connection was no longer valid) do an automatic rollback. It does so by using log files and various tricks that guarantee the operation will either succeed completely or fail completely. All serious modern databases are very good at this task.

14.1.1 Example results

Figure 14.1 shows the state of the data before the transaction took place.

	TeacherID	TeacherName	Classroom	Subject
▶	1	Mr. Biddick	A1	Math
	2	Ms. Fortune	B2	English
	3	Mr. Kriefels	C3	Physics
*				

Figure 14.1 Before the transaction

Figure 14.2 shows the data after the transaction has been committed.

	TeacherID	TeacherName	Classroom	Subject
▶	1	Mr. Biddick	B2	Math
	2	Ms. Fortune	A1	English
	3	Mr. Kriefels	C3	Physics
*				

Figure 14.2 After the transaction

Note the values in the Classroom field for the first two rows. Had the rollback been called, or the operation been interrupted, the data would have looked exactly the same as in the *before* table. If you don't believe me, try running the sample code, but replace the conditional commit/rollback with a forced call to `Rollback`.

14.2 MULTIPLE SIMULTANEOUS TRANSACTIONS?

Several times in the previous example, I referred to the fact that all the commands created after the call to `BeginTransaction()` were associated with the transaction, regardless of whether the command was explicitly associated to the transaction. This not only seems counterintuitive, but implies that extra work is being done that is unnecessary, given that it has no effect.

It also seems, based on the existence of a transaction object and the methods for using it, that you could create several transactions on the same connection, associate some commands with one and some with another, and have the engine roll back one transaction while committing the other.

The problem is that the database engine simply does not support this process. SQL Server, and most other databases, can handle only a single transaction per connection at a time. No matter what you do with the connection, the transaction will be associated with everything.

Why did Microsoft go to all of the effort, then, of creating transaction objects and requiring their use? The answer is that there are plans for a future version of SQL Server to support this capability. As soon as that happens, ADO.NET will automatically be able to support it. Of course, if you write your database code assuming it doesn't matter, your code will break when that support is added!

If you are familiar with OLE DB, you might recall that it did have support for multiple transactions, via the use of sessions. However, this support was mostly fake—it relied on the creation of multiple connections behind the scenes. Not only was it hard for providers to handle, it tended to be somewhat flaky.

If you need support for multiple simultaneous transactions today, you can get it in a fairly simple way—create multiple connections. This technique is rather resource intensive, but it is not as bad, particularly if you have connection pooling enabled.

14.3 SAVEPOINTS

Transactions are fairly straightforward—you start a transaction, do some work, and then either commit or roll back your changes. Consider a scenario, though, where you want to either commit or roll back an entire transaction, but you may want to roll back *pieces* of the transaction as you go.

For example, imagine setting up a class within a transaction. First, the teacher needs to be assigned, then each student is added to the class, and then an update to their billing information is made. If, however, a particular student is rejected by the billing procedure, then we want to roll back the piece of the transaction related to adding the student without giving up on the entire class. Of course, we want the entire class to be set up before committing so we don't end up with a partially assigned set of information.

The example here is simpler—it updates two records with a Savepoint in between, and then rolls back to that Savepoint before committing. Note that this functionality is specific to the SQL Server data provider—it is not exposed via the OLE DB data provider. This is a pity, because several other engines, such as Sybase, also support this capability:

```
public void TestSavepoint(SqlConnection conn)
{
    SqlTransaction tran = conn.BeginTransaction();

    SqlCommand comm = new SqlCommand();
    comm.Connection = conn;
    comm.Transaction = tran;

    // Statement 1
    comm.CommandText = "UPDATE Teachers SET Classroom='G9' WHERE "
                        +"TeacherName='Mr. Biddick'";
    comm.ExecuteNonQuery();

    tran.Save("AfterFirst");              ❶ Set savepoint

    // Statement 2
    comm.CommandText = "UPDATE Teachers SET Classroom='H9' WHERE "
                        +"TeacherName='Ms. Fortune'";
    comm.ExecuteNonQuery();

    tran.Rollback("AfterFirst");          ❷ Roll back to
    tran.Commit();                          savepoint
}
```

❶ This statement creates a Savepoint and gives it the name AfterFirst. It doesn't really matter what the Savepoint is called, but the name needs to be remembered for the rollback. Note that this Savepoint is created after the first command has been executed, but before the second command.

Savepoints are fairly efficient, so it doesn't hurt to create a number of them— within reason. Hundreds may be a problem, but a couple of dozen should cause no trouble.

❷ This call to Rollback() does not roll back the entire transaction—it just restores the transaction to its state when the AfterFirst Savepoint was created. Unlike a standard call to Rollback(), it does not end the transaction. It is still possible to call Rollback() to roll back the entire transaction, to call Commit() to save the changes as they exist, or even to roll back to another Savepoint.

14.3.1 Example results

Before this code was run, the state of the Teachers table was the same as at the end of the last example (figure 14.3).

TeacherID	TeacherName	Classroom	Subject
1	Mr. Biddick	B2	Math
2	Ms. Fortune	A1	English
3	Mr. Kriefels	C3	Physics
*			

**Figure 14.3
Table before the transaction**

Figure 14.4 shows the table after the transaction has been committed.

TeacherID	TeacherName	Classroom	Subject
1	Mr. Biddick	G9	Math
2	Ms. Fortune	A1	English
3	Mr. Kriefels	C3	Physics
*			

**Figure 14.4
Table after the transaction**

Notice that the update on the first row happened as expected, but that the second row is unchanged, even though an update command was executed. This is the case because the rollback to the Savepoint undid that change.

14.4 ISOLATION LEVELS

In talking about transactions so far, the assumption has been that one client has been making changes to the database and may want to commit or roll back the changes. But what happens when another client attempts to access the data that is being changed within the transaction?

Imagine a scenario where you are using the database to generate a unique identifier, perhaps using the following SQL:

```
UPDATE IDTable SET IDValue=IDValue+1 WHERE IDName='SomeID'
SELECT IDValue FROM IDTable WHERE IDName='SomeID'
```

It's fairly straightforward. Of course, some interesting situations could occur with this SQL. What happens if two clients attempt to execute the code at more or less the same time? There are two equally likely possibilities:

- The first client finishes executing both statements and gets back a value before the second client begins. Everything is OK.

- The first statement is executed by the first client, and then the first statement is executed by the second client, before the select can take place. The value is incremented by 2, and both clients end up with the same value.

This classic client/server problem gets worse as more users are added. It is less of an issue with a three-tier application, but it can still occur—and this is just one scenario. Consider an inventory application where quantity is decremented—could two people both order the last item in stock? There are many such situations.

The important thing to understand is exactly what rules will apply when multiple users hit the same data. Maybe it is OK for two different clients to change the same data, or for clients to read the same data as long as only one makes a change at a time, and so forth. It really depends on the business problem to be solved. This is where isolation levels come in—literally, how isolated should one client's transaction be from another client's?

When you create a transaction, you can specify the isolation level. For example:

```
SqlTransaction tran =
        conn.BeginTransaction(IsolationLevel.ReadCommitted);
```

You can also set the `IsolationLevel` property on the transaction directly. The isolation level has a number of different settings, each with a slightly different behavior. There are also fancy names for the problems that can occur at each level and a potential performance cost associated with the level.

14.4.1 Isolation issues

Three problems tend to come up, based on the way the isolation level is set:

- *Dirty read*—One client sees data based on another client's incomplete transaction, which can be rolled back. For example, Client A marks a student as owing money as part of a transaction. Client B does a check to see if the student can register for classes, and rejects the student. Client A then rolls back the transaction, marking the student as paid up.

- *Nonrepeatable read*—When the same client does the same query twice within a transaction, the results change from one execution to the next. For example, Client A successfully checks to make sure that a student's total bill is not above his limit. In the meantime, Client B adds $300 to the value in the total column. A moment later, Client A refers to the total again, but gets a different result.

- *Phantom records*—Similar to a nonrepeatable read, except at a row level; the rows that meet a selection criteria change. For example, a query for classes returns five classes the first time, but then returns six classes the next time because a new row was added. This can also happen if data is changed that makes a row suddenly become part of the criteria or stop being part of the criteria.

Whether these problems are *your* problems depends entirely on the type of application being written and the specific data being worked on at any given time.

14.4.2 Isolation levels

Table 14.1 shows the legal isolation levels that you can set. The values are listed in order, starting with the one that provides the least protection and, therefore, has the lowest cost (performance overhead). An additional value in the `IsolationLevel` enum, `Unspecified`, means that the isolation level cannot be determined. However, you should never set the isolation level to this value.

Table 14.1 Values in the `IsolationLevel` enum

Isolation Level	Meaning	Potential Issues
Chaos	If the isolation level is set to chaos, it is almost as if no transaction is going on at all. If a rollback takes place, the results are likely to be arbitrary. At this level, all clients can see all the data immediately and can change data arbitrarily.	Dirty reads Nonrepeatable reads Phantom records Chaos!
ReadUncommitted	Other clients can see all the changes made inside a transaction, but cannot directly change the same data. Although all the standard problems can take place, a rollback will happen successfully.	Dirty reads Nonrepeatable reads Phantom records
ReadCommitted	Changes made inside a transaction are not visible to other clients until the transaction is complete. However, there is no guarantee that data read inside the transaction will not be changed by other clients.	Nonrepeatable reads Phantom records
RepeatableRead	The database guarantees that once data has been read from a record within a transaction, the same data will be seen for the duration of that transaction. So, for example, if a total value is read once from a record, that value will not change. However, if a select returns multiple records, there is no guarantee that the select might not pick up other records that have changed outside the transaction.	Phantom records
Serializable	The database acts as though each transaction must be completed in its entirety before another transaction can be started or any of the associated data can be read. This method guarantees that everything stays consistent within the transaction. However, this isolation level has the highest overhead—other clients are literally blocked from accessing the touched data until the entire transaction has been completed. Although behavior might vary on different engines, on SQL Server, if you set the isolation level to Serializable and two users attempt to update the same data, one of those users will get an exception. You will have to build your own retry code to handle this appropriately. This is also the solution to the unique identifier problem stated earlier.	

The default value for both the SQL Server and OLE DB data providers is Read-Committed. It is often a good compromise between performance overhead and data protection.

14.5   SUMMARY

This chapter has been heavy on database theory. These concepts have a habit of tripping up the unwary—although database engines do a good job of handling many of the issues associated with supporting multiple users, some effort is still required on the part of the programmer.

Using transactions is relatively straightforward in ADO.NET, even with the added complexity of separate transaction objects to support the future ability for simultaneous transactions. ADO.NET also exposes other transaction-related capabilities, such as Savepoints and isolation levels, in a nonintrusive and simple manner.

This chapter brings part 2 to a close. Part 3 will introduce the DataSet and its capabilities. The discussion will require the use of a couple of data provider objects we haven't touched on—the DataAdapter and the CommandBuilders. There was little point talking about these classes earlier, because they are specifically provided for working with DataSets. The DataSet can do a lot for you, and as you will see later in the book, you can even do a lot of the work with the DataSet using drag-and-drop; but many times, straight SQL and low-down database coding are required.

The DataSet

Part 3 explores the DataSet in detail, explaining its purpose and showing how to use it for various different tasks. Chapter 15 provides an overview of the DataSet, and Chapter 16 provides examples of various basic operations.

Chapter 17 explores the DataTable (the most important class within the DataSet), DataColumn, and DataRow classes, which make up a DataTable. Chapters 18 through 20 that explain how to set up relationships and constraints within a DataSet, and how to run queries against the DataSet.

The final chapter in part 3, chapter 21, demonstrates how to remote a DataSet—that is, how to work with a DataSet across multiple tiers of an application.

CHAPTER 15

What are DataSets?

Up until now, this book has concentrated on how to do low-level database work: inserting data, querying data, that sort of thing. For anyone working seriously with database technologies in the last decade or so, that was really all you had—a basic toolkit for communicating with a database.

ADO.NET goes one step further. One of the major new pieces provided by ADO.NET is the DataSet, which allows for database independent manipulation of your data.

15.1 WHY DATASETS?

The ADO.NET low-level database classes get you the access to your database that you need. If you're building a modern application with this basic toolkit, though, you generally have a lot more to do. Once data is read, it is common to need to be able to store it for manipulation, to display it to the user for modification, and to store back changes to the database. To display it, you need some sort of graphical widget, such as a grid, that can be filled with the data.

Then, of course, there are three-tier and n-tier applications, where the user is not working on the same machine that is connected to the database; and stateless web applications, where the server cannot even hold onto the data between calls.

Past developers were not entirely on their own. Data-bound ActiveX controls allowed some tie-in between the database and the visual display, and ADO disconnected

Recordsets allowed for some capabilities to deal with multi-tier applications. However, these solutions all seemed like afterthoughts (which, in many cases, they were), and it showed in the complexity of their creation and, frequently, in their use.

Fortunately, the ADO.NET developers had the opportunity to learn from past problems and design a solution that addressed these issues in a clean and straightforward manner—the DataSet. A DataSet, in its simplest form, is just a collection of data. That data is broken down into tables, columns, and rows, and can have relationships, and so forth. This doesn't sound very revolutionary—in fact, it sounds a lot like an ADO Recordset.

There is one major difference, though, between a Recordset and a DataSet—the DataSet does not, in any way, have any association with a database! This may seem counterintuitive, but it is a major benefit for several reasons:

- Because the DataSet doesn't have to worry about a database, it is not loaded down with all the code necessary to talk to a database. Also, because it is not dependent on any such code, it won't have to change when the database code changes.

- Because the DataSet is not tied to the database, once it has been loaded, no association exists with a database or a connection; so, the database connection can be freed.

- The DataSet can be passed around to different tiers or machines without worrying about the connection to the database. In fact, you can even pass a DataSet over the Internet with no particular issues.

- Because a DataSet must be filled externally, it doesn't necessarily have to be filled from a database. It can be used with any data that can be put into tables and rows.

You might be thinking that this is all very well; but if a DataSet doesn't know anything about a database, how do you get data into it from a database, or data from the DataSet back to the database? The answer is that all the data providers have objects specifically designed to work with DataSets. These objects know how to put data into a DataSet and how to get data back out. You will see how this is done in the next several chapters.

Another advantage of the DataSet is that it is a core component of .NET. That means other core pieces of .NET were aware of the DataSet from the beginning, and were specifically designed to work with it. These components include such things as GUI and web components for displaying and manipulating data. Part 4 of this book is dedicated to using these data-bound controls.

DataSets are also very much XML aware, and they provide a lot of functionality for working with data as XML, and XML as data. This topic forms much of part 5.

From my glowing description of DataSets so far, you may think that they are the solution to all problems up to and possibly including world peace. Well, not quite—there are some downsides to using DataSets.

First, DataSets are fairly *heavy*. Using them has an overhead just because of all the data and capabilities they contain. The importance of this issue depends on the way you intend to use DataSets. For many applications, this will be a nonissue; but in a heavy transaction environment, it could cause trouble.

Second, DataSets assume that they contain all the data you might need related to a particular table. For example, you can set up a constraint on a DataSet that prevents a duplicate ID from being entered into a field. However, this technique works only if all the records from the table are loaded into the DataSet—not a good idea if there are a couple of million of them!

This is not so much a DataSet issue as a three-tier programming issue, for which DataSets were explicitly created. A trade-off always exists between the amount of functionality on the client versus the server. Nonetheless, it is an issue that must be addressed when using DataSets in situations where they cannot contain all of your data.

Aside from these few issues, DataSets are an incredibly handy construct and can dramatically simplify development of data-aware applications.

15.2 PARTS OF A DATASET

The DataSet is made up of a number of different classes that are part of the `System.Data` namespace. The chart in figure 15.1 shows these classes and their relationships to each other.

The next sections briefly explain each of these classes and their purpose. You will see the classes in use in the next several chapters.

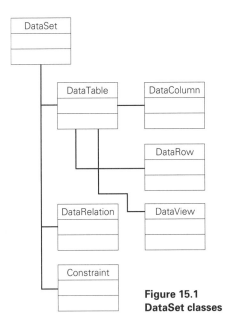

**Figure 15.1
DataSet classes**

15.2.1 The DataSet class

As you might imagine, the DataSet is the main controlling class. It doesn't hold any data itself, but contains a collection of DataTables that do. It also contains a collection of DataRelations that control how the different tables are connected with one another.

The DataSet contains a number of properties that control the way in which the contained data is treated, such as whether constraints are enforced. The DataSet also knows that it is "dirty" if one or more of the contained tables' data has been changed.

You can do a number of handy things with a DataSet. For example, you can convert the contained data to XML, or merge the DataSet with another DataSet. Of course, when you do these things, the operations are tied to the objects the DataSet contains. I think of the DataSet as little more than a container that conveniently allows operations to be performed on its contents.

15.2.2 The DataTable class

A DataTable represents a single table of data. It is synonymous with a database table. Actually, it is more like a database view than a table, because the data it contains is usually based on an SQL Select statement, which might select a subset of the fields, might include a where clause limiting the rows that are returned, and might, in fact, include data from several different tables via the use of a join.

Once the data is placed in a DataTable, though, it can be treated like a table—you can add, remove, and change data, as you might expect. You can also have rules (constraints) applied to the data that can maintain the DataTable's integrity. You can also navigate, via relations, to other DataTables contained within the DataSet.

The fact that the data is not *necessarily* all of the data from a table is both a plus and a minus. On the plus side, it allows for the manipulation of only the data that is appropriate. On the minus side, it can be misleading—you might, for example, have a constraint requiring that a value in a column be unique. The DataSet will enforce this constraint, but only within the data contained by the DataTable. If a couple of thousand other rows are sitting on the database server, the DataTable doesn't know or care whether the value is unique within that data.

As I already stated, the data held in a DataTable can be the product of one or more joins. Again, this has some benefits—it allows for modeling data appropriately for your application. But it also means that storing changes to the data back to the database becomes much more complicated. This topic is explored in more detail in chapter 19, as part of the discussion on custom DataAdapters.

A DataSet can contain virtually any number of DataTables,[1] which can be accessed via the Tables property of the DataSet object.

---

[1] Limited only by memory and common sense.

15.2.3 The DataColumn class

If you think of a DataTable as an in-memory representation of a table, it should probably come as no surprise that the DataTable is made up of columns and rows. Each column defines things like the name of the column, the data type and size, and so forth.

DataColumns also have some useful properties that can make the DataTable act more intelligently. For example, you can set a default value for a column that will be used when a new row is created, or an incrementing value. This feature, along with other capabilities of the various DataSet objects, allows the DataSet to act like a little in-memory database.

When you fill a DataSet from a database, the columns will automatically be created for you with their basic information (although things such as default values will not be created automatically). If you want to manually create a DataTable, then you must create columns before you can put data into the table.

15.2.4 The DataRow class

There are no prizes for guessing the purpose of a DataRow. It is a good thing, really, that most of the ADO.NET classes have fairly sensible names, but it does mean there is a certain lack of revelation in some of my explanations!

Just as the DataTable has a collection of columns, it also has a collection of rows, which contain the data for the table. However, unlike a real database, manipulating the data is much more straightforward—you can access the individual rows just as you would in an array. You can access the data in each column within the row in a similar way—either numerically or by using the name of the column.

Adding and removing rows is just as straightforward—it's simply a matter of adding and removing data from the array. Under the hood, however, the process is more complex. After all, the goal of a DataSet is rarely just to edit data in memory—at some point, the data needs to go back to the database, so the DataSet must remember what has changed. Section 15.3 discusses how this process works.

There is a limit to the number of rows that can be held in a table, but given that this number is over 15 million, it shouldn't be a problem. If you need to store more rows than that in memory, I would suggest a re-evaluation of your design!

15.2.5 The DataRelation class

A DataRelation defines a relationship between two DataTables contained within a DataSet. So, for example, a Teacher table might be related to a Classes table, via a relationship. DataRelations are handy because once the relationship has been established, you can enforce the relationship as a foreign key or have changes in the parent cascade to the child.

Another nice thing about relations is that many of the data-aware controls understand them. So, for example, you can display a grid of data, and then click on a button that will expand and show the child rows from the related table—all automatically.

15.2.6　The Constraint class

A *constraint* is a rule that can be enforced against the data in a DataSet. Currently, ADO.NET provides two different constraints:

- *UniqueConstraint*—Requires that the value entered into a column must not be the same as the value in that column in any other rows. As I mentioned earlier, this constraint works against the data contained in the DataSet; so if the table contains additional data that was not sucked into the DataSet, it will not be checked.

- *ForeignKeyConstraint*—Allows the enforcement of the link between a parent and a child table. For example, if a Classes table contains a TeacherID column, the value entered into that column *must* be a legal value from the Teachers table.

These objects can be used to make the DataSet act more like a stand-alone database representation.

15.2.7　The DataView class

Just as a view in a database allows for a different way of looking at a table, a DataView allows a different way of looking at a DataTable. DataViews are primarily used when working with data-bound controls, such as the DataGrid—you can change the way the data is viewed without messing up the DataTable. You can also have multiple DataViews on the same DataTable, which means different controls can display the data in different ways.

Although the DataView is part of the DataSet, it is *mostly* used for working with data-bound controls. So, it is not discussed until part 4, which is dedicated to the topic of data-bound controls.

15.3　*WORKING WITH DATASETS*

The paradigm for working with a DataSet is fairly straightforward. First, the DataSet is filled in some manner, usually from a number of database queries. The data within the DataSet is manipulated—items are added, removed, and changed; then, at some later time, the changes are written back out.

We need to answer a few interesting questions about how this process works. First, how does data get into the DataSet? And second, how does it get back to the database? On top of that, how does the DataSet determine what has changed, so it will know what information to write back to the database?

15.3.1　Filling a DataSet

On several occasions, I have mentioned that the DataSet is not tied in any way to the database. I won't go over the reasons again, except to say that it makes for a much cleaner design. Still, at some point you do need to get data into the DataSet for it to be useful.

You can fill a DataSet manually—create a new DataTable and add it to the DataSet, and then add DataColumns and DataRows to the DataTable. In fact, in some situations you might want to do just that, to take advantage of the DataSet's capabilities (and the controls that understand DataSets). However, when you are working with a database, you need to use a more straightforward technique.

A data provider communicates with a DataSet via a DataAdapter. The DataAdapter is part of a particular data provider, and just as with most data provider classes, there are different versions (see table 15.1).

Table 15.1 DataAdapter implementations

Class	Provider	Interface
SqlDataAdapter	SQL Server	IDbDataAdapter
OleDbDataAdapter	OLE DB	IDbDataAdapter

I have already said that the DataSet does not know anything about data providers, which of course means that the DataSet cannot know about the DataAdapters. That does not, however, mean that the DataAdapters cannot know about the DataSet!

I will leave the code examples to chapter 16, but in principle a DataAdapter is given the command required to retrieve data from a database. It retrieves the data using the same mechanisms you would use to retrieve data—DbCommand and DbDataReader objects—but then it uses these objects to define and populate the DataTables within a DataSet.

You can use multiple DataAdapters to read in a number of different tables. You can also mix and match, creating some DataTables by hand and using DataAdapters to create others. You could also use DataAdapters from different data providers to fill the same DataSet!

This approach is a little more work than, say, setting up an ADO Recordset, where the Recordset is responsible for retrieving data and is also responsible for the manipulation of the data. It is worth the extra couple of lines, though, to have a completely disconnected model for that data manipulation.

You might notice that the DataAdapter has created DataTables, DataColumns, and DataRows automatically, but I haven't mentioned the creation of DataRelations or constraints. The DataAdapters do *not* automatically create these objects. However, a mechanism exists that has the DataAdapter fill in at least some of this information, by retrieving schema and setting information as a separate call. This technique will be demonstrated in chapter 17, "DataTables, DataColumns, and DataRows." Alternatively, you can specify this information yourself.

Using a DataAdapter to fill a DataSet is pretty straightforward. The next several chapters will present a number of examples.

15.3.2   Storing changes to a DataSet

Okay, so you have filled your DataSet and used its various methods to make changes to the data. Now it is time to put that data back into the database. It should come as no surprise that this process, once again, involves the DataAdapters.

A DataAdapter has four interesting properties that control how it transfers data. Each of these properties is a command object, like those used extensively in part 2 of this book to send commands to the database:

- `SelectCommand`—Used to retrieve data from the database to populate the DataTable
- `UpdateCommand`—Used when data in a DataRow has changed
- `InsertCommand`—Used when a new DataRow has been added to the DataTable
- `DeleteCommand`—Used when a DataRow has been removed from a DataTable

If you picture the adapter stepping through the rows in a DataTable, it will use the `UpdateCommand` to change each individual row that has been modified, the `InsertCommand` to insert rows that are new, and so on. The nice thing is that you have a great deal of flexibility in the way these commands operate—you can use stored procedures, custom SQL, multiple SQL commands, or even commands that don't write to the database at all!

Of course, a lot of the time you want to have the data written back to the database without having to worry about it. To make this process straightforward, the ADO.NET data providers both have CommandBuilder classes that you can use to set up the `Update`, `Insert`, and `Delete` commands automatically. There *are* some limitations on what they can do (discussed in chapter 19), but they address most simple cases.

As usual, there is a CommandBuilder for each provider (see table 15.2).

Table 15.2   CommandBuilder implementations

Class	Provider	Interface
SqlCommandBuilder	SQL Server	n.a.
OleDbCommandBuilder	OLE DB	n.a.

CommandBuilders have no base interface—not every data provider will provide this functionality, and the ones that do may choose a completely different mechanism. The CommandBuilders for SQL Server and OLE DB both operate in more or less the same way—you create a CommandBuilder and pass the adapter to it, and it fills in the command methods.

This process might again seem like extra work, especially compared with ADO Recordsets or other mechanisms that do almost everything for you. But, for one extra line of code in the simple case, ADO.NET provides a huge amount of extra flexibility and does not force a single, hard-coded mechanism.

15.3.3 Keeping track of changes

The last two sections have discussed how to get data into a DataSet and how to store changes back to the database. You might wonder how the DataSet keeps track of what has changed.

The answer is that the DataSet, or rather the DataTables and DataRows, store additional information. For example, each DataRow has a property called `RowState` that indicates whether the row has been added, deleted, or modified, and each field within the row knows whether it has been changed. With just this information, you can determine what needs to be done with a particular row.

Each field within a row stores more information. In fact, each field can have up to four values:

- *Original*—The original value that was stored in the field, before any changes took place.

- *Current*—The current value for the field.

- *Proposed*—When in a special edit mode, the value that will *become* the current value, after validation. The edit mode on DataRows lets you change several items without causing validation to take place. Imagine a situation where several rows' values depended on each other. In edit mode, all of those fields can be changed. The validation will not happen until after you exit edit mode. In the meantime, the value that will eventually become the current value, as soon as it has been validated, is stored as a proposed value.

- *Default*—The most appropriate version of the field value—original, current, or proposed, depending on the state of the DataRow and DataTable. This is the value you will get if you ask the DataRow for a particular value without specifically asking for a version.

Although keeping all this information may seem like overhead, it has some benefits. For one thing, you can roll back changes without ever touching a database transaction. Also, the current value may be necessary to properly store the new values back to the database, as part of an update statement.

Normally you will keep all this information until the DataSet is stored back to the database. In fact, the DataAdapter will automatically mark the changes as applied, and make all the changes current—the current value will also become the original value, all the rows will be marked as unchanged, and so forth. You can also do this yourself: tell the DataSet to accept all changes and treat the data as current, or tell it to abandon all changes and revert the DataSet back to its original state. You have complete control over the DataSet's life cycle.

15.4 SUMMARY

This chapter has been heavy on text and high-level information. I think it is useful to have a high-level overview of a topic before diving into the details. Don't worry, though—the following chapters are much more practical and hands-on.

Working with a DataSet is slightly more complex than using a pre-packed object, such as an ADO Recordset, although doing so doesn't compare in complexity to older technologies that provided no built-in support for working with result sets—except perhaps some low-level cursor support. In actual use, the complexity disappears quickly. You need to do a handful of things, and they are not exceptionally onerous.

On the flip side, if you need to work with more complex manipulations, the DataSet can handle them easily. By separating the implementation of the DataSet completely from the data providers, it becomes much more powerful and, once loaded with data, much more straightforward to manipulate.

This separation makes it easy to move the DataSet onto other tiers of an application—something that was, at best, a nuisance with previous technologies. It also makes data-aware controls more consistent; once the data is contained in a DataSet, the control never has to worry about the underlying database implementation.

As useful as a DataSet can be, remember that performance and memory overheads are associated with its use. For many applications this will not be an issue, but if you are planning to build high-traffic applications or pass very large amounts of data, you should think carefully about using the DataSet. At the least, you should do some performance testing to make sure the overhead will not be a problem.

Now that I have talked your ear off [2] about the theory behind DataSets, it is time to put them to some use. The next chapter demonstrates how to use a DataSet.

---

[2] Or written your eye off?

C H A P T E R   1 6

Using DataSets

Now that we are done with the theoretical stuff, let's see the DataSet in action. This chapter will present a number of examples of using the DataSet, although most of them will be fairly simple.

The next several chapters will go into detail about different facets of the DataSet and its capabilities, such as the DataTable, custom DataAdapters, and querying the DataSet. The last chapter in part 3, chapter 21, shows how to transfer a DataSet between different tiers of an application.

Part 4 continues talking about the DataSet, but concentrates on its use with data-bound controls, both for rich (GUI) applications and for web applications.

Most of the examples in this chapter use SQL Server to fill the DataSet, although I will also throw in an OLE DB example. It doesn't matter, though, because the DataSet is not tightly bound to the data providers. The differences in implementation are specific to the data provider (using an SqlCommand versus an OleDbCommand, for example), and part 2 should have given you the information necessary to deal with such issues.

16.1 GETTING DATA INTO A DATASET

The first example simply loads data into a DataSet and then prints it. In the real world, this would be a poor use of a DataSet—if all that is going to happen is data being written out, then a DataReader would be a much better choice. Assume, though, that this is just a first step; once the DataSet is filled, then more work will been done. In fact, this additional work will be demonstrated in the next example.

The example in listing 16.1 loads the data from the Teachers table into a DataSet and then writes it out to the console.

Listing 16.1 Loading data into a DataSet and printing it out

```
using System.Data;                          ❶ Namespaces
using System.Data.SqlClient;

public void TestDataSetSQL(SqlConnection conn)
{
    string strSQL = "SELECT * From Teachers";      ❷ Select statement

    // Create the data adapter and initialize it with
    // the select statement
    SqlDataAdapter sda = new SqlDataAdapter(strSQL,conn);   ❸ Create
                                                               DataAdapter

    // Create and fill the dataset
    DataSet ds = new DataSet();               ❹ Create and
    sda.Fill(ds,"Teachers");                     fill DataSet

    // Get the specific table out of the dataset
    DataTable dt = ds.Tables["Teachers"];     ❺ Retrieve DataTable

    foreach ( DataRow dr in dt.Rows )
    {                                         ❻ Write data
        foreach ( DataColumn dc in dt.Columns )
        {
            if(dc.Ordinal > 0)  Console.Write(", ");

            Console.Write(dr[dc].ToString().Trim());
        }
        Console.WriteLine("");
    }
}
```

❶ All the DataSet classes exist in the System.Data namespace, so it is necessary to use that namespace. Of course, in reality this using statement would appear at the top of the source file, not above a particular method. The System.Data.SqlClient namespace is for the various SQL Server data provider methods.

❷ The Select statement used in this example is pretty simple, but it didn't have to be—it could have been as complex as desired, including subqueries, joins, and so on. However, there are issues associated with returning data from multiple database tables into a single DataTable:

- The built-in support for writing data *back* to the database cannot handle joins. So, if you use a join, you *must* customize the behavior of the DataAdapter or you will not be able to save changes.

- You lose some of the abilities of the DataSet to understand and represent relationships between data. You can still create relationships between your selected data, but then the DataSet will no longer model the data in the database. Of course, sometimes this is an advantage.

Another issue is whether the data you selected has enough information about a row to be able to write it back to the database. For example, if you do not select the table's primary key, you might get some odd results when doing updates.

❸ The DataAdapter is the liaison between the data provider and the DataSet. The DataAdapter is a part of the data provider and must be passed the connection object.

This example uses one of the specialized constructors of the DataAdapter class that takes the `Select` command as a string. This constructor will automatically create an SqlCommand object and set the CommandText to be the passed string.

The example could have just as easily, though rather more verbosely, created an SqlCommand object itself, and set the SqlDataAdapter's `SelectCommand` property:

```
SqlCommand commSelect = new SqlCommand(strSQL,conn);
sda.SelectCommand = commSelect;
```

It's important to realize that this is a fully fledged command object—it can use parameters, specify a name of a stored procedure, or operate using any of the capabilities of a command object. Still, it is nice to have a quick way to set up the DataAdapter to use a simple SQL statement.

❹ Creating a DataSet is simple. We could have passed a name to the DataSet to refer to it more easily, but that is about it. Of course, the DataSet that is created is completely empty. To be useful, it must be populated with tables and data. We *could* do this manually, but the DataAdapter can also do it.

The `Fill()` method tells the DataAdapter to fill the DataSet. Notice that the DataSet is passed to the adapter, and not the other way around—the DataSet doesn't know anything about how the data is loaded.

Philosophically, the DataAdapter does the following when the `fill` command is called:

1 Executes the SelectCommand and gets back a data reader.

2 Creates a DataTable and adds columns based on the results from the data reader.

3 Steps through all the rows of data that are returned and creates a new DataRow for each, populated with the data from the reader. Each row is then added to the DataTable.

4 Adds the DataTable to the Tables collection of the DataSet.

You may have noticed that the code is passing a name for the selected table—Teachers. This name will be used as the name of the DataTable that is created. If the name was not specified, then the DataTable would have been given an arbitrary name, such as Table1.

It would seem reasonable that the adapter could determine the name from the SQL; but doing so is harder than it sounds, especially considering that the SQL could have included joins or any amount of complexity. Still, it would be nice if the adapter at least determined the name for simple cases.

As you may recall from the discussion about DataReaders, it is possible for the reader to return multiple result sets, using batch SQL or stored procedures. In that case, more than one DataTable would be created and added to the DataSet.

❺ Because a name was specified for the table when filling the DataSet, we can immediately retrieve that table using the name. However, the `Tables` property of the DataSet exposes the list of tables like an indexed collection. The table could have been accessed using a numeric indexer:

```
DataTable dt = ds.Tables[0];
```

Or the code could have just stepped through them all:

```
foreach(DataTable dt in ds.Tables)
```

In this example we only want the one table, and know what it is called, so we can access it simply by name.

❻ The next piece of code steps through all the data in the DataTable and writes it out to the console with some minimal formatting. The code is generic enough that it will work with virtually any DataTable. Because this is the first example using a DataSet, I have broken down this piece of the code into even more pieces to highlight some of the nuances. The following sections demonstrate this.

16.1.1 Accessing the rows

The first `foreach` statement steps through each row in the DataTable:

```
foreach ( DataRow dr in dt.Rows)
```

Each DataTable has a collection of the rows it contains, which can be accessed via the `Rows` property. Thus data in the DataTable can be accessed by stepping through the rows or by using an index to arbitrarily get rows. Unlike with other technologies, we don't need to worry about *skip* commands, or whether a cursor is set up that allows for bidirectional or arbitrary movement. Pretty cool.

16.1.2 Accessing the columns

The second `foreach` statement steps through each column in the DataTable:

```
foreach ( DataColumn dc in dt.Columns )
```

Each DataTable also has a `Columns` property that contains the collection of columns within the data. Each DataColumn has information about the column, such as the column name and its data type.

16.1.3 Accessing the value in a field

There is no Fields collection on a data row. Instead, the DataRow exposes an indexer for accessing each of the fields. The indexer is overloaded so that the field can be retrieved by using the field's ordinal position. For example,

```
dr[2]
```

retrieves the third field. We can also retrieve the field by using its name

```
dr["TeacherName"]
```

or by specifying the DataColumn, as in the example:

```
dr[dc]
```

In any case, the indexer returns an object, so that it can handle any data type generically. The object will be the appropriate type based on the data (string, Int, DateTime, and so forth). The `ToString()` and `Trim()` are just there for formatting—first the object is converted to a string, and then spaces that might be in the data are removed.

16.1.4 Example summary

The example's output looks remarkably like the output from a DataReader example (see figure 16.1).

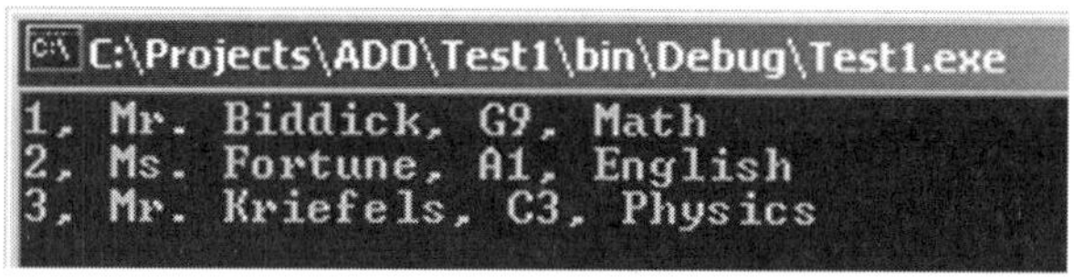

Figure 16.1
Output from listing 16.1

To get here may have seemed like a lot more work than using a DataReader. For this example, that is true—if we were using the DataSet for nothing more than reading and stepping through data, it would have been overkill. However, in the next few examples, you will see where the DataSet really comes into its own.

16.2 CHANGING DATA IN A DATATABLE

The previous example showed how to get data into a DataTable, but was otherwise not terribly enlightening. The real power of a DataSet is in its ability to allow data to be changed and then saved back out. The next example demonstrates.

Because the DataSet is disconnected from the database, it is up to the DataAdapter to write the data back to the database; but, by default, the DataAdapter doesn't know how to do this! You must teach the DataAdapter what to do for each type of modification—

Insert, Update, and Delete. This is nice, because it means you have a great deal of flexibility. On the other hand, it would be a real pain to do so for every simple use.

That is where the CommandBuilder comes in. It is a utility that can teach the DataAdapter how to do these operations. Of course, the CommandBuilder has some limitations—for example, it can't handle DataTables that are built using joins, and the approach it takes for updating is fairly brute force. Chapter 19 goes into detail about these limitations and shows how to customize DataAdapter updates.

For the moment, though, the automatic behavior is fine. The example in listing 16.2 retrieves the information from the Classes table, updates a row, inserts a row, and deletes a row.

Listing 16.2   Updating data in a DataSet

```
public void TestDataSetUpdate(SqlConnection conn)
{
    string strSQL = "SELECT * From Classes";

    // Initialize data adapter with command builder
    SqlDataAdapter sda = new SqlDataAdapter(strSQL,conn);
    SqlCommandBuilder sqb = new SqlCommandBuilder(sda);      ❶ Set commands using
                                                               CommandBuilder
    // Create and fill the dataset
    DataSet ds = new DataSet();
    sda.Fill(ds,"Classes");

    // Get the specific table out of the dataset
    DataTable dt = ds.Tables["Classes"];

    // Update a row
    dt.Rows[2]["TeacherID"] = 1;        ❷ Change data in a row

    // Delete a row
    dt.Rows[3].Delete();        ❸ Delete a row

    // Add a row
    DataRow drNew = dt.NewRow();        ❹ Add a row
    drNew["TeacherID"] = 2;
    drNew["ClassName"] = "Philosophy";
    drNew["Period"] = 5;
    dt.Rows.Add(drNew);

    // Save the changes back to the database
    sda.Update(ds,"Classes");        ❺ Save changes
}
```

❶ I mentioned that using a CommandBuilder was easy. Well, this single line of code is all that is required! The CommandBuilder is created, and is passed the DataAdapter as a parameter. From that point, the CommandBuilder takes over—when the Data-Adapter is told to save data back to the database, the CommandBuilder provides all the plumbing necessary to make everything happen correctly.

❷ Accessing and changing data in a DataSet is nothing more than accessing an array. The `Rows` property holds an array of rows, and the first indexer (`[2]`) specifies that the third row should be accessed. The second indexer (`["TeacherID"]`) references that particular column within the row. It would have been just as legal to specify the column's ordinal position (for example, `dt.Rows[2][2]`); but because the data was retrieved using a `"Select *"` command, it would have been necessary to look up the column first to determine its position.

Once the row and column has been specified, the value basically acts like any other property—we can set and get the data at will. Of course, we must use the correct data type, or an exception will be thrown.

❸ Deleting a row is handled simply by calling the `Delete()` method on that row. Because `Rows` is a collection, you might think we could remove the row using the `Remove` or `RemoveAt` method on the collection. Doing so *will* work, sort of—it will remove the row from the collection. However, when we finally save our changes back to the database, the row will not be deleted!

The reason is that the DataAdapter knows what it has to do by stepping through the rows within the DataTable. When it finds a row whose state has changed to Deleted, it knows to delete the row using the `delete` command. However, if the row has been removed from the `Rows` collection, the DataAdapter will not see it and will not know to delete it.

We can also recover a row that has been marked for deletion, either by changing the state or using the `RejectChanges()` method on the row. If the row has really been removed from the collection, however, there is no easy way to recover it.

❹ In most respects, adding a row to a DataTable is as simple as adding a new DataRow to the `Rows` collection. The one proviso is that a new row must be created, and the row must be appropriate for the DataTable; that is, it must have the appropriate columns in it for each column in the table.

Fortunately, there is an easy way to create such a row: the `NewRow()` method on the DataTable, which returns a new DataRow already set up with all the columns. You might wonder why the method is on DataTable, rather than on the `Rows` collection. It is probably because the DataTable knows about the `Rows` collection, but the `Rows` collection doesn't necessarily know about the table that contains it.

Once the row has been created, the items can be set just as with any existing row. Finally, the row is added to the `Rows` collection. Actually, there is no reason why the new row is added last—we can add it to the `Rows` collection immediately after it is created. However, if constraints or rules were set up on the DataTable, they would be enforced as soon as the row was added. If a blank row violated any rules, then an exception would be thrown.

❺ This is where the DataAdapter comes back into the picture. The DataAdapter fills the DataTable but does not hold onto it. When we want the DataAdapter to write the changes back out, we must pass in the changed data, in the form of the DataSet. We also must pass in the name of the table to update, because a DataAdapter is associated with a particular table, and the DataSet can contain a number of tables.

We can pass the DataTable to the `Update()` method, instead of the DataSet and the name of the table:

```
sda.Update(dt);
```

For this example, that approach might have been a better choice.

16.2.1 Example summary

Figure 16.2 shows the state of the Classes table before the example code was run.

ClassID	TeacherID	ClassName	Period
1	2	Basket-weaving	1
3	3	Physics	2
4	2	Chemistry	3
5	3	Geometry	4
*			

Figure 16.2
State of the Classes table before running Listing 16.2

And figure 16.3 shows the Classes table after the example code was run.

ClassID	TeacherID	ClassName	Period
1	2	Basket-weaving	1
3	3	Physics	2
4	1	Chemistry	3
7	2	Philosophy	5

Figure 16.3
State of the Classes table after running Listing 16.2

Notice that the TeacherID for class 4 changed from 2 to 1, class 5 has been removed, and class 7 has been added. Basically, the code worked as advertised!

In some ways, this example is as spurious as the first—if the goal is to do a bunch of specific adds, updates, and deletes, then we might have well have used the lower-level data provider methods. However, if you extend the mechanism shown here to an interface where the data is presented to a user, and the user can interactively change data, including adding and removing rows, you can see how useful the DataSet can be.

16.3 OTHER DATASET CAPABILITIES

Considering that the DataSet is the focus of part 3 of this book, it is interesting to note that much of the functionality is not so much in the DataSet itself, but in the objects it contains, such as DataTables and Constraints. Nonetheless, the DataSet offers several other points of interest. Some capabilities, such as remoting DataSets or converting a DataSet to and from XML, are covered in their own chapters. However, some things are worth breaking out here.

16.3.1 Dealing with changes

Several handy methods in the DataSet let you determine whether any of the contained data has changed, rolling back changes or committing changes. These methods are generally straightforward. For example, to determine if the DataSet has been modified in any way (since the last time changes were saved), you can use the `HasChanges()` method:

```
bool bChanged = ds.HasChanges();
```

Saving changes

I pointed out that `HasChanges()` specifies whether changes have occurred since the last time changes were saved. In fact, a DataSet is similar to a transaction in that you can either make all the changes permanent or roll them back. *Permanent* does not necessarily mean stored to the database—don't forget that the DataSet knows nothing about the database. Instead, it means the changes are rolled into their respective locations. For example:

- Rows that were added are no longer marked as *new*, but are just considered rows.
- Rows that were deleted are removed from the `Rows` collection.
- The original value for each field is set to the current value, and the field is considered to be unchanged.

This is accomplished via a call to the `AcceptChanges()` method of the DataSet. This method runs through all the DataTables and calls the *DataTable's* version of `AcceptChanges()`. As you might expect, the DataAdapter calls this method after it has finished writing all the changes to the database.

This process is nice, because you can save changes and then continue working with the DataSet, making more updates, saving changes again, and so on. You don't need to reload the DataSet. Of course, other users could have made changes to the data, and the DataSet will not reflect those changes; but, depending on the type of data, that might not matter.

Rolling back changes

If a number of changes have been made, and you decide you do not want to save the changes, but you want to keep working with the DataSet, you can call `Reject-Changes()`. It is the equivalent of calling `Rollback()` on a transaction—it restores the DataSet to its state when it was created, or to the point when `Accept-Changes()` was last called.

Retrieving changes

For various reasons, you might want to get a DataSet that only contains the data that has changed. For example, you might want to prompt the user with the list of changes before applying them, or you might want to make sure that there are no errors in the changes. The main reason you might want to do this, though, is if you are working in a three-tier application. Once changes have been made, you want to send them to the server to be saved, but there is no point sending back all the data—you only want to send the data that has changed.

The DataSet has a method that creates a new DataSet that contains only those DataRows in those DataTables that have changed in some manner:

```
DataSet dsChanged = ds.GetChanges();
```

The new DataSet will only contain rows that have been modified. You can make additional changes to this data, remove items from it, and so forth. Once you are happy with the DataSet containing the changes, you can pass it to a DataAdapter, just as if it were the original DataSet, and save the changes. Of course, the original DataSet will still think that it has the changes to be saved. You will need to call `AcceptChanges()` if you intend to keep working with the original.

When you call `GetChanges()`, you can filter the returned data to one or more particular type of change. For example, you can ask just for rows that have been added:

```
DataSet dsChanged = ds.GetChanges(DataRowState.Added);
```

Using this method, you can specify data that has been added, deleted, or modified, or even data that is unchanged. However, you must consider one issue when retrieving deleted data.

Imagine you want to display a list of records to be deleted before finally applying the changes. You can easily get the rows that have been deleted by calling `Get-Changes(DataRowState.Deleted)`. To display information, though, you will have to access data from one or more columns of the row. When you do this, the row will throw an exception! It does so because you are not allowed to access data in a row that has been deleted.

Fortunately, as you will see in chapter 17, the DataRow maintains multiple versions of itself, including the original values for each column. Although you cannot access the *current* value of the column (because it doesn't currently have a value, having been deleted), you can access the *original* value, from before the delete took place.

16.3.2   Merging DataSets

DataSets also have the ability to merge together two different DataSets. Although doing so might be useful in a number of reasonable scenarios, the main purpose is the support of three-tier applications—instead of sending an entire DataSet to a client or to the server, only differences are sent, and then merged into the rest of the data.

Although using the `Merge` method of a DataSet is fairly straightforward, the merge process is not quite so simple. There are several issues:

- How does the DataSet determine which rows are associated with each other, to deal with the merge?

- What happens if the DataSet has been modified—should those changes be kept?

- What happens if the schema is not the same between the two DataSets?
- What happens if the data is not legal after the merge?

The following sections address each of these issues in order.

Determining associated rows

Although you do not normally need to worry about how this happens, it is important to be aware of the mechanism so you can make sure your data appropriately supports merging. The way in which rows are matched depends on how the DataSet was generated. If the DataSet was generated using the `GetChanges()` method, then the DataSet automatically puts a unique ID in every row, which it can later use to match up differences. If the DataSet was generated any other way, however, then no such unique identifier exists. In that case, the DataSet matches rows by comparing the values in the primary key columns. For this reason, it is important to make sure that you have a primary key field *and* that it is included in the data retrieved from the database.

Dealing with modifications

The `Merge()` method has a number of overloads, including some that let you specify a Boolean value that indicates whether the merge should maintain changes:

```
Merge(DataSet source,bool PreserveChanges);
```

If the `PreserveChanges` flag is set to `false`, or if an overloaded version of `Merge()` is used that doesn't take that flag, then changes to merged rows on the original DataSet are lost—they are overwritten by the changes in the DataSet being merged.

Dealing with schema differences

Most of the time when DataSets are being merged, you can assume that the structure of the contained tables are the same. What happens, though, if they are not? For example, one version may have added an additional column to store the results of a calculation.

The answer is, it depends. You can control what happens by specifying the `MissingSchemaAction` enum, which can be passed to various overloads of the `Merge` method:

```
Merge(DataSet source,bool PreserveChanges, MissingSchemaAction action);
```

This enum specifies what should happen if a column is found in the source DataSet that doesn't exist in the target DataSet. The legal values for `MissingSchema-Action` are shown in table 16.1.

Table 16.1 Legal values for the `MissingSchemaAction` enum

MissingSchemaAction value	Behavior
Add	The extra columns from the source DataSet are added to the target DataSet. This is the default behavior.
Ignore	The extra columns and their data are ignored.
Error	An exception is thrown.
AddWithKey	The extra columns are added, just as with add, plus any primary key information is transferred.

Handling errors

Although we won't get deep into this topic until chapter 18, you can put constraints onto DataTables to limit what data is legal. For example, you can specify that a value in a particular column must be unique. But what happens when you try to merge two DataTables such that you end up with duplicate values in that column?

The DataSet has a property called `EnforceConstraints`. When it is set to `true`, attempting to add data that violates a constraint throws an exception. When it is set to `false`, the DataSet will allow data to be entered that is invalid.

This property is handy when, for example, work is going on in the DataSet, such as a merge. When the merge begins, the `EnforceConstraints` property is turned off; this allows the data to be merged even if problems occur. As soon as the merge is complete, the `EnforceConstraints` property is set back to `true`. At this time, all the existing constraints are checked.

One of two things can happen: either the data is legal, and everything is okay, or the data is not legal. In that case, `EnforceConstraints` is turned back off and an exception is thrown. The idea is that you will catch the exception and fix the problems, and then turn `EnforceConstraints` back on manually.

16.3.3 Example of DataSet changes

Having talked the `Merge()` and `GetChanges()` topics more or less to death, it is time to show some code. The example in listing 16.3 is a modified version of the previous one—it retrieves the same data and modifies it. However, instead of saving the changes back out to the database, it creates a new DataSet containing changes, resets the original DataSet, and then merges the two back together.

The contents of the DataTables are written out at various different points to show the state of the data. We do so using a `PrintDataTable()` method. This method is not shown in the example, but it steps through each row and writes it out, along with a title. It also writes the current state of the row.

The example is slightly artificial in that we are clearing out changes from a DataSet, and then putting them back in. If you imagine that instead of doing this, the DataSet was sent from a server and then returned to the server, it makes more sense.

Listing 16.3 **Merging DataSet changes**

```
public void TestDataSetMerge(SqlConnection conn)
{
    string strSQL = "SELECT * From Classes";

    // Initialize data adapter with command builder
    SqlDataAdapter sda = new SqlDataAdapter(strSQL,conn);
    SqlCommandBuilder sqb = new SqlCommandBuilder(sda);

    // Create and fill the dataset
    DataSet ds = new DataSet();
    sda.Fill(ds,"Classes");

    // Get the specific table out of the dataset
    DataTable dt = ds.Tables["Classes"];

    // Make the ClassID column the primary key column.
    DataColumn[] dcPrimaryKey = new DataColumn[1];
    dcPrimaryKey[0] = dt.Columns["ClassID"];
    dt.PrimaryKey = dcPrimaryKey;

    PrintDataTable("Just after loading",ds.Tables["Classes"]);

    // Update a row
    dt.Rows[2]["TeacherID"] = 1;

    // Delete a row
    dt.Rows[3].Delete();

    // Add a row
    DataRow drNew = dt.NewRow();
    drNew["TeacherID"] = 2;
    drNew["ClassName"] = "Philosophy";
    drNew["Period"] = 5;
    dt.Rows.Add(drNew);

    PrintDataTable("After making changes",ds.Tables["Classes"]);

    // Get the changes
    DataSet dsChanged = ds.GetChanges();
    DataTable dtChanged = dsChanged.Tables["Classes"];
    PrintDataTable("Just changes",dtChanged);

    ds.RejectChanges();
    PrintDataTable("Throw away changes - should look like original",
        ds.Tables["Classes"]);

    // Merge the changes back in
    ds.Merge(dsChanged);
    PrintDataTable("After merging changes",ds.Tables["Classes"]);
}
```

❶ **Specify key information**

❷ **Unchanged data**

❸ **After changes**

❹ **Retrieve changes**

❺ **Clear out original DataSet**

❻ **Merge changes**

❶ By default, when you fill a DataTable, the DataTable contains only basic information about the data. However, in order for a merge to work correctly, the table needs to know which column or columns make up the primary key for the table. The Data-Table stores this information in a `PrimaryKey` property, which is an array of columns.

In our example, the column ClassID is the primary key, so we create an array containing that one column and assign it to the `PrimaryKey` property.

A mechanism exists for automatically retrieving `PrimaryKey` information from the database; chapter 17 explains.

❷ Everything up to now has been straightforward—data has been read out of the database into the DataSet. Figure 16.4 shows what `PrintDataTable` writes out at this point.

```
Just after loading
-------------------
<Unchanged>1, 2, Basket-weaving, 1
<Unchanged>3, 3, Physics, 2
<Unchanged>4, 2, Chemistry, 3
<Unchanged>7, 2, Geometry, 4
```

Figure 16.4
Example output just after loading data

❸ Again, nothing is new here—it's just a bunch of changes to the DataSet. The DataT-able now looks like figure 16.5.

```
After making changes
--------------------
<Unchanged>1, 2, Basket-weaving, 1
<Unchanged>3, 3, Physics, 2
<Modified>4, 1, Chemistry, 3
<Deleted>7, 2, Geometry, 4
<Added>, 2, Philosophy, 5
```

Figure 16.5
Example output after making some changes

The first column in the added row is blank because it is an identity column; SQL Server will assign a unique ID for that column when the data is written to the database.

❹ A new DataSet is being created here that contains just the changes in our original DataSet via the use of the `GetChanges()` method. Because no parameter is being passed to `GetChanges()`, all modified rows are returned, as shown in the output of the new DataSet's table (figure 16.6).

```
Just changes
------------
<Modified>4, 1, Chemistry, 3
<Deleted>7, 2, Geometry, 4
<Added>, 2, Philosophy, 5
```

Figure 16.6
Example output of the DataSet
containing only changed data

❺ In order to merge data into a DataSet, we need to have a clean DataSet. Normally this would be the original DataSet sitting on a server. However, for the sake of the example, we are rolling back all the changes in the DataSet by calling `RejectChanges()`. Of course, our changes are preserved in the `dsChanged` DataSet.

Just to prove that the DataSet is back to its original state, figure 16.7 shows the output.

```
Throw away changes - should look like original

<Unchanged>1, 2, Basket-weaving, 1
<Unchanged>3, 3, Physics, 2
<Unchanged>4, 2, Chemistry, 3
<Unchanged>7, 2, Geometry, 4
```

Figure 16.7
Example output of the original DataSet restored to its original state

❻ Finally, we merge back in the changes using the `Merge()` method. We don't need to worry about schema changes, and so on, because we know the DataSets have the same structure. Figure 16.8 shows the DataSet after calling `Merge()`.

```
After merging changes

<Unchanged>1, 2, Basket-weaving, 1
<Unchanged>3, 3, Physics, 2
<Modified>4, 1, Chemistry, 3
<Deleted>7, 2, Geometry, 4
<Added>, 2, Philosophy, 5
```

Figure 16.8
Example output after `Merge()`

Notice that the contents of the DataSet are exactly the same as after step 3, when the changes were made. This may not seem like much of a trick—doing the same thing with additional code—but if you consider that this process could have happened on a server running elsewhere with the same results, it is fairly impressive.

16.4 SUMMARY

This chapter has given you a taste of the power of the DataSet. It still requires some imagination at this point, because we haven't dealt with remoting or data-bound controls, but the concepts shown here really shine when these other things are thrown into the mix.

As with many facets of .NET, it is easy to immediately make use of the DataSet; but a lot more depth waits beneath the surface. This functionality is demonstrated by some of the change and merge functionality shown in this chapter, and will become even more clear as we plumb the depths of the different pieces of the DataSet over the next several chapters.

The benefit of this depth is that it makes the DataSet both powerful and flexible. The drawback is that you can trip over some of the complexity. For example, if you don't set the primary key information on a DataTable, the merge functionality will not act as expected. As these pitfalls come up, I will point them out and explain how to appropriately navigate around them.

The next chapter discusses the DataTable, DataColumn, and DataRow classes in depth; they are bound to one another quite tightly.

C H A P T E R   1 7

DataTables, DataColumns, and DataRows

As you may have noticed in chapter 16, although part 3 is all about DataSets, much of the focus is on the DataTable. In some ways, you can think of the DataSet as a rather elaborate container for DataTables. A DataTable is a collection of columns that define the data that can be contained, and rows that contain the data.

This chapter explores some of the capabilities of the DataTable, DataColumn, and DataRow classes. It begins by talking about how the DataTable keeps track of what has changed, and what changes took place. It also talks about the ways in which you can automatically set the values for columns by using default values, increments, or calculations. DataTables can also be made responsible for enforcing rules, as we'll discuss.

There is much more to these three classes, however. For an in-depth look at their properties and methods, refer to appendices E, F, and G.

17.1 ROW STATE

In chapter 16, you saw that you could ask a DataSet if it contained any changes via the `HasChanges()` method, and you could accept those changes using the `AcceptChanges()` method, after saving the changes using the DataAdapter. Just knowing that there are changes, though, is obviously not enough information when saving changes. For one thing, the DataAdapter needs to know which rows have changed, which rows have been deleted, and which rows have been added.

You can determine this information using of the `RowState` property on each row contained by the DataTable. This property indicates the state of the row at the current time. Table 17.1 shows the legal values for this property.

Table 17.1   Values of the `DataRowState` enum

Value	Meaning
Unchanged	The row has not been changed since it was loaded, or since the last time `AcceptChanges()` was called.
Modified	The row has been changed in some manner, such as a change to one or more columns.
Added	This is a new row.
Deleted	The row has been marked for deletion. When the row is in this state, data is not allowed to be read from the row.
Detached	The row is not associated with a DataTable. This is the case when a row has been created using the `NewRow()` method but has not yet been added to the DataTable's row collection.

Once the changes to the rows have been saved, `AcceptChanges()` will eventually be called; it will set all the rows back to the `Unchanged` state—all rows, that is, except for those that have been deleted. Those rows will be removed from the `Rows` collection altogether.

The method in listing 17.1 prints out all the rows of data within a passed Data-Table. It uses the `Rows` property and the `Columns` property to retrieve the data, and it also writes out the state of the current row. This method will be used in a number of future examples.

There is one problem, with printing out data: If a row has been deleted, you are not allowed to access its current data. This method provides a workaround, which is explained in the code-notes that follow. Although this code is similar to previous examples, it is explained in more detail.

Listing 17.1   Printing out a DataSet using the Columns and Rows properties

```
public void PrintDataTable(DataTable dt)
{
  foreach(DataRow dr in dt.Rows )          ❶  Access Rows collection
  {
    // Write the state of the row                        ❷  Get row's
    Console.Write("({0})",                                   state
      Enum.Format(typeof(DataRowState),dr.RowState,"g"));
```

```
    // Step through each column in the row and write it out
    foreach(DataColumn dc in dt.Columns)          ❸ Access Columns
    {                                                collection
      if(dc.Ordinal > 0)
        Console.Write(", ");

      if(dr.RowState == DataRowState.Deleted)        ❹ Handle
      {                                                 deleted
        Console.Write(                                  rows
          dr[dc,DataRowVersion.Original].ToString().Trim());
      }
      else
      {
        Console.Write(dr[dc].ToString().Trim());    ❺ Access field value
      }
    }
    Console.WriteLine("");
  }
}
```

❶ The Rows property on a DataTable returns a DataRowCollection, which is really just a type-safe collection of rows. The code uses the `foreach` notation to step through each item in the collection in turn.

TYPE-SAFE COLLECTION   A collection that works with a specific type of object.

Most of the collection classes in .NET are designed to work with the *object* class. This is handy, because everything is derived from object, so the array can hold anything. Sometimes, however, it is nice to guarantee that a collection holds only objects of a specific type, such as a DataRow or a DataColumn. To do so, a derivation of a standard collection is made whose methods work only with objects of the specific type.

This technique is handy because only objects of the specified type can be put in, meaning that the collection is *safe* from having other, illegal, objects added. Also, no typecasting is required, because all the methods return objects of the appropriate type. Finally, you can also put specialized methods on the specialized collection, which only make sense in relation to the type of objects contained in the collection.

❷ This line is fairly ugly, but it just gets the enumerated value indicating the current state of the row (Unchanged, Modified, Deleted, and so on) and converts that value into a string.

❸ Just as with the Rows collection, the Columns property returns a type-safe collection, this time called—wait for it—a DataColumnCollection. The code uses a nested `foreach` statement to step through each column in turn.

❹ As explained in chapter 16, you cannot access the current data in a deleted row. However, you *can* access the original value of the column. The next section explains the different versions of a row's values. For the moment, though, just know that this code is checking to see if the row is deleted; if it is, the code asks for the original version of the data (before any changes), rather than the current version. Asking for the current value of a deleted row will throw an exception.

⑤ To get to the field value, an indexer is used on the DataRow. The DataRow allows for several different indexers—it can access the field numerically

```
dr[3]
```

or by name

```
dr["Classname"]
```

or you can pass the DataColumn object for the desired field. This is the indexer that is used in the example.

17.1.1   Example summary

The example includes a little formatting code to make things look better. Figure 17.1 shows the final output, run against a DataTable with a few changes made.

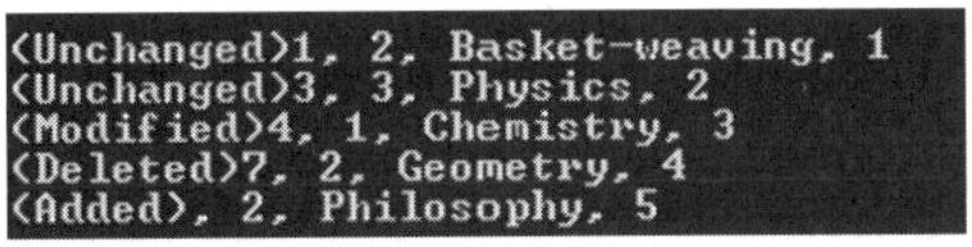

```
<Unchanged>1, 2, Basket-weaving, 1
<Unchanged>3, 3, Physics, 2
<Modified>4, 1, Chemistry, 3
<Deleted>7, 2, Geometry, 4
<Added>, 2, Philosophy, 5
```

Figure 17.1
Output from listing 17.1

17.2   COLUMN VERSIONS

We have talked about the fact that you can call AcceptChanges() to make your changes permanent. However, you can also call RejectChanges() to restore the data to its original state. How does the DataTable roll back to data that has already changed? For that matter, when saving back to the database, an update statement might need to be able to refer to the original value of a column to do a proper update. Again, where is that information stored?

The answer is that each column in each row can store multiple versions of itself. There is the version of the data as it currently appears, which is called the *default* version of the data because it is what you expect to get back by default when asking the column for its value. The column also keeps an *original* value—the value of the column before changes were made, or since the last time AcceptChanges or Reject-Changes was called. This original value is not always available; it is set when AcceptChanges or RejectChanges is called, or when a DataAdapter loads a row, but it is not necessarily set when a new row is created.

A column might contain a couple of other versions. The DataRow supports a special edit mode in which multiple changes can be made and then accepted or rejected together. When you're in this edit mode, the value is stored as the *proposed* version of the data. At this point, though, you can retrieve the value as it existed before the edit, which is referred to as the *current* value. This edit mode is used extensively by the DataBound controls, such as the DataGrid, to allow changes to be made and then saved or abandoned.

The naming of these modes can be quite confusing. Table 17.2 shows the meanings of the different versions.

Table 17.2   Versions of data in a column, using the `DataRowVersion` enum

Value	Meaning
Default	This rather confusingly named value is the default value that will be returned when the column is normally accessed—that is, if you ask for the data in the column.
Current	This is the official value for the column. If some changes are in progress but have not been made permanent, then the current value will not have that proposed value, but will have the official version of the data prior to the change taking place.
Original	If the value in a column has been changed, but changes have not yet been accepted, this is the original value within the column.
Proposed	When you're using the specialized edit mode, described in the next section, the value is not made permanent (set as the current value) until the edit mode is ended. In the meantime, the new value is stored as proposed.

You can determine if a particular row has a particular version using the `HasVersion()` method:

```
dr.HasVersion(DataRowVersion.Original)
```

Notice that the check is at the row level, not at the column level—if there is an original value for the row, then there is an original value for every column in the row. You can access the particular version of the value in a column using a special version of the indexer:

```
dr[dc,DataRowVersion.Original]
```

The second argument to the indexer specifies a particular version to retrieve.

The example in listing 17.2 creates a DataRow and does various things to demonstrate the different versions. A method called `WriteVersions()` uses the `HasVersion()` method and the special indexer to write out all available versions of the value. This method is shown at the end of the code example.

Listing 17.2   Different versions of a value

```
public void DoTestVersions()
{
    // Create the table and the row
    DataTable dt = new DataTable("Test");           ❶ Basic
    DataColumn dc = new DataColumn("Value1",typeof(string));   setup
    dt.Columns.Add(dc);
    DataRow dr = dt.NewRow();
    dt.Rows.Add(dr);
```

```
    // Write out versions before making any changes          ❷ Initial
    Console.WriteLine("Initial values");                         values
    Console.WriteLine("--------------");
    WriteVersions(dr,dc);

    // Start an edit and make a change                     Edit mode and ❸
                                                           make change
    dr.BeginEdit();
    dr[dc] = "New value";
    Console.Write("\r\nValues after edit,");
    Console.WriteLine(" before ending the edit");
    Console.WriteLine("----------------------------------------");
    WriteVersions(dr,dc);

    // End editing                                           ❹ Leave edit
    dr.EndEdit();                                               mode
    Console.WriteLine("\r\nAfter edit has been ended");
    Console.WriteLine("------------------------");
    WriteVersions(dr,dc);
}

public void WriteVersions(DataRow dr,DataColumn dc)        ❺ Retrieve
{                                                            values
    Console.WriteLine("Value = {0}",dr[dc]);

    if(dr.HasVersion(DataRowVersion.Default))
        Console.WriteLine("Default value = {0}",
                        dr[dc,DataRowVersion.Default]);

    if(dr.HasVersion(DataRowVersion.Current))
        Console.WriteLine("Current value = {0}",
                        dr[dc,DataRowVersion.Current]);

    if(dr.HasVersion(DataRowVersion.Original))
        Console.WriteLine("Original value = {0}",
                            dr[dc,DataRowVersion.Original]);

    if(dr.HasVersion(DataRowVersion.Proposed))
        Console.WriteLine("Proposed value = {0}",
                            dr[dc,DataRowVersion.Proposed]);
}
```

❶ This code creates the DataTable with a single column and a single row.

❷ Before any changes have been made, this code writes out the various "values of the values"—if any of the different values have, well, values, then it writes them to the screen. It does so using the WriteVersions() method (explained later), but basically just prints out any values that are set.

   The output from WriteValues() at this point is shown in figure 17.2.

Figure 17.2
Values before any changes

As you might expect, all of the available values are blank. The first line `Value` = is the value retrieved if no special value is specified. You will notice as the explanation continues that the `Value` and the `Default` value are always the same—the default value is the value you get by default when you don't specify any other value!

❸ The next section of code enters edit mode by calling the `BeginEdit()` method. Theoretically, the change will not become the real current value until after we exit edit mode. After entering edit mode, we change the value to be equal to `New value`. Figure 17.3 shows the values as they now exist.

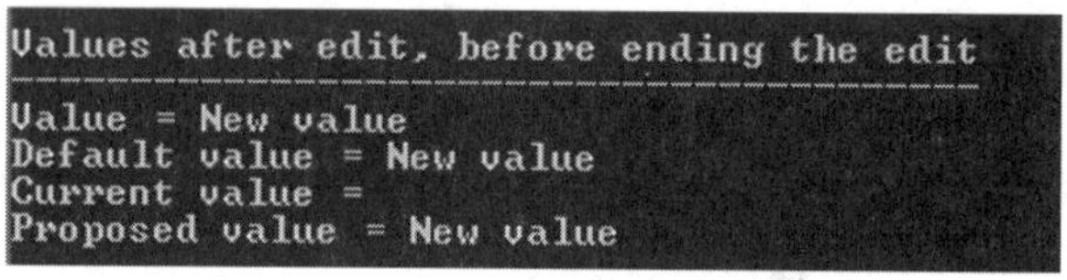

```
Values after edit, before ending the edit
Value = New value
Default value = New value
Current value =
Proposed value = New value
```

Figure 17.3
Values after entering edit mode

As before, the straight value is the same as the default value, which is the value we have set. So, for all intents and purposes, just accessing the data will make it look as though the change has already taken place.

This is not really the case, though, as you can see—the current value is still blank, and the proposed value shows the new value. Not until we leave edit mode will the change become permanent.

❹ The call to `EndEdit()` makes our proposed change permanent. We could also have called `CancelEdit()` to throw away the proposed value. Figure 17.4 shows the values after calling `EndEdit()`.

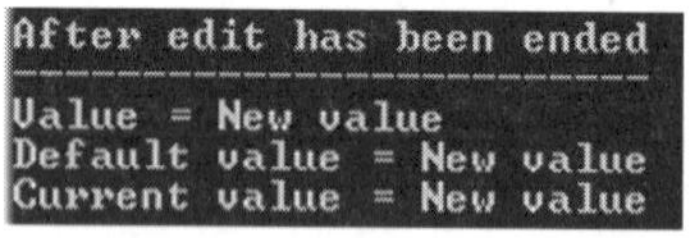

```
After edit has been ended
Value = New value
Default value = New value
Current value = New value
```

Figure 17.4
Values after leaving edit mode

As expected, the current value has now become the value that was previously proposed, and there is no longer a proposed value. The default value remains unchanged.

❺ This method writes out each value that is present. It first uses the `HasValue()` method to determine if the value is present, and then uses the special notation on the indexer to specify that a particular value is desired. The indexer takes a second argument, which is a value from the `DataRowVersion` enum. The first value could be any of the legal indexes. For example, it could have used the column's ordinal position:

```
dr[0,DataRowVersion.Current]
```

17.2.1 The original value

You may have noticed that there never seems to be an original value at any point in the process. That is the case because the original value is set when Accept-Changes() is called. It will also be set if the data is retrieved via a DataAdapter. In my opinion, the creation of the row should count as a first call to AcceptChanges(), but it doesn't, which accounts for its absence from the example. Listing 17.3 shows the original value in use.

Listing 17.3 Working with the original value

```
public void DoTestOriginalVersion()
{
    // Create the table and the row
    DataTable dt = new DataTable("Test");
    DataColumn dc = new DataColumn("Value1",typeof(string));
    dt.Columns.Add(dc);
    DataRow dr = dt.NewRow();
    dt.Rows.Add(dr);

    dr.AcceptChanges();
    Console.WriteLine("Original value = {0}",
                    dr[dc,DataRowVersion.Original]);          ❶

    dr[dc] = "A value";
    Console.WriteLine("Original value = {0}",
                    dr[dc,DataRowVersion.Original]);          ❷
    dr.AcceptChanges();

    dr[dc] = "A different value";
    Console.WriteLine("Original value = {0}",
                    dr[dc,DataRowVersion.Original]);          ❸
    dr.AcceptChanges();
    Console.WriteLine("Original value = {0}",
                    dr[dc,DataRowVersion.Original]);          ❹
}
```

This code calls AcceptChanges(), then sets the data, and writes out the original value each step of the way. Figure 17.5 shows the output.

```
C:\Projects\ADO\Test1\bin\Debug\Test1.exe
Original value =
Original value =
Original value = A value
Original value = A different value
```

Figure 17.5
Output from listing 17.3

❶ The first line is after AcceptChanges() has been called, but no data has been set. The output shows that the original value is blank.

❷ The second line is after the value has been changed, but before AcceptChanges() is called again. Note that the original value is still blank. This makes sense because we are looking at the value from the last `AcceptChanges()`. The A value string has not yet been committed.

❸ The third line is called after the value has been changed to `A different value`. This happens after a call to `AcceptChanges()`, though, which *commits* the A value, making it original.

❹ The final line does not involve a change to the value, but one last change to `AcceptChanges()`. It commits the final value (`A different value`), so that it now becomes the original value.

17.3 *GETTING THE SCHEMA FOR A DATATABLE*

We've talked a lot about the different states for rows and how DataRows keep track of changes. In one respect, a DataTable is really just a collection of rows and columns, but the DataTable has the ability to enforce rules about the data that can be entered. You can manually set up all sorts of rules on a DataTable and its rows and columns. Alternately, you can use the DataAdapter to determine some of the information for you.

When you use the `Fill()` method on a DataAdapter, the DataTable picks up certain pieces of information about the structure of the underlying table—for example, it creates a column for each column in the table, and retrieves its name and data type.

The DataAdapter has a `FillSchema()` method, which can read even more information about the underlying database and transfer that to the DataTable. For example, you can get the primary key information and information about various rules on the table—whether a column allows nulls, and so forth. In the next section, we will look at the various rules and the effects of breaking them; for now, I will run through the list of what `FillSchema()` can read from the database, and then show an example of using `FillSchema()`.

Table 17.3 shows the various properties and items that `FillSchema()` can retrieve from the database.

Table 17.3 Items filled in by `FillSchema()`

Item	Level	Description
PrimaryKey	Table	Fills the primary key collection of the DataTable, which indicates how a row can be uniquely identified.
UniqueConstraint	Table	Normally, `FillSchema()` does not set up any constraints. However, in one circumstance a constraint will be created, and it is a little odd, so bear with me. If the following conditions are `true`, the DataTable will automatically create a `Unique-Constraint` for the field: —There is no primary key on the table. —The table has a field that requires unique values. —The field *also* allows null. Constraints are discussed in detail in chapter 18.
AllowDbNull	Column	Controls whether null values are allowed in the column.

continued on next page

CHAPTER 17 DATATABLES, DATACOLUMNS, AND DATAROWS

Table 17.3   Items filled in by `FillSchema()` *(continued)*

Item	Level	Description
AutoIncrement	Column	Indicates whether the column is set up to automatically create its own value that is incremented. `FillSchema()` will set the flag indicating that incrementing is enabled, but it will not set the next value or the amount the increment should increase each time—this must be done manually.
MaxLength	Column	For text fields, the maximum length of the field.
ReadOnly	Column	If the column does not allow a value to be set.
Unique	Column	Indicates whether the value in the column must be unique compared to any other values in that column.

You can set these properties yourself, and you are not tied to the database when you do so; if you do not want a column to be modified, you can, for example, set the ReadOnly property on the column to prevent it, even if the database allows the value to be changed. This mechanism is handy, though, if you want to model the database. Be aware that calling FillSchema() causes a round-trip to the database, so if you are performance wary, you should use it sparingly. Fill the schema once and then copy the structure, rather than calling it every time you create a new DataTable.

The primary keys can also be specified manually, as demonstrated in chapter 16, by building an array of fields and setting the information:

```
DataColumn[] dcPrimaryKey = new DataColumn[1];
dcPrimaryKey[0] = dt.Columns["ClassID"];
dt.PrimaryKey = dcPrimaryKey;
```

The primary key was used for merging DataTables together. It would be nice, though, to get the primary keys automatically. Listing 17.4 uses FillSchema() to do just that. Of course, the other properties are set too, but listing the primary keys is a good demonstration.

Listing 17.4   Reading the schema from the database

```
public void TestDataSetFillSchema(SqlConnection conn)
{
    string strSQL = "SELECT * From Classes";        ❶ SQL statement

    // Create and fill the dataset schema information
    SqlDataAdapter sda = new SqlDataAdapter(strSQL,conn);
    DataSet ds = new DataSet();
    sda.FillSchema(ds,SchemaType.Mapped,"Classes");    ❷ Fill schema

    // Write out the list of primary keys
    DataTable dt = ds.Tables["Classes"];
    ICollection coll = dt.PrimaryKey;              ❸ Write out primary keys
    foreach(DataColumn dc in coll)
    {
        Console.WriteLine("Primary key field: {0}",dc.ColumnName);
    }
}
```

① This code asks for all the fields in a single table, but we could also SELECT just those fields in which we have an interest. Keep in mind, though, that if we don't select all the fields, we won't get back information on those columns we do not select.

② Using the FillSchema() method on the DataAdapter is fairly straightforward. It determines what schema information is needed based on the Select SQL. It is important to know, however, that this method makes a call to the database to retrieve the schema, so you don't want to do this any more than necessary if performance is an issue. If you are likely to use the same information multiple times, you can create a DataTable holding just the schema, and then use the Clone method to copy the structure to a new DataTable.

Also note that the FillSchema() call doesn't retrieve any data. To do that, you must call Fill(), as before.

③ This code retrieves the primary keys as a collection, and then steps through each column in the collection and writes it out. As you can see from the output in figure 17.6, there is only one primary key column on this table.

```
C:\Projects\ADO\Test1\bin\Debug\Test1.exe
Primary key field: ClassID
```

Figure 17.6
Listing primary keys

17.4   *BREAKING THE RULES*

By using the FillSchema() method, you can set a number of properties that define rules for the data—this column must be unique, that column doesn't allow nulls, and so on. You can also set up these rules manually to control what the DataSet considers legal. What happens, though, when you try to violate those rules? The example in listing 17.5 sets up a column with a number of these rules in place, and then demonstrates what happens when the rules are broken.

To save space, all the errors are coded in a row—of course, once the first error has occurred, the next error will never take place. For the output, though, I commented out each error in turn to show the results.

Listing 17.5   Violating rules on a DataColumn

```
public void DoTestDataColumnErrors()
{
    DataTable dt = new DataTable("Test");

    DataColumn dc =
        new DataColumn("StringData",typeof(string));
    dt.Columns.Add(dc);
```

① Manually create table and column

CHAPTER 17   DATATABLES, DATACOLUMNS, AND DATAROWS

```
    try
    {
        DataRow dr = dt.NewRow();          ❷ Create and
        dt.Rows.Add(dr);                       add row

        // Exceed length                                           ❸ Length
                                                                      violation
        dc.MaxLength = 10;
        dr[dc] = "This value is longer than ten characters!";

        // Set value to null            ❹ Null value
        dr[dc] = "Test";                    violation
        dc.AllowDBNull = false;
        dr[dc] = null;


        // Unique value            ❺ Unique
        dc.Unique = true;              violation
        dr[dc] = "Value1";
        dr = dt.NewRow();
        dt.Rows.Add(dr);
        dr[dc] = "Value1";

        // Read-only                   ❻ Read-only
        dc.ReadOnly = true;               violation
        dr[dc] = "Set a value";


        Console.WriteLine("Test completed");
    }
    catch(Exception ex)
    {
        Console.WriteLine(ex.ToString());
    }
}
```

❶ In most of the examples to this point, the DataTables and DataColumns have been
created using a DataAdapter. Nothing stops us from creating them directly, though.
This code creates the table and the column, and adds the column to the table.

❷ We can work with a row without adding it to a table. However, until a row is part of
a table, none of the rules on any of the columns will be enforced. For the purpose of
this example, the row is being added up front so that each error is generated when its
code is hit. If the row had *not* yet been added to the table, then there would not have
been any exceptions.

That is, there would not have been any exceptions until the row was added to the
table. At that point, the validity of each column would have been checked, and the
add call would have thrown the exception. The exception, however, would have been
the same as shown in the direct examples we'll see later.

❸ This piece of code sets the maximum length of the text in the column to 10, and then tries to put considerably more than 10 characters into the column. The result is an `ArgumentException`:

```
System.ArgumentException: Cannot set Column 'StringData' to
'This value is longer than ten characters!'. The value violates
MaxLength limit of this column.
```

❹ This violation presents a chicken-and-egg problem. Normally, we would define the rules for a column up front, or have that information set based on the properties of the database table. Of course, the moment we create the row, the uninitialized row will have `null` for *all* the columns, including those that do not permit it.

This is usually not a problem because the row is not added to the table until after the data has been set. That is one reason why rows do not check their validity until after the row has been added to the table.

For the purposes of this example, though, we want to simulate a situation where the column is still `null` after the row has been added. To do so, we first put a value into the column, set the rule, and then set the value to `null`.

If the value was not put in first, then just setting the column to not allow `null`s would have immediately thrown an exception. Instead, we don't get an exception until the value is set to `null`. The exception looks like this:

```
System.Data.NoNullAllowedException:
Column 'StringData' does not allow nulls.
```

In the example, the column was set to an explicit `null`. We could have also used the special database `null` object shown in part 2. Doing so would be useful if the value should be `null`, but will also cause an exception when `null`s are not allowed:

```
dr[dc] = DBNull.Value;
```

❺ In order to test this rule, we need more than one row. This code sets the value in the row we have been using all along, then creates a new row and attempts to set the value to be the same. As you probably expect by now, an exception is thrown:

```
System.Data.ConstraintException: Column 'StringData' is constrained to be
unique.  Value 'Value1' is already present.
```

❻ It doesn't get more straightforward than this—the column is read only, and the code attempts to set a value, with the expected result:

```
System.ArgumentException: Column 'StringData' is read only.
```

17.4.1 Example summary

It isn't friendly to throw exceptions at your user all the time. However, this mechanism can allow for a fairly flexible interactive experience—the user edits the row, and then, when the code tries to add the row to the table, you catch the exception, give the user a formatted version of the exception to tell them the row is not legal, and let them try to fix the problem.

This is the default mechanism used by some of the GUI components, such as the DataGrid. Depending on your application and its audience, this default behavior may be perfectly acceptable. Of course, you might want to make the error messages a little more pleasant.

The point is that DataTables and their columns can take care of themselves—once you have set up the proper rules, the DataTable will prevent the data from becoming illegal.[1] In chapter 18, you will see how to set up even more complicated constraints based on multiple columns and other tables.

17.5   DATATABLE EVENTS

So, you can use the built-in exception mechanism to prevent the violation of some very database-centric rules—not allowing `nulls`, checking for unique, and so on. Later, in chapter 18, you will see how to also enforce relationships in the data—for example, specifying that the data in a particular column must be a legal value from another column. What about situations when your application requires that data follow rules beyond the scope of these built-in rules?

You can put in your own handling to catch when an attempt is made to change particular data, and add your own logic to do additional things. This ability is not limited to enforcing data rules; you can update GUI elements, do additional calculations—anything you like.

You do so by subscribing to events that the DataTable exposes. Table 17.4 shows the list of DataTable events.

Table 17.4   DataTable events

Event	Purpose
ColumnChanging	A column in a particular row is about to be changed.
ColumnChanged	A column in a particular row just changed
RowChanging	A row is about to be changed in some way.
RowChanged	A row was just changed.
RowDeleting	A row is about to be deleted.
RowDeleted	A row has been deleted.

Unfortunately you cannot use the `Changing` events to prevent the action from taking place. However, you can make changes to the data if you need to, including restoring the data to its original value (which has the same effect). You can also do arbitrary other things to the data that's being changed. For example, the code in listing 17.6 catches changes to a column and uppercases the value in that column.

---

[1]   Although it can't control whether the data is sensible.

Listing 17.6   Subscribing to a column-changing event

```
public void TestDataTableEvent(SqlConnection conn)
{

    // Create and fill the dataset
    string strSQL = "SELECT * From Classes";
    SqlDataAdapter sda = new SqlDataAdapter(strSQL,conn);
    DataSet ds = new DataSet();
    sda.Fill(ds,"Classes");
    DataTable dt = ds.Tables["Classes"];

    // Register for the column changing event          Subscribe to event ❶
    dt.ColumnChanging +=
            new DataColumnChangeEventHandler(OnColumnChanging);

    // Update a column in a row
    dt.Rows[2]["ClassName"] = "Astro-physics";    ❷  Change value

    PrintDataTable("Display the data",dt);
}

public void OnColumnChanging(object sender,DataColumnChangeEventArgs e)
{
    // Upper-case the value
    if(e.Column.ColumnName == "ClassName")                    ❸  Catch
        e.ProposedValue = e.ProposedValue.ToString().ToUpper();        event
}
```

❶ As with any event, a new event handler is created and assigned to the event. The event handler takes as an argument the name of the method to handle the event. That method must match the expected signature, returning the appropriate data type (in this case void), and taking the appropriate arguments (the sender of the event—the DataTable—and an object that holds event-specific information).

The ColumnChanging event will be fired every time a value in *any* column is changed. We will have to make sure in the event handler that we make changes only to the columns we care about.

❷ This code is just like any other to change the value of a column. However, because we have subscribed to the event, the OnColumnChanging method will be called automatically.

❸ The OnColumnChanging method is called whenever any column is changed, and is passed a DataColumnChangeEventArgs object that contains three important properties:

- Column—The column that is changing
- Row—The row that is changing
- ProposedValue—The value to which the column within the row will be changed

The `Column` property is used in this example to make sure the column we care about is the one changing. If this code didn't check, it would try to run against any column, even if the data type was not `string`, which would cause problems.

The `ProposedValue` is the value that was set earlier. All the example does with it is take the value, uppercase it, and put it back into the `ProposedValue`.

17.5.1 Example summary

As you can see in the example's output (figure 17.7), which was created using the `Print-DataTable()` method developed for other examples, the value is now capitalized.

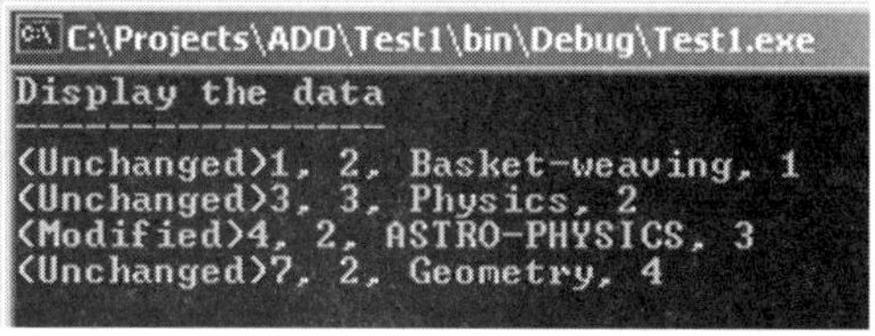

Figure 17.7
Output from listing 17.6

The other events work in more or less the same way as this one. The only difference is that most of the other events take a `DataRowChangeEventArgs` parameter rather than the `DataColumnChangeEventArgs` parameter. This parameter is similar, but has only two properties:

- `Row`—The row being changed or deleted
- `Action`—What is happening to the row; an enumerated value whose possible values are `Add`, `Change`, `Commit`, `Delete`, and `Rollback`

17.6 AUTOMATIC VALUES

You've seen how the DataTable can take care of rules, or allow you to hook in and add your own rules. These operations, though, are all based on data being set externally. In a number of situations, it would be handy if the value in a column could be determined automatically. In at least three situations, a column can do exactly that:

- *Default value*—Specifies the value that a column will contain when a row is first created, instead of being empty.
- *Auto-increment*—When the row is created, places a value in the column based on a counter that continues to increase. You can specify the initial value and also the amount by which the value will increase.
- *Expression*—The most powerful mechanism of all: calculates the value in the column based on an expression. The expression can include values from other columns, mathematical expressions, and so on.

As you might expect, these three mechanisms are mutually exclusive; you cannot have a default value and *also* auto-increment.

The expression mechanism is powerful, and can also be used for other things—for example, you can calculate a total for all rows in a table. This and the other mechanisms are each demonstrated in the following sections.

17.6.1 Default values

The following code sets a default value for a column, and then creates a new row and displays the value in the column. It's not particularly complicated, but it shows that the property functions as advertised:

```
public void DoTestDefaultValue()
{
    DataTable dt = new DataTable("Test");
    DataColumn dc = new DataColumn("StringData",typeof(string));
    dc.DefaultValue = "A default!";
    dt.Columns.Add(dc);

    DataRow dr = dt.NewRow();
    Console.WriteLine("Value in column = {0}",dr[dc]);
}
```

I won't go into a lot of detail about this example. As you can see, the `DefaultValue` property for the column is set to `A default!`. When the new row is added, the value written out should be "A default!" even though it was not set directly, as you can see in the output (figure 17.8).

Figure 17.8
Output from the default value test

17.6.2 Automatic increments

This next example uses the auto-increment properties to create an identifier value. Again, it is fairly self-explanatory:

```
public void DoTestAutoIncrement()
{
    DataTable dt = new DataTable("Test");
    DataColumn dc = new DataColumn("Counter",typeof(int));
    dc.AutoIncrement = true;
    dc.AutoIncrementSeed = 20;
    dc.AutoIncrementStep = 10;
    dt.Columns.Add(dc);

    DataRow dr = dt.NewRow();
    Console.WriteLine("Value in column = {0}",dr[dc]);

    dr = dt.NewRow();
    Console.WriteLine("Value in column = {0}",dr[dc]);

    dr = dt.NewRow();
    Console.WriteLine("Value in column = {0}",dr[dc]);
}
```

When the Counter column is created in this example, the `AutoIncrement` property is set to `true`, and the value is seeded at 20, with an incremental step of 10. The code then creates three rows and writes out the value in the column (figure 17.9).

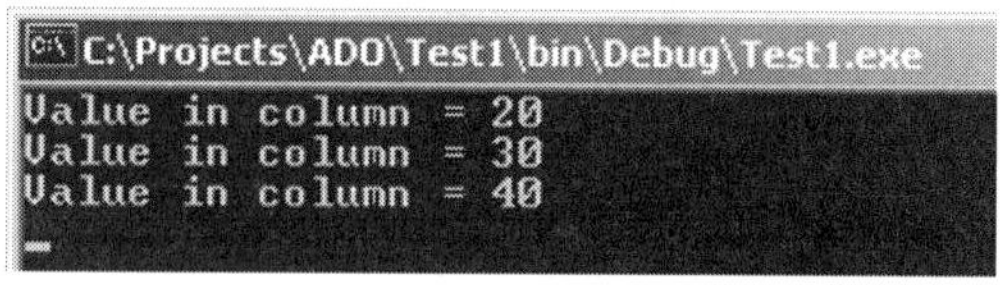

Figure 17.9
Output from the auto-incrementing test

You must be careful when setting up an auto-incrementing column in a table that already contains data. Just because the last value in a row in the table is already set doesn't mean the increment will take that into account! You have to manually set the seed to match the last value *plus* the value of the increment. I understand that making assumptions about data can be a bad thing, but I think that, at the very least, there should be a method to automatically determine the seed, even if the behavior isn't automatic. If I ruled the world. . .

17.6.3   Calculated columns

One of the cool features of a data column is its ability to calculate its value based on an expression. The details of what is and is not legal in an expression are covered in detail in chapter 20, but the example in listing 17.7 shows how to set up a simple expression where the value in a column is the sum of two other columns.

Listing 17.7   A calculated column

```
public void DoTestExpression()
{
    DataTable dt = new DataTable("Test");             ❶ Setup
    DataColumn dc = new DataColumn("Value1",typeof(int));
    dt.Columns.Add(dc);
    dc = new DataColumn("Value2",typeof(int));
    dt.Columns.Add(dc);
    dc = new DataColumn("Value3",typeof(int));
    dt.Columns.Add(dc);

    dc.Expression = "Value1 + Value2";        ❷ Set expression

    DataRow dr = dt.NewRow();
    dt.Rows.Add(dr);                ❸ Adding the row

    dr["Value1"] = 42;                        ❹ Get
    dr["Value2"] = 49;                           result

    Console.WriteLine("Value3 = {0}",dr["Value3"]);

    dr["Value2"] = 100;                       ❺ Change
    Console.WriteLine("Value3 = {0}",dr["Value3"]);   value
}
```

There is enough going on in this example to make it worth breaking out.

❶ This code sets up three columns: Value1, Value2, and Value3, all of type `integer`. There is no particular limitation on the data types that can be involved in expressions, but for this simple example, `integers` are convenient. This is also a good example of how easy it is to build a DataTable without using a DataAdapter.

❷ This expression on the Value3 column adds the values in the Value1 and Value2 columns. Again, this expression could be quite a bit more complicated, as you will see in chapter 20. The column names can be used to reference their contained value.

❸ Calculating the expression is another capability of a column that is not activated until the row has been added to the DataTable. Unlike the validation rules listed earlier, though, if the value cannot yet be calculated, the DataTable does not throw an exception.

❹ Yes—pretty complicated—this code puts a couple of values into the Value1 and Value2 columns. The code then writes out the value in the Value3 column, which we hope will be the sum of the two values. The output is shown in the summary.

❺ Just to show that the expression is updated when the values change, the value in one of the columns is changed and the result is written out again.

Example summary

Figure 17.10 shows the output from the example.

```
C:\Projects\ADO\Test1\bin\Debug\Test1.exe
Value3 = 91
Value3 = 142
```

Figure 17.10
Output from Listing 17.7

As you can see, the initial value is 91, which (assuming my basic math skills are up to speed) is the sum of 42 and 49. The value then changes to 142 when the second value is changed from 49 to 100.

This is a painful way to do math, but it's handy if you are working with a whole table full of rows—especially if you are using a DataGrid that can show the calculated value for each row. Chapter 20 discusses the details of the other types of calculations you can do here.

17.6.4 Computing values against a DataTable

The previous section showed how to calculate a value in a column for each row, but there is also a mechanism for doing summary calculations against an entire table. For example, you can sum up all the values in a particular column. This functionality is fairly limited; for instance, you cannot do calculations that involve more than one column. However, for certain types of operations, it can be quite useful.

The following example uses the `Compute()` method to determine the last period for which there is a class from the Classes table:

CHAPTER 17 DATATABLES, DATACOLUMNS, AND DATAROWS

```
public void TestDataSetCompute(SqlConnection conn)
{
    string strSQL = "SELECT * From Classes";

    // Create and fill the dataset
    SqlDataAdapter sda = new SqlDataAdapter(strSQL,conn);
    DataSet ds = new DataSet();
    sda.Fill(ds,"Classes");

    // Compute the last class
    DataTable dt = ds.Tables["Classes"];
    int iTotal = (int)dt.Compute("Max(Period)","");

    Console.WriteLine("Last class is {0}",iTotal);
}
```

Using the Compute method

Two strings can be passed to the Compute method. The first is the expression to evaluate, and the second is a filter that limits which row will be sent.

The format for both the expression and the filter is fairly SQL-like. However, there are some limitations. The expression is limited to a single column; and the filter can use multiple columns, but not joins. The valid expressions that can be used are discussed in more detail in chapter 20, which examines querying the DataSet in detail.

Just to be complete, figure 17.11 shows the output from the code.

Figure 17.11
Output from the summary
calculation example

17.7 SUMMARY

This chapter is long, but considering that it covers three really important classes, it could have been a lot worse! You can do many things with the DataTable, DataColumn, and DataRow classes—both directly and indirectly. Appendices E–G present all the properties and methods of these three classes and provide additional examples.

At one level, a DataTable is simply a holder for a bunch of data, broken down into rows, where each row contains some columns. If you choose, though, you can take advantage of a lot more functionality within the DataTable, making it emulate many of the behaviors of a database. For example, a DataRow keeps track of various versions and can roll back data. DataColumns can define all sorts of rules about the data that is legal, and can even determine their own values.

Beyond these capabilities, these classes are powerful because of the other classes with which they work, such as relationships and constraints (discussed in chapter 18); and also because of the way they can be loaded and saved via DataAdapters (the topic of chapter 19).

CHAPTER 18

DataRelations and constraints

The idea behind a DataSet is very powerful—instead of working directly with a database, you can take a slice out of that database, work on it offline, and then have the changes written back to the database. This concept is at the heart of the stateless application model and is currently the best model for making applications scaleable.

How far does a DataSet really go, though, in supporting this functionality? So far, we have seen representations of tables, columns, and rows, but they are only one piece of what a relational database provides—the key word being *relational*. Tables are related to one another in various ways, and those relationships make the data model complete. In the same way, a DataSet can contain DataRelations and constraints to more accurately model the database.

This functionality does not mean that you can completely model your business logic in the DataTable, any more than you can do so in the database—of course, with stored procedures and triggers, some systems try to do so, but it is not a good idea. Burying an application's logic in a database is almost as bad as burying the logic within the user interface! However, it is convenient to model some basic aspects of data relationships within a database, and, likewise, it is convenient to do so in the DataSet that represents your database on the client tier.

As well as being able to provide some reasonable sanity checks via relationships and constraints, the DataSet can also provide automatic behavior for dealing with relationships, like removing invalid data via a foreign key. Also, some of the data-aware controls can traverse the relationships to display parent/child data.

This chapter will demonstrate how to set up relationships and constraints, and how to use them to update data. Later, in part 4, you will see how the DataGrid can automatically show parent/child relationships.

18.1 SETTING UP A RELATIONSHIP

There is no automatic way for a DataAdapter to set up relationships within a DataSet, even if the relationships have been defined in the back-end database. FillSchema() will fill in some constraint information under very specific circumstances, but for relationships you are on your own. Fortunately, it is fairly easy to set up a relationship.

The example in listing 18.1 relates the Teachers and Classes table, such that the TeacherID of the Classes table is related to the Teachers table's TeacherID. It then writes out the teacher information, followed by the classes for that teacher. This example is fairly lengthy, partially because it includes a generic method for displaying a table and its children.

Listing 18.1 Setting up and writing out a relationship

```
public void TestRelationshipDataSetSQL(SqlConnection conn)
{
    // Create and fill the dataset with two tables
    DataSet ds = new DataSet();
    string strSQL1 = "SELECT * From Classes";
    SqlDataAdapter sda1 = new SqlDataAdapter(strSQL1,conn);
    DataTable dtClasses = ds.Tables.Add("Classes");
    sda1.Fill(dtClasses);

    string strSQL2 = "SELECT * From Teachers";
    SqlDataAdapter sda2 = new SqlDataAdapter(strSQL2,conn);
    DataTable dtTeachers = ds.Tables.Add("Teachers");
    sda2.Fill(dtTeachers);

    // Set up the DataRelation
    DataRelation dr = new                              ❶ Create
            DataRelation("TeacherClasses",               relationship
                    dtTeachers.Columns["TeacherID"],
                    dtClasses.Columns["TeacherID"]);
    ds.Relations.Add(dr);

    // Write out the Teachers table, and show related data
    DisplayDataTableWithChildren(dtTeachers);
}

// Generic method for writing out a data-table and
// one level of children
```

```
public void DisplayDataTableWithChildren(DataTable dt)
{
    // Write out each row in the passed table
    foreach(DataRow dr in dt.Rows)
    {
        foreach(DataColumn dc in dt.Columns)               ❷ Write out
        {                                                      main table
            if(dc.Ordinal > 0) Console.Write(", ");
            Console.Write(dr[dc].ToString().Trim());
        }
        Console.WriteLine("");

        // Now step through all child-relationships for this row
        foreach(DataRelation rel in dt.ChildRelations)
        {                                                  ❸ Step through
            Console.WriteLine("      {0}",                    child relationship
                            rel.ChildTable.TableName);
            Console.WriteLine("      -------");

            ICollection coll = dr.GetChildRows(rel);       ❹ Step through
            foreach(DataRow drChild in coll)                   child rows
            {

                foreach(DataColumn dcChild in drChild.Table.Columns)
                {
                    if(dcChild.Ordinal == 0)            Write out ❺
                        Console.Write("      ");        child table
                    else
                        Console.Write(", ");
                    Console.Write(drChild[dcChild].ToString().Trim());
                }
                Console.WriteLine("");
            }
        }
        Console.WriteLine("");
    }
}
```

❶ All the code up until this point should be familiar: two different DataTables are loaded with data from the database using a couple of DataAdapters. Right now, though, they do not have any knowledge of each other. For that to happen, a DataRelation needs to be created and added to the DataSet.

A DataRelation can be created a number of different ways, but the practical goal is to specify which columns in the parent table are related to which columns in the child table. In this example, a single column in each table forms the relationship: the TeacherID column. The Teacher table is the parent in the relationship, so it's specified first, followed by the TeacherID column in the Classes table, which identifies the child. The relationship is also given a name: TeacherClasses.

We can use more than one column on each side to identify the relationship, either by passing an array of columns to the constructor, rather than a single column, or by directly accessing the ChildColumns or the ParentColumns properties of the DataRelation. We are using the convenient override for specifying a single-column relationship, which will often be the case for relationships.

Once the relationship has been created, it must be added to the DataSet, which is done simply by adding it to the DataSet's Relations property. Doing so will automatically associate the relationship with the appropriate tables' parent and child relationships.

One important fact about this relationship is that the relationship itself does not provide any enforcement. However, by default, a ForeignKeyConstraint is created as well, which does enforce that the value is legal. ForeignKeyConstraints and enforcement are discussed in section 18.2. Writing out the data based on the relationship is done in the DisplayDataTableWithChildren method.

② The DisplayDataTableWithChildren method steps through each row in the passed DataTable. The first thing it does with each row is write out each column. This process is no different from the innumerable previous examples.

③ The DataTable has two collections of relationships:

- ChildRelations—The collection of all relationships where the current table is the *parent* and the other table is a child
- ParentRelations—The collection of all relationships where the current table is the *child* and the other table is the parent

Because we want to display child information, we are using the ChildRelations property. In the example, there will be only one child relationship, but this method will work no matter how many relationships have been defined.

Once the relationship has been retrieved (via the loop), the name of the child table is retrieved and written out via the DataRelation's ChildTable property, which is a reference to the child table. As you have probably already assumed, there is also a property called ParentTable.

④ The DataRow is used to access the child rows from the child table, using the Get-ChildRows() method. The argument to this method is the relationship that should be navigated to retrieve the rows. The method returns a collection of rows from the child table that are related—that is, all rows where the values in the parent columns within the relationship match the values in the child columns within the relationship.

⑤ This code is no different from the code that wrote out the main table's rows, except that it indents the output slightly for readability.

In fact, those of you who are into such things might wonder why we didn't just make the code recursive. Not only would doing so have let us reuse the row output, it would have also displayed the children's children, and so on. To be honest, I had to fight the urge to do just that, because it would have made the example much harder to follow. The super-recursive, ultra-efficient version of this method is left as an exercise to the more adventurous (or bored) reader.

18.1.1 Example summary

Figure 18.1 shows the output from listing 18.1.

```
C:\Projects\ADO\Test1\bin\Debug\Test1.exe
1, Mr. Biddick, G9, Math
    Classes
    ---------

2, Ms. Fortune, A1, English
    Classes
    ---------
        1, 2, Basket-weaving, 1
        4, 2, Chemistry, 3
        7, 2, Geometry, 4
3, Mr. Kriefels, C3, Physics
    Classes
    ---------
        3, 3, Physics, 2
```

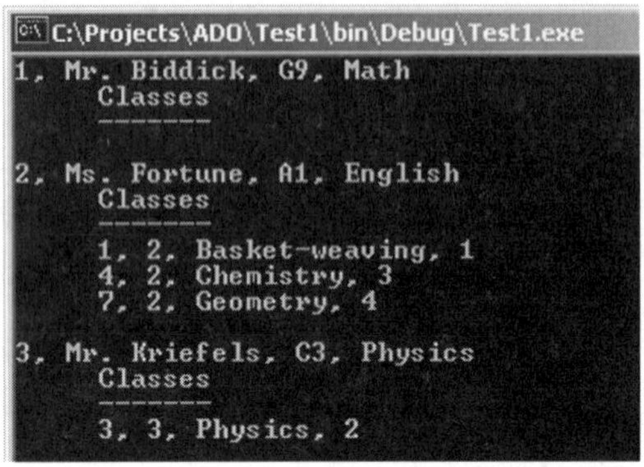

Figure 18.1
Output from listing 18.1

Notice that some rows in the Teachers table have no children, whereas others have several. Of course, this sample data is designed to be more brief than realistic.

18.2 SETTING UP CONSTRAINTS

Using relationships to associate tables is useful for navigation, but it would also be nice if there was a way to enforce that the relationship was maintained—that no illegal values were set on one side or the other of the relationship.

You can do this by using a `ForeignKeyConstraint`. In addition, another type of constraint, called a `UniqueConstraint`, can be used to enforce that the value within a particular column is unique for the table. This section will demonstrate the use of both constraints, and will also explore some of their options.

18.2.1 Foreign key constraints

FOREIGN KEY A foreign key is a constraint placed on a column or columns that requires the value within that column or columns to be a value that exists in another table.

By putting a foreign key on a column in a database, the database will only allow the value in the column be a legal value from a column in the referenced table. In figure 18.2, a foreign key is defined for the Classroom field in the Classes table.

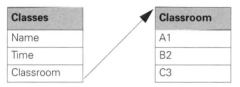

Classes		Classroom
Name		A1
Time		B2
Classroom		C3

Figure 18.2   Foreign key

When a new row is added to the Classes table, the value in the Classroom field *must* be a legal value from the Classroom column of the Classroom table. If it is not, the database will prevent the row from being saved.

By setting up a foreign key constraint on a DataTable, you can prevent an illegal value from being placed into a field, and control what happens when the data associated with the constraint is modified or removed. Note that although a relationship can exist that matches the foreign key, no such relationship is required—the constraint works entirely independently.

Let's look at the foreign key in a couple of different pieces: first, requiring a legal value; and second, dealing with changes in the dependent values.

Enforcing a foreign key

The code in listing 18.2 reads the Teachers table and the Classrooms table into a DataSet, and then sets up a constraint on the Classroom field of the Teachers table such that the value must be a legal value from the Classrooms table.

Listing 18.2   Violating a foreign key constraint

```
public void TestForeignKeyConstraint(SqlConnection conn)
{
    // Load the tables into the data set
    DataSet ds = new DataSet();
    string strSQL1 = "SELECT * From Teachers";
    SqlDataAdapter sda1 = new SqlDataAdapter(strSQL1,conn);
    DataTable dtTeachers = ds.Tables.Add("Teachers");
    sda1.Fill(dtTeachers);

    string strSQL2 = "SELECT * From Classrooms";
    SqlDataAdapter sda2 = new SqlDataAdapter(strSQL2,conn);
    DataTable dtClassrooms = ds.Tables.Add("Classrooms");
    sda2.Fill(dtClassrooms);
                                           Define and add ❶
    // Create and add the foreign key constraint    constraint
    ForeignKeyConstraint fkc = new
        ForeignKeyConstraint(dtClassrooms.Columns["Classroom"],
                             dtTeachers.Columns["Classroom"]);
    dtTeachers.Constraints.Add(fkc);
    ds.EnforceConstraints = true;        ❷ Enforcing
                                           constraints
    try
    {
```

```
    DataRow dr = dtTeachers.Rows[0];
    dr["Classroom"] = "U7";    // Illegal value
}
catch(Exception ex)
{
    Console.WriteLine(ex.Message);
}
}
```

❸ **Set illegal value**

❶ The code prior to these lines sets up and read the two tables: Teachers and Classrooms. Classrooms contains a list of the legal classrooms in the building.

The `ForeignKeyConstraint` has two important properties that we set via the constructor: the columns in the table being constrained and the columns in the related table that provide the list of legal values:

- The *second* argument to the `ForeignKeyConstraint` constructor being used in this example specifies the column being constrained. This could have been a collection of columns rather than just one, and could have also been set directly via the `Columns` property of the constraint. In this example, the column being constrained is the Classroom column of the Teachers table, because we want to ensure that the value entered in that column is a legal value from the Classrooms table.

- The *first* argument to the constructor specifies the column (or columns) that contains the values to which we are limited—in this case, the Classroom column of the Classroom table. The related columns can also be accessed via the `RelatedColumns` property of the constraint.

Note that if you want to use multiple columns to make up the constraint, a one-to-one mapping must exist—if there are three columns in the main table, then there must be three columns in the related table.

Once the constraint has been created, it must be added to the DataTable's constraint collection. It doesn't really matter which DataTable the constraint is added to—it will automatically be added to the other.

❷ By specifying that constraints will be enforced, we are telling the DataSet that we want it to throw an exception if a constraint is violated. Actually, this value defaults to `true`, so setting it explicitly is not strictly necessary; but it is always a good idea to specify the desired behavior in case the default changes later.

We could set the `EnforceConstraints` property to `false` here, in which case setting the value to an illegal value would succeed. If we later attempt to set the property to `true` (after putting in the illegal value), the set will fail and throw an exception indicating that a constraint has been violated. This process is shown a little later.

❸ Just to prove that the constraint is working, the code sets the Classroom column in one of the rows to an illegal value. Doing so immediately throws an exception (figure 18.3).

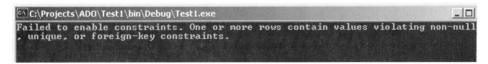

```
C:\Projects\ADO\Test1\bin\Debug\Test1.exe                          _ □
ForeignKeyConstraint Constraint1 requires the child key values (U7) to exist in
the parent table.
```

Figure 18.3   Output from listing 18.2

The constraint is of type `InvalidConstraintException`, so it could have been caught explicitly to provide a custom message. We did not do that in the example because we'll change the code in a minute to generate a different type of exception.

Note that the constraint has a name—`Constraint1`. Because we did not explicitly give the constraint a name, the system provided one for us automatically.

Enabling constraints later

As I mentioned, the sequence of the code could have been changed. If we changed the initial set to

```
ds.EnforceConstraints = false;
```

and the code in the `try`, `catch` block to enable it

```
try
{
   DataRow dr = dtTeachers.Rows[0];
   dr["Classroom"] = "U7";   // Illegal value
   ds.EnforceConstraints = true;
}
```

we would have been passed the line setting the value. However, as soon as we attempted to set the `EnforceConstraints` property to `true`, we would have received an exception (figure 18.4).

```
C:\Projects\ADO\Test1\bin\Debug\Test1.exe                          _ □
Failed to enable constraints. One or more rows contain values violating non-null
, unique, or foreign-key constraints.
```

Figure 18.4   Output from example that enables constraints later

The type of this exception is a straight `ConstraintException`. Both this and the `InvalidConstraintException` are derived from `DataException`, so the catch could have caught that, rather than just a generic exception.

Because there is data that violates the constraint, the `EnforceConstraints` property remains set to `false`.

Once you have caught the exception, you can determine which rows have errors via the `GetErrors()` method:

```
catch(ConstraintException ex)
{
   Console.WriteLine(ex.Message);
   Console.WriteLine("");
```

```
    ICollection coll = dtTeachers.GetErrors();
    foreach(DataRow dr in coll)
        Console.WriteLine(dr.RowError);
}
```

This code will get all the rows in the table with an error and write out the error for that row (figure 18.5).

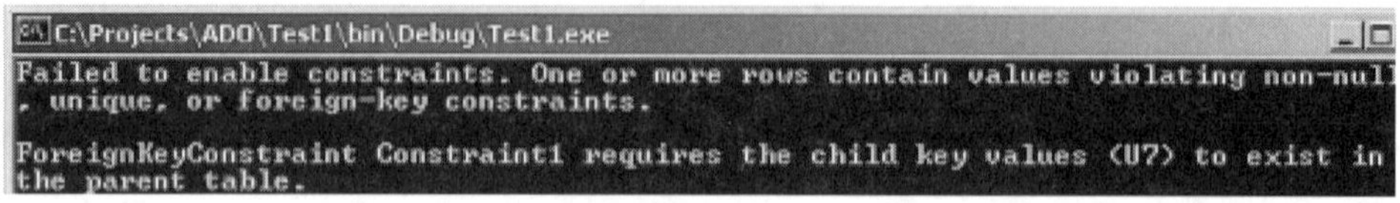

Figure 18.5   Output that writes out row errors

The nice thing about this result is that you can determine which rows have problems and respond accordingly. Unfortunately, there is no direct way of determining which constraint has the problem. This is okay in our example because we have a single constraint, but would be problematic if we had multiple constraints.

Notice that the code is explicitly catching the `ConstraintException`. Given that this is a fairly explicit constraint, I don't know why Microsoft did not add a member that referenced the constraint, or at least the name of the constraint (which would avoid marshalling problems across tiers). As it is, the best that you can do is to check the `RowError` string for the name of the constraint, which is not a clean process and could be inconsistent (giving the constraints unique names that are unlikely to appear in the rest of the text would help).

In some circumstances, disabling and then enabling constraint enforcement is a useful procedure, such as when you are making a series of changes to data that will eventually all be legal.

Dealing with changes with foreign keys

So far, we have used foreign key constraints to prevent an illegal value from being entered into a column. Foreign keys can also be used to provide automatic behavior when the referenced value changes—for example, if a classroom is renumbered.

The example in listing 18.3 sets up a rule such that when the referenced value changes, the value in the main table changes as well.

Listing 18.3   Changing the related table with a constraint

```
public void TestForeignKeyConstraint(SqlConnection conn)
{
    // Load the tables into the data set
    DataSet ds = new DataSet();
    string strSQL1 = "SELECT * From Teachers";
    SqlDataAdapter sda1 = new SqlDataAdapter(strSQL1,conn);
    DataTable dtTeachers = ds.Tables.Add("Teachers");
    sda1.Fill(dtTeachers);
```

CHAPTER 18   DATARELATIONS AND CONSTRAINTS

```
string strSQL2 = "SELECT * From Classrooms";
SqlDataAdapter sda2 = new SqlDataAdapter(strSQL2,conn);
DataTable dtClassrooms = ds.Tables.Add("Classrooms");
sda2.Fill(dtClassrooms);

// Create and add the foreign key constraint
ForeignKeyConstraint fkc = new
    ForeignKeyConstraint(dtClassrooms.Columns["Classroom"],
                         dtTeachers.Columns["Classroom"]);
fkc.UpdateRule = Rule.Cascade;        ❶ Set up rule
dtTeachers.Constraints.Add(fkc);
ds.EnforceConstraints = true;

try
{
    PrintDataTable("Before change",dtTeachers);

                                      Make changes ❷
    DataRow dr = dtClassrooms.Rows[0];
    Console.WriteLine("Current classroom: {0}",dr["Classroom"]);
    dr["Classroom"] = "A5";
    Console.WriteLine("New classroom: {0}\r\n",dr["Classroom"]);

    PrintDataTable("After change",dtTeachers);
}
catch(DataException ex)                ❸ Catch exceptions
{
    Console.WriteLine(ex.Message);
}
}
```

❶ My apologies for repeating so much of the code from the earlier example, but I wanted the example to be complete. The same tables are loaded, and the same constraint is created. There is, however, one difference: we are setting the behavior on the constraint to indicate what should happen when the related data is updated. In this case, we are specifying that the change should be cascaded to dependent tables.

Several other things can be done, other than cascading; they are explained a little later.

❷ This code changes one of the classrooms from A1 to A5 in the Classrooms table and prints out the data before and after, using the `PrintDataTable()` method created in chapter 16. Notice that absolutely no change is made to the Teachers table (nothing up my sleeves. . .). The output is shown in figure 18.6.

Even though no change was made to the Teachers table directly, the value was updated, and the row was marked as modified. Pretty cool, no? If the value had been used in more rows, it would have been changed in those rows as well.

❸ Although this code doesn't throw an exception, I wanted to take the opportunity to show yet another variant for the `try`, `catch` block. In this case, we are catching a `DataException`, which is the base class for most of the DataSet exceptions. By being more specific with the exception code, we can build something that catches only data problems and let other problems pass to a more general exception mechanism.

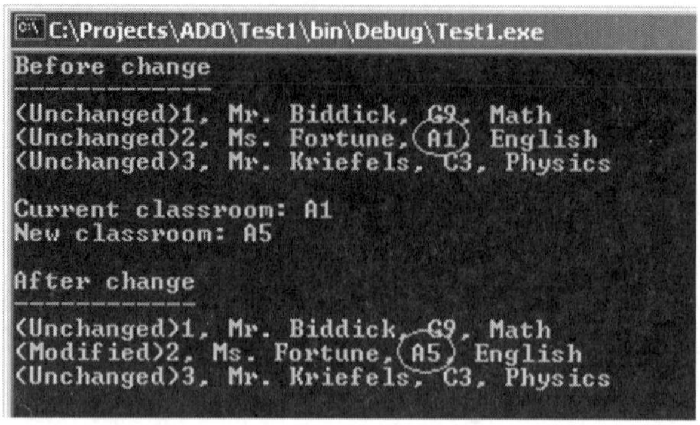

Figure 18.6
Output from Listing 18.3

The exceptions for database errors are not derived from `DataException`, but are data-provider specific. For example, SQL Server Provider exceptions are all based on `SqlException`. There is no base class for database exceptions (an unfortunate oversight on Microsoft's part).

Other rules

The previous code demonstrates one option for dealing with an update in the related table, but the `UpdateRule` property has several other legal values, contained in the `Rule` enum; see table 18.1.

Table 18.1 `Rule` **enumeration**

Value	Result
None	No action is taken in the main table.
Cascade	As you have already seen, this value changes the value in all dependent rows to match the new value in the related table.
SetDefault	The value in the column is set back to the default value for the column.
SetNull	The value in the column is set to `null`.

Keep in mind when using these rules that if constraints are being enforced, then the behavior of the row can cause an exception to be thrown. For example, if a value is changed in the related table that is being used in the main table, and the `Update-Rule` is set to `None`, then those values will suddenly be in violation of the constraint.

The `UpdateRule` property on the constraint is responsible for handling changes to rows in the related table, but does not handle deletes from that table—that is the responsibility of the `DeleteRule`. The value of the `DeleteRule` property is also based on the `Rule` enum, and for most of the values, the behavior is the same as for the `UpdateRule`. `Cascade`, however, is a different story. If the `DeleteRule` property is set to `Cascade`, and a row is removed from the related table, all rows in the main table that use the value from the deleted row will be *deleted*!

This is a powerful capability and should be used with care. I know that schools have a lot of problems these days, but eliminating a teacher simply because a classroom stops being available is a bit draconian!

18.2.2 Unique constraints

The other type of constraint provided by ADO.NET is the unique constraint, which simply guarantees that the value entered into a column (or columns) hasn't been used in any other rows. This constraint is useful for identifiers or for avoiding duplicates.

The example in listing 18.4 makes sure that no teacher is teaching more than one class at the same time.

Listing 18.4 Violating a unique constraint

```
public void TestUniqueConstraint(SqlConnection conn)
{
    // Load the table into the data set
    DataSet ds = new DataSet();
    string strSQL1 = "SELECT * From Classes";
    SqlDataAdapter sda1 = new SqlDataAdapter(strSQL1,conn);
    DataTable dtClasses = ds.Tables.Add("Classes");
    sda1.Fill(dtClasses);

    // Define the constraint
    UniqueConstraint uc = new UniqueConstraint(         ❶ Define unique
        new DataColumn[]                                  constraint
            {dtClasses.Columns["TeacherID"],
                dtClasses.Columns["Period"]});
    dtClasses.Constraints.Add(uc);
    ds.EnforceConstraints = true;

    // Set some data
    try
    {
        // Legal add
        DataRow drNew = dtClasses.NewRow();             ❷ Add legal row
        drNew["TeacherID"] = 1;
        drNew["ClassName"] = "Bowling";
        drNew["Period"] = 2;
        dtClasses.Rows.Add(drNew);

        // Illegal add
        drNew = dtClasses.NewRow();                     ❸ Add illegal row
        drNew["TeacherID"] = 3;
        drNew["ClassName"] = "French";
        drNew["Period"] = 2;
        dtClasses.Rows.Add(drNew);
    }
    catch(DataException ex)
    {
        Console.WriteLine(ex.Message);
    }
}
```

❶ One of the constructors for the unique constraint allows us to pass an array of columns that should be used for the constraint, which can be accessed via the `Columns` property. The notation creates the array in-line. If the constraint was only a single column, then we could have passed the column without creating the array at all, by using a different constructor.

Setting up a unique constraint is pretty simple—all the constraint really needs is the list of columns.

❷ Figure 18.7 shows the current layout and data from the Classes table.

ClassID	TeacherID	ClassName	Period
1	2	Basket-weaving	1
3	3	Physics	2
4	2	Chemistry	3
7	2	Geometry	4

Figure 18.7
The Classes table

Notice that although there is a class already for period 2, there is no class for teacher 1 during that period. Therefore, this add is completely legal.

❸ On the other hand, there *is* already a class for teacher 3 during period 2. He is already teaching physics, so he cannot take on the French class at the same time (unless he wants to talk about Marie Curie, maybe). Therefore, as soon as the row is added, an exception will be thrown (figure 18.8).

Figure 18.8   Output from Listing 18.4

The wording of the exception is a little awkward, but the effect is as desired.

An important caveat about the unique constraint is that it can only guarantee uniqueness between the values in memory. If there had been a `where` clause on the `select` that filled the DataTable, then it would have conceivably been possible to put in data that was legal for the values in memory, but that caused duplicates at the point where the data was written to the database.

18.3 USING RELATIONSHIPS TO SET UP CONSTRAINTS

So far we have set up relationships by themselves and we have set up constraints by themselves. However, you can automatically set up constraints based on the relationships. If you recall earlier when we created the relationship, all we passed were the name and the columns:

```
DataRelation dr = new
        DataRelation("TeacherClasses",
                    dtTeachers.Columns["TeacherID"],
                    dtClasses.Columns["TeacherID"]);
```

You can pass an additional argument to the constructor, which specifies whether to create a matching foreign key constraint that matches the relationship:

```
DataRelation dr = new
        DataRelation("TeacherClasses",
                     dtTeachers.Columns["TeacherID"],
                     dtClasses.Columns["TeacherID"],true);
```

This is the default behavior—if the parameter is omitted, the constraint will be created automatically. You only need to specify this parameter if you do not want the constraint to be created.

18.4 SUMMARY

Although they are very powerful, relationships and constraints are quite straightforward to set up and use. The tricky part comes when you want the code to work with exceptions and interact with the user to correct problems. Of course, if you are using one of the built-in data-bound controls, such as the DataGrid, then it does much of this work for you, as you will see starting with chapter 22.

When you're developing applications, it's important to decide how much automatic behavior you want; you must also decide whether to build an application around data rules throwing exceptions or whether you want to have the application understand the data and respond appropriately. In the first case, the application tends to be more flexible and easier to update—all you have to do is customize your rules, and the application will respond appropriately. On the other hand, it takes a lot of work to do this in a way that provides users with a good interactive experience. The second route generally provides a better user experience, but requires the application to change when the data changes.

Chapter 19 shows how to control the way in which changes to data in a DataSet are written out to the database.

Customizing DataAdapters

Starting with chapter 15, we offered several examples of writing data back to a database using a CommandBuilder to generate the statements for inserts, updates, and deletes. Although this automatic behavior is convenient, it does not always work exactly as desired. The CommandBuilder's statements cannot do some things, like deal with joins. In addition, the SQL it generates is generic and might not do what you expect. Finally, these statements cannot take advantage of the knowledge *you* have of your database, such as the use of stored procedures.

This chapter explains how you specify your own commands for doing updates, either partially or completely, providing specific examples for updates that are more efficient, updates that involve joins, and updates that use stored procedures.

19.1 COMMANDBUILDER STATEMENTS

In earlier examples, the CommandBuilder was used with the DataAdapter to create the `insert`, `update`, and `delete` commands. For example:

```
string strSQL = "SELECT * From Classes";
SqlDataAdapter sda = new SqlDataAdapter(strSQL,conn);
SqlCommandBuilder sqb = new SqlCommandBuilder(sda);
DataSet ds = new DataSet();
sda.Fill(ds,"Classes");
```

You know the CommandBuilder creates the commands for you, but what do they look like? By interrogating the CommandBuilder, you can find out; see table 19.1.

Table 19.1   Auto-generated Command SQL

Command	Generated SQL
Update	UPDATE Classes SET TeacherID = @p1 , ClassName = @p2 , Period = @p3 WHERE (ClassID = @p4 AND TeacherID = @p5 AND ClassName = @p6 AND Period = @p7)
Insert	INSERT INTO Classes(TeacherID , ClassName , Period) VALUES (@p1 , @p2 , @p3)
Delete	DELETE FROM Classes WHERE (ClassID = @p1 AND TeacherID = @p2 AND ClassName = @p3 AND Period = @p4)

The @p1, @p2 notation indicates parameters that will be bound with values when the statement is updated.

You may notice in the `update` and `delete` commands that the WHERE clauses reference every field, although some fields will be excluded, such as binary and large text fields. This is referred to as *pessimistic updating*.

PESSIMISTIC UPDATE   An update statement that will fail if any of the columns in the table being updated have changed since the data was initially retrieved.

Imagine a situation where multiple users are working on data from the same table. If two users retrieve the same row of data, then both make changes to it and attempt to save to the database, the first user's updates will succeed, but the second user's updates will not. This result happens because one or more of the values used to specify the WHERE clause have changed, so no rows match the original row.

The alternative is an *optimistic update*, in which the WHERE clause only references the table's key. In this case, the system optimistically assumes that no one else has changed the table, and so will overwrite any changes made by another user. This approach is more efficient, but can potentially lead to lost data.

A compromise is to just update fields changed by the user, which will cause overwrites only if the same fields have been changed.

In addition to setting up the statements to execute, a number of parameters are also created: one each for each field's value and for each field's original value. Notice, for example, that the update statement uses parameter @p2 to specify the new value for the ClassName field and @p6 to specify the original value. How is this done? For that matter, how is the @p2 or @p6 parameter associated with a particular field? The answers are based on two properties of the Parameter class that we have not yet explored:

- SourceColumn—This property, when set, indicates the column from which it should derive its value. So, @p2 and @p6 both have their SourceColumn property set to ClassName.

- SourceVersion—This property specifies which version of the column's value should be used when binding. As you'll recall from chapter 17, a column in a DataRow has up to four different versions of its value. For @p2 in the example, we would expect the version to be set to DataRowVersion.Current to retrieve the new value to store, and we would expect the version for @p6 to be DataRowVersion.Original to specify that we want to update based on the original value of the column.

These properties exist in the Parameter object for no other reason than to provide this information to the DataAdapter when updating data. A purist would argue that this arrangement violates the separation between the database-specific code and the DataSet code. Fortunately, Microsoft is smart enough to know when taking the pure approach is appropriate and when practicality should be taken into account. In this case, this simple modification hurts nothing and makes the code considerably more straightforward. (The purists frequently forget that the concept is meaningless if it cannot be applied.[1])

Just to prove our assumptions correct, I wrote a couple of lines of code to write out the values for all the parameters in the example's update command. The results are summarized in table 19.2.

Table 19.2   Update command parameters from the example

Name	DataType	Source Column	Source Version
@p1	Int	TeacherID	Current
@p2	Char	ClassName	Current
@p3	Int	Period	Current
@p4	Int	ClassID	Original
@p5	Int	TeacherID	Original
@p6	Char	ClassName	Original
@p7	Int	Period	Original

[1] Yes, as you may have gathered, this is one of my personal soap-boxes. I consider myself a serious object-oriented developer, but I don't take it to be a religion.

As expected, the first set of parameters uses the current version to write the new values, and the second set uses the original versions. ClassID appears only once because it is an auto-generated column, updated by the database. In the next section, you will see how to customize the statement.

19.2 CUSTOMIZING THE STATEMENTS

The DataAdapter keeps track of four different commands: `select`, `update`, `insert`, and `delete`. The `select`, of course, must be provided. Whether the other three need to be set depends—if you know that you are only adding data, or only updating existing data, then you only need to provide the corresponding commands.

Also, if you only need to provide special behavior for one of the commands (say that you want to use a stored procedure for doing deletes, but are okay with default behavior for the other commands), then you can use the CommandBuilder to create your initial commands, and then specify the one special command.

In this section, we will customize the `update` command to use an optimistic update rather than a pessimistic update. The first version takes advantage of the fact that we already know the structure of the Classes table (listing 19.1).

Listing 19.1 Customizing the update command

```
public void TestCustomDataAdapter(SqlConnection conn)
{
    // Create and fill the dataset
    string strSQL = "SELECT ClassID,TeacherID,ClassName,Period"
                        + " From Classes";
    SqlDataAdapter sda = new SqlDataAdapter(strSQL,conn);
    SqlCommandBuilder sqb = new SqlCommandBuilder(sda);
    DataSet ds = new DataSet();
    sda.Fill(ds,"Classes");

    // Create a custom update command                          ❶ Define
    SqlCommand commUpdate = new SqlCommand();                     command
    commUpdate.Connection = conn;
    commUpdate.CommandText = "UPDATE Classes "
            + "SET TeacherID=@p1,ClassName=@p2,Period = @p3 "
            + "WHERE (ClassID = @p4)";

    // Add the parameters                                      ❷ Add update
    SqlParameter p1 =                                            parameters
        new SqlParameter("@p1",SqlDbType.Int,0,"TeacherID");
    p1.SourceVersion = DataRowVersion.Current;
    commUpdate.Parameters.Add(p1);

    SqlParameter p2 =
        new SqlParameter("@p2",SqlDbType.Char,30,"ClassName");
    p2.SourceVersion = DataRowVersion.Current;
    commUpdate.Parameters.Add(p2);
```

```
        SqlParameter p3 =
            new SqlParameter("@p3",SqlDbType.Int,0,"Period");
        p3.SourceVersion = DataRowVersion.Current;
        commUpdate.Parameters.Add(p3);

        SqlParameter p4 =                                          ❸ Add where
            new SqlParameter("@p4",SqlDbType.Int,0,"ClassID");        clause
        p4.SourceVersion = DataRowVersion.Original;
        commUpdate.Parameters.Add(p4);

        // And make it be the update statement for the adapter
        sda.UpdateCommand = commUpdate;    ❹ Set update clause

        // Update the data table
        DataRow dr = ds.Tables["Classes"].Rows[0];    ❺ Change some data
        dr["Period"] = 5;
        sda.Update(ds,"Classes");
}
```

❶ Defining the update command is no different from creating any other command object—we literally just provide the SQL to execute. We have followed the naming convention of the CommandBuilder, but you can name the parameters any way you choose.

The only real difference between our version of the update statement and the auto-generated one is that the where clause only contains the ClassID field, which is the primary key for the table.

❷ For each field that needs to be updated, a parameter needs to be created. The constructor we are using takes the parameter name, data type, length (which is ignored except for the char field), and source column (the column from which the column the data should be retrieved).

The SourceVersion is set on the following line, and for all the update columns, we want the current version of the data. It would be handy if a constructor took this parameter as well as the source column (it makes little sense to set one without the other). The documentation lists such a constructor—but, alas, it is not present.

❸ The last parameter, @p4, defines the where clause. It references the ClassID field, but references the original value rather than the current value. Because this field is the primary key and will not change, it would have worked if we had set this parameter to use the current value; but it is clearer to specify the original value (it would have worked even if the field was not an primary key, but was just an identifier).

❹ The last step tells the DataAdapter to use our new command for doing updates. We used the CommandBuilder to set up our original commands, so there is already technically an update command in place, which we are replacing.

❺ This code gets a row out of the table, modifies it, and then does an update. The first test we did ran the code and checked the database. We then did the same thing, but this time we manually modified the value in one of the other columns so that a pessimistic update would have failed, and confirmed that the change still took place.

Just to be thorough, we also did the test using the CommandBuilder's version of the statement, and got an exception thrown telling us that the row had changed and could not be updated.

I could spend the next several pages showing the results from these various tests, but I'm hoping you will trust me—or run the tests on your own.

19.3 CUSTOMIZING A LITTLE MORE GENERICALLY

The last section's example works fine for a very specific case, but let's make the code a little less specific. Listing 19.2 shows the same example, but this time the code is written to generate an appropriate optimistic statement for most tables. You may notice that rather more code is involved with this example, which is generally the case with generic code—however, this code only needs to be written once, no matter how many different types of statements use it.

Listing 19.2 More generic optimistic update

```
public void TestCustomDataAdapter(SqlConnection conn)
{
    // Create and fill the dataset
    string strSQL = "SELECT ClassID,TeacherID,ClassName,Period"
                        + " From Classes";
    SqlCommandBuilder sqb = new SqlCommandBuilder(sda);
    DataSet ds = new DataSet();
    sda.FillSchema(ds,SchemaType.Mapped,"Classes");     ❶ Get schema info
    sda.Fill(ds,"Classes");

    // Create a custom update command
    sda.UpdateCommand =                                 ❷ Encapsulate
       CreateCustomUpdateCommand(ds.Tables["Classes"],conn);    command
                                                                 creation


    // Update the data table
    DataRow dr = ds.Tables["Classes"].Rows[0];
    dr["Period"] = 7;
    sda.Update(ds,"Classes");
}
public SqlCommand CreateCustomUpdateCommand(DataTable dt,
                                           SqlConnection conn)
{
    // Create the new command
    SqlCommand commUpdate = new SqlCommand();
    commUpdate.Connection = conn;

    StringBuilder sb = new StringBuilder();             ❸ Build SQL
    sb.AppendFormat("UPDATE {0} SET ",dt.TableName);
```

```
// Step through each field, update the SQL and create a parameter
SqlParameter p = null;
int iParmCount = 1;
foreach(DataColumn dc in dt.Columns)              ❹  Add fields
{
    if(dc.AutoIncrement == true)
        continue;

    // Update the SQL
    if(iParmCount > 1) sb.Append(",");
    sb.AppendFormat("{0}=@p{1}",
            dc.ColumnName,iParmCount.ToString().Trim());

    // Create the parameter
    p = new SqlParameter();
    p.ParameterName = string.Format("@p{0}",
                        iParmCount.ToString().Trim());
    p.DbType = (DbType)Enum.Parse(typeof(DbType),dc.DataType.Name);
    if(dc.MaxLength >= 0)
        p.Size = dc.MaxLength;
    p.SourceColumn = dc.ColumnName;
    p.SourceVersion = DataRowVersion.Current;
    commUpdate.Parameters.Add(p);

    iParmCount++;
}

// Add in the where clause based on the primary key
sb.Append(" WHERE ");
int iPosition = 1;
foreach(DataColumn dcKey in dt.PrimaryKey)        ❺  Add where clause
{
    if(iPosition > 1) sb.Append(" AND ");
        sb.AppendFormat("({0}=@p{1})",
            dcKey.ColumnName,iParmCount.ToString().Trim());

    // Create the parameter
    p = new SqlParameter();
    p.ParameterName = string.Format("@p{0}",
                        iParmCount.ToString().Trim());
    p.DbType = (DbType)Enum.Parse(typeof(DbType),
                            dcKey.DataType.Name);
    if(dcKey.MaxLength >= 0)
        p.Size = dcKey.MaxLength;
    p.SourceColumn = dcKey.ColumnName;
    p.SourceVersion = DataRowVersion.Original;
    commUpdate.Parameters.Add(p);

    iParmCount++;
}

commUpdate.CommandText = sb.ToString();           ❻  Set command text

return commUpdate;
}
```

❶ The method for building the optimistic update relies on the table's knowing its own primary key information, which can be determined via the call to `FillSchema()`. Don't forget, though, that this approach adds an additional call to the database. If you expect to use the same table multiple times, then try to set up the code to use the same DataTable, or copy the schema from a table for which you have already done a `FillSchema()` call.

❷ The creation of the `update` command has been moved into its own method to make the code more readable. In fact, were this a real-world application, I would have moved all of this code into its own class—a custom CommandBuilder, or perhaps even a derivation of Command that builds the command text.

❸ We use a StringBuilder to create the SQL text, because it is more efficient than appending strings together. All that is happening, though, is that the string is adding each element in turn. For this technique to work, we must put a `using System. Text` statement at the top of the file.

❹ This loop steps through each column in the DataTable and adds it, provided that the column is not auto-incremented. This limit avoids our adding the primary key field to the SQL, which would cause a database error. There are two distinct parts to adding each field: adding the SQL and adding the parameter.

The SQL for each field will look like this:

```
ClassName=@p2
```

The field name is read from the column. The parameter name is created via the use of an ever-increasing variable, `iParmCount`.

Creating the parameter requires a number of steps. The name is determined by using the same counter we used in the SQL string—@p1, @p2, and so forth. Determining the data type, however, is more complex. The column knows the data type based on the *type* of the data: the .NET underlying data type, returned as a Type object. Parameters, however, know their type based on the value in the `DBType` enum, because the `DBType` enum can hold values other than basic system types.

Fortunately, though, because the system types that can be used are a subset of the `DBTypes`, and the names on the common types are the same, we can use a little .NET magic to convert. We get the name of the type and use the enum's `Parse()` method to get the enum value.

The length is retrieved from the column's maximum length, which is also part of the schema. However, this value will be set to −1 for columns that don't support a maximum length (such as integer columns), which is the reason for the check.

The source information includes the name of the column and the `DataRowVersion.Current` value, because we know that we want to update using the current value.

Be aware that this code is not all-encompassing. Several situations are not handled, such as dealing with precision and scale appropriately for decimal fields.

The last step is to add the parameter to the `Command` object's parameter collection.

❺ This code is very similar to the code for adding the set statements, except that it steps through the collection of columns that make up the primary key. Also, the parameter's source version is set to `DataRowVersion.Original`, rather than the current value. Note that the same variable is used to name the parameter, so the parameters just keep counting up.

Another situation that is not handled by this code is what to do when there is no primary key. A more robust solution might look at standard indexes, or resort to a pessimistic update as a last resort.

❻ The final step puts the built string into the command's `CommandText` property. In the example, the code looks like this:

```
UPDATE Classes SET TeacherID=@p1,ClassName=@p2,Period=@p3
        WHERE (ClassID=@p4)
```

If you run the code, you will see that it works exactly the same way as the manually built statement. However, this function can be used for virtually any single-table SQL, provided there is a primary key. The same technique can be used to create the other commands, although I would suggest moving the code into another class and adding handling for some of the special cases.

19.4   DEALING WITH JOINS

I have repeatedly used the join example as a reason why you might want to build your own custom commands. This has been a bit of a red herring, however, because it is really not a good idea to use joins with DataTables that you intend to update. You lose the ability to have the DataTable understand and enforce the relationships between the joined tables, and updating data in a join is not straightforward. Consider the following example:

```
SELECT Classes.ClassID,Teachers.TeacherName,
       Classes.ClassName,Classes.Period FROM Classes,Teachers
       WHERE (Classes.TeacherID = Teachers.TeacherID)
```

Executing the statement inside SQL Server will return the data shown in figure 19.1.

ClassID	TeacherName	ClassName	Period
1	Ms. Fortune	Basket-weaving	7
3	Mr. Kriefels	Physics	2
4	Ms. Fortune	Chemistry	3
7	Ms. Fortune	Geometry	4

Figure 19.1
Data from a join

This result is better than just having a TeacherID, but what happens when we try to update the TeacherName column? It depends on what task we are trying to accomplish:

- We are providing the information for reference, and don't expect it to be changed. In other words, we want the change to be ignored.

- We want to change the name of the teacher—basically updating both tables.

- We want to change which teacher is teaching the class—updating the reference in the Classes table.

Each of these scenarios must be handled in a different manner, assuming you are sure which operation is being attempted. I will not show the complete code for any of the cases, but is should be obvious from the explanation how to customize the commands.

19.4.1 Ignoring the field

In the last case, even if the TeacherName has changed, we don't want to do anything about it. The CommandBuilder won't help us, because it sees the join and will not create commands. Really, though, our update is straightforward:

```
UPDATE Classes SET ClassName=@p1,Period=@p2 WHERE (ClassID=@p3)
```

Notice that this SQL is identical to the case in which we didn't do a join, except that the TeacherID field is excluded. Once we set up the parameters, any updates to any of the other fields will work as normal. You just cannot change the TeacherName or the TeacherID.

The code could also be written generically to only include fields from one of the tables.

19.4.2 Updating both tables

This task would be a little unusual in the example, but in some scenarios it makes more sense (for example, if another table contained extended properties). The easiest way to deal with this situation is to use the database's ability to do batch SQL. On SQL Server, that would look like this:

```
UPDATE Classes SET ClassName=@p1,Period=@p2 WHERE (ClassID=@p3);
UPDATE Teachers SET TeacherName=@p4 WHERE TeacherName=@p5
```

The semicolon separates it into two separate SQL statements. One flaw is that the update of the Teachers table is based on the TeacherName, rather than the TeacherID field, because we never retrieved the TeacherID field. However, nothing prevented us from doing so; if we had retrieved the value from the Teachers table, we could have used it to do a more reliable update.

The code shown here, though, should work, provided that @p4 uses the current value and @p5 uses the original value, per the code example.

19.4.3 Updating a reference

This is the most likely desired scenario for doing an update, but it turns out to be the hardest to accomplish. The code is simple and follows the previous examples. The complexity comes from the SQL:

```
UPDATE Classes SET ClassName=@p1,Period=@p2,
    TeacherID=(SELECT TeacherID
            FROM Teachers WHERE TeacherName=@p3)
        WHERE ClassID=@4
```

The subquery resolves the TeacherName back to a TeacherID before storing it to the Classes table. Nothing to it—right?

While I am all for generic code, this is a special case, and I don't know that I would try to do this generically. It comes down to what you are ultimately trying to accomplish.

19.5 USING STORED PROCEDURES

Under certain circumstances, you might want to use a stored procedure as one of your commands, rather than a straight `update` statement. I don't want to revisit the efficiency issue, but perhaps additional processing needs to take place. For example, the following stored procedure inserts a new row into the Classes table, and also creates another version of the class in which the period is multiplied by 10—a study period (just play along):

```
CREATE PROCEDURE
    InsertClasses(@TeacherID int,@ClassName char(30),@Period int) AS
INSERT INTO Classes(TeacherID,ClassName,Period)
                    Values (@TeacherID,@ClassName,@Period)
INSERT INTO Classes(TeacherID,ClassName,Period)
                    Values (@TeacherID,@ClassName,@Period * 10)
```

There is an issue with doing things this way, as you will see later. However, it should be fairly straightforward to customize the `Insert` command to use this procedure (listing 19.3).

Listing 19.3   Using a stored procedure in a custom insert command

```
public void TestCustomDataAdapter(SqlConnection conn)
{
    // Create and fill the dataset
    string strSQL = "SELECT ClassID,TeacherID,ClassName,Period
                     From Classes";
    SqlDataAdapter sda = new SqlDataAdapter(strSQL,conn);
    SqlCommandBuilder sqb = new SqlCommandBuilder(sda);
    DataSet ds = new DataSet();
    sda.Fill(ds,"Classes");

    // Create a custom Insert command
    SqlCommand commInsert = new SqlCommand();                    ❶ Create
    commInsert.Connection = conn;                                   command
    commInsert.CommandText = "InsertClasses";
    commInsert.CommandType = CommandType.StoredProcedure;
    sda.InsertCommand = commInsert;

    // Create the parameters
    SqlParameter pTeacherID = new                                ❷ Create
        SqlParameter("@TeacherID",SqlDbType.Int,0,"TeacherID");     parameters
    pTeacherID.SourceVersion = DataRowVersion.Current;
    commInsert.Parameters.Add(pTeacherID);
```

```
    SqlParameter pClassName = new
            SqlParameter("@ClassName",SqlDbType.Char,0,"ClassName");
    pTeacherID.SourceVersion = DataRowVersion.Current;
    commInsert.Parameters.Add(pClassName);

    SqlParameter pPeriod = new
            SqlParameter("@Period",SqlDbType.Int,0,"Period");
    pTeacherID.SourceVersion = DataRowVersion.Current;
    commInsert.Parameters.Add(pPeriod);

    // Create the new row
    DataTable dt = ds.Tables["Classes"];
    DataRow dr = dt.NewRow();
    dr["TeacherID"] = 1;
    dr["ClassName"] = "History";
    dr["Period"] = 9;
    dt.Rows.Add(dr);
    sda.Update(ds,"Classes");

    PrintDataTable("Classes",dt);
}
```

❶ This code is not much different than before, except that the command text is the
name of the stored procedure and the command type is set to StoredProcedure.
Also, this time we are customizing the Insert command rather than the Update
command.

❷ Again, very little is different. The parameter name, however, must match the expected
name within the stored procedure.

Some odd results

Everything runs as expected. If we look in the database, we see the two new rows
(figure 19.2).

ClassID	TeacherID	ClassName	Period
1	1	Basket-Weaving	5
3	3	Physics	2
4	2	Chemistry	3
7	2	Geometry	4
18	1	History	9
19	1	History	90

Figure 19.2
Rows added to the
Classes table

However, we also added a PrintDataTable call at the end of the code to write out
the structure of the DataTable. There are some interesting differences (figure 19.3)

First, notice that there is no TeacherID value for the newly added row, because the
database added that value, not the DataTable. Second, the specially added "study
period" row *is missing altogether!* If you think about how the update of the DataTable

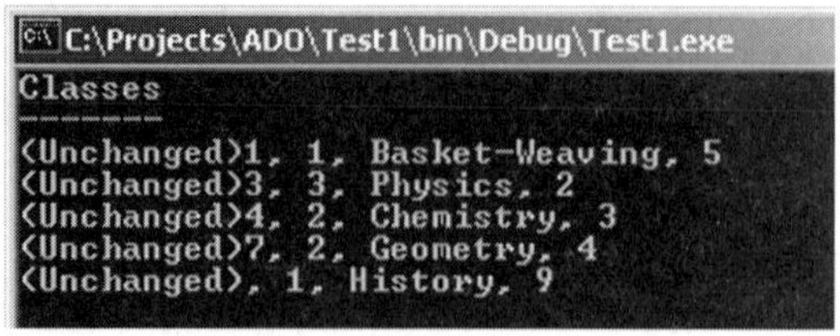

Figure 19.3
DataTable version of the data

works, this result makes sense—the DataAdapter sent some SQL to the database to do various updates, but it doesn't have any idea of anything that happened on the database side.

It might have been possible for Microsoft to make the DataAdapter automatically determine the changes and update the DataTable, but doing so would have required at least one additional database call. Considering that, for the majority of cases, the DataTable can determine the data, this approach would have been inefficient. If you want to update the DataTable, you must do it yourself.

The simplest, though most painful, way to do so is to re-query for all the data:

```
dt.Clear();
sda.Fill(ds,"Classes");
PrintDataTable("Classes",dt);
```

You can also do some custom work based on your own knowledge of what the stored procedure will do, and perhaps use the merge capabilities described in chapter 16.

19.6 CUSTOMIZING THE STATEMENT FOR EACH USE

Earlier I mentioned the idea of updating only those columns that have changed. The problem with doing this is that the SQL in the command will change for each row you update. Some efficiency issues arise, but they may not matter, depending on your code. There are other reasons, of course, to customize the statement on a per-usage basis, but the approach is more or less the same.

I won't include all the code, because it is quite involved, but I will explain the general approach. The code is available with the samples on the book's web site.

The approach is relatively straightforward: before each row is updated, the command text and the parameters are re-created. The first trick, of course, is to get a chance to make a change before each row is updated. We can do so by subscribing to the RowUpdating event on the DataAdapter:

```
sda.RowUpdating += new
        SqlRowUpdatingEventHandler(SqlRowUpdatingEventHandler);
```

This subscription will cause our method to be called before each row is updated. The event handler looks something like this:

```
protected void SqlRowUpdatingEventHandler(object sender,
                                        SqlRowUpdatingEventArgs e)
    {
```

```
    DataRow dr = e.Row;
    if(dr.RowState == DataRowState.Modified)
        CustomizeUpdateCommand(e.Command,dr);
}
```

This event will be called for *every* row that will potentially be saved, whether via an insert, update, or delete. Another event, `RowUpdated`, can also be caught if you are trying to do something different, such as having an additional operation happen every time a row is updated.

This code does little more than check to make sure the row is being modified, rather than added or deleted, and then call a method to build the custom command. It retrieves the row and command object from the `SqlRowUpdatingEventArgs` parameter.

One neat trick you can do here is prevent the row from being updated, by setting the `Status` of the parameter:

```
e.Status = UpdateStatus.SkipCurrentRow;
```

You can also skip all remaining rows:

```
e.Status = UpdateStatus.SkipAllRemainingRows;
```

Back to the example. The `CustomizeUpdateCommand` method is just a variant of the `CreateCustomUpdateCommand` method from listing 19.2, which builds SQL for an update. However, there are a few of differences:

- The `Parameters` collection must be cleared each time so that new parameters can be added:

  ```
  public SqlCommand CustomizeUpdateCommand(SqlCommand commUpdate,
                                              DataRow dr)
  {
      DataTable dt = dr.Table;
      commUpdate.Parameters.Clear();
  ```

- Rather than adding in all the columns, we only want to add in those columns that have changed:

  ```
  foreach(DataColumn dc in dt.Columns)
  {
      if(!dr.HasVersion(DataRowVersion.Original) ||
          !dr.HasVersion(DataRowVersion.Current) ||
          (dr[dc,DataRowVersion.Original] ==
                              dr[dc,DataRowVersion.Current]))
          continue;
  ```

  This code determines whether there are different versions of the value in the column, and that they are different. If not, it continues to the next column.

- The parameter's values must be explicitly set, because the values have already been put into the parameters by the time the row-updating event is called. Of course, the first thing we do is blow away the parameters collection, and our new parameters don't yet have values. To rectify this situation, after we create each new parameter, we have to set its value:

```
commUpdate.Parameters.Add(p);
p.Value = dr[dc];
```

Although there is a fair amount of other code, the rest is much the same as in previous examples. You have numerous opportunities to optimize this code, as well. For example, you could check to see if the current command and parameters would work for the new row, or cache the commands for reuse. However, this code will never be superefficient. Its advantage is that it won't touch columns that have not been changed by the user.

This is just one example of customizing the commands on the fly. You could do various other things, including custom calculations or even other SQL commands.

19.6.1 Updating identity columns

I want to mention identity columns, because they cause so much consternation. You can use customization approaches shown in this chapter, along with the techniques from chapter 13, to update the identity column in the table as you do updates. The difference is that you will need to customize the insert statement, and you will also have to catch the OnRowUpdated event to retrieve the special parameter.

19.7 SUMMARY

One of the things that demonstrates a good design, in my opinion, is a system that works in a straightforward manner with little work but is flexible enough to allow for complex customization if required. Of course, the perfect design would imply that even the customization is extremely simple, but that may be pushing our luck! In any case, I think the design around the DataAdapters is a pretty good compromise between ease-of-use and flexibility.

An enormous number of things can be done with the DataAdapter, and this chapter has given you a flavor for the techniques and mechanisms that are available. If you intend to do a lot of customization, I encourage you to build some support classes, or perhaps even derive your own custom Command objects. Most of the sample code in this chapter (and, indeed, in this book) is written to highlight a particular technique or capability. Rarely is that the best way to implement real-world applications!

Chapter 20 explores the DataSet's querying capabilities, and also goes into more detail about the ability to have calculated columns and summaries. That completes our discussion of the topics directly related to the capabilities of the DataSet. Chapter 21 demonstrates how easy it is to transport DataSets between tiers via .NET's remoting capabilities.

C H A P T E R   2 0

Queries and expressions

At first blush, it may seem a little odd to combine queries and expressions into a single chapter. I have a good reason, however: the format for commands to query a DataSet and the format for creating expressions is the same.

The ADO.NET "expression language" is fairly SQL-like. The advantage is that it seems familiar and has a small learning curve. The disadvantage is that the differences are more likely to trip you up. For example, queries within a DataSet are against a single DataTable and can only return results from that table—although you can reference related data.

You can do a query against a DataSet another way: use XML and XPath, as demonstrated in part 5. Each approach has advantages and disadvantages.

This chapter is broken into two main sections: one on queries, and one on expressions. Throughout these sections, you will get a feel for the expression language, including a fair number of details.

20.1   QUERIES

In order to explore the query capabilities of DataTables, I've written a couple of methods to set up data and write out results. This approach will avoid repeating code over and over just to change a single line. The first method (listing 20.1) builds a DataSet, populates the Teachers and Classes DataTables, and sets up a relationship between them.

```
DataSet BuildQueryDataSet(SqlConnection conn)
{
   // Create the data adapters
   string strSQL1 = "SELECT * From Classes";
   SqlDataAdapter sdaClasses = new SqlDataAdapter(strSQL1,conn);
   string strSQL2 = "SELECT * From Teachers";
   SqlDataAdapter sdaTeachers = new SqlDataAdapter(strSQL2,conn);

   // Create and fill the dataset
   DataSet ds = new DataSet();
   DataTable dtClasses = ds.Tables.Add("Classes");
   sdaClasses.FillSchema(ds,SchemaType.Mapped,"Classes");
   sdaClasses.Fill(dtClasses);

   DataTable dtTeachers = ds.Tables.Add("Teachers");
   sdaTeachers.FillSchema(ds,SchemaType.Mapped,"Teachers");
   sdaTeachers.Fill(dtTeachers);

   DataRelation dr = new
     DataRelation("TeacherClasses",dtTeachers.Columns["TeacherID"],
                                    dtClasses.Columns["TeacherID"]);
   ds.Relations.Add(dr);

   return ds;
}
```

This code should look familiar, so I won't bother with explanations. The next method (listing 20.2) takes an array of DataRows and writes them out to the console. It takes an array of DataRows because that is what will always be returned when we do a query.

```
public void DisplayResults(DataRow[] aDR)
{
   Console.WriteLine("Results");
   Console.WriteLine("=======");

   foreach(DataRow dr in aDR)
   {
      foreach ( DataColumn dc in dr.Table.Columns )
      {
         if(dc.Ordinal > 0) Console.Write(", ");
         Console.Write(dr[dc].ToString().Trim());
      }
      Console.WriteLine("");
   }
}
```

Once again, there should be no surprises here. Now, let's create a simple query example.

20.1.1   Simple query

The following code uses the methods that we just created and executes a very simple
query against the DataTable to return all classes being taught by teacher 2:

```
public void TestQuery(SqlConnection conn)
{
   DataSet ds = BuildQueryDataSet(conn);
   DataTable dtClasses = ds.Tables["Classes"];

   DataRow[] aDR = dtClasses.Select ("TeacherID = 2");

   DisplayResults(aDR);
}
```

The first two lines of this code use our existing method to build the query and
retrieve the Classes DataTable. The last line writes out the results. It is the middle line
that we care about.

All queries against a DataTable are done using the Select() method, which has
several overrides. The version we are using takes a query string and returns a collection
of DataRows in the DataTable that match. The output appears in figure 20.1.

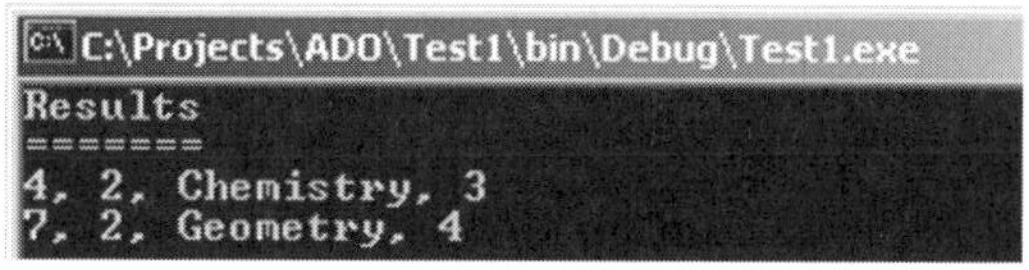

**Figure 20.1
Output from the simple query**

There are several additional overloads of the Select() method. For example, you
can specify a sort order:

```
DataRow[] aDR = dtClasses.Select("TeacherID = 2","Period");
```

The sort order clause is much like an SQL clause and can specify ascending or
descending and multiple columns. For example, the following would have been perfectly legal:

```
DataRow[] aDR =
      dtClasses.Select("TeacherID = 2","Period desc,ClassName");
```

A third argument that can be passed to the Select() method allows you to filter
based on the state of the row:

```
DataRow[] aDR = dtClasses.Select("TeacherID = 2","Period",
                                 DataViewRowState.Added);
```

This particular example would only return rows whose state was Added. You can also
filter for deleted rows, unchanged rows, and several other combinations.

This approach allows you to extend the filter, but the filter itself provides the most
power when specifying what data to return. The next section talks about some of the
options with a filter.

20.1.2 Query elements

You can reference any column within the DataTable by name, although you must put the column in brackets if, for some reason, the column name has any sort of special character in it (such as a space, or punctuation):

```
"[My strange!field] = 'Hello'"
```

The operators supported are the standard comparison operators (<=, <, =, >, =>, and <> for not-equal), plus LIKE and IN. IN checks for one of a set of values:

```
"TeacherID IN (2,3)"
```

LIKE does a lookup with a wildcard:

```
"ClassName LIKE 'B%'"
```

or

```
"ClassName LIKE 'B*'"
```

Notice that with the LIKE statement, you can use either % or *; they are interchangeable. There is no single character wildcard, like the underscore (_) in SQL. Also, you cannot put the wildcard in the middle of the string—only at either end. So the following are legal:

```
"ClassName LIKE 'B*'"
"ClassName LIKE '*B'"
"ClassName LIKE '*B*'"
```

But this is not legal:

```
"ClassName LIKE 'B*sket'"
```

As with SQL, strings are single-quoted, and numbers are not. You can also specify a date by putting the value between pound signs:

```
"SomeDate > #9/10/2001#"
```

For the record, I dislike this format for specifying dates, because it is locale specific—in the U.S., this date is September 10, 2001; but in the U.K., the same string becomes October 9, 2001.

A number of functions can be used within the filter, although some of them don't make much sense for filters and are present mainly for expressions. They are covered in section 20.2.

20.1.3 Compound statements

Just as with SQL, you can build query expressions with multiple pieces joined together with ANDs and ORs, and also use parentheses to group statements:

```
@"(ClassName LIKE 'B*' OR ClassName LIKE 'C*')
                                AND (TeacherID = 2)"
```

Order of operations is the same as for SQL, so AND takes precedence over OR, unless parentheses change the grouping. You can also negate a statement, the same as with SQL:

```
@"(ClassName LIKE 'B*' OR ClassName LIKE 'C*')
                            AND NOT (TeacherID = 2)"
```

20.1.4   Dealing with relationships

I have already said that you can only do a query against a single DataTable—but you can reference related tables to a limited extent. For example, you can refer to related fields in the Parent table. Consider the example we have been using, where the Teacher table is the parent of the Classes table, via the TeacherID. Therefore, we can refer to fields in the parent table:

```
public void TestQuery(SqlConnection conn)
{
    DataSet ds = BuildQueryDataSet(conn);

    DataTable dtClasses = ds.Tables["Classes"];
    DataRow[] aDR =
        dtClasses.Select("Parent.TeacherName = 'Ms. Fortune'");

    DisplayResults(aDR);
}
```

The Parent keyword indicates that the field should come from the record in the table associated as the parent via a relationship. As you can see in figure 20.2, the results are the same as when we used the TeacherID directly.

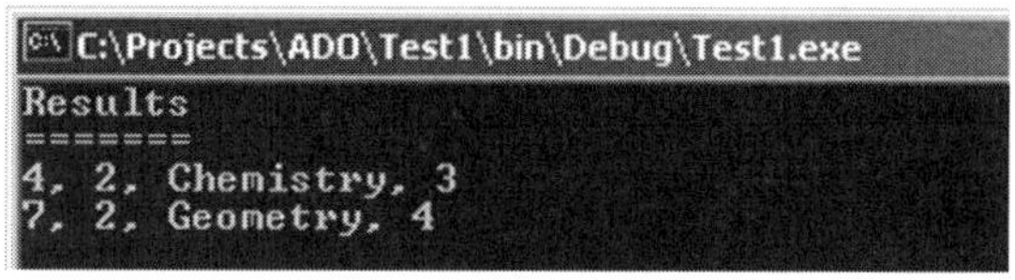

Figure 20.2
Output from the relationship example

This technique works because a one-to-one relationship exists between the record and its parent—a parent can have any number of children, so the reverse doesn't work the same way. This example also assumes that only one parent relationship exists between the tables. If there were more, then a special notation would have been used to specify the relationship:

```
"Parent(TeacherClasses).TeacherName = 'Ms. Fortune'"
```

The name of the relationship appears in parentheses after the Parent keyword, to be more explicit.

With child relationships, it would be nice if you could reference fields in the same way:

```
public void TestQuery(SqlConnection conn)
{
    DataSet ds = BuildQueryDataSet(conn);
```

```
DataTable dtTeachers = ds.Tables["Teachers"];

// Illegal!
DataRow[] aDR = dtTeachers.Select("Child.Period = 3");

DisplayResults(aDR);
}
```

Unfortunately, this code will throw an exception. There is a `Child` keyword, but it can't be used this way because there is an ambiguity: should this code return rows where any of the children meet the criteria, or should it return only rows where all rows meet the criteria? Neither scenario is supported, which is a shame; the functionality would have been useful, and I hope it will be added in a future release.

You *can* do queries that reference the child relationship, but you must do so on summary information—sums, averages, and the like. Although a little bogus, the following example is legal:

```
public void TestQuery(SqlConnection conn)
{
    DataSet ds = BuildQueryDataSet(conn);
    DataTable dtTeachers = ds.Tables["Teachers"];

    DataRow[] aDR = dtTeachers.Select("Min(Child.Period) = 5");

    DisplayResults(aDR);
}
```

Table 20.1 Aggregate functions

Function	Explanation
Avg	Averages the values in the column
Count	Counts the number of child items
Max	Returns the largest value from the column
Min	Returns the smallest value from the column
StDev	Calculates the standard deviation (fun for accountant types)
Sum	Adds all the values in the column in all the rows
Var	Calculates the statistical variance (another fun accountant-type function)

This code is legal because it can resolve the formula to a minimum value and then do the comparison. Because these functions return a single value, they are referred to as *aggregates*. Table 20.1 shows a list of the legal aggregates. Don't forget that these functions can also be used in calculations.

As with a `Parent` reference, you can explicitly specify the relationship to use with a `Child` reference if necessary:

```
"Min(Child(TeacherClasses).Period) = 5"
```

20.1.5   Case sensitivity

By default, DataSet queries, and DataSets in general, are not case sensitive. So, the following two queries would return the same result:

```
DataRow[] aDR = dtClasses.Select("Classname = 'Basket-Weaving'");
```

or

```
DataRow[] aDR = dtClasses.Select("Classname = 'basket-weaving'");
```

This is usually a highly desirable trait of a query. However, sometimes you want to be able to do a case-sensitive query, or to have the DataSet work in a case-sensitive manner in general. This is particularly the case if you are using a case-sensitive database engine, and you want the DataSet to mirror the database as much as possible. It is easy to make the DataSet case sensitive:

```
ds.CaseSensitive = true;
```

Once you have set this property, the second query will no longer return any data, because the casing does not match.

20.2   EXPRESSIONS

An expression is a string that can be evaluated to return a value based on certain input. If you think about it, the filters used for querying are basically just expressions—if you evaluate the expression against each row's data, you collect all the rows where the expression returns `true`! Of course, a real query engine is smart enough to use indexes and other information to avoid this rather tedious and slow approach, but the concept is still valid.

There is no reason an expression can return only `true` or `false`—it can return a string, a number, or another data type. So, for example, you could evaluate an expression that totals all the values in a column, or have a column whose value is calculated based on data in other columns.

You could do this programmatically, of course, stepping through the data and sending it to a function, but using the built-in mechanism offers a couple of advantages:

- The expression can be changed at runtime without recompiling.
- It is already written. Microsoft has done the work, so why waste it?

You might worry about performance when using the expression evaluator, which is a reasonable concern. However, expressions are optimized before use, so they are fairly efficient. In some situations there can be a performance hit; but for most situations, performance is pretty good.

Expressions can be used in several places in the DataSet:

- *Calculated columns*—You can create a column in a DataTable whose value is calculated based on other items within the row.

- *Computed values*—You can ask the DataTable to compute a summary value for you, such as the average of a column.
- *Display name*—You can calculate the display name of a DataTable.

You have seen some of these techniques in previous chapters. The most useful is probably the calculated column, so I will demonstrate it first. Although calculating a display name is a legitimate use of expressions, it is not something that comes up often, so I have not provided an example here (it is discussed in appendix E with the properties of a DataTable). The format is much the same as other uses of expressions.

20.2.1 Calculated columns

The example in listing 20.3 adds a column that calculates the time of a class based on the period. It makes a couple of questionable assumptions—it assumes all classes are one hour long and the first class starts at 9:00 A.M., but you get the basic idea

Listing 20.3 Adding a calculated column

```
public void TestExpression(SqlConnection conn)
{
    DataSet ds = BuildQueryDataSet(conn);
    DataTable dtClasses = ds.Tables["Classes"];

    DataColumn dc = new
        DataColumn("Class Time",typeof(int),"9 + (Period - 1)");       ❶ Set
                                                                           expression

    dtClasses.Columns.Add(dc);

    DisplayResults(dtClasses.Select());       ❷ Display results
}
```

❶ We're using the functions created for setting up the DataSet in the previous sections to save time and space. The first new thing happening here is the creation of a new DataColumn to contain the data. The constructor takes a name for the column, a data type, and an expression. We could also have supplied the expression by setting the Expression property directly:

```
dc.Expression = "9 + (Period - 1)";
```

The constructor is just a convenient way of doing it all in one step. The only other thing that has to be done is to add the column to the data table, and we are done. The expression follows the same rules as query filters—"Period" refers to the Period column. We can also reference Parent or Child related data, following the same rules, if we desire. No math was done in any of the query examples, but it would have been completely legal to do so.

❷ We're also reusing the method from the query examples to write out the results. However, that method takes an array of DataRows, so we need a way to get all the rows.

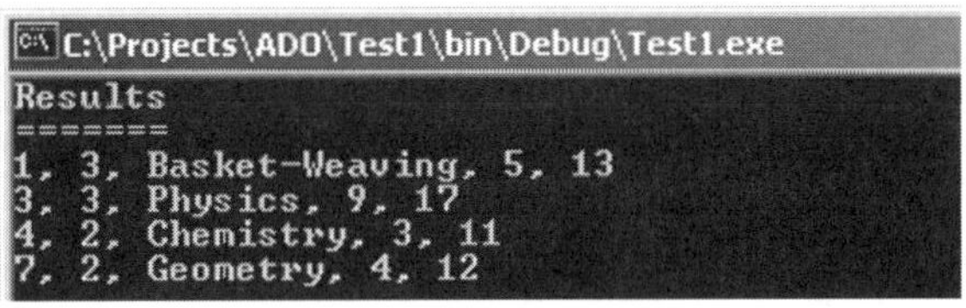

Figure 20.3
Output from listing 20.3

We do this simply by using a special overload of the `Select()` method that takes no arguments and returns all the rows in the table. The output looks like figure 20.3. The output is ugly, but you get the idea—the last column shows the number of hours, but as an integer. In the next section, I will demonstrate how to make the output a little prettier.

20.2.2 Expression functions and prettier output

As you are using a method to write out the data from the DataTable, nothing stops you from updating the output code to format the columns any way you like. However, as you will see in part 4, when you are working with GUI controls, you are more constrained in the way you control the output.

Aside from this, it would be more flexible to have a way to set up the column to deal with its own data. This desire provides a good opportunity to demonstrate some of the other things you can do with expressions. The following example does a little more formatting:

```
public void TestExpression(SqlConnection conn)
{
    DataSet ds = BuildQueryDataSet(conn);
    DataTable dtClasses = ds.Tables["Classes"];

    DataColumn dc = new DataColumn("Class Time",typeof(string));
    dc.Expression =
            "Convert(9 + (Period - 1),'System.String') + ':00'";
    dtClasses.Columns.Add(dc);

    DisplayResults(dtClasses.Select());
}
```

A couple of things are of interest here. First, the column we are creating is now of type `string`, rather than `int`. Second, the expression uses a function to convert the numeric calculated value to a string, and then appends a string containing the minutes section of the number—the ":00". Figure 20.4 shows the slightly prettier output.

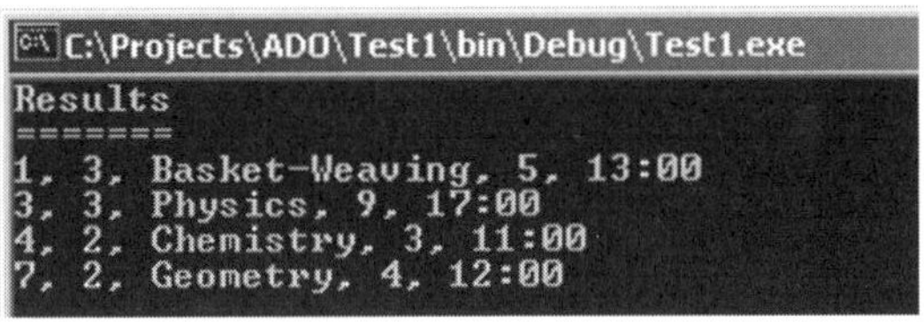

Figure 20.4
Output from the more advanced expression

The expression syntax supports several fairly useful functions, of which some are shown in table 20.2.

Table 20.2 Expression functions

Function	Explanation and example
ABS()	Returns the absolute value of a number. The following example returns the absolute value of the value in the IntValue column: `"ABS(IntValue)"`
CONVERT()	Converts from one data type to another. Only certain conversions are permitted. For example, you cannot convert from a bool to a DateTime. The method takes two arguments: the value to convert and the data type to which the value should be converted. One example was shown in the previous code listing. The following example converts a string (stored in a column called StringValue) to an integer: `"Convert(StringValue,'System.Int32')"`
IIF()	Evaluates a condition and returns one value if the condition is true, or a different value if the condition is false. An example is shown in the next code listing. The following example returns the absolute value of a number stored in the IntValue column: `"IIF(IntValue > 0,IntValue,-IntValue)"`
ISNULL()	Allows a substitute value if the condition's value (usually the name of a column) is null. This is sort of a special case of the IIF() function. The following example returns the word *Blank* if the column's value is null: `"ISNULL(StringValue,'Blank')"` If the column is *not* null, then the first argument (in the example, StringValue) will be returned.
LEN()	Returns the length of a string expression. An example using LEN is shown with the description for SUBSTRING.

SUBSTRING()	Returns a piece of a string. The following example returns the first 30 characters of a column, followed by an ellipsis. If the column is fewer than 30 characters, then the value of the column is returned. This example demonstrates the use of the IIF, LEN, TRIM, and SUBSTRING functions:
	
	`"IIF(LEN(TRIM(StringValue)) < 30,StringValue,"`
	`+ "SUBSTRING(StringValue,30)+'...')"`
	
	The TRIM is necessary to make sure the extra spaces after the value are not considered.

TRIM()	Removes the spaces from the end of a string. An example is shown with the description for SUBSTRING.

Although the code improved the format of the class time, we'd like to include an A.M./P.M. display. By using the IIF function, doing so is relatively easy:

```
dc.Expression =
"Convert(9 + (Period-1) - IIF(Period<=4,0,12),'System.String')"
+ " " + ':00' + IIF(Period<4,'am','pm')";
```

The output is a little ugly, but it's what we wanted (figure 20.5).

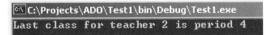

```
Select C:\Projects\ADO\Test1\bin\Debug\Test1.exe
Results
=======
1, 3, Basket-Weaving, 5, 1:00pm
3, 3, Physics, 9, 5:00pm
4, 2, Chemistry, 3, 11:00am
7, 2, Geometry, 4, 12:00pm
```

Figure 20.5
Prettier time format output

20.2.3   Computed values

As I mentioned earlier, you can do a couple of other useful things with expressions. For example, you can compute a value against a set of rows. The format for the computation is the same expression language we have been using; you can also specify a filter to limit the records to return, using the expression language.

The following example returns the last class of the day for teacher 2:

```
public void TestCompute(SqlConnection conn)
{
    DataSet ds = BuildQueryDataSet(conn);
    DataTable dtClasses = ds.Tables["Classes"];

    int iLast =
        (int)dtClasses.Compute("MAX(Period)","TeacherID = 2");

    Console.WriteLine(
            "Last class for teacher 2 is period {0}",iLast);
}
```

Once again, we're using the existing method to retrieve data.

The Compute() method takes two parameters: the expression to evaluate and the filter. The expression generally must use some form of aggregate function that returns a single value. The filter is a standard query filter. If you want to compute against all rows, you can pass an empty string for this parameter.

You may have noticed that we are type-casting the result of the Compute() method to an int. The return type of the Compute() method is an object, but because we know that the expression will return an integer, we can safely cast from object to integer. If we were not sure of the result, we might have put in a ToString() call, or perhaps test the type of the object using GetType(). Figure 20.6 shows the output.

```
C:\Projects\ADO\Test1\bin\Debug\Test1.exe
Last class for teacher 2 is period 4
```

Figure 20.6
Output from the computed value example

20.3   SUMMARY

One of the goals for the DataSet is to be able to emulate some basic database functionality on a client that is not tied to the database. To make this goal practical, a mechanism was required for querying a DataSet. In fact, this is just one way of retrieving data. Aside from manually stepping through the DataSet, you can also convert the data to XML and use XPath to retrieve results, as you will see in part 5.

One caution about the query mechanism within the DataSet: it will not always return the same results as a database query, especially taking into account different database engines, different character sets, and the more advanced capabilities that most major database engines provide. Depending on your application, this could be a serious issue.

Being able to create calculated columns is a handy capability that is especially valuable when you're working with data-bound controls. Although there are limitations on what you can do, this functionality covers a large number of cases. Where it falls down, you can always step in by catching DataSet events and doing your own, more complex calculations.

This chapter brings to a close our exploration of the DataSet. We have covered all the major DataSet classes and their capabilities. Chapter 21 shows how to use the remoting capabilities of .NET to transfer DataSets between different application domains or computers, which is surprisingly easy.

C H A P T E R   2 1

Remoting DataSets

Prior to .NET, building multi-tier applications under Windows frequently required bringing together a hodge-podge of different technologies, combined under the Microsoft marketing term DNA. I can only assume that the DNA term was used because, as with genes, the smallest changes brought about strange and unexpected results! That is not to say there weren't some great apps written using DNA, but it certainly wasn't straightforward, especially if you were building a commercial application designed to be shipped to end-users, rather than just built in place.

In this chapter, you will get a glimpse of some of the cool abilities .NET provides for multi-tier applications. In particular, you will learn how to transfer DataSets between different tiers of your application.

21.1   *.NET* REMOTING

.NET is a whole new world when it comes to building distributed applications. Even though the focus is on building web-facing applications, the concepts for building strong distributed applications are built in throughout the framework. One key part of this capability is the remoting support built into .NET. Remoting is all about components talking to one another, on the same box or across multiple boxes, even if those boxes are strewn across the Internet.

This book isn't an in-depth guide to using remoting in .NET.[1] However, DataSets were built to work with .NET's remoting capabilities. Not only are DataSets designed to be marshaled across process boundaries (a fancy way of saying *remotable*), but they also have capabilities specifically designed to make multi-tier development more efficient.

One more thing—you may have heard a lot about web services. Although web services and remoting are related, they are not the same thing. Web services are designed to expose data to any client via HTTP and SOAP,[2] whether the client is using .NET or something else. Thus web services can expose only a subset of the types and classes that are available within .NET. Remoting, however, is based on the assumption that both client and server are using .NET, and so can trust that the information being sent back and forth will be understood. Remoting can use HTTP and SOAP, but it can also use other protocols.

21.2 SENDING A DATASET "ACROSS THE WIRE"

All I've done is write a title for the section, and I'm already lying! This section explains how to set up a server and a client, and have the client retrieve data from the server. However, both client and server will be running on the same box. Actually, the code shown here will work across multiple machines almost unchanged. (I leave trying that as an exercise for the reader.)

.NET really does make remoting easy. However, some details must be set up correctly and, unfortunately (at least in the version I am using), when something goes wrong, it is not always obvious what it is. Work is going on to improve this situation, and I expect the final release to be much easier to troubleshoot. In many ways, remoting issues are already easier to troubleshoot because you can literally step across process boundaries while debugging. (As someone who has worked without this capability, I can tell you that it is really cool!)

We need to set up a lot of little pieces to work through this example. The first thing we need is a server object that does something. This is the object on the server that will be called by the client to do things for us.

21.2.1 Creating a server object

This new class needs to be in a DLL that can be called by the server and can also be referenced by the client (so that the client knows what methods are available to call). There are other ways of doing this step, but the following is the most straightforward for our purposes. We create a class library (a DLL) called ArFServer, using the Visual Studio new project wizard (figure 21.1).

---

[1] Manning has a good book on the subject by Don Browning (.*NET Remoting*).

[2] HTTP stands for Hypertext Transfer Protocol, and is the way in which web pages are sent across the Internet. SOAP stands for Simple Object Access Protocol, and is a way of calling objects and methods across the Internet and getting back results.

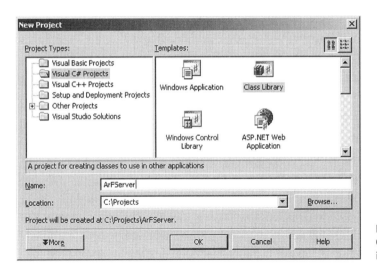

Figure 21.1
Creating a DLL
in Visual Studio

We then create a new class in the project called DataSetServer. Listing 21.1 shows the code for DataSetServer after a few changes.

Listing 21.1   Server object for remoting a DataSet

```csharp
using System;
using System.Data;                          ❶  Use the right namespaces
using System.Data.SqlClient;

namespace ArFServer          ❷   Namespace
{
    /// <summary>
    /// Arlen's simple server object for
    /// passing DataSets
    /// </summary>                                ❸  Derive from
    public class DataSetServer : MarshalByRefObject     MarshalByRefObject
    {
        public DataSet GetSomeData()     ❹   Return data
        {
            string strConnect =
                "server=localhost;database=ADONetSamples;user id=sa";
            SqlConnection conn = new SqlConnection(strConnect);
            conn.Open();

            string strSQL = "SELECT * From Teachers";
            SqlDataAdapter sda = new SqlDataAdapter(strSQL,conn);
            DataSet ds = new DataSet();
            sda.Fill(ds,"Teachers");

            conn.Close();
            return ds;
        }
    }
}
```

❶ Nothing is new here, but we are using DataSet classes that are in System.Data and SQL Server classes, which are in System.Data.SqlClient.

❷ The namespace that shows up here was automatically added by Visual Studio when it created the class, based on the name of the class library. So far we haven't paid much attention to the namespace being used for our code, but we will need to know it to set up remoting later.

❸ Deriving from MarshalByRefObject tells .NET how this class should be transferred between tiers. Section 21.2.2 explains the different marshaling options.

❹ Nothing in the GetSomeData() method should be unfamiliar. In some ways, that is what makes the remoting mechanism so powerful—the fact that there is nothing special in this code. I just stated the one caveat: all the parameters and the return value must be marshalable. There are no parameters to GetSomeData(), so no problem there, and the return value is a DataSet, which is serializable.

21.2.2   Marshaling

In listing 21.1, we derived DataSetServer from MarshalByRefObject, which tells .NET how to transfer the object from tier to tier.

An object can be passed from one place to another two ways. When you pass something like a number or a string from one context to another, you usually only want to pass the *value*. If you are using two different computers, for example, computer A doesn't care where computer B stored the value of a number; it just wants the value of the number. This process is referred to as *marshaling by value*.

In figure 21.2, when the value has been passed from machine to machine, no association remains. The value has been copied and is stored in different variables on each machine.

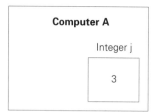
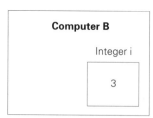

Figure 21.2
Marshaling by value

The other way of passing an object is by *reference* (figure 21.3). Instead of just copying the data within an object, a reference to the object is passed. The receiver of the object can then call methods on the object directly. This is how most objects in C# are passed—if you pass a DataTable to a method, you are passing a reference to that DataTable, not making a copy of it.

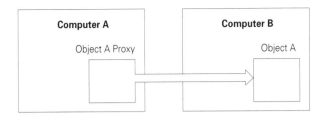

Figure 21.3
Marshal by reference

This approach is all well and good when you are in your own memory space, but what happens when you aren't? You could be calling a different process (another executable running), a different Application Domain (a .NET concept that allows different process-like actions to happen in the same process), or even a different computer. Windows goes to some effort to prevent you from touching the memory of other processes. Basic physics pretty much stops this from happening between machines.

You can do these things, though—it just takes some specialized code. For example, if you are calling a method on another machine, the call needs to be wrapped up via some network protocol and transported to the other machine. The other machine must then find the object that has the method, unwrap the arguments, and pass them to the method. Once the method has finished running, the return value needs to be wrapped up, and the process reversed.

It has not been a million years since you had to do that yourself for every method call. The code still needs to exist, but .NET builds it for you. .NET automatically builds a *proxy* object to represent the object on another machine (or process or application domain) you are calling. The proxy object has all the same methods as the object, so when you call it, it seems as though you are talking directly to the object. What happens, though, is that the proxy does all of the work just described. Except for perhaps a slight delay while your packets go shooting around the world, your code looks no different than if you were calling a local object.

This automatic creation of the proxy is a nice feature of .NET remoting. Previous technologies, like DCOM or CORBA, required the proxy to be created and maintained as a separate class. Although tools were available to do this, it was still a pain in the neck, especially when you had to make changes. With .NET, all you have to do is write your class and specify a particular base class.

You must follow some rules to be able to marshal objects. To marshal an object by value, that object must be *serializable*. That means it can write itself out and re-create itself later from the information it wrote out. Basically, the server makes the object write itself out in a manner that can be passed to another machine (if you think of an XML string, you won't be far off). When the client gets the serialized version of the object, it uses the information to rebuild the object.

All the basic types in .NET (strings, integers, and so on) are directly serializable. A number of classes can also be serialized. It should come as no surprise that the DataSet and all its supporting classes are serializable. The framework can determine if an object can be serialized if it derives from an interface called ISerializable.

This concept is important because we will pass a DataSet between a server and a client; if the DataSet was not serializable, then we could not do this.

To be able to marshal a class by *reference*, the class must derive from a special class called MarshalByRefObject. This class provides all the underlying support for automatically creating proxies, and so forth. As you can see in the example, our server object is derived from MarshalByRefObject.

One more rule: all the public methods of our class must take as arguments, or return, only values that can be marshaled in some manner. That means the arguments and return values must either be serializable or they must be derived from MarshalBy-RefObject.[3] Otherwise, the remoting code won't know how to pass the data.

21.2.3 Hosting the server

We now have an object designed to be called as a server. It is not enough, however—we can't just compile the code and wait for .NET to find it. (Maybe that ability will be a feature of version 3.) .NET has several options for hosting objects to be called for remoting, including using IIS.[4] For our purposes, though, we will build a little server that sits on the computer and waits for requests. Our server has two parts: a small console application and a configuration file.

Let's look at the application first. We create a new console application called ConsoleServerHost. (The word *console* appears in the name because I also have a GUIServerHost, and I wanted to be able to tell them apart easily.)

Once the application is created, we add a reference to the ArFServer DLL so that the server can create the appropriate object—the DataSetServer object. After that, it is just a matter of adding a couple of lines of code. Listing 21.2 shows the entire Class1 code. (I have bolded the lines I added.)

Listing 21.2 Server host application

```
using System;
using System.Runtime.Remoting;          ❶ Remoting
                                            namespace

namespace ConsoleServerHost
{
    class Class1
    {
        static void Main(string[] args)
        {
```

---

[3] Often abbreviated MBR.

[4] Internet Information Server—Microsoft's web server.

```
        string strConfigFile =
            "C:\\Projects\\ServerHost\\ServerHost.exe.Config";
        RemotingConfiguration.Configure(strConfigFile);        ❷ Configure remote
                                                                    server

        Console.WriteLine("Press enter to shut down server");
        Console.ReadLine();
    }                                                          Keep application ❸
  }                                                                     running
}
```

❶ Because we are using remoting code, we need to use the namespace.

❷ These two lines specify that the remoting code should load a particular configuration file and use the information it contains to set up a server. This is all there is to the server! The contents of the configuration file are discussed later.

Two lines of code—one, really, if you ignore the string assignment—and we have set up a multithreaded server listening to HTTP requests.

❸ Once the server has been configured, it will deal with requests until it goes away. Of course, with a console application, it will go away as soon as the Main function has finished executing. To stop the server from going away, we stop the Main function from ending until someone presses Enter. In the real world, your server would probably be an NT service, or possibly be hosted by IIS, but this simple console application is fine for our sample.

21.2.4   The configuration file

As you have probably surmised, the configuration file contains the heart of what the server is supposed to do (listing 21.3). The configuration file's name follows the remoting convention—the executable name followed by *.Config*. I won't explain every detail of this file (such an explanation is far beyond the scope of this book), but the file defines several things:

- The name of the "application" as it will be exposed to the outside world: ArF-Server. Although the names are the same in this case, the name does not need to match the name of the application or the namespace.

- The object that should be accessed and how it should be presented. In this case, it's the DataSetServer object, as a singleton.

- The protocol to use and information relevant to the protocol. Here we specify the use of HTTP on port 8086.

Listing 21.3   ServerHost.exe.Config file

```
<configuration>
  <system.runtime.remoting>
    <application name="ArFServer">        ❶ Application name
      <service>
```

```
            <wellknown mode="Singleton"
                    type="ArFServer.DataSetServer, ArFServer"
                        objectUri="DataSetServer.soap" />
        </service>
        <channels>
            <channel ref="http" port="8086"/>
        </channels>
    </application>
  </system.runtime.remoting>
</configuration>
```

❷ **Object to create and how**

❸ **The protocol**

❶ This code identifies the name of the application that will be exposed.

❷ This line is important. The first attribute, mode, indicates how the object should be accessed. The options are:

- Singleton—One and only one object will be created, and all calls from all clients will go to that object.

- SingleCall—Every call made to this server will create a new object.

As you can see in this example, the object is a singleton—we want to have only one server running.

The next argument, type, identifies the type of object to create. The first part of the argument (before the comma) is the class name, along with its namespace. The second part of the argument (after the comma) is the name of the assembly that contains the class. In this example, the assembly and the DLL are one and the same, so the assembly has the same name as the DLL.

The objectUri specifies how the object will be referenced; this value will become part of the URL that will be used to find and communicate with the server later.

❸ This information says that the server will be available via HTTP, using port 8086. We are using that port rather than, say, 80 (the normal port for HTTP access) to avoid conflicting with other servers that are running on the machine.

21.2.5   Testing the server

Although we don't yet have a client, we now have everything we need to run the server. Of course, we should test to make sure the server is working correctly. Fortunately, we have a generic client we can use that already knows how to talk HTTP: the web browser.

The remoting services automatically create a special call for describing the interface of a remoted application. The format for the description is called WSDL (Web Service Description Language), which is XML based. You can access it directly from a web browser (figure 21.4)—of course, you must start the server application running first. Although you can go through the output to determine information about our server, the important thing is that, by getting any response back, we know the server is running.

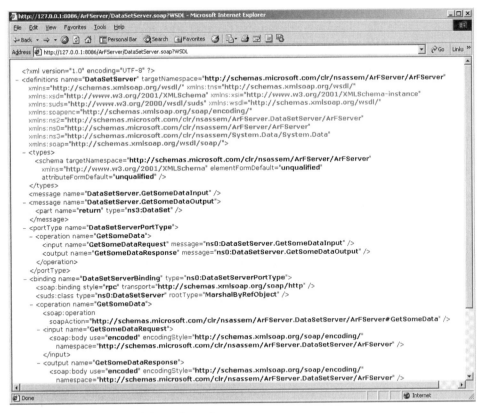

Figure 21.4 Description of the web service

Let's look at the URL in a little more detail: http://127.0.0.1:8086/ArFServer/
DataSetServer.soap?WSDL

Here are the pieces one at a time:

- *http*—The protocol we are using (standard for a web request).

- *127.0.0.1*—The IP address indicating the machine that is hosting our server. This is a special IP address, though, that always loops back to the calling machine. It says the server we want is our own machine.

- *:8086*—The port to use. By default, HTTP will use port 80, but we specified in the configuration file that the server should be exposed on port 8086.

- */ArFServer*—The name of the application, as specified in the configuration file.

- */DataSetServer.soap*—The URI of the object we want to talk to, again from the config file.

- *?WSDL*—An argument we want passed to our server. WSDL is a special command that requests a description of the exposed interface.

This is a handy trick—not only can you confirm that a web service is running at a particular place, but you can also discover what methods it contains. Notice the `Get-SomeData()` method at the bottom of figure 21.4.

21.2.6 Creating the client

Now that we have proven that the server is working, the last step is to build a client application to talk to the server. We do this with yet another console application. It needs to have a reference to the ArFServer DLL so that it knows what methods are available. There are ways of calling the interface without this knowledge, but this is the most straightforward way.

The code in listing 21.4 shows most of the main class for the client application.

Listing 21.4 Remoting client

```
using System;
using System.Runtime.Remoting.Channels;            ❶  Use appropriate
using System.Runtime.Remoting.Channels.Http;           namespaces
using System.Data;
using ArFServer;

namespace ArFClient
{
    class Class1
    {
        static void Main(string[] args)
        {
            HttpChannel ch = new HttpChannel(8087);    ❷  Register a
            ChannelServices.RegisterChannel(ch);           channel

            try

            {
                DataSetServer dss =
                  (DataSetServer)                    Get reference ❸
                  Activator.GetObject(typeof(DataSetServer),   from server
                    "http://localhost:8086/ArFServer/DataSetServer.soap");

                DataSet ds = dss.GetSomeData();      ❹  Call object via proxy
                DisplayDataTable(ds.Tables[0]);
            }
            catch(Exception ex)
            {
                Console.WriteLine(ex.ToString());
            }

            Console.WriteLine("\r\nPress enter to exit");
            Console.ReadLine();
        }
            .
            .
            .
```

❶ There are a bunch of namespaces here. `Channels` contains classes for setting up a channel—a channel is used to transport messages. The `Http` namespace has the specific channel capabilities for using HTTP, as you would expect. `System.Data` is required for the use of the DataSet, and `ArFServer` provides access to the DataSet-Server class so we know what methods can be called.

❷ This code creates a new HTTP channel and registers it for use. The argument to the HttpChannel's constructor is the port on which communication should occur. You may have noticed that this port number is not the same as the one we used for the server. That difference is deliberate—messages go out on one port and return on another. You cannot use the same port for both sides on the same machine, although you can use the same port on multiple machines.

All that is required to use the port is for it to be registered. Once that has happened, the port will be used for HTTP traffic automatically.

❸ This is the magic line. The call to the Activator `GetObject()` method creates a proxy object that looks like the requested object, but is really just set up to call to that object remotely. The information we are providing includes the type of object we want and the location of the real object. The Activator does the rest. We must typecast the result to be a DataSetServer, though, because `GetObject()` returns a regular object.

One interesting point here: even though this code has created the proxy for us, it has in no way connected to the server or confirmed that the real object exists. Doing so would be inefficient, because it would require a round-trip. The connection won't be tested until we call a method on the object.

❹ Even though we know the reference returned to us is not the DataSetServer, but is, in fact, a proxy, we can treat it as though it really were the object. The code simply calls methods on the object as though it were local.

In this case, the server is asked to generate a DataSet and return it. The client, with no code of its own to create a DataSet, nonetheless is handed one. This code would work even if there were no way for the client to talk to the database, because the client never talks to the database.

The code for `DisplayDataTable()` is omitted, but it's basically the same as the version from previous chapters.

Results

After all that, the output from the client is a little disappointing. However, the example doesn't matter as much as the power behind the concepts. Before running the client, the server must be started. Figure 21.5 shows the output.

When running this for the first time, you may notice a slight delay; the first call has to do a lot of setup work. A second call to the same object would be a little faster.

```
C:\Projects\ArFClient\bin\Debug\ArFClient.exe
1, Mr. Biddick, G9, Math
2, Ms. Fortune, A1, English
3, Mr. Kriefels, C3, Physics

Press enter to exit
```

Figure 21.5
Output from client application

We've come a long way to get a fairly simple result. A real three-tier application would have to do quite a bit more; but, once communication between client and server has been set up, it becomes trivial to pass data back and forth using DataSets.

The next section talks about ways to do some slightly more elaborate work with the DataSet and remoting.

21.3   *RESULTS, CHANGES, AND MERGES*

So far, we have been able to pass data from a server to a client. At some point, though, the client will make changes and want to save them. In the meantime, other changes may have occurred on the server, which need to be passed back to the client.

We could do all these things by passing the DataSet back and forth, but the DataSet might contain a large amount of data, whereas only a few rows might have changed. Fortunately, the DataSet has capabilities that make it possible to perform these tasks far more efficiently: the GetChanges() and Merge() methods. GetChanges() retrieves a DataSet containing anything that has been modified within the DataSet, and Merge() allows for two DataSets to be merged together.

I won't give a three-tier example because doing so would require a fair amount of code. However, chapter 16 shows how to use these methods via some simple examples. Figure 21.6 shows the flow in a three-tier environment.

This scenario (or pieces of it) may or may not make sense, depending on your application. At the very least, being able to send just the data that has changed back to the server is almost always a good approach.

The beauty of the remoting capabilities within .NET is that accomplishing these tasks is no more complex than it would be if the code were all local—once the small piece of remoting code is written. For example, you could add a method to the DataSetServer for saving changes:

```
public bool SaveChanges(DataSet dsChanges);
```

You could then call it from your client just like a regular method:

```
    .
    .
    .
DataSet dsChanges = ds.GetChanges();
if(dss.SaveChanges(dsChanges))
   Console.WriteLine("Changes have been saved!");
    .
    .
    .
```

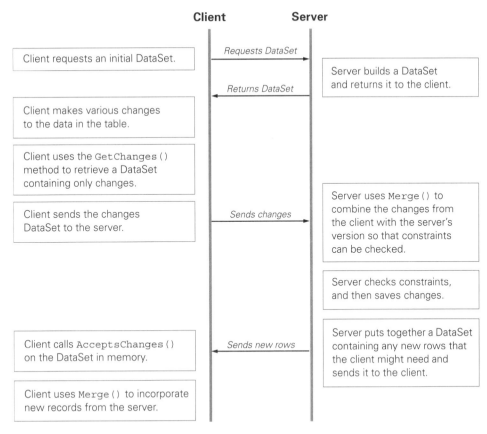

Figure 21.6   Possible client/server scenario for DataSets

21.4 SUMMARY

Remoting is a complex topic, but it is only one of the pieces of multi-tier development that we need to consider. This chapter has shown that it is fairly straightforward to pass data between different tiers, and that the DataSet can make the task easier.

This is a place where the DataSet shines over older technologies like disconnected Recordsets. The DataSet fits cleanly into the cohesive model and goals of .NET.

This is the last chapter of part 3; you should now have all the information you need to make effective use of DataSets. The DataSet is a useful tool that can simplify development in many ways. That said, the DataSet, like any tool, can be used poorly. A solid design is required before you move forward with a multi-tier application.

The next part of this book is also related to the DataSet. Instead of being directly about DataSets and their capabilities, however, it focuses on .NET's various GUI and web controls that can use the DataSet directly.

DataBound controls

One of the great things about .NET is that it is a cohesive framework, rather than a jumble of unrelated pieces. The DataSet, for example, is a powerful component unto itself, but it has also been built to work with other parts of the framework, such as the remoting services seen in chapter 21. The DataSet has also been built to understand a concept called *data binding*.

Data binding simply means that data is exposed in a consistent manner that is understood by certain controls. The controls can therefore present data from any source that exposes the appropriate interfaces. The DataSet is not the only source for data in .NET; for example, you can use data-bound controls with a number of the different collection classes, such as the ArrayList, although they may not provide the same rich functionality you get when binding to a DataSet.

The first chapter in part 4 talks about the DataGrid, which is a powerful Windows grid control that can display data from a DataSet. Chapter 23 discusses the web version of the DataGrid. Chapter 24 describes other data-bound web controls. Finally, chapter 25 looks at DataViews, which allow for custom views of the data, similar to a database view.

CHAPTER 22

The DataGrid WinForm control

The DataGrid WinForm control is a powerful user interface control that allows data to be displayed and edited in a grid, as you'll see in this chapter. The control was designed to work with the DataSet, and it allows data from a DataSet to be displayed easily and quickly. It can even show related data in a subgrid for each row.

22.1   USING THE DATAGRID

The good news is that using the DataGrid is straightforward—once you set up some basic associations, the grid does all the rest for you. In some ways, this is also the bad news—if you want more power over what the control does and how it does it, it is not always intuitively obvious how to do so.

The DataGrid has some other limitations, which may or may not matter, depending on your application. The biggest issue is that there is currently no *virtual mode*. Consider a scenario where you are looking at a list of a couple of million customers. A virtual mode would load the first page or so of data into the control, and would load the remaining data only when you scrolled down.

The DataGrid expects you to load all the data it needs up front. For many scenarios this is no big deal, but for the customer list scenario, it can be a major problem. In some ways, though, this is a problem of the three-tier architecture that .NET is built around—you cannot rely on techniques such as using a server-side cursor to maintain your position in the data, so dealing with large lists in a multi-tier environment is quite a challenge. Rather than not be able to deliver a control in time, Microsoft pragmatically chose to not support this model—at least not for the first release of .NET.

There are a couple of different approaches to using the DataGrid. You can use the built-in Form Designer to configure your data sources and the grid, similar to the VB 6 approach, or you can do the work programmatically. Personally, I find it much more straightforward to do everything programmatically—the autocreation is OK, but it generates code in a manner that is harder to maintain. Nonetheless, I will demonstrate both approaches in this chapter.

22.2 SETTING UP A DATAGRID IN THE DESIGNER

Using the designer involves more than setting up the grid—the Visual Studio designer is set up to configure your data connections and specify the contents of a DataSet. This approach is fairly convenient if you are slapping together a program, but it feels somewhat sloppy when you're building a production system. My concern is that using the designer this way builds an enormous reliance on the development tool to manage what I consider to be core parts of the system. Then again, I am probably old-fashioned—a whole generation of developers has used 4GL tools like VB 6 and PowerBuilder this way and has turned out some great applications. Once you have gone through the steps to automatically set up a data source and configure the DataGrid, we will look at the code that is generated, and you might begin to share some of my misgivings!

Although the underlying designer does a lot for you, a surprising number of steps are required to set up a DataGrid—largely because you need to do more than just set up a grid. You need to:

1 Create a new project.

2 Connect to the database.

3 Set up a DataSet.

4 Put the DataGrid on the form.

5 Set up a DataAdapter.

6 Reference the DataSet from the form.

7 Associate the DataSet with the DataGrid.

8 Write some code to load the data from the adapter—say, at the click of a button.

See—nothing to it! It doesn't help that inconsistencies exist in the way some operations are done, and that if you do certain steps out of order it is unclear why some options aren't available that seem like they should be. Don't worry, though—we'll go through the whole process step by step. Once you have run through it once or twice, it is fairly straightforward, and it gets easier to extend once the initial pieces are set up. I know some Microsoft developers are concerned with these issues, and I expect the process to be much smoother in the next version of .NET.

22.2.1 Creating the project

This step is straightforward: we create a new Windows application project. Call the project DataGridDemo (figure 22.1).

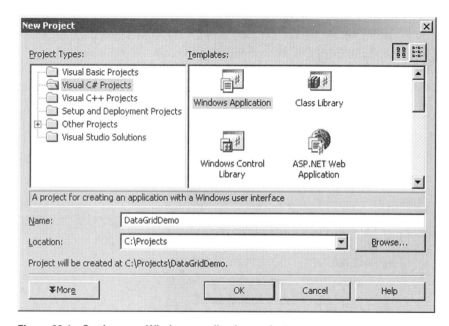

Figure 22.1   Setting up a Windows application project

22.2.2 Connecting to the database

Visual Studio has a lot of different components and tools for different purposes. One of these is the Server Explorer. The Server Explorer keeps track of various databases and other system services. Unlike many of the other windows in Visual Studio, it is not tied to the current project, but is global—once you have told it about a server, that server's items will be available in any project.

The Server Explorer can be used to connect to the ADO.NET test database that has been used throughout the book. To bring up the Server Explorer, select Server Explorer from the View menu. Before we add a database server to it, it will look something like figure 22.2.

Figure 22.2
Server Explorer

We can add a database to the Server Explorer by right-clicking on Data Connections and selecting Add Connection. This option will bring up the Data Link Properties dialog box, which is actually the OLE DB data connection dialog box. By default, it opens ready to set up a SQL Server connection, but you can choose a different type of data source from the Provider tab. However, this example uses SQL Server, so we don't need to change anything.

Even though the Server Explorer uses OLE DB to access data, it doesn't mean we have to use the OLE DB data provider in our code. We will have the option of specifying the appropriate data provider later.

The Data Link Properties looks like figure 22.3 after we fill them in.

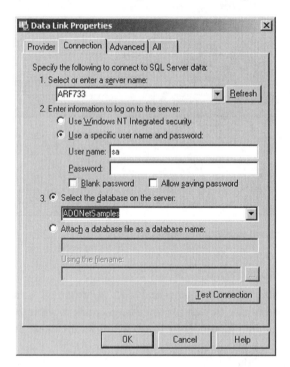

Figure 22.3
Data Link Properties dialog box

The server name in the figure is the name of my computer—you should have a different name here.[1] We have specified the *sa* account (system administrator) with no

---

[1] Barring a strange coincidence.

password,[2] and we have specified the ADONetSamples database. You should recognize these arguments from the standard SQL Server connection string in early examples. When we click OK, the new connection will show up in the Server Explorer (figure 22.4).

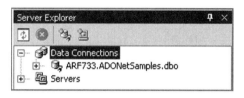

Figure 22.4
Server Explorer with the new connection

This connection will be used in a second, both to configure the DataSet and to set up the connection. Because the Server Explorer is global, we won't need to add this particular database again. That step would be necessary only if we wanted to point to a different data source.

22.2.3 Setting up a DataSet

So far, all the DataSets used in examples have been created by writing code, but there is another way. Visual Studio provides a handy utility for building DataSets. It is a fairly nice tool—it includes a visual tool in which you can drag-and-drop tables and relationships, and so forth. The visual tool then generates an XSD file (an XML schema) that contains the definition. You can edit the schema for the DataSet using either the visual tool or by modifying the schema directly.

One more file is created as part of this process, although it is hidden by default. This C# file contains code for setting up a DataSet. If you look in this file, you will see that it contains a class derived from DataSet that represents *your* DataSet, and a nested class for each contained DataTable and relationship. So, for example, if we add the Teachers table to the DataSet via the designer, then a class called Teachers will be added to the TeacherInfo DataSet class:

```
class TeacherInfo : DataSet
{
    class Teachers : DataTable
    .
    .
    .
```

The C# file is important, because it contains the class that represents the DataSet. However, this file will be regenerated every time you modify the schema via the editor, so you cannot change it directly (at least not safely). Because the code is generated by the designer, it is fairly ugly; so you probably wouldn't want to edit it directly anyway. (By the way, this is referred to as a *strongly typed DataSet*. Strongly typed DataSets are discussed in more detail in chapter 27.)

---

[2] Yes, I know—very naughty.

To add the DataSet, we need to add a new item to the project. The easiest way to do this is to go to the Solution Explorer, right-click on the project, and select Add New Item (figure 22.5).

Figure 22.5
Right-click on the project to add a new item.

One of the choices lets items add a new DataSet. Select this option and give the DataSet the name TeacherInfo.xsd (figure 22.6).

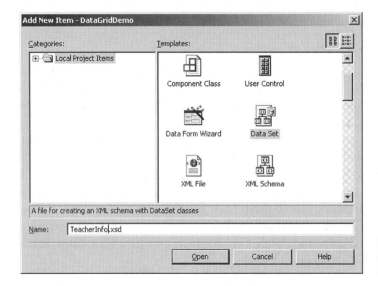

Figure 22.6
Creating a new DataSet

When we create the file, we are taken to the DataSet designer screen. At first it will be blank, except for some instructions.

To set up the DataSet, we drag items onto the designer screen. We can drag tables from the Server Explorer, and we can also drag things like constraints and relationships from the toolbox. For the moment, though, we want the DataSet to contain the Teachers table. Go back to the Server Explorer and expand the data source added earlier, and then expand the Tables node (figure 22.7).

Drag-and-drop the Teachers table onto the designer. When we do, the table will appear with all its fields (figure 22.8). The big *E* stands for Entity, because we are really building an Entity-Relationship diagram.

Notice that the fields in the Teachers table all appear here. This is an important point, because the XSD file will explicitly contain a reference to the fields that are

CHAPTER 22   THE DATAGRID WINFORM CONTROL

Figure 22.7
Expanded Server Explorer

shown—if we add or remove fields, we will have to come back to the designer to make the XSD file reflect the changes.

Of course, if you write DataSet code, you may frequently set up specific, hard-coded DataSets. But you also have the choice of reading the schema and setting up the DataSet more flexibly, or storing a definition in some manner that can be updated without writing code. If you use the designer, you must recompile your code to make a change. This may or may not matter, depending on your application.

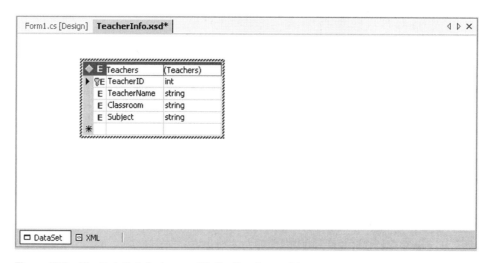

Figure 22.8   The DataSet designer with the Teachers table

22.2.4 Putting the DataGrid onto the form

This step is straightforward. We'll set up our main form to contain a DataGrid. Considering that this chapter is supposed to be about the DataGrid, we have covered a lot of ground before seeing one! The fact is, the setup of the DataGrid is trivial—the real work is setting up the data to associate with the DataGrid.

All we need to do to set up the DataGrid is to drag a DataGrid from the Windows Forms section of the toolbox. If you don't have the toolbox up, you can get to it from the View menu. You will need to switch back to the Form1 design view (figure 22.9).

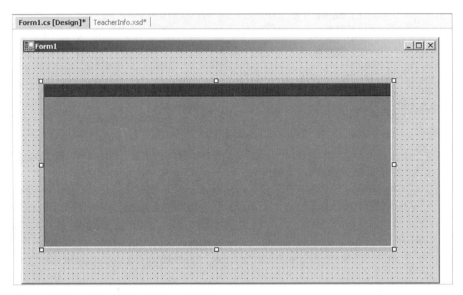

Figure 22.9   Putting a DataGrid on the form

Make the DataGrid a reasonable size, and leave a little space above it for some buttons that we will add later.

The DataGrid has a lot of properties. I will not discuss them, because this is not a book about user interface controls; however, we will set some properties later to specify the data source. The properties give you reasonable control over the look and feel of the DataGrid, with some limitations. You can set up specialized handling for different columns, although doing so is far from intuitive. You can also add custom columns with controls, such as buttons or combo boxes. Again, these topics are beyond the scope of this book.

22.2.5 Setting up a DataAdapter

In earlier examples, filling the DataSet from the database required the use of a DataAdapter. That is still true with the designer. Instead of setting up a DataAdapter manually, though, we will do it using a wizard from within the designer. The toolbox has a Data section. One of the items in that section is an SqlDataAdapter— we can drag and drop it onto the form. When we do, we will immediately be taken to a wizard for configuring the DataAdapter.

The first page of the wizard is introductory. When we click Next, we will be asked to specify the data source from which the data should be retrieved (figure 22.10).

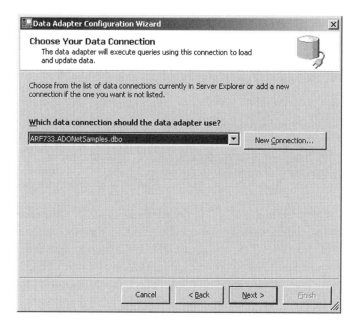

**Figure 22.10
Specifying a
data connection**

The combo box lists data sources from the Server Explorer. The selection shown in the dialog box is the sample database. The next page of the wizard specifies how data should be retrieved, and also how the data should be written back to the data source. For our purposes, we want to use SQL statements, the default choice. The other choices are explained clearly on the dialog box.

It is interesting to know how this wizard works. As with most things in the designer, it will generate code to match what you request—that means it will put SQL into the code that sets up the form. Although the wizard might use the Command-Builder internally, it pulls out the statements, parameters, and so forth, and basically hard-codes them into the application; the generated code does not use the Command-Builder. The danger here, as with much of this auto-generated mechanism, is that the code is now reliant on the current structure—if you change the structure of your table, you must reconfigure the adapter along with all the other pieces.

The next page we see expects us to enter the SQL for our select. We can either type in a select statement or click the Query Builder button. If we do that, we will be asked to select tables. Choose the Teachers table and then close the Add Table dialog box. The Query Builder will appear (figure 22.11).

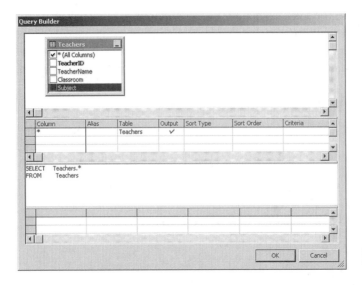

Figure 22.11
The Query Builder

For the purposes of this example, selecting the All Columns checkbox is appropriate, although we could be more selective. We could also add a filtering criteria (such as a `where` clause). When we click OK, the query will be transferred into the wizard.

There is nothing else we need to do. We can click Finish or click Next, which will bring up a summary page. Once we click Finish (here or on the final page), we will be back in the Form Designer. Two new items will appear at the bottom of the window (figure 22.12).

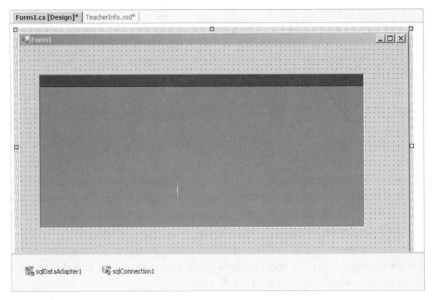

Figure 22.12   Form Designer after setting up an adapter

Even though we only set out to configure a DataAdapter, the wizard automatically created a connection as well. You can change the names if you like, but for this exercise the default names are OK.

Another word about using the designer for these tasks: the code for the Data-Adapter and the connection are now part of the form. Basic design 101 tells you that you should always separate your data access code from your user interface. Even within the designer, there is a way to accomplish this—you can create a component that has the connection and the adapter, and use the component from your user interface. You can also choose to use the designers for some of the steps, as will be shown in section 22.5.

22.2.6 Referencing the DataSet from the form

We have defined the DataSet already, and we have a way to fill the DataSet (the Data-Adapter we just created). Now we need to bring them together. This next step is incredibly simple but conceptually a bit strange. Let's start with the simple part—setting up the DataSet.

On the Data menu is an option labeled Generate DataSet. When we select it, a dialog box comes up that includes a Choose a DataSet option. Choose the TeacherInfo DataSet that was created earlier (figure 22.13).

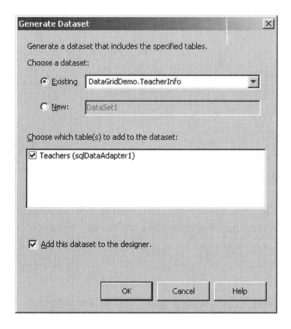

Figure 22.13
Generating a DataSet

When we click OK, a new item is added to the bottom of the Form Designer (figure 22.14).

 sqlDataAdapter1   sqlConnection1   teacherInfo1

Figure 22.14   Form Designer with an added component

This step may seem odd—after all, we already created a DataSet, but now we are "generating a DataSet." The conceptual issue is not helped by some rather confusing terminology.

The DataSet we created earlier—TeacherInfo—is now a class, which is derived from DataSet. The teacherInfo1 DataSet we just "generated" is an instance of the TeacherInfo class. The code within the form will now contain a variable called `teacherInfo1`, with is of type TeacherInfo—the basic difference between a class and an object!

22.2.7   Associating the DataSet with the DataGrid

We have all the elements we need. It is now a matter of bringing them together. First, the DataGrid needs to be told about the DataSet, and told which table in the DataSet to use. Bring up the properties for the DataGrid (we can do this easily by right-clicking on the DataGrid and selecting Properties). One of the sections of the properties is titled Data (figure 22.15).

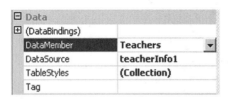

Figure 22.15
Data section of the
DataGrid properties

We need to set the `DataSource` property first—`teacherInfo1` will show up in the drop-down as a possible DataSource. We also see `teacherInfo1.Teachers` in the list, because a DataTable is also a legal DataSource for a DataGrid, as well as a DataSet. We want to use the DataSet so that later we can reference other items.

The `DataMember` specifies the item in the DataSource that should be associated with the DataGrid—in this case, the Teachers table, which will be in the drop-down. As soon as we have specified this value, the DataGrid takes on properties of the Teachers table (figure 22.16).

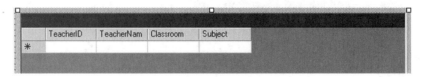

Figure 22.16   DataGrid is now tied to the DataTable

22.2.8 Putting data into the DataGrid

If we run the application at this point, the grid will come up, but it won't contain any data. Although we have set up an adapter that knows how to read the data, and we have a DataSet tied to the DataGrid, some action needs to make the DataAdapter fill the DataSet, which will in turn fill the DataGrid. We'll need to write some code.

Given that everything else has used wizards and designers, it is almost a shame that there isn't one last automatic step. However, such an approach would have some issues. In this example program, we will set up a button that, when clicked, loads the data. In a real application, though, we would have to figure out the appropriate place to connect to the database and the appropriate spot to load the data. Another option would have been to fill the grid when the application is run.

For the test program, we want to put a Fill Grid button on the form. Drag a button off the Windows Form section of the toolbox onto the form, and then change its `Text` property to read "Fill grid" (figure 22.17).

If we double-click on the button, the designer will create a method that will be called when the button is clicked, and then will take us to that code. We need to add a few lines of code to the method:

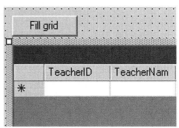

Figure 22.17
The Fill Grid button on the form

```
private void button1_Click(object sender, System.EventArgs e)
{
    sqlConnection1.Open();
    sqlDataAdapter1.Fill(teacherInfo1);
    sqlConnection1.Close();
}
```

The member variables referenced here were created in the designer. This code opens the connection, fills the DataSet using the DataAdapter that was already created, and then closes the connection. Of course, in a real application you would probably not open and close the connection like this, but doing so is convenient for the moment.

22.2.9 Running the application

After all that work, we hope the results will be as expected. Compile and run the application. We see the form with an empty DataGrid. When we click the Fill Grid button, the grid fills with data (figure 22.18).

We can click on headers to sort the data, size the headers, and edit the data as we like. Of course, there is currently no way to save the data, but we will add that functionality in a while. The DataGrid will also handle all the rules on the DataSet—if there are constraints, unique rules, and so forth, the DataGrid will pop up a message any time we try to violate any of them, and give us a chance to fix the problem.

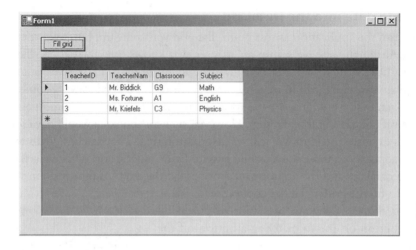

**Figure 22.18
The running
application**

Although a lot of steps were required to get to this point, they shouldn't have taken you too long. Also, now that everything is set up, you can modify things and add functionality easily. In the next section, for example, we will add a related table to our DataSet.

22.3 ADDING RELATIONSHIPS TO THE GRID

The DataGrid was built with the DataSet in mind. That means it must be able to handle relationships, because they are a major component of DataSets. To demonstrate this fact, we'll add the Classes table to the DataSet and set up the relationship between Teachers and Classes. The first step is to add the Classes table to the DataSet, which we do the same way you added the Teachers table—bring up the TeacherInfo DataSet designer and drag the Classes table from the Server Explorer (figure 22.19).

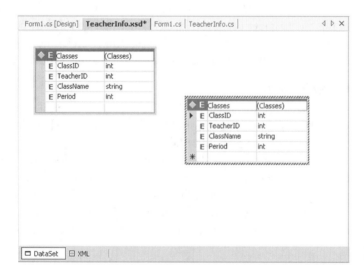

**Figure 22.19
Adding the Classes
table to the DataSet**

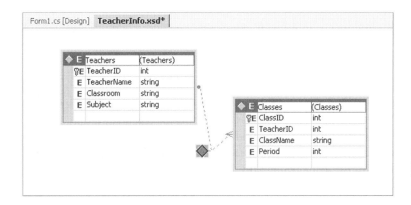

**Figure 22.20
Relating the
Teachers and
Classes tables**

Next, we need to add the relationship. The easiest way to do that is to drag a Relation from the XML Schema section of the toolbox *onto* the Teachers table—if we don't drop the Relation onto one of the entities, it will disappear!

When we drop the Relation, a dialog box appears that lets us configure the Relation. All we need to do is set the Parent element to Teachers and the Child element to Classes. Once we exit the dialog box, the relationship appears between the two entities (figure 22.20).

Even though the TeacherInfo DataSet now knows about the Classes table and the relationship, we still need to set up a DataAdapter to fill the Classes table. We do so the same way we did for the Teachers table—go to the Form Designer and drag another SqlDataAdapter. As before, we must set up the select statement. Using the Query Builder, choose the Classes table and then choose all columns (figure 22.21).

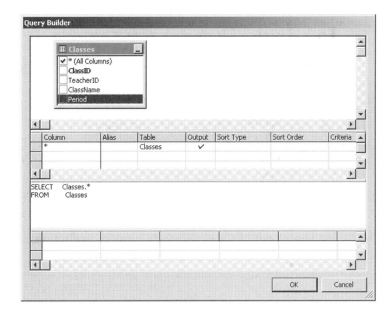

**Figure 22.21
Building the
query for the
Classes table**

ADDING RELATIONSHIPS TO THE GRID

sqlDataAdapter1   sqlConnection1   teacherInfo1   sqlDataAdapter2

Figure 22.22   Components in the form

Once we have built the query and exited the wizard, a new SqlDataAdapter is added at the bottom of the form (figure 22.22).

There is still only a single connection and one DataSet, but now there are two different DataAdapters. The last step is to have the new DataAdapter fill the Classes table. We do so with the same code that fills the Teachers table when the Fill Grid button is clicked:

```
private void button1_Click(object sender, System.EventArgs e)
{
    sqlConnection1.Open();
    sqlDataAdapter1.Fill(teacherInfo1);
    sqlDataAdapter2.Fill(teacherInfo1);
    sqlConnection1.Close();
}
```

You may have noticed that neither of the Fill() calls specifies which table to fill. The adapter finds the table with the same name, so it is not necessary to specify.

That is the last step. If we run the application again and click the Fill Grid button, we will get the same grid as before, but expansion + icons appear next to each row (figure 22.23).

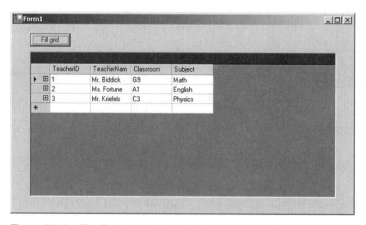

Figure 22.23   The Teachers table with the expansion icons

If we click the + sign next to one of the rows, we see a link named for the relationship (figure 22.24).

CHAPTER 22   THE DATAGRID WINFORM CONTROL

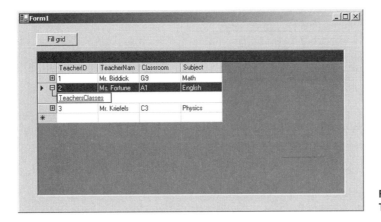

Figure 22.24
The relationship link

Clicking on the button takes the control to a subgrid of the related data, with the parent row shown at the top (figure 22.25).

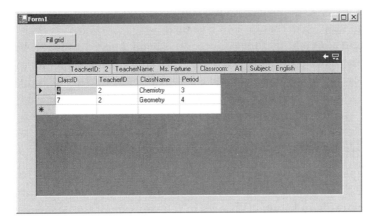

Figure 22.25
A subgrid

This is pretty cool. Depending on whether you are allowing editing, you can edit the subdata right here. This may not be the way you want to expose data in your application, but it is quite impressive for automatic behavior!

22.4 SAVING CHANGES

Now that we can edit data, both in the main table and in the subtable, it would be nice to be able to save changes. Doing so is fairly easy—it's a matter of saving the DataSet changes via the adapters, the same as if we were not using a grid. The only thing we need is something to trigger the save—like a button (figure 22.26).

Figure 22.26
Adding a Save button

Drag the button onto the form and change its label to "Save". Then, double-click to create an on-click handler. The code shouldn't be any surprise:

```
private void button2_Click(object sender, System.EventArgs e)
{
    sqlConnection1.Open();
    sqlDataAdapter1.Update(teacherInfo1);
    sqlDataAdapter2.Update(teacherInfo1);
    sqlConnection1.Close();
}
```

The connection needs to be opened because we closed it after reading the data. The Update() calls save the changes to the appropriate DataTables. That is all we need to do. We can now make changes and save them!

It may seem a bit odd that the connection is being opened and closed every time. Remember, though, we are living in a multi-tier world. In most three-tier applications, the connection would be retrieved from a pool and then released after use. Of course, the designer approach you just took would not work *exactly* the same as in this example, although you could use pieces of it.

22.5 TO USE DESIGNERS OR NOT TO USE DESIGNERS?

In this example, we built a tightly coupled application—the user interface was tied tightly to the data access code. Also, the data access code was quite specific—it would not lend itself easily to handling changes in the structure of the database or, for that matter, talking to a different data source. At some point, take a look at the automatically generated code created as part of this example—it will be buried in the Form1.cs file in the section labeled "Windows Form Designer generated code."

Do these issues condemn the designer approach? Not at all—in some scenarios, the approach, or pieces of it, make perfect sense. At the most obvious end, if you are building a prototype, for example, these factors don't really matter. But what about a production two-tier or three-tier application?

When you create a dialog box that contains a DataGrid, you can easily set it to point to a particular DataSet and table that you have created:

```
dataGrid1.DataSource = dsPassedInDataSet;
dataGrid1.DataMember = "Teachers";
```

That's it—really! The DataSet could be created the way you created DataSets in previous chapters, or you could use the DataSet designer.

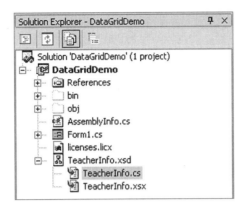

Figure 22.27
The Solution Explorer with hidden files

The DataSet designer lets us build a DataSet derivation that is already tailor-made with a particular set of tables, relationships, constraints, and so forth. It is tied to a particular structure, but that may not be a problem. The designer works by creating a hidden .cs file based on the XML. We can see this file by telling the Solution Explorer to show hidden files—a button at the top shows all files.

When we click this button, we see an expansion button (+) next to the XSD file. Expand it to see the hidden file (figure 22.27).

The code is automatically generated, and we shouldn't change it—if we do, it will be overwritten when we change the XSD file in the designer. The point is that we can create an instance of the specific DataSet by creating an instance of the derivation:

```
TeacherInfo TeacherDataSet = new TeacherInfo();
```

We can use this derivation on the client or on the server. It is not tied to a particular database—after all, a DataSet is never tied to a database. We need a DataAdapter to load and save the data.

We can create a DataAdapter the old-fashioned way, perhaps using a Command-Builder:[3]

```
public DataSet GetTeacherDataSet(SqlConnection conn)
{
   // Create and initialize the adapter
   string strSQL = "SELECT * From Teachers";
   SqlDataAdapter sda = new SqlDataAdapter(strSQL,conn);
   SqlCommandBuilder sqb = new SqlCommandBuilder(sda);

   // Create and fill the dataset
   TeacherInfo TeacherDataSet = new TeacherInfo();
   sda.Fill(TeacherDataSet,"Teachers");

   return TeacherDataSet;
}
```

---

[3] Microsoft (and I) seriously suggest that you do not use CommandBuilders for anything other than the most trivial uses—the SQL created tends to be quite inefficient and ugly. For more on this topic, see the discussion in chapter 19.

Again, this could be on the client in a two-tier application, or on the server in a three-tier application. We could also use the DataAdapter designer to create the adapter. In most cases it would not be appropriate to do this as part of a form or other user interface element, but a special element is specifically designed for handling such cases—a component. We can add a new component to the project just as we would add any new element (figure 22.28).

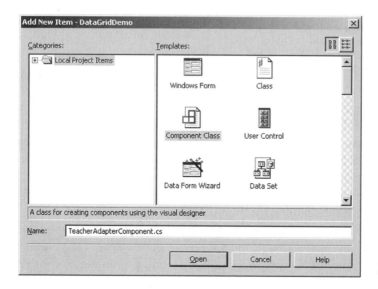

**Figure 22.28
Adding a Component
to the project**

A Component is a special class that works with the designers. When we bring up the new Component in design mode, we are presented with a blank designer screen. We can drag an adapter onto that screen and go through the wizard, exactly the same way we did with the form. Once it is set up, we have a similar result (figure 22.29).

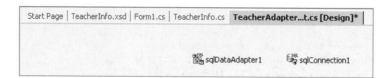

**Figure 22.29
Component with
components**

Notice that we get a connection as well as a DataAdapter. Of course, we can rename either of them.

The Component is a class with some autogenerated code, the same as the form. We can bring up the code by right-clicking on the file in the Solution Explorer and selecting View Code. Then, we can add a method for filling the DataSet directly to the component class. It is really not much different from the manually generated code, except that the connection and the adapter are already defined for you (listing 22.1).

Listing 22.1 **Returning a filled DataSet from within the component**

```
using System.Data;                    ❶ Add data namespaces

public TeacherAdapterComponent()
{
    /// <summary>
    /// Required for Windows.Forms Class Composition Designer support
    /// </summary>
    InitializeComponent();

    sqlConnection1.Open();            ❷ Connect in the
}                                        constructor

public DataSet GetTeacherDataSet()                          ❸ Get DataSet
{
    TeacherInfo TeacherDataSet = new TeacherInfo();
    sqlDataAdapter1.Fill(TeacherDataSet);

    return TeacherDataSet;
}
```

❶ This code to add the Data namespace is in the wrong place, of course—it should be at the top of the file. We need to add it because the component doesn't know anything about DataSets.

❷ We have a component that knows about our connection, so we might as well use it. The constructor is a good place to open the connection, depending on the way the application will operate. The constructor is already in place—all we do is add the Open() call.

❸ The adapter already is configured, so all we need to do is create a new DataSet and fill it from the adapter.

22.5.1 Example summary

This method allows you to use the various designers but still end up with some reasonably well-organized code. You need to be aware, however, that the code in the component is fairly specific—both the connection information and the adapter are hard-coded and must be updated if either change.

22.6 *BINDING TO OTHER CONTROLS*

The DataGrid is not the only control that can be bound to a DataSet or other data source. In fact, most of the Windows Form controls have the ability to be bound. For example, you can have the values that show up in a combo box or list control be filled from a DataSet. It is easy to set this up. All you have to do is set the properties for a combo box appropriately (figure 22.30).

⊟ **Data**		
⊟ (DataBindings)		
(Advanced)		...
SelectedItem	(None)	
SelectedValue	(None)	
Tag	(None)	
Text	(None)	
DataSource	**teacherInfo1**	
DisplayMember	**Teachers.TeacherNan**	
Items	**(Collection)**	
Tag		
ValueMember		

Figure 22.30
Binding a combo box

The figure shows the Data section of a combo box's properties. Notice that the `DataSource` has been set to our DataSet, and the `DisplayMember` has been set to `Teachers.TeacherName`—which indicates the TeacherName field from the Teachers table.

Once the DataSet has been filled, the list of selections in the combo box will reflect the list from the Teachers table (figure 22.31).

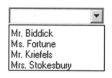

Figure 22.31
Drop-down filled
by the DataSet

Be aware, though, that binding multiple items to the same DataTable in the same DataSet has some implications. If, for example, we put this drop-down list on the same form as the DataGrid, then the selection in the combo box will change as we move through the different items. We can make use of this action. For example, we could put labels or text boxes on the form and have them change with the DataGrid (figure 22.32).

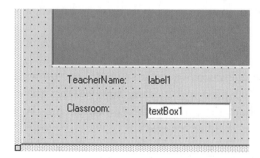

Figure 22.32
Some additional data-bound
controls on the form

As you can see, a few controls have been added at the bottom of the form below the DataGrid. The labels on the left are what they appear, but the label and text box on the right will be bound directly to the DataSet. Because this is not a common operation for a label or text box, the DataSource options are usually collapsed in the property designer. If we click the + sign next to the (DataBindings) option, we can specify some additional options. The drop-down that appears next to `Text` lets us choose an item to which to bind (figure 22.33).

CHAPTER 22 THE DATAGRID WINFORM CONTROL

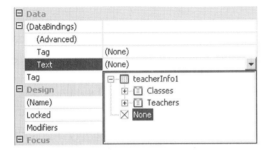

Figure 22.33
Binding the `Text`
property to a field

For the label, expand Teachers and choose the TeacherName field. For the text box, choose the Classroom field. Now, if we run the application and move through the DataGrid, the values on those controls will change automatically (figure 22.34).

Not only will the values update as you move through the grid, but if we change the value in the Classroom text box, the value will change automatically in the DataSet and the DataGrid. Again, not bad for automatic functionality!

If you want to tie multiple controls to the same data but have them work independently, you can use DataViews, which are discussed in chapter 25.

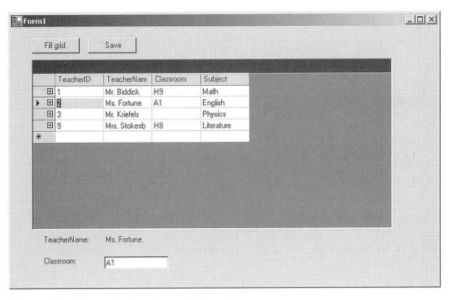

Figure 22.34   Controls changing with the grid

22.7 SUMMARY

This chapter has covered a lot of ground and has shown several different ways to get to the same place. The chapter's title mentions the DataGrid, and you did see the DataGrid, but it was sometimes lost in the details of the designers.

Although you may have picked up the impression that I am not a fan of designers in general, that is not true. What I don't like is *reliance* on designers, without taking into account the repercussions of their use—it is easy to end up with tightly coupled, hard-to-maintain code by letting the designers take over. In their proper place, though, and with an understanding of their limitations, they can be useful.

Okay—enough of my lecturing. The DataGrid is a cool control, and I encourage you to explore its properties. (I would have liked to spend more time exploring the properties of the control, but it is not the topic of this book. Maybe the next book I write will be about WinForms. . . .)

The next chapter is also about a DataGrid: the web version, rather than the Windows version.

C H A P T E R   2 3

The DataGrid web control

OK—I know what you are thinking. Why is the writer spending all this time talking about Windows and Windows Forms? Doesn't he know that the Web is everything now? Well, for those of you have waded patiently through the Windows Form stuff, this chapter finally addresses using it from the Web. I will even forgo my usual rant about web interfaces, except to say that the two types of interfaces—web and GUI— have different purposes, and each has its place.

ASP.NET, the .NET technology for building web sites, is quite impressive and makes great strides in moving general web development from scripting to programming. Some great pre-.NET web sites were developed with a true programming model, but the nature of the web development tools, including such things as the original ASP, tended to encourage a model that was less than ideal.

ASP.NET is another topic beyond the scope of this book; but in this chapter I will run through enough steps to set up an ASP.NET project, so we can explore the data-bound web controls. In particular, I will demonstrate the web version of the DataGrid. The web DataGrid has a similar purpose to the Windows DataGrid, but there are a fair number of differences in the way in which it is used.

As with the previous chapter, we will begin by using the designers to create the application, and then explore different approaches and options that are available via code.

23.1 USING THE WEB DATAGRID WITH DESIGNERS

One of the great things about WebForms in ASP.NET is that they work in a parallel manner to WinForms. I hope you didn't skip the last chapter, because many of the steps are the same, and I do not intend to go into quite as much detail about topics that have already been covered.

23.1.1 Setting up the project

The first thing we need to do is create a new project. In this case, it will be an ASP.NET web application (figure 23.1). To do this in the most straightforward manner, Microsoft Internet Information Server (IIS) must be up and running on our machine.

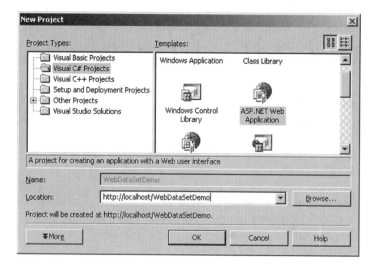

**Figure 23.1
Creating an ASP.NET
web application**

When we create the project, we are presented with a blank web form. We will come back to this stage later; we first need to set up a few other things, starting with a DataSet definition.

23.1.2 Creating a DataSet

Instead of creating a DataSet manually, we can use the built-in DataSet/Schema editor within Visual Studio to create a custom derivation of a DataSet that contains the appropriate definitions, simply by dragging objects into the editor. The process is the same as with the GUI application, and chapter 22 provides a much more complete explanation.

As with the previous chapter, we can create the new DataSet by adding a new item to the project of type DataSet; you will probably have to expand the tree in the Add New Item dialog box (figure 23.2).

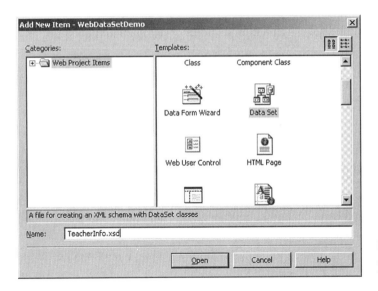

Figure 23.2
Adding a DataSet
to the project

We want the Teachers table again, so drag it from the Server Explorer onto the DataSet editor (figure 23.3). Notice that the data source is still set up from the example in chapter 22—once we put something in the Server Explorer, it should stay there indefinitely.

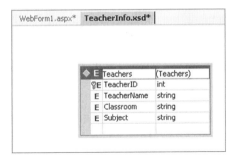

Figure 23.3
TeacherInfo DataSet with the Teachers table

23.1.3 Setting up the web form

The next few steps are virtually the same, as well—go to the web form and drag on a DataGrid from the Web Forms section of the toolbox. Then, drag on an SqlDataAdapter from the Data section—we are immediately taken to the Data Adapter wizard to configure the DataAdapter. As before, we use the SQL builder to build a select statement that returns the rows in the Teachers table. When we are done with the wizard, we have a DataAdapter and a connection at the bottom of the form (figure 23.4).

Figure 23.4
A Data Adapter and a connection for the form

A new class called TeacherInfo was created in the DataSet designer; it is derived from DataSet. On the form, we need to create an *instance* of the TeacherInfo DataSet, which we do by selecting Generate DataSet from the Data menu. Select TeacherInfo, and the new DataSet will show up at the bottom of the form (figure 23.5).

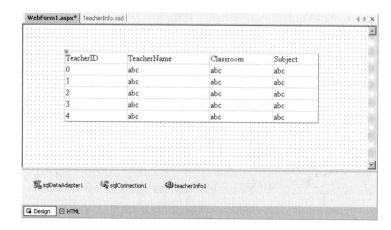

Figure 23.5
The form and
components

23.1.4   Associating the DataGrid with the DataSet

The last step to take in the designer is to associate the DataSet with the DataGrid. We do so from the DataGrid's properties. We have to set the `DataSource` before we set the `DataMember`. Unfortunately these are backward; they are in alphabetical order within the section, rather than a more logical order (figure 23.6).

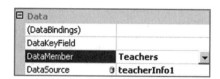

Figure 23.6   DataGrid properties

As with the GUI example, we need to put in some code to do the load. However, the code is a little different. First, we will load the data when the HTML page is first loaded, rather than when a button is clicked; second, an extra step is required when working with the web version of the DataGrid.

To edit the code, right-click on the form and select View Code. A `Page_Load` method will already be in place; it will be called when the page is loaded. We need to add a few lines to it:

```
private void Page_Load(object sender, System.EventArgs e)
{
    if(!IsPostBack)
    {
        sqlConnection1.Open();
        sqlDataAdapter1.Fill(teacherInfo1);
        sqlConnection1.Close();
        DataGrid1.DataBind();
    }
}
```

The `IsPostBack` check makes sure this is the creation of the page, rather than a reload of the page after data was sent back. For the moment this is not an issue, because there is no way to post data back to the page; but that will change as the example is extended.

The next three lines are as normal—open the connection, load the DataSet, and close the connection. The last line—the `DataBind()` call—is specific to the fact that we are using controls on the Web. In the GUI world, the DataGrid can subscribe to events on the DataSet to know when the contents of the DataSet have changed. The web version cannot do this, so we have to explicitly tell the grid to talk to its data source.

That is the last step for setting up the example. All that is left is to run the application. When we do so from Visual Studio, it launches our browser and brings up the page (figure 23.7).

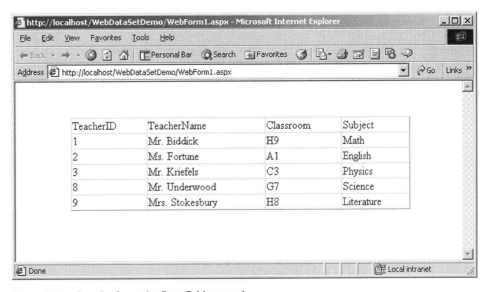

Figure 23.7   Results from the DataGrid example

I realize this window is pretty ugly, but a bunch of DataGrid properties let you customize the appearance. In fact, the web DataGrid has more options than the GUI version. That is not the focus of this book, so I won't go into detail; but it would be worth your time to explore some of the options.

23.2   EDITING DATA ON THE WEB

As you probably already know, the Web doesn't work the same way as a rich client. For example, the WinForms version of the DataGrid has an automatic edit mode in which you can click in a cell and start editing. This paradigm is not appropriate for a disconnected web client. However, there *is* a built-in edit mode available for the web version of the DataGrid; it just works slightly differently.

ASP.NET lets you write code as if you were writing regular code, responding to events, and so forth. It then figures out how to implement this code on the appropriate browser, and does post-backs to the server to execute the code when appropriate.

You will use this functionality to add an edit link to each row; the link will allow the data in that row to be edited. You have a huge amount of flexibility in the way in which this technique works, but this example will take advantage of a default mechanism that is provided by the DataGrid.

23.2.1 Columns on the DataGrid

Currently, the grid contains a column for each column in the DataSet. We want an additional column that has an Edit link for each row. The user will be able to click on that link to access an editable version of the particular row. While we are at it, we can also remove the TeacherID field from the grid—there is no value in displaying it, because it is read-only and really for internal use. Both of these changes can be accomplished via the Property Builder. The Property Builder is a special editor that lets you edit the properties of the DataGrid in a more convenient way. There are several ways to bring it up, including a button that appears at the top of the standard property editor (illustrated on the left).

We can also right-click on the DataGrid on the WebForm and select Property Builder. A dialog box will appear with a menu down the left-hand side for various different pages. Select the Columns page (figure 23.8).

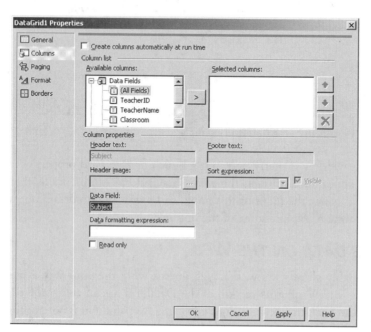

Figure 23.8
The Property Builder

We will look at some of the other pages later. For the moment, we are interested in defining what columns appear on the DataGrid. This page lets us choose the columns to display and set a number of properties for each column. You may notice that no columns are currently listed. That is the case because the columns are being added at runtime—the Create Columns Automatically at Run Time checkbox is checked! (Sometimes the user interface makes sense.)

An advantage of the autocreate columns option is that it handles changes to the DataSet automatically. However, to remove columns via the editor, we need to explicitly specify which columns to include, so we uncheck that checkbox. Instead, we will specify the columns to display by moving them into the Selected Columns list. We do this by selecting the column in the Available Columns list and then clicking the > button to move to the field into the Selected Columns list. Add the TeacherName, Classroom, and Subject fields (figure 23.9).

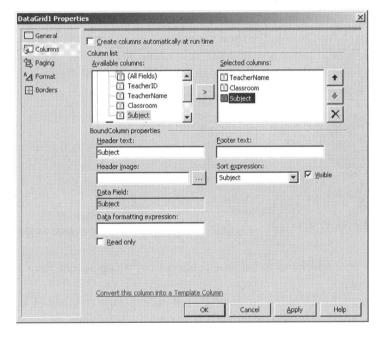

**Figure 23.9
Adding some
columns to the grid**

If we click OK right now, the grid will show the columns in the list. We can also do things like specify a different header or a specialized expression for formatting the text. We need to add one more column, though—a specialized column that contains an Edit option.

The DataGrid allows for several different types of columns. We can add a hyperlink column, for example, or a column that gets its content from another URL. Basically, we can create a column that contains anything that is legal on the Web. One of the special columns we can add is an Edit, Update, Cancel column. This special column initially will have an Edit link; when the row is in edit mode, it will have two links—an Update link and a Cancel link. The user can click Update to save changes or Cancel to abandon them.

We add this column just like a field, except that we have to expand the Button Column option in the Available Columns list; then select the Edit, Update, Cancel option and use the > button to add it to the list (figure 23.10).

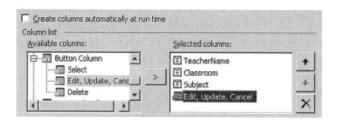

Figure 23.10
Adding the Edit, Update,
Cancel column

The order of the columns in the list is the order in which they will appear on the grid. It would be nice to put this special edit column on the left. We can easily do so by using the up and down arrows to the right of the list, which allow the columns to be rearranged (figure 23.11).

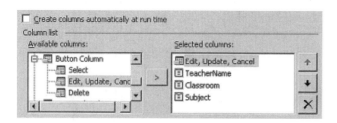

Figure 23.11
Rearranged column order

Of course, we could have added that column first, which would have avoided the need to move it.

One important to thing to remember is that a *huge* number of options and approaches are possible with this control. You could easily change the text that appears to something besides Edit, for example, or use the value in one of the columns as the link that lets you edit. You can explore these options on your own, or pick up a book on ASP.NET.

If we click OK on the Property Builder, we have a grid with an Edit option (figure 23.12).

So far, so good. If we run this code now, though, the grid will be filled, but the Edit link will do nothing. We need to hook up some events to make something happen.

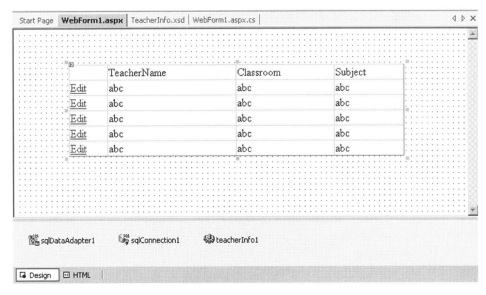

Figure 23.12   The DataGrid with the Edit column

23.2.2   Catching the Edit event

You might be wondering about this step. After all, with the WinForm DataGrid, we didn't have to worry about anything like this—the event handling just *happened*. With the Web, though, the situation is a lot more complicated. It is not just a matter of setting up some different parts of a control—the whole page needs to be rebuilt, providing a place to edit data. The nice thing is that most of the complexity is hidden.

The more web-savvy already know that you don't necessarily have to rebuild everything—there are ways within ASP.NET to be more efficient. However, that is another topic that needs its own book. For our purposes, the whole page is the DataGrid, which has built-in mechanisms for rebuilding itself appropriately.

The methods aren't added automatically because there are simply too many different ways you might want to use the DataGrid and, for that matter, the DataSet that sits beneath the DataGrid. Still, the ASP.NET model makes it easy to add code in the appropriate places. A click on the Edit link is converted into an event that you can catch.

As with many things in .NET, there are several different ways to hook up an event. The easiest is to use the property editor. If we bring up the properties for the DataGrid and click the lightning bolt, we get a list of all the events on the DataGrid. At the top is a section labeled Action (figure 23.13).

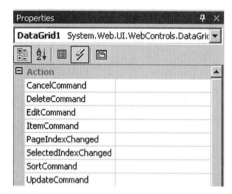

Figure 23.13
Action events on the DataGrid

If we type in a name of a method next to the event we care about, an appropriate method will automatically be created. Pressing Enter then takes us to the code. The first event we care about is the EditCommand event. I added an event handler called OnDataGridEdit (figure 23.14).

The file to which we are taken is called WebForm1.aspx.cs. This is the code "behind" the web page; it runs on the server and creates the page. This code will also be called when an event happens on the web page. In this respect, the WebForm code works the same way as the WinForm code. However, with the WinForm, the code catches a Windows message. With the WebForm, the event causes the server to be called, which, in turn, converts the activity on the web page into an actual event.

We now have an event handler for when the Edit link is clicked. We need to make it do something:

```
private void OnDataGridEdit(object source,
                  System.Web.UI.WebControls.DataGridCommandEventArgs e)
{
    DataGrid1.EditItemIndex = e.Item.ItemIndex;
    DoBind();
}
```

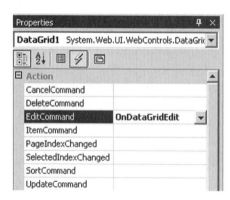

Figure 23.14
Creating an EditCommand event handler

CHAPTER 23   THE DATAGRID WEB CONTROL

Add the bolded lines to the automatically generated method.

The first new line tells the DataGrid that a particular row should be put into edit mode when the page is regenerated. The row that needs to be in edit mode is determined from the event arguments passed to the method. The `Item.ItemIndex` contains the row on which the Edit link was clicked.

The second line calls a method we can add, called `DoBind()`. It looks like this:

```
private void DoBind()
{
    // Reload the DataSet
    sqlConnection1.Open();
    sqlDataAdapter1.Fill(teacherInfo1);
    sqlConnection1.Close();

    // Regenerate the DataGrid
    DataGrid1.DataBind();
}
```

Wait a minute, I hear you say—why are we reloading the DataSet? Welcome to the world of stateless coding. You have to imagine that your server is serving a huge number of clients, and you don't want to hold onto any information from call to call. This is the same WebForm code in which we originally loaded the data, but it is not the same instance. Every time the WebForm is needed, a new instance is created. It has the same variables, such as the `teacherInfo1` DataSet, but it is a new instance that has not yet been loaded.

You don't have to do things this way; a couple of other approaches will let you hold onto the data, and I will discuss them later. For the moment, though, you will do proper stateless coding, which means the DataSet needs to be refilled before it can be used.

The last line of the method calls `DataBind()`, which regenerates the DataGrid. If we did not have this call, then nothing would seem to happen—we would not go into any sort of edit mode, and the DataGrid would remain unchanged.

You might wonder how the DataGrid manages this trick—after all, doesn't the page have to be re-created? The answer is that enough information is sent back to the server when it is called that it can return the DataGrid in its original state. If we didn't reload the DataSet with the adapter, but did call `DataBind()`, we would end up with a DataGrid that had some headers but no data, and certainly no edit capabilities.

Adding this code now lets the user enter edit mode for the row, although we cannot yet appropriately leave edit mode. Still, it would be nice to run what we have so far and see how it works (figure 23.15).

The row on which Edit was clicked now has edit controls for each of the columns and Update and Cancel links in place of the Edit link. There are not yet any handlers for Update and Cancel, though. That is the next step.

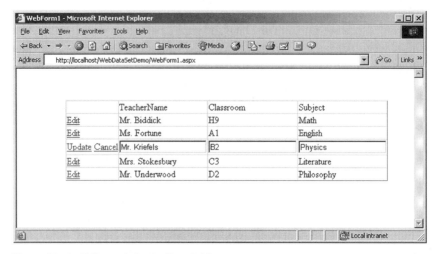

Figure 23.15 Edit mode in the DataGrid

23.2.3 The Cancel handler

We'll add the Cancel handler first because it is simple. We need to add an event handler for the CancelCommand. We can do this the same way we added the Edit-CommandHandler, in the property editor (figure 23.16).

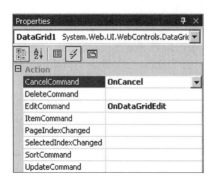

Figure 23.16
Adding the CancelCommand handler

Again, pressing Enter takes us to the code:

```
private void OnCancel(object source,
            System.Web.UI.WebControls.DataGridCommandEventArgs)
{
    DataGrid1.EditItemIndex = -1;
    DoBind();
}
```

The added lines are virtually the same as for the EditCommand handler, except that the EditItemIndex is set to -1, rather than an actual row. This special value indicates that no rows should be in edit mode. The DoBind() call is the same as before—it rebuilds the DataSet and then rebuilds the DataGrid from the DataSet.

23.2.4 The Update handler

The Update event handler is rather more complex, because it needs to retrieve the DataSet, get the changes from the web page, update the DataSet, and then save the changes. Adding the handler is the same as always—go through the property editor.

The code in listing 23.1 handles the update, but it has a few issues we will address later.

Listing 23.1 The Update event handler

```
private void OnUpdateGrid(object source,
        System.Web.UI.WebControls.DataGridCommandEventArgs e)
{
    // Reload the table                           ❶ Reload      Retrieve
    sqlConnection1.Open();                           DataSet     data from
    sqlDataAdapter1.Fill(teacherInfo1);                          WebForm ❷
    // Get hold of the controls that contain the edited data
    TextBox ctlTeacherName = (TextBox)e.Item.Cells[1].Controls[0];
    TextBox ctlClassroom = (TextBox)e.Item.Cells[2].Controls[0];
    TextBox ctlSubject = (TextBox)e.Item.Cells[3].Controls[0];

    // Set the values in the appropriate row in the DataTable
    DataTable dtTeachers = teacherInfo1.Tables["Teachers"];
    DataRow dr = dtTeachers.Rows[e.Item.ItemIndex];
    dr["TeacherName"] = ctlTeacherName.Text;
    dr["Classroom"] = ctlClassroom.Text;           Update ❸
    dr["Subject"] = ctlSubject.Text;               dataset

    // Save changes and close the connection      ❹ Save
    sqlDataAdapter1.Update(dtTeachers);               data
    sqlConnection1.Close();

    // Update the page              ❺ Update
    DataGrid1.EditItemIndex = -1;      DataGrid
    DataGrid1.DataBind();
}
```

❶ Just as with the Edit and Cancel event handlers, we need to reload the data into the DataSet; we must assume this is a whole new world. However, we don't want to close the connection immediately—we will use it when we save data. Also, we don't yet want to rebuild the DataGrid.

❷ These lines get hold of the edit controls that were modified by the user, so that we can get the data from them. The Item property of the DataGridCommandEventArgs is a DataGridItem—the equivalent of a row. We can access each cell via the Cells property of the DataGridItem. A cell refers to the specific column within the row. From that, we can access the control that contains the data. Again, this is from another array—a cell can contain multiple controls, but we know in this case that it only contains the one.

Although this code will work for the time being, it is pretty specific to our grid and our data. We will address that issue a little later.

❸ This code is more or less a standard update of a row within a DataSet. We are retrieving the data for each column from the text controls. It has one problem: what row are we updating? We are using the `ItemIndex` property to determine the row that is being edited. That should work, assuming this is a one-person web site! Don't forget that we reload the DataSet every time an event occurs. If another user happens to add or remove a row, or, for that matter, does something that changes the order, then we will be saving our changes in the wrong place.

For the moment, though, we *are* dealing with a single-user web site, so the code is OK. In the next section, we will address this issue in a way that is more appropriate for the real world.

❹ This code is nothing special—we are using the DataAdapter to save our changes, and then closing the connection.

❺ We are no longer in edit mode, and we want the DataGrid to reflect this fact. So, we set the `EditItemIndex` to −1 to indicate that we are not editing, and then tell the DataGrid to update itself.

Example summary

Now that we have added these two handlers, we can run the code again. This time, when we are done editing, we can click Update to save our changes or Cancel to abandon them. Those of you who have implemented this type of functionality using ASP will probably appreciate the power here the most.

23.3 IMPROVING THE EXAMPLE

I pointed out several flaws in the previous section. For example, the mechanism for identifying the row to retrieve will not stand up in the real world, and the code for updating a row is hard-coded. Also, you are allowing the ability to update, but what about inserts and deletes? The next several sections address these issues.

23.3.1 Getting the proper row

Because the code we are using reloads the DataSet every time for a database that might be changing underneath us, we obviously cannot rely on the position of the row being edited on the Web to decide which row in the DataSet is being changed. Imagine a situation where one person goes into edit mode for the fifth row in the grid, and then another user adds a row that appears before the current row. When the first user goes to save the changes, the row that needs to changed is now the sixth row, but the `ItemIndex` will still be 5. The changes will be made to the wrong row!

The best way to address this issue is not to rely on position, but instead to rely on a key field of the DataTable, such as the primary key. In fact, the DataGrid has some capabilities to help you do this.

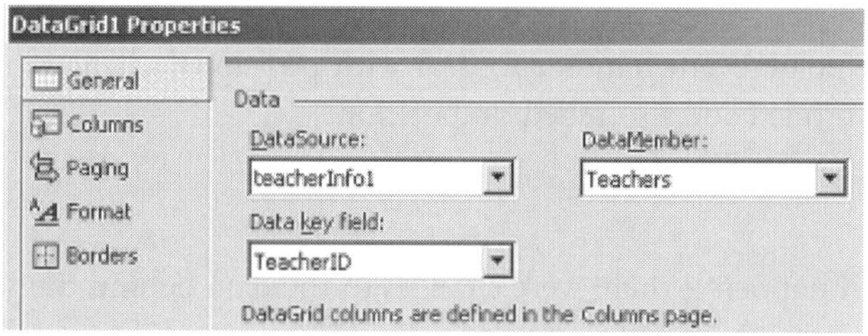

**Figure 23.17
Part of the Property
Builder General page**

If we bring up the Property Builder (by right-clicking on the DataGrid) and stay on the General page, notice an option to set the Data key field (figure 23.17).

This option is used to specify the column from the DataTable that uniquely identifies the row. As in the figure, select the TeacherID, which is the primary key for the Teachers table.

Although we could have retrieved a particular field's value from the row that is returned to use to identify a row, this built-in mechanism offers several advantages. First, there doesn't need to be a column containing the field, which means that it is still OK to exclude the TeacherID field from the grid. Second, if the field were editable, the value wouldn't necessarily be useful to you as a key—we must have the original value for the key to do an appropriate update.

When we specify a Data key field, we are asking the DataGrid to keep track of the original value for that field for every row. We can then retrieve that value later to locate that row.

Several more steps are necessary to make use of this new setting. Take the original positional code that was used to retrieve the row

```
DataTable dtTeachers = teacherInfo1.Tables["Teachers"];
DataRow dr = dtTeachers.Rows[e.Item.ItemIndex];
```

and replace it with code that uses the relation:

```
DataTable dtTeachers = teacherInfo1.Tables["Teachers"];
DataRow dr =
    dtTeachers.Rows.Find(DataGrid1.DataKeys[e.Item.ItemIndex]);
```

Because we told the DataGrid to use the TeacherID column as a key, it maintained the value for each row in an array property called `DataKeys`. All we are doing is accessing the data key for the particular row that was being edited in the DataGrid.

The `Find` method on the Rows collection of a DataTable allows us to do a lookup for a field based on its primary key. We use this method to do the lookup here.

Of course, it would be possible for the row not to be found—for example, someone may have deleted the row while we were looking at it. As you can see, this code doesn't handle that situation, and in a proper application it would be a real concern.

There is nothing magical to show here as a result. The code should work exactly the same as before—except now it will continue to work if other users are working in the system.

23.3.2 Entering edit mode

We just fixed the Update event handler to deal with positional changes; but, if you remember, the edit mode code also relied on position:

```
DataGrid1.EditItemIndex = e.Item.ItemIndex;
DoBind();
```

Imagine what would happen if there were changes to the data behind the scenes—we would click Edit on one row, but end up editing a different row. To fix this problem, we need to change the code to use our new method. Unfortunately, that means we cannot use the DoBind() method any more, because it retrieves the data and rebuilds the DataGrid in one step. Listing 23.2 shows the new version of the OnData-GridEdit method. It is longer than before and also has to do something fairly ugly to deal with a limitation of the Rows collection.

Listing 23.2   More accurate OnDataGridEdit method

```
private void OnDataGridEdit(object source,
        System.Web.UI.WebControls.DataGridCommandEventArgs e)
{
    // Refill the DataSet                      ❶ Reload
    sqlConnection1.Open();                        DataSet
    sqlDataAdapter1.Fill(teacherInfo1);
    sqlConnection1.Close();
                                               Find row
                                               to edit
    // Find the row we want to edit                    ❷
    DataTable dtTeachers = teacherInfo1.Tables["Teachers"];
    DataRow dr =
       dtTeachers.Rows.Find(DataGrid1.DataKeys[e.Item.ItemIndex]);

    // Now figure out the row's position
    int iPos = 0;
    foreach(DataRow drFind in dtTeachers.Rows)
    {                                          ❸ Figure out
        if(drFind == dr)                          row's position
           break;
        iPos++;
    }
    DataGrid1.EditItemIndex = iPos;

    // Rebuild the DataGrid           ❹ Rebuild
    DataGrid1.DataBind();                DataGrid
}
```

❶ Because we are no longer relying on the DoBind() method to refill the DataSet, we need to do it ourselves. Of course, it would be trivial to move these lines into a "Refill DataSet" method.

❷ This code is the same as in the `OnUpdateGrid()` method to find the row that needs to be edited. However, just determining the row is not enough—we need to know the *position* of the row in the DataTable so that we can figure out the DataGrid row on which editing should be allowed.

❸ This is where things get ugly. Although we know which row is being edited, we need to get the position of that row; and there is no method on the DataRow or the DataRowCollection to retrieve this information! We are forced to step through the rows one at a time to find the position of the one we care about. This is an unfortunate oversight, which I hope will be addressed in a future version of .NET.

❹ The last step is to rebuild the DataGrid, as usual, with a call to `DataBind()`.

If everything is working correctly, then the behavior should be unchanged. (Rather sad, really!)

23.3.3 Generic row update

In the previous code, we retrieved the changed data for the data row by explicitly referencing cells to retrieve controls. Although this approach will work, it is a bit brittle—it would be nice if the code would work even if we changed the order of columns or added other columns.

Listing 23.3 shows a new version of the `Update` event handler that is a little more robust.

Listing 23.3 More flexible Update event handler

```
private void OnUpdateGrid(object source,
        System.Web.UI.WebControls.DataGridCommandEventArgs e)
{
    // Reload the table
    sqlConnection1.Open();
    sqlDataAdapter1.Fill(teacherInfo1);

    DataTable dtTeachers = teacherInfo1.Tables["Teachers"];
    DataRow dr = GetUpdateRowFromIndex(dtTeachers,e.Item.ItemIndex);

    // Get data out of the controls that
    // contain the edited data
    for(int i = 0;i < DataGrid1.Columns.Count;i++)          ❶ Step through columns
    {
        if(DataGrid1.Columns[i] is BoundColumn)             ❷ Find bound columns
        {
            string strFieldName =                           ❸ Identify matching field
                ((BoundColumn)DataGrid1.Columns[i]).DataField;

            // Update text fields
```

```
        if(dr[strFieldName].GetType() == typeof(string))        ❹ Retrieve
        {                                                           data
            TextBox ctlTextBox =
                (TextBox)e.Item.Cells[i].Controls[0];
            dr[strFieldName] = ctlTextBox.Text;
        }
    }
}

// Save changes and close the connection
sqlDataAdapter1.Update(dtTeachers);
sqlConnection1.Close();

// Update the page
DataGrid1.EditItemIndex = -1;
DataGrid1.DataBind();
}
```

❶ This loop steps through the collection of columns in the DataGrid. We use a for loop, rather than a foreach statement, because we will need to know the position later.

❷ The columns in a DataGrid can be of several different types. For example, the first column in the example grid is an EditCommandColumn. We only want to get data out of the columns that are bound to fields. Fortunately, these are easily identified—they are instances of the BoundColumn class. This line checks the class type to see if the object is of the type, or is a derivation.

❸ One of the properties of a BoundColumn is DataField, the name of the field to which the data is bound. We have to cast the column to a BoundColumn to be able to access this property, but then it is just a matter of getting the value from the property.

❹ We happen to know that in this example all the fields are text, but that is not necessarily guaranteed for other code. This check is slightly lazy—it sees if the DataRow's data is a string, and if it is, it knows that it can act as though the column is a text box and get the value as Text.

In this code, if there had been a nontext column, it would be skipped. We would need to write some code to do any necessary conversions—for example, converting the string to an integer. If the column *is* a string, then we retrieve the TextBox control and store its value directly into the DataRow.

As with the last section, the code will continue to work exactly as it did before. However, it is now more resilient.

23.3.4   Deletes

Handling a delete is quite easy. It is similar to the way we handled editing.

Just as we added an Edit, Update, Cancel column before, we can add a Delete column to the grid (figure 23.18). The easiest way to do this is to go to the Property Builder and select it the same way we did with any other column.

		TeacherName	Classroom	Subject
Edit	Delete	abc	abc	abc
Edit	Delete	abc	abc	abc
Edit	Delete	abc	abc	abc
Edit	Delete	abc	abc	abc
Edit	Delete	abc	abc	abc

**Figure 23.18
The DataGrid with an
added Delete column**

We can add an event handler in the property editor, just as with the other events. The code to handle the event will eventually look something like this:

```
private void OnDelete(object source,
            System.Web.UI.WebControls.DataGridCommandEventArgs e)
{
    // Reload the table
    sqlConnection1.Open();
    sqlDataAdapter1.Fill(teacherInfo1);

    // Find the row and delete it
    DataTable dtTeachers = teacherInfo1.Tables["Teachers"];
    DataRow dr = GetUpdateRowFromIndex(dtTeachers,e.Item.ItemIndex);
    dr.Delete();

    // Save changes and close the connection
    sqlDataAdapter1.Update(dtTeachers);
    sqlConnection1.Close();

    // Update the page
    DataGrid1.EditItemIndex = -1;
    DataGrid1.DataBind();
}
```

The start and end of this code are the same as for the update event handler. The big difference is that, instead of having to pull data from each column and write it back to the DataSet, all we have to do is mark the column for deletion. Not too tough.

23.3.5   Inserts

You do not need to use the grid control to do inserts. For example, you could create an Add New link that goes to an entirely different page for adding a new item. However, you can allow a new row to be created directly within the grid control. There are a couple of different approaches to consider, but they are similar:

- A button or link on the form can be presented to do an add. When it's clicked, a blank row is added to the bottom (or top) of the DataGrid and automatically placed in edit mode.

- A blank row is presented all the time. If the Edit button next to the row is clicked, then the DataGrid goes into edit mode to allow the new row to be added.

In either case, the first important step is to create a blank row. We do this by creating a blank DataRow and adding it to the DataSet:

```
DataRow drNew = dtTeachers.NewRow();
dtTeachers.Rows.Add(dr);
```

If we want to put the row immediately into edit mode, we can make use of the fact that we know it is at the end of the Rows collection to specify the row to put into edit mode:

```
DataGrid1.EditItemIndex = dtTeachers.Rows.Count - 1;
DataGrid1.DataBind();
```

Of course, we need a mechanism for adding the new row to the database appropriately. There is not a special handler for this step, though—when the user has finished editing, he will click on the Update link to save. If clicking on Update doesn't seem intuitive enough, we can easily change the text for the Update link to say something like Add:

```
EditCommandColumn ecc = DataGrid1.Columns[0] as EditCommandColumn;
ecc.UpdateText = "Add";
```

We need to make sure we change this text back when editing.

The Update handler needs some modifications. Instead of updating an existing row, it needs to create a new row to be updated. The biggest issue is determining if the row is new.

Again, you can take a couple of different approaches, depending on the setup of your code:

- If you always have an empty row to edit, then you can rely on its position to determine that it is new.

- If you are using an autogenerated primary key, you can check the `DataKey` value for the row. If it is blank, then you know it is a new row.

- If you changed the label on the Update text, you can check to see if the value says *Add* versus *Update*.

In the following code snippet, if the primary key is not found, we will assume that the update is really an add. This is not necessarily a great approach. After all, someone might have deleted the row while we were editing. However, adding the data back may be an appropriate response to that event:

```
  .
  .
    // Find the row we want to edit
    DataTable dtTeachers = teacherInfo1.Tables["Teachers"];
    DataRow dr = null;
    try
    {
       dr =
         dtTeachers.Rows.Find(DataGrid1.DataKeys[e.Item.ItemIndex]);
    }
    catch(Exception)
    {
       // Row not found - create new
       dr = dtTeachers.NewRow();
       dtTeachers.Rows.Add(dr);
    }
  .
  .
```

By making these changes, we can provide a pretty robust editable grid with support for adding, editing, and deleting data. Although there is some code to write, it is extremely simple compared to what would have been required to provide this functionality prior to ASP.NET and ADO.NET. This is also the tip of the iceberg. The DataGrid provides innumerable options, and there are also other DataSet-aware web controls, as you will see in chapter 24.

23.4 THE STATE OF THE STATE

The previous example was stateless—that is, the server did not in any way hold on to the data being displayed on the client. In fact, we had to do several special things to make it work reliably. The benefit of this approach is that it is highly scalable. However, it is certainly not the only way to go.

ASP.NET has some easy-to-use mechanisms for handling session state. That means we can store the DataSet once it has been built, and then retrieve it every time we need to access it. To store the DataSet, we can modify the Page_Load method:

```
private void Page_Load(object sender, System.EventArgs e)
{
   if(!IsPostBack)
   {
      sqlConnection1.Open();
      sqlDataAdapter1.Fill(teacherInfo1);
      sqlConnection1.Close();
      DataGrid1.DataBind();
      Session["TeacherInfo"] = teacherInfo1;
   }
}
```

This method puts the DataSet into a "slot" in the session called TeacherInfo. IIS will automatically keep track of the object for you and make it available to the appropriate user.

Accessing the item later (say in one of the event handlers) is trivial:

```
teacherInfo1 = (TeacherInfo)Session["TeacherInfo"];
```

23.4.1   Why would you want to do this?

This approach makes all the code simpler. For example, you don't need to worry about the DataSet being reloaded every time, so you can rely on positions and check things like the status of a row to determine whether a row is new.

This approach also can be faster. I hear you say, "What about all that talk about scalability and the stateless model?" Scalability is *not* the same thing as speed. The rule for scalability is that the *n*th user will have the same basic performance as the first. That doesn't mean performance will be super fast! If you don't have a huge number of users, then keeping data in memory is likely to be faster—that is, until the *n*th user crashes your server.

23.4.2   Why wouldn't you want to do this?

Scalability is the first issue. If you expect a huge number of users, then this approach tends to break down; if the amount of data for each user tends to be large, you are also likely to run into difficulties. Also, by default, the state is available only on the one server; if you intend to use a web farm where one of several machines will catch each request, this approach will break down. ASP.NET can store state in a SQL Server database, which can be pointed to by a number of servers, but this arrangement increases complexity and has an impact on performance; after all, one reason to use state in the first place was to avoid hitting a database.

The other issue is that state *times out*. The server will eventually throw away the state data if the user doesn't come back to the server for a while. By default, the time-out is 20 minutes. That may be acceptable to you, but you will still need to make sure your code is robust enough to handle a request where the session has timed out, even if you just redirect the user to an error page.

23.4.3   Other options

There are more options to consider, as well—for example, you can set up the state to be written to a database to be retrieved later, or possibly on a different machine in a web farm. It might seem a bit strange with this example to read data from a database only to write it back to a database, but doing so would deal with some of the positioning issues and might make sense for more complex applications.

Also, you might not store the DataSet in its entirety, but might, for example, just store information about the currently edited row.

You must consider these and many other options when building a web-facing application. It would be highly presumptuous (and incorrect) for me to suggest a particular approach. It comes down to the nature of your application and its target.

23.4.4 Using the web page to hold state

One other option presented by ASP.NET is to keep the data on the web page. ASP.NET can take data or information about a control and embed it in the web page. You can then retrieve the data from the page when it returns—although demonstrating this technique is beyond the scope of the book. With this approach, you could store the entire DataSet or just some key information.

Storing the entire DataSet is potentially dangerous—if you imagine a user dialing up at modem speeds, you are now increasing (possibly by a lot) the amount of data to send back and forth. Also, the DataGrid has a paging mode in which only a certain number of rows from the DataSet are displayed on each page. The DataSet might be considerably bigger than the amount of data being displayed.

Another approach is to use the DataGrid itself as a state mechanism. After all, it contains all the data from the DataSet. You could take the same approach you used to build the update row in the earlier example, except that you would rebuild the entire DataSet.

That approach has a couple of dangers, though. First, the data displayed on a particular page might only be a subset of the data in the DataSet. That may not matter, except if you are relying on constraints or other rules to protect your data.

Second, you might not have all the columns from the DataSource in the DataGrid. However, you can have columns in the DataGrid that are not visible. On the web page, the column will not be present; but in the code it will be present and have data. The DataGrid does this using the technique described earlier, by storing the data in a hidden manner on the web page.

Again, these are several more options for you to consider.

23.5 *AVOIDING THE EDITORS*

In some ways, coding directly versus relying on the editor is easier with ASP.NET than with the WinForm example. You are already doing so much code directly—opening and closing connections, filling data sets, and so forth.

Imagine that we have built a component for accessing the Teacher DataSet. All we need to do is add a member variable that points to our component

```
TeacherAdapterComponent m_TeacherComponent =
                        new TeacherAdapterComponent();
```

and then use that component when we need to access our data:

```
private void Page_Load(object sender, System.EventArgs e)
{
    if(!IsPostBack)
    {
        teacherInfo1 = m_TeacherComponent.GetTeacherDataSet();
        DataGrid1.DataBind();
    }
}
```

We can put all our various methods for connecting, accessing, and modifying data into the component. Refer to chapter 22 for one approach to building such a component.

As a general rule of thumb, you should never tie your data access code tightly to the user interface. Also, the more flexible you make your user interface code, the less likely that you will be to change it when you make minor changes to your data access code.

23.6 SUMMARY

This has been another long chapter, and we have barely scratched the surface of the DataGrid, let alone the issues involved in building a robust, scalable web application.

A number of good books about ASP.NET are on the market, and you will probably want to pick one up before embarking on the creation of a web-facing application. In this chapter, I have brought to the forefront some of the issues relating to the DataSet and data access from the Web in general. Although this topic is touched on by several ASP.NET authors, it is not often the major focus.

The DataGrid is not the only web control that can be hooked up to data. In chapter 24, you will see several more.

C H A P T E R   2 4

Other data-bound web controls

The DataGrid is a great control if you want to present data as a grid, but there are a number of other ways you might want to present data. In fact, you might want to present data as a grid, but in a way other than the DataGrid allows. The DataGrid is a fairly formal control. If you think of the many shopping cart applications that are now available, you can, for example, imagine the DataGrid as the perfect control for showing your invoice. When you want to show the list of available products, though, perhaps with pictures and descriptions, the standard rows and columns of a grid are a bit limiting. We'll discuss some other options in this chapter.

24.1   *OTHER DATA-BOUND CONTROLS*

ASP.NET provides a couple of other controls that might be more appropriate—they still are designed to work with a DataSet or other data source and to display different information for each separate DataRow in a DataTable, but they are not so row-and-column oriented. The two controls are the DataList and the Repeater, and each has a slightly different focus:

- *Repeater*—The Repeater can display each item in the DataSet based on a template that you define. It is not particularly tied to a grid layout, like the grid control. You specify HTML that is used to represent each item, and the Repeater fills in the details. The Repeater has no support for selection or editing; it just allows data to be displayed.

- *DataList*—You can think of the DataList as a slightly more advanced Repeater. You still define a template for each item to be displayed, but the DataList also has built-in support for selection, editing, and other operations. As with the Repeater, you specify a template for the display of an item. You can also specify templates for other situations, such as for the selected item, or for an edit mode. Unlike the Repeater, though, you can use the editor to set up the template.

These are not the only data-bound controls available for WebForms. In fact, most of the web controls support data binding. For example, you can have the contents of a drop-down list fill from a DataSet. Even controls like labels and buttons support data binding, although they can only display a single value, such as the value from a field in a row. You will use this capability of regular controls with the DataList a little later.

As well as using data binding to determine the value displayed in a control, you can use data binding to determine the value for other properties of a control. For example, you can set the colors of an item based on a column's data. Although I have not provided a demonstration of this capability in this chapter, it is reasonably straightforward once you have seen how to bind the Text property to data.

Data binding is not limited to the DataSet or the DataTable. You can bind to any object that implements one of several list-based interfaces. For example, you can bind to an array or any number of different collection classes. You can also create your own data-bindable classes, although doing so is beyond the scope of this book. As you will see in chapter 25, you can also bind to a DataView, which allows you to create a database-like view of a particular DataTable with a subset of the rows.

This chapter is fairly short, because it builds on examples from chapter 23. In most cases, I assume you have set up a WebForm and a DataSet on that WebForm already, although with each example I will explain which setup steps need to have taken place.

24.2 *BINDING TO SIMPLE CONTROLS*

Just as we can use data binding to fill the grid, we can use it to fill other controls. For example, if we want to populate the values in a drop-down list, all we need to do is put the DropDownList on our form and set the DataBindings properties (figure 24.1). The project we set up is the same as in the previous chapter, with the same DataSet, and so forth. All we've done is specify a DataSource (the teacherInfo1 DataSet) and the field (TeacherName) from which values should be retrieved. There is one more step, though—we need to tell the control to explicitly bind data. For example, in the Page_Load method of the form, we can add a single call:

```
DropDownList1.DataBind();
```

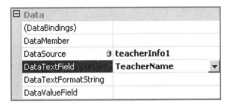

Figure 24.1
Setting properties for
a drop-down list

That's it—the control is now bound (figure 24.2). Of course, if the data in the DataSet changes, we will need to call `DataBind()` again to refresh the data.

It is logical to be able to data-bind a control such as a drop-down list that, after all, is a list. As you will see with the DataList and the Repeater, though, you can also bind the controls that only handle a single value, like labels and text boxes. In chapter 25, you will also see some things you can do with DataViews to allow a single row to be represented.

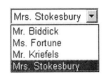

Figure 24.2
Values in the drop-down list

24.3   THE REPEATER

The Repeater control allows you to use data binding to retrieve data, but gives you the ability to specify the HTML for each item. You are not limited to raw HTML, though—you can specify the use of various server-based web form controls. So, for example, you can use labels and buttons in each row, and have their text and other properties reflect information from the current row.

One unfortunate thing about the Repeater control is that you cannot set up the template for each item in the designer—you have to switch to the HTML view of the form. I'm guessing that the team at Microsoft ran out of time, because the DataList, which has a similar model, *does* allow you to define the template in the editor.

24.3.1   Demonstrating the Repeater

To use the Repeater, first create a web application and set up the adapter and the DataSet exactly as we did for the DataGrid example. We can drag the Repeater control onto the form from the Web Forms section of the toolbox. It will snap to the top corner of the page (figure 24.3).

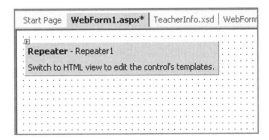

Figure 24.3
The Repeater control

If we want to position the Repeater elsewhere on the form, we need to put it into another control, such as a Layout Panel.

Before setting up the template for the Repeater, we need to bind it to the DataSet and, in particular, to the Teachers table. We can do so easily via the Repeater's properties, either in the editor or by writing some code to set the properties at runtime. The DataSet is already associated with the form (based on the earlier example), so we might as well use the property editor (figure 24.4.)

⊟ Data	
(DataBindings)	
DataMember	**Teachers**
DataSource	ⓘ **teacherInfo1**

Figure 24.4
Binding the Repeater

With the DataGrid, this was sufficient information for the control to know what to display—one column for each field, although we could customize it. With the Repeater, though, the whole point is that we don't want a grid display, so there is no way for the Repeater to automatically set up its contents. We need to define the template for each item in the Repeater. The template will be used to create the actual HTML to send to the browser for each DataRow in the Teachers DataTable.

As I said before, we can't set up the template for the Repeater in the graphical designer. Instead, we need to switch to the HTML view of the form. The editor maintains the HTML and designer modes in parallel. We can switch by using the tabs at the bottom of the WebForm (figure 24.5).

Figure 24.5   WebForm tabs

Once we have switched to the HTML mode, find the Repeater's definition:

```
<asp:repeater id="Repeater1" runat="server" DataMember="Teachers"
                        DataSource="<%# teacherInfo1 %>">
</asp:repeater>
```

The more web-savvy among you may have noticed that this is not quite traditional HTML. In fact, the HTML behind a WebForm is a blending of straight HTML and ASP.NET directives that will be resolved before the page is sent to the browser. In this respect, ASP.NET works similarly to ASP. The mechanism for building the templates, and the code-behind concepts, on the other hand, are fairly different.

This particular tag describes the Repeater control and its data-binding attributes. The designer has automatically put some tags in place:

- runat="server"—This tag indicates that the control will be set up on the server before being sent to the browser, rather than on the browser itself. This is important because the DataSet from which the control is being loaded is only available on the server.

CHAPTER 24   OTHER DATA-BOUND WEB CONTROLS

- DataSource—This tag specifies that the data will be retrieved from the instance of the TeacherInfo DataSet that is associated with the form. This is here because we set the DataSource property in the property editor. It also highlights an important point about the way ASP.NET works: although some properties and setup for the web form are defined in the code behind, most of the control's properties are embedded in the HTML.

- DataMember—This tag provides the data from the DataMember property that was also set via the property editor, and tells the control that the data comes from the Teachers table within the TeacherInfo DataSet.

Before the Repeater will display any data, we need to add some subtags to define the template for displaying items. In this case, we'll display each teacher as a hyperlink:

```
<asp:repeater id="Repeater1" runat="server" DataMember="Teachers"
                             DataSource="<%# teacherInfo1 %>">
    <ItemTemplate>
        <asp:HyperLink Runat="server"
            Text=
            '<%#  DataBinder.Eval(Container.DataItem,"TeacherName") %>'
            NavigateUrl='www.manning.com'>
        </asp:HyperLink>
        <br>
    </ItemTemplate>
</asp:repeater>
```

The Repeater can have several different templates, as you will see later. For the moment, though, we just need to define the template for each item to display—the ItemTemplate.

The contents of the template can be any legal HTML, and it can also include server-side controls whose values will be determined before the page is sent to the client. In this example, we use the HyperLink control, which will present a link on which the user can click.

The important bit in the definition for the HyperLink is the value for Text—the text to display as the link. The DataBinder.Eval call resolves the passed arguments, which specify the source of the data (the current data item in the repeater) and the particular item to retrieve (the TeacherName). This will happen on the server before the page is sent to the client.

The NavigateUrl is the URL to which the link will take us when we click on the link. In this example it is hard-coded, but it could easily have been made to refer to another column in the DataSet (although there isn't an appropriate column in the Teachers table). If there were a HomePage field, for example, we could reference it directly:

```
NavigateUrl='<%# DataBinder.
                    Eval(Container.DataItem,"HomePage") %>'
```

You can use this technique to specify just about any attribute. For example, you might have a Favorite Color column that you bind to the text color of the item.

Don't forget that columns in a DataSet can be calculated, so you could change the color if a particular condition was true.

Now that we have specified the HTML for each item, we need to bind the Repeater to the DataSet. This is much the same mechanism we used for the DataGrid—we put some code in the Page_Load method:

```
private void Page_Load(object sender, System.EventArgs e)
{
    if(!IsPostBack)
    {
        sqlConnection1.Open();
        sqlDataAdapter1.Fill(teacherInfo1);
        sqlConnection1.Close();
        Repeater1.DataBind();
    }
}
```

Nothing new here—we're filling the DataSet and then calling DataBind() on the repeater. If we run the page now, we should see a link for each teacher (figure 24.6).

Figure 24.6
The repeater output

24.3.2   Other templates

The Item template lets you specify how each item should be displayed, but you can specify several other templates for the Repeater:

- HeaderTemplate—Specifies the HTML that should be written before writing out any items. You can put in header info, or do things like set up a table.

- FooterTemplate—The reverse of the HeaderTemplate, this template specifies the HTML to appear at the end of the Repeater.

- AlternatingItemTemplate—If you want every other row to appear differently, you can specify an AlternatingItemTemplate to define how the alternating row should appear, perhaps with a different color.

- SeparatorTemplate—Defines HTML to be placed between each item.

We define these other templates much the same way we defined the Item template. The following HTML includes some boring but functional examples of all of the templates:

```
<asp:Repeater id="Repeater1" runat="server"
        DataSource="<%# teacherInfo1 %>" DataMember="Teachers">
   <HeaderTemplate>
      <Font style="FONT-SIZE: x-large; TEXT-DECORATION: underline">
      Repeater example
      </Font>
      <br>
   </HeaderTemplate>
   <ItemTemplate>
      <asp:HyperLink Runat="server"
         Text='<%#
            DataBinder.Eval(Container.DataItem,"TeacherName") %>'
         NavigateUrl='www.manning.com' ID="Hyperlink1">
      </asp:HyperLink>
      <br>
   </ItemTemplate>
   <AlternatingItemTemplate>
      (Alternate)
      <asp:HyperLink Runat="server"
         Text='<%#
            DataBinder.Eval(Container.DataItem,"TeacherName") %>'
         NavigateUrl='www.manning.com' ID="Hyperlink1">
      </asp:HyperLink>
      <br>
   </AlternatingItemTemplate>
   <SeparatorTemplate>
      <hr>
   </SeparatorTemplate>
   <FooterTemplate>
      <hr>
      <font style="FONT-SIZE: xx-small">
         (This is the end of the Repeater's output) </font>
   </FooterTemplate>
</asp:Repeater>
```

I will not go into all of the details of the HTML in each section here—I am using some common tags. Be aware, though, that I have formatted this code for printing— you will have to compensate in your editor to avoid problems with spacing.

The new, much uglier output appears in figure 24.7.

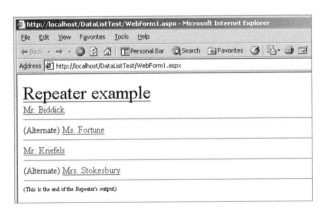

Figure 24.7
The Repeater with more templates being used

24.4　THE DATALIST

The DataList works similarly to the Repeater. However, there are two significant differences:

- The DataList supports selection and editing.
- You can use the WebForm designer to specify the contents of the templates.

That is not to say you *have* to edit the templates using the designer—WebForms can always be edited directly in HTML. If your HTML skills are as rotten as mine, though, you will appreciate the ability to edit in a friendlier environment.

As with the Repeater, your templates can be as unique as you like. Added to that, though, is the ability to define templates for a selected item and to have an item in edit mode. Just as with the DataGrid, the DataList generates events for you to let you specify which mode a particular row should enter; but you are not limited to the columnar edit mode, so, for example, you can present a form for editing a particular item.

24.4.1　Demonstrating the DataList

Setup for using the DataList is much the same as in the other examples. Again, we will be use the Teachers table in the DataSet. This time, though, we need to drag a DataList from the toolbox onto the form (figure 24.8).

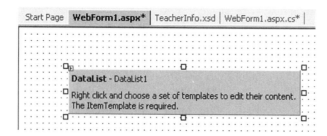

**Figure 24.8
The DataList control
on the form**

Unlike the Repeater, we can position the DataList normally, as long as the page layout is set to grid layout.

As before, the data-binding properties need to be set to bind the DataList to the DataSet (figure 24.9).

Now we need to set up the various templates for the DataList. We can do this the same way we did with the Repeater—switch to the HTML view and manually add HTML for each template—or we can put the DataList into Template Edit mode (figure 24.10).[1]

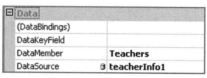

**Figure 24.9
Binding the DataList to the DataSet**

---

[1]　It really depends on how masochistic you are feeling.

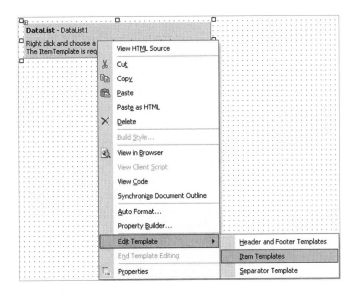

Figure 24.10
Putting the DataList
into template
editing mode

The templates are divided into three sets, as you can see from the menu. For the moment, we are interested in the Item Templates. When we select this option from the menu, the DataList's representation on the WebForm changes (figure 24.11).

The DataList has all the same templates as the Repeater—Item, Alternating Item, Header, Footer, and Separator.[2] In addition, though, there are two more templates—Selected and Edit. When we put a particular row into select mode, it will use the SelectedItemTemplate to display the item. Likewise, when we put the row into edit mode it will use the EditItemTemplate.

To put the DataList into these other modes, we have to provide a mechanism ourselves—for example, we can put a button or

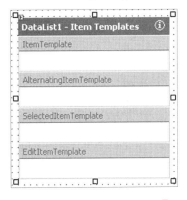

Figure 24.11 Editing the Item Templates

link in the ItemTemplate that, when clicked, puts that row into another mode. Once we have to set up the control, we can specify the DataList event that the control should generate.

Let's start by setting up a template for the item that has a link for selection. We can define the template by dragging and dropping items into the band for that item. We will put the teacher's name in the list as a link, and make the link put you in select mode.

---

[2] To edit the Header, Footer, and Separator templates, you must select one of the other options from the Edit Template menu.

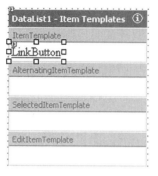

Figure 24.12
Putting a Link button
in the ItemTemplate

Drag a LinkButton from the toolbox onto the ItemTemplate band of the DataList (figure 24.12).

We need to do two things to set up this Link button: set its text to be tied to the DataSet, and set up an action to take place when the link is clicked. Let's talk about the binding first. Because this is a simple, single-item control, binding it to data is not quite the same as with other controls; although there is a `DataBindings` option in the property editor for the control, we can't set the details directly there. Instead, we need to select the `(DataBindings)` property (figure 24.13), and then click the ellipsis button to bring up the Data-Bindings dialog box.

The DataBindings dialog box is available for the other controls as well, and can be used to bind other properties to a data source. This secondary dialog box allows all these properties to be available but not clutter up the property editor with a bunch of properties that are rarely used.

Figure 24.13
The DataBindings option
in the property dialog box

We want to bind the `Text` property to the appropriate DataItem. Select Text in the Bindable Properties list on the left if it is not already selected. Then, expand Container, DataItem in the tree control on the right and select the TeacherName field (figure 24.14).

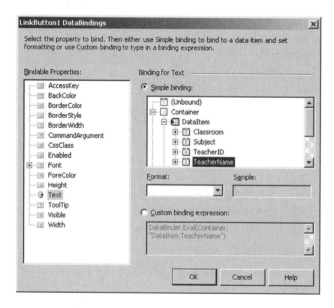

Figure 24.14
The DataBindings dialog box

     CHAPTER 24 OTHER DATA-BOUND WEB CONTROLS

We can bind to several things in the tree control. One option is the page, which provides access to components on the WebForm. Another is the teacher1 DataSet. We can select items from the DataSet directly, including the TeacherName field, but we will not get the results we might expect; because we are linking to a single-item control, we will end up with every row showing the value from the first row in the DataSet.

In order to get the appropriate row's data, we need something that moves through the data—in this case, the DataList. The DataList is the container, and it will step through the data for us.

We also need to set up the action for when the link is clicked. To do this, set the CommandName for the button to select (figure 24.15).

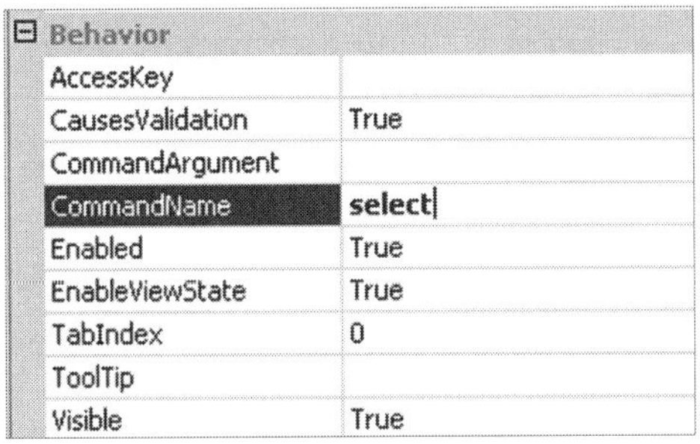

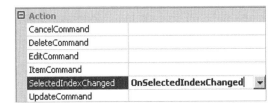

Figure 24.15
Setting the CommandName

This select value is a special command that the DataList understands. Now, when the link is clicked, the DataList will raise the SelectedIndexChanged event. Of course, we need some code to make something happen when the event is fired. We can add the event handler via the properties of the DataList. However, we cannot edit the events for the DataList while the DataList is in template editing mode.

Exit template editing mode by right-clicking on the DataList and selecting End Template Editing. Once we have exited the mode, select the DataList and then click the lightning bolt in the property editor to get the list of events. After these contortions, we can add a handler for the SelectedIndexChanged event (figure 24.16).

Figure 24.16
Putting in a handler for the
SelectedIndexChanged event

Press Enter to edit the code:

```
private void OnSelectedIndexChanged(object sender, System.EventArgs e)
{
    FillDataSet();
    DataList1.DataBind();
}
```

This code first fills the DataSet, then this functionality is moved to a function so the code doesn't have to repeat. Finally, the DataList needs to be told to refresh itself, via the `DataBind` call. We don't need to tell the DataList which row is the current selection—that is handled automatically by the fact that the event was raised for a particular selection.

Here is the `FillDataSet()` method:

```
private void FillDataSet()
{
    sqlConnection1.Open();
    sqlDataAdapter1.Fill(teacherInfo1);
    sqlConnection1.Close();
}
```

While we are in the code, make sure the `Page_Load` method is initializing the DataList:

```
private void Page_Load(object sender, System.EventArgs e)
{
    if(!IsPostBack)
    {
        FillDataSet();
        DataList1.DataBind();
    }
}
```

This method is also simple—it loads the data and binds. In fact, it does the same thing we do when the selection index changes.

If we ran the code at this point, we would get a list of links. However, clicking on those links would not do anything, because we have not yet defined a template for the selected item. That is the next step.

Switch back to the WebForm and put the Data-List back into item template edit mode via the context menu. Now, instead of putting things into the `ItemTemplate`, we will set up the `Selected-ItemTemplate` (figure 24.17).

This layout is fairly ugly—we've put some labels on the left for each field and a label on the right to contain the value. We bound each label's[3] `Text` property to the appropriate field, exactly the same way the LinkButton's text property was linked. Finally, as a vague attempt to improve appearances, we put a line at the top and the bottom of the template.

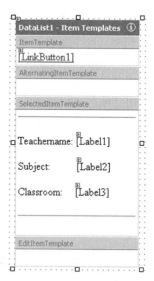

Figure 24.17 Setting up the `SelectedItemTemplate`

___

[3] Just the labels on the right—the ones on the left are simple labels that identify the name of the field.

You can, of course, do anything you like with this template, making it simple or fancy. For example, you could have the same basic template as for the item, but with an image to indicate the selected mode, or an extra link.

If we run the code now and click on one of the links, we will put that row into select mode (figure 24.18).

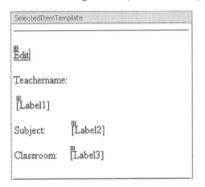

Figure 24.18
A row in select mode

24.4.2 Edit mode

The selection mode can be useful for a number of different operations, such as indicating a current selection or, as in the previous example, displaying more information about the current item. The selection mode is designed as a read-only state. If you want to change data, you need to provide an edit mode.

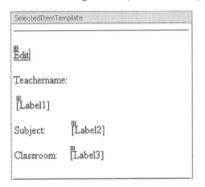

Figure 24.19
Adding an Edit link to the
`SelectedItemTemplate`

Setting up the DataList to take you into edit mode is much the same as the setup for select mode. Some sort of action needs to be defined, such as clicking on a link. Although in the example we can only go to edit mode from select mode, there is no such requirement—we could, for example, have an Edit link for each item, and not even have a select mode.

In this example, we will put an Edit link into the `SelectedItemTemplate`. When we click on the link, we will be taken into edit mode. The major difference between this link and the one that took us into selected mode is that the command name will be `edit` versus `select`.

First, drag a link button onto the `SelectedItemTemplate` band (figure 24.19). Change the `Text` property of the link to `Edit` and also set the `CommandName` property to `edit` (figure 24.20).

Figure 24.20
Setting properties for the Edit link

That's all we have to do the template, but we need to put in an event handler for the EditCommand:

```
private void OnEditMode(object source,
            System.Web.UI.WebControls.DataListCommandEventArgs e)
{
    FillDataSet();
    DataList1.EditItemIndex = e.Item.ItemIndex;
    DataList1.DataBind();
}
```

Once again, the code is basically the same—the control rebuilds itself. Unlike the select mode, we must explicitly specify which row is being edited. For the moment, use the index for the selected item. However, as you saw in the previous chapter, this technique is not reliable for a real application.[4]

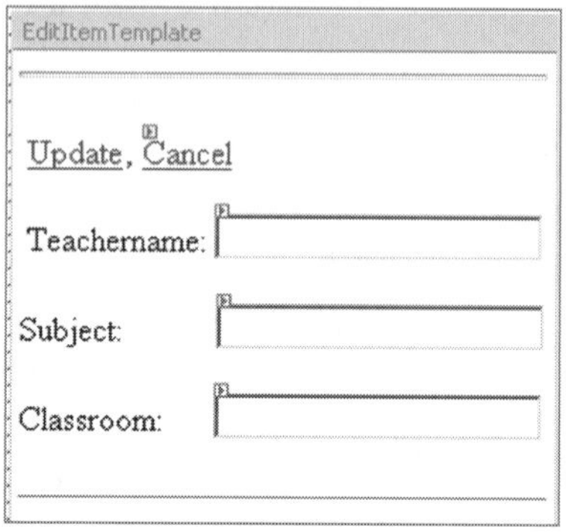

Now we need to define the template for edit mode. We can basically copy the SelectedItemTemplate, but replace the Edit link with Update and Cancel links and replace the label controls with text box controls (figure 24.21).

Figure 24.21 The `EditItemTemplate`

If we now run the code, select a row, and select Edit, we will see the template in action (figure 24.22).

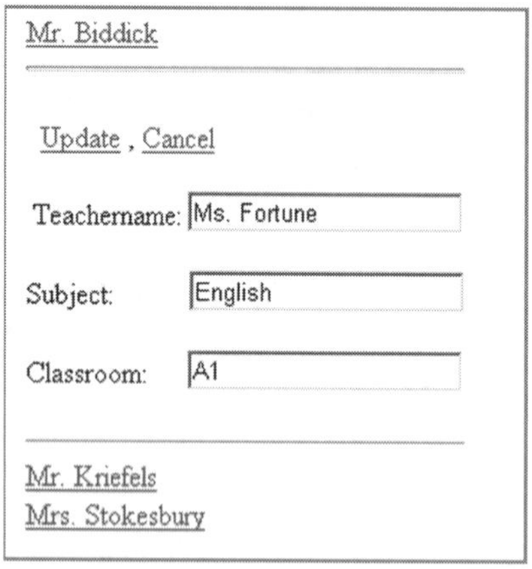

Figure 24.22 Edit mode

Of course, there are a few more steps. We need to hook up the update and cancel events. The CommandName properties for the buttons are respectively update and cancel. We hook up the events as we did the edit event. In fact, the handling for these events is virtually identical to the handling for update and cancel in the Data-Grid. To cancel, for example, we set the edit item to −1:

---

[4] I will not go into detail about the steps required to make this work reliably in a real-world application, but you can refer to chapter 23 for the various issues and steps for avoiding the problems.

```
private void OnCancelEdit(object source,
              System.Web.UI.WebControls.DataListCommandEventArgs e)
{
    FillDataSet();
    DataList1.EditItemIndex = -1;
    DataList1.DataBind();
}
```

I won't show the code for the update command, although it is available on the web site. The handling is virtually the same as for the DataGrid and has the same complications, such as requiring a more appropriate mechanism for identifying the current row.

24.5   SUMMARY

This chapter has brushed the surface of some of the data-bound controls. It has shown how you can quickly get these controls up and running with some powerful functionality, and has also suggested some other uses.

The data-binding concept can be powerful, especially in its ability to let you get functionality working quickly. This was one of the forces behind the success of Visual Basic, and it is now available in .NET. Over the next year or two, I expect to see a huge number of data-bound controls coming onto the market.

We have not delved into how to more carefully control the data presented in a particular control. For example, perhaps you only want some records from a DataTable to be shown, but you want the entire DataSet to enforce constraints and so forth. You can accomplish this by using DataViews, the topic of the next chapter.

C H A P T E R   2 5

Using DataViews

A DataTable is a convenient mechanism for storing data, especially when used in conjunction with constraints and relationships to make sure the data is legal. Sometimes, though, you don't really want to work with all the available data. That is where the DataView comes in: it allows you to limit the data from a DataTable, in a similar manner to a database view, as we'll discuss in this chapter.

25.1   WHY USE A DATAVIEW?

The DataTable *does* provide several other mechanisms for limiting data. For example, you can add a select statement to the SQL that builds the DataTable, but then you don't have all the data—which means your various constraints might not be correct. Also, if you wanted to change the data you are displaying, you would have to requery the database.

Another possible solution is to use the query capabilities of the DataTable to select just the rows you want to display, and put those rows into a new DataTable. However, if you want to allow editing, you must manually merge changes.

You might also have a problem if you try to bind two different controls to the same DataTable—if you bind both controls to the same DataSet, then actions in one control will directly affect the other. That might be what you want, but then again it might not be.

The DataView resolves all of these problems—you can specify which rows appear in the DataView and bind controls to the DataView instead of the DataSet or Data-Table. You can also have multiple DataViews of the same DataTable that work independently.

A DataView isn't quite like a database view. A DataView currently can't do several things:

- The data in a DataView comes from a single DataTable. You cannot do joins as you can with a database view.

- The columns in the DataView will be the same as the columns in the Data-Table. You cannot eliminate columns or add your own columns to a DataView.

You can, however, control which rows appear in a DataView, and you can also control the sort order of a DataView.

25.2 WORKING WITH DATAVIEWS

This part of the book has included a lot of GUI work; but to cover the basics of Data-Views, we are back to the console. Creating a DataView is simple. The code in listing 25.1 creates a DataView that contains a subset of the rows in the Teachers DataTable. It also includes a method for printing out the contents of a DataView.

Listing 25.1 Setting up a simple DataView

```
public void TestDataView(SqlConnection conn)
{
   DataSet ds = BuildQueryDataSet(conn);           ❶ Setup
   DataTable dt = ds.Tables["Teachers"];

   DataView dv = new DataView(dt);                  ❷ Create data
   dv.Sort = "Classroom";                              view
   dv.RowFilter = "Classroom <> 'A1'";

   DisplayView(dv);        ❸ Print data view
}

public void DisplayView(DataView dv)
{
   for(int i = 0;i < dv.Count;i++)
   {
      foreach(DataColumn dc in dv.Table.Columns
      {
         if(dc.Ordinal > 0) Console.Write(", ")      ❹ Data view
         Console.Write(dv[i][dc.Ordinal].ToString().Trim());  display
      }                                                   method
      Console.WriteLine("");
   }
}
```

❶ This code uses a method from chapter 20 that builds a DataSet containing the Teachers and Classes tables.

❷ Creating a DataView is simple. All we have to do is pass the DataTable to be viewed to the new DataView. You can set several other properties that control the DataView:

- Sort—Specifies the sort order for the DataView. In the example, we are specifying the Classroom column as the sort order. We can also specify multiple comma-separated columns and use the keyword desc to indicate a descending sort order.

- RowFilter—Specifies a query string used to determine which rows should appear in the DataView. The filter follows the standard rules for querying DataTables, explained in chapter 20. In the example, we eliminate any Teacher in the A1 classroom.

- RowStateFilter—Although it is not being used in this example, we can choose to include rows based on their state. For example, we can ask for only added rows or only unchanged rows. The next section talks about this option.

❸ This is a call to the method to write out the DataView to the console. In reality, it is unlikely that we would do this directly—the DataView is more likely to be used with a data-bound control for displaying its contents.

❹ This method takes a DataView as an argument and writes it out to the console. It is not much different from the methods for writing out a DataTable, but there are a few differences:

- The individual rows are directly accessed from the DataView, rather than via a Rows collection, so we access a row dv[i] instead of dv.Rows[i].

- There is no direct exposure of the columns collection in the DataView. However, because the columns are the same as for the DataTable, we can access the columns collection of the associated DataTable via the Table property.

The output from the display method appears in figure 25.1.

Figure 25.1
Example output

It is not much of a filter, but the row containing the A1 classroom is missing, as per our filter.

25.2.1 The RowStateFilter

I mentioned earlier that you can filter the DataView based on the state of rows. Beyond limiting the rows that are returned, you can use this filter to control which version of the rows are returned. Table 25.1 shows you the options for what you can pass for the `RowStateFilter` property.

Table 25.1 Values from the `DataViewRowState` enumeration

Value	Meaning
None	No filter (returns all rows).
Unchanged	Returns all rows that have not been modified.
Added	Returns all rows that have been added to the DataTable.
Deleted	Returns all the rows that have been deleted from the DataTable.
CurrentRows	Returns all the rows that are currently present, including added, changed, and unchanged rows; does not include deleted rows.
OriginalRows	Returns all the rows that were originally in the DataTable and returns them with their original values, even if changes have been made. If you have deleted rows, those rows will show up in the DataView and will not be seen as deleted.
ModifiedCurrent	Returns all rows that have been modified. The data in the view will reflect the changes.
ModifiedOriginal	Returns all rows that have been modified, but the data in the view will be the original versions of all changes. However, the same rows will be returned as with `ModifiedCurrent` (just a different version).

Setting the row state filter is trivial:

```
dv.RowStateFilter = DataViewRowState.Unchanged;
```

You can also combine values to get back a combination:

```
dv.RowStateFilter =
        DataViewRowState.Added | DataViewRowState.Deleted;
```

25.2.2 Modifying data via the view

You can usually modify data via a DataView. When you do, your changes are automatically reflected in the DataTable. After all, this is just a view of the data. You can control what activities are allowed via the DataView using a few properties:

- `AllowEdit`—If `true`, then you can modify values via the view
- `AllowDelete`—If `true`, then you can delete values via the view
- `AllowNew`—If `true`, you can add new rows to the DataTable via the view

By default, these properties are all set to `true`. The example in listing 25.2 does an edit, a delete, and an add via the DataView. It creates the view the same way as the previous example.

Listing 25.2   Edit, delete, and add via a DataView

```
public void TestDataView(SqlConnection conn)
{
    DataSet ds = BuildQueryDataSet(conn);
    DataTable dt = ds.Tables["Teachers"];

    DataView dv = new DataView(dt);
    dv.Sort = "Classroom,TeacherName desc";
    dv.RowFilter = "Classroom <> 'A1'";

    // Edit example
    dv[0]["Classroom"] = "T2";              ❶ Editing

    // Delete example
    dv[1].Delete();            ❷ Deleting

    // Add example
    DataRowView drv = dv.AddNew();                    ❸ Adding
    drv["TeacherName"] = "Mrs. Martell";
    drv["Subject"] = "Algebra";
    drv["Classroom"] = "Y3";
    drv.EndEdit();

    DisplayView(dv);
}
```

❶ Editing via a view is similar to editing the DataTable directly. This code does accesses a particular row (row 0) and then accesses a particular field and set its value. The row is not a DataRow as with a DataTable, but is instead a DataRowView. If we wanted to, we could retrieve the row first, and then set the data:

```
DataRowView drv = dv[0];
drv["Classroom"] = "T2";
```

We can also access the column ordinally, just as with a DataRow:

```
drv[2] = "T2";
```

❷ Deleting is just as simple—we call the `delete` method on the DataRowView. Again, we could have retrieved the row first and then called the method, but there was no need.

❸ To add a row, we call the `AddNew()` method on the DataView, which returns a DataRowView whose values we can set. There are a couple of differences from adding a row to a DataTable:

- The row was automatically added to the view—we do not need to manually add it to a collection.

- The new row was put directly into edit mode, the equivalent of calling `BeginEdit()`. Until we call `EndEdit()`, the row will not seem to exist in the DataTable. When we are using a data-bound control, it will handle this detail for you.

Figure 25.2
Example output

Figure 25.2 shows the output from the example.

The last couple of sections have shown you the major pieces of the DataView. It is not a big class. The next two sections show examples of using the DataView with Windows-based data-bound controls and with web-based data-bound controls.

25.3 DATAVIEWS AND WINDOWS FORMS

As with the earlier examples of the DataGrid, there is a designer way and a non-designer way of working with the DataView. You'll begin by creating the DataView as part of the form, and then look at manipulating the DataView via code. The Data-View is one data component I don't mind having tied directly to the form. After all, its major purpose is to act as an intermediary between data and display.

This example works with the WinForms DataGrid example from chapter 22. Reload that example and bring up the main form. Next, drag a DataView onto the form from the Data section of the toolbox (figure 25.3).

Figure 25.3
Putting a DataView on the form

Not much is involved in configuring a DataView. For this example we only need to set two properties:

- `Table`—The table for which this DataView is a view. The drop-down shows the DataSet that is on the form in a tree format. We can expand it to select a particular table.

- `RowFilter`—The condition that will limit what data is displayed. In this case, the filter is a little silly; we will provide a better example later. The filter here limits the display to those rows whose `TeacherID` is greater than two (figure 25.4).

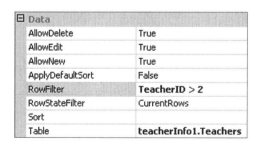

Figure 25.4
DataView properties

Only one more step. Currently, the DataGrid is pointing to the `Teachers` Data-Table inside the DataSet on the form. We need to change it to point to the DataView. Doing so is simply a matter of changing the `DataSource` property on the DataGrid. If we select the DataGrid, the DataView should now appear in the drop-down list for the `DataSource` property (figure 25.5).

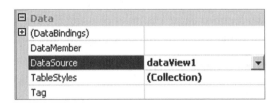

Figure 25.5
The `DataSource` property of the DataGrid

Now all we need to do is run the program and fill the grid (figure 25.6).

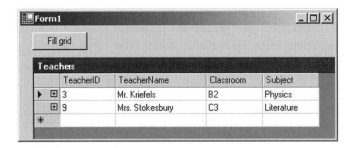

Figure 25.6
Grid filtered by DataView

25.3.1 Coding the DataView directly

Setting up a specific DataView is straightforward via the designer, but the result may not be what we want. We might want to create and manage several different Data-Views and manipulate them separately. This next example will put several radio buttons on the form to choose between displaying all the teachers or just the male or just the female teachers.

We can take a couple of different approaches. We could change the filter on a single DataView, which may provide the functionality we desire. Alternatively, we could switch between different DataViews; we'll take this approach in this example. We might hold onto the different views normally, but this sample creates the view as it needs it and relies on the garbage collector to clean up.

The first step of this process is to get rid of the DataView that we put on the form. Once that is done, the DataSet will no longer be pointing at a DataSource, so we need to change the `DataSource` property of the DataGrid back to the DataSet and change the `DataMember` property back to the Teachers table.

After that, put three radio buttons labeled All, Male Teachers, and Female Teachers on the form (figure 25.7).

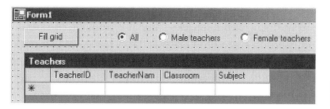

Figure 25.7
Form with radio buttons

Set the `Checked` property of the All radio button to `true`, because that is the default view of the grid when it comes up.

Next, we need to add handlers for each of the radio buttons being clicked. The easiest way to do this is to double-click on each radio button on the form to create a `CheckedChanged` event. This method will be called every time the state of the radio button changes (whether it is selected or unselected). Listing 25.3 shows the auto-generated code, along with the code to make the buttons work appropriately.

Listing 25.3   Radio button handlers

```
private void radioButton1_CheckedChanged(object sender,
                                         System.EventArgs e)
{
    if(radioButton1.Checked)
    {                                                    ❶ All radio
        dataGrid1.DataSource = teacherInfo1;               buttons
        dataGrid1.DataMember = "Teachers";
    }
}

private void radioButton2_CheckedChanged(object sender,
                                         System.EventArgs e)
{
    if(radioButton2.Checked)
    {                                                    ❷ Male radio
        DataView dv =                                      button
            new DataView(teacherInfo1.Tables["Teachers"]);
        dv.RowFilter = "TeacherName like 'Mr.%'";
        dataGrid1.DataSource = dv;
    }
}

private void radioButton3_CheckedChanged(object sender,
                                         System.EventArgs e)
{
    if(radioButton3.Checked)
    {
        DataView dv =                                    ❸ Female radio
            new DataView(teacherInfo1.Tables["Teachers"]);  button
        dv.RowFilter = "TeacherName not like 'Mr.%'";
        dataGrid1.DataSource = dv;
    }
}
```

❶ This handler first sees if the radio button is checked. This method will be called when the button changes state from unchecked to checked and also from checked to unchecked.

For the All button, we don't need to create a DataView—we can point the Data-Grid at the teacher1 DataSet and the Teachers table, which contains all the data.

We could have set the `DataSource` property to point directly to the `Teachers` DataTable and skipped setting the `DataMember`:

```
dataGrid1.DataSource = teacherInfo1.Tables["Teachers"];
```

❷ Again, this code makes sure the radio button is clicked. If it is, then we create a new DataView and associate it with the Teachers table.

The `RowFilter` determines if the teacher is male by the reasonably reliable method[1] of looking for *Mr.* at the beginning of the teacher's name. The last step sets the DataGrid's data source to the newly created view.

❸ This radio button works almost exactly the same as the Male Teachers radio button, but the query looks for teachers whose names do *not* start with *Mr.* We could have checked for *Mrs.*, but then we would also need to check for *Ms.* and *Miss.*

If we now run the code, we can switch back and forth between the modes by clicking on the radio buttons (figure 25.8).

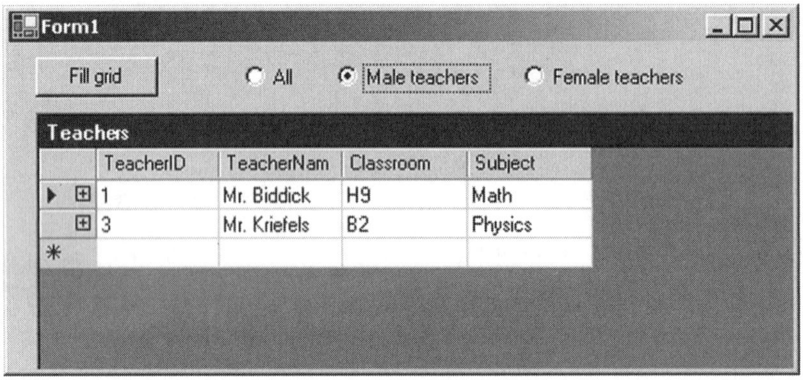

Figure 25.8   Filtering the DataGrid based on gender

Although particular filters are hard-coded, we could pop up a dialog box in which a user could enter or build a filter string, or provide any number of other mechanisms for specifying a filter. The important thing is that we can adjust the data in the grid without ever having to go back to the database.

---

[1] At least, reasonable given my bogus data.

25.3.2 Default view

One of the things we can do with a DataTable is set a *default view*. This view will be used automatically by data-bound controls if no other view is specified. Such a view might be handy if you normally limit the display to a particular set of data, but want all the data to be present. Setting a default view is easy:

```
SomeDataTable.DefaultView = SomeView;
```

25.4 DATAVIEW AND WEB FORMS

You can use a DataView on a web form exactly the same way you used it on the Windows Form. However, if you are writing a stateless application, this approach is less useful—you might as well change the DataTable, because you have to read it anyway. Of course, if you are keeping the DataSet in the session, it is more useful.

There is another use for a DataView on a web form: you can use it to tie other controls to a particular row in a grid control. For example, if you want to display the details of the currently selected record, you can set up a DataView that is limited to the currently selected row, then use data binding to tie other controls to the DataView.

If you think about how the DataList works, this technique makes sense—you can tie the controls in the template to a particular row because the DataList provides the context for the current row. However, that only works in the template. In the following example, you will pull out some data from the currently selected row in the DataGrid.

In order to set up this example, create a new ASP.NET project and set it up more or less the same way as the example from chapter 23. Follow these steps:

1 Create the TeacherInfo DataSet schema via the editor.

2 Drag an SQLDataAdapter onto the form and configure it to read the Teachers table.

3 Generate an instance of the TeacherInfo DataSet via the Data menu.

4 Drag a DataGrid onto the form.

Next, use the Property Builder to specify the data binding for the DataSource, Data-Member, and DataKey (figure 25.9).

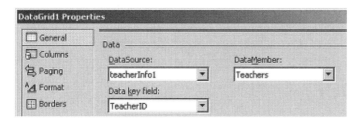

**Figure 25.9
Setting the data
properties for the
DataGrid**

Also set up columns in a manner similar to the earlier example, but instead of an Edit, Update, Delete column, add a Select button (another option from the Button columns; see figure 25.10).

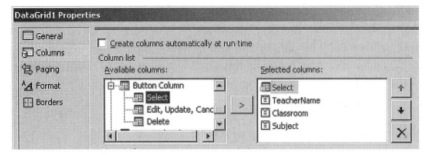

Figure 25.10 Specifying the columns

Set up the code on page load to fill the DataSet and bind the DataGrid:

```
private void Page_Load(object sender, System.EventArgs e)
{
   if(!IsPostBack)
   {
      LoadData();
      DataGrid1.DataBind();
   }
}

private void LoadData()
{
   sqlConnection1.Open();
   sqlDataAdapter1.Fill(teacherInfo1);
   sqlConnection1.Close();
}
```

There is nothing new in the code, except the DataSet being filled has been moved to its own method. Now we need to set up a DataView and use it to fill in some simple controls.

We can drag the DataView onto the WebForm and then set the `Table` property to `teacherInfo1.Teachers`. The `RowFilter` property will stay blank—it will be set programmatically when the selection changes.

Drag a label control onto the form. In this example, set the font to XX-Large (figure 25.11).

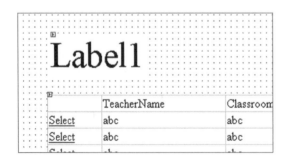

Figure 25.11
Putting a label on the form

Now, we need to bind the label to the DataView. If we bring up the properties for the label, a `(DataBindings)` property appears under Data. When we select it, we see an ellipsis button that will bring up the DataBindings dialog box (figure 25.12).

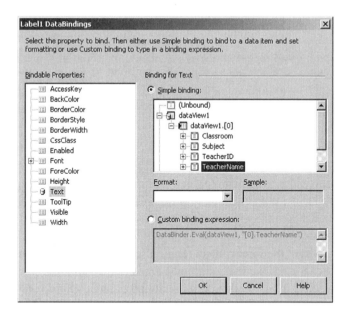

The DataView is now available as an option for binding a property. If we expand the tree, we can select the TeacherName field under the first element (`dataView1.[0]`) in the DataView. Why bind to the first element? The goal is to set up the DataView to just contain the selected row, so the first item in the DataView will be the *only* row in the DataView.

The last step is to set up the code to set the DataView to contain the selected row. This needs to happen whenever the selection changes, so we need to add a handler for the `SelectedIndexChanged` event of the DataGrid. To add a handler, select the DataGrid, switch to the event view of the property editor (using the lightning bolt), and then type in a name for the handler and press Enter (figure 25.13).

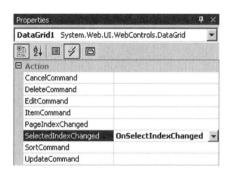

Figure 25.13
Handling the `SelectedIndexChanged` event

Here is the code for the `OnSelectIndexChanged` method:

```
private void OnSelectIndexChanged(object sender, System.EventArgs e)
{
    LoadData();
    int iIndex = DataGrid1.SelectedIndex;
    if (iIndex != -1)
    {
        string strKey = DataGrid1.DataKeys[iIndex].ToString();
        dataView1.RowFilter = "TeacherID = " + strKey;
    }

    Label1.DataBind();
}
```

The code first calls `LoadData()` to reload the DataSet. Then it gets the index of the item that was selected and makes sure it is an actual item.

Because the DataGrid knows that TeacherID is the DataKey for the data, it has a list of the TeacherIDs. We use the index to get the TeacherID from the selected row. We then use it to build the filter expression for the DataView, limiting the data to the currently selected row.

The last step is to have the label control rebind itself to the data. If we run the code now, the label will change as we select different items (figure 25.14).

This may seem like a lot of work to change the text of a label. After all, we could retrieve the data from the DataSet—or even from the DataGrid—and set the label directly. However, if you were setting a whole series of labels or edit controls, this approach makes more sense.

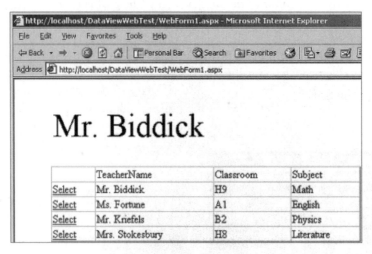

Figure 25.14
Bound label

25.5　SUMMARY

The DataView is a handy and simple class to use. It is designed for use with the data-bound controls. Although you can use DataViews for straight manipulation, you can do much the same thing by selecting data out of the DataTables directly. When you're using controls like the Windows or web DataGrids, though, the DataView makes filtering data much simpler.

This chapter brings to a close the discussion of data-bound controls. I could probably write an entire book on the foibles of the handful of controls discussed here, along with their myriad properties and capabilities; but this brief introduction to their use is enough to get you started, and should make the data binding concepts clear.

XML and ADO.NET

Although this is far from being a book on XML, ADO.NET has a number of XML related features that require a discussion of XML in order to make sense. This part of the book talks about some of the tasks you can perform with XML and ADO.NET; it begins with the basics, and then talks about schemas, queries, and taking advantage of SQL Server–specific XML functionality via ADO.NET.

Part 5 uses a number of terms related to XML. Chapter 3 provides an overview of the terminology, and you will see some of the XML mechanisms used here. XML itself is fairly simple, but the surrounding technologies such as schemas and transforms can be quite complex; I highly recommend that you check out a book on XML if you want to go beyond basics with XML.

C H A P T E R 2 6

DataSets and XML

This first chapter of part 5 begins by showing some of the most basic operations between a DataSet and XML: writing out data from a DataSet as XML, and also reading XML into a DataSet. It then goes on to show how you can link a DataSet to an XML document and manipulate the two in parallel.

Before getting into the details, the first big question to answer is how the data in a DataTable gets translated into XML. After all, a DataTable contains relational data, whereas XML is hierarchical. Well, both have one thing in common philosophically: a schema. A Database schema is all about tables and how those tables relate to one another, and an XML schema talks about nodes and what they can contain. At one level, these are quite different uses of the word *schema*, but at another level they are much closer in meaning.

Chapter 27 is all about the use of schemas and controlling how data is transferred back and forth between DataSets and XML. This chapter, however, relies on built-in behaviors and defaults. By default, when a DataSet is converted to XML it will look at a Database's schema, such as the one represented by figure 26.1.

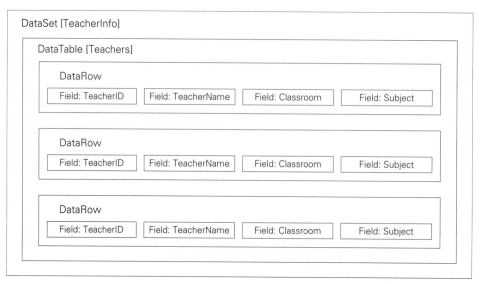

Figure 26.1   The layout of a DataSet

Of course, the DataSet can include multiple DataTables, which can relate to one another (a topic we will get to later). For the meantime, though, if you look at this relational table, it is hierarchical: a DataSet contains a DataTable, which contains rows, which contain fields. As you will see in the first example, this is essentially how the data is written out to XML.

26.1   WRITING OUT A DATASET AS XML

This first example does little more than load a DataSet and then tell the DataSet to write out to a file. You might want to do this because the major story behind XML is interoperability—being able to export data in a format that can be read by other applications or other mediums. Another application might be interested in your data but not interested in learning about your database structure, or you might want to send the XML as a *data island*[1] to a web page.

XML is handy for other uses, as well; as long as .NET has gone to all the effort to build support for handling XML, you might as well use it. In the system on which I primarily work, for example, we use XML to store our system definitions, our settings, and our archive files, and for a host of other operations.

The code in listing 26.1 reads the Teachers table into a DataSet, and then has the DataSet write itself out as XML to a file. This code is amazingly short, primarily because the XML support within .NET is so pervasive.

---

[1]   A data island is a chunk of XML included in an HTML page that can be referenced by controls in the page.

Listing 26.1   Writing out a DataSet to XML

```
public void XmlWriteTest(SqlConnection conn)
{
    string strSQL = "SELECT * From Teachers";
    SqlDataAdapter sda = new SqlDataAdapter(strSQL,conn);

    // Create and fill the dataset
    DataSet ds = new DataSet();
    ds.DataSetName = "TeacherInfo";
    sda.Fill(ds,"Teachers");

    // Write out the XML from the dataset
    ds.WriteXml("XmlWriteTest1.XML");
}
```

The first part of the code should be very familiar—it's the same old stuff for loading a DataTable.[2] The only new aspect is the call to WriteXml(). That is literally all there is to writing out the XML to a file. Let's look at the contents of the file, in listing 26.2; note that I removed a couple of lines that represented more rows to save space.

Listing 26.2   The XML output from listing 26.1

```
<?xml version="1.0" standalone="yes"?>        ① XML header

<TeacherInfo>        ② DataSet node

    <Teachers>                        ③ Rows from DataTable

        <TeacherID>1</TeacherID>
        <TeacherName>Mr. Biddick              </TeacherName>     ④ Fields in
        <Classroom>H9         </Classroom>                          each row
        <Subject>Math              </Subject>
    </Teachers>
    <Teachers>
        <TeacherID>2</TeacherID>
        <TeacherName>Ms. Fortune              </TeacherName>
        <Classroom>A1         </Classroom>
        <Subject>English           </Subject>
    </Teachers>
        .
        .
</TeacherInfo>
```

[2] I have added a new line to set the name of the DataSet, so the name will be specific and not the automatically generated name NewDataSet.

❶ The first line in any XML file should be an XML declaration. It indicates that the file is using version 1.0 of the XML standard and that the document is completely self-contained or *stand-alone*.

❷ The `<TeacherInfo>` node represents the DataSet in the XML. Anything contained in the DataSet will be contained within this node. TeacherInfo is the name we explicitly gave the DataSet. This is the *root* node of the document—for an XML document to be valid or *well-formed*, it must have one and only one root node.

❸ If you look at the XML, you will see that each row is contained within an element with the same name as the table—in this case, Teachers. You might expect a node representing each DataTable in the DataSet, which would then contain the individual rows—something like this:

```
<Teachers>
   <Row>
      <TeacherID>1</TeacherID>
      <TeacherName>Mr. Biddick                </TeacherName>
      <Classroom>H9        </Classroom>
      <Subject>Math            </Subject>
   </Row>
      .
      .
      .
</Teachers>
```

There are some issues with that approach, though. For example, if you are using a DTD to define the validity of the XML, you can specify which elements are legal below which other elements. So, you could say that `<Teachers>` must contain one element each of `<TeacherID>`, `<TeacherName>`, `<Classroom>`, and `<Subject>`. If, however, you insert the generic `<Row>` tag, there is no way to say that it sometimes contains those elements and sometimes contains elements from another table.

Workarounds are available, of course. For example, we could have a `<TeachersRow>` element below, but it would require the building of a string to determine the elements for which to search—never a good idea, especially when you're considering internationalization issues.

So rows in the different tables are, by default, kept at the same level. If the DataSet contained another table, say the Classes table, the rows in the Classes table would probably be at the same level as the Teachers nodes, but would be `<Classes>` nodes instead of `<Teachers>` nodes.

❹ As you can see in the XML, there is a node for each field. The name of the element is the name of the field, and the *inner-text* is the value from the field. The text fields have a lot of spaces after their value, because the data in the DataTable represents the whole width of the field. In section 26.3, I will show some ways of getting rid of these spaces.

26.1.1 Example summary

One line of code to write out our data to XML. Pretty neat, eh? Next time your CEO comes to you and demands that your applications use XML because they read about it and heard it was the future of everything,[3] you can show that you are already taking care of it!

This functionality is just the tip of the iceberg—you can do a great deal more with XML, but in some instances this may be enough.

26.1.2 Writing to places other than a file

In the previous example, the code just created and wrote to a file; but you may want more control. The DataSet can write out in a couple of different ways. For example, you can write to a stream.

STREAM   A *stream* is an abstraction that takes or returns a sequence of data. It could represent a file, a chunk of memory, or even a low-level socket.

The DataSet can also write to a TextWriter, another abstraction that is focused on writing character data rather than binary data like the stream. Some of the derivations of a TextWriter automatically format the data or do other setup work for their target. The following code snippet shows how to have the DataSet write out to a string using a StringWriter—a derivation of TextWriter:

```
    .

    .
using System.IO;
using System.Text;
    .

    .
    StringBuilder sb = new StringBuilder();
    StringWriter sw = new StringWriter(sb);
    ds.WriteXml(sw);

    Console.WriteLine(sb.ToString());
    .

    .
```

The using statements should appear with your other using statements at the top of the file. The IO namespace is required for the StringWriter, and the Text namespace is for the StringBuilder.

A StringWriter writes to a *StringBuilder*. Although you can build up a string by appending strings to one another, doing so is inefficient because you must continually allocate new memory to contain the longer string. The StringBuilder allocates a large buffer up front, which doesn't have to be reallocated until that buffer is full. You can also tell the StringBuilder how big it is likely to get, to make it even more efficient.

---

[3] Oops—are my personal experiences leaking into my manuscript?

Once you have created the StringWriter, you pass it to the `WriteXml()` method of the DataSet. The data will be written to the StringBuilder. The string can easily be extracted from the StringBuilder by calling `ToString()`. In this snippet, the string is being written to the console.

26.2 LOADING A DATASET FROM XML

Writing out the DataSet is easy. What about loading a DataSet from an XML file? Let's start with the simplest case first: XML that looks exactly like the file we just wrote out. In fact, we'll use the file that was written out. The following code is the reverse of the earlier example, and is just as straightforward:

```
public void XmlReadTest()
{
   // Create the dataset from the XML
   DataSet ds = new DataSet();
   ds.ReadXml("XmlWriteTest1.XML");

   // Write out the DataSet
   PrintDataSet(ds);
}
```

Notice that there is no database access code here (nothing up my sleeves). The reverse call to `WriteXml()`—`ReadXml()`—can read from a file, a stream, a TextReader, and so forth. The output is generated using the `PrintDataSet` method that steps through the DataTables in the DataSet and writes them out; I won't show the code, because it is basically the same method used in part 3 for writing out DataSets. The output appears in figure 26.2.

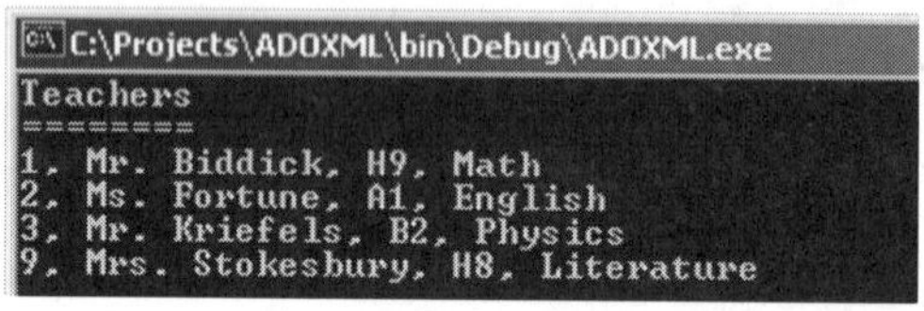

Figure 26.2
Output from example that loads a DataSet from an XML file

The DataSet and its DataTable have been reconstructed exactly as before. This result may give you a hint about how the remoting mechanisms shown in chapter 21 work—the remoting mechanisms use XML to transfer data.

26.2.1 Other formats for the XML

It is all well and good to be able to read in XML in the exact format in which it was written out, but what about other formats? The `ReadXml()` method can do fairly well without help. For example, we can store the data in attributes versus elements:

```
<?xml version="1.0" standalone="yes"?>
<TeacherInfo>
  <Teachers TeacherID="1" TeacherName="Mr. Biddick"
                        Classroom="H9" Subject="Math"/>
```

```
<Teachers TeacherID="2" TeacherName="Ms. Fortune"
                        Classroom="A1" Subject="English"/>
<Teachers TeacherID="3" TeacherName="Mr. Kriefels"
                        Classroom="B2" Subject="Physics"/>
<Teachers TeacherID="9" TeacherName="Mrs. Stokesbury"
                        Classroom="H8" Subject="Literature"/>
</TeacherInfo>
```

If we run this XML through the `ReadXml()` method, we get the same output (figure 26.3).

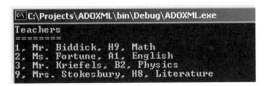

Figure 26.3
Output from example that uses other XML formats

You can also combine the approaches—have some attributes and some elements. Doing so is especially useful if most of the fields contain simple data, but some of the fields are more involved—possibly containing characters that are not legal in attributes (such as carriage returns). Here is an example where the Subject field is an element, but all the other fields are attributes:

```
<?xml version="1.0" standalone="yes"?>
<TeacherInfo>
    <Teachers TeacherID="1" TeacherName="Mr. Biddick"
                                            Classroom="H9">
        <Subject>Math</Subject>
    </Teachers>
    <Teachers TeacherID="2" TeacherName="Ms. Fortune"
                                            Classroom="A1">
        <Subject>English</Subject>
    </Teachers>
    <Teachers TeacherID="3" TeacherName="Mr. Kriefels"
                                            Classroom="B2">
        <Subject>Physics</Subject>
    </Teachers>
    <Teachers TeacherID="9" TeacherName="Mrs. Stokesbury"
                                            Classroom="H8">
        <Subject>Literature</Subject>
    </Teachers>
</TeacherInfo>
```

I won't show the output because it is, again, the same as in the previous examples. This result raises an interesting question: what happens when the contents of a field contain things that would mess up the XML?

26.2.2 Handling XML inside XML

In the examples so far, all the data has been quite simple. But in the real world, data can be complex—for example, the field might contain XML, which would cause serious problems reading in the XML. This situation might come up if you were storing user settings as XML inside the database.

A more spurious but simpler example using the test data might be if Mr. Biddick's subject was (for some unknown reason) `<Math>`. If this subject were just dumped out, it would look as though an unclosed tag called `Math` appeared in the middle of the XML, which would generate an error. We can handle this situation two ways in XML. The first is to *escape* the characters that might cause confusion:

```
<Subject>&lt;Math&gt;</Subject>
```

The less-than symbol has been replaced with `&lt;` and the greater-than symbol with `&gt;`. The XML reader understands this notation and knows to convert the symbols back to < and > automatically. This process works, but it makes the XML harder to read.

The other mechanism is to use CData, which stands for Character Data. When you use CData you specify that everything contained in the special `CData` tag is literal character data that must be left alone and kept exactly as it appears, including white space, up to the tag indicating the end of the CData:

```
<![CDATA[<Math>]]>
```

This code has three pieces:

- *The start of the CData tag*—`<![CDATA[`—Everything after this is considered to be data, until the end tag.
- *The data*—`<Math>`—The data to be represented. It can include XML, multiple lines, or just about anything *except* the end of the CData tag.
- *The end of the CData tag*—`]]>`—Indicates the end of the CData and a return to regular XML processing.

26.2.3 Other formats to the XML

You have seen that the `ReadXml()` method of the DataSet is fairly flexible—it can handle, for example, data that is stored as attributes or as elements. However, the data in the XML file could be represented in an infinite number of ways. The previous examples have only dealt with a single DataTable, but the data could represent multiple tables and their relationships.

The DataSet can deal with this variety of data two ways:

- You can tell it by providing a schema. Schemas are the primary topic of chapter 27.
- You can convert the data, either manually or by using XSL Transforms. Chapter 28 includes an example of using a transform.

The great thing about XML is that it is incredibly flexible, and it even provides flexible mechanisms for dealing with the flexibility.

26.3 LINKING DATASETS AND XML DOCUMENTS

So far, we've discussed converting from one format to another—starting with a DataSet and converting it to XML or vice versa. But sometimes you'll want to work in both forms at the same time. One reason you might want to do this is there are different mechanisms for manipulating the data in each form that might be appropriate for different operations, and you might not want the overhead of moving back and forth between formats. For example, you can display your data in a DataGrid via the DataSet, but still search and manipulate the data in XML using XPath or stylesheet transformations (XSLT).

The other reason to link a DataSet and an XML document has to do with one of the behaviors of an XML document. In the previous examples, all the data in the XML was transferred into the DataSet. However, the XML might include data that is not important to the DataSet, but that is still important in the XML. Ideally, you could leave that data alone in the XML but work with the data that is relevant to the DataSet *in* the DataSet.

This is an important tenet of XML. If you think about several companies agreeing on a format for a particular type of XML, the XML might include elements specific to one company versus another. Using the Teachers example, perhaps one teacher-management system tracks whether the teacher has tenure, but that is not part of the standard agreed-on definition for a teacher. The rule is that any system that does not recognize the extended features must leave them alone, even if they modify the commonly agreed-on elements.

In order to have the DataSet contain a subset of the data, you must use schemas (a demonstration appears in chapter 27). The next sections demonstrate linking an XmlDocument to an existing DataSet and linking a DataSet to an existing XmlDocument.

26.3.1 Starting with a DataSet

In the example in listing 26.3, we load the DataSet with the Teacher table as usual, and then link it to an XmlDocument. The code then uses XPath to select all the Subject nodes and uppercases them. Finally the DataSet is printed out, demonstrating that the change to the XmlDocument is synchronized with the DataSet.

Listing 26.3 Synchronizing an XmlDocument to an existing DataSet

```
using System.Xml;          ① Xml namespace

public void XmlLinkTest(SqlConnection conn)
{
    string strSQL = "SELECT * From Teachers";
    SqlDataAdapter sda = new SqlDataAdapter(strSQL,conn);

    // Create and fill the dataset
    DataSet ds = new DataSet();
    ds.DataSetName = "TeacherInfo";
    sda.Fill(ds,"Teachers");
```

```
       ds.EnforceConstraints = false;              ② Turn off constraints

       // Create a synchronized XmlDocument
       XmlDataDocument xdd = new XmlDataDocument(ds);   ③ Create synchronized
                                                           document
       // Use XPath to select all of the Subject nodes
       XmlNodeList xnl = xdd.SelectNodes("//Teachers/Subject");   ④ Select
                                                                     nodes
       // Step through all of the nodes
       // and uppercase their contents
       foreach(XmlElement xe in xnl)                 ⑤ Modify
          xe.InnerText = xe.InnerText.ToUpper();          XmlDocument

       // Print out the DataSet
       PrintDataSet(ds);
    }
```

❶ To use an XmlDocument, we must first tell .NET to use the Xml namespace so that the various classes are available. As usual, this declaration must appear at the top of our file with the other using statements, but it's shown here for convenience.

❷ Normally, when we work with a DataSet, we want it to enforce the various constraints that have been set up. However, if we want to *modify* data via an XmlDocument, we must turn off the enforcement of constraints. If we don't, then any operation that modifies data via the XmlDocument will fail, even if it doesn't break a constraint. This happens because the model for data manipulation in a relational database is so different from XML manipulation. We can, however, synchronize the two and read data without disabling constraints; or we can turn off enforcement prior to making an XML-based change, and then turn enforcement back on.

❸ XmlDataDocument is a derivation of XmlDocument, which is the class used in .NET to represent the DOM (the Document Object Model). The primary difference between the two classes is that the XmlDataDocument is specifically designed to work with the DataSet. To create a synchronized XmlDocument, all we have to do is create a new instance of the XmlDataDocument derivation and pass it the DataSet to which we want to be synchronized.

Once we have the XmlDataDocument, we can do virtually anything with it that we can do with an independent XmlDocument. One exception is that we cannot load new XML data—the document is already populated from the DataSet.

❹ This statement executes an XPath query against the XmlDocument. The details of XPath are left until chapter 28, but this statement basically asks for any elements called Subject whose parent element is called Teachers. The result is an XmlNodeList— a collection of nodes that meet the criteria.

❺ The XmlNodeList is a collection, so you can step through it using the foreach statement. The items in the collection are derivations of the XmlNode class, which includes a number of classes, such as the document itself, elements, attributes, and several special cases. However, we happen to know that our query will only return objects of class XmlElement, so we can have the `foreach` statement automatically type-cast to that type.

The inner-text of an element in this case is the value, so it is easy to uppercase the value and store it. Fair warning, though—if the element contains child elements as well as text, then setting the `InnerText` will overwrite these elements.

Results

The last step is to print out the DataSet. Notice in figure 26.4 that although no code directly modifies the DataSet, the Subject field is now uppercase.

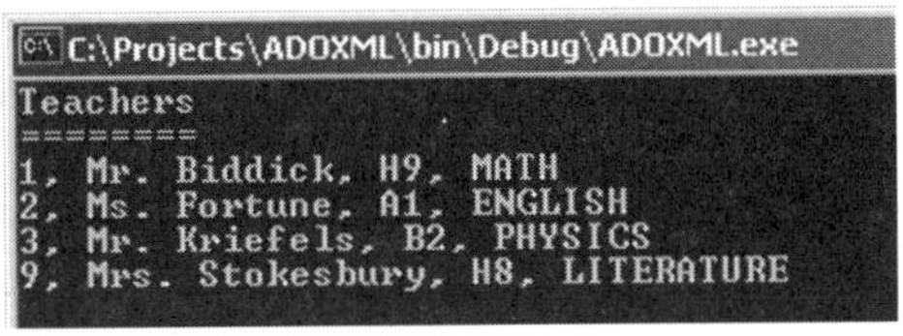

Figure 26.4
Output from listing 26.3

26.3.2 Starting with an XmlDocument

The previous example started with a DataSet and then created the XmlDocument. Going the other way is not quite as easy, because you must provide a schema for the DataSet before loading in the data. This process can happen a number of ways:

- The XML file can contain the schema in-line.
- You can tell the DataSet specifically which schema to use.
- You can manually configure the DataSet's structure by adding tables and columns appropriately for the data.
- You can use a strongly typed DataSet—that is, a derivation of a DataSet whose structure is predefined.
- You can ask the DataSet to try to figure out the schema based on the XML.

You will see examples of several of these techniques in chapter 27, but for the moment we will use the last method—we'll ask the DataSet to figure out the structure from the XML, because we do not have a schema.

Once the schema has been set, the example in listing 26.4 loads the data from the XML file and then synchronizes it with the DataSet. To make a change, we run through all the columns and trim the text to remove spaces. Finally, we print out the XmlDocument, showing the change.

Listing 26.4 Synchronizing a DataSet to an XML document

```
public void XmlLinkTestFromXml()
{
    // Create the DataSet and infer the schema from the XML
    DataSet ds = new DataSet();
    ds.InferXmlSchema("XmlWriteTest1.XML",new string[] {});        ❶ Infer
                                                                       schema

    // Put the XML into an XML document
    // linked to the DataSet
    XmlDataDocument xdd = new XmlDataDocument(ds);                  ❷ Load XML
    xdd.Load("XmlWriteTest1.XML");

    // Go through all fields in all rows and trim
    // any data of type string
    foreach(DataRow dr in ds.Tables["Teachers"].Rows)              ❸ Trim
    {                                                                  data
        foreach(DataColumn dc in ds.Tables["Teachers"].Columns)
        {
            if(dc.DataType == typeof(string))
                dr[dc] = dr[dc].ToString().Trim();
        }
    }

    // Write out the XML
    Console.WriteLine(FormatXml(xdd.OuterXml));                     ❹ Write out XML
}
```

❶ When we hook up an XMLDocument to an existing DataSet, the XMLDocument automatically takes on the structure of the DataSet. Going the other way is a problem, however—the DataSet must have a structure into which the XML data will be loaded. You could argue that this should happen automatically, as when you are loading XML into a DataSet. You could also argue that you might be able to specify a property or flag to get that automatic behavior. (Arguing is bad for you, though—it builds up your stress level!)

My guess is that there was no elegant way to provide the default behavior without confusing the more likely scenarios in which you have a schema. In any case, we must explicitly specify the schema before we can link the document.

This leaves us with a problem: the XML with which we are working does not have a schema. Fortunately, the DataSet includes a mechanism that can look at an XML file and attempt to determine the schema based on the contents of the file. This mechanism is reasonably robust—in fact, it is the same mechanism used when loading the data. However, if the data is not laid out reasonably clearly, we will have to create a schema.

The InferSchema() method can take a filename, as in the example. It can also take a stream or a TextReader to read in the data. The second argument is an array of strings indicating namespaces to ignore from the XML file. In the example, we are not worried about namespaces, so we pass an empty array.

❷ This code creates an XmlDocument, or rather the XmlDataDocument derivation of an XmlDocument that understands linking to DataSets. The XmlDataDocument is initialized with the DataSet that we already created, and then the XML is loaded, which automatically fills the DataSet.

❸ Here, the code steps through all the fields in the Teachers table and trims any fields that contain strings. We could have made the code more generic to step through all the tables that were retrieved, but this code is less verbose.

❹ To write out the XML, we simply need to access the XML in the XmlDocument. However, to make it output more prettily, we added a call to a method we wrote to format the output. Figure 26.5 shows the output without the formatting.

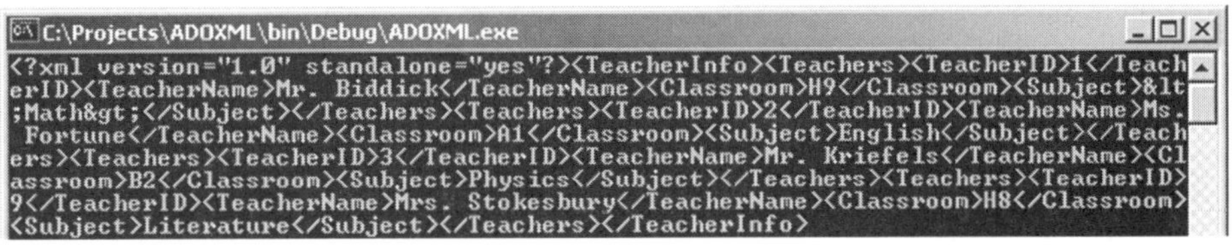

Figure 26.5 Ugly output from the sample

And figure 26.6 shows the output (slightly abbreviated for space) using the simple formatting method.

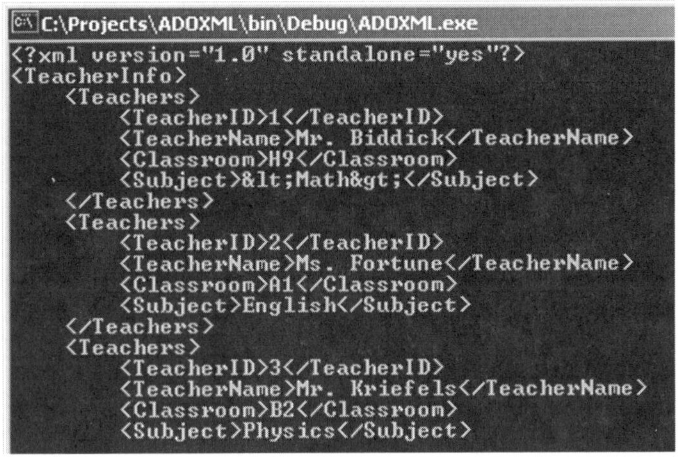

**Figure 26.6
Pretty output
from listing 26.4**

Just for reference, here is the code for the `FormatXml()` method:

```
public string FormatXml(string strXml)
{
    // Put the XML into an XML document for manipulation
    XmlDocument doc = new XmlDocument();
    doc.LoadXml(strXml);

    // Create an XML text writer for writing the XML, initialized
    // with a StringWriter to actually capture the data
    StringWriter sw = new StringWriter();
    XmlTextWriter xtw = new XmlTextWriter(sw);

    // Set formatting options
    xtw.Formatting = Formatting.Indented;
    xtw.Indentation = 4;

    // Actually write out the XML
    doc.WriteTo(xtw);

    return sw.ToString();
}
```

You can see that the extraneous spaces have been removed from the fields.

26.4 WORKING WITH DIFFGRAMS

In earlier chapters, I showed how to work with changes to a DataSet, as well as use remoting to send those changes to another tier and merge them back into an original DataSet. In this chapter, you have seen how a DataSet is represented as XML, and you can easily see how a DataSet could be transferred, as XML, between tiers. But what if you want to capture changes to the data, or be able to merge the changes into an existing DataSet?

A *DiffGram* is an XML representation of the data in a DataSet that includes additional information:

- The current value of the data
- Order information about the data
- A unique identifier for each row
- Whether a row has been changed
- If a row has changed, the original values of that row

This XML is obviously more verbose than just the raw data, but all this information is needed to properly recreate the DataSet. Listing 26.5 shows the DiffGram for the Teachers DataSet (after I made a couple of modifications to the data and removed a couple of rows to save space).

Listing 26.5   XML DiffGram

```xml
<?xml version="1.0" standalone="yes"?>
<diffgr:diffgram
        xmlns:msdata="urn:schemas-microsoft-com:xml-msdata"
        xmlns:diffgr="urn:schemas-microsoft-com:xml-diffgram-v1">
  <TeacherInfo>
    <Teachers diffgr:id="Teachers1" msdata:rowOrder="0"
                                    diffgr:hasChanges="modified">
      <TeacherID>1</TeacherID>
      <TeacherName>Mr. Biddick                </TeacherName>
      <Classroom>H9        </Classroom>
      <Subject>History</Subject>
    </Teachers>
    <Teachers diffgr:id="Teachers2" msdata:rowOrder="1">
      <TeacherID>2</TeacherID>
      <TeacherName>Ms. Fortune               </TeacherName>
      <Classroom>A1         </Classroom>
      <Subject>English           </Subject>
    </Teachers>
    .
    .   (Omitted for space)
    .
  </TeacherInfo>
  <diffgr:before>
    <Teachers diffgr:id="Teachers1" msdata:rowOrder="0">
      <TeacherID>1</TeacherID>
      <TeacherName>Mr. Biddick               </TeacherName>
      <Classroom>H9         </Classroom>
      <Subject>Math              </Subject>
    </Teachers>
  </diffgr:before>
</diffgr:diffgram>
```

As you can see, the DiffGram is not much different from the straight XML export. The <Teachers> tag contains quite a bit more information, though, especially for the first row, which includes the hasChanges attribute. There is also a new section at the bottom: the <before> tag, which has the original version of the changed row.

By the way, you may have noticed that a number of the tags and attributes have a clause in front of them, such as diffgr: or msdata:. These are namespaces, indicating that the tag comes from a specific schema. You can see these defined at the top of the document. For example, the following line indicates that the XML namespace msdata is associated with the schema that can be found at the specified location:

```
xmlns:msdata="urn:schemas-microsoft-com:xml-msdata"
```

I won't spend much time on DiffGrams, because reading and writing them is trivial. To write a DiffGram, all you have to do is add an argument to the WriteXml() call:

```
ds.WriteXml("XmlDiffGram.XML",XmlWriteMode.DiffGram);
```

Reading is equally complicated:

```
ds.ReadXml("XmlDiffGram.XML",XmlReadMode.DiffGram);
```

When you are reading in XML, you have a handful of other options, shown in table 26.1.

Table 26.1 The `XmlReadMode` enumeration

Value	Description
Auto	Determines the best thing to do based on the incoming XML. If there is no schema, it attempts to determine the schema from the XML, and so on. Interestingly, if the mode is default (which it is if you don't specify a value), then the DataSet will automatically recognize a DiffGram and read it appropriately.
DiffGram	As already discussed, reads in the data as a DiffGram.
InferSchema	Explicitly instructs the DataSet to try to determine the schema.
ReadSchema	Tells the DataSet to determine its schema based on the schema included in-line in the XML.
IgnoreSchema	Assumes that you have already set up the DataSet's structure (its schema). Any schema information in the XML is ignored, and the structure of the XML itself is ignored. However, any data in the XML that does not match the structure is *thrown away.*
Fragment	One of the rules for well-formed XML is that the XML has one and only one root node. However, sometimes you might have mostly legal XML that contains multiple root nodes. An example is using the FOR XML clause against SQL Server—you get back XML, but each row of data is held under a separate root node. This option allows you to read in that XML. To give you an idea how much this option is designed to work with SQL Server, this read mode used to be called SqlXml.

26.5 SUMMARY

This chapter has demonstrated some of the basic operations you can do with DataSets and XML. Already, you should see the power in these approaches. I like the fact that although Microsoft is highly focused on XML, it does not force you to be aware of the XML options; you can work with relational data just as you have always done, but if you want to bring XML into the equation, it is immediately and easily available with the full power of the various standards.

Up to now, although schemas have been mentioned, we have not done much with them. Although XML is useful by itself, schemas and the concepts behind them give XML its power. Chapter 27 will talk about schemas and then show how you can use them with ADO.NET.

C H A P T E R   2 7

DataSets and schemas

So far we have talked about using XML by itself. XML has rules, which must be followed—end tags for every start tag, and so on—but that is all. With schemas, you can define what is and is not legal in a great deal more detail, such as the elements and attributes to be found, and how many. This chapter explores schemas and the ADO.NET features available for working with them.

27.1   SCHEMAS

You can use a schema to specify exactly what elements and attributes should be allowed in your XML. For example, the following schema defines a definition for a class:

```
<?xml version="1.0"?>
<xs:schema xmlns:xs="http://www.w3.org/2001/XMLSchema">
<xs:element name="Class">
    <xs:complexType>
      <xs:sequence>
      <element name="Teacher" type="xs:string"/>
      <element name="Classroom" type="xs:string"/>
      <element name="Period" type="xs:number"/>
      </xs:sequence>
    </xs:complexType>
</xs:element>
</xs:schema>
```

This fairly simple example defines a *complex type* called Class as being made up of several *simple types*: Teacher, Classroom, and Period. A complex type contains other types, and a simple type is one of the primitive types, like string, number, or date. An XML file that conforms to this schema might look something like this:

```
<?xml version="1.0"?>
<Class xmlns:xsi="http://www.w3.org/2001/XMLSchema-instance"
            xsi:noNamespaceSchemaLocation="TeacherSchema.XSD">
   <Teacher>Mr. Biddick</Teacher>
   <Classroom>A1</Classroom>
   <Period>2</Period>
</Class>
```

We don't want a way to define an XML document, though—we want a way to represent a DataSet. If you think about it, the two are not far apart. For example, the complex type called Class could easily represent a table, whereas the simple types could represent fields.

Microsoft took that approach in defining a DataSet's schema—it takes some parts of an XML schema and maps them to tables, fields, and even relationships and constraints. The schema definition language (XSD) has similar constructs, so the mapping works well.

By using the same definition language for DataSets and XML, it becomes easy to transfer data back and forth between XML and a DataSet or link the two together, as you saw in chapter 26. In this chapter, we will look at the automatic schema generated by a DataSet for tables, fields, and relationships and constraints. We will also examine how you can use the schema to have data in the XML document that is not included in the DataSet, but that is still maintained. Finally, we will discuss strongly typed DataSets—classes generated from schemas that contain properties and members that directly mirror the elements of the schema.

27.2 DATASET SCHEMAS

In chapter 26, you saw how easy it was to export data from a DataSet as XML. It is just as easy to export a schema. All you have to do is call the XmlWriteSchema() method:

```
ds.WriteXmlSchema("XmlSchemaWriteTest1.XML");
```

I have done this on the Teachers DataSet from the previous chapter, which contains the Teachers table. Listing 27.1 shows the result.

| Listing 27.1   Schema for the Teachers DataSet |

```
<?xml version="1.0" standalone="yes"?>
<xsd:schema id="TeacherInfo" xmlns=""
       xmlns:xsd="http://www.w3.org/2001/XMLSchema"
       xmlns:msdata="urn:schemas-microsoft-com:xml-msdata">
   <xsd:element name="TeacherInfo" msdata:IsDataSet="true">
     <xsd:complexType>
```

① XML, schema and namespaces

② First complex type

```
<xsd:choice maxOccurs="unbounded">                  ❸ MaxOccurs

   <xsd:element name="Teachers">                    ❹ Teachers
     <xsd:complexType>                                  complex type
       <xsd:sequence>
         <xsd:element name="TeacherID"                ❺ Simple
                 type="xsd:int" minOccurs="0" />         types

         <xsd:element name="TeacherName" type="xsd:string"
                                     minOccurs="0" />
         <xsd:element name="Classroom" type="xsd:string"
                                     minOccurs="0" />
         <xsd:element name="Subject" type="xsd:string"
                                     minOccurs="0" />
       </xsd:sequence>
     </xsd:complexType>
   </xsd:element>
  </xsd:choice>
 </xsd:complexType>
 </xsd:element>
</xsd:schema>
```

I won't explain every detail about schemas (doing so would require an entire book on its own), but I do want to point out several things about this schema.

❶ One of the cool things about a schema is that it is defined in XML, which is why the first line of the schema indicates the use of XML. Also, because it is XML, we can validate the schema with a schema! The `schema` tag identifies the schema and also references the schema that defines what a schema should look like.[1] This well-known schema is referenced using the URI http://www.w3.org/2001/XMLSchema, so we can use standard XML tools to validate and edit the schema.

The first part of the reference to the schema says `xmlns:xsd`. *Xmlns* stands for XML NameSpace. In XML, it indicates a way of scoping items to guarantee uniqueness. By convention, schema elements based on the XMLSchema schema are always defined with the letters *xsd*, so you know that any items in the text that begin with xsd are based on the schema definition within XMLSchema.

Another schema is referenced here as well: urn:schemas-microsoft-com:xml-msdata, whose elements will all be prefixed with *msdata*. This schema adds several tags to the standard schema to make it easier to associate with a DataSet.

That is another cool thing about schemas and XML—you can extend the legal XML easily, which means you can extend the way a schema is defined easily. In this case, the schema is referenced, but you can also define additional elements directly in the file.

---

[1] You may have to read that sentence twice.

Namespaces are designed to avoid conflicts where two items might have the same name. They become part of the name to make it more unique. If you do not specify a namespace in front of an element, then that element will not be in a namespace—or will be in the default namespace for the document, if one has been specified.

❷ In the XML schema world, a complex type is a type that contains other types. In this case, the TeacherInfo complex type contains the remaining contents of the DataSet—just the Teachers table in this case, but a more complex schema could include any number of other elements. When transferring this information into a DataSet, how does the DataSet know this is the main group? The special attribute `msdata:IsDataSet` is a good clue—it's an attribute that comes from the Microsoft schema that is extending the basic schema.

❸ Using `MaxOccurs`, we can limit the number of times a particular child appears. Normally the value will be either 1 (the item can occur at most one time) or, as in the example, unbounded, meaning that any number of occurrences can appear. However, you can also set this value arbitrarily (say, to 7).

❹ In this schema, the complex type Teachers contains a TeacherID, TeacherName, Classroom, and Subject. This information is clear from an XML point of view. When it is mapped to a DataSet, the complex type is automatically converted into a DataTable, so this complex type contains the definition for the Teachers table.

❺ The items within the Teachers complex type are all of simple types, and so are fully defined by their tags. The information for each element includes:

- `name`—The name of the element.
- `type`—The data type. All the data types shown here are simple types from the lengthy list of schema-supported types—`int`, `string`, and so on. This value could also refer to a complex type made up of other types, or even to a custom type that specifically limits the contents based on a regular expression.
- `minOccurs`—The minimum number of times this element can appear in the XML within the `Teachers` tag. The default is 1, meaning that the item is required. Specifying 0 means the element is optional.
- `maxOccurs`—The maximum number of times this element can appear in the XML within the `Teachers` tag. Notice that this tag is not present; it defaults to 1, so we don't need to specify it. Basically, each field in the example can be absent or can appear at most one time.

We could specify a number of other pieces of information here, but this is all we need for the moment.

27.3   VALIDATING AGAINST A SCHEMA

Defining a schema is well and good, but it would be handy to have a way to check
and see if the data in the XML file matched the schema. Many tools can do this, and
you can also do it programmatically. This discussion is a little off-topic, because it is
not really related to the use of schemas and ADO.NET. However, the process is
tricky, and so is worth covering.

.NET has a built-in XML Validator called the XmlValidatingReader. It is designed
to validate XML as it is read in from a stream or a file; it can make sure that the XML
is well-formed (all the tags match, and so forth) and, if the XML references a schema,
that the XML conforms to the schema.

The XmlValidatingReader does not check everything—for example, you can
define some complex rules such as requiring an element's value to be unique in a document. The XmlValidatingReader will *not* check for this rule, but it will make sure
all the elements are where they are supposed to be, with the correct number of occurrences.

27.3.1   Straight validation

Let's set up the XmlValidatingReader to read in our XML *without* the schema. Then
we can break the XML and make sure the validator catches the problem. Next, we'll
add in the reference to the schema. The first step is to break the XML. I have made a
copy of the XML with which we have been working, and messed up an end-tag:

```
<Teachers>
  <TeacherID>2</TeacherID>
  <TeacherName>Ms. Fortune                </TeacherName>
  <Classroom>A1            </Class>
  <Subject>English            </Subject>
</Teachers>
```

Notice that the Classroom tag does not have a proper matching closing tag, so the
XML is not well-formed. The code in listing 27.2 will check for us.

> **Listing 27.2   Code to test for errors in the XML**

```
public void TestXML()
{
    try
    {
        XmlTextReader tr = new XmlTextReader("XMLWithError.XML");

        XmlValidatingReader reader =                    ❶ XmlValidatingReader
            new XmlValidatingReader(tr);

        reader.ValidationEventHandler += new
            ValidationEventHandler(XmlValidationHandler);   ❷ Register for
                                                              validation event
        XmlDocument doc = new XmlDocument();
```

```
        doc.Load(reader);          ❸  Load data
    }
    catch(XmlException e)                            ❹  Catch
    {                                                    exception
        Console.WriteLine(e.ToString());
    }
}

public static void XmlValidationHandler(object sender,
                                ValidationEventArgs args)
{                                                     ❺  Display
    Console.WriteLine("Error found in XML");              errors
    Console.WriteLine("------------------");
    Console.WriteLine("Severity: {0}", args.Severity);
    Console.WriteLine("Message:  {0}", args.Message);
    Console.WriteLine("");
}
```

❶ The XmlValidatingReader is a specialized XmlReader—a class designed to read in XML. It is initialized with an XMLTextReader—a class that can read in XML from a file. Once we have a reader, you can step from tag to tag and read in the XML in a forward-only manner.

❷ The XmlValidatingReader can work two ways. If we don't do any special setup, then it will throw an exception whenever it encounters a problem with the XML. The alternative is to register a ValidationEventHandler—a function that will be called whenever an error is found. This code says "call the function called XmlValidationHandler whenever the XML does not conform to the schema."

❸ The XmlDocument class can read in XML using an XmlReader. In fact, it always uses an XmlReader to read in XML, the same way a DataAdapter uses a DataReader under the covers. In this case, though, we are explicitly telling the XmlDocument to load using the provided XmlReader—the one that validates. It will step through all the data and notify us of any problems.

❹ The default behavior of the XmlValidatingReader is to throw an exception when it finds an error unless we register a handler for errors. But we did register a handler, so why are we also catching the exception? We are also telling the XmlDocument to load the XML—even though the validating reader would notify us of the problem, the Xml-Document cannot load bogus data, and so the exception is thrown for invalid XML. On the other hand, the XmlDocument can load data that doesn't match a schema, as long as it is well formed; so when we try to validate against a schema, the validating method will be used.

❺ As long as the XmlDocument can handle the error, even if it violates the schema, we will be notified by a call to this method that prints out the details of the error. The method will be called once for every error found.

Results

When we load the messed-up XML using this code, an exception is thrown telling us of the problem. The error message that appears is as follows:

```
System.Xml.XmlException: The 'Classroom' start tag on line '12'
doesn't match the end tag of 'Class' in file 'file:///C:/Projects/
ADOXML/   bin/Debug/XMLWithError.XML'.
Line 12, position 28.
```

This error message is pretty good; it tells us exactly what was wrong, and where. I should warn you, though, that not all the error messages you might receive are as clear.

27.3.2   Validating against a schema

Now we want to make the XML be validated against a schema. The first step (after fixing the mismatched tag) is to make the XML document reference the schema. This is a little trickier than it sounds. Here is what the XML will look like:

```
<?xml version="1.0" standalone="yes"?>
<TeacherInfo xmlns:xsi="http://www.w3.org/2001/XMLSchema-instance"
             xsi:noNamespaceSchemaLocation="TeacherSchema.XSD">
  <Teachers>
    <TeacherID>1</TeacherID>
    <TeacherName>Mr. Biddick               </TeacherName>
    .
    .
```

We are modifying the root node of the document to refer to the schema. There are two formats for specifying the location of the schema: an `xsi:schemaLocation` attribute that specifies the namespace associated with the schema, and the `xsi:no-NamespaceSchemaLocation` attribute that indicates the location and no namespace (we're using this format).

These attributes are defined in the schema that defines how XML documents (or Instances of Xml Schemas—the reason for *xsi* in the namespace declaration) reference schemas. To use these attributes, we need to reference that schema, which is why we declare the `xsi` namespace before using them. (This process gets even trickier when you are using multiple namespaces, but, again, that is the topic of another book.)

The next step is to make the data violate the schema in some way. To do so, we add a new tag to one of the teachers:

```
<Teachers>
  <TeacherID>2</TeacherID>
  <TeacherName>Ms. Fortune               </TeacherName>
  <Classroom>A1        </Classroom>
  <Subject>English          </Subject>
  <ChalkColor>Blue</ChalkColor>
</Teachers>
```

Even though the new ChalkColor might be a perfectly legitimate thing to track (work with me here), it is not defined in any included schema, and so it's not legal. If we now run the code, we get the output shown in figure 27.1.

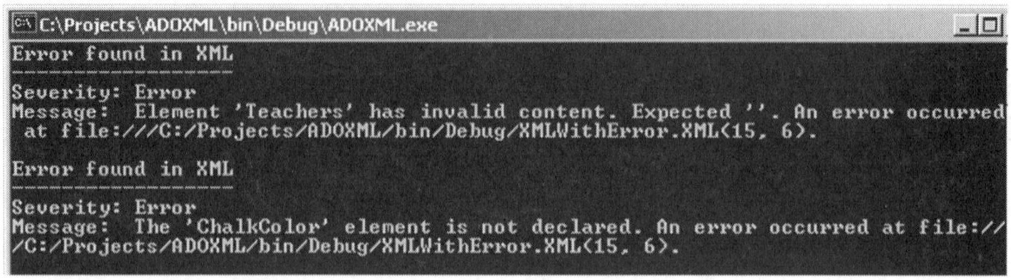

Figure 27.1 Schema errors

Notice that the error was found. In fact, multiple errors were generated from the same mistake—one indicating that the ChalkColor was not declared, and one indicating that the Teachers element has invalid content. Over time, the processor might get smart enough to realize that these are the same error![2]

27.4 *EXCLUDING INFORMATION*

So far in our examples, all the content of the DataSet has been represented in the XML, and vice-versa. However, you might want to have some items in the XML that do not appear in the DataSet. Imagine this scenario: several schools get together and agree on a common schema for defining Teachers. Some schools might then extend this schema to include additional information. Teachers can be transferred back and forth in XML, so you don't want to lose the extra information; but your database doesn't handle the extra information.

Let's simulate this situation. We have taken the previous schema and removed the definition for Classroom:

```
    .
    .
    .
<xsd:sequence>
  <xsd:element name="TeacherID" type="xsd:int" minOccurs="0" />
  <xsd:element name="TeacherName" type="xsd:string"
                                        minOccurs="0" />
  <xsd:element name="Subject" type="xsd:string" minOccurs="0" />
</xsd:sequence>
    .
    .
    .
```

Now, with the following code, we will link an XmlDocument (that contains Classroom tags) to a DataSet, making use of the schema missing the Classes data:

───────────────────────

[2] To be fair, it is a nontrivial problem to solve.

```
public void XmlMissingLinkTestFromXml()
{
    // Create the DataSet and infer the schema from the XML
    DataSet ds = new DataSet();
    ds.ReadXmlSchema("SchemaMinusClasses.XSD");

    // Put the XML into an XML document linked to the DataSet
    XmlDataDocument xdd = new XmlDataDocument(ds);
    xdd.Load("XmlWriteTest1.XML");

    // Display the data in the DataSet
    PrintDataSet(ds);

    // Confirm that the XML still contains the Classroom data
    Console.WriteLine(FormatXml(xdd.OuterXml));
}
```

This example is very similar to the linking sample in chapter 26, but instead of inferring a schema from XML, we are reading in a schema—in this case, the schema that does not contain the Classroom field. The rest of the link process is exactly the same: it creates an XmlDataDocument associated with the DataSet and loads the XML.

Let's look at the data in the DataSet (figure 27.2).

Figure 27.2
The DataSet part of the output

Notice that the Classroom field is missing. Now, figure 27.3 shows the XML.

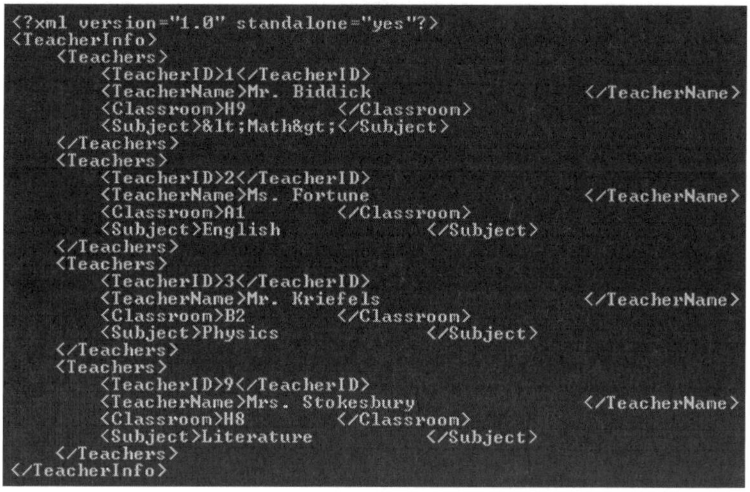

Figure 27.3
The XML part of the output

And the Classroom information is still there! These two can be manipulated separately, and the changes will be reflected in both places appropriately—however, the extra information in the Classroom elements will be untouched.

The official way of referring to this process is to say that the XML document maintains its *fidelity*. The exact order of the data in the XML document is not guaranteed, however, so don't be surprised if your tags end up being moved around.

27.5 DEFINING CONSTRAINTS

DataSets can contain constraints that force the data to be unique or to be based on a foreign key. XML schemas similarly have ways to define constraints. The DataSet can pick up these constraints and enforce them by creating Constraint objects.

Unfortunately, the schema validation mechanism of .NET does not currently have the ability to enforce these constraints, which means they are just definitions for the DataSet. For that reason, I will not spend a lot of time on them, but I will show the format they take in the XML.

27.5.1 Unique constraints

A unique constraint indicates that the value in a field must be either unique against all other values in a field or null. XSDs also have a unique concept, which is similar, except that the value must be unique—there is no concept of null. The following XSD is the same schema with which we have been working, but with a unique constraint added to the end:

```
<?xml version="1.0" standalone="yes"?>
<xsd:schema id="TeacherInfo" xmlns="" xmlns:xsd="http://www.w3.org/2001/
XMLSchema"
              xmlns:msdata="urn:schemas-microsoft-com:xml-msdata">
  <xsd:element name="TeacherInfo" msdata:IsDataSet="true">
    <xsd:complexType>
      <xsd:choice maxOccurs="unbounded">
        <xsd:element name="Teachers">
          <xsd:complexType>
            <xsd:sequence>
              <xsd:element name="TeacherID" type="xsd:int"
                                          minOccurs="0" />
              <xsd:element name="TeacherName" type="xsd:string"
                                          minOccurs="0" />
              <xsd:element name="Classroom" type="xsd:string" />
              <xsd:element name="Subject" type="xsd:string"
                                          minOccurs="0" />
            </xsd:sequence>
          </xsd:complexType>
        </xsd:element>
      </xsd:choice>
    </xsd:complexType>
    <xsd:unique name="UniqueClass" msdata:PrimaryKey="true">
      <xsd:selector xpath=".//Teachers" />
      <xsd:field xpath="Classroom" />
```

```
      </xsd:unique>
    </xsd:element>
  </xsd:schema>
```

I want to avoid talking too much about XPath until chapter 28, but you probably noticed that the constraint uses XPath to identify the item that must be unique; it indicates that within the `Teachers` elements, the `Classroom` element must be unique.

You might also have noticed the `msdata:PrimaryKey` attribute. The DataSet uses this extension to the schema definition to determine if the unique tag should be converted to a primary key or to a regular constraint. If you are not indicating a primary key, then you can exclude this tag.

27.5.2 Other constraints

As you know, a unique constraint is not the only type of constraint—you can, for example, create foreign key constraints. XSD provides a notation that supports this functionality, using a `keyref` tag. However, to be useful, the schema must include the definition for another table. I will present an example in the next section, when we work with multiple tables.

If you need to create constraints via XSD, I recommend that you set up the scenario using a DataSet, and then use the `WriteXmlSchema()` method of the DataSet to see what the constraint should look like in XML.

27.6 REPRESENTING RELATIONSHIPS

So far we have been working with a single table of data, but one of the powerful things about DataSets is their ability to represent relationships. It is equally useful to be able to represent relationships with XML.

You can represent relationships without using schemas. The first example in this section does just that—it lets the DataSet determine the relationship from the XML. After that, I will show how that relationship would be represented in a schema, and finally I will show you a Microsoft-specific way to specify a relationship in the schema.

27.6.1 Relationships without a schema

A DataSet is relational, meaning that a relationship can be defined as a relationship between tables. XML is hierarchical, however, so you can represent a relationship more naturally in XML by using *nesting*—showing the child data beneath the parent data. For example, the data for Teachers and Classes could be represented in the following way:

```
<?xml version="1.0" standalone="yes"?>
<NewDataSet>
  <Teachers>
    <TeacherID>1</TeacherID>
    <TeacherName>Mr. Biddick</TeacherName>
    <Classroom>H9</Classroom>
```

```
      <Subject>Math</Subject>
    </Teachers>
    <Teachers>
      <TeacherID>2</TeacherID>
      <TeacherName>Ms. Fortune</TeacherName>
      <Classroom>A1</Classroom>
      <Subject>English</Subject>
      <Classes>
        <ClassID>4</ClassID>
        <TeacherID>2</TeacherID>
        <ClassName>Chemistry</ClassName>
        <Period>3</Period>
      </Classes>
      <Classes>
        <ClassID>7</ClassID>
        <TeacherID>2</TeacherID>
        <ClassName>Geometry</ClassName>
        <Period>4</Period>
      </Classes>
    </Teachers>
    .
    . (removed for space)
    .
</NewDataSet>
```

Notice how the data for the Classes table is nested beneath the data for the Teachers table. The following code will load the data into a DataSet and print out the DataSet. We're using the `PrintDataSet()` method from earlier, but it has been modified to list relationships at the bottom:

```
public void XmlReadRelatedTest()
{
    // Create the dataset from the XML
    DataSet ds = new DataSet();
    ds.ReadXml("XmlRelated.XML");

    // Write out the DataSet
    PrintDataSet(ds);
}
```

Figure 27.4 shows the output.

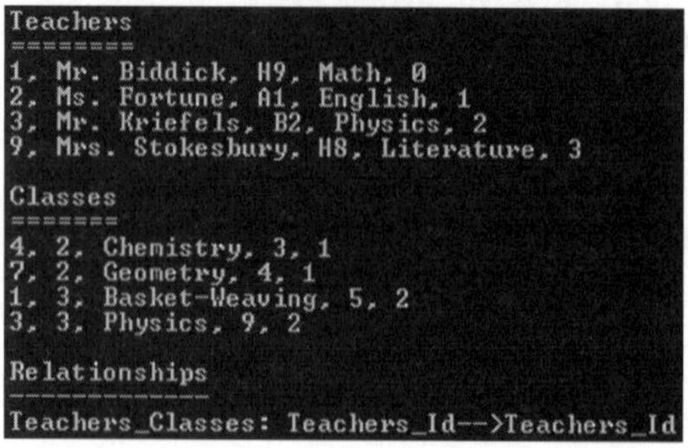

Figure 27.4
Hierarchical output

Notice that not only did the DataSet figure out the data for the two different tables, it also created the relationship for us. At first glance, it appears to have used the TeacherID to link the fields. But if you look closely, you will see that both tables have an additional field—rather than try to guess which field or fields provided the link, the DataSet added a new field (coincidentally named Teacher_id) and used it to define the link.

27.6.2 Nested schema

Let's look at the schema from the XML in the previous example, generated by calling WriteXmlSchema on the DataSet (listing 27.3).

Listing 27.3 Nested schema

```xml
<?xml version="1.0" standalone="yes"?>
<xsd:schema id="NewDataSet" xmlns="" xmlns:xsd="http://www.w3.org/2001/
XMLSchema"
            xmlns:msdata="urn:schemas-microsoft-com:xml-msdata">
  <xsd:element name="NewDataSet" msdata:IsDataSet="true">
    <xsd:complexType>
      <xsd:choice maxOccurs="unbounded">
        <xsd:element name="Teachers">
          <xsd:complexType>
            <xsd:sequence>
              <xsd:element name="TeacherID" type="xsd:string"
                           minOccurs="0" msdata:Ordinal="0" />
              <xsd:element name="TeacherName" type="xsd:string"
                           minOccurs="0" msdata:Ordinal="1" />
              <xsd:element name="Classroom" type="xsd:string"
                           minOccurs="0" msdata:Ordinal="2" />
              <xsd:element name="Subject" type="xsd:string"
                           minOccurs="0" msdata:Ordinal="3" />
              <xsd:element name="Classes"
                           minOccurs="0" maxOccurs="unbounded">

                <xsd:complexType>                    ❶ Nested complex type
                  <xsd:sequence>
                    <xsd:element name="ClassID" type="xsd:string"
                                 minOccurs="0" msdata:Ordinal="0" />
                    <xsd:element name="TeacherID" type="xsd:string"
                                 minOccurs="0" msdata:Ordinal="1" />
                    <xsd:element name="ClassName" type="xsd:string"
                                 minOccurs="0" msdata:Ordinal="2" />
                    <xsd:element name="Period" type="xsd:string"
                                 minOccurs="0" msdata:Ordinal="3" />
                  </xsd:sequence>
                  <xsd:attribute name="Teachers_Id"      ❷ New classes
                          type="xsd:int" use="prohibited" />     attribute
                </xsd:complexType>
              </xsd:element>
            </xsd:sequence>
```

```
            <xsd:attribute name="Teachers_Id"
                  msdata:AutoIncrement="true" type="xsd:int"
                              msdata:AllowDBNull="false"
                              use="prohibited" />        ❸ New teachers
          </xsd:complexType>                                 attribute
        </xsd:element>
      </xsd:choice>
    </xsd:complexType>
    <xsd:unique name="Constraint1" msdata:PrimaryKey="true">   ❹ Unique
      <xsd:selector xpath=".//Teachers" />                        constraint
      <xsd:field xpath="@Teachers_Id" />
    </xsd:unique>
    <xsd:keyref name="Teachers_Classes" refer="Constraint1"   ❺ Foreign key
                      msdata:IsNested="true">                     constraint
      <xsd:selector xpath=".//Classes" />
      <xsd:field xpath="@Teachers_Id" />
    </xsd:keyref>
  </xsd:element>
</xsd:schema>
```

All sorts of things are going on here. I will highlight some of the more pertinent ones.

❶ Earlier I said that complex types are generally turned into tables. That is still true, even if the complex type is defined to exist beneath another complex type.

❷ Here is the field that was autocreated for us; it's called Teacher_Id, and it's of type integer. Notice that it is an attribute rather than an element.

❸ And here is the Teachers version of the new field. Notice that several additional Microsoft-specific tags indicate that this element is autoincremented and doesn't allow nulls. This information is present purely for the DataSet.

❹ The new field that was automatically created has a constraint on it indicating that it must be unique. In addition, the schema indicates that this is the primary key for the table.

❺ The relationship between the two tables has been defined as a foreign key, which is mapped to the schema as a keyref element. The information here indicates how to find the information that is limited by the constraint.

27.6.3   Using the existing key via a schema

The automatic behavior is impressive, but it would be nice to make the DataSet use the key that already exists (confusingly called TeacherID rather than Teachers_Id, but still quite different). To accomplish this, we will need to modify the schema and then make the DataSet use the new schema. Listing 27.4 shows the schema modified to handle the ID in the desired way.

Listing 27.4   Modified schema

```xml
<?xml version="1.0" standalone="yes"?>
<xsd:schema id="TeacherInfo" xmlns=""
   xmlns:xsd="http://www.w3.org/2001/XMLSchema"
   xmlns:msdata="urn:schemas-microsoft-com:xml-msdata">
  <xsd:element name="TeacherInfo" msdata:IsDataSet="true">
    <xsd:complexType>
      <xsd:choice maxOccurs="unbounded">
        <xsd:element name="Teachers">
          <xsd:complexType>
            <xsd:sequence>
              <xsd:element name="TeacherID" type="xsd:string" />
              <xsd:element name="TeacherName" type="xsd:string"
                                                minOccurs="0" />
              <xsd:element name="Classroom" type="xsd:string"
                                                minOccurs="0" />
              <xsd:element name="Subject" type="xsd:string"
                                                minOccurs="0" />
              <xsd:element name="Classes" minOccurs="0"
                                      maxOccurs="unbounded">
                <xsd:complexType>
                  <xsd:sequence>
                    <xsd:element name="ClassID" type="xsd:string"
                                                minOccurs="0" />
                    <xsd:element name="TeacherID" type="xsd:string"
                                                minOccurs="0" />
                    <xsd:element name="ClassName" type="xsd:string"
                                                minOccurs="0" />
                    <xsd:element name="Period" type="xsd:string"
                                                minOccurs="0" />
                  </xsd:sequence>
                </xsd:complexType>
              </xsd:element>
            </xsd:sequence>
          </xsd:complexType>
        </xsd:element>
      </xsd:choice>
    </xsd:complexType>
    <xsd:unique name="Constraint1" msdata:PrimaryKey="true">
      <xsd:selector xpath=".//Teachers" />
      <xsd:field xpath="TeacherID" />
    </xsd:unique>
    <xsd:keyref name="Teachers_Classes" refer="Constraint1"
                                      msdata:IsNested="true">
      <xsd:selector xpath=".//Classes" />
      <xsd:field xpath="TeacherID" />
    </xsd:keyref>
  </xsd:element>
</xsd:schema>
```

The first big change is the removal of the `Teachers_Id` attribute from the Classes and Teachers tables—we deleted the tags. We also changed the constraints to reference the `TeacherID` element versus the `@Teachers_Id` attribute (the @ sign in front of the reference indicates an attribute versus an element).

The next step is to make the DataSet use this schema instead of inferring the schema from the XML. It would be convenient if we could put the reference to the schema into the XML:

```
<TeacherInfo xmlns:xsi="http://www.w3.org/2001/XMLSchema-instance"
             xsi:noNamespaceSchemaLocation="XMLRelatedSchema.XSD">
```

This is perfectly reasonable. Unfortunately, the `ReadXml()` method of the DataSet does not have the capability of picking up the schema from this code. The method can read the schema if it is in-line—that is, if it is part of the XML, which is legal and would look something like this:

```
<?xml version="1.0" standalone="yes"?>
<TeacherInfo>
  <xsd:schema id="TeacherInfo" xmlns=""
      xmlns:xsd="http://www.w3.org/2001/XMLSchema"
xmlns:msdata="urn:schemas-microsoft-com:xml-msdata">
    <xsd:element name="TeacherInfo" msdata:IsDataSet="true">
      <xsd:complexType>
        <xsd:choice maxOccurs="unbounded">
          <xsd:element name="Teachers">
            <xsd:complexType>
              <xsd:sequence>
                <xsd:element name="TeacherID" type="xsd:string" />
                <xsd:element name="TeacherName" type="xsd:string"
                                             minOccurs="0" />

        .
        .        (excluded for space)
        .
    </xsd:element>
  </xsd:schema>
  <Teachers>
    <TeacherID>1</TeacherID>
    <TeacherName>Mr. Biddick</TeacherName>
    <Classroom>H9</Classroom>
    <Subject>Math</Subject>
  </Teachers>
  <Teachers>
    <TeacherID>2</TeacherID>
    <TeacherName>Ms. Fortune</TeacherName>

    .
    .
```

As you can see, the schema is buried in the XML. Although this solution would solve the problem, it is messy. A more straightforward way is to modify the code to read in the schema first, and then read in the XML. The following code does so, and then prints out the data:

```
public void XmlReadRelatedTest()
{
    // Create the dataset from the schema, then read in the XML
    DataSet ds = new DataSet();
    ds.ReadXmlSchema("XmlRelatedSchema.XSD");
    ds.ReadXml("XmlRelated.XML");

    // Write out the DataSet
    PrintDataSet(ds);
}
```

The highlighted call will set up the schema of the DataSet based on our modified
XML. Figure 27.5 shows the output.

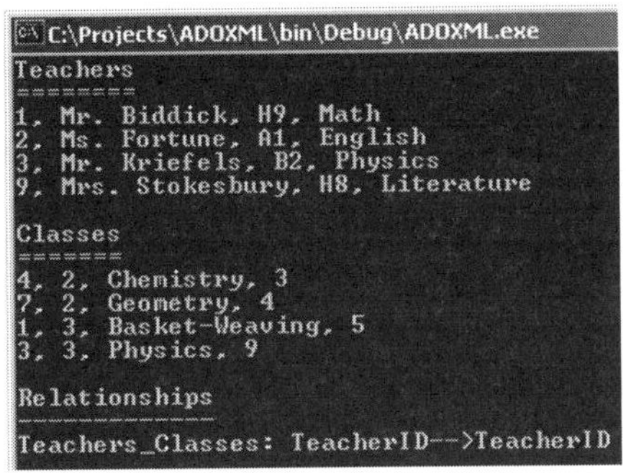

Figure 27.5
**Output from reading in the
schema and then the XML**

As you can see, the extra column is gone and the relationship is now properly on the
TeacherID field.

27.6.4   Un-nesting the data

Although nesting the data helps by automatically implying the schema for relationships, it is not the only way to set up a relationship. As you saw in the last example,
the details of the relationship can be specified separately anyway, so it will work even
if the data is not nested. If we wanted to (and we were feeling masochistic), we could go
through by hand and modify the schema and the data appropriately. However, given
that we have a computer that can do it for us, let's make .NET do the work. It is easy:

```
public void XmlUnnestSchema()
{
    // Read in the schema and the data
    DataSet ds = new DataSet();
    ds.ReadXmlSchema("XmlRelatedSchema.XSD");
    ds.ReadXml("XmlRelated.XML");

    // Make the relationship non-nested
    DataRelation dr = ds.Relations[0];
    dr.Nested = false;

    // Write out the new schema and data
    ds.WriteXml("XmlRelatedUnnested.XML");
    ds.WriteXmlSchema("XmlRelatedSchemaUnnested.XSD");
}
```

This code reads in the schema and data into a DataSet, sets the relationship to be non-nested, and then writes out new versions. The new data looks like this:

```xml
<?xml version="1.0" standalone="yes"?>
<TeacherInfo>
  <Teachers>
    <TeacherID>1</TeacherID>
    <TeacherName>Mr. Biddick</TeacherName>
    <Classroom>H9</Classroom>
    <Subject>Math</Subject>
  </Teachers>
  .
  . (Excluded for space)
  .
  <Teachers>
    <TeacherID>9</TeacherID>
    <TeacherName>Mrs. Stokesbury</TeacherName>
    <Classroom>H8</Classroom>
    <Subject>Literature</Subject>
  </Teachers>
  <Classes>
    <ClassID>4</ClassID>
    <TeacherID>2</TeacherID>
    <ClassName>Chemistry</ClassName>
    <Period>3</Period>
  </Classes>
  .
  . (Excluded for space)
  .
  <Classes>
    <ClassID>3</ClassID>
    <TeacherID>3</TeacherID>
    <ClassName>Physics</ClassName>
    <Period>9</Period>
  </Classes>
</TeacherInfo>
```

As you can see, the tables are back to being side-by-side, an arrangement that is easier to read and edit. The relationship still exists, though—it is just buried in the schema (listing 27.5).

Listing 27.5   Un-nested schema

```xml
<xsd:schema id="TeacherInfo" xmlns=""
    xmlns:xsd="http://www.w3.org/2001/XMLSchema"
    xmlns:msdata="urn:schemas-microsoft-com:xml-msdata">
  <xsd:element name="TeacherInfo" msdata:IsDataSet="true">
    <xsd:complexType>
      <xsd:choice maxOccurs="unbounded">
        <xsd:element name="Teachers">          ❶ Teachers element/table
          <xsd:complexType>
            <xsd:sequence>
              <xsd:element name="TeacherID" type="xsd:string" />
              <xsd:element name="TeacherName" type="xsd:string"
                                              minOccurs="0" />
```

```
                    <xsd:element name="Classroom" type="xsd:string"
                                                minOccurs="0" />
                    <xsd:element name="Subject" type="xsd:string"
                                                minOccurs="0" />
                </xsd:sequence>
              </xsd:complexType>
            </xsd:element>
          <xsd:element name="Classes" minOccurs="0"          ❷ Classes element/table
                maxOccurs="79228162514264337593543950335">
            <xsd:complexType>
              <xsd:sequence>
                <xsd:element name="ClassID" type="xsd:string"
                                            minOccurs="0" />
                <xsd:element name="TeacherID" type="xsd:string"
                                            minOccurs="0" />
                <xsd:element name="ClassName" type="xsd:string"
                                            minOccurs="0" />
                <xsd:element name="Period" type="xsd:string"
                                            minOccurs="0" />
              </xsd:sequence>
            </xsd:complexType>
          </xsd:element>
        </xsd:choice>
      </xsd:complexType>
      <xsd:unique name="Constraint1" msdata:PrimaryKey="true">
        <xsd:selector xpath=".//Teachers" />
        <xsd:field xpath="TeacherID" />                     ❸ Constraint
      </xsd:unique>
      <xsd:keyref name="Teachers_Classes" refer="Constraint1">
        <xsd:selector xpath=".//Classes" />
        <xsd:field xpath="TeacherID" />
      </xsd:keyref>
    </xsd:element>
</xsd:schema>
```

❶ Here is the definition for the Teachers element. It is basically the same as before, but it no longer contains the Classes definition.

❷ The Classes definition is now broken out. An interesting problem with the .NET version with which I am working (which I am sure will be fixed in the final release) is that the maxOccurs attribute is set to an incredibly huge number. The code should really look like this:

```
maxOccurs="unbounded"
```

❸ These Constraints should look familiar; they are virtually the same as in the nested example. The one difference is that there is no nested attribute on the keyref constraint:

```
msdata:IsNested="true"
```

The data is not nested, so this value is false (the default) and the entire attribute is excluded.

If we now load this schema and XML into a DataSet, the results appear the same as with the data, so I won't show them. You can either trust me, or run it yourself.

27.7 STRONGLY TYPED DATASETS

You have seen throughout this chapter that the schema and DataSet concepts are quite related. Once you load a schema into a DataSet, it represents that schema, and you can access data based on that schema:

```
ds.Tables["Teachers"].Columns["Classroom"]
```

You can think of this code as *late-bound.* That is the case because the names of the items, Teachers and Classroom in the example, are just strings at compile-time. Not until the code runs do you know if the code is correct, or if it refers to an illegal element.

Much of the time this behavior is appropriate—after all, databases are somewhat transitory and can change. On the other hand, many databases are set up ahead of time and will not change. In that case, it would be better to have a way to make the code explicitly aware of the constructs within the DataSet. Then we could do things like this:

```
ds.Teachers.ClassroomColumn
```

The major advantage would be that this code is *early bound*—that is, the compiler checks to make sure the items are referenced long before the code ever runs. Some other advantages include an easier-to-read format and, of course, the benefit of intellisense to autofill the items as you type.

As I am sure you have guessed, .NET has the ability to do this. In fact, we made extensive use of the capability in part 4, when talking about data-bound controls. However, we didn't discuss the mechanism involved.

Visual Studio has a built-in schema editor. This editor gives you a visual representation of the entities and relationships within a schema (figure 27.6).

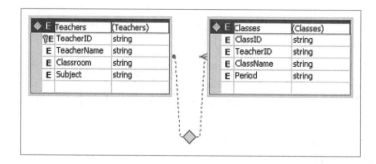

Figure 27.6
Visual schema editor

This visual representation sits on top of the XSD. In fact, at the bottom of the window are some tabs that let you switch back and forth between the visual view and the XSD itself (figure 27.7).

The tab for the XSD is labeled XML. (Don't forget that an XSD is also legal XML.) Interestingly, the other tab, which shows the visual representation of the schema, is labeled DataSet. This is no mistake— it is easy to make this schema create a DataSet.

Figure 27.7 Switching between the visual view and the XSD view

There are a number of ways to create this specific DataSet, which is called a *strongly typed* DataSet because all the types (tables, fields, and so forth) are strongly associated with the code and thus can be enforced by the compiler. The easiest way is to right-click on your project and add a new item. Under the Data node of the tree is an option to add a new DataSet (figure 27.8).

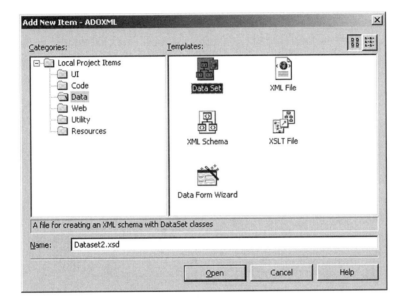

**Figure 27.8
Creating a
new DataSet**

After you have added this item, you can edit visually by dragging database elements, relationships, and so on onto the visual designer (as you did in part 4) or by editing the schema directly.

Alternatively, if you already have a schema, you can add it to your project. There is one caveat, however—even though the schema will be added, and you can edit it visually, it will not by default generate a strongly typed DataSet. To make it do this, you must edit the properties of the schema. Right-click on the XSD file in the Solution Explorer and choose Properties (figure 27.9).

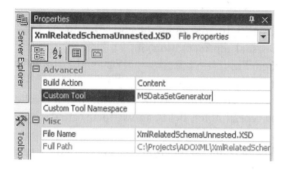

Figure 27.9
XSD properties

When you first bring up this properties list for an XSD you have manually added, the Custom Tool property will be empty. Type in "MSDataSetGenerator" to tell the environment that when you build the project, you want the XSD to be run through this special tool to generate a DataSet. Once you have built, go back to the Solution Explorer and click on the Show All Files button at the top. Now you can open a tree of files underneath the XSD (figure 27.10).

Figure 27.10
The files related to the schema

Two files show up under the XSD. The .xsx file is nothing more than some hint info for the visual designer—where items are located and so forth. The .cs file, however, is the implementation of the strongly typed DataSet. If you open this file, you will see that it has created a class named appropriately, based on your schema, which has subclasses and elements to match the content of the schema:

```
public class TeacherInfo : System.Data.DataSet {

    private TeachersDataTable tableTeachers;

    private ClassesDataTable tableClasses;

    private DataRelation relationTeachers_Classes;

    public TeacherInfo() {
        this.InitClass();
    }

    private TeacherInfo(SerializationInfo info,
                                  StreamingContext context) {
    .
    .
    .
```

This code is ugly, as is often the case with autogenerated code. That is not a problem, though, because you should never edit this file directly. If you do, you will probably regret it, because any changes to the schema, or even a standard rebuild, will completely overwrite this file.

The important thing to know is that this new class exists, and that it is derived from DataSet. Thus you can use it the same way as a DataSet—except that its schema is already set up for you. You can also use the strongly typed notation, directly referencing the contents of the schema. So, the notation we talked about earlier

```
ds.Teachers.ClassroomColumn
```

will work as advertised. Intellisense will work, and the compiler will catch errors—as long as the schema is up to date.

27.7.1 Creating strongly typed DataSets from the command line

You do not have to use Visual Studio to generate a strongly typed DataSet. A command-line tool called XSD can do it for you. The syntax looks like this:

```
XSD /d XMLRelatedSchema.XSD
```

This will generate a DataSet derivation (that is what the /d is for) based on the XML-RelatedSchema.XSD file. The derivation will be in C# by default and will have the same name as the XSD file, but with a .cs extension.

The tool will also generate code in other languages and has a handful of other options. If you type "XSD" at the command line, the tool will list its options.

In addition to benefiting those people who do not generally use the Visual Studio environment, this tool offers some other advantages. If you want to edit the derivation without its being overwritten, you can use this tool to generate the .cs file, and then add the .cs file to your project without involving the schema. You lose the ability to have the system automatically update the .cs file when the schema changes, but you gain the surety that the file will not be overwritten.

27.7.2 Extending a strongly typed DataSet

Using the command-line tool to create your DataSet is one way to make a strongly typed DataSet that you can edit, but you lose the ability to update the schema and have the DataSet mirror your changes. Also, the autogenerated code is ugly, and you might have to spend a lot of time cleaning it up.

A simple mechanism for extending a strongly typed DataSet is to create a derivation:

```
public class ExtendedTeacherInfo : TeacherInfo
```

You can then add as many methods as you like.

27.8 SUMMARY

In some ways, this chapter has covered a lot of ground. But it has also demonstrated that there is a lot to schemas—far more than could conveniently be covered in a book on ADO.NET. I've shown you specifically how schemas can be used with ADO.NET and also given you a starting point for understanding schemas.

There are still a few holes in the way in which ADO.NET interacts with XML, as you have seen. For example, referenced schemas are not automatically picked up. Nonetheless, I cannot think of any other environment that gives you so much flexibility when working with XML and databases. Even the few holes have some fairly straightforward workarounds.

The next chapter gives a brief introduction to querying using XPath and transforming data using XSL Transforms.

C H A P T E R   2 8

XPath queries and XSL Transforms

I went back and forth about whether to include a chapter on XPath and XSLT. This is not a book about XML, and it could not possibly cover the complexities of these two technologies. On the other hand, a brief introduction might provide enough information on the topic for the purposes of using XML with ADO.NET, and might make it clear whether the technology is appropriate and worth exploring in more depth.

In the end I compromised. This chapter provides a brief introduction to XPath and demonstrates one XSLT Transform against an XML document linked to a DataSet. This is a fairly short chapter, but it will give you a feel for XPath and XSLT.

XPath is a mechanism for querying XML documents. It was originally part of XSLT, which is a way of transforming an XML document from one schema to another. XPath provided the mechanism for identifying what elements in the document needed to change. It was quickly realized that XPath was useful by itself, and it was separated into its own standard.

This chapter begins by showing how to do XPath queries against an XMLDocument. The XML document I will use will be linked to a DataSet. After showing this technique, I will talk about some of the syntax of XPath, although this won't be a complete reference. Finally, I will demonstrate how to use XSLT to make changes to an XML document that is linked to a DataSet.

28.1 USING XPATH

Just as SQL lets you query against a relational database, XPath lets you query against an XML document. Of course, the syntax is completely different; after all, an XML document is hierarchical and not relational. Thus you not only search for particular values, as you do with SQL, but you can also search for particular structures—for example, all the Subject elements that are directly below a Teachers element.

There are several ways of using XPath against an XmlDocument. In the simplest model, you can send an XPath query in one of two methods that return either an individual node or a collection of nodes. The following code sets up an XMLDocument linked to a DataSet, and then does two different XPath queries—one for a set of results, and one for a single result:

```
// These should really appear at the top of your file
using System.Data;
using System.Data.SqlClient;
using System.Xml;

public void XPathTest(SqlConnection conn)
{
    // Create and fill the dataset
    string strSQL = "SELECT * From Teachers";
    SqlDataAdapter sda = new SqlDataAdapter(strSQL,conn);
    DataSet ds = new DataSet();
    sda.Fill(ds,"Teachers");

    // Create a synchronized XmlDocument
    XmlDataDocument xdd = new XmlDataDocument(ds);

    // Use XPath to select all of the Subject nodes
    XmlNodeList xnl = xdd.SelectNodes("//Teachers/Subject");

    // Use XPath to select the first Subject node
    XmlNode xn = xdd.SelectSingleNode("//Teachers/Subject");
}
```

Don't worry about the syntax of the XPath query for the moment. The point is that you can do one of the two types of query to return a list of nodes or a single node.

This technique is handy if you want to do a quick and dirty query, but it has a couple of problems. First is performance. XPath is very fast—it gains its speed by compiling the query into a highly efficient format. The problem is that when using these simple select mechanisms, the expression is recompiled every time you make the call. Unless you have a large document, the speed advantages of XPath are lost in the compile step.

The second problem is positional. Using these methods, the query is like an SQL query—you are querying against the entire document every time. XPath, however, was designed around the idea of maintaining position. You do a query that positions you to a certain place within the document; then you do another query from that position, and the query is done relative to your new position.

To handle these issues, .NET provides a number of useful classes, including:

- *XPathNavigator*—Specifically designed to move through XML using XPath and other methods. You can navigate through the document and also query for particular results. You can retrieve an XPathNavigator from an XmlDocument quite easily:

```
XPathNavigator navigator = xdd.CreateNavigator();
```

- *XPathExpression*—Used to contain a compiled XPath query or expression. The methods on XPathNavigator that take an XPath query generally will take either a string or an XPathExpression as an argument. If you intend to reuse the same expression, it is a good idea to compile it for efficiency. This is also fairly straightforward:

```
XPathExpression exp = navigator.Compile("//Teachers/Subject");
```

If you want to use these classes, you need to use the appropriate namespace:

```
using Sytem.Xml.XPath;
```

When we do a transform later in this chapter, these classes will be used under the covers, although you will not see them directly. To explain the model behind XPath, however, using the simple `Select` methods on the document will suffice.

28.2 BASIC XPATH SYNTAX

The easiest way to demonstrate how XPath works is to show a lot of examples. For the examples, I will use a portion of the Teachers XML from the earlier chapters. I have added some attributes and some elements for some of the examples:

```
<TeacherInfo>
  <Teachers>
    <TeacherID>1</TeacherID>
    <TeacherName>Mr. Biddick</TeacherName>
    <Classroom Floor='1'>H9</Classroom>
    <Subject>Math</Subject>
    <Teachers Student='TRUE'>
      <TeacherID>1A</TeacherID>
      <TeacherName>John</TeacherName>
    </Teachers>
  </Teachers>
  <Teachers>
    <TeacherID>2</TeacherID>
    <TeacherName>Ms. Fortune</TeacherName>
    <Classroom Floor='2'>A1</Classroom>
    <Subject>English</Subject>
  </Teachers>
</TeacherInfo>
```

Before starting on the details, I should tell you that XPath uses two formats: a long notation and a short notation. For example, these two statements are equivalent:

```
short: // Classroom[@Floor='1']
long:  //child::Classroom[attribute::Floor='1']
```

I will stick to the short notation, except where referring to an explicit axis.[1]

28.2.1 Absolute and relative paths

Just as with a directory path, you can specify an absolute path and a relative path to a particular item. A single forward slash (/) at the front of an expression indicates an absolute path, whereas two slashes (//) indicate a relative path. Here are some examples.

The expression

```
/TeacherInfo/Teachers/TeacherName
```

selects all nodes whose root path starts with TeacherInfo, followed by Teachers, followed by TeacherName:

```
<TeacherInfo>
  <Teachers>
    <TeacherID>1</TeacherID>
    <TeacherName>Mr. Biddick</TeacherName>
    <Classroom Floor='1'>H9</Classroom>
    <Subject>Math</Subject>
    <Teachers Student='TRUE'>
      <TeacherID>1A</TeacherID>
      <TeacherName>John</TeacherName>
    </Teachers>
  </Teachers>
  <Teachers>
    <TeacherID>2</TeacherID>
    <TeacherName>Ms. Fortune</TeacherName>
    <Classroom Floor='2'>A1</Classroom>
    <Subject>English</Subject>
  </Teachers>
</TeacherInfo>
```

This expression

```
//Teachers/TeacherName
```

selects all nodes whose parent is Teachers, no matter what the parent of the Teachers node is. In the example XML, this expression will return the same teachers as before, but will also now pick up the nested student teacher:

```
<TeacherInfo>
  <Teachers>
    <TeacherID>1</TeacherID>
    <TeacherName>Mr. Biddick</TeacherName>
    <Classroom Floor='1'>H9</Classroom>
```

---

[1] Yes, I will explain what that means in a little while (section 28.2.6).

```
      <Subject>Math</Subject>
      <Teachers Student='TRUE'>
        <TeacherID>1A</TeacherID>
        <TeacherName>John</TeacherName>
      </Teachers>
    </Teachers>
    <Teachers>
      <TeacherID>2</TeacherID>
      <TeacherName>Ms. Fortune</TeacherName>
      <Classroom Floor='2'>A1</Classroom>
      <Subject>English</Subject>
    </Teachers>
</TeacherInfo>
```

When you use either of those notations, the entire document is searched, which is always the case anyway with the `SelectNodes` or `SelectSingleNode` methods. If you are using the navigator, though, you can ask for items relative to the current selection by excluding either the / or the //:

```
Classroom/@Floor
```

This expression says to find the Classroom child below the current node, and the `Floor` attribute below that. There is no current node per se using the `Select-Nodes` methods, so the expression will not return anything; but if you are using the navigator and had previously done a select that made a Teachers node current, then the Classroom would be found below it. You will see this technique in action later when we do the XSL Transform.

28.2.2   Using the wildcard

The asterisk (*) can be used to indicate any pattern. So, for example, the expression

```
//Teachers/*
```

will select everything under a Teachers node:

```
<TeacherInfo>
  <Teachers>
    <TeacherID>1</TeacherID>
    <TeacherName>Mr. Biddick</TeacherName>
    <Classroom Floor='1'>H9</Classroom>
    <Subject>Math</Subject>
    <Teachers Student='TRUE'>
      <TeacherID>1A</TeacherID>
      <TeacherName>John</TeacherName>
    </Teachers>
  </Teachers>
  <Teachers>
    <TeacherID>2</TeacherID>
    <TeacherName>Ms. Fortune</TeacherName>
    <Classroom Floor='2'>A1</Classroom>
    <Subject>English</Subject>
  </Teachers>
</TeacherInfo>
```

You can use the wildcard in other positions in the expression as well. Thus the expression

```
/TeacherInfo/*/TeacherID
```

would return any `TeacherID` elements below any element that was directly below `TeacherInfo`.

28.2.3 Selecting attributes

So far, all the expressions have selected elements, but you can also select attributes—attributes are also considered to be nodes. To indicate attributes, precede them with an at sign (@). The expression `//@Floor` will select all `Floor` attributes:

```
<TeacherInfo>
  <Teachers>
    <TeacherID>1</TeacherID>
    <TeacherName>Mr. Biddick</TeacherName>
    <Classroom Floor='1'>H9</Classroom>
    <Subject>Math</Subject>
    <Teachers Student='TRUE'>
      <TeacherID>1A</TeacherID>
      <TeacherName>John</TeacherName>
    </Teachers>
  </Teachers>
  <Teachers>
    <TeacherID>2</TeacherID>
    <TeacherName>Ms. Fortune</TeacherName>
    <Classroom Floor='2'>A1</Classroom>
    <Subject>English</Subject>
  </Teachers>
</TeacherInfo>
```

You can also be more explicit and say you want only `Floor` attributes that are part of the `Classroom` elements that are part of `Teachers` elements:

```
//Teachers/Classroom/@Floor
```

Of course, you might want to select elements that contain the attribute, rather than the attribute itself. XPath has a notation for specifying additional criteria: you specify what nodes you want in the normal way, and then add the extra criteria in square brackets ([]) after the clause. So, for example, you could specify any elements that have a `Floor` attribute:

```
//Classroom[@Floor]
```

This expression will give the entire element:

```
<TeacherInfo>
  <Teachers>
    <TeacherID>1</TeacherID>
    <TeacherName>Mr. Biddick</TeacherName>
    <Classroom Floor='1'>H9</Classroom>
    <Subject>Math</Subject>
    <Teachers Student='TRUE'>
```

```
      <TeacherID>1A</TeacherID>
      <TeacherName>John</TeacherName>
    </Teachers>
  </Teachers>
  <Teachers>
    <TeacherID>2</TeacherID>
    <TeacherName>Ms. Fortune</TeacherName>
    <Classroom Floor='2'>A1</Classroom>
    <Subject>English</Subject>
  </Teachers>
</TeacherInfo>
```

In this example, both instances of Classroom have the attribute; but if the attribute were not present, then the node would not have been selected.

28.2.4 Using expressions

Checking for the existence of an attribute is handy, but it would be better if you could look for a particular value. The following expression

```
//Classroom[@Floor='1']
```

looks for any Classrooms on the first floor:

```
<TeacherInfo>
  <Teachers>
    <TeacherID>1</TeacherID>
    <TeacherName>Mr. Biddick</TeacherName>
    <Classroom Floor='1'>H9</Classroom>
    <Subject>Math</Subject>
    <Teachers Student='TRUE'>
      <TeacherID>1A</TeacherID>
      <TeacherName>John</TeacherName>
    </Teachers>
  </Teachers>
  <Teachers>
    <TeacherID>2</TeacherID>
    <TeacherName>Ms. Fortune</TeacherName>
    <Classroom Floor='2'>A1</Classroom>
    <Subject>English</Subject>
  </Teachers>
</TeacherInfo>
```

You can also check to see if an element has a particular value. The following expression

```
//Teachers[Subject='Math']
```

looks for any teacher whose subject is math:

```
<TeacherInfo>
  <Teachers>
    <TeacherID>1</TeacherID>
    <TeacherName>Mr. Biddick</TeacherName>
    <Classroom Floor='1'>H9</Classroom>
    <Subject>Math</Subject>
    <Teachers Student='TRUE'>
```

```
      <TeacherID>1A</TeacherID>
      <TeacherName>John</TeacherName>
    </Teachers>
  </Teachers>
  <Teachers>
    <TeacherID>2</TeacherID>
    <TeacherName>Ms. Fortune</TeacherName>
    <Classroom Floor='2'>A1</Classroom>
    <Subject>English</Subject>
  </Teachers>
</TeacherInfo>
```

28.2.5 Using functions in expressions

Just as with SQL, expressions can contain various functions. For example, a function returns the number of occurrences of a particular type of element:

```
//Teachers[count(Teachers) > 0]
```

This expression will give us all Teachers that contain at least one Teachers node below. The argument can even contain nesting of its own:

```
//Teachers[count(Teachers[@Student='TRUE']) > 0]
```

This version more explicitly states that there must be at least one Teachers element that has a Student attribute whose value is TRUE. Of course, with our simple XML, both of these expressions will return the same Teachers node as the last example.

A number of functions are supported, including mathematical expressions and some positional functions. Another useful function is position(), which yields the position of the potentially selected node. For example, we can ask for only the first three elements that meet a criteria:

```
//Teachers[position() < 3].
```

This is slightly different XML, but it shows the results:

```
<TeacherInfo>
  <Teachers Name='Mr. Biddick' Classroom='A1'/>
  <Teachers Name='Mrs. Fortune' Classroom='B2'/>
  <Teachers Name='Mr. Underwood' Classroom='C3'/>
  <Teachers Name='Mr. Kriefels' Classroom='A1'/>
  <Teachers Name='Mrs. Martell' Classroom='A1'/>
</TeacherInfo>
```

28.2.6 Specifying axes

The examples so far have not specified the axis of any of the nodes. The axis indicates the relationship relative to your current location. I've omitted it because we always wanted the child axis, which is the default; but we can include a number of other axes.[2] Table 28.1 shows some of the most important.

---

[2] Yes, this is the plural of axis, pronounced ax-ees.

Table 28.1   Different XPath Axes

Axis	Description
child	Indicates a node directly below the current node. This is the default if no axis is specified.
descendant	Indicates any node that is a child, or a child of that child, and so on—the whole tree of nodes below the current position.
parent	The parent of the current node. This axis can also be abbreviated with two dots (..).
ancestor	The parent or the parent's parent, and so on—the reverse of descendant.
following-sibling	All elements at the same level following the current node.
preceding-sibling	All elements at the same level preceding the current node.

Let's look at some examples. The expression

```
/TeacherInfo/descendant::TeacherName
```

returns any descendants of the TeacherInfo root of type TeacherName:

```
<TeacherInfo>
  <Teachers>
    <TeacherID>1</TeacherID>
    <TeacherName>Mr. Biddick</TeacherName>
    <Classroom Floor='1'>H9</Classroom>
    <Subject>Math</Subject>
    <Teachers Student='TRUE'>
      <TeacherID>1A</TeacherID>
      <TeacherName>John</TeacherName>
    </Teachers>
  </Teachers>
  <Teachers>
    <TeacherID>2</TeacherID>
    <TeacherName>Ms. Fortune</TeacherName>
    <Classroom Floor='2'>A1</Classroom>
    <Subject>English</Subject>
  </Teachers>
</TeacherInfo>
```

The next one returns the TeacherName of any Teacher whose Classroom is on the first floor:

```
//TeacherName[following-sibling::Classroom[@Floor='1']]
```

It seems complicated, but you can break it into pieces. We are selecting any Teacher-Name nodes that meet a particular criteria. The criteria is that a following sibling called Classroom also has a condition—the Floor attribute is equal to 1:

```
<TeacherInfo>
  <Teachers>
    <TeacherID>1</TeacherID>
    <TeacherName>Mr. Biddick</TeacherName>
    <Classroom Floor='1'>H9</Classroom>
```

```
    <Subject>Math</Subject>
    <Teachers Student='TRUE'>
      <TeacherID>1A</TeacherID>
      <TeacherName>John</TeacherName>
    </Teachers>
  </Teachers>
  <Teachers>
    <TeacherID>2</TeacherID>
    <TeacherName>Ms. Fortune</TeacherName>
    <Classroom Floor='2'>A1</Classroom>
    <Subject>English</Subject>
  </Teachers>
</TeacherInfo>
```

28.2.7 Combining expressions

You can combine expressions to get multiple results. For example, you can use the expression

```
//TeacherID | //TeacherName
```

to ask for TeacherID nodes and TeacherName nodes:

```
<TeacherInfo>
  <Teachers>
    <TeacherID>1</TeacherID>
    <TeacherName>Mr. Biddick</TeacherName>
    <Classroom Floor='1'>H9</Classroom>
    <Subject>Math</Subject>
    <Teachers Student='TRUE'>
      <TeacherID>1A</TeacherID>
      <TeacherName>John</TeacherName>
    </Teachers>
  </Teachers>
  <Teachers>
    <TeacherID>2</TeacherID>
    <TeacherName>Ms. Fortune</TeacherName>
    <Classroom Floor='2'>A1</Classroom>
    <Subject>English</Subject>
  </Teachers>
</TeacherInfo>
```

You can also put ors into the narrowing clause:

```
//TeacherName[following-sibling::Classroom[@Floor='1'] |
             following-sibling::Classroom[@Floor='2']]
```

This expression extends the example from the previous section, but looks for either the first or second floor:

```
<TeacherInfo>
  <Teachers>
    <TeacherID>1</TeacherID>
    <TeacherName>Mr. Biddick</TeacherName>
    <Classroom Floor='1'>H9</Classroom>
    <Subject>Math</Subject>
```

```
      <Teachers Student='TRUE'>
        <TeacherID>1A</TeacherID>
        <TeacherName>John</TeacherName>
      </Teachers>
    </Teachers>
    <Teachers>
      <TeacherID>2</TeacherID>
      <TeacherName>Ms. Fortune</TeacherName>
      <Classroom Floor='2'>A1</Classroom>
      <Subject>English</Subject>
    </Teachers>
</TeacherInfo>
```

28.2.8   XPath summary

This has been a whirlwind tour of XPath, covering a number of highlights but not
going into much depth. It should provide enough information to let you get past any
simple tasks, and serve as a stepping-stone toward an XPath reference when you get to
the point of needing it.

28.3   *Transforming a DataSet using XSLT*

This section is not intended to teach you XSLT, but rather is designed to give you a
brief taste of what you can do with it. Normally, you use stylesheets[3] to convert one
XML document to another, or to another format such as HTML. You can transform
XML that is linked to a DataSet, but the transformation always creates a new document, so the data in the DataSet is not affected in any way.

So, why would you want to transform the XML? Because doing so saves a step—
instead of converting the DataSet to an XML document and an XSD schema and then
transforming them, you can use the XmlDataDocument's contents directly.

The prototypical example of XSLT is to convert XML into HTML. Not wishing
to be left out, I will provide a similar example: we'll take the contents of a DataSet containing the Teachers table and convert it to an HTML table.

28.3.1   The code

First, let's look at the code for doing the transform (listing 28.1).

> **Listing 28.1   Code to transform XML to HTML**

```
using System;
using System.Data;
using System.Data.SqlClient;
using System.Text;
using System.Xml;
using System.Xml.Xsl;
```

❶ Namespaces

---

[3] A stylesheet is another name for an XSL Transform.

```
public void XmlTransformTest(SqlConnection conn)
{
    // Create and fill the dataset
    string strSQL = "SELECT * From Teachers";
    SqlDataAdapter sda = new SqlDataAdapter(strSQL,conn);
    DataSet ds = new DataSet();
    ds.DataSetName = "TeacherInfo";
    sda.Fill(ds,"Teachers");

    // Create a synchronized XmlDocument                    ❷ Synchronize
    XmlDataDocument xdd = new XmlDataDocument(ds);             DataSet and XML

    // Create and load the transform
    XslTransform xsl = new XslTransform();                 ❸ Load transform
    xsl.Load("TeachersToHtml.XSL");

    // Write out the XML document to a new file via the transform
    XmlTextWriter writer =
        new XmlTextWriter("Teachers.html",Encoding.ASCII);  ❹ Perform
    xsl.Transform(xdd,null,writer);                            transform
    writer.Close();
}
```

❶ As usual, these `using` statements should appear at the top of the file but are shown here for convenience. Most of the namespaces are familiar, but two are worth separating out:

- `System.Xml.Xsl`—The `Xsl` namespace contains classes for working with XSL, including the XslTransform class.

- `System.Text`—We've used this one before, but we need it here for the `Encoding` enum used when initializing the XmlTextWriter.

❷ Everything to this point is the same as in the DataSet/XML linking example from chapter 26. We create and fill the DataSet, and then create the XmlDataDocument and initialize it with the DataSet.

❸ Here we are creating a new XslTransform and initializing it from the file containing the transform. In this example, we load from a file, but all the usual suspects are permissible—stream, TextWriter, and so on. We will look at the transform in a moment.

❹ The last step is to perform the transform. First we create a place to write the output, via an XmlTextWriter. The transform is a simple call on the XslTransform to which we pass the source XML (from our XmlDocument) and the destination (the XmlTextWriter). The middle argument, to which we pass `null`, specifies namespace options, which we don't care about for the example.

28.3.2 The XSL file

The code is straightforward. The real magic happens within the XSL file. Listing 28.2 shows the XSL, with some explanation of what is going on.

Listing 28.2 The stylesheet

```
<xsl:stylesheet version='1.0'
    xmlns:xsl='http://www.w3.org/1999/XSL/Transform'>      ❶ Stylesheet
                                                              declaration
  <xsl:template match="TeacherInfo">
    <HTML>
    <BODY>
    <TABLE BORDER="1">
      <xsl:apply-templates select="Teachers"/>             ❷ Build main
    </TABLE>                                                   body of HTML
    </BODY>
    </HTML>
  </xsl:template>

  <xsl:template match="Teachers">
    <TR>                                                   ❸ Build rows
    <TD><xsl:value-of select="TeacherName"/></TD>             of table
    <TD><xsl:value-of select="Classroom"/></TD>
    <TD><xsl:value-of select="Subject"/></TD>
    </TR>
  </xsl:template>

</xsl:stylesheet>
```

❶ Just about any XSL file will begin with a line like this. The notation should look familiar, because XSL files are also XML files. This is good because it means the XSL is validatable, but it is occasionally problematic when your final output is not entirely well-formed. It isn't a problem in this case, and rarely is a problem when you are converting XML to XML.[4]

❷ Three distinct things are going on this section:

- The `match` option tells the transform to search for the TeacherInfo node and use the provided template for all instances that are found. In our case, this will happen once, because TeacherInfo is the root node. Note that the match expression, `"TeacherInfo"`, is an XPath expression, indicating that a TeacherInfo node should be found as a child below the current node. This expression can be any legal XPath, but it needs to be relative to the current position, rather than to the document (so `TeacherInfo/SomeOtherNode` would be fine, but `//TeacherInfo` could cause problems).

---

[4] One issue with HTML is that, although it is tag-based, it is not always well-formed according to XML rules. This fact has led to the creation of XHTML, which is HTML that is also legal XML.

- It indicates raw text that will be included as part of the template. The HTML commands HTML, BODY, and TABLE will be put into the document every time TeacherInfo is found, which, in this example, will be just once.

- It indicates template elements that require additional processing. In this case, the apply-templates command says that the results from the Teachers template should be included. This is similar to the way the server-side bound controls worked in part 4.

❸ This template will search for every instance of Teachers relative to the current node and generate the results. Because it is called from inside the TeachersInfo match, it will look for "Teachers" below TeachersInfo. Again, this is XPath. Some of the items are raw content, such as the HTML for setting up the columns. Other items indicate that data should be retrieved from the document, selecting the subitems from the XML. The select statements are, you guessed it, more XPath.

Results

When we run the code using this stylesheet, we get an HTML file that looks like this (with some manual formatting on my part):

```
<HTML>
    <BODY>
        <TABLE BORDER="1">
            <TR><TD>Mr. Biddick</TD><TD>H9</TD><TD>Math</TD></TR>
            <TR><TD>Ms. Fortune</TD><TD>A1</TD><TD>English</TD></TR>
            <TR><TD>Mr. Kriefels</TD><TD>B2</TD><TD>Physics</TD></TR>
            <TR><TD>Mrs. Stokesbury</TD><TD>C3</TD><TD>Literature</TD></TR>
        </TABLE>
    </BODY>
</HTML>
```

For the more visually oriented, figure 28.1 shows the output in a browser.

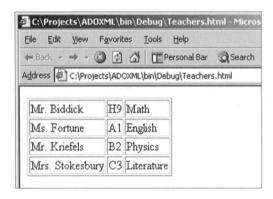

Figure 28.1
Visual output of the HTML

28.3.3 Example summary

This example uses only the simplest examples of XSL. XSL is very powerful, with looping constructs and various other real-language features. Even so, this example is fairly impressive—it shows how you can make your data work for you.

28.4 SUMMARY

I hope I have whetted your appetite for XPath and XSL Transforms. This chapter could do little more than that, but it should be enough to point you in the right direction and help you decide whether you want to use these technologies.

This chapter has gone a little off-topic for the book, with only the slightest tie-in to the use of ADO.NET. Chapter 29 is more on-topic and talks about using SQL Server's XML-related functionality from ADO.NET.

C H A P T E R   2 9

SQL Server XML features

When SQL Server 2000 was released (in September 2000), there was quite a focus on XML and support for the Internet. As a result, SQL Server 2000 shipped with several interesting features. For example, you can set up SQL Server 2000 to respond directly to HTTP requests (via IIS): the URI contains the details of a query which can then be returned as XML. A request might look something like:

```
http://ArF733/ADONetSamples?
            sql=SELECT+*+FROM+Teachers+FOR+XML+AUTO&root=root
```

Assuming, of course, that you exposed SQL Server appropriately. Queries via this mechanism are not limited to SQL; you can specify annotated schemas as part of the URL and do XPath queries against the relational data as though the data was stored as XML. Full-blown schemas were not yet standardized when SQL Server 2000 was released, so the schemas supported are XDR schemas (a subset of XSD schemas).

This chapter won't discuss this capability of SQL Server. First, it is a double-edged sword feature—yes, it provides a powerful mechanism, but I'm not entirely keen on the idea of exposing database engines directly over the Internet. Second, given the functionality of .NET, including web services and ASP.NET, this capability probably will be a technological dead-end (although I wouldn't be surprised if the next version of SQL Server allows you to directly expose web services).

I would like to discuss some XML features of SQL Server 2000. SQL Server has some capable mechanisms for returning data directly as XML, and it provides a mechanism for updating data using XML. Of course, given the DataSet's ability to convert back and forth to XML, you won't take advantage of these features as often; but they still certainly have their place.

29.1   RETRIEVING DATA AS XML

Given that the DataSet is so capable of converting data to XML, why would you want to directly read XML from SQL Server? First, using a DataSet involves overhead. The DataSet is a relatively bulky class, and you might not need its functionality. Second, for the DataSet to work with XML, it must first read all of the XML. Perhaps you only need to begin reading the XML until you have what you need, or perhaps you want to immediately begin using the XML before you have pulled it all down for the server. Finally, when retrieving nested data, it might be more efficient to pull the XML than individually joined rows.

The SQL Server data provider has a convenient mechanism for reading XML from SQL Server 2000, via the use of an XmlReader. Not only does it avoid the overhead of the DataSet, but it uses a stream, meaning that it only pulls data from the server as you request it.[1] To read data from SQL Server as XML, you must specify in your query that you want the results to be returned as XML, as well as the way you want the XML to be set up. SQL Server 2000 supports three modes for retrieving data as XML:

- *Raw*—Much like a traditional result set, each row that is returned from the database becomes an element, with each field represented as an attribute. If fields are joined, then the fields will show up as additional attributes.

- *Auto*—The data is returned as nested XML elements. If two tables are joined (say, Classes and Teachers), each Teacher will be returned as an element, and each associated Class will be returned as an XML element nested within the Teacher. The fields can be returned as either attributes or child elements of these nodes. This mode is called Auto because it automatically figures out how to nest the children.

- *Explicit*—This mode lets you specify in great detail how the XML should be returned. It gives you the most flexibility but is the hardest to use.

---

[1]   It will pull reasonable blocks from the server for efficiency, so it will read a little more than you ask for; but the data is presented as though it is retrieved as you ask.

29.1.1 Auto mode versus Raw mode

The explanation for Auto versus Raw is a little confusing—it is easier to understand the difference between the two modes by looking at an example. The difference is important when you are joining tables, so let's use the following query to return teachers and their classes:

```
SELECT Teachers.TeacherID,
       Teachers.TeacherName,
       Teachers.Subject,
       Teachers.Classroom,
       Classes.ClassID,
       Classes.ClassName,
       Classes.Period
       FROM Teachers LEFT OUTER JOIN Classes ON
       Teachers.TeacherID = Classes.TeacherID
```

Note that we are doing an outer join (You might also have seen this done using the older syntax, with *= in the where clause). If we executed this query and read the results, we would get a tabular result where each row contained fields from both tables; but because of the outer join, in some cases the results would be null (table 29.1).

Table 29.1 Results from an outer-join

Teachers table				Classes table		
Teacher ID	TeacherName	Subject	Classroom	Classes	ClassName	Period
1	Mr. Biddick	Math	H9	null	null	null
2	Ms. Fortune	English	A1	4	Chemistry	3
2	Ms. Fortune	English	A1	7	Geometry	4
3	Mr. Kriefels	Physics	B2	1	Basket-Weaving	5
3	Mr. Kriefels	Physics	B2	3	Physics	9
9	Mrs. Stokesbury	Literature	C3	null	null	null

Note that some data is repeated in the Teachers table because there are multiple Classes for the join, and some of the Teachers have null values for the Classes fields because there is no matching class for those teachers. This result is similar to the way XML is returned using the RAW keyword:

```
SELECT Teachers.TeacherID,
       Teachers.TeacherName,
       Teachers.Subject,
       Teachers.Classroom,
       Classes.ClassID,
       Classes.ClassName,
       Classes.Period
       FROM Teachers LEFT OUTER JOIN Classes
       ON Teachers.TeacherID = Classes.TeacherID
       FOR XML RAW
```

The FOR XML RAW clause is all we need to tell SQL Server 2000 that we want our results to be returned as XML. (We will look at code for retrieving the data a little later, in section 29.1.2.) Here is the way the XML is returned using the RAW keyword:

```
<row TeacherID="1" TeacherName="Mr. Biddick" Subject="Math"
                                                Classroom="H9" />
<row TeacherID="2" TeacherName="Ms. Fortune" Subject="English"
     Classroom="A1" ClassID="4" ClassName="Chemistry" Period="3" />
<row TeacherID="2" TeacherName="Ms. Fortune" Subject="English"
     Classroom="A1" ClassID="7" ClassName="Geometry" Period="4" />
<row TeacherID="3" TeacherName="Mr. Kriefels" Subject="Physics"
     Classroom="B2" ClassID="1" ClassName="Basket-Weaving"
                                                Period="5" />
<row TeacherID="3" TeacherName="Mr. Kriefels" Subject="Physics"
     Classroom="B2" ClassID="3" ClassName="Physics" Period="9" />
<row TeacherID="9" TeacherName="Mrs. Stokesbury"
     Subject="Literature" Classroom="C3" />
```

Notice that for every row that appears in the table, there is an element in the XML. We also have the same duplication where the child exists in multiple situations (two rows for TeacherID 2 and two rows for TeacherID 3). For those places where we got null in the table, the attributes are simply excluded from the XML.

This might be exactly the result you want; but a relationship exists between the Teachers and Child table, and it would be nice if the XML could represent that. That is where Auto mode comes in. Here is the same query, but using Auto instead of Raw:

```
SELECT Teachers.TeacherID,
       Teachers.TeacherName,
       Teachers.Subject,
       Teachers.Classroom,
       Classes.ClassID,
       Classes.ClassName,
       Classes.Period
       FROM Teachers LEFT OUTER JOINClasses
       ON Teachers.TeacherID = Classes.TeacherID
       FOR XML AUTO
```

Not much difference in the query, but the result are quite different:

```
<Teachers TeacherID="1" TeacherName="Mr. Biddick" Subject="Math"
                                                Classroom="H9">
  <Classes />
</Teachers>
<Teachers TeacherID="2" TeacherName="Ms. Fortune" Subject="English"
                                                Classroom="A1">
  <Classes ClassID="4" ClassName="Chemistry" Period="3" />
  <Classes ClassID="7" ClassName="Geometry" Period="4" />
</Teachers>
<Teachers TeacherID="3" TeacherName="Mr. Kriefels"
                              Subject="Physics" Classroom="B2">
  <Classes ClassID="1" ClassName="Basket-Weaving" Period="5" />
  <Classes ClassID="3" ClassName="Physics" Period="9" />
```

```
    </Teachers>
    <Teachers TeacherID="9" TeacherName="Mrs. Stokesbury" Subject="Literature"
                                                  Classroom="C3">
      <Classes />
    </Teachers>
```

First, the rows returned are identified by their names, rather than the boring and unhelpful row from the raw output. Second, rather than having duplicate rows, the Classes table rows are split out into child elements nested beneath the Teachers, so there is no duplication of the Teachers data. If there are no children (as with the first and last Teachers), then there is a single empty placeholder.

You should be asking a couple of questions at this point. How did the query know which was the parent and which was the child? And how did it know which rows could be rolled up?

The hierarchy is decided by seeing which table's columns were referenced first. If we had asked for a Classes field first, then it would have shown up as the parent. To decide which rows can be combined, SQL Server relies on the primary key of the table: if the primary key is the same, then it is the same row. If you do not have a primary key, then all the fields are compared (except binary and very large fields, which cannot be compared). If the data is identical, then it is assumed to be the same row.

This mode is pretty cool. Not only is the XML returned by Auto much cleaner, but it is more efficient—no duplicate data is sent. The Auto mode has an additional option, as well—we can ask for the fields to be returned as elements instead of as attributes:

```
SELECT Teachers.TeacherID,
       Teachers.TeacherName,
       Teachers.Subject,
       Teachers.Classroom,
       Classes.ClassID,
       Classes.ClassName,
       Classes.Period
       FROM Teachers LEFT OUTER JOIN Classes
       ON (Teachers.TeacherID = Classes.TeacherID)
       FOR XML AUTO, ELEMENTS
```

Here is the output based on using the Elements keyword, although I have excluded some of the data for space:

```
    <Teachers>
      <TeacherID>1</TeacherID>
      <TeacherName>Mr. Biddick</TeacherName>
      <Subject>Math</Subject>
      <Classroom>H9</Classroom>
      <Classes />
    </Teachers>
    <Teachers>
      <TeacherID>2</TeacherID>
      <TeacherName>Ms. Fortune</TeacherName>
      <Subject>English</Subject>
```

```
      <Classroom>A1</Classroom>
      <Classes>
         <ClassID>4</ClassID>
         <ClassName>Chemistry</ClassName>
         <Period>3</Period>
      </Classes>
      <Classes>
         <ClassID>7</ClassID>
         <ClassName>Geometry</ClassName>
         <Period>4</Period>
      </Classes>
   </Teachers>
      .
      .
      .
```

The only difference is that the fields are now elements instead of attributes.

Well-formedness

You may have noticed that in all the examples so far, the XML was not well-formed. That is, it was not legal XML. The reason is that multiple root nodes are returned. In the data returned as raw XML, for example, six root nodes are called *row*. In the Auto examples, there are four root nodes, all called *Teachers*.

Does this matter? It depends on what you intend to do with the XML. If you just want to step through it, then the lack of well-formedness is not a big deal; the Xml-Reader doesn't do any validation, so will let you go through the XML. If you want to use the XML with an XMLDocument or a DataSet, though, you might have trouble. One simple solution is to read the XML into a string and stick a root element at the front and the closing element at the end. Alternately, DataSets have a special mode for reading in this type of XML, which I will demonstrate a little later (section 29.1.4) when I show you how to read XML directly into a DataSet.

Aliases

In SQL, you can specify an alias for certain things, like fields and tables. The XML functionality works with these aliases and will modify the XML appropriately. Here is the same query, but with a field and a table alias:

```
SELECT Torturer.TeacherID,
       Torturer.TeacherName,
       Torturer.Subject,
       Torturer.Classroom as HidingPlace,
       Classes.ClassID,
       Classes.ClassName,
       Classes.Period
       FROM Teachers as Torturer LEFT OUTER JOIN Classes
       ON Torturer.TeacherID = Classes.TeacherID
       FOR XML AUTO, ELEMENTS
```

Notice that we are aliasing Teachers as Torturers,[2] and we also aliased Classroom as HidingPlace. The changes are reflected in the resulting XML:

```xml
<Torturer>
    <TeacherID>1</TeacherID>
    <TeacherName>Mr. Biddick</TeacherName>
    <Subject>Math</Subject>
    <HidingPlace>H9</HidingPlace>
    <Classes />
</Torturer>
<Torturer>
    <TeacherID>2</TeacherID>
    <TeacherName>Ms. Fortune</TeacherName>
    <Subject>English</Subject>
    <HidingPlace>A1</HidingPlace>
    <Classes>
        <ClassID>4</ClassID>
        <ClassName>Chemistry</ClassName>
        <Period>3</Period>
    </Classes>
    <Classes>
        <ClassID>7</ClassID>
        <ClassName>Geometry</ClassName>
        <Period>4</Period>
    </Classes>
</Torturer>
    .
    .
    .
```

Pitfalls

There are a handful of things you cannot do with the FOR XML clause, or that you must handle specially.

If your field or table names contain special characters (like spaces) that SQL Server allows but XML does not, the name will be munged—you will end up with something like My_x0020_Field instead of My Field. SQL Server puts in the code for the special character in place of the character. In general, it is a good idea to avoid names like this anyway, but if you are using them, you should provide an alias for the field or table name.

Also, if your data is not legal for an attribute (if, for example, it contains XML), it will be escaped. So if for some strange reason my subject was <Math>, the attribute would look like:

```
ClassName="&lt;Math&gt;"
```

SQL Server 2000 cannot handle queries that do group-bys or use aggregate functions (Count(), Avg(), and so on). If you use these with FOR XML, then you will get an error.

---

[2] Not really—I loved all my teachers. . .

SQL Server *does* support retrieving binary data as XML, but if you use the normal queries you have seen so far, you will get an odd result:

```
<BigBinary ID="3"
           BigData="dbobject/BigBinary[@ID='3']/@BigData" />
```

BigData is the field that contains the binary data, but the content of the `BigData` attribute is not the value in the field. Instead, this is a reference to the location of the data, relative to the root of the database. Huh? Remember that I said in the introduction to this chapter that SQL Server supports accessing data via HTTP, and you can do queries directly against it. If you were using that mechanism, this reference could be used to retrieve the data. Unfortunately (or fortunately, depending on your point of view), we are not using that mechanism, so this reference is useless. However, a keyword tells SQL Server to *Base64 encode* the binary data.

Base64 encoding is a way of converting binary data (that can have all sorts of difficult things in it, like `nulls` and illegal characters) into a legal (albeit longer) text string. .NET provides a great deal of support for Base64 encoding; for example, you can take a Base64 string and turn it into an image or back into a binary array. To make SQL Server Base64 encode binary data, add a clause to the query:

```
SELECT * FROM BigBinary FOR XML AUTO,BINARY BASE64
```

The XML will then look like this:

```
<BigBinary ID="3" BigData="VGhpcyBpcyBsYXJnZSBiaW5hcnkgZGF
                  0YQAAAAAAAAAAAAAAAAAAAAAAAAAAAAAA=" />
```

This result isn't particularly illuminating, I know, but the data is a Base64 representation of the binary data (although I had to put a line-break in the middle that would not normally be present).

29.1.2 Code to read XML

I've shown a bunch of examples of querying SQL Server for XML, but I haven't yet demonstrated how to write code to accomplish this. Doing so is incredibly simple. The code in listing 29.1 executes one of the earlier queries and retrieves the XML data. The sample steps through the XML and writes it to the console, but you could do anything appropriate with the XML as you read it.

Listing 29.1 Reading XML from SQL Server

```
public void XmlQueryTest(SqlConnection conn)
{
    string strSQL = @"SELECT Teachers.TeacherID,
                      Teachers.TeacherName,
                      Teachers.Subject,
                      Teachers.Classroom,
                      Classes.ClassID,
                      Classes.ClassName,
                      Classes.Period
```

```
                        FROM Teachers LEFT OUTER JOIN Classes
                        ON
                        Teachers.TeacherID = Classes.TeacherID
                        FOR XML AUTO";

    // Create the command and get back an XmlReader
    SqlCommand comm = new SqlCommand(strSQL,conn);
    XmlReader reader = comm.ExecuteXmlReader();          ❶ ExecuteXmlReader

    // Step through the XML
    reader.Read();
    while(!reader.EOF)                                   ❷ Step through XML
        Console.WriteLine(reader.ReadOuterXml());
}
```

❶ The SQL Server data provider's version of a command, `SqlCommand`, has a method on it explicitly designed to handle XML output from SQL Server. The `ExecuteXml-Reader()` method returns an XmlReader that is designed to step through a stream of XML in a forward-only manner. This process is similar to the `ExecuteReader()` method that returns a DataReader for stepping through relational data.

❷ The XmlReader lets us step through the XML, reading it in pieces. We can read element by element or attribute by attribute, or read the entire contents of the current element. For well-formed XML, to read the entire content of the document, all we have to do is get the root node and then ask for the *outer XML*. The outer XML includes the current element and all XML contained within that element, as opposed to the inner XML, which includes only the XML inside the element.

The problem is that the XML returned by SQL Server is not well-formed—it can include multiple root nodes. This code handles the situation by calling `Read()` to move to the first element, and then calling `ReadOuterXml()` repeatedly to return the XML and position the stream after the item it has read. This process will continue until the stream is positioned past the end, at which point the loop will exit.

Results

Although earlier I showed the cleaned-up XML from this particular query, figure 29.1 shows the output directly from the code.

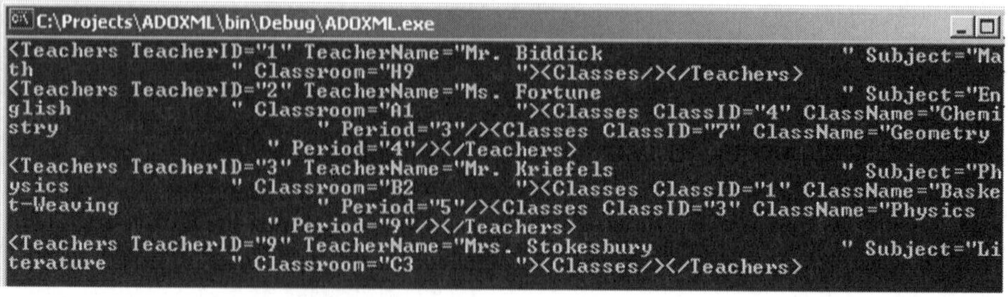

Figure 29.1   Output from listing 29.1

CHAPTER 29   SQL SERVER XML FEATURES

29.1.3　Reading the schema of the results

The results returned by a FOR XML query are XML, which means that, in theory, they could be defined by a schema. Having a schema can be useful; you can turn it into the basis of a strongly typed DataSet, or use it for convenience when communicating with other systems. You can easily have SQL Server return the schema along with the data by adding the XMLDATA clause to your query. SQL Server will add the schema in-line to the return results:

```
SELECT Teachers.TeacherID,
       Teachers.TeacherName,
       Teachers.Subject,
       Teachers.Classroom,
       Classes.ClassID,
       Classes.ClassName,
       Classes.Period
       FROM Teachers LEFT OUTER JOIN Classes
       ON Teachers.TeacherID = Classes.TeacherID
       FOR XML AUTO, XMLDATA
```

There are problems, though. First, SQL Server 2000 was released before the standard for schemas was finalized, so it doesn't write XSD schemas—it writes XDR schemas. XDR is a subset of XSD, so it should be compatible, but some minor differences exist. For example, in an XSD schema, you would see

```
maxOccurs="unbounded"
```

whereas in the XDR format, you see

```
maxOccurs="*"
```

You may also notice that the location of the schema is different. The XDR schema sets up a namespace pointing to the old spec

```
xmlns:dt="urn:schemas-microsoft-com:datatypes"
```

instead of the reference to

```
xmlns:xs="http://www.w3.org/2001/XMLSchema"
```

The second problem is that the XML returned from SQL Server is not legal XML, because of the multiple root nodes. The schema that is returned reflects this fact in its definition, so it is appropriate for the returned data; but it might cause problems when the XML is read into another program.

Listing 29.2 shows the results from the last query, with a little formatting.

Listing 29.2   XML data with in-line schema

```
<Schema name="Schema1" xmlns="urn:schemas-microsoft-com:xml-data"
                     xmlns:dt="urn:schemas-microsoft-com:datatypes">
  <ElementType name="Teachers" content="eltOnly"
     model="closed" order="many">
     <element type="Classes" maxOccurs="*"/>
     <AttributeType name="TeacherID" dt:type="i4"/>
     <AttributeType name="TeacherName" dt:type="string"/>
     <AttributeType name="Subject" dt:type="string"/>
     <AttributeType name="Classroom" dt:type="string"/>
     <attribute type="TeacherID"/>
     <attribute type="TeacherName"/>
     <attribute type="Subject"/>
     <attribute type="Classroom"/>
  </ElementType>
  <ElementType name="Classes" content="empty" model="closed">
     <AttributeType name="ClassID" dt:type="i4"/>
     <AttributeType name="ClassName" dt:type="string"/>
     <AttributeType name="Period" dt:type="i4"/>
     <attribute type="ClassID"/>
     <attribute type="ClassName"/>
     <attribute type="Period"/>
  </ElementType>
</Schema>
<Teachers xmlns="x-schema:#Schema1" TeacherID="1"
                              TeacherName="Mr. Biddick"
                 Subject="Math " Classroom="H9 ">
  <Classes/>
</Teachers>
<Teachers xmlns="x-schema:#Schema1" TeacherID="2"
                              TeacherName="Ms. Fortune"
                 Subject="English " Classroom="A1 ">
  <Classes ClassID="4" ClassName="Chemistry " Period="3"/>
  <Classes ClassID="7" ClassName="Geometry " Period="4"/>
</Teachers>
<Teachers xmlns="x-schema:#Schema1" TeacherID="3"
                              TeacherName="Mr. Kriefels"
                 Subject="Physics " Classroom="B2 ">
  <Classes ClassID="1" ClassName="Basket-Weaving " Period="5"/>
  <Classes ClassID="3" ClassName="Physics " Period="9"/>
</Teachers>
<Teachers xmlns="x-schema:#Schema1" TeacherID="9"
     TeacherName="Mrs. Stokesbury" Subject="Literature "
                              Classroom="C3 ">
  <Classes/>
</Teachers>
```

The schema is the first part of the return results, followed by the data—which now refers to the schema in each of its roots. We can read this XML from the database using the XmlReader, just as we read the XML by itself; after all, a schema must be legal XML.

29.1.4 Reading XML directly into a DataSet

You saw in previous chapters that you can create a DataSet directly from XML. Likewise, you can use the XML returned from an XML query and create a DataSet from it. Why would you want to do that? After all, one of the reasons given for using the XML queries was that you didn't have to use a DataSet to transform your data. Doing an XML query and reading it directly into a DataSet offers at least one advantage.

Using XML Auto, you can do a query that involves a join, and then feed that data into a DataSet. Normally, when you do a join to fill a DataSet, you end up with a single table that is a view of the data. Via the XML Auto query, however, you get back nested XML that represents the data and its relationships. Thus you can get back the data you want via a join and a single query, but still build a DataSet that understands the relationships.

The code in listing 29.3 performs the same query as the previous example; but instead of writing the data out, it puts the data into a DataSet. It then uses the method we created earlier to write out the contents of the DataSet.

Listing 29.3 Reading XML directly into a DataSet

```
public void XmlQueryToDataSetTest(SqlConnection conn)
{
    string strSQL = @"SELECT Teachers.TeacherID,
                       Teachers.TeacherName,
                       Teachers.Subject,
                       Teachers.Classroom,
                       Classes.ClassID,
                       Classes.ClassName,
                       Classes.Period
                       FROM Teachers LEFT OUTER JOIN Classes
                       Teachers.TeacherID = Classes.TeacherID
                       FOR XML AUTO, XMLDATA";        ❶ Retrieve schema

    // Create the command and get back an XmlReader
    SqlCommand comm = new SqlCommand(strSQL,conn);
    XmlReader reader = comm.ExecuteXmlReader();

    // Build the DataSet from the XML, then write it out
    DataSet ds = new DataSet();
    ds.ReadXml(reader,XmlReadMode.Fragment);        ❷ Load DataSet
    PrintDataSet(ds);
}
```

❶ Notice that we explicitly ask for the schema, using the XMLDATA clause on the query. The DataSet will build its structure from that schema. If we didn't do this, then we would have to make the DataSet first infer the schema from the XML and then read in the XML itself; so, we would either have to store the XML to a string or read the data twice.

❷ The ReadXml() method of the DataSet can take an XmlReader directly, which is quite convenient. One problem, though, is the recurring issue that the returned data is not well-formed (remember, multiple root nodes). Fortunately, a special mode on the ReadXml() method, which we specify using the XmlReadMode.Fragment flag, tells the DataSet that the XML being read in can contain multiple nodes. (I'm not saying the Fragment mode was created explicitly for handling the output from a FOR XML query, but before it was called Fragment, the flag was called SqlXml.)

Results

Figure 29.2 shows the output from the code. Notice that we have two tables and a relationship between them, even though we queried using a join.

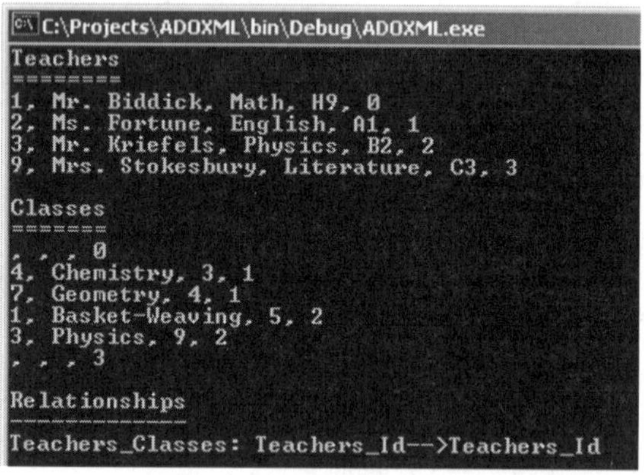

Figure 29.2
Output from listing 29.3

This result is pretty cool. But notice the first and last rows of the Classes table: they are there because we ended up with a couple of empty Classes nodes, due to the outer join. You will have to deal with problems like that manually, by either removing the rows from the XML or removing them from the DataTable later. Alternatively, you can use Explicit mode to get more control over the output.

29.1.5 Explicit retrieval

Early in the chapter, I said you can use the FOR XML clause three ways. We've explored two of them, Auto and Raw, in some depth. I've left the third, Explicit, until last. The idea behind the Explicit mode is that you can explicitly control the way the XML is returned, rather than limiting yourself to the behavior of the Raw or Auto mode. I should warn you, though, that it is not for the faint of heart—both the mechanism and the notation are quite complex.

The major reason for the complexity is that you are trying to specify a schema and a mapping of relational data to that schema, all within a query. You do so by making the columns be returned in a specific way, with specific names. For example, there must be a Tag column that is a number indicating the depth of the tag. There must also be a Parent column specifying the depth of the parent tag.

This requirement is a little odd, because generally, if the Tag's depth is 3, you can assume that the Parent's depth is 2, and so forth. But in some situations, you might want to skip levels—for example, if you have XML in a column you are reading that will fill in the space. If the Tag is 1, then the Parent will be `null`.

Wait a bit, I hear you say—I don't have columns in my database called Tag and Parent. Where do I get them? You use aliases. For example, if we want to read in Teachers as level 1 elements, we could do the following:

```
SELECT 1 as Tag,
       NULL as Parent
       FROM Teachers
```

We have Parent set to NULL, indicating that it is at the top of the document. If we looked at the raw results, we would have a fairly odd looking table (table 29.2).

Table 29.2 Select providing hard-coded values for each row

Tag	Parent
1	NULL
1	NULL
1	NULL
1	NULL

There is one row for every Teacher, but no data from the Teachers table. We need to add columns to the table that contain useful data, and we have to tell SQL Server how to represent the columns as XML. We do so via aliased column names. The column name uses a special format to specify its representation:

```
ElementName!TagNumber!AttributeName![Directive]
```

Here is what each of these pieces means:

- `ElementName`—The name of the element that will contain this item.
- `TagNumber`—The depth of the element. This value is associated with the Tag column, so every place this number matches the Tag value, the *ElementName* will be used for the tag.
- `AttributeName`—The name of the attribute that will hold this particular piece of data, unless a directive is specified. In that case, the *AttributeName* might be used to mean something else.
- `Directive`—An optional instruction to specify that the data should be stored in some manner other than as an attribute. For example, you can have the data stored as a child element, in which case the *AttributeName* becomes the name of the child element; or you can specify that the data should be stored as CData, or in several other ways.

Those explanations are probably as clear as mud. Let's look at some examples. The expression

```
Teachers!1!TeacherName
```

says that the tag associated with level 1 should be called Teachers, and that the attribute should be called `TeacherName`. Here is an expression that specifies that the Subject should be stored as a child element rather than as an attribute:

```
Teachers!1!Subject!element
```

Before going any deeper, let's look at how the query would be formatted to retrieve data this way, and also at our slightly more involved result table:

```
SELECT 1 as Tag,
       NULL as Parent,
       Teachers.TeacherName as [Teachers!1!TeacherName],
       Teachers.Subject as [Teachers!1!Subject!element]
       FROM Teachers
```

Note that we have to put the fancy column names in square brackets ([]) because otherwise the exclamation marks will cause an error. Table 29.3 shows what the table will look like now.

Table 29.3   Select adding our strange rows

Tag	Parent	Teachers!1!TeacherName	Teachers!1!Subject!element
1	NULL	Mr. Biddick	Math
1	NULL	Ms. Fortune	English
1	NULL	Mr. Kriefels	Physics
1	NULL	Mrs. Stokesbury	Literature

Now we have some data, although the structure is odd. (By the way, SQL Server refers to this as a *universal* table.) If we add the FOR XML EXPLICIT clause onto this query, SQL Server will know how to interpret the column names and map them to XML:

```
SELECT 1 as Tag,
       NULL as Parent,
       Teachers.TeacherName as [Teachers!1!TeacherName],
       Teachers.Subject as [Teachers!1!Subject!element]
       FROM Teachers
       FOR XML EXPLICIT
```

Here is the resulting XML:

```
<Teachers TeacherName="Mr. Biddick">
   <Subject>Math</Subject>
</Teachers>
<Teachers TeacherName="Ms. Fortune">
   <Subject>English</Subject>
```

```
</Teachers>
<Teachers TeacherName="Mr. Kriefels">
   <Subject>Physics</Subject>
</Teachers>
<Teachers TeacherName="Mrs. Stokesbury">
   <Subject>Literature</Subject>
</Teachers>
```

Already we have done something we couldn't do before: we have some fields coming back as elements and others as attributes. The real power of this mechanism doesn't appear until we start nesting other data. This is also where the real complexity comes in.

The problem is that we need additional rows to represent the nested data—say, the data from the Classes table. We could build another query that specifies the nesting level (the tag level of the items), but it won't contain our parent data:

```
SELECT 2 as Tag,
       1 as Parent,
       Classes.ClassName as [Classes!2!ClassName]
       Classes.Period as [Classes!2!Period]
       FROM Classes
```

This query gets us the children but doesn't include the parent info; nor does it associate the children with the appropriate parents. Fortunately, SQL provides a way to combine two queries: a union. These two queries can be combined, but we need to rearrange a few things and add a couple of new items (listing 29.4).

Listing 29.4   The union

```
SELECT 1 as Tag,
       NULL as Parent,
       Teachers.TeacherID as [Teachers!1!TeacherID],         ❶ Add TeacherID
       Teachers.TeacherName as [Teachers!1!TeacherName],
       Teachers.Subject as [Teachers!1!Subject!element],
       NULL as [Classes!2!ClassName],
       NULL as [Classes!2!Period]                            ❷ Create NULL columns
       FROM Teachers                                            for union

UNION ALL        ❸ Union

SELECT 2          ❹ Second select
       1,
       Teachers.TeacherID,
       NULL,
       NULL,                                ❺ Other NULL columns for union
       Classes.ClassName,
       Classes.Period                       ❻ Classes fields
       FROM Teachers,Classes
       WHERE Teachers.TeacherID = Classes.TeacherID      ❼ Join
ORDER BY [Teachers!1!TeacherID],[Classes!2!ClassName]     ❽ Order data
```

❶ In order to relate the two queries, we needed a common item to associate them. As you would expect, this is the TeacherID, which is present in both tables. We add it to the query and tell SQL Server that we want it to be an attribute.

❷ In order to join the two SQL statements, they need to have the same basic structure; so we must put placeholders in the Teachers query for the data from the Classes table. These placeholders will always be NULL in the first select, but will hold data for the second. We also alias them using the special Explicit naming convention, indicating that they are level 2 items.

❸ This code simply says to combine the results of both select statements into a single result set, which is reasonable as long as the structure of the two result sets are the same (they have the same number of columns, and so on).

❹ This select retrieves data from the Classes table and also some data from the Teachers table, so that it can join on the TeacherId field and eliminate unassociated data. Notice that the Tag field for all rows will contain the value 2, and the Parents field will contain the value 1. We don't have to bother with the aliases here, because they will be automatically picked up from the first select in the union.

❺ In the first select, we had to make sure the columns from the Classes tables were represented, although empty. Likewise, for the second select, we must make sure the columns for the Teachers table are represented, even though their value will be NULL for all of these rows.

❻ These are the data fields from the Classes table. Again, we don't have to put in the alias because it is assumed from the first select.

❼ The second select joins the Teachers and Classes table, so only Classes that should show up below particular Teachers will be included. In our data, all the Classes are associated with Teachers, so we could have skipped this step; but it is more correct to include it for the common case.

❽ Specifying the order of the results is very important because the XML will be built based on the order of the rows. This order by clause is for the entire result set, not just for one of the selects; it orders everything first by TeacherID to keep Teachers and their Classes together, and then by ClassName to make sure the first item to show up will be the Teachers row, where the ClassName is NULL. The order by must use the aliases for the columns, which explains the odd format.

The universal table

If we execute this SQL, the universal table will look like table 29.4.

Table 29.4   Universal table with join

Tag	Parent	Teachers!1! TeacherID	Teachers!1! TeacherName	Teachers!1! Subject!element	Classes!2! ClassName	Classes!2! Period
1	NULL	1	Mr. Biddick	Math	NULL	NULL
1	NULL	2	Ms. Fortune	English	NULL	NULL
2	1	2	NULL	NULL	Basket-weaving	5
2	1	2	NULL	NULL	Physics	9
1	NULL	3	Mr. Kriefels	Physics	NULL	NULL
2	1	3	NULL	NULL	Chemistry	3
2	1	3	NULL	NULL	Geometry	4
1	NULL	9	Mrs. Stokesbury	Literature	NULL	NULL

Notice the NULL values where we have put rows into one or the other select in order to make the structure match. If you look at the Tag field and the column names, you can see how this table will turn into XML. Here is the XML output after we add the FOR XML EXPLICIT clause onto the query:

```
<Teachers TeacherID="1" TeacherName="Mr. Biddick">
   <Subject>Math</Subject>
</Teachers>
<Teachers TeacherID="2" TeacherName="Ms. Fortune">
   <Subject>English</Subject>
   <Classes ClassName="Chemistry" Period="3" />
   <Classes ClassName="Geometry" Period="4" />
</Teachers>
<Teachers TeacherID="3" TeacherName="Mr. Kriefels">
   <Subject>Physics</Subject>
   <Classes ClassName="Basket-Weaving" Period="5" />
   <Classes ClassName="Physics" Period="9" />
</Teachers>
<Teachers TeacherID="9" TeacherName="Mrs. Stokesbury">
   <Subject>Literature</Subject>
</Teachers>
```

I hope this is what you were expecting. This mechanism is very powerful, but it is also something of a mind-bender.

Adding in a root node

All this time, I have been mentioning that the XML returned is not legal because of the lack of a root node. Well, with an Explicit query, you can add one. The mechanism is fairly obvious: just fake a row of data that has the appropriate join in it specifying a root. For space reasons, I will demonstrate using the first Explicit query we did, which only gets data from a single table, but the mechanism will work the same for the more complex case:

```
SELECT 1 as Tag,
       NULL as Parent,
       NULL as [Root!1],
       NULL as [Teachers!2!TeacherName],
       NULL as [Teachers!2!Subject!element]

UNION ALL

SELECT 2,
       1,
       NULL,
       Teachers.TeacherName,
       Teachers.Subject
       FROM Teachers
FOR XML EXPLICIT
```

All we are doing is creating a select that will return a single level 1 row called Root, with NULL for all the other values, and then unioning[3] it to the original query, which has changed just slightly (it is now set to level 2 and has a null placeholder for the Root column).

Here is the output:

```
<Root>
    <Teachers TeacherName="Mr. Biddick">
       <Subject>Math</Subject>
    </Teachers>
    <Teachers TeacherName="Ms. Fortune">
       <Subject>English</Subject>
    </Teachers>
    <Teachers TeacherName="Mr. Kriefels">
       <Subject>Physics</Subject>
    </Teachers>
    <Teachers TeacherName="Mrs. Stokesbury">
       <Subject>Literature</Subject>
    </Teachers>
</Root>
```

As you can see, there is now a root node. This XML is now well-formed, and the associated schema would also be legal.

Other directives

As you have seen, one of the things you can specify on the column name is a directive indicating how the data should be put in the XML. If no directive is specified, the data is represented as an attribute. We also used the element directive to make the data appear as a child element, but a number of other legal directives are available. Table 29.5 lists some of the more useful ones.

---

[3] And making up words while I do it!

Table 29.5 Legal Explicit mode directives

Directive	Description
element	Makes the data show up as a child element.
xml	Does the same thing as the element directive, but the content of the data is left alone. If the data contains XML, using element, the < and > symbols would be escaped; but using the xml directive, they would not. Used carefully, this direction can be pretty cool. You can have some of the XML structure built based on the universal table, and some of it built based on the content of fields that contain XML data.
cdata	Leaves the content untouched, but puts it inside a CData directive. That is an XML way of including arbitrary unescaped text that does not mess up the rest of the XML.
hide	The attribute is not shown in the XML. You might want to do this if you need to include the column for ordering or joining, but you don't want it to show up.

29.2 SETTING DATA USING OPENXML

We have spent a huge amount of time getting XML data out of SQL Server 2000. The obvious follow-on question is whether you can put data *into* SQL Server using XML. The answer is yes, it is possible, but it is not necessarily the most useful or convenient way of getting XML data back into SQL Server.

Prior to .NET and the DataSet, you didn't have many options for getting XML data into SQL Server. You could parse the XML yourself and split it out into tables, or you could use some features of the OLE DB provider designed for handling streams of XML. Other than that, you could use the OPENXML mechanism that I will describe in this section.

With ADO.NET, however, it is a different world. You can easily take XML and convert it into relational data for storage in a database. Sometimes, though, it's handy to pass a lump of XML to SQL Server and let it parse it and store the data to various tables. Doing so makes the most sense when the XML changes would lead to a number of separate SQL calls.

SQL Server 2000 has a couple of specialized stored procedures for working with XML data. The first, sp_xml_preparedocument, is used to load an XML document into SQL Server such that it can be manipulated. The second, sp_xml_removedocument, clears the XML document out of SQL Server.

It is important to understand that sp_xml_preparedocument does not parse the XML, put it into relational tables, and so forth. It simply holds onto it so you can do SQL Server operations against it, via the OPENXML keyword. An example of using an XML document might be something like this:

```
sp_xml_preparedocument @DocId OUTPUT, <Root>My XML here</Root>

some various SELECT statements that reference the
prepared SQL using OPENXML and the @DocId

sp_xml_removedocument @DocId
```

You wouldn't want to do this from ADO.NET—basically, you would be using SQL Server as an XPath query engine (OPENXML uses XPath), which is silly given that .NET has direct XPath support. However, you might want to use this mechanism inside a stored procedure. You can create a stored procedure that takes an XML document as an argument, prepares it, pulls out the data, inserts it in the appropriate places, and then removes the document.

This mechanism can be quite efficient, depending on your data and the complexity of the conversion between XML and relational data (for example, if the XML was fairly small but generated a large number of rows of data). You should be cautious about the approach, but if it is appropriate, then by all means use it.

Enough soap-boxing. The following is a simple example, which should give you an idea of the approach. Imagine that we have the following XML, which defines some classes to insert into the Classes table:

```
<Root>
   <Class TeacherID="1" ClassName="History" Period="5"/>
   <Class TeacherID="9" ClassName="Shakespeare" Period="6"/>
</Root>
```

This XML has multiple Class elements, each representing a new Class to add, and it has the data stored as attributes. As I said, this is a simple example; we could have some data stored as elements and some as attributes, we could have nested data designed to be stored in multiple tables, and so on. The mechanism is flexible, as it relies on XPath to retrieve the data.

Now we need a stored procedure that takes the XML and puts it into the Classes table. We can either manually create the stored procedure in SQL Server using Enterprise Manager, or use the technique from chapter 13 and write some code to put it in place. Just for variety, I created this stored procedure directly in SQL Server. An explanation follows listing 29.5.

Listing 29.5   Stored procedure that takes XML and puts data into a table

```
CREATE PROCEDURE AddClassesFromXml(@ClassesXml varchar(1000)) AS      ❶ Stored
                                                                        procedure
--Prepare the XML document
DECLARE @idoc int
EXEC sp_xml_preparedocument @idoc OUTPUT, @ClassesXml      ❷ Load XML into
                                                            SQL server
--Insert all classes found in the XML
INSERT INTO Classes (TeacherID,ClassName,Period)           ❸ Insert
  SELECT TeacherID, ClassName, Period                        statement
  FROM OPENXML (@idoc, '//Class',1)
  WITH (TeacherID int,                                      ❹ OPENXML query
        ClassName varchar(30),
        Period int)

--Remove the XML document from memory
EXEC sp_xml_removedocument @idoc          ❺ Remove XML from SQL server
```

① We call the stored procedure `AddClassesFromXml` and give it a single argument: a string to contain the XML. We arbitrarily limit it to 1,000 characters, but you can specify a longer length if required.

② Before we can work on XML inside SQL Server, we must prepare the document for manipulation. We do so by calling the system stored procedure `sp_xml_prepare-document`, which returns an integer ID that we will use to refer to the document.

③ We are doing a standard SQL Insert into the Classes table, but instead of providing values, we provide the data from a query. Normally it would be a standard SQL query, but we are doing an `OPENXML` query.

④ This, as they say, is the clever bit. `OPENXML` is a special keyword that indicates the query should retrieve data from an XML document rather than via a relational query. Several things are going on here. First, here are the arguments on the `OPENXML` statement (following `OPENXML` in parentheses):

- *Document ID*—The integer returned from the `sp_xml_preparedocument` call, which is sort of handle to the document. Basically, it tells `OPENXML` which XML document to access.

- *Row Pattern*—An XPath query that specifies the element within the document that represents a row. As you'll remember from chapter 27, you have tremendous flexibility with this command. In this case, we're saying, "Find any elements named `Class`, no matter what their parent is."

- *Flags*—Specifies how the various fields should be found under the element for each row. If it is omitted or set to `1`, then the fields are expected to be attributes of the element, as they are in the example. Later (in section 29.2.1), I will talk about some of the other values you can use here.

The next part of the `OPENXML` syntax, following the `WITH` statement, specifies the fields to be retrieved. Because the flags indicated that the fields are represented by attributes, SQL Server will attempt to find an attribute of the `Class` element with the same name as the field. (You can also explicitly identify how to retrieve the XML for each field, as I will discuss in section 29.2.2.)

As you can see, we have specified that three fields should be created: TeacherID, ClassName, and Period. Their values will be retrieved from the attributes of the same name. Because the XML contains two `<Class>` elements, two rows will be inserted into the Classes table.

⑤ Once the XML has been loaded into SQL Server, it will stay there until explicitly removed—which is done via the `sp_xml_removedocument` stored procedure. The only argument is the integer `handle` that we got from the `sp_xml_prepare-document` stored procedure.

Calling the stored procedure

Now that we have our fancy stored procedure, we need to call it. The code is straightforward:

```
public void XmlStoredProcTest(SqlConnection conn)
{
    // The XML
    string strXml = @"
      <Root>
        <Class TeacherID=""1"" ClassName=""History"" Period=""5""/>
        <Class TeacherID=""9"" ClassName=""Shakespeare""
                                                Period=""6""/>
      </Root>";

    // Call the stored procedure using the XML as a parameter
    string strSQL = "AddClassesFromXml";
    SqlCommand comm = new SqlCommand(strSQL,conn);
    comm.CommandType = CommandType.StoredProcedure;
    comm.Parameters.Add("@ClassesXml",strXml);

    // Actually does the insert
    comm.ExecuteNonQuery();
}
```

This code is standard for calling a stored procedure, but any other way of calling a stored procedure (see chapter 13) would work as well.[4]

Figure 29.3 shows the Classes table after we call this code.

ClassID	TeacherID	ClassName	Period
1	3	Basket-Weaving	5
3	3	Physics	9
4	2	Chemistry	3
7	2	Geometry	4
27	1	History	5
28	9	Shakespeare	6

**Figure 29.3
The Classes table
after inserting XML**

As you can see, the two new rows from the XML were added.

29.2.1 Other flags

I mentioned earlier that you can specify other flags in the OPENXML arguments to get different behavior. The value 1 indicates attribute-wise retrieval. You can also specify a 2 to indicate element-wise retrieval:

```
FROM OPENXML (@idoc, '//Class',2)
WITH (TeacherID int,
      ClassName varchar(30),
      Period int)
```

---

[4] Notice that we are using double quotes around the values of the attributes. In XML, single and double quotes are both legal, but SQL Server will not accept single quotes. Normally this would not be an issue, because you would rarely define XML in a string—you would load it from a file or other source.

Doing so would be desirable if the XML looked something like this:

```
<Root>
    <Class>
        <TeacherID>1</TeacherID>
        <ClassName>History</ClassName>
        <Period>5</Period>
    </Class>
</Root>
```

You can also combine the flags, indicating that the data might be stored as attributes or as elements. SQL Server will check attributes first, then elements. You *bitwise-or* the flags together to combine them, which gives you the value 3:

```
FROM OPENXML (@idoc, '//Class',3)
WITH (TeacherID int,
      ClassName varchar(30),
      Period int)
```

The XML might look something like this:

```
<Root>
    <Class TeacherID="1">
        <ClassName>History</ClassName>
        <Period>5</Period>
    </Class>
</Root>
```

29.2.2 Customizing the WITH field retrieval

The flags give you a reasonable amount of flexibility, but you can get explicit with the way each field is retrieved. For each field you want to retrieve, you can specify an XPath expression identifying the location of the data. Imagine that the XML (for some reason) looked like this:

```
<Root>
    <Class TeacherID="1">
        <ClassDetails Value="History">
            <Period>5</Period>
        </ClassDetails>
    </Class>
</Root>
```

The TeacherID is straightforward, but the name of the class is now an attribute of the subelement `ClassDetails`, and the Period is a subelement of the `ClassDetails` element. Obviously, the flags won't help us. Instead, we need to provide an XPath query for these special items:

```
FROM OPENXML (@idoc, '//Class',1)
WITH (TeacherID int              '@TeacherID',
      ClassName varchar(30)      'ClassDetails\@Value',
      Period int                 'ClassDetails\Period')
```

For each field, we have now provided an XPath expression:

- `@TeacherID`—Retrieves the `TeacherID` attribute from the current nod
- `ClassDetails\@Value`—Retrieves the `Value` attribute from the `Class-Details` element below the current node
- `ClassDetails\Period`—Retrieves the `Period` element from beneath the `ClassDetails` element below the current node

Note that these mappings override the flag on the `OPENXML` parameters indicating attribute-wise retrieval. Obviously, with the power of XPath, you have considerable flexibility in the way the data is retrieved.

29.2.3   Edge tables

If you don't specify a `WITH` clause, SQL Server will build up what it calls an *edge table* that has a row for each edge—every attribute and element ends up in a row. Although it is interesting to do queries that return this data, doing so is not likely to be useful when you're doing an `Insert-Select`. I mention edge tables here only to be complete.

29.3   SUMMARY

SQL Server 2000 hit the streets at the top of the hype-curve for XML, and the SQL Server team did a good job of providing useful XML-based functionality, both for retrieving and inserting data using XML. Of course, that was a while ago in computer time, and XML and its surrounding technologies have changed and stabilized. I expect that the next version of SQL Server (codenamed Yukon and slated for a 2002 release) will include considerably updated XML support.

The next version of SQL Server will also be much more .NET aware. For instance, you will be able to write stored procedures in any .NET-compatible language and get the associated advantages from security and managed code. This functionality may not be quite the panacea it sounds—the stored procedures will have to be compiled and added by an administrator, so they are more akin to SQL Server's current ability to have stored procedures call external DLLs. However, because .NET uses managed code, the chance of this DLL causing your server to crash is greatly diminished.

This chapter ends the discussion of XML and ADO.NET. If you are not an XML person, these chapters have provided a taste of what XML can do and have given you enough information to get by until you feel like reading an entire book on XML. If you are an XML person, I hope you had the sense to skip over those bits that you already knew! In either case, you can see that ADO.NET has some great features that lower the bar for bringing XML and relational data together.

PART 6

Useful extras

Most of the chapters in this part of the book explain how to accomplish fairly specific tasks, such as reading schema information from the database or setting up a distributed transaction—tasks that might otherwise take some time to figure out. These chapters are fairly short, because they are so targeted, but they provide enough information to get you started on each task.

Chapter 34 is a little different. Throughout the book, I have given somewhat simplistic examples to highlight various concepts. Although I have sprinkled suggestions through the book about how to approach an ADO.NET project, I have reserved the last chapter as a soapbox for my thoughts on design and implementation.

CHAPTER 30

Connection pooling

Connection pooling is simply a method for sharing a limited number of connections with a larger number of users. Instead of a connection being maintained for each user, when the user makes a request of the server, a connection is taken out of the pool, used for the operation, and then returned to the pool for the use of the next user.

There are a number of different mechanisms for pooling connections. Some engines, such as SQL Server, have built-in support. Others can use system services, such as OLE DB resource pooling or COM+ object pooling. This chapter explores all of these methods and explains the rationale and issues of connection pooling in general.

30.1 WHY POOL?

In traditional client/server database applications, you get a connection to a database, you use it for the duration of the application's lifetime, and then you release the connection. This is a reasonable model—after all, getting a connection is relatively expensive,[1] and most client/server applications only have so many users. Client/server database applications tend to top out around 200 to 300 users, although if you are stubborn enough (and can spend enough money on hardware, and have a simple enough application), you can probably get close to the 1,000-user mark.

---

[1] Resourcewise, not moneywise!

The world has moved on, though. Especially when you start talking about web applications, you can have applications that literally serve millions of users at more or less the same time. Trying to have a connection for each of those users would not be practical. Connections are expensive resources; plus, in the web world, you have no idea if the user will come back any time soon. You don't want to maintain a connection for everyone who has ever hit your site, in case they come back.

This situation has given rise to a new model of coding referred to as *stateless*, which is very efficient for web applications and also applicable for general three-tier applications. The steps go something like this:

1 User makes a request to the server

2 Server connects to the database

3 Server does whatever work it needs to do to fulfill the request

4 Server disconnects from the database

5 Server passes results back to the user

6 Server forgets it has ever heard of the user until the next request

This process sounds horribly inefficient. For one thing, you have to figure out all sorts of things about the user every time they connect. For another, you have to connect to the database and disconnect, which, as we have already said, is expensive.

This model works so well because of the nature of the web, and because of well-designed three-tier applications. Think about the common interaction with a web application. You go to a page, which involves talking briefly to a server. You interact with the page for some amount of time, which generally doesn't involve the server; then, at some later point, you hit Submit and send information back to the server, involving the server again.

If the server keeps track of you for the entire time you are messing around with the page, it is holding onto expensive resources that it is not using and that could be better spent on users who are actively hitting the server at the current moment. Worse, if the user closes the browser and goes home, the server is are wasting resources on someone who doesn't even care.[2]

That is not to say this model is always appropriate; as with everything, it depends on your application and the amount of interaction with the server that is required. However, for web applications, and for three-tier applications that can offload processing to the client, it is a very efficient model.

We're still left with the problem of getting those connections. You may have noticed that there is frequently a significant delay when you first connect to a database. As I said, creating the connection is expensive, whereas using a connection that you already have is cheap.

---

[2] Rather sad, really.

Pooling is a mechanism that helps with this problem. The idea behind it is very simple: instead of connecting and disconnecting every time, you hold onto a bunch of connections and "check out" those connections to each user. Of course, there is more to it than that, but conceptually we can change the earlier process to take pooling into account:

1 User makes a request to the server

2 Server requests a connection from the pool

3 Server does whatever work it needs to do to fulfill the request

4 Server returns the connection to the pool

5 Server passes results back to the user

6 Server forgets it has ever heard of the user until the next request

This process gives you the best of all worlds. You don't have to worry about users wasting your resources, and you don't have to worry about the cost of retrieving connections. However, you need to consider a few caveats, provisos, and so forth. . .

30.2   CONNECTION POOLING ISSUES

The first thing to worry about with a connection pool is the size of the pool. After all, connections are quite expensive—if the pool is holding onto 1,000 connections when you have only 3 users, you are wasting resources. Likewise, if the pool has only 10 connections and you have 1,000 users, the pool is definitely out of its depth.

You need to think about three general options with a connection pool: maximum connections, minimum connections, and connection lifetime. You may or may not be able to control them, depending on the pooling mechanism you are using. Although connection pooling can get more complicated than dealing with these issues, worrying about these three will get you a long way toward understanding the issues of connection pooling.

30.2.1   Maximum connections

You must consider the maximum number of connections the pool can be responsible for at any one time. What happens when you exceed this number? Say the pool has a maximum of 10 connections. The first 10 people will get their connections as expected, but the eleventh person will have to wait. The request for the connection will lock up until one of the first 10 people releases a connection.

A good pooling algorithm will deal with this situation well, making sure the next person in line gets the next connection. A good user of a pool (your application) will make sure they hold onto a connection for the absolute minimum amount of time possible.

30.2.2   Minimum connections

Suppose you set your pool maximum to 100 connections. Does it automatically make sense for you to create 100 connections right at that moment? Maybe, or maybe not. Perhaps 10 connections are enough to handle your average traffic, but you will allow up to 100 connections to be created before blocking people.

This is where the minimum pool size comes in. If you set the minimum to 10, then 10 connections will be allocated immediately and never dropped. Any requests above 10 will cause a new connection to be allocated and handed out, but those extra connections (beyond 10) will be dropped as soon as they are released back to the pool.

There are a couple of different algorithms for handling the minimum connection pool size. The most common approach is to automatically allocate the minimum number of connections when the first request is made. Another is to wait for each request before allocating any connections, but not release any connections until you have the minimum count that you need.

30.2.3   Connection lifetime

Based on the way a pool works, any given connection in a pool might be held onto indefinitely. This scenario presents some problems. Let's say you hold onto 10 connections overnight, while nobody is hitting your web site. Many engines have a timeout on connections—if nothing has happened on the connection for X amount of time, then the engine drops the connection. Doing so could cause quite a problem in the morning, when the system attempts to use the dropped connection!

The other problem with holding onto connections indefinitely has to do with high-scale environments in which, perhaps, you have a cluster of servers. If a server is taken out of the cluster, you could have trouble if some of the held connections still point to it. Likewise, if a new server is added, it might not be properly utilized because you are pooling connections off the other servers. To combat this situation, you would like to control the lifetime of a connection, such that old connections are retired in favor of new ones.

30.3   AVAILABLE POOLING APPROACHES

You can take a number of approaches to add connection pooling to your application, depending on your needs and the particular engine with which you are working. Here are some of the options that are available:

- *ADO.NET SQL Server data provider connection pooling*—If you are using SQL Server 7 or later, the ADO.NET data provider has built-in support for connection pooling. If you can get away with requiring SQL Server, this is the way to go—the mechanism is robust and incredibly easy to use. Section 30.4 explains how to use it.

- *OLE DB resource pooling*—OLE DB has support for connection pooling, which you can take advantage of via the OLE DB data provider. It is not as flexible, and it often requires you to do things like update the registry to configure details. Also, it relies to an extent on the underlying engine, so it won't necessarily be available all the time. It's discussed in section 30.5.

- *COM+ object pooling*—COM+ provides a number of services for managing components, including object pooling. It can pool COM objects in general, which means that it can pool connections. .NET exposes COM+, so you can use it in your code. However, COM+ is available only on Windows 2000 and up, which can be a limiting factor.[3] An example of COM+ pooling is shown in section 30.6.

- *Roll your own*—If you want the ultimate control over how the pooling works, independent of everything, you can build your own pooling mechanism. I should warn you, though, having recently designed a pooling mechanism, that doing so is more involved than it sounds. Details of how to do this are beyond the scope of this book.

30.4 SQL SERVER CONNECTION POOLING

I said earlier that the SQL Server connection pooling in ADO.NET is robust and easy to use. For robustness, the ADO.NET team, uh, borrowed the code for COM+ object pooling. That means the pooling is very robust indeed, and it is available on any Microsoft .NET platform, including Windows 98.

To set up pooling, you provide the appropriate parameters as part of your connection string. So, for example, your connection string might look like this:

```
server=localhost;database=ADONetSamples;user id=sa;pwd=secret;
    Pooling=true;Min Pool Size=10;Max Pool Size=100
```

This connection string indicates that pooling is enabled, with a minimum of 10 connections and a maximum of 100. The connection string automatically creates and manages the pool. For other connections to participate in the pool, they simply connect with exactly the same parameters. The pooling mechanism identifies another request for the same pool by comparing the exact text of the connection string—if they are the same, then it is the same pool. Otherwise it is a different pool.

To release the connection back to the pool, you close the connection, as you would normally. When the close takes place, the underlying code checks to see if the connection is participating in a pool. If it is, the code acts as though the connection has been closed, but really puts it back into the pool.

Let's look at an example. The following code might show up as the handler for a click from a server-side web control (see chapter 23 for examples):

---

[3] Some capabilities are available on Windows NT under the guise of MTS.

```
private void Page_Load(object sender, System.EventArgs e)
{
   if(!IsPostBack)
   {
      string strConnect =
         "server=localhost;database=ADONetSamples;"
       + "user id=sa;pwd=secret;"
       + "Pooling=true;Min Pool Size=10;Max Pool Size=100";

      SqlConnection conn = new SqlConnection(strConnect);
      conn.Open();
      sqlDataAdapter1.Fill(teacherInfo1);
      conn.Close();
      DataGrid1.DataBind();
   }
}
```

This code will be called every time a new user hits the web page with which it is associated. The important code is bolded. Literally all we do is connect, use the connection, and then close the connection. The SQL Server data provider takes care of everything else. The first 10 people to hit the page simultaneously will get a connection immediately. After that, the eleventh through one-hundredth users will get a connection allocated for them. Simultaneous user 101 will end up waiting until at least one user releases a connection.

As I said, using this mechanism is very simple.

30.4.1 Connection pooling arguments

In addition to the three arguments shown in the example, you can pass a few other arguments to control the connection pooling behavior. Table 30.1 shows all the arguments.

Table 30.1 SQL Server connection pool arguments

Argument	Meaning
Pooling	Controls whether connection pooling is enabled on this connection. This parameter defaults to true.
	Examples: Pooling=true, Pooling=false
Min Pool Size	Specifies the minimum number of connections in the pool. This many connections will be created up front, even if they are not immediately being used. This parameter defaults to 0.
	Example: Min Pool Size = 10
Max Pool Size	Specifies the maximum number of connections in the pool. When this many connections have been hit, the next user to request a connection will have to wait. This parameter defaults to 100.
	Example: Max Pool Size = 50

continued on next page

Table 30.1   SQL Server connection pool arguments *(continued)*

Argument	Meaning
Connection Lifetime	Used to make the connection pool retire old connections after a set amount of time (in seconds). It is sometimes useful if a server might not be hit for a long time, causing the connection on the server to timeout, and to help make more efficient use of resources. This value defaults to 0, which means the connection has no lifetime limit. Example: `Connection Lifetime=120`
Connection Reset	Controls whether the connection is reset before being handed out of the pool. Doing so causes a performance hit (because the connection must make a call to the database engine) but guarantees that the connection is in a clean state before use. This value defaults to `true`. Example: `Connection Reset=false`
Enlist	If set to `true`, and the user of the connection is enrolled in a COM+ transaction, automatically associates the connection with that transaction. This value defaults to `true`. Example: `Enlist=false`

The default behavior is to have pooling enabled. If you don't specify a pooling argument, the result is the same as if you said the following:

```
server=localhost;database=ADONetSamples;user id=sa;pwd=secret;
    Pooling=true;Min Pool Size=0;Max Pool Size=100;Enlist=true;
    Connection Lifetime=0;Connection Reset=0
```

This default behavior gives you many of the advantages of pooling, but without much overhead. After all, the minimum pool size is set to 0, so you are not allocating any connections by default; but up to 100 connections will be allocated and handled by the pool if the requests come in.

This behavior might seem like a bit of a contradiction—the assumption is that released connections above the minimum are freed, causing new connections to be allocated. The pooling algorithm is smarter than that, though. It doesn't immediately release the connections above the minimum: it holds onto them for about six minutes. If another request for a connection comes up within that time, it will quickly get a new connection. This behavior is almost always desirable in a real-world scenario.

30.4.2   Connection pool lifetime

With a connection pool, you must worry about the pool's lifetime. The pool exists as long as there are participants in the pool, but what happens if all the connections are released? Imagine a lull in activity on your web site.[4] There are no longer any participants in the pool, so what stops it from going away?

With SQL Server, once a pool is created by a process, that pool will exist until the process goes away. As a result, you don't have to worry about keeping the pool alive.

---

[4]   Obviously, there wouldn't be lulls in *your* web site's activity—but maybe on some other site.

However, to reconfigure the pool (change the minimum or maximum entries, for example), you must restart your process. There is currently no manual way to make a pool go away.

30.4.3 Monitoring connections

To see how the connection pooling is operating, you can use the Performance Monitor snap-in. In Windows 2000, from the Administrative Tools of the control panel, select Performance (figure 30.1).

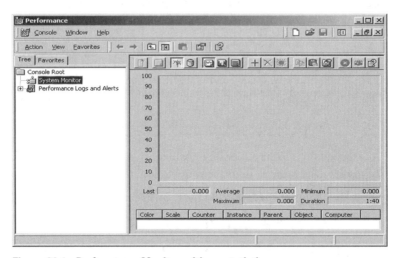

Figure 30.1 Performance Monitor with no statistics

Right-click anywhere on the chart on the right and select Add Counters. A dialog box will pop up in which you can choose items to monitor (figure 30.2).

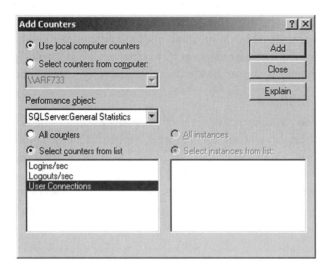

**Figure 30.2
Adding a counter**

Select the local computer counters (or the server where SQL Server is running). For the Performance Object, choose SQLServer.General Statistics—one of a number of SQL Server items you can monitor. Then select User Connections from the list of counters and click the Add button.

Doing so will take you back to the chart, but the bar will now be moving. If you run some code that allocates connections, you will see the graph change to show you the active number of connections at the current moment (figure 30.3).

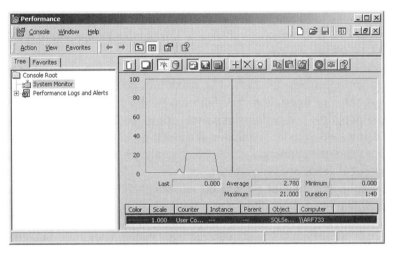

Figure 30.3 Performance Monitor showing active connections

30.5 *OLE DB* RESOURCE POOLING

OLE DB has some built-in support for connection pooling. I should warn, you, though, that it is not nearly as flexible or easy to use as SQL Server connection pooling. Also, OLE DB connection pooling relies on underlying MTS/COM+ support, so it will work only on Windows NT, 2000, or XP.

In some respects, OLE DB connection pooling is straightforward. In fact, by default it is turned on and operating. As with SQL Server, it identifies members of the same pool by exactly matching the connection string. However, in the connection string, you cannot set any properties, such as the minimum or maximum pool size. The only thing you can do in the connection string is turn off pooling. To disable pooling on a connection, you specify which OLE DB services you want enabled:

```
Provider=MSDAORA;Data Source=ADONETOR;
        User ID=scott;Password=tiger;
        OLE DB Services = -2";
```

This may seem like an odd notation, and to be fair, it is. Table 30.2 shows some of the values you can pass to enable/disable various OLE DB services.

Table 30.2   Values for the `OLE DB Services` connection string property

OLE DB Services value	Meaning
0	All services are disabled.
-1	All services are enabled. This is the default if you do not include the `OLE DB Services` setting in the connection string.
-2	All services are enabled *except* for connection pooling.
-4	All services are enabled *except* for connection pooling and auto-enlistment.
-5	All services are enabled *except* for client cursor support.
-6	All services are enabled *except* client cursor and connection pooling.

If you can't set any of the properties about the pool in the connection string, then how can you set them? You can't. The maximum pool size is determined automatically without your input, and the minimum pool size doesn't have any meaning for OLE DB pooling—the mechanism is purely time-based. Once a connection has been released, it is held onto for X amount of time. If no one asks for a new connection in that time, then the connection is closed. If someone asks for a connection, though, they get one that has not yet been released.

By default, this timeout is set to 60 seconds. You can change this value, but you cannot do it programmatically—you must do it through the Registry.[5] The value is associated with the particular OLE DB provider, so you cannot control it for different applications; but you can specify different values for different providers. The timeout is specified in the oh-so-convenient GUID key identifying the provider. For the Microsoft Oracle driver, that would be

```
HKEY_CLASSES_ROOT\CLSID\{e8cc4cbe-fdff-11d0-b865-00a0c9081c1d}
```

If you find this key in the registry, you can add a new DWORD entry called SPTimeout and set it to the number of seconds you want the timeout to be (figure 30.4).

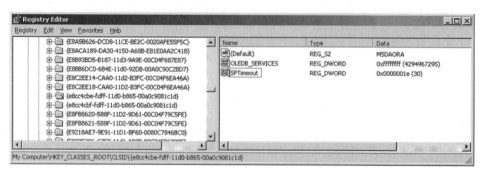

Figure 30.4   Setting the pooling timeout for Oracle

---

[5]   Okay, so you could programmatically set the value in the Registry.

If you can't find the key in the Registry, then pooling will also not function appropriately. You can add the key, and add the OLEDB_SERVICES DWord with the value shown in figure 30.4. The value 0xffffffff is the default value for `OLE DB Services` (the value you are specifying in the connection string). 0xffffffff is the same value as −1. To change the default behavior for `OLE DB Services`, change the value here.

In the figure, we changed the value to 30 seconds, so connections will last 30 seconds and then be released if no one asks for a new connection in that time period.

30.5.1 Debugging the connection pool

In early beta versions of VS.NET, you could not debug pooling code; that is, when you ran your code by pressing F5 (rather than Ctrl-F5), the pooling was automatically disabled. This no longer happens; you can now debug pooling code. However, in some situations (particularly with uncooperative drivers), repeated debugging may not work correctly. In those cases, you can disable pooling when you are debugging the surrounding code.

30.5.2 Releasing the pool

OLE DB connection pooling can do one thing SQL Server cannot: it lets you explicitly ask OLE DB to release the pool. You need to have first released (closed) all the connections you were using. Then, you can call the static method on the OleDbConnection class:

```
OleDbConnection.ReleaseObjectPool();
```

However, this is just a hint to OLE DB to release the pool. At least on the version of .NET with which I am working, this method has no noticeable effect. The pool will go away when your application closes, though, the same as with SQL Server.

30.6 COM+ OBJECT POOLING

If you are running Windows 2000 or later, you can use the powerful COM+ features, including object pooling. (Object pooling is also available under Windows NT, although with a few less options, via MTS.) COM+ can be thought of as a newer version of MTS (Microsoft Transaction Server).[6]

Whereas connection pooling and resource pooling are all about pools of connections, COM+ object pooling lets you keep arbitrary objects within the pool, with COM+ doing all the pool management for you. Prior to .NET, the "objects" you could manage with COM+ were, as the name implies, COM components. With .NET, you can set up a .NET class as a COM+ object by doing little more than adding an attribute to the code.[7]

---

[6] In my opinion, the name MTS was never good, because it emphasized transactions and downplayed all the other great features of MTS.

[7] Although under the hood, the .NET class is being exposed as a COM component.

If you can create a .NET class that uses COM+ object pooling, that object can hold onto a database connection—and, voila, you have a database connection pool. Compared to the other mechanisms, if you are exclusively using SQL Server, this type of pooling is more work to use and doesn't buy you much unless you were using COM+ for some other reason. If you are using OLE DB, though, it is as much as 50% faster and gives you much more control.

All the ins and outs of COM+ are beyond this book, but I will provide a simple example of using COM+ object pooling. The example creates a pooled COM+ object in .NET and uses it from .NET, using automatic registration to configure the object. The object creates a connection to an Oracle database when it is started. We will create only one instance of the object, but because we have set up the object to use pooling, the number of objects equal to the minimum pool size will be created. We'll see this result by looking at the active connections in Oracle.

Before we can use the pool, we have to create a poolable object, which involves several steps:

- We need a DLL to hold the poolable object.

- We need to create the class for the pool.

- The DLL must be given a *strong name*. For security reasons, you cannot put a .NET class into COM+ until it is clearly identified.

We'll go through each of these steps in turn.

30.6.1 Creating a DLL for the pooled object

Creating the DLL is straightforward: create a new project in the environment as a C# class library. We'll call it ADONetPoolTest (figure 30.5).

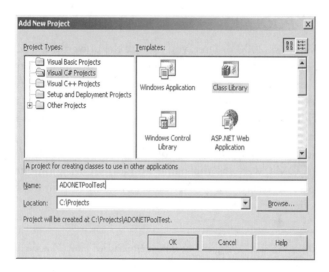

Figure 30.5
Creating a DLL

CHAPTER 30 CONNECTION POOLING

30.6.2   Creating the class for the pool

The class for the pool can be easily created by right-clicking on the project and choosing Add Class. Let's create a class called ADONetTestComponent. The class needs to be modified, though. Listing 30.1 shows the code for the entire class.

Listing 30.1   Creating a poolable .NET class

```
using System;                                          ❶ Using statements
using System.EnterpriseServices;
using System.Data;
using System.Data.OleDb;


namespace ADONetPoolTest
{

/// <summary>
/// ADONetTestComponent for testing connection pooling
/// </summary>
[ObjectPooling(MinPoolSize=20, MaxPoolSize=100)]       ❷ ObjectPooling attribute

                    Deriving from serviced component ❸

public class ADONetTestComponent : ServicedComponent, IDisposable

                            Deriving from IDisposable ❹
{
    private OleDbConnection m_Conn = null;

    /// <summary>Constructor</summary>
    public ADONetTestComponent()
    {
        // Connect to the database on connection - note that
        // OLE DB connection pooling is disabled.             ❺ Constructor
        string strConnect =
            "Provider=MSDAORA;Data Source=ADONETOR;" +
            "User ID=scott;Password=tiger;OLE DB Services = -2";
        m_Conn = new OleDbConnection(strConnect);
        m_Conn.Open();
    }

    /// <summary>Finalizer</summary>
    ~ADONetTestComponent()
    {                                                  ❻ Finalizer
        CloseConnection();
    }

    /// <summary>Explicit clean-up</summary>
    protected override void Dispose(bool disposing)
    {
        CloseConnection();                             ❼ Dispose
        base.Dispose(disposing);                          method
        GC.SuppressFinalize(this);
    }
```

```
/// <summary>Does actual clean-up work for class</summary>
protected void CloseConnection()
{
    m_Conn.Close();
}


/// <summary>
/// Indicates that pooling is allowed
/// </summary>
public override bool CanBePooled()
{                                                    ❽ CanBePooled
    return true;
}


/// <summary>Method to see if a teacher exists</summary>
public bool TeacherExists(string strName)
{
    // Create a command, and select data
    string strSQL =
        "SELECT * FROM Teachers WHERE TeacherName=?";
    OleDbCommand comm = new OleDbCommand(strSQL,m_Conn);
    comm.Parameters.Add("@Teacher",strName);          ❾ Check for
                                                         teacher
    IDataReader reader = comm.ExecuteReader();

    // True if at least one record found
    bool bRetval = reader.Read();
    reader.Close();

    return bRetval;
}
}
}
```

❶ The only namespace here that might not be familiar is System.EnterpriseSer-
vices. It is required in order to access COM+ services. One problem, though—this
namespace references a DLL that is not loaded by default. If we try to compile this
code, we will be told that System.EnterpriseServices doesn't exist, and the
various items we are using from that namespace will be treated similarly.

To remedy this situation, we need to add a reference to the appropriate DLL. In
the Solution Explorer, right-click on References under our project and select Add Reference. Scroll down the .NET list to find System.EnterpriseServices. Select it, and
then click OK in the dialog box (figure 30.6). System.EnterpriseServices will now
show up in the list of references in the Solution Explorer.

❷ If you are not familiar with the attribute capabilities of .NET and C#, then this statement may look odd. It is *decorating* our class with an attribute. The information in
the attribute becomes extra metadata associated with the class that can be read by
external mechanisms (such as the COM+ registration mechanism).

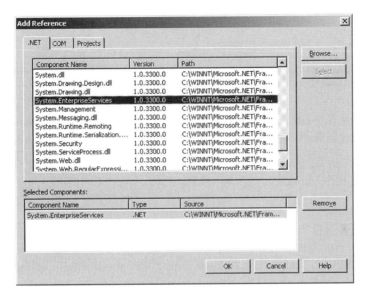

Figure 30.6
Referencing
EnterpriseServices

The primary thing being specified here is that the object should be set up for object pooling. In addition, we specify a couple of default parameters: the minimum and maximum pool sizes. Note that these are defaults that will be used when the component is registered, but the administrator of the system can go to the component service's Activation tab and change these values.

❸ In order for the class to work with COM+, it must be derived from ServicedComponent, which provides all the underlying support for COM+ in .NET.

❹ This interface indicates that the class has a method on it called `Dispose()`, which will clean up resources if called.

❺ This is the standard object constructor. In this case, the constructor is connecting to Oracle and storing the connection in a member variable for later use. Notice that we disable the OLE DB connection pooling (using the `OLE DB Services = -2` notation). We don't want two different mechanisms fighting to pool our connections.

❻ Although, if you are C++ person, this looks like a destructor, it is a *finalizer*, which will be called when the object is garbage-collected. We need to have a finalizer to make absolutely sure the connection is released when the object goes away. Of course, if we didn't do this, the connection would eventually be garbage-collected anyway, but we have no way to know when this might happen. We don't know when the pooled object will go away either, but at least we can make sure the connection is not held any longer than the pooled object.

This is a short-hand mechanism built into C#. You can also create a finalizer like this:

```
protected override void Finalize()
{
    base.Finalize();
    CloseConnection();
}
```

Using the tilde (~) named method automatically calls the base class, so you cannot forget to do it. On the other hand, the explicit `Finalize()` method is easier to read.

❼ This method can be called to explicitly free resources from the object. When it is called, it does three things:

1 Releases the connection.

2 Gives any base classes the opportunity to clean up.

3 Tells the runtime that the class does not need to be finalized. An overhead is associated with finalization, because the object cannot simply be thrown away. We know, though, that if `Dispose()` has been called, we don't need to finalize because we have already released the connection.

❽ This method is an override of the base class, indicating that the object is allowed to be pooled. Given that we set up the attribute at the top of the class, this code is somewhat redundant, but it is more explicit.

❾ For the object to be useful, it has to do something with the connection. This method uses the connection to query for a teacher, and returns `true` if the teacher exists.

30.6.3 Giving the DLL a strong name

One of the major focuses of .NET is security. Given the current state of the Internet, you want to be able to limit what different applications can do[8] and make sure the applications you are running are really the applications you think they are.

This last issue is addressed via the use of public/private key encryption. The mechanism works something like this:

• When you create an assembly (say, a DLL), you use your private key to create an encrypted signature that becomes part of the name of the assembly. An assembly that does this is said to have a *strong name*. This can *only* be done when the assembly is created—there is no way to do it after the fact.

• When another piece of code attempts to access the assembly, it uses the public key to decrypt the strong name. This process will work *only* if the signature was encrypted using the private key. If the decryption works, then it is the expected file, and not a pretender.

---

[8] As opposed to the ActiveX mechanism—allow nothing or allow *everything*.

This topic comes up in a discussion about connection pooling because COM+ requires an assembly to have a strong name in order to be registered. For a real-world deployed application, you would go to a company such as Verisign to get a public/private key assigned to your company. For our purposes, though, we can use a .NET command-line utility to generate a public/private key for testing.

Generating a key

The strong name utility is a command-line utility, so we need to open a command window. Use the Visual Studio.NET Command Prompt under Visual Studio.NET Tools on the menu, because it will set up the path to the various utilities automatically. At the prompt, enter the following command:

```
sn -k ADONETTest.snk
```

It will generate a new key with the name ADONETTest.snk. Copy this file to the directory with the test component DLL (in our case, c:\projects\ADONetPoolTest).

Referencing the key

We now need to make the assembly use the key, which we can do by adding a reference to it in the AssemblyInfo.cs file that was automatically created as part of the project. While we are at it, we should give our component a name, rather than relying on .NET to generate it. I have added the lines close to the bottom of the AssemblyInfo.cs file:

```
[assembly: AssemblyDelaySign(false)]
[assembly: AssemblyKeyName("")]
[assembly: ApplicationName("ADONetTestComponent")]
[assembly: AssemblyKeyFile(@"..\..\adonettest.snk")]
```

The bolded lines are ones I added.[9] The ApplicationName attribute is used to indicate the name COM+ will use to refer to components in this assembly. The AssemblyKeyFileAttribute tells the assembly to read the key information out of the file AdoNetTest.snk. Notice that we are using a relative directory to reference the file, because the assembly will be built in either the bin\debug or bin\release directory. We need to back up to the project directory to access the key.

Component version

The strong name is not the only thing that becomes part of the name of the assembly. One of the features of .NET is its ability to run different versions of an application and its DLLs side by side. It does so by modifying the name of the various DLLs to contain the version of the component. The version is also stored in the Assembly-Info.cs file. If you look, you will see an attribute like this:

```
[assembly: AssemblyVersion("1.0.*")]
```

---

[9] There might already be an AssemblyKeyFile attribute in the file, set to a blank string. If so, then use it rather than creating a new one.

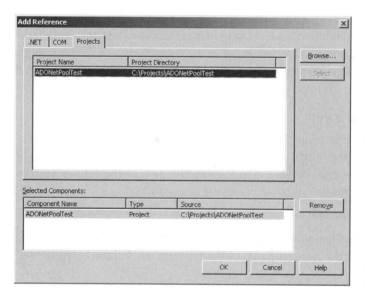

Figure 30.7
Referencing a project

The version has a major, minor, build, and revision component. In this case, major is 1, minor is 0, and build is an asterisk. Currently there is no revision number. The asterisk is the reason I brought up the topic: it is a handy feature of .NET that says "automatically increment this build number every time I build." Remember that the version number becomes part of the name of the DLL we intend to register with COM+.

The problem is, every time you build and run the component, .NET will see if it has already been registered with COM+, and it will *not* see it because it has a different name (the version number piece will be different). So, it will re-register the component, and you will end up with a new version of the component from every different build.

Your code will still work (the component will be in place), but you will have a couple of problems:

- Running the code will take longer; the registration process is a little slow.
- You will end up with a bunch of different copies of the component in COM+.

The easiest way to remedy these problems is to stop the version number from changing, by modifying the `AssemblyVersion` attribute:

```
[assembly: AssemblyVersion("1.0.0.1")]
```

30.6.4 Registering/using the component

We will use the ability of .NET COM+ components to register themselves. Doing so is simple—the first time we attempt to use the component, it will be registered with COM+! To use the component from .NET, use it exactly the same way you would use any other class.

To test this, I created a new console application. For simplicity, I created it in the same workspace as the component, by right-clicking on the solution in the Solution Explorer, choosing Add → New Project, and then selecting a C# console application.

The console application does, however, need to reference the component; so under the console application (mine is called ADOPoolHost), right-click on References, choose Add Reference, and then switch to the Projects tab and select the component project (figure 30.7).

Now we need to modify the code to reference the component. Listing 30.2 shows the entire code, with the parts I added in bold.

Listing 30.2 Using the component

```
using System;
using ADONetPoolTest;                 ❶ Use component's namespace

namespace ADOPoolHost
{
    /// <summary>Test the ADONetPool component</summary>
    class Class1
    {
        static void Main(string[] args)
        {
            try
            {                                           ❷ Create
                ADONetTestComponent antc                    component
                    = new ADONetTestComponent();
                                                        ❸ Call
                bool bFound =                              method
                    antc.TeacherExists("Mr. Biddick");

                Console.WriteLine(
                        bFound ? "Teacher found" : "Teacher not found");
                Console.WriteLine("Press enter");
                Console.ReadLine();
            }
            catch(Exception ex)
            {
                Console.WriteLine(ex.ToString());
            }
        }
    }
}
```

❶ The component is in another namespace, so we must reference it here to be able to use it.

❷ This code creates an instance of the object, as with any other object; but behind the scenes, COM+ is doing some significant work. First, it checks to see if the component is registered with COM+, and if not, it registers it. Second, it uses the behavior we specified for pooling.

❸ Here we invisibly call the pooled component.

30.6.5 Running the application

As with the other pooling mechanisms, we will not get reliable pooling services if we are running in the debugger, so we must run the application directly (Ctrl-F5 instead of F5). It will probably run slowly the first time; the COM+ registration takes a little while, plus the initial connection to Oracle is generally slow.

Even though we are expecting pooling behavior, we do not have to wait for all the connections to be made—just the first one. COM+ will make the other connections for us in the background.

To see that this process is working, look in Component Services to see that the application was registered. From the Control Panel, in Administrative Tools, select Component Services. Expand the tree through the following nodes; Component Services → My Computer → COM+ Applications → ADONetTestComponent → Components. The test component appears (figure 30.8).

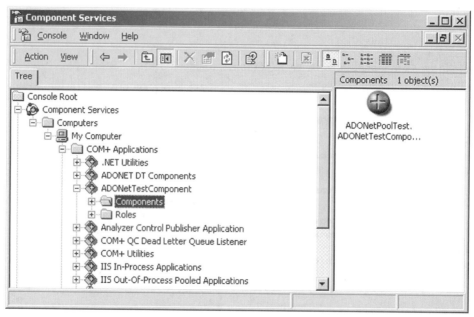

Figure 30.8   Component Services showing the COM+ application

Right-click on the component and choose Properties, and a multipage property sheet will come up. Go to the Activation tab to see our settings (figure 30.9).

As you can see, the minimum and maximum pool sizes are set as expected. Further, if you look in Oracle's sessions, you will see that 20 connections have been made, even though we only created one instance of the component (figure 30.10).

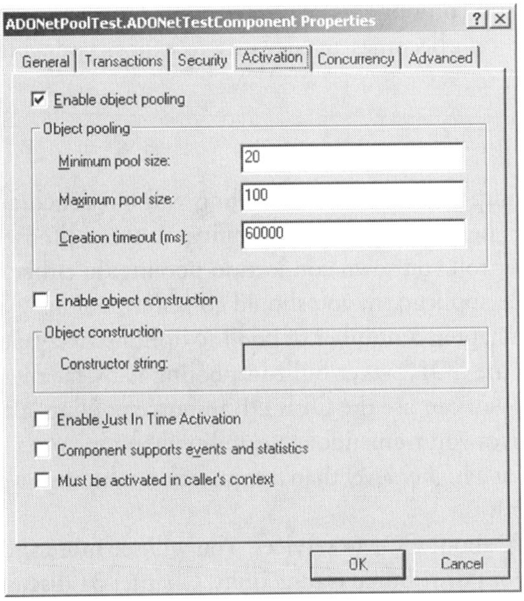

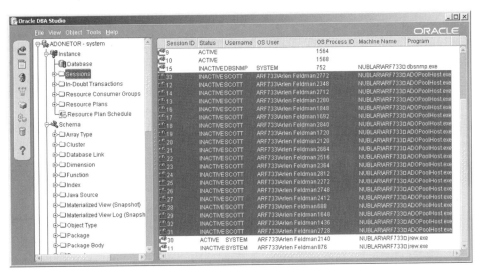

**Figure 30.9
Component pooling settings**

30.6.6   COM+ object pooling summary

The COM+ object pooling mechanism is by far the most powerful technique for pooling connections or other objects. It lets you do your pooling at a higher level than a connection, so you can tie the pool to your business logic in a more meaningful way. COM+ will also notify your component every time an object is activated (taken out of the pool) or deactivated (returned to the pool), giving you much finer control over your use of resources.

Figure 30.10   Oracle connections

One last benefit is that .NET components registered with COM+ can be used by non-.NET code, via COM. This becomes an easy way to expose your .NET code to legacy applications.

30.7 SUMMARY

Few things you can do as simply as connection pooling will have such a significant impact on your application's performance and scalability. You can choose to use the approaches presented here, or roll your own connection pooling; in either case, if you are planning a highly scalable application, you should consider pooling.

As you have seen in this chapter, a number of pooling options are available. If you are using SQL Server, then the SQL Server built-in pooling is by far the fastest and best choice. With OLE DB, you can use the OLE DB resource pooling, although you have few options. COM+ gives you tremendous flexibility when it comes to pooling, including the ability to pool at a higher level than a connection (although a lot of auto-magical behavior is going on).

This chapter talked a little about COM+ services. You will see more about COM+ in chapter 32, when I talk about distributed transactions. Chapter 31 discusses reading schema information from your database.

CHAPTER 31

Reading database information

This chapter explains how to retrieve information about your database schema using ADO.NET. This topic may or may not be of interest to you, depending on the type of applications you write. Certain types of applications, such as general utilities, depend on being able to read information about the database in order to function (for example, a tool for creating ER diagrams, or a generic import tool). Other applications don't need to read database information; for example, many business applications are hard-coded to talk to a particular database structure, and they assume the database will be set up in the expected manner.

For these types of applications, it is *fairly* reasonable to trust that the database is configured appropriately, and this assumption gives job security to legions of DBAs. However, it is not a bad practice to build your applications such that they confirm the expected database setup, or have a mode for checking for problems. It's good practice to provide an administrative utility that can check the structure and has the ability to create the expected structures in a new database or fix certain problems.

For SQL Server, the main way of determining structural information is via stored procedures. If you're used to working with SQL Server, there is little difference in the way this is done with ADO.NET versus older technologies, although I will discuss a few procedures.

437

For OLE DB users, the situation is different. You can use the various system tables and stored procedures for your engine, but you also have the option of using OLE DB's capability of reporting information via the `GetOleDbSchemaTable()` method on the OleDbConnection class. Many OLE DB providers support reading information this way, so you can generically read structural information without having intimate knowledge of the underlying engine.

31.1 SQL SERVER STRUCTURAL INFORMATION

As well as holding a user's data, a database must also hold information about the database itself—what tables are present, how they are indexed, and so forth. SQL Server does this by the recursive but powerful mechanism of maintaining a series of *system* tables. These tables operate in the same way as any user table, but they are specific to the system; you cannot delete them or change their structure. If SQL Server needs to know something about the structure of the database, it can query one of these system tables to get the information.

Because the information is stored in tables, you can write queries against these tables to determine information about tables, indexes, and so on. Doing so works, but has a couple of problems:

- These tables are designed for the convenience of SQL Server, not for you, so the organization of the data is not optimal for retrieval.

- There is no guarantee that the structures won't change. Microsoft is within its rights to add or remove system tables or change their layout. Although these tables tend not change dramatically, even a patch might make a change.

Still, regular users needed a way to access this data, so Microsoft created a series of stored procedures that access the system tables for you. These procedures solve both problems:

- Because Microsoft has a detailed understanding of the data in the system tables, the company can expose the data in a more useable format, even if it requires multiple queries, joins, and so forth.

- Even if the underlying system tables change, the stored procedure can still expose data the same way. This is the case even if under the hood, the stored procedure now hits completely different tables.

As you saw in chapter 13, calling stored procedures is trivial, and the stored procedure can return data or can return a result set as though you had done a classic query. In the next several sections, we will look at a number of these procedures.

31.1.1 Getting a list of tables

Once you know the name of a table, you can get a lot of information about that table. By the expedient of doing a query, you can determine all the columns, their data types, and more:

```
SELECT * FROM SomeTable
```

You can also call `FillSchema()` on a DataSet to retrieve information about the primary keys and some rules about the table.

Doing so is predicated on the fact that you know the name of the table. To first find out the list of tables, you can use the `sp_tables` stored procedure:

```
public void SqlGetTables(SqlConnection conn)
{
    SqlCommand comm = new SqlCommand("sp_tables",conn);
    comm.CommandType = CommandType.StoredProcedure;

    IDataReader reader = comm.ExecuteReader();

    DisplayReaderResults(reader);
}
```

This code should be familiar. The only new aspect is that we are using a system stored procedure rather than one we created. The `DisplayReaderResults()` method writes out the results from the reader, which I have pulled out to show here:

TABLE_QUALIFIER	TABLE_OWNER	TABLE_NAME	TABLE_TYPE
ADONetSamples	dbo	syscolumns	SYSTEM TABLE
ADONetSamples	dbo	syscomments	SYSTEM TABLE
ADONetSamples	dbo	sysdepends	SYSTEM TABLE
ADONetSamples	dbo	sysfilegroups	SYSTEM TABLE
ADONetSamples	dbo	sysfiles	SYSTEM TABLE
ADONetSamples	dbo	sysfiles1	SYSTEM TABLE
ADONetSamples	dbo	sysforeignkeys	SYSTEM TABLE
ADONetSamples	dbo	sysfulltextcatalogs	SYSTEM TABLE
ADONetSamples	dbo	sysfulltextnotify	SYSTEM TABLE
ADONetSamples	dbo	sysindexes	SYSTEM TABLE
ADONetSamples	dbo	sysindexkeys	SYSTEM TABLE
ADONetSamples	dbo	sysmembers	SYSTEM TABLE
ADONetSamples	dbo	sysobjects	SYSTEM TABLE
ADONetSamples	dbo	syspermissions	SYSTEM TABLE
ADONetSamples	dbo	sysproperties	SYSTEM TABLE
ADONetSamples	dbo	sysprotects	SYSTEM TABLE
ADONetSamples	dbo	sysreferences	SYSTEM TABLE
ADONetSamples	dbo	systypes	SYSTEM TABLE
ADONetSamples	dbo	sysusers	SYSTEM TABLE
ADONetSamples	dbo	BigBinary	TABLE
ADONetSamples	dbo	Classes	TABLE
ADONetSamples	dbo	ClassName	TABLE
ADONetSamples	dbo	Classrooms	TABLE
ADONetSamples	dbo	Customers	TABLE
ADONetSamples	dbo	dtproperties	TABLE

```
ADONetSamples    dbo         Employees          TABLE
ADONetSamples    dbo         LargeDataTest      TABLE
ADONetSamples    dbo         Orders             TABLE
ADONetSamples    dbo         Shippers           TABLE
ADONetSamples    dbo         Table1             TABLE
ADONetSamples    dbo         Table2             TABLE
ADONetSamples    dbo         Teachers           TABLE
ADONetSamples    dbo         sysconstraints     VIEW
ADONetSamples    dbo         syssegments        VIEW
```

The stored procedure returns five columns. The first four are shown in this listing and are self-explanatory. I have excluded the fifth column, named Remarks, to conserve space. This column is always empty; it is provided for compatibility with ODBC.

A number of the tables are system tables—the tables SQL Server uses to manage the database. You can filter the returned list based on the table type. In fact, you can filter based on any of the fields (except remarks) by passing parameters. For example, to list only items where the table type is TABLE, you would do the following:

```
public void SqlGetTables(SqlConnection conn)
{
    SqlCommand comm = new SqlCommand("sp_tables",conn);
    comm.CommandType = CommandType.StoredProcedure;

    comm.Parameters.Add("@table_type","'TABLE'");

    IDataReader reader = comm.ExecuteReader();

    DisplayReaderResults(reader);
}
```

The stored procedure has an optional parameter called @table_type to which you can pass one or more tables on which to filter. Note that the value TABLE is in single-quotes: this is required. To filter on multiple items (say, TABLE or VIEW), you do the following:

```
comm.Parameters.Add("@table_type","'TABLE','VIEW'");
```

Here are the results from the TABLE filter:

```
TABLE_QUALIFIER TABLE_OWNER       TABLE_NAME      TABLE_TYPE
--------------- -----------       ----------      ----------

ADONetSamples   dbo               BigBinary       TABLE
ADONetSamples   dbo               Classes         TABLE
ADONetSamples   dbo               ClassName       TABLE
ADONetSamples   dbo               Classrooms      TABLE
ADONetSamples   dbo               Customers       TABLE
ADONetSamples   dbo               dtproperties    TABLE
ADONetSamples   dbo               Employees       TABLE
ADONetSamples   dbo               LargeDataTest   TABLE
ADONetSamples   dbo               Orders          TABLE
ADONetSamples   dbo               Shippers        TABLE
ADONetSamples   dbo               Table1          TABLE
ADONetSamples   dbo               Table2          TABLE
ADONetSamples   dbo               Teachers        TABLE
```

As expected, the result set contains only TABLEs.

I won't show the result sets from the remaining options, but you can filter on the other columns as well via the following parameters:

- @table_name—Filters the list based on the table name.

- @table_owner—Filters the list based on the owner of the table (usually the user who created the table, although a different creator can be specified).

- @table_qualifier—In SQL Server, generally filters on the name of the database. It is included here for compatibility with other engines (via mechanisms such as ODBC). You can always refer to a table with a fully qualified name—the qualifier plus the owner plus the name: ADONetSamples.dbo.Classes.

To filter on the owner, for example, you would set the @table_owner parameter:

```
comm.Parameters.Add("@table_owner","dbo");
```

You can also use wildcards on these parameters. If you wanted all tables whose name started with the letter *C*, you would set the parameter like this:

```
comm.Parameters.Add("@table_name","C%");
```

31.1.2 Index and key information

You might also want to read the list of indexes on a particular table. You can do this using the sp_statistics stored procedure. This seems like a silly name for a procedure to return column names, but it does more than return the list of indexes—it also provides various statistics about the way the index is set up. Here is the code to call the procedure:

```
public void SqlGetIndexes(SqlConnection conn)
{
    SqlCommand comm = new SqlCommand("sp_statistics",conn);
    comm.CommandType = CommandType.StoredProcedure;

    comm.Parameters.Add("@table_name","Classes");

    IDataReader reader = comm.ExecuteReader();

    DisplayReaderResults(reader);
}
```

As with the sp_tables stored procedure, you can pass a number of parameters. Unlike sp_tables, though, at least one of the parameters is not optional: you must specify a table name, and you cannot use wildcards. This procedure returns a bunch of columns—I have pulled out a few of the relevant ones:

NON_UNIQUE	INDEX_NAME	TYPE	SEQ_IN_INDEX	COLUMN_NAME	COLLATION
0	PK_Classes	1	1	ClassID	A
1	IX_Classes	3	1	ClassName	A
1	IX_Classes	3	2	Period	A

The Non_Unique column returns 0 if the index is unique and 1 if it is not. The name is self-explanatory, but you may notice that the same index name shows up in multiple columns—that happens because the particular index IX_Classes, indexes multiple columns. The IX_Classes index looks something like this:

```
ClassName Asc, Period Asc
```

If you look at the SEQ_IN_INDEX (short for sequence in index) and the column name, you can see how the index can be reconstructed. The Collation column indicates ascending or descending.

The Type indicates, amazingly enough, the type of the index. Values include:

- 1 (Clustered)
- 2 (Hashed)
- 3 (Other)

Primary and foreign keys

Stored procedures are available to retrieve information about primary and foreign keys. To get the primary key, use sp_pkeys:

```
public void SqlGetIndexes(SqlConnection conn)
{
    SqlCommand comm = new SqlCommand("sp_pkeys",conn);
    comm.CommandType = CommandType.StoredProcedure;

    comm.Parameters.Add("@table_name","Classes");

    IDataReader reader = comm.ExecuteReader();

    DisplayReaderResults(reader);
}
```

As with the sp_statistics stored procedure, you have to provide the table name. Here is the output:

```
TABLE_QUALIFIER TABLE_OWNER TABLE_NAME COLUMN_NAME KEY_SEQ PK_NAME
--------------- ----------- ---------- ----------- ------- -------
ADONetSamples   dbo         Classes    ClassID     1       PK_Classes
```

These fields should be familiar.

You can get a list of foreign keys using the sp_fkeys stored procedure:

```
SqlCommand comm = new SqlCommand("sp_fkeys",conn);
comm.CommandType = CommandType.StoredProcedure;
```

As with the other stored procedures, you can supply a number of parameters. You must provide one of the following two parameters:

- pktable_name—The table with the primary key
- fktable_name—The table with the foreign key

31.1.3 Other useful stored procedures

SQL Server includes hundreds of system-provided stored procedures related to various different sets of functionality, such as using the fast text search capabilities, dealing with distributed queries (queries that cross multiple engines), and working with replication. I can't do justice to them all here, but calling them is generally as straightforward as the ones we have been working with. I recommend you look at the SQL Server documentation for a full list.

31.2 OLE DB STRUCTURAL INFORMATION

If you are only working with a single database engine via OLE DB, and you are familiar with the way that engine stores structural information, then you can access that information directly. Many engines have stored procedures similar to SQL Server, or have system tables designed to be accessed to read schema information.

However, if you are not sure what engine you are using, you can use an OLE DB mechanism that is exposed by the ADO.NET OLE DB data provider: `GetOleDb-SchemaTable()`. This method provides access to the various different sets of schema information the provider has available. Be aware, though, that not all providers implement support for this method. For example, the Microsoft Oracle driver supports this method, but the Oracle driver does not.

The `GetOleDbSchemaTable()` method had to be relatively generic to map to the underlying functionality. Depending on the type of schema data you want, you might have any number of arguments to pass, of various data types. To handle this variety, `GetOleDbSchemaTable()` takes two arguments:

- *Schema identifier*—A value indicating which data you want to retrieve. The values to pass can be retrieved from the OleDbSchemaGuid class.

- *Array of arguments*—An array of objects (usually strings) that are passed to the underlying mechanism to indicate the type of data you require. These are referred to as *restrictions*, because they limit the data that is returned.

The method returns a DataTable configured to hold the appropriate return data. Let's look at an example.

31.2.1 Getting a list of tables

The following code gets a list of tables from an OLE DB data source:

```
public void OleDbGetTables(OleDbConnection conn)
{
    object[] aRestrictions = new object[4];
    aRestrictions[3] = "TABLE";

    DataTable dt = conn.GetOleDbSchemaTable(OleDbSchemaGuid.Tables,
                                            aRestrictions);

    PrintDataTable(dt);
}
```

The value `OleDbSchemaGuid.Tables` indicates that we want to get a list of tables. When asking for a list of tables, you can pass up to four arguments restricting the data. The order is important. For tables, each argument has the following meaning:

- *First argument*—Catalog name
- *Second argument*—Schema name
- *Third argument*—Table name
- *Fourth argument*—Table type

In the example, we are setting the fourth argument (array position 3) only, to indicate that we want only tables included in the result set. As with SQL Server, we can pass a number of values, such as `View`, `Alias`, or `System Table`.

The other arguments are `null` (because we never set them); we don't want to limit the data based on them. Here is the output from this method when run against an Oracle data source, with some columns removed for space:

```
TABLE_SCHEMA    TABLE_NAME    TABLE_TYPE
------------    ----------    ----------
MDSYS           CS_SRS        TABLE
MDSYS           MD$DICTVER    TABLE
SCOTT           ACCOUNT       TABLE
SCOTT           BONUS         TABLE
SCOTT           DEPT          TABLE
SCOTT           EMP           TABLE
SCOTT           RECEIPT       TABLE
SCOTT           SALGRADE      TABLE
```

To limit the data in any other way—say, to see only the tables owned by Scott—we could set the restrictions:

```
aRestrictions[1] = "SCOTT";
```

Unlike with the SQL Server stored procedure, however, we cannot use wildcards. So, for example, we cannot do something like `"SCO%"`.

31.2.2 Reading index information

You can pass several arguments to `GetOleDbSchemaTable()` to retrieve various sets of index information. These arguments include the following:

- `OleDbSchemaGuid.Indexes`—To read index information
- `OleDbSchemaGuid.Primary_Keys`—To read the primary key on a particular table
- `OleDbSchemaGuid.Foreign_Keys`—To read the foreign key on a table or the list of foreign keys in which the table is participating

Let's look at some examples. First, we'll read an index. This time we will hit an Access database:

```
public void OleDbGetIndexes(OleDbConnection conn)
{
    object[] aRestrictions = new object[5];
    aRestrictions[4] = "Teachers";

    DataTable dt = conn.GetOleDbSchemaTable(OleDbSchemaGuid.Indexes,
                                            aRestrictions);

    PrintDataTable(dt);
}
```

The list of restrictions for `OleDbSchemaGuid.Indexes` contains up to five items:

- *Table catalog (0)*—The catalog, if supported.
- *Table schema (1)*—The schema or owner name
- *Index name (2)*—A particular index
- *Type (3)*—The type of index. You can specifically ask for indexes that are BTrees, hash tables, and so on.
- *Table name (4)*—The name of the table.

Unlike the SQL Server stored procedure, you can exclude the table name to get a list of all indexes. We don't do that here, but instead specifically ask for the indexes on the Teachers table. Here are the somewhat pruned results:

TABLE_NAME	INDEX_NAME	PRIMARY_KEY	UNIQUE	CLUSTERED	ORD[1]	COLUMN_NAME
Teachers	PrimaryKey	True	True	False	1	TeacherID
Teachers	TeacherID	False	False	False	1	TeacherID

The information is very similar to that returned from SQL Server. There are no multicolumn indexes on this table; but if there were, that index would have multiple rows, with just the ordinal position column and column name columns changed

You probably have a good idea how the `GetOleDbSchemaTable()` method works now. I'll list the options for the other two index requests.

Primary keys

To get a list of primary keys on a table, pass the `Primary_Keys` ID:

```
DataTable dt =
        conn.GetOleDbSchemaTable(OleDbSchemaGuid.Primary_Keys,
                                            aRestrictions);
```

---

[1] Abbreviated from ORDINAL_POSITION.

The restrictions contain up to three arguments to limit the return result (information to identify the table):

- *Table catalog (0)*—If catalogs are supported, the name of the catalog containing the table
- *Table schema (1)*—The schema or owner of the table
- *Table name (2)*—The name of the table

To get the primary key from the Teachers table, we would set the restrictions like this:

```
aRestrictions[2] = "Teachers";
```

Don't forget that you can get back multiple rows for the primary key—one row for each field that participates in the key.

Foreign keys

The call to retrieve foreign keys should look like this:

```
DataTable dt =
        conn.GetOleDbSchemaTable(OleDbSchemaGuid.Foreign_Keys,
                                        aRestrictions);
```

For foreign keys, the restrictions collection can include up to six arguments:

- *Primary key table catalog (0)*—If catalogs are supported, the catalog containing the table with the primary key
- *Primary key table schema (1)*—The schema or owner of the table with the primary key
- *Primary key table name (2)*—The name of the table containing the primary key
- *Foreign key table catalog (3)*—If catalogs are supported, the catalog containing the table with the foreign key
- *Foreign key table schema (4)* —The schema or owner of the table with the foreign key
- *Foreign key table name (5)*—The name of the table containing the foreign key

To ask for any foreign keys that were using the Classroom table to validate their entries, we would set the primary key table name:

```
aRestrictions[2] = "Classroom";
```

31.2.3 Other schema tables

You can pass a large number of other values of greater or lesser value to `GetOleDb-SchemaTable()`, depending on your needs. For example, you can pass `OleDb-SchemaGuid.Procedures` to get a list of stored procedures. I recommend looking at the members of the OleDbSchemaGuid class for a fuller list.

31.3   SUMMARY

For certain types of applications, the ability to determine the underlying schema of the database is absolutely critical. For others, it is merely a handy confirmation mechanism, or completely unimportant. Whatever the case, ADO.NET provides mechanisms for accessing the information, both via the use of the specialized `Get-OleDbSchemaTable()` method, and by giving you full access to the underlying support of your database engine.

C H A P T E R 3 2

Distributed transactions

You normally do a transaction in a database to make sure multiple operations are considered to be atomic—either they all happen, or none of them happen. A distributed transaction is no different, except:

- The operations that must be atomic are not all necessarily in the same database.
- The operations are not necessarily database operations.

Technically speaking, distributed transactions have little to do with ADO.NET—as I said, the objects involved in the transaction do not necessarily even have anything to do with a database. Also, the basics of using COM+ and distributed transactions are straightforward, but many details delve deep into COM+. I feel that it is a worthwhile topic to include in this book. However, I will only provide a single, straightforward example. To go into more depth, you should pick up a good COM+/.NET book.

32.1 USING DISTRIBUTED TRANSACTIONS

When Microsoft Transaction Server (MTS) was first released for NT 4.0, a lot of noise was made about its ability to do distributed transactions—after all, MTS even has *Transactions* in its name. This was a shame, because MTS is much more than a tool for doing distributed transactions. It is a component management system that can be used to control the life cycle of components, make them accessible, deal with threading issues and pooling, and provide a number of other services. When the next release of MTS came out with Windows 2000, the name had changed to COM+, which wasn't as misleading.

Not that being able to do distributed transactions isn't useful and powerful, but I suspect it is not close to being the most-used COM+ feature. When you need it, though, COM+ makes distributed transaction very easy.

The classic example of a distributed transaction is a money transfer. Money is taken out of one account in one system and added to an account in another system (possibly controlled by a different organization). It is important that both operations succeed or fail together. You would be annoyed if the money was removed from your account but not put into the account where it was going.

Another common use of distributed transactions is with legacy applications, when data is being transferred from/to an old mainframe application into a COM+ application. You need to guarantee that the data went into the new system before removing it from the old.

The mechanism for accomplishing this task is extremely complex. With the banking example, for instance, think about all the points in the operation where something could go wrong: power going out on one of the machines, an account's being unavailable, and so forth. COM+ hides all this complexity behind a couple of simple methods.

32.2 DISTRIBUTED TRANSACTION CONCEPTS

Before getting too deep into an example, you need to have a basic understanding of what goes on during a distributed transaction. COM+ does a lot of the work for you—enough, in fact, that the process seems a bit like magic. The first issue is determining whether a particular object[1] is participating in a transaction. When an object is created (via COM+), it specifies whether it should participate in a transaction. In fact, one of the properties that you can specify on a COM+ object is how it will work with a transaction:

- `Required`—This object requires a transaction. If a transaction has already been started, then this object will participate in the existing transaction. If not, a new transaction will be created.

---

[1] Remember COM+ is all about objects, not database connections.

- Supported—If a transaction exists, then this object will participate in the transaction. If there is no transaction, then the object will work anyway.

- RequiresNew—Not only must the object be in a transaction, but a new transaction must be created for this object, even if a transaction already exists.

- NotSupported—The object must not be involved with any existing transaction.

- Disabled—The object doesn't care one way or the other, and doesn't have any interaction with the transaction.

The diagram in figure 32.1 provides an example.

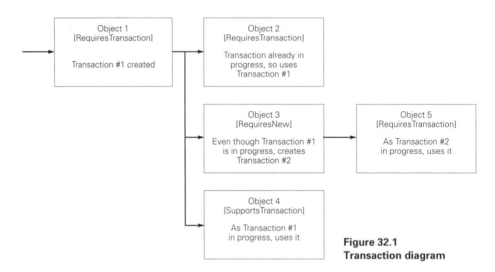

Figure 32.1
Transaction diagram

When the first object is called there is not yet a transaction; but Object 1 requires a transaction, so one is created. When Object 2 is called, it also requires a transaction; but because one exists, it uses that transaction. Object 3 not only requires a transaction, but demands a new one; so, a second transaction is created, which is then used by Object 5. Object 4 can use a transaction if one exists, so it uses transaction 1.

Let's consider what it means to "use a transaction." When methods are called within each component, they can either succeed or fail. If any object within a transaction indicates a failure, then the entire transaction (for all objects) is rolled back. However, if all objects complete without indicating an error, then all transactions are completed.

Think about this for a minute. You have some code to do something in each object. It does something and succeeds or fails. At some point in the future, COM+ will come back to your component and say either "yes, the rest of the transaction was successful, too; go ahead and commit your changes" or, "something went wrong; roll back your transaction."

Here is where the magic comes in—you don't have to do anything to handle this process (normally, anyway). Assuming you are talking to SQL Server or any upper-end database engine that supports distributed transactions (via the Distributed Transaction Coordinator), the fact of connecting and talking to the database automatically enlists the DTC. Even if you are not talking to a database, but are talking to a legacy system, you can use tools such as COMTI (COM Transaction Integrator) to provide similar services for various mainframe applications such as CICS and IMS.

This is fortunate, because managing a distributed transaction appropriately can be complicated. As you will see in the example, though, you have to do very little yourself. I talked about MTS/COM+ issues in chapter 30, when discussing COM+ object pooling. You might want to read that section before working on this example, because I do not go into the same level of depth here.

32.3 DISTRIBUTED TRANSACTION EXAMPLE

The following example is based on the idea that we want to integrate the Teacher system with a legacy application. The Teacher part inserts a new row into the Teachers table. The legacy piece asks whether the transaction should be allowed. If the answer is yes, the transaction succeeds; otherwise it is rolled back.

In order to make this work, we need three components that are involved in the transaction:

- The SQL Server component that inserts the record
- The legacy component that confirms the transaction is okay
- A component that calls each of these in turn

We need the third component to make sure the other two are put in the same transaction. If we called the components independently, they would each return, which would end their individual transactions. We could have the SQL Server component call the legacy component, but that approach doesn't seem very clean.

All these components will be in the same DLL. We'll create the DLL, and then the individual classes in the DLL.

32.3.1 Creating and setting up the component DLL

The first step is to create a new DLL. We do this by creating a new project of type Class Library. I called mine (unoriginally) DistributedTransComponents. Before we can use it, though, we need to do some housekeeping.

Referencing EnterpriseServices

The COM+ support resides in a system assembly called EnterpriseServices, which is not referenced by default. To reference it, right-click on the References folder under the project and select Add Reference. Choose System.EnterpriseServices from the list (figure 32.2).

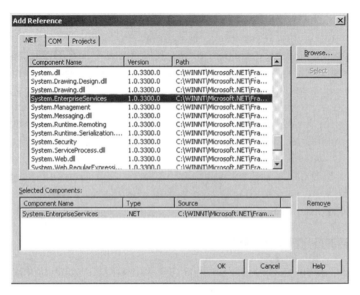

Figure 32.2   Adding a reference to System.EnterpriseServices

Giving the assembly a strong name

In order for COM+ to talk to the components in the DLL, the DLL must be given a strong name; it's a way of ensuring that the component is the component it is supposed to be, and not a pretender. (Refer to chapter 30, section 30.6.3 for an explanation of what strong names are and why they are necessary.)

To create a key for use in the test application, go to the command prompt (ideally the Visual Studio.NET Command Prompt under Visual Studio.NET Tools on the menu, because it has the path set for referencing Visual Studio tools). Change to the directory where the project exists (in my case, c:\projects\DistributedTransComponents) and type the following command:

```
sn -k DistributedTransComponents.snk
```

This command uses the strong name utility to generate a public/private key, which will be stored in the file DistributedTransComponents.snk.

Now we have to tell the assembly (the DLL in this case) to use the key. We can most easily do so from the AssemblyInfo.cs file that was automatically created as part of the assembly. We need to make a couple of changes:

```
using System.Reflection;
using System.Runtime.CompilerServices;
using System.EnterpriseServices;

.   (Bunch of lines removed for space)
.

[assembly: AssemblyVersion("1.0.0.1")]
.
```

. (Bunch of lines removed for space)
.

```
[assembly: AssemblyDelaySign(false)]
[assembly: AssemblyKeyName("")]
[assembly: ApplicationName("ADONET DT Components")]
[assembly: AssemblyKeyFile(@"..\..\DistributedTransComponents.snk")]
```

We need to add the System.Enterprises using statement at the top because the ApplicationName attribute is stored there. ApplicationName is the name COM+ will use to identify the application containing the components.

The AssemblyKeyFile attribute tells the assembly that it should pull the key information out of the passed filename and use it to generate a strong name. The relative path backs up two directories because the build takes place in either the bin\debug or bin\release directory below the project, where the strong name key file is located.

Notice that we changed the AssemblyVersion to 1.0.0.1 from 1.0.*. The full explanation can be found in chapter 30, but basically we did so to prevent a new component being generated for every build (because the version number becomes part of the component's name).

32.3.2   The SQL Server component

The first component to create inserts a record into SQL Server. Add a new file to the project, called SQLServerComponent.cs. Listing 32.1 shows the source.

Listing 32.1   SQLServerComponent source

```
using System;                           ❶ Namespaces
using System.EnterpriseServices;
using System.Data.SqlClient;

                                        Indicate involve-
                                        ment with
namespace DistributedTransComponents    transactions
{
    [Transaction(TransactionOption.Required)]  ❷
    public class SQLServerComponent : ServicedComponent  ❸
    {                                   Derive from
        private SqlConnection m_Conn = null;  ServicedComponent

        public SQLServerComponent()
        {
            string strConnect =
                "server=localhost;database=ADONetSamples;"  ❹ Create
                + "user id=sa";                                connection
            m_Conn = new SqlConnection(strConnect);
            m_Conn.Open();
        }

        ~SQLServerComponent()
        {                               ❺ Finalizer
            m_Conn.Close();
        }
```

```
                        AutoComplete
    [AutoComplete]       6
    public void AddTeacher()    7  The actual method
    {
        string strSql =
            "INSERT INTO Teachers(TeacherName,Classroom,Subject)"
              + " VALUES ('Mr. Underwood','D2','Philosophy')";

        SqlCommand comm = new SqlCommand(strSql,m_Conn);
        comm.ExecuteNonQuery();
    }
  }
}
```

1 The only namespace that might not be familiar is System.Enterprise-Services, which contains all the support for using COM+.

2 This attribute, placed above the class declaration, becomes associated with the class itself, as a sort of decoration; it indicates that we want to get some special behavior. In this case, the attribute indicates that we want this object to be set up to use transactions, and that we require a transaction—if one doesn't exist, one should be created. This information will be used to auto-register the object with COM+ later.

3 In order for an object to be used with COM+, it must be derived from ServicedComponent, which contains all the base class support required.

4 We create the connection in the constructor for the object and hold onto it in a member variable.

5 Because we are holding onto a resource, we need to make sure we release that resource when the object is destroyed. The finalizer will be called when the garbage collector goes to free up this object after it is no longer being used.

6 We can indicate whether a call within a transaction was successful or whether it failed (causing a rollback of the entire transaction) two ways. The method used here is AutoComplete, which means the operation is assumed to be successful unless the method throws an exception. The other approach will be shown in the next section, when we create the legacy component.

7 This method does something within the component; in this case, it inserts a teacher into the Teachers table. Of course, more than one method could be called.

32.3.3 The legacy component

Our legacy component is another class that will interact with the transaction and pretend to talk to a mainframe. (We get to play the part of the mainframe, by approving or denying the transaction.) Create a new class called LegacyComponent. The code is in listing 32.2, but I will only highlight those items that are different from the SQL Server component.

Listing 32.2   The LegacyComponent code

```
using System;
using System.EnterpriseServices;

namespace DistributedTransComponents
{
    [Transaction(TransactionOption.Required)]
    public class LegacyComponent : ServicedComponent
    {
        public LegacyComponent()
        {
        }

        public void CheckLegacySystem()
        {
            Console.WriteLine(
                    "Press Y to allow transaction or N to prevent "
                + "transaction, then press Enter");
            string strLine = Console.ReadLine();

            if(string.Compare(strLine,"Y",true) == 0)// Yes!
            {
                ContextUtil.SetComplete();        ❶ SetComplete
            }
            else
            {
                ContextUtil.SetAbort();           ❷ SetAbort
            }
        }
    }
}
```

❶ The bulk of the code is the same as for the SQLServerComponent, except that, not having a database connection, the code is simpler. The first divergence is that we are not using AutoComplete.

I said earlier that there are two ways to indicate success or failure of the operation within the transaction. Using AutoComplete, the code is considered successful unless an exception is thrown. Alternatively, you can use the SetComplete() method to indicate that the operation succeeded.

❷ If something went wrong, then we can call SetAbort() to indicate that the entire transaction should fail and rollback. This is the equivalent of throwing an exception when using AutoComplete. As you can see, this method will be called in the code if the user presses anything other than Y.

32.3.4 Managing component

The last component we need is the managing component that starts the transaction and then calls each of the other two components in turn. The class name I am using is TestTransManager. Listing 32.3 shows the code.

Listing 32.3 The TestTransManager class

```
using System;
using System.EnterpriseServices;

namespace DistributedTransComponents
{
    [Transaction(TransactionOption.Required)]
    public class TestTransManager : ServicedComponent
    {
        public TestTransManager()
        {
        }

        public void DoTest()
        {
            SQLServerComponent ssc = new SQLServerComponent();
            LegacyComponent lc = new LegacyComponent();
            ssc.AddTeacher();
            lc.CheckLegacySystem();
        }
    }
}
```

As you can see from the attribute, this class also requires a transaction. The DoTest() method does nothing more than create instances of the other classes, and then executes the two methods in those classes. Because they all require transactions, however, they will all end up participating in the same transaction.

32.3.5 Test application

In order to use these components, we need a test application. Create a console application in the same solution as the components. I called mine TransTest. A couple of steps will get the test application up and running.

Adding references

For the test application to use the test components, it has to have a reference to the DLL containing the components. We can most easily have accomplished this by right-clicking on References beneath the console application project in the Solution Explorer, selecting Add Reference, and choosing the DistributedTransComponents project from the list (figure 32.3).

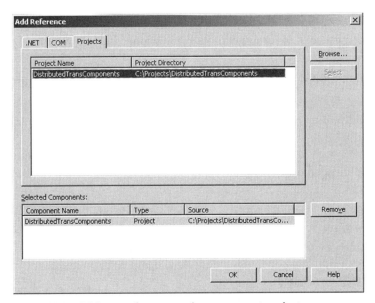

Figure 32.3   Adding a reference to the component project

Before we leave this dialog box, we also need to add a reference to System.Enterprise-Services. Do this by switching to the .NET tab and selecting System.Enterprise-Services from the list (figure 32.4).

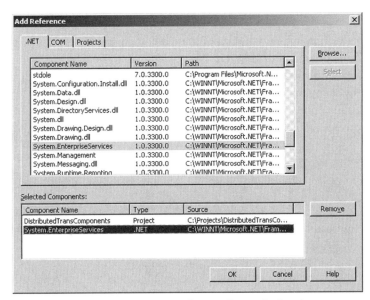

Figure 32.4   Adding a reference to System.EnterpriseServices

Calling the component

The following is the code for the console application. I bolded the lines that I added:

```
using System;
using DistributedTransComponents;

namespace TransTest
{
    class Class1
    {
        static void Main(string[] args)
        {
            TestTransManager ttm = new TestTransManager();
            ttm.DoTest();
        }
    }
}
```

There is not much to do—we reference the namespace containing the components, and then create the component and call the test method.

Running the example

All that is left to do is to run the application. Let's look at the data in the database for a point of comparison (figure 32.5).

TeacherID	TeacherName	Classroom	Subject
1	Mr. Biddick	H9	Math
2	Ms. Fortune	A1	English
3	Mr. Kriefels	B2	Physics
9	Mrs. Stokesbury	C3	Literature

Figure 32.5
Database before the transaction

Now run the application. It will take a little while the first time, because it is registering all the components with COM+. To see this registration, select ComponentServices from the Administrative Tools of the Control Panel, and then navigate through the tree to the following node: Component Services → Computers → My Computer → COM+ Applications → ADONET DT Components.

As you can see in figure 32.6, the three components have been created.

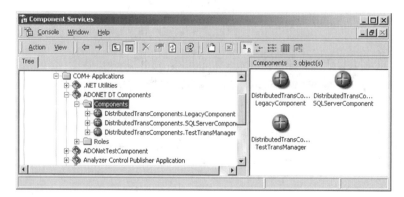

Figure 32.6
Transaction components

Further, if you right-click on any of these components and bring up the Transactions tab, you will see that the component is configured for transactions (figure 32.7).

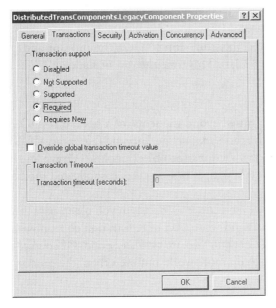

Figure 32.7
Transaction settings on one of the components

Now, the program is asking us to do our duty as a legacy application and approve or deny the transaction (figure 32.8).

Figure 32.8   Pretending to be a legacy application

Go ahead and say no the first time, and then check with SQL Server. The transaction has been rolled back (figure 32.9).

	TeacherID	TeacherName	Classroom	Subject
▶	1	Mr. Biddick	H9	Math
	2	Ms. Fortune	A1	English
	3	Mr. Kriefels	B2	Physics
	9	Mrs. Stokesbury	C3	Literature
*				

Figure 32.9
Database after abort

Think about this for a moment. The SQL Server component had zero code for rolling back the transaction, and the legacy component was called after the insert had taken place; but the transaction was still automatically canceled.

TeacherID	TeacherName	Classroom	Subject
1	Mr. Biddick	H9	Math
2	Ms. Fortune	A1	English
3	Mr. Kriefels	B2	Physics
9	Mrs. Stokesbury	C3	Literature
19	Mr. Underwood	D2	Philosophy

Figure 32.10
Database after completion

Run the application again, and this time enter "Y" at the prompt and press Enter. Now look at the table (figure 32.10). This time the row was added.

32.4 SUMMARY

Distributed transactions are a little beyond the scope of a book on ADO.NET, but I figure that because they use the term *transaction*, they are fair game. COM+ involves much more than distributed transactions (or object pooling, shown in chapter 30). The cool thing about COM+, though, is how it takes complicated mechanisms and makes them trivial to use.

.NET has taken this ability even further. Whereas in yon olden days (say, last year) you had to create COM objects and write a bit of registration code, now all you have to do is put an attribute on a class and you are basically done. Of course, to do more complicated things, you have to do more work; but even then, the process is straightforward.[2]

---

[2] I can't say this many nice things about Microsoft without taking at least one potshot. Someone, somewhere, thought that COM, COM+, and .NET were great names to use for these technologies. I dare you to search for them from your favorite web search engine. . .

CHAPTER 33

Using ADO Recordsets with ADO.NET

When a new technology comes out, it would be great if you could immediately drop support for all your existing source and build a new project from scratch. Unfortunately, in the real world, doing so is rarely an option.

The architects of .NET provided a number of mechanisms for working with legacy applications,[1] such as being able to call into DLLs or interoperate with COM objects. They also knew that a lot of people had written applications that used ADO Recordsets, and that considerable logic might be involved in their use.

For this reason, ADO.NET has the ability to take a Recordset and suck it into a DataSet. This is a one-way mechanism—you can't automatically put data back into the Recordset from the DataSet, but at least you can write a .NET consumer of your existing middle-tier logic.

This chapter briefly demonstrates how to get at a Recordset from ADO.NET. Doing so involves three major steps:

---

[1] That's right—the brand-spanking-new DNA application you just shipped is now a legacy application!

1 Create a COM component that exposes a Recordset. Presumably, you already have such a component that you want to talk to, because this is a legacy access mechanism.

2 Make the COM component available to .NET.

3 Get the Recordset from the component, and suck it into the DataSet.

33.1 CREATING THE COM COMPONENT

We'll create a COM component in Visual Basic 6.0 to set up this example. I am not a Visual Basic person, and would normally do this in C++, but it is a more straightforward in VB.

The component selects all the records from, you guessed it, the Teachers table, and stores them in a disconnected Recordset, which it then returns. I won't go into the details of how to set up and create the VB component, but listing 33.1 shows the VB code.

Listing 33.1 VB code to return a Recordset in RSTest

```
Public Function GetRecordset() As ADODB.Recordset

' Connect to the database
Dim conn As New ADODB.Connection
conn.Open "Provider=SQLOLEDB;Data Source=localhost;" & _
        "Initial Catalog=ADONetSamples;UID=sa;PWD="

Dim rs As New ADODB.Recordset

'To use disconnected Recordset you must use client side cursors
rs.CursorLocation = adUseClient

' Create and initialize the recordset
rs.Open "Teachers", conn

'Disconnect the recordset
rs.ActiveConnection = Nothing

' Set the function's return value to be the recordset
Set GetRecordset = rs

' Clean up
conn.Close
Set conn = Nothing

End Function
```

This code is inside a new VB ActiveX DLL project, which we compile. Set the VB project name to RSTestComponent, which will become the name of the component (figure 33.1).

We named the class RSTest, so the function listed earlier is RSTest.GetRecordset().

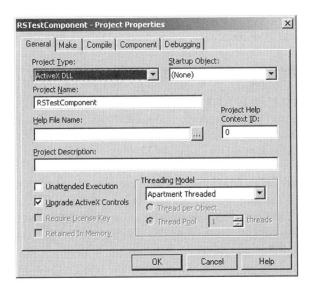

Figure 33.1
Setting the VB project name

33.2 ACCESSING THE *COM* OBJECT FROM *C#*

To use the component we created is simple, especially when using Visual Studio. Create a console application to call the code (or use one of the test applications from a previous chapter). Now, right-click on the References folder, and select Add Reference.

One of the tabs on the Add Reference dialog box is labeled COM. When we go to that tab (after a short delay while the list is filled), we see all available COM objects in the system. Scroll down to RSTestComponent and select it (figure 33.2).

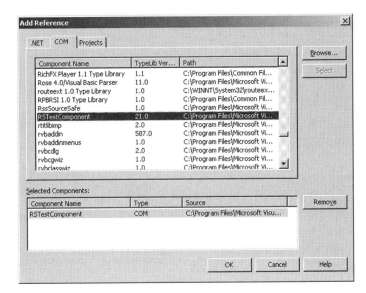

Figure 33.2
Referencing a COM
Component from .NET

Click the OK button. A dialog box pops up, telling us that there is currently no wrapper for the COM object (figure 33.3).

Figure 33.3 Dialog box asking to generate a wrapper

.NET cannot directly talk to a COM object—we have to generate a wrapper for the COM object that .NET *can* talk to. You do so using a command-line utility called TlbImp (Type LiBrary IMPort); or, if you are using Visual Studio, you can basically say Yes to this dialog box and let the environment do all the work for you. (In case I was being too subtle, click the Yes button.)

This is not quite all we need to do. We will use the RSTestComponent COM object and have a reference to it, but the RSTestComponent returns an ADO Recordset—another COM object. In order to use the ADO Recordset, we need to also reference ADO. The mechanism is the same—bring up the Add Reference dialog box, and then find the Microsoft ActiveX Data Objects Library. There will probably be several versions. I have included the latest version (2.7)on my machine (figure 33.4).

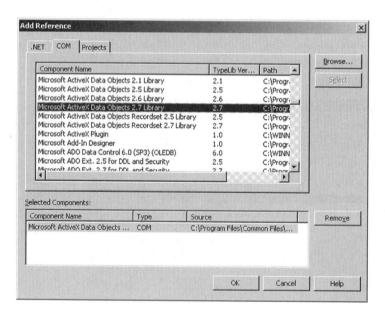

Figure 33.4
Referencing ADO

Be careful not to select the Microsoft ActiveX Data Objects Recordset Library; despite the name, that is not what we need.

When we click OK, we're prompted to generate a wrapper. Once again, let the environment do the work—click Yes.

The C# code can now access both our component (RSTestComponent) and ADO. If you are an ex–VB coder, then accessing COM objects this way should seem obvious and boring. However, if you come from the C++ world, you will probably be more impressed with this capability.

33.3   ACCESSING THE RECORDSET

The last step is to write the code that accesses the Recordset and sucks it into a DataSet. Listing 33.2 shows the entire console application except the Print-DataSet method, which appears in a number of other chapters and prints out the contents of the DataSet. I have bolded the code I added (versus the automatically created code).

Listing 33.2   C# code to access the ADO Recordset

```
using System;
using System.Data;                          ❶ Namespaces
using System.Data.OleDb;

using RSTestComponent;

namespace TestADORecordset
{
    class Class1
    {
        static void Main(string[] args)
        {
            Class1 aClass = new Class1();
            aClass.DoStuff();
        }
    }

    public void DoStuff()                        Create
    {                                            component
        RSTest test = new RSTest();  ❷
        object oRecordset = test.GetRecordset();        ❸ Call VB method

        DataSet ds = new DataSet();                     ❹ Fill DataSet
        OleDbDataAdapter da = new OleDbDataAdapter();      from Recordset
        da.Fill(ds,oRecordset,"Teachers");

        PrintDataSet(ds);
    }
    .
    .
    .
```

❶ We need the `Data` namespace for the DataSet. We also need the `OleDb` namespace, even though we are not directly accessing OLE DB, because we will use an OleDb-DataAdapter to convert the Recordset.

The other `using` statement is for a reference to our COM component: RSTest-Component. When we agreed to let Visual Studio generate a wrapper for the COM object, it created a wrapper DLL that, among other things, contained this namespace and a wrapper for each object in the component (in this case, just RSTest).

❷ Because we are creating a wrapper for the object rather than the actual COM component, the notation is the same as the creation of any .NET object. Under the hood, however, the wrapper is creating the COM object for us.

❸ Again, because of the wrapper, we call the method exactly as if it were a .NET object. The one caveat is that because the method doesn't return a simple type, the return type is an object.

❹ We have used the `Fill` method extensively on the OleDbDataAdapter to load data into a DataSet. One of the overrides of `Fill` takes an object argument, which is expected to be a COM wrapper of a Recordset. We are using this override and passing our object, which we know is a Recordset wrapper. The DataAdapter does the rest of the work for us.

33.4 RESULTS

The last thing to do is run the code and check the results (figure 33.5).

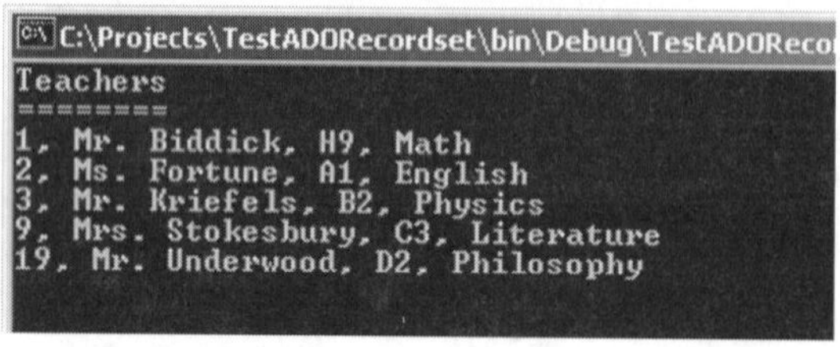

Figure 33.5
Results from the DataSet
built from a Recordset

This should be exactly what you were expecting.[2]

33.5 SUMMARY

This approach is a convoluted way to get at data, and you would never do this in a new application. However, if you have a lot of legacy code that uses ADO Recordsets, this technique makes it possible to leverage that code and still use .NET.

This is the last chapter in the book that talks about how to do something specific. The next chapter, chapter 34, is a summary of suggestions I have made throughout the book, along with some ideas and recommendations for using ADO.NET moving forward.

---

[2] Unless you are a pessimist, in which case you probably expected flames to shoot out of your hard-drive. For that result, please refer to the example in chapter 35.

C H A P T E R   3 4

Recommendations and advice

I have tried to make this book as practical and focused as possible. Especially with the examples, I concentrated on showing the specific concepts being discussed, rather than muddying the point with other bits of code. I believe this is a good approach; generally you are trying to solve a particular problem, and you don't want to dig through a bunch of unrelated code and guess which bit matters. The only problem, though, is that this approach doesn't provide a framework for how the various pieces should be used.

Providing a cohesive set of guidelines and recommendations is difficult. For one thing, every application is different, and it would be silly of me to presume that the same approaches apply to any project. For another, .NET is very new. Several people who reviewed this book asked for case studies, but the truth is, there aren't any. A handful of applications have been deployed, but there has not been enough time to get anything more than superficial results.

However, I can still talk about the approaches to take when you're using ADO.NET. Many of the things I talk about here are common sense or good practices, no matter what the environment, but they will be helpful for developers who are relatively new to database development. The points I express are, to some extent, my own practices and opinions, and there is certainly room for differences of opinion. The most important point I can make is that, because every application is different, no set of rules can *always* be applied.

34.1 SECURITY

One of the goals of .NET was to provide a programming model that could be secured. Given the numbers of viruses, buffer-overrun issues, and so forth, that have occurred in the past few years, it is no longer possible to take security for granted. Despite all that Microsoft has done, however, it is still beholden to the individual programmers to expend some effort, or all the security within .NET is for naught.

Here's an example. A large software company recently set up a major ASP.NET web site with hundreds of servers and millions of users. A minor problem cropped up, as frequently happens. Of course, ASP.NET has a feature to help in debugging: when an error occurs, it shows the code that was attempting to be executed along with the error. In this case, the code included a hard-coded connection string! It gave all of the millions of users specific information on how to attach to the company's database.

So, the security points I list may sound like common sense, but trust me—they are often missed by some of the big guys. Here are some guidelines I see broken the most often:

- Never put database connection information into an ASP.NET page. Always store it in a configuration file or, better still, create a separate component that connects to the database that is called by your ASP.NET code.

- Change the default account information on your database. I cannot tell you the number of SQL Server databases where the user ID *sa* with no password gets you complete administrative access. Oracle creates a number of accounts, and you need to disable or change the password on them all.

- Throughout the book, I have relied on the databases' being set up with no administrative password. I did so because I don't mind if anyone breaks into my Teachers database. However, even if I don't care about a particular database, an intruder who accesses that database can do more than you would think—they could load data or connect to other services.

- When you set up accounts for your application (or, as is more common in the three-tier stateless world, a single account), do your best to limit the accounts' permissions. Most applications do not need full administrative rights, and you might as well avoid opening a potential hole to your data.

- When you set up user accounts and passwords, remember the basic rules about passwords; plenty of programs out there are ready to try to crack your passwords. In a nutshell, a good password should not be a common name or word that can be found in a dictionary. It should be reasonably long (at least six characters, preferably longer), and ideally should include numbers and punctuation if allowed.
- If at all possible, don't expose any mechanism by which a user can enter SQL or part of an SQL string directly (for example, a mechanism that lets you type in a criteria for records you want to return, which becomes your Where clause). Anyone who is good with SQL can add the odd subquery or batch command and possibly gain more access than you'd expect.

You need to worry about a billion and one other security issues, especially if you are building a web application. Numerous articles and books are available on these topics, and Microsoft has provided a lot of underlying support. Just remember, it does little good to know that you are immune from buffer-overrun attacks if anyone can access your list of credit card numbers!

34.2 ENCAPSULATION

Object-oriented programming has been around for quite a long time. (Smalltalk, the first popular OO language, came out in 1981!) For some reason, though, even serious practitioners of OO concepts seem to forget the basics when they start talking to a database.

The most fragile parts of applications are generally where they interact with external systems—file I/O, the web, devices, and, of course, talking to databases. I strongly recommend isolating your database code as much as possible from the rest of the system. ADO.NET provides a great facilitator for doing this: the DataSet. You can put all your data-access code in one or more objects, and you can pass data back and forth using DataSets.

If you support a number of applications from the same database, coming up with a standard set of objects for accessing that database can be very beneficial. Even if the structure of your database changes, you can still build a DataSet that looks like the old structure; so, you can continue to support old applications that call your original interfaces, and also provide newer interfaces that handle your new structures. Then you can update the other applications at your leisure.

34.3 CONNECTION POOLING

If you are building a three-tier application or a web application (which is basically a three-tier application by default), few things you can do are as simple as enabling connection pooling and will have such a major impact on the performance of your application.

Chapter 30 goes into detail about the options you have for connection pooling and how to configure it. SQL Server is the easiest to use and is quite flexible. OLE DB has less flexibility but still has usable capabilities. Alternatively, you can use COM+ to get the most complete control over pooling.

34.4 GENERIC CODE

Early in this book, I emphasized the steps required to make your code more database-agnostic. Even if you are fairly sure that your application will only ever be run against a single database engine, the possibility exists that you might someday move it or test it against a different engine.

Making your application work against virtually any database engine without changes can be a major hassle, and I am not recommending that you go to that much effort unless you are explicitly building a utility designed to talk to different engines. Although engines generally have much in common, little differences can cause problems, such as variations in SQL syntax, different default behaviors for transactions, and so forth. Also, the DDL commands (Data Definition Language—used for modifying the database structure) often differ from engine to engine.

However, you can make your code fairly generic with little work—generic enough that modifying the system later to handle another engine should be more straightforward than if you had, say, coded everything to Oracle or SQL Server. Genericizing your code also tends to improve its encapsulation, which is never a bad thing.

Chapter 8 discusses some of the details required to make your code work with any data provider with virtually no changes. Genericizing can go considerably beyond that, though. There is almost always a specific and a generic way to do anything. For example, whenever I wrote out the data contained in a DataSet in the book, I could have written code that knew about the specific tables and columns. Instead, I wrote a generic method that looked inside the DataSet and wrote out what it found.

However, even if I only plan to use a method one time, I often code it generically for two reasons:

- The way in which the method is used may change slightly, and a generic method is more likely to handle the change.

- I may find another use for the method and save myself having to build another hard-coded method.

Of course, these techniques require more work up front, and sometimes, building a generic mechanism can require a massive effort whereas writing a hard-coded method would be quick. You have to use your judgment about when to be generic, but you should consider the approach in your future projects.

34.5 CREATION UTILITIES

I'm constantly amazed, especially in the web development world, that some developers assume the machine they are working on is the only machine they ever need to worry about. This assumption leads to hard-coded paths and a database structure built up over time that is undocumented and that relies completely on the knowledge of its creator to maintain it.

Tools are available that let you export a database structure, and you can move it to other machines. However, then you are also moving everyone's test data and tables, all the bad assumptions that were made at some point and never corrected, and possibly tables that have nothing to do with your application.

I strongly believe that you should always have a way to create specific tables and other database elements from scratch in a clean database. I have a number of reasons:

- This mechanism becomes the de facto documentation for your structures. ER diagrams are nice, but the only thing you can rely on being up to date is your code.

- When you move to a new system, you guarantee that only those elements you need are moved. If something ends up not being moved, you know that your assumptions aren't quite correct.

- If you are building a deployed application, you dramatically reduce the complexity of the install.[1]

- This approach encourages more testing. If it is trivial to set up a new engine, then you don't have to worry about taking down the development or production server with a test.

- The mechanism allows for easier distributed development. Rather than having a dozen developers all hitting the same server, they can easily set up their own databases without breaking everyone else's. When the developer is sure of the structures and artifacts they require, they just have to encode those elements into the creation utility, rather than trying to replicate their local changes manually.

You can take a number of different approaches when building a creation utility. The simplest is to create a script, which is infinitely better than hacking at the database structure directly. I make more complex creation tools that involve code, for several reasons:

- I tend to work with applications that support multiple database engines. I would have to maintain a different script for each engine.

- Ideally, the creation tool also has the ability to correct problems, which is harder to do in a script.

---

[1] I have reviewed commercial applications that had a dozen pages of installation instructions for setting up the database prior to running the app. Guess what my review looked like?

For a simple example of a creation tool, look at the LoadSQLServer and the LoadOracle utilities that are available with the sample code for the book. If you examine the code closely, you will see that they are the same program with a single piece designed to handle the engine-specific details.

You can also combine the creation code directly into your application, although you need to take into account the rights you will have to expose to create tables, and so forth, rather than the rights required to run your application. You might require a special login for this functionality.

34.6 SUMMARY

Much of what I have put into this chapter is common sense and is a recap for the experienced database programmer. However, if you are new to writing database code, it is easy to fall into some of the traps I've described. My comments should help you to steer clear of these issues.

Except for the appendices, this chapter brings the book to a close. I hope the material I've provided will help you with your ADO.NET coding endeavors. Thank you for sticking with me to the end!

Appendices

These appendices either cover topics that didn't fit naturally within the flow of the book or dive into more depth on particular classes (beyond the detail in the chapters). Most of these appendices began as chapters, so you will see a lot of common material and examples. However, the appendices discuss every property and method of the classes they discuss, even if those items are rarely used; this explanation would have been a distraction in the main text.

APPENDIX A

The ODBC data provider

Throughout the book, I have talked about using native data providers. SQL Server is currently the only one available; the OLE DB data provider gives access to the OLE DB providers already available.

OLE DB has been around for a few years, and there are a number of drivers; but ODBC has been around longer, and many more drivers are available for ODBC. On top of the sheer quantity of drivers, using ODBC offers other advantages:

- ODBC drivers can be faster than OLE DB. Believe it or not, because of the C-style interface and the large amount of time available for optimizations, this is often the case. The SQL Server ODBC driver is faster than the OLE DB driver, although neither is as fast as the native .NET driver.

- ODBC drivers frequently support features the OLE DB drivers do not. For example, the Oracle ODBC driver supports the CLOB data type, which the OLE DB driver does not.

Originally, supporting ODBC was a nonissue for ADO.NET. One of the first OLE DB data providers gave access to ODBC, so you could use either mechanism via the

OLE DB data provider. However, there were problems with the way the OLE DB ODBC driver worked with .NET. Microsoft could have fixed these problems, but chose a different route: it created an ODBC data provider, which provides direct access to ODBC.

This is a far better solution—using the OLE DB provider inserted a lot of layers that weren't necessary. However, the decision to go this direction was made too late in the development cycle for .NET version 1, so the ODBC data provider didn't make it into the release. Waiting for version 2 to get access to ODBC was not acceptable either, so Microsoft released the ODBC data provider as a separate installable piece shortly after the release of .NET.

This appendix will briefly cover the major points of using the ODBC driver. I assume that you have already read enough about the SQL Server and OLE DB data providers to pick up the details quickly.

A.1 INSTALLING THE ODBC DATA PROVIDER

The official .NET release was in January 2002, and the ODBC data provider became available in February. You can download it from Microsoft's web site at: http://msdn. microsoft.com/downloads/. Enter a search for ODBC, and you should be able to find it.

Download the installation package called odbc_net.msi. Installing is simply a matter of running the installer and following the instructions. However, you need to reference the ODBC functionality from your application to make it available, because you have to reference any other .NET functionality that is not loaded by default.

The easiest way to add a reference is to right-click on References under your project in the Solution Explorer and select Add Reference. You'll find Microsoft.Data.Odbc. dll in the list of .NET references (figure A.1).

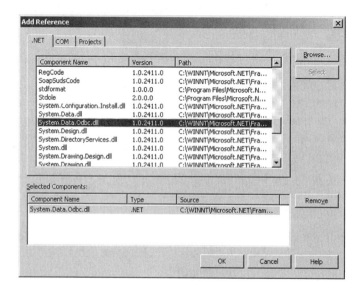

Figure A.1
Referencing the
ODBC DLL

A.2 THE ODBC DATA PROVIDER NAMESPACE AND CLASSES

Once you have installed and referenced the ODBC data provider, a new namespace will be available:

```
Microsoft.Data.Odbc;
```

The classes exactly mirror the other data providers. Table A.1 shows the important classes.

Table A.1   Important ODBC classes

Class	Purpose
OdbcConnection	Used to connect to an ODBC data source
OdbcCommand	Used to execute a command against a connection.
OdbcDataReader	Steps through result sets.
OdbcParameter	Binds parameters on a command.
OdbcDataAdapter	Fills a DataSet from an ODBC data source
OdbcCommandBuilder	Quickly creates default Insert, Update, and Delete statements for a Data Adapter

A.3 CONNECTING TO ODBC

Generally, with ODBC, you create a data source to which you connect. One way to do this is via the ODBC Data Source control panel applet available in Administrative Tools (figure A.2).

If you intend to use an ODBC driver from ADO.NET, you are probably familiar with setting up drivers. You don't have to do anything special for SQL Server—just set up your data source. The connection string you would have used from any other tool is the same connection string you use in ADO.NET:

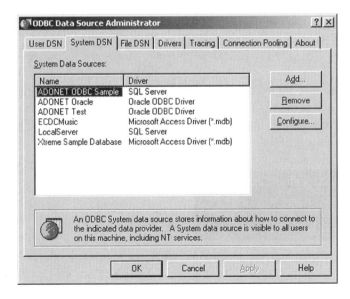

**Figure A.2
ODBC Data
Source applet**

```
OdbcConnection conn =
        new OdbcConnection("DSN=ADONET ODBC Sample;UID=sa");
```

All the other options you would expect are available. Refer to the ODBC documentation if you need more information.

A.4 AN EXAMPLE

The following code accesses the SQL Server database we have been using, via ODBC, and reads the list of teachers:

```
using Microsoft.Data.Odbc;

public void TestOdbc()
{
    OdbcConnection conn =
            new OdbcConnection("DSN=ADONET ODBC Sample;UID=sa");
    conn.Open();

    string strSql = "SELECT * FROM Teachers";
    OdbcCommand comm = new OdbcCommand(strSql,conn);

    OdbcDataReader reader = comm.ExecuteReader();

    int iCount = reader.FieldCount;
    while(reader.Read())
    {
        for(int i = 0;i < iCount;i++)
        {
            if(i > 0) Console.Write(", ");
            Console.Write(reader.GetValue(i).ToString().Trim());
        }
        Console.WriteLine("");
    }

    reader.Close();
    conn.Close();
}
```

This code should look incredibly familiar—it mirrors the other providers exactly.[1] The only difference is the notation for connecting (which, frankly, isn't very different). The ADONET ODBC Sample data source points to the same SQL Server database used throughout the book. Figure A.3 shows the output.

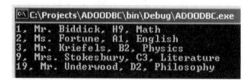

Figure A.3
Example output

---

[1] I show the namespace in the code above the method, but it should appear at the top of the file.

A.5 SUMMARY

Although I have not gone into much detail about ODBC, you shouldn't have any trouble using it if you have made it through either the SQL Server or OLE DB sections of the book.

I am a fan of ODBC. I have been working with it since it first was released, and I believe that it is one of the better mechanisms available for accessing data. Over the next few years, we should see a proliferation of ADO.NET data providers, and they should be used from ADO.NET once they are available. In the meantime, you must resort to OLE DB or ODBC, and you shouldn't discount using ODBC simply because it is older.

Connection classes

The connection object has been a key component of all the examples in this book. In many ways, the connection is a simple class to understand and use, but it has some useful properties and some gotchas; for example, correctly building a connection string can be troublesome.

This appendix describes the important (and not so important) properties and methods of connections, and also discusses connection strings, both for SQL Server and for OLE DB. This appendix covers ground similar to chapter 9, but is more complete: it lists all the properties and methods, no matter how esoteric. You may notice that it includes a lot of tables; tables provide a good mechanism for presenting lists of properties. At the same time, when you are not explicitly looking for a piece of data, it is easy to find yourself skimming over tables in their entirety (I tend to do that).

I have organized the tables so that the most important information is at the top, and I have also broken out some tables into multiple pieces to make the data easier to digest. Much of the useful information in this appendix is in the tables, so I suggest you read the first few entries.

This appendix is one of several that goes into detail about a particular set of classes. I will not explore every class in this fashion, but it is helpful to explore the main classes thoroughly.

B.1 DATA PROVIDER-SPECIFIC CLASSES

Considering that you can't do anything with a data source without first getting a connection, the connection object is relatively simple. This is especially true of the IDbConnection interface, which provides the basic methods any connection object must provide. The specific derivations, however, provide additional data provider-specific functionality (table B.1).

Table B.1 Connection implementations

Class	Provider	Interface
SqlConnection	SQL Server	IDbConnection
OleDbConnection	OLE DB	IDbConnection

B.2 CONNECTION PROPERTIES

When you look at a .NET class, two major sets of items form the class's interface: properties and methods. A property is generally *passive*—setting a property or reading the value from a property usually does not do something immediately, but potentially changes the behavior of the object when a method is called. Methods are generally *active*—calling a method does something.

A good example on the connection object is the ConnectionString property and the Open() method. Setting the connection string does not do anything, but the connection string is used to determine how the connection will take place when the Open() method is called.

The connection string is an interesting property because it contains a number of pieces of information that eventually show up in other properties. For example, you can't set the ConnectionTimeout property directly on a connection—that property is read-only. But you can include a connection timeout value in the connection string that will, after the connection is made, become the value you read from the ConnectionTimeout property.

You will notice that many of the properties of a connection are read-only. They are either set by specifying a value in the connection string or are read from the underlying database engine.

The rest of this section is broken into three parts: the properties of the base interface for connections, and the properties of the two data provider–specific connection classes. The connection methods will be covered in the next section.

B.2.1 IDbConnection properties

The IDbConnection interface is the base interface for the data provider-specific connection implementations. It has only five properties, of which just one (the connection string) is modifiable. Even then, the connection string can only be modified before the connection has been opened.

The other properties are read from the database engine, although some of them can be set as part of the connection string. Setting connection information is discussed in great detail later in this appendix, in section B.5. Table B.2 shows the five properties that are available in the IDbConnection interface and are therefore also available for the two derivations.

Table B.2 IDbConnection properties

Property	Purpose
ConnectionString	The information required to connect to the data source. This information can include such things as the name of the database, and the user ID and password to use. An extensive discussion about connection strings appears in section B.5. This property can only be set before the connection has been opened. Once it has been opened, it is read-only.
ConnectionTimeout	The amount of time (in seconds) to spend attempting to connect before considering the attempt a failure. By default, this value is 15 seconds. If the timeout is set to 0, then the connection will not time out. You cannot set this property directly; it must be specified as part of the connection string.
Database	The name of the database to which the connection object is connected. This property is read-only and will be blank until the connection has been opened.
State	The current condition of the connection. Possible values include: | Connection state	Meaning
Open	There is currently a connection to the data source.
Closed	There is not currently a connection to the data source.
Connecting	The connection is currently in the process of attempting to connect to the data source.
Executing	A command object associated with the connection is currently executing a command.
Fetching	Data is currently being read via the connection object.
Broken	Something has caused a problem with a connection that was previously open. The connection must be explicitly closed and then reopened to continue. | The states are stored in an enum called ConnectionState. The values are bit-flags, and so can be combined. (For example, the state can be Open and Executing at the same time). This property is, of course, read-only. Most of these states are reserved for future use by Microsoft, such as Connecting, Executing, Fetching, and Broken. You should not have to worry about them in version 1.

This snippet of code prints out the values of all these properties:

```
public void WriteConnectionInfo(IDbConnection conn)
{
    Console.WriteLine("ConnectionString = {0}",
                                    conn.ConnectionString);
    Console.WriteLine("ConnectionTimeout = {0}",
                                    conn.ConnectionTimeout);
```

```
Console.WriteLine("Database = {0}",conn.Database);
Console.WriteLine("State = {0}",
          Enum.Format(typeof(ConnectionState),conn.State,"g"));
}
```

This code is straightforward, except for the `State` property; that code converts the enumerated value to a string. Figure B.1 shows the output from the code.

Figure B.1 Output from IDbConnection properties example

B.2.2   SqlConnection properties

The SqlConnection class is a good example of the way a data provider implementer can extend its implementation beyond the basics. The SqlConnection class supports all the IDbConnection properties shown previously, but also adds several SQL Server–specific properties. Table B.3 shows these properties.

If you look in the help for this class, you'll notice a handful of additional properties that are derived from base classes. I have excluded them from the table because they are not relevant to database coding.

All of these properties are read-only. They are read from the database engine, although their values can be modified as part of the connection string.

Table B.3   SqlConnection properties

Property	Purpose
DataSource	Returns the name of the data source to which SQL Server is connected. This will probably be the name of the server containing the database, or localhost if the current machine was specified.
PacketSize	Specifies how much data will be sent in each packet from the server. By default, this value is 8K, but it can be changed by specifying a different size in the connection string.
	Changing the packet size can increase efficiency if you know up front that the data being sent will either be smaller than the default (lots of small selects) or larger (for sending large blocks of text, images, and so on).
ServerVersion	Returns the version of SQL Server to which the connection object is connected. For example, on my machine, this property returns
	`08.00.0194`
	which is SQL Server 2000, build 194. The format is
	`Major Version.Minor Version.Build`
WorkstationId	A string that identifies the client machine connecting to the database. This is how SQL Server keeps track of different users. Typically, this string will be the name of the computer that is connecting.

The following method writes out these properties to the console:

```
public void WriteSqlConnectionInfo(SqlConnection conn)
{
    Console.WriteLine("DataSource = {0}",conn.DataSource);
    Console.WriteLine("PacketSize = {0}",conn.PacketSize);
    Console.WriteLine("ServerVersion = {0}",conn.ServerVersion);
    Console.WriteLine("WorkstationId = {0}",conn.WorkstationId);
}
```

Figure B.2 shows the output when run against the ADO.NET sample database from the examples.

Figure B.2
Example output showing SqlConnection properties

B.2.3   OleDbConnection properties

The OleDbConnection also has a handful of properties that extend the basic interface, although, as you would expect, the connection implements all the IDbConnection properties as well. As with the extended SQL Server properties, these properties are all read-only (see table B.4).

A couple of the properties, DataSource and ServerVersion, exist on both OleDbConnection and SqlConnection. They are not moved up into the base class because Microsoft assumes these properties may not be required for all data providers, and because the data they return is not quite the same. For example, the server version for OLE DB can include additional, provider-specific information.

Table B.4   OleDbConnection properties

Property	Purpose
DataSource	Returns the name of the data source to which the connection is connected. The value that appears here can vary depending on the OLE DB provider. This property will be empty until the connection has been opened, and is read-only.
Provider	The name of the OLE DB data provider that is being used. For example, if the Oracle data provider is being used, this value will be MSDAORA. This property will be empty until the connection has been opened, and is read-only.
ServerVersion	The version of the database to which the connection is connected. The format of this value will be Major Version.Minor Version.Build However, additional information may be appended to the string that is data provider-specific. This property will be empty until the connection has been opened, and is read-only.

Figure B.3
Output showing
OleDbConnection propertie

Here is the code to display these properties for an OLE DB connection:

```
public void WriteOleDbConnectionInfo(OleDbConnection conn)
{
    Console.WriteLine("DataSource = {0}",conn.DataSource);
    Console.WriteLine("Provider = {0}",conn.Provider);
    Console.WriteLine("ServerVersion = {0}",conn.ServerVersion);
}
```

Figure B.3 shows the output when run against the Access test database.

B.3   CONNECTION METHODS

As with the connection properties, the base interface, IDbConnection, specifies a number of methods that are implemented by the two derivations, OleDbConnection and SqlConnection. Unlike the properties, though, there are virtually no data provider-specific extensions.

If you look at the OleDbConnection or SqlConnection class, you will see a number of additional methods. These methods, with one exception, are inherited from base classes, and they're beyond the scope of this book. The exception is the GetOleDb-SchemaTable() method on OleDbConnection, which can be used to retrieve advanced information about the data source (it's shown in use in chapter 31).

You have already seen several of the IDbConnection methods in previous chapters, such as Open(), Close(), and CreateCommand(). They are defined in table B.5, along with the couple of other methods on IDbConnection.

Table B.5   IDbConnection methods

Method	Purpose
Open	Opens the connection to the database specified by the Connection-String property. If the connection string is not valid, or if the connection cannot be made, then this method will throw an exception.
Close	Closes an open connection.
CreateCommand	Creates an appropriate new command object, which can then be used to execute commands against the data source. The command object will automatically be initialized with the connection object that created it. CreateCommand is demonstrated in chapter 6.
ChangeDatabase	Switches the data source to use a different database, if possible.
BeginTransaction	Creates a new transaction object that can then be associated with one or more command objects. All commands that are executed after the transaction is started are considered to be an *atomic* set of operations. The transaction can later be *committed*, which will make all the changes permanent, or *rolled back*, which will make the system seem as though none of the commands were executed. Transactions are discussed in detail in chapter 14.

Both objects also implement a method called `Dispose()`. This is the standard name of the function within an object that cleans up resources used by that object. If the object has cleanup work to do (such as cleaning up connections), then the `Dispose` method is the place where it should be done. You can call `Dispose()` instead of `Close()` on a connection, but it is considered more correct to call `Close()` for objects like connections that have semantics for being opened and closed.

If neither `Dispose()` nor `Close()` is called directly, `Dispose()` will eventually be called by the garbage collector, via finalization. However, relying on this call can be problematic. First, you have no idea when garbage collection will take place, meaning that you are holding a database connection open indefinitely. Second, finalization is inefficient because of the way the garbage collector works. As a rule of thumb, close or dispose of objects as soon as you can.

B.4 EVENTS

In addition to methods and properties, classes can define events to which other objects can subscribe. These events are not part of the IDbConnection interface, but both existing data providers have essentially the same event capabilities on their connection classes.

Events can be part of interfaces, because they are essentially just special properties, but again Microsoft chose not to make them part of the base class. This is sensible, considering that other data providers could work in substantially different ways.

> **EVENT** An event is a message that an object can send to indicate that some predefined *thing* has occurred.
>
> In .NET, objects can have event properties. Other objects can subscribe to that event and will be notified when the event is raised.
>
> The classic example for an event is a button on a form. When the button is clicked, a button-pushed event is generated that can be caught so the application can do something. It is legal for more than one object to subscribe to the same event, in which case all the subscribers will be notified about the event.

Table B.6 shows the events that can be raised by the connection objects (they are fundamentally the same for the OleDbConnection and the SQLConnection, with only a minor change in the syntax).

Table B.6 Connection event handlers

Event	Event handler signature
StateChange	`void StateChangeEventHandler(object,StateChangeEventArgs);`

InfoMessage	SQL Server version:
	`void SqlInfoMessageEventHandler(object,`
	`                    SqlInfoMessageEventArgs);`
	OLE DB version:
	`void OleDbInfoMessageEventHandler(object,`
	`                    OleDbInfoMessageEventArgs);`

B.4.1 The state change event

The state change event is fired every time the connection goes from open to closed or closed to open. You might catch it to update a screen icon showing whether there is currently a connection, or to monitor the behavior of connections in a pool.

Listing B.1 shows how to catch a state change event.

Listing B.1 Subscribing to the state change event

```
public void ConnectToSqlServer(string strConnect)
{
    SqlConnection conn = new SqlConnection(strConnect);

    conn.StateChange +=
            new StateChangeEventHandler(OnStateChange);        ❶ Subscribe to event
    conn.Open();
}
                                                     Define event handler method ⌐
protected void OnStateChange(object sndr,StateChangeEventArgs e)    ❷
{
    Console.WriteLine("State is now {0}",e.CurrentState);
}
```

❶ This line of code creates a new handler for the event that points to the `OnState-Change()` method and adds it to the list of subscribers for the event. Notice the `+=` notation, where you might have expected an `=`. We use this notation because the code is adding a subscriber to the list of subscribers. Any number of objects can subscribe to the same event.

❷ The function that handles the event must have the specific signature expected by the event handler. For this event, that means it must have a void return value and two parameters: the sender and an object of type StateChangeEventArgs:

- *Sender*—The sender is the object that sent the event—in this case, the connection object. Of course, to use the object as a connection object, it must be type-cast back to a connection, rather than a generic object:

  ```
  SqlConnection conn = sndr as SqlConnection;
  ```

- *StateChangeEventArgs*—This object contains the state to which the connection was changed (in the `CurrentState` property and the original state of the connection before the change (in the `OriginalState` property).

B.4.2 The info message event

This event is fired whenever something of consequence happens to the connection (for example, if a different database is selected). It is also fired for certain types of errors. It might be useful to subscribe to this event in order to provide logging functionality.

The code sample in listing B.2 demonstrates how to subscribe to this event using SQL Server. The syntax is slightly different for the OLE DB version, but should be easy enough to extrapolate.

```
public void ConnectToSqlServer(string strConnect)
{
    SqlConnection conn = new SqlConnection(strConnect);

    conn.InfoMessage +=
        new SqlInfoMessageEventHandler(OnInfoAdd);        ❶ Subscribe to event
    conn.Open();
}                                                    Define event handler function ─┐
                                                                                    ❷
protected void OnInfoAdd(object sndr,SqlInfoMessageEventArgs e)
{
    foreach(SqlError se in e.Errors)                      ❸ Look
        Console.WriteLine("Message: {0}",se.ToString());      at info
}
```

❶ As with the previous example, this line creates an event handler pointing to our event-handling member function and adds it as a subscriber to the event.

❷ The event handler for this event must look like the function shown in the sample, although it can have a different scope (public, protected, private, and so forth). It must, however, have a void return type and the two arguments shown:

- *Sender*—This the connection object, although it must be typecast back to a connection in order to be used.

- *SqlInfoMessageEventArgs*—This object contains the "info message." If this had been an OLE DB connection, then an OleDbInfoMessageEventArgs object would have been used instead, which contains some additional information about the message.

❸ Both InfoMessageEventArgs objects (SQL Server and OLE DB) contain a property called `Errors` that contains a collection of one or more messages. It is mildly confusing that this property is called `Errors`, because not all the info messages are errors. For example, it could contain information about a change in the connection.

The code steps through all the error objects in the collection and prints them out to the console as strings.

B.5 CONNECTION STRINGS

We have spent a lot of time exploring the connection object's methods, properties, and events. Before the connection object can be used for anything practical, though, it must first connect to the database. The connection string contains all the instructions for how to do this, such as the location of the database, the user ID and password to use, and instructions on how to connect.

Although there are some similarities, the connection strings for SQL Server are not the same as for OLE DB. In fact, for OLE DB, different OLE DB providers can have different parameters. For this reason, I'll discuss the SQL Server and OLE DB connection strings separately.

B.5.1 SQL Server connection strings

Because the SQL Server data provider only has to worry about a single database engine, it is easy to talk about all the legal values that can appear in a connection string. With OLE DB, this discussion is more difficult. This section first talks about the formatting rules for connection strings and then breaks down the legal parameters. I do so by category to make the discussion more digestible; the last category consists of settings that will almost never be used.

Connection string format

The SQL Server connection string is made up of a series of name/value pairs separated by semicolons:

```
Data Source=localhost;Initial Catalog=ADONetSamples;UID=sa;PWD=
```

In this example, not all the parameters have values. For example, `PWD=` specifies no password, which is the same as excluding the argument from the string. However, you should never have a blank password in any production system.

It is also legal to put quotes around the values, which is necessary if the argument has a quote in it. For example:

```
Data Source="Arlen's Server"
```

or

```
Data Source='my "favorite" server'
```

You can use either single or double quotes, as long as the string does not include the same type of quote. The name of the parameter is not case sensitive, and, except in the string, all white space is ignored. So,

```
Data Source = localhost
```

is the same as

```
Data Source=localhost
```

but

```
Data Source=local host
```

is not legal.

Basic parameters

Table B.7 shows the primary set of legal connection string parameters. You are apt to use these parameters all the time, and they appear in most of the book's examples. Many of the parameters have multiple aliases to accommodate formats that have gathered over the years. There is no behavioral difference between the parameter and its aliases.

Table B.7   Basic SQL Server connection parameters

Parameter	Meaning
Data Source	Specifies the name of the server where the SQL Server is located. If SQL Server is running on the local machine, then the special value `localhost` can be used.
	Aliases: `Server, Address, Addr, Network Address`
	Examples: `Data Source = localhost` `Data Source=MyServer`
	`Address = 127.0.0.1`
Initial Catalog	Specifies the name of the database.
	Alias: `Database`
	Example: `Initial Catalog=ADOTestDB`
User ID	Specifies the user login account to use.
	Alias: `UID`
	Examples: `User ID = Bob` `UID=Fred`
Password	Specifies the password for the user login account to use.
	Alias: `PWD`
	Examples: `Password=secret` `PWD=hello`
Connect Timeout	Specifies how much time the connection should spend attempting to connect before giving up and generating an error, specified in seconds. The connection timeout defaults to 15 seconds if it is not set. If the value is set to 0, then the connection will attempt to connect forever (it will never timeout).
	Alias: `Connection Timeout`
	Example: `Connect Timeout=60`

Here is an example that uses all these values:

```
SqlConnection conn = new SqlConnection("data source=localhost;" +
"Initial Catalog=ADONetSamples; UID=sa;PWD=;" +
"Connect Timeout=20");
```

Connection pooling parameters

The next set of parameters is used to control connection pooling. Connection pooling is a mechanism for efficiently reusing connections, and is discussed in detail in chapter 30. The settings that can be specified in the connection string are shown in table B.8.

Table B.8   SQL Server connection pool parameters

Parameter	Meaning
`Pooling`	Controls whether connection pooling is enabled on this connection. This parameter defaults to `true`. Examples: `Pooling=true` `Pooling=false`
`Min Pool Size`	Specifies the minimum number of connections in the pool. This many connections will be created up front, even if they are not immediately being used. This parameter defaults to `0`. Example: `Min Pool Size = 10`
`Max Pool Size`	Specifies the maximum number of connections in the pool. When this many connections have been hit, the next user to request a connection will have to wait. This parameter defaults to `100`. Example: `Max Pool Size = 50`
`Connection Lifetime`	Used to make the connection pool retire old connections after a set amount of time (in seconds). This parameter is sometimes useful if a server might not be hit in a long time, causing the connection on the server to timeout, and to help make more efficient use of resources. This value defaults to `0`, which means that there is no lifetime limit on the connection. Example: `Connection Lifetime=120`
`Connection Reset`	Controls whether the connection is reset before being handed out of the pool. It causes a performance hit (because the connection must make a call to the database engine), but guarantees that the connection is in a clean state before use. This value defaults to `true`. Example: `Connection Reset=false`
`Enlist`	If set to `true`, and the user of the connection is enrolled in a COM+ transaction, then automatically associates the connection with that transaction. COM+ transactions are discussed in chapter 32. This value defaults to `true`. Example: `Enlist=false`

An interesting point about these settings is that, by default, connection pooling is turned on. This is a clue about how seriously ADO.NET is aimed toward building distributed applications, where connection pooling is critical.

Security parameters

SQL Server has several options that can make its connections more secure; they are shown in table B.9. I have not duplicated the password parameter here, although it is obviously security related.

Table B.9 SQL Server security parameters

Parameter	Meaning
Integrated Security	Indicates that instead of using the user ID and password values, the user information should be determined by determining the authenticated current user of Windows. For example, if user AFeldman is logged in to a trusted Windows Domain, then that would be the user for the SQL Server database.
	Integrated Security is more secure than passing a user ID and password in the clear to the server, and, based on SQL Server's configuration, it is possible that the connection will be encrypted to prevent snooping on the data passing back and forth. However, it assumes that the user is logged in to a valid NT Domain, and that SQL Server has been configured for integrated security.
	This value defaults to false.
	Alias: Trusted_Connection
	Example: Integrated Security=true
Persist Security Info	Normally, once the connection has been made, the connection string contains all of the parameters that were passed, including the user ID and password. Sometimes, though, you do not want this information to be available to all users of the connection object.
	By setting this parameter to false, SQL Server will strip security information from the connection string after the connection has been made.
	This value defaults to false, meaning that security information will be removed.
	Example: Persist Security Info=true

Other parameters

This final set of parameters consists of values that are either used very rarely, or are rarely changed from their default value (table B.10).

Table B.10 Other SQL Server parameters

Parameter	Meaning
Application Name	If you specify an application name, then this information will be tracked by SQL Server to make it easier to identify who is responsible for which activities. For example, you can sort log files based on the application name.
	Example: Application Name=My cool program
AttachDBFilename	Normally, connecting to a database is done by its name. However, you can connect to a database based on its path. SQL Server still requires a database name to be specified.
	Aliases: Extended properties, Initial File Name
	Examples: Database=MyDB;
	AttachDBFilename=C:\\Data\\MyDB.MDF
	(The double slashes are used in C# because a backslash is an escape character.)

continued on next page

Table B.10 Other SQL Server parameters *(continued)*

Parameter	Meaning
Current Language	Specifies the default language to use with this connection. This value controls, for example, formatting dates, times and numbers, and error messages.
	Example: Current Language=French
Network Library	Specifies a different low-level mechanism for connecting to the database. The specified library needs to be installed on the client, and the server must be configured appropriately to use it. This value defaults to dbmssocn, which indicates the use of TCP/IP.
	Alias: Net
	Examples: Net=dbnmpntw (Named pipes) Network Library=dbmsspxn (IPX/SPX)
Workstation ID	Specifies the name of the computer connecting to SQL Server. This value is used by SQL Server to tell if a connection is from the same machine. This value defaults to the local name of the computer.
	Example: Workstation ID=Fred PC

B.5.2 OLE DB connection strings

Connecting to an OLE DB provider can be challenging. As with SQL Server, you can pass a number of parameters, but the parameters to pass are different for different providers. And, because providers can be used to talk to multiple data sources, the parameters for the data sources may be different as well.

The most important parameter on an OLE DB connection string is the provider, which specifies which OLE DB data provider needs to be used. Table B.11 shows some common providers and the value of the provider parameter, which is not always obvious.

Table B.11 Commonly used OLE DB providers

Type of data	Provider string
Microsoft Access (MDB)	Provider=Microsoft.Jet.OLEDB.4.0
Microsoft SQL Server	Provider=SQLOLEDB
Microsoft provider for Oracle	Provider=MSDAORA
Oracle provider for Oracle	Provider=OraOLEDB.Oracle
Data shaping provider (a utility provider that allows access to other relational data sources in a hierarchical manner)	Provider=MSDataShape

There are other OLE DB providers, including many with very specific syntax. The ADO.NET OLE DB provider will not talk to all drivers—it is smart enough to know, to some extent, which drivers are compatible with it. So, for example, you cannot use the OLE DB provider for ODBC.

The following sections show how to connect to the providers described earlier. Other providers will be similar.

Microsoft Access

The primary parameter you must provide is the data source, which identifies the name and location of the MDB file. Optional parameters include a user name and password:

```
strConnect = @"Provider=Microsoft.Jet.OLEDB.4.0;" +
  @"Data Source=c:\ADOSample\ADONetSamplesAccess.MDB;User ID=;Password=";
```

The data source is the path and filename. If the Access file was located in the current directory, then the path could be omitted. Note that single slashes instead of double slashes appear in the path, unlike previous examples, because we put an at sign (@) in front of the string; it tells C# to treat the entire string literally.

This example includes no user ID and password, so those parameters could have been omitted. If any Access-specific parameters needed to be specified, they could be added to the end of the string, separated by semicolons (;).

Microsoft SQL Server

It is relatively unnecessary to connect to SQL Server via OLE DB when an ADO.NET data provider is specifically written to SQL Server. However, doing so might be useful in a couple of situations:

- Talking to an older version of SQL Server (The SQL Server data provider requires SQL Server version 7 or later.)
- Using OLE DB generic functionality to talk to arbitrary data sources.

The connection arguments, except for the provider, are basically the same as for the ADO.NET SQL Server data provider:

```
strConnect = "Provider=SQLOLEDB;Data Source=localhost;" +
  "Initial Catalog=ADONetSamples;UID=sa;PWD=";
```

This example will create a connection to the same database we have been using via the ADO.NET SQL Server data provider.

Oracle

Two different Oracle data providers are listed in table B.11: one provided by Microsoft and one provided by Oracle. Each has pluses and minus. The Microsoft data provider has support for more features and behaves more like the SQL Server data provider. The Oracle data provider supports Oracle-specific capabilities better and theoretically performs better. To be honest, I haven't seen much difference in performance between the two.

Whichever provider you choose, the notation is similar, aside from the provider. Here is the format for the Microsoft provider:

```
strConnect = "Provider= MSDAORA;Data Source=ADONETOR;" +
  "User ID=scott;Password=tiger";
```

And here is the format for the Oracle provider:

```
strConnect = "Provider= OraOLEDB.Oracle;Data Source=ADONETOR;" +
"User ID=scott;Password=tiger";
```

The `Data Source` in both cases refers either to the name of a server or to a value in a text file called tnsnames.ora. This file specifies how the data source maps to a particular database. Here is the entry for ADONETOR in the tnsnames.ora file on my machine (Oracle is installed locally):

```
ADONETOR =
  (DESCRIPTION =
    (ADDRESS_LIST =
      (ADDRESS = (PROTOCOL = TCP)(HOST = arf733)(PORT = 1521))
    )
    (CONNECT_DATA =
      (SERVICE_NAME = ADONETOR)
    )
  )
)
```

The user ID and password shown (*scott* and *tiger*) are for one of several default accounts on an Oracle sample database. As with the user ID *sa* on SQL Server with no password, many Oracle databases in the world still use the default *scott/tiger* values (a good thing to know if you feel like hacking into some web sites). If you are planning to expose your database, don't forget to remove those defaults!

Data Shaping

Data Shaping is a Microsoft concept that lets data be retrieved from a relational database but be returned as a hierarchy (like a tree). For example, if a teacher teaches a number of classes, the list of classes might be represented as a single item for each teacher that contains multiple items (table B.12).

Table B.12   Hierarchical data

Teacher	Classes
Ms. Fortune	Basket Weaving Chemistry
Mr. Kriefels	Physics Geometry

Notice how there are multiple rows in the Classes column for each row in the Teacher column. Of course, you can get this information using a join, but you end up with redundantly repeated information. You could also pull back the data using multiple queries and combine the results in memory, or do a query as you move to each new row. This is all the Data Shaping provider does, but it saves you from having to do all the work yourself.

The connection string for the Data Shaping provider is interesting, because you have to specify an additional provider for the location of the data:

```
string strConnect = "Provider=MSDataShape;Data Provider=SQLOLEDB;" +
    "Data Source=localhost;Initial Catalog=ADONetSamples;user id=sa";
```

The provider being specified is for the Data Shaping service. It then uses the value specified in the `Data Provider` parameter to connect to the source of the data—in this case, the SQL Server OLE DB provider. The rest of the information should look familiar; it is the information required to connect to SQL Server.

Data Shaping is complicated and beyond the scope of this book. However, chapter 11 includes an example of reading hierarchical data with the Data Shaping provider.

ODBC

Most anyone who has worked with OLE DB is aware that there is an OLE DB provider that lets you talk to ODBC. You might think you could specify the appropriate provider (MSDASQL) and connect to the huge number of existing ODBC drivers.

However, this is not the case. ADO.NET will throw an exception if you attempt to use this driver. Because of the way ODBC works, there were problems with allowing access to ODBC via OLE DB from ADO.NET.[1] Although Microsoft could have fixed these problems, it decided that a better solution was to provide an ODBC data provider.

This is a much better solution. ODBC is extremely fast (one reason you might choose to use it), but adding in the OLE DB provider layer slows it down and adds unnecessary complexity. Unfortunately, Microsoft did not have time to include the ODBC data provider in the first version of .NET, but the company made it available on its web site shortly after the release. Appendix A talks about the installation and use of this data provider.

B.6 SUMMARY

For a relatively small class, there is a lot to know about connections and connection strings. Much of the time you can get by with the basics of connections; but every now and then, knowledge of the more involved information is an absolute necessity.

Appendix C discusses the command class and the data reader in manner similar (although somewhat shorter) to this appendix's approach to connections.

---

[1] Aren't acronyms wonderful?

Command classes

Appendix B talked about connecting to a data source. Although doing so is certainly a critical step, it isn't useful by itself—unless you can do something with that connection. That is where the command classes come in. Virtually all work you do with a data source is done directly or indirectly via the use of a command object.

Chapter 10 provides an overview of the command classes. This appendix examines the ins and outs of the command object and looks at some of the more involved or esoteric things you can do with a command.

There are two aspects of the command classes that I won't discuss in detail, because they are large enough topics to justify into their own chapters. These topics are parameters (covered in detail in chapters 12 and 13) and transactions (discussed in chapter 14). Technically, they are their own classes and should be covered separately anyway; but they are very much tied to the command objects.

As in the previous appendix, several tables contain information about the properties and methods of the command classes. Don't worry, though; the command classes are quite a bit smaller, so you'll have to wade through less information.

C.1 COMMAND INTERFACES AND IMPLEMENTATIONS

The command object, as the name implies, is the way commands are sent to the database. If you are trying to do basic database operations, execute stored procedures, retrieve data, fill DataSets, and so forth, you will end up using a command object, either directly or indirectly.

As with most database objects, a base interface provides common functionality, and each data provider includes an implementation (table C.1).

Table C.1 Command implementations

Class	Provider	Interface
SqlCommand	SQL Server	IDbCommand
OleDbCommand	OLE DB	IDbCommand

C.2 COMMAND PROPERTIES

All the relevant properties of command objects are defined in the IDbCommand interface. You'll see several additional properties on the specific implementations (SqlCommand and OleDbCommand), but they are there because of base classes, and have nothing to do with the database side.

Table C.2 shows the properties available in the IDbCommand interface. As expected, these methods are available on the two data provider-specific implementations.

C.2.1 Command text

The command text that can be passed is any legal SQL for the underlying data source. This includes the standard DML (Data Manipulation Language) commands, such as:

```
SELECT * FROM MyTable
INSERT INTO MyTable (Field1,Field2) VALUES ('Bob',1)
UPDATE MyTable SET Field1='Fred' WHERE Field2=1
DELETE FROM MyTable WHERE Field1='Bob'
```

These commands are similar from database to database, based on the SQL standards. However, there are some minor differences. For example, the format for an outer join differs from engine to engine. SQL Server uses the following format:

```
SELECT Field1,Field2 FROM MyTable1,MyTable2 WHERE
MyTable1.Field3 *= MyTable2.Field3
```

The Oracle format is as follows:

```
SELECT Field1,Field2 FROM MyTable1,MyTable2 WHERE
MyTable1.Field3 = MyTable2.Field3 (+)
```

Table C.2   IDbCommand properties

Property	Purpose
Connection	The connection object that the command will use. This property must be set before the command can be executed. If the command is created directly from a connection object, then this property will be set already.
CommandText	The SQL command to be executed. Command text is discussed in more detail in section C.2.1.
CommandType	The type of command contained in the CommandText property. Legal values include:

Command Type	Meaning
Text	Indicates that the command text contains an SQL string to execute. This is the default value for the CommandType property.
StoredProcedure	Indicates that the command text contains the name of a stored procedure to execute.
TableDirect	A special type that is currently supported only by the OleDbCommand implementation. When this setting is used, it indicates that the command text contains the name of a table. When the command is executed, all the rows in the table will be returned. This is equivalent to setting the command type to Text and the command text to `SELECT * FROM MyTable`

Property	Purpose
Parameters	A collection of arguments that are required to complete the statement, or to pass to a stored procedure. Parameters are discussed in detail in chapters 12 and 13.
Transaction	Associates multiple commands with a transaction, to bind them together so they either succeed or fail as a group. Transactions are discussed in detail in chapter 14.
CommandTimeOut	The amount of time (in seconds) the command should spend attempting to complete before giving up. The default timeout is 30 seconds. Setting this value to 0 means the command will keep trying to execute forever.
UpdatedRowSet	Controls how a DataSet is updated based on the command. This property is specifically provided for working with DataSets. DataSets are discussed in detail starting in chapter 15.

OUTER JOIN   A type of join where one side of the join always appears, even if no records meet the join expression.

When two tables are joined together through a normal join statement, the result is *multiplicative*—that is, all matching columns are joined in all combinations:

Student	
Name	**StudentID**
Bob	1
Fred	2

Languages	
Language	**StudentID**
English	1
French	1

The results of a standard join would be:

StudentID	Name	Language
1	Bob	English
1	Bob	French

There are two interesting things about the result. First, the first record of student Bob is repeated, because the Student ID 1 appears twice in the join; the second record (Fred) never appears, because there is no match in the second table. If, however, an outer join is used, then all the values will appear from either the first table specified (a left outer join) or the second table specified (a right outer join):

StudentID	Name	Language
1	Bob	English
1	Bob	French
2	Fred	(null)

We still get the two rows for each combination of the first row, but now we also get an instance of the second row from the first table. Of course, the Language field is null for that row because there is no matching row in the second table.

For the specific details of the appropriate syntax for your database engine, you will need to refer to the appropriate documentation. This is just a warning that the same SQL will not always transparently transfer.

Commands can also send DDL (Data Definition Language) to the database:

```
CREATE TABLE MyTable (Field1 VARCHAR(15), Field2 INTEGER)
DROP TABLE MyTable
ALTER TABLE MyTable ADD Field3 VARCHAR(20)
```

These types of statements are usually quite different from engine to engine, if they are present.

You can also call stored procedures. When you do this, you can specify the command type to be StoredProcedure. This tells the provider that the CommandText contains nothing more than the name of a stored procedure. You can also use the data provider-specific syntax for calling a stored procedure, and leave the CommandType set to Text. For example, using the Oracle provider, you could send the following text:

```
BEGIN someprocedure(42); END;
```

This technique is important, because the Oracle OLE DB provider does not support calling stored procedures directly using the StoredProcedure value for CommandText, although the Microsoft provider does.

C.3 EXECUTE METHODS ON COMMANDS

The most important methods on the command classes are the methods for executing the command. There are a number of different execute methods (table C.3), although not all of them are available in both data providers.

Table C.3 Execute methods

Execute Method	Purpose
ExecuteNonQuery	This execute method is used to execute statements that are not expected to return results, such as an Insert or an Update. This method usually returns the number of rows that were changed by the statement, but in some circumstances will only return a nonzero result (usually –1), indicating success.
ExecuteReader	This method is used when a result set is expected back, usually from a Select or a stored procedure. The return value is a data reader that can be used to step through results.
ExecuteScalar	This method is used when a result is expected—but only a single value (for example, when a count was selected).
ExecuteXmlReader	(SQL Server only) SQL Server has the ability to return results as XML. Using the ExecuteXmlReader method, the returned results can be put directly into an XML reader that allows easy navigation through the XML.

C.3.1 ExecuteNonQuery example

Any time you want to execute SQL that does not return a result set, you can use the ExecuteNonQuery() method. It is specifically designed for this purpose. Generally, it will return the number of rows affected by executing the SQL, although for some commands (such as a Create Table) it will return a -1 to indicate that something was done.

The following code does a simple insert into the Teachers table using Execute-NonQuery():

```
public void TestExecuteNonQuery(SqlConnection conn)
{
    string strSQL = "INSERT INTO Teachers"
        + " (TeacherName,Classroom) VALUES ('Mr. Dewitt','D4')";

    SqlCommand comm = new SqlCommand(strSQL,conn);

    int iReturn = comm.ExecuteNonQuery();

    Console.WriteLine("ExecuteNonQuery returned {0}",iReturn);
}
```

The output is shown in figure C.1.

Figure C.1
Output from the ExecuteNonQuery example

C.3.2   ExecuteReader example

To execute SQL that returns results, you will most often use the ExecuteReader()
method, which returns a DataReader for stepping through results. The DataReader is
a powerful class; it is discussed in chapter 11 and in great detail (all properties and
methods) in appendix D. The following simple example selects data out of the Teachers table and writes it out to the console:

```
public void TestExecuteReader(SqlConnection conn)

    string strSQL = "SELECT TeacherName,Classroom,Subject"
                        + " FROM Teachers";

    SqlCommand comm = new SqlCommand(strSQL,conn);

    SqlDataReader reader = comm.ExecuteReader();

    while ( reader.Read() )
    {
        Console.WriteLine( reader.GetString(0) + ", " +
                    reader.GetString(1) + ", " +
                    reader.GetString(2));
    }

    reader.Close();
```

The output appears in figure C.2.

**Figure C.2
Output from the
ExecuteReader
example**

Command behavior

When you call ExecuteReader, you can also pass an additional parameter that is
either a special order or a hint to execute the SQL in a certain way. You can also combine these command behaviors. For example, the call

```
comm.ExecuteReader(CommandBehavior.SingleRow |
    CommandBehavior.CloseConnection);
```

tells the database that we are expecting back a single row as a result only, and that
once the reader has finished executing, we want the connection to be closed.

Table C.4 shows the legal CommandBehavior flags you can use.

Table C.4 CommandBehavior flags

CommandBehavior	Purpose
CloseConnection	If this flag is set, then the connection associated with the command will be shut down as soon as all the data has been read from the data reader.
	This flag can be useful if you have only opened the connection for the express purpose of reading a single set of data, or you are using connection pooling and want to make sure you release connections back to the pool as soon as possible.
SchemaOnly	Using this flag returns a DataReader that doesn't contain any rows of data, but contains the structure of the various columns that would have been used had the query been resolved.
	This is one way to read the structure of a table. If you do a SELECT * on the table with this flag set, you can get the information on the columns without having to read any data.
SingleResult	This flag indicates that only a single result value is expected (for example, from a SELECT Count(*) call). In theory, the engine can use this flag to make the query more efficient. It is semantically similar to using the ExecuteScalar() method described in the next section.
SingleRow	This flag indicates that only a single row of data is expected back. The database engine can use this information to make the query more efficient.
KeyInfo	(SQL Server only) When this behavior is specified, information on the indexes and primary keys of the table is returned.
SequentialAccess	This flag is used when you want to read large binary or text data fields using the GetChars() or GetBytes() method, so that you can read a piece of the image or text at a time.

C.3.3   ExecuteScalar example

Sometimes you want to execute some SQL that returns a single value. You can use the ExecuteReader() method, but it is a little heavy if you are expecting a single result. The ExecuteScalar() method is specifically provided to handle situations in which you either are expecting one simple result or don't care about the results that are returned as long as something is returned.

The following example gets a count of records in the Teachers table and returns a single integer value:

```
public void TestExecuteScalar(SqlConnection conn)
{
    string strSQL = "SELECT COUNT(*) FROM Teachers";
    SqlCommand comm = new SqlCommand(strSQL,conn);

    int iCount = (int)comm.ExecuteScalar();

    Console.WriteLine("ExecuteScalar returned {0}",iCount);
}
```

The out put appears in figure C.3.

The result from ExecuteScalar() is typecast to an integer in the example. The return type from ExecuteScalar() is an object. However, we know that the SQL we are passing will return an integer because we asked for a count. If we executed SQL

Figure C.3
Output from the `ExecuteScalar` example

that we expected to return, for example, a `DateTime` value (for example, the maximum `DateTime` value from a particular table), then we would have to typecast the object to a `DateTime`.

If we had no way of knowing the return type, we could rely on the basic behavior of any object, which always allows us to turn a result into a string. Alternatively, we could look at the object's type to determine how to use the value.

C.3.4   ExecuteXmlReader example

The `ExecuteXmlReader()` method only exists on the SQL Server data provider's version of command, SqlCommand, and relies on XML functionality built in to SQL Server. Microsoft has gone to considerable lengths to support XML in its products. In fact, with SQL Server, you can read and write data via XML, change schemas, and perform other tasks with XML. (Chapter 29 talks about SQL Server's support for XML.) The following example reads data from SQL Server as XML and then outputs it:

```
using System.Xml;

public void TestExecuteXmlReader(SqlConnection conn)
{
    string strSQL = "SELECT * FROM Teachers FOR XML AUTO";
    SqlCommand comm = new SqlCommand(strSQL,conn);

    XmlReader reader = comm.ExecuteXmlReader();

    while(reader.Read())
        Console.WriteLine(reader.ReadOuterXml());

    reader.Close();
}
```

The `using System.Xml` directive should appear above the class, but is shown here to indicate that it must be included to access the XmlReader class.

The output appears in figure C.4.

In its simplest format, SQL Server returns each field as an XML attribute. Chapter 29 shows other ways the data can be returned.

Figure C.4   Output from the `ExecuteXmlReader` example

C.4 OTHER COMMAND METHODS

Although the Execute methods are by far the most important methods of the command classes, a handful of other methods may come in useful (see table C.5). Most of them are defined on the IDbCommand interface. The exception is Reset-CommandTimeout(), which is present on both of the implementations of IDbCommand (SqlCommand and OleDbCommand) but is not part of the interface. (Someone at Microsoft must have decided that this method was needed for both current implementations, but not necessarily for new data providers.)

Table C.5   Other command methods

Method	Purpose
Cancel	Cancels the current command. For example, if a data reader has been returned, but not all of the data has yet been stepped through, calling Cancel will throw out the remaining data.
CreateParameter	Creates a new parameter and adds it to the Parameters collection. Parameters are discussed in detail in chapters 12 and 13.
Prepare	If the same command will be used multiple times with different parameters, Prepare is used to set up the command before it is executed with each set of parameters. This method is explained in more detail in chapter 12.
ResetCommandTimeout	This method is available on both the SqlCommand and the OleDbCommand, but is not part of the IDbCommandinterface. When this method is called, it resets the timeout to the default, which is 30 seconds.

C.4.1   Canceling asynchronous commands

You might think, because of the presence of a Cancel method, that you can cancel a command that is in progress (for example, if you send a complex query to the database that might take some minutes to execute, and then the user clicks a cancel button). This functionality has shown up, in one form or another, in many of the previous Microsoft database access technologies.

However, the Cancel method does not currently cancel a command this way. In fact, many of the previous engines that supposedly supported this capability, did not—the command was sent, but the engine did not respond until it had finished running the original query. When the method did work, its functionality was frequently being faked by the driver, which eventually led to problems.

What you *can* do with the Cancel method is interrupt the return of results from a large query. So, for example, if you are retrieving a few thousand rows from the database engine, calling this method will interrupt the return of that data.

It would be very handy if you could cancel a complex database operation in the middle, even with the understanding that support for such a capability would have an effect on performance. However, for the moment, you should understand the limitations of most engines when it comes to this capability.

C.5   SUMMARY

Considering the importance of the command classes, this is a short appendix. The complexity of what you can do with a command object comes down to the SQL you pass (and possibly the use of parameters) rather than the capabilities of the object.

One useful feature of the command classes is the way they split up the execution of different types of SQL. For example, you don't have to mess around with a Data-Reader if you are executing an `update` statement, or go through similar overhead when you are reading XML directly from SQL Server. This functionality not only makes your code significantly cleaner, but it allows the writer of the data provider to make the code considerably more efficient.

The command objects are used in ever more complex examples throughout the book. The next appendix explores the DataReader, which is returned from a call to the command's `ExecuteReader()` method.

DataReader classes

ADO.NET has two distinct mechanisms for dealing with result sets of data: the DataSet and the DataReader. A DataSet (discussed in part 3) is a highly flexible class—or rather, set of classes—that allows data to be viewed and manipulated in complex ways and later stored back to its source. In comparison, the DataReader is simplistic: it allows data to be read, with no ability for manipulation. In fact, when reading, you must read through the data in a forward-only manner; you start at the beginning of the data and move forward a record at a time until you are done.

Why would you use the much simpler DataReader, then, when you have access to the apparently more functional DataSet? First, a DataSet doesn't have the ability to read data at all—it must be filled with data. You can do so using a DataAdapter, which uses the DataReader to access the data to fill the DataSet.

Second, the DataReader is a much lighter object than a DataSet. A cost is associated with the added functionality of a DataSet, which may be an issue depending on the type of application you are building. Because of the added costs, the DataReader can be significantly faster than using a DataSet; if you consider that all the work the Data-Reader might potentially do must take place to fill a DataSet, in addition to the work and storage that takes place for the DataSet, the DataSet is guaranteed to be slower.

That is not to say you should avoid using the DataSet. If you need to manipulate data or transmit it to another tier of your system, the DataSet is an excellent mechanism. However, if you just need to step through a result set of data, the DataReader is the way to go.

Most of the time, you will get a DataReader by calling `ExecuteReader()` on a command object. (The command object was discussed in detail in appendix C and also in chapter 10.) This appendix continues from chapter 11, which showed many uses of the DataReader. I'll go into more detail about all the properties and methods.

As with the other in-depth appendixes, this appendix is heavy on tables. Some list useful properties and methods, and you should read them in detail. Others, such as the list of `Get` methods on the `IDataRecord` interface, are for reference; feel free to do a quick scan.

D.1 DATAREADER CLASSES AND INTERFACES

Unlike most of the other ADO.NET objects, two interfaces are associated with each data reader:

- *IDataReader*—This interface is responsible for stepping from record to record and from result set to result set.

- *IDataRecord*—This interface is responsible for accessing the data in the current row.

You usually don't need to worry about which interface contains which methods or properties. Even if you are writing generic code that passes the interface around, you do not need to worry about casting back and forth between the interfaces, because the IDataReader interface is derived from the IDataRecord interface; so, you can call any IDataRecord methods on an IDataReader reference. Of course, if you pass an IDataRecord interface reference, you will have to typecast it to an IDataReader interface if you need to call any `IDataReader` methods. Table D.1 shows the interfaces and the data provider–specific implementations.

Table D.1   DataReader implementations and interfaces

Class	Provider	Interface
SqlDataReader	SQL Server	IDataReader, IDataRecord
OleDbDataReader	OLE DB	IDataReader, IDataRecord

D.2 EFFICIENCY

The methods on a DataReader make it appear as though one row at a time is read from the database and transferred to the client. In practice, that process would be very inefficient. The DataReaders bring over data in efficient lumps, based on the network packet size, and so forth. However, the DataReader makes it seem that only one row is sent at a time. The underlying code is efficient, but the DataReader is still easy to use.

It is also possible for less than an entire row to be brought over at a time. Imagine a situation where a column contains a very large picture as binary data. Although you can have the DataReader read it in its entirety, methods are available that allow the pieces of the image to be read; for example, they would let the image begin to be displayed before the whole image had been retrieved from the server.

D.3 INTERFACE PROPERTIES

When talking about DataReader properties, I need to describe two different sets: those on the IDataReader interface, and those on the IDataRecord interface. Both implementations of IDataReader implement both interfaces. Although each interface has a handful of properties, the important aspects of each are their methods. I'll quickly present the properties first.

D.3.1 IDataReader properties

The IDataReader interface is responsible for moving through records and sets of records, as opposed to the IDataRecord interface, which is responsible for reading data from each individual record.

The IDataReader interface has only three properties, which you are only likely to use in special circumstances. The properties are shown in table D.2. As usual, these methods are all present on the two implementations (SqlDataReader and OleDb-DataReader).

Table D.2   IDataReader properties

Property	Purpose
IsClosed	Indicates whether the reader is open or closed. You might occasionally want to check to make sure a reader has been closed, although you'll usually close the reader explicitly when you are done reading.
Depth	Specifies how many levels deep into the hierarchy the DataReader is returning data. This property is used when you're looking at hierarchical information, either from a hierarchical database (such as Raima) or when using a mechanism for returning data in a hierarchical format from a relational database. Most of the time, this property will return 0.
	An example later in this appendix, in section D.5, demonstrates reading hierarchical data and uses the Depth property and methods specifically designed to work with this type of data.
RecordsAffected	The number of records that were changed by the execution of the SQL. This property is not set until after all data has been read and the Data-Reader has been closed. This property might be useful if a stored procedure is executed that changes data and returns results.

The RecordsAffected property

The `RecordsAffected` property can be handy if you are doing batch SQL or calling a stored procedure that both modifies data and returns results. It's valuable when you are trying to minimize round-trips to the database by doing several related tasks together, you need to know how many records were modified, and you want to get some records back as well.

The following example is a little spurious, but it demonstrates the property. The code inserts a row into the Teachers database and then returns all the records:

```
public void TestSelectSQL(SqlConnection conn)
{
    string strSQL =
            "INSERT INTO Teachers (TeacherName,Classroom,Subject) "
        + " VALUES ('Mr. Underwood','A1','French'); "
        + "SELECT TeacherName,Classroom,Subject FROM Teachers";

    SqlCommand comm = new SqlCommand(strSQL,conn);
    SqlDataReader reader = comm.ExecuteReader();

    // Using our existing method to display data
    DisplayReaderResults(reader);

    //always call Close when done reading.
    reader.Close();

    Console.WriteLine("RecordsAffected = {0}",reader.RecordsAffected);
}
```

The SQL here uses SQL Server's ability to execute multiple statements by separating them with a semicolon. The `RecordsAffected` property is not written out until after the reader has been closed. Technically, this property is not guaranteed to be set until after the reader has been closed. However, for simple cases like this, the value is available immediately. Figure D.1 shows the output from the sample code.

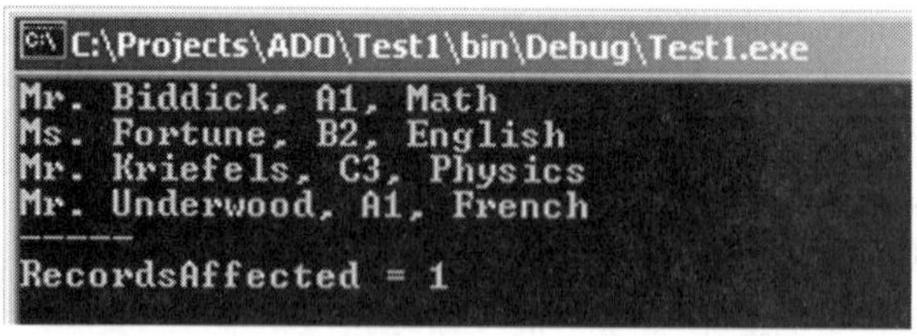

Figure D.1
Results from the
`RecordsAffected` **example**

As you can see, one record is affected, because we inserted a single row.

D.3.2 IDataRecord properties

The IDataRecord is responsible for providing information about the current record. It does so mostly via methods that are shown later in section D.4.3. However, the IDataRecord has two properties (table D.3). Unlike the properties on the IData-Reader, you'll probably use the IDataRecord properties.

Table D.3   IDataRecord properties

Property	Purpose
FieldCount	The total number of fields in the current row.
Item	An indexer that returns the value in the specified column as an object. Note that there is no property called Item that you will use. Rather, an indexer is used directly on the object, as if you were accessing an item in an array. There are two versions of this property: one that takes an integer specifying the column number, and one that takes the name of the column:
	`reader[1]   // Second column (0-based)` `reader["TeacherName"]`
	In both versions, reader is the name of the DataReader.

Although the following example is not necessarily the most efficient way, you can read all the data from a reader using these two properties:

```
public void DisplayReaderResults(IDdataReader reader)
{
    IDataRecord record = reader as IDataRecord;

    int iCount = record.FieldCount;
    while(reader.Read())
    {
        for(int i = 0;i < iCount;i++)
        {
            Console.WriteLine(record[i].ToString());
        }
    }
}
```

This example does not waste time making the output pretty, but you can see how the loop is based on the number of fields, determined from the FieldCount property. It accesses each item in turn using the indexer (record[i]).

The indexer also allows you to asks for a particular field by its name:

```
record["TeacherName"]
```

This method of access is slightly slower because the field name must be looked up. This is not a big deal if you are only getting a little data, but you should avoid this approach if you are stepping through a large result set, accessing columns for each row.

D.4 INTERFACE METHODS

Although the properties on the two interfaces are interesting, you cannot do anything with the data without using some of the IDataReader methods. As with the properties, I have broken the discussion between the two interfaces, even though IDataReader implements IDataRecord, and, of course, the two main implementations (SqlDataReader and OleDbDataReader) implement both.

D.4.1 IDataReader interface methods

The IDataReader interface is responsible for moving through result sets. Generally when you execute SQL for a reader, you only get back one set of results, and only need to use the Read() and Close() methods. However, you can execute SQL that returns multiple result sets, either by using batch SQL or by executing a stored procedure. For this reason, the DataReader has the ability to step to new result sets, using the NextResult() method.

Another method on IDataReader can be used to return the structure of the data: GetSchemaTable(). This is odd, considering that all other methods and properties for describing the data are part of the IDataRecord interface.

Table D.4 shows the methods on the IDataReader interface.

Table D.4   IDataReader methods

Method	Purpose
Read	Moves to the next row of results. The DataReader starts above the first row, so Read must be called before the first row can be read. This method returns true until there is no more data, at which point it returns false.
Close	Closes the reader and releases resources. Because .NET is a garbage-collected environment, it is always a good idea to call Close() rather than waiting for the garbage collector to clean up resources.
NextResult	Moves to the next result set, which can then be read as normal. It is possible for the SQL being executed to return more than one result set; for example, a stored procedure might contain multiple selects.
	Unlike the semantics of the Read() method, the DataReader starts out positioned on the first result set, so it is only necessary to call NextResult() to move to additional result sets.
	NextResult() returns true if it positioned to a new result set, or false if there are no more result sets.
GetSchemaTable	Returns a DataTable that contains the structure of the result set. DataTables are discussed in detail when I talk about the DataSet, starting with chapter 15.

D.4.2 Reading multiple result sets

You have already seen numerous examples that return a single result set. The code in listing D.1 can be used to read multiple result sets from the same command.

Although this example uses a stored procedure to retrieve the data, it could have used batch SQL—with SQL Server you can execute multiple statements simultaneously using a semicolon between each command.

```
public void DoubleSelect(SqlConnection conn)
{
    string strSQL = "GetClassesAndTeachers";
    SqlCommand comm = new SqlCommand(strSQL,conn);
    comm.CommandType = CommandType.StoredProcedure;          ❶ Execute stored
                                                               procedure

    SqlDataReader reader = comm.ExecuteReader();

    do
    {
        int iCount = reader.FieldCount;         ❷ Data reading loop
        while(reader.Read())
        {
            for(int i = 0;i < iCount;i++)
            {
                if(i > 0)        Console.Write(", ");
                Console.Write(reader.GetValue(i).ToString().Trim());
            }
            Console.WriteLine("");
        }
        Console.WriteLine("-----");
    } while (reader.NextResult());              ❸ NextResult

    reader.Close();
}
```

❶ The command type has been set to StoredProcedure because we are executing a stored procedure. In fact, this setting does not matter with SQL Server—the command would be executed even if the type were set to Text. But there are advantages to letting the provider know a stored procedure is being executed, as discussed in chapter 13.

❷ As with all the previous DataReader examples, this loop steps through each row and writes out data. A little formatting code makes the output more readable.

❸ This is the special handling for multiple results. Calling NextResult() will move the reader onto the next result set if there is one. Note that this call is done inside a do loop, rather than a while loop, as with the Read() command. We do so because NextResult() works slightly differently than Read()—the first call to Read() moves the reader to the first row of data, whereas the reader is automatically positioned on the first result set.

Although this behavior is inconsistent, it is convenient. It is rare for multiple result sets to be returned. If the reader started life before the first result set, every piece of code using a reader would end up having to call `NextResult()` at least once, even though few would care about the call. However, it is convenient to use the reader within a `while` loop. If it started on the first row, additional logic would have to be put in place every time to see if the result set was empty before starting a loop.

Output

The stored procedure does two selects: one from the Classes table and one from the Teachers table. Figure D.2 shows the output from the code.

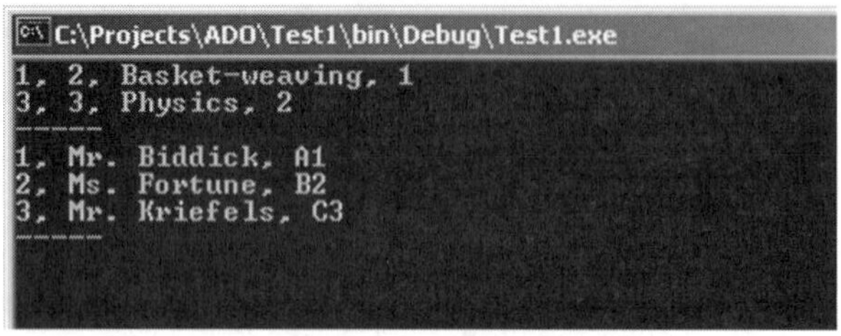

Figure D.2
Output from listing D.1

D.4.3   IDataRecord interface methods

The methods on IDataReader make it possible to step through the data contained in a reader. This ability is not useful, however, unless you can access the data in some way. You do so through the methods and properties on the `IDataRecord` interface. IDataRecord has a large number of methods, and I have broken them into several topics. Earlier I said this appendix contained some tables that should be read in detail, and some that should be skimmed; most of the tables in this section are in the skim category. For each set of methods, I will point out any to which you should pay special attention.

IDataRecord simple data access methods

The set of methods in this section all operate more or less the same way. Given the ordinal position of a column, the data is returned as the appropriate data type (table D.5). For example, the following call

```
int iValue = reader.GetInt32(2);
```

returns the value in the third column (columns start at 0) as an integer. Note that if the data in that column was not numeric, but was a string, then an exception would be thrown. If you are not sure of the position of the column containing the specific field you want (for example, if you did a `Select *`), you can use the `GetOrdinal()` method, described in the "Methods for Finding Out about Data" section.

Table D.5   IDataRecord data-retrieval methods

Method	Purpose
GetBoolean	Returns the value in the specified column as a Boolean value (`true`/`false`).
GetByte	Returns the column's value as a byte.

GetBytes	Allows a number of bytes to be retrieved from the column at an arbitrary position within the data. An example might be when you're reading a large image from a database in pieces—enough can be requested each time to display the next part of the image:
	
	`byte[] buffer = new byte[1024];`
	`reader.GetBytes(1,1000,buffer,0,1024);`
	
	This example reads up to 1,024 bytes from the second field (zero-based) into the buffer. If there were fewer than 1,024 bytes left, then the data would be read up to the end of the field.

GetChar	Returns the column's value as a single `char`.
GetChars	Similar to `GetBytes`, but retrieves character data in pieces, rather than binary data. It allows for efficient retrieval of large amounts of text in pieces, which can be used to display part of the text before the whole field has been retrieved from the server.
GetDateTime	Returns the column's value as a `DateTime`.
GetDecimal	Returns the column's value as a `Decimal`.
GetDouble	Returns the column's value as a `double`.
GetFloat	Returns the column's value as a `float`.
GetGuid	Returns the column's value as a GUID. A GUID is a Globally Unique IDentifier—a value that is guaranteed to be unique from any other GUID, no matter who generated it or when. SQL Server has a specific data type for holding GUIDs.
GetInt16	Returns the column's value as a 16-bit integer (`Int16`).
GetInt32	Returns the column's value as a 32-bit integer (`Int32`).
GetInt64	Returns the column's value as a 64-bit integer (`Int64`).
GetString	Returns the column's value as a `string`.
GetValue	Returns the column's value as an `object`. Using this method is the same as using the `Item` property with an integer indexer. Although the returned result is of type `object`, it is an instance of the specific type of object for the data it contains; so, for example, it might be an `Int32` or a `string`. The value can be cast to the appropriate type, or it can be used generically as an object (put into a collection, or converted to a `string` via `ToString()`).

A couple of the `get` methods, such as `GetBytes()` and `GetChars()`, are designed to read pieces of data, rather than the entire record at a time. Listing D.2 shows the use of `GetChars()` to read in the data from a large text field in 8K chunks, allowing them to be written out in pieces. The Description field in the example contains the numbers from 1 to 100,000 as a string.

```
public void TestReadPieces(SqlConnection conn)
{
    string strSQL = "SELECT Name,Phone,Description FROM LargeDataTest";
    SqlCommand comm = new SqlCommand(strSQL,conn);
    SqlDataReader reader = comm.ExecuteReader();
    while(reader.Read())
    {
        Console.WriteLine("Name = {0}",reader.GetString(0));
        Console.WriteLine("Phone = {0}",reader.GetString(1));
        Console.Write("Description = ");
        // Read the description in 8K chunks
        int iChunk = 8192;
        char[] buffer = new char[iChunk];          ❶ Set up buffer
        long lPos = 0;
        long lRead = 0;
        while(true)
        {
            lRead = reader.GetChars(2,lPos,buffer,0,iChunk);   ❷ Get part
            if(lRead > 0)        // we read some data                of data
            {
                Console.Write(buffer);
                lPos += lRead;
            }
            if(lRead < iChunk) // No more data to read    ❸ Exit loop
                break;
        }
        Console.WriteLine("");
    }
}
```

I won't show the output from this method, because it would take up a lot of pages. However, a description of the pieces of the code will be useful. Most of the code should be familiar. The explanation starts with the section related to reading the data.

❶ This code sets up a character buffer that is 8K in size, which will be used to hold each chunk of data. We're creating the buffer inside the `while` loop because it makes the example easier to read, and because we know there is only one row in the result set. Obviously, in a real-world case, you would create the buffer outside the loop.

❷ This call to `GetChars()` specifies the next chunk of the data to read. The arguments passed here include the position in the data that is desired and the location in the buffer where the data should be placed, as well as the maximum amount of data to read.

We could have done several different things here. We could have created a huge buffer capable of holding all the data and filled it in pieces, or we could have skipped the beginning of the buffer and read a chunk from the end. For the purpose of the example, though, the code reads a chunk at a time and writes it to the console.

You may wonder how the information is brought over from the server when this method is used. That is purely at the discretion of the data provider—it could be reading significantly larger chunks at a time, or it could wait until you ask for data before retrieving it. The worst case would be if the entire contents of the column were read over before filling the first request, which would negate the benefits of the call.

❸ Each time the `GetChars()` method is called, it returns the number of characters that were read. This should always be the same number as the quantity we requested (8,192), until the end of the data is reached. At this point, however many characters are left will be read, and the number of characters left will be fewer than that requested. We use this fact to know when to jump out of our loop.

Data provider-specific get methods

All the methods in the previous section are available in both providers. The specific derivations also add some of their own methods to get data specific to them:

- *OleDbDataReader get methods*—The OleDbDataReader adds only one additional data retrieval method: `GetTimeSpan()`, which can be used if the underlying data source exposes data as a duration of time. This may or may not be useful, depending on the engine to which the provider is connected.

- *SqlDataReader get methods*—SQL Server adds a number of additional data retrieval methods for SQL Server–specific data types. Some of these methods return values that are not as easily represented using native types, such as `Bit` or `Money`. The main advantage of these data types is that they understand `null` values. Any of these data types can have a `null` value and behave properly when compared with other values—that is, any comparison with a `null` will return `false`.

  These data types, shown in table D.6, can be used in client code, but they were created for use inside SQL Server; a future version of SQL Server will allow .NET code to run inside the engine. So, for example, you could write a function or stored procedure in C# or any other .NET language. When you're doing that, having data types for native comparison is very important.

Table D.6 SqlDataReader additional data-retrieval methods

Method	Purpose
GetSqlBinary	Returns an SqlBinary object that holds a stream of bytes
GetSqlBit	Returns an SqlBit that holds either a 0 or a 1
GetSqlByte	Returns an SqlByte that holds a single byte of data
GetSqlDateTime	Returns an SqlDateTime that holds a date/time value
GetSqlDecimal	Returns an SqlDecimal that holds a decimal value
GetSqlDouble	Returns an SqlDouble that holds a double value

continued on next page

Table D.6   SqlDataReader additional data-retrieval methods *(continued)*

Method	Purpose
GetSqlGuid	Returns an `SqlGuid` that holds a GUID value
GetSqlInt16	Returns an `SqlInt16` that holds a 16-bit integer value
GetSqlInt32	Returns an `SqlInt32` that holds a 32-bit integer value
GetSqlInt64	Returns an `SqlInt64` that holds a 64-bit integer value
GetSqlMoney	Returns an `SqlMoney` object, which can hold a very large value with a guaranteed precision to four decimal places
GetSqlSingle	Returns an `SqlSingle`, which holds a floating-point number but is somewhat smaller than an `SqlDouble`
GetSqlString	Return an `SqlString`, which holds a string
GetSqlValue	Returns an `object`, which is cast from one of the above SQL Server-specific data types

Methods for finding out about data

All the previously shown methods assume you already know about the data contained in the DataReader. In addition, several methods on IDataRecord let you determine information about the data (table D.7).

Both data providers contain methods for providing information about the data in each column.

Table D.7   IDataRecord schema methods

Method	Purpose
GetName	Returns the name of the field at the specified index.
GetOrdinal	Given the name of a column, returns the integer position of the column in the results. This method is the reverse of `GetName`. It is useful if you want to use any of the earlier `Get` methods but don't know which column contains the specific field you need. If the column is not found, then this method will throw an exception.
GetFieldType	Returns the Type of the object at the specified index. A Type object represents the information about all instances of a certain type of object. The type will always be of a known class, no matter what database type was used to store the data, and so can be used to classify the type of the data.
	You could use this method and the reflection mechanism built into .NET to create an appropriate object to contain the data you need. However, this approach would not be very fast.
GetDataTypeName	Returns a string identifying the database type of the field at the specified index. This is an important distinction, because the database data type name might be `varchar` when the object in memory is a string.

Other methods

This section shows a handful of methods that don't fit well into any of the other categories but are worth knowing about (table D.8). `IsDBNull()` is a handy method to use when you are about to read data from a column whose value might be `null`; if the value is null, and you use a get method, the code will throw an exception. GetValues() is useful to transfer all the data returned into an array. GetData() is a specialized method that will be used only when retrieving hierarchical data.

Table D.8 IDataRecord additional methods

Method	Purpose
GetValues	This method fills an array with all the columns in the row. The array should be set up ahead of time with the appropriate number of slots. If the array has fewer elements than there are columns, then only the first *x* columns will be returned:
	`object[] oData = new object[3];` `reader.GetValues(oData);`
	This is a very efficient way to read data, if appropriate.
IsDbNull	This method returns true if the specified column contains a null value. If a column allows null values as well as data, it is wise to check this value before reading the column using one of the data access methods; a null value will cause an exception to be thrown:
	`If(!reader.IsDbNull(2))` `iValue = reader.GetInt32(2);`
	If the value was null and there was no check, the GetInt32 call would throw an exception.
GetData	Some data providers can return complex data within a field that requires another DataReader to step through. Imagine a field that contains a number of columns and rows. If one of the returned fields is of this type, then GetData will return an IDataReader that can then be used to step through the data in the field. An example of using this method to read hierarchical data appears in section D.5.

The SqlDataReader has an additional version of the GetValues() method, called GetSqlValues(). The difference between the methods is that the GetSql-Values() version returns objects as SQL Server–specific types (SqlInt32, SqlString, and so on) rather than standard objects (Int32, string, and so forth).

D.5 *READING HIERARCHICAL DATA*

Several references to reading hierarchical data have appeared throughout this appendix, but I had no good place to put the example. Although this is not a commonly used capability, it is important enough that an example is warranted.

Most of the time, the data being retrieved by ADO.NET will be relational: tables that relate to other tables. Sometimes, though, you'll want to work with data that is hierarchical (in a tree-type structure). Some specialized databases, such as Raima, are explicitly designed to work in a hierarchical manner. Microsoft also has a special OLE DB provider that allows data to be retrieved from a relational database and then treated as hierarchical. This mechanism is called Data Shaping.

A more thorough (although still brief) explanation of Data Shaping appears in chapter 9. This mechanism allows the results of a query to be returned as a single data column of another query. You can then drill down into that data column and step through the results it contains.

The example in listing D.3 uses the Microsoft Data Shaping provider to read the list of teachers, along with their classes. The classes are returned as a single data item, which is then read separately. This example demonstrates the use of the Depth property of IDataRecord, as well as the GetData() method of IDataRecord.

Listing D.3   Reading hierarchical data

```
public void DoShapeRead()
{
  string strConnect = "Provider=MSDataShape; "        ❶ Connect via
    + "Data Provider=SQLOLEDB;Data Source=localhost;"    Data Shaping
    + "Initial Catalog=ADONetSamples;user id=sa";        provider

  OleDbConnection conn = new OleDbConnection(strConnect);

  string strSQL=@"SHAPE
    {SELECT TeacherID,TeacherName,Classroom FROM Teachers}    ❷ Request
    APPEND ({SELECT TeacherID,ClassName,Period FROM Classes}    data
    AS ClassInfo
    RELATE TeacherID TO TeacherID)";

  OleDbCommand comm = new OleDbCommand(strSQL,conn);

  OleDbDataReader reader = comm.ExecuteReader();
  Console.WriteLine("Depth = {0}",reader.Depth);    ❸ Initial depth

  IDataReader reader2 = null;
  while(reader.Read())
  {
    Console.WriteLine("{0}, {1}",reader.GetString(1).Trim(),    ❹ Basis
                        reader.GetString(2).Trim());            info

    reader2 = reader.GetData(3);    ❺ Access nested data
    while(reader2.Read())
    {

      Console.WriteLine("Depth ({0})-->{1}, {2}",    ❻ Nested depth
                          reader2.Depth,
                          reader2.GetString(1).Trim(),
                          reader2.GetInt32(2));
    }
    reader2.Close();    ❼ Close inner reader
    Console.WriteLine("-----");
  }
}
```

❶ This connection string specifies the Microsoft Data Shaper as the provider and tells the Data Shaper provider how to connect to a different provider (the SQL Server OLE DB provider) to read data. Although we use the OLE DB provider to connect to SQL Server, the parameters should look familiar from the SQL Server data provider.

❷ Understanding the details of the Microsoft Data Shaper is beyond the scope of this book. Although the statement contains some SQL, the format of the command is unique to the data provider. Suffice to say that this command says to read information from all the rows of the Teachers table and, in addition, to create an additional column in each row, called ClassInfo, that contains the associated rows from the Classes table.

Notice the way the string has been specified. Rather than joining together a number of separate strings, the code uses the @ notation; it indicates that all text up to the closing quote should be considered part of the same string, even if it crosses multiple lines.

❸ The reader returned from ExecuteReader() is a standard reader, as in the other examples. To prove it, this line prints out the Depth of the reader, which is 0.

❹ Again, like most other examples, this code prints out a couple of elements from the reader—nothing special.

❺ This line uses the specialized GetData() method on IDataRecord. Instead of returning a simple value, as with most of the Get methods, it returns a new Data-Reader that can be used to step through the associated data.

The DataReader could also have been accessed a couple of other ways, such as referencing the column using the indexer:

```
reader2 = (IDataReader)reader["ClassInfo"];
```

However, the GetData() method is built specifically to return a column that contains nested data. Once the reader has been returned, we can use it like our other reader to step through rows and access data.

❻ This line prints out the individual rows in our special column. To show that this data is nested, it also prints out the Depth property, which is 1, indicating that this is an additional level deep (the first level is level 0).

The Data Shaper allows multiple levels of nesting, so one of the columns in the nested DataReader could contain nested data, and so on.

❼ It is very important to close the inner reader before attempting to continue stepping through the data in the outer reader. In fact, if we do not do this, the next time the code attempts to move to a new row in the outer reader, an exception will be thrown.

D.5.1   Example output

All that work seems extreme, but using the Data Shaper can have some significant benefits if it is appropriate. Figure D.3 shows the output of the code.

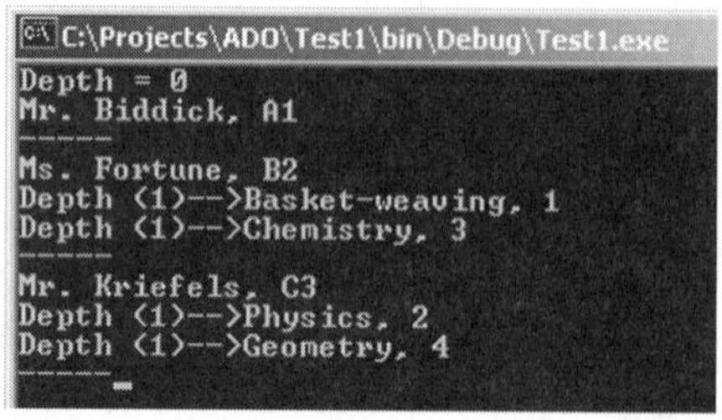

Figure D.3
Output from Listing D.3: nested data

D.6   SUMMARY

This has been a long appendix. A significant reason is not the complexity of the DataReader, per se, but the large number of special cases it must handle. In fact, considering how useful the DataReader is, its interfaces are surprisingly simple to use. In my opinion, this is the hallmark of a good design and good separation of functionality. Although there are more advanced ways of dealing with results (specifically, the DataSet), in innumerable situations the lightweight DataReader will be exactly what you need.

APPENDIX E

The DataTable

Chapter 17 talked a lot about the DataTable, DataColumn, and DataRow classes. I didn't discuss a fair number of details, though, either because they seemed out of place or because they were esoteric. Nevertheless, these details are potentially relevant, and the next three appendices examine all the methods and properties of these three classes. I begin in this appendix with the DataTable.

A lot of talk goes on about the power of the DataSet, but the DataTable is the most important part of the DataSet. In some ways, you can think of the DataSet as an elaborate container for DataTables.

This appendix is heavy on tables. Again, I will indicate which tables should be read in detail and which tables are safe to skim. As usual, I have arranged the tables so that the most important information is listed toward the top. After each table, I include examples that show how to do common tasks related to items in that table, or techniques that are complex or confusing.

E.1 DATATABLE PROPERTIES

Besides base-class properties that are beyond the scope of this book, the DataTable has quite a few properties. I have broken these properties into three categories:

- *Basic state and information*—These properties include the basic information about a DataTable, such as its name and flags controlling its behavior.
- *Collections*—These properties include things like the collection of rows and columns.
- *Other*—These other properties are used in special circumstances.

E.1.1 Basic state and information properties

These four simple properties provide information about the DataTable and the way it will behave (table E.1). Most of these properties are static, but the `HasErrors` property can change as the data within the data table is manipulated.

Table E.1 Basic DataTable properties

Property	Purpose
TableName	The name of the table. If you don't explicitly give the table a name, then a default name will be assigned.
DataSet	The DataSet that contains this DataTable.
HasErrors	`True` if any of the contained rows have errors. This value can either be determined by the system via constraints, and so forth, or can be manually set by the application.
CaseSensitive	How the DataTable should handle string comparisons. This is an issue when you're dealing with a UniqueConstraint, or when you're running queries against the DataSet. By default, this property is set to the value of the `CaseSensitive` property of the DataSet in which the DataTable is created.

These properties are straightforward to understand and use. For example, displaying the table name is like accessing any other property:

```
Console.Writeline("Table name = {0}",dt.TableName);
```

E.1.2 Collection properties

As the DataSet's most important property is the collection of DataTables, so a DataTable's most important properties are `Rows` and `Columns`, because they contain the useful information that forms the table. In addition, the DataTable has several other collection and array properties, shown in table E.2.

Table E.2 DataTable collection and array properties

Property	Purpose
Rows	The collection of rows of data within the DataTable. You can access each row as you would elements from an array—there is no navigation (next, previous, and so on) that you might have had to use with other data-access technologies. DataRows and their properties and methods are discussed in detail in appendix G.
Columns	A collection of columns that are present within the DataTable. Each column contains basic information about the column, such as its name and data type. DataColumns and their properties and methods are discussed in detail in appendix F.
PrimaryKey	An array of columns that make up the primary key for the DataTable. It can either be populated manually or determined via the `FillSchema()` method demonstrated later in this section. If this property has not been set, then its value will be `null`.

continued on next page

Table E.2   DataTable collection and array properties *(continued)*

Property	Purpose
Constraints	The collection of constraints on this table. Constraints can either require that the value in a particular column be unique or enforce that the value be a legal value from another DataTable (a foreign key). Constraints are discussed in detail in chapter 18.
ChildRelations	A collection of all child relationships for this DataTable. Child relationships are those in which the current DataTable acts as the parent of the other Data-Table. For example, a Teacher DataTable might have a child relationship to a Classes DataTable that contains multiple classes for that teacher.
ParentRelations	A collection of all parent relationships for this DataTable. Parent relationships are those in which the current DataTable is the child for another DataTable. In the Teacher/Classes example, it's the same relationship, but for the Classes table. Relationships are discussed in detail in chapter 18.

Reading columns and rows

The example in listing E.1 uses the Columns and Rows properties to write out all the data in a DataTable. This is more or less the method used throughout the book for printing out results, but with a couple of lines taken out for brevity.

Listing E.1   Printing out a DataSet using the Columns and Rows properties

```
public void PrintDataTable(DataTable dt)
{
  foreach(DataRow dr in dt.Rows )                    ❶ Access Rows collection
  {
    // Write the state of the row
    Console.Write("({0})",                           ❷ Get row's
      Enum.Format(typeof(DataRowState),dr.RowState,"g"));    state

    // Step through each column in the row and write it out
    foreach(DataColumn dc in dt.Columns)             ❸ Access Columns
    {                                                  collection
      if(dc.Ordinal > 0)
        Console.Write(", ");

      if(dr.RowState == DataRowState.Deleted)        ❹ Handle
      {                                                deleted
        Console.Write(                                 rows
          dr[dc,DataRowVersion.Original].ToString().Trim());
      }
      else
      {
        Console.Write(dr[dc].ToString().Trim());     ❺ Access field value
      }
    }
    Console.WriteLine("");
  }
}
```

❶ The `Rows` property on a DataTable returns a DataRowCollection, which is a type-safe collection of rows. The code uses the `foreach` notation to step through each item in the collection in turn.

❷ This line is ugly, but it gets the enumerated value indicating the current state of the row (`Unchanged`, `Modified`, `Deleted`, and so on) and converts that value into a string.

❸ As with the `Rows` collection, the `Columns` property returns a type-safe collection, this time called a DataColumnCollection. The code uses a nested `foreach` statement to step through each column in turn.

❹ One issue with rows is that if a row has been marked as deleted, you cannot access its current value (because there is no current value). However, you can access the original value of the column. Appendix G talks about the different versions of a row's values. For the moment, know that this code checks to see if the row is deleted, and if it is, asks for the original version of the data (before any changes) rather than the current version. Asking for the current value of a deleted column will throw an exception.

❺ To get to the field value, an indexer is used on the DataRow. The DataRow allows for several different indexers. It can access the field numerically

```
dr[3]
```

or by name

```
dr["Classname"]
```

or you can pass the DataColumn object for the desired field. This indexer is used in the example.

The example also includes a little formatting code to make things look better. Figure E.1 shows the final output, run against a DataTable with a few changes made.

```
<Unchanged>1, 2, Basket-weaving, 1
<Unchanged>3, 3, Physics, 2
<Modified>4, 1, Chemistry, 3
<Deleted>7, 2, Geometry, 4
<Added>, 2, Philosophy, 5
```

Figure E.1
Output from listing E.1

Primary keys

The primary keys collection on a table can be important, because you can use this information to save data efficiently; it's also important when you're doing merges of DataTables.

The primary keys can be specified manually by building an array of fields and setting the information:

```
DataColumn[] dcPrimaryKey = new DataColumn[1];
dcPrimaryKey[0] = dt.Columns["ClassID"];
dt.PrimaryKey = dcPrimaryKey;
```

This example requires only a single column, but there is no limitation—we just create an array with multiple items to specify a multicolumn key.

Given that the data was read from a database along with basic column information, it would be handy to be able to automatically have the primary key set up for us. In fact, this is possible. The DataAdapter has a `FillSchema()` method that can retrieve this and other information. The example in listing E.2 uses `FillSchema()` to retrieve schema information, including the primary key information.

Listing E.2 Reading the schema from the database

```
public void TestDataSetFillSchema(SqlConnection conn)
{
    string strSQL = "SELECT * From Classes";

    // Create and fill the dataset schema information
    SqlDataAdapter sda = new SqlDataAdapter(strSQL,conn);
    DataSet ds = new DataSet();
    sda.FillSchema(ds,SchemaType.Mapped,"Classes");        ❶ Fill schema
    // Write out the list of primary keys
    DataTable dt = ds.Tables["Classes"];
    ICollection coll = dt.PrimaryKey;              ❷ Write out
    foreach(DataColumn dc in coll)                    primary keys
    {
        Console.WriteLine("Primary key field: {0}",dc.ColumnName);
    }
}
```

❶ Using the `FillSchema()` method on the DataAdapter is straightforward. It determines what schema information is needed based on the `Select` SQL. It is important to know, however, that this method makes a call to the database to retrieve the schema, so we don't want to do this any more than necessary. If you are likely to use the same information multiple times, you can create a DataTable holding the schema, and then use the `Clone` method (described in section E.2.1) to copy the structure to a new DataTable.

Another important thing to know is that the `FillSchema()` call doesn't retrieve any data. To do that we must call `Fill()`, as before.

❷ This code retrieves the primary keys as a collection, and then steps through each column in the collection and writes it out. As you can see from the output (figure E.2), there is only one primary key column on this table.

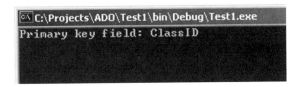

Figure E.2
Listing primary keys

E.1.3 Other properties

A handful of other properties on the DataTable may be useful, depending on your application (table E.3). It is worth skimming through them to know they exist, in case a situation comes up where you need one of them.

A couple of these properties are quite handy, such as `ExtendedProperties` and `MinimumCapacity`; I recommend skimming the others for reference.

Table E.3 Other DataTable properties

Property	Purpose
DefaultView	DataTables can have views that allow for filtering of data or selecting specific columns. Doing so is useful when you're working with data-bound controls and you want to display a subset of data. The DefaultView is a view you can specify to be used by default by such controls. DataViews are discussed in detail in chapter 25.
DisplayExpression	When a user interface control wants to display the name of a DataTable, it will generally use the name of the DataTable. However, you can customize the display value by using a `DisplayExpression`. Not only can you specify a name to use, but you can have that name be calculated on-the-fly by providing an expression.
	This mechanism can also be used to create specialized columns in a DataTable. The format for `DisplayExpression` for columns and for the table is the same.
ExtendedProperties	Sometimes it is convenient to store additional, application-specific information with a DataTable. `ExtendedProperties` is a specialized hash table where you can place such information. You can add a property to this collection and reference it later, even if the DataSet has been remoted to another machine.
Locale	When you're doing queries and comparisons within a DataTable, the comparisons will be done using the current default locale for the machine—for example, `en-us` for US English. If for some reason you want to override this behavior, you can specify a different locale to use.
MinimumCapacity	When a DataTable is being loaded, it doesn't normally know how much memory it will require. This can cause memory to be allocated and reallocated as more items are added. If you know how many items will be put into the DataTable (or even have a rough idea), you can set the `Minimum-Capacity` property. It will allow the DataTable to optimize its allocations. This property can be helpful if you are writing a performance-critical application.
	You can always add more items than the minimum capacity, and memory will be allocated as usual. Likewise, if you add fewer, there is no problem—although you will have allocated some memory that will not be used.
Namespace	DataSets and DataTables have a lot of support for working with XML. When you convert to XML, you can use this property to have the data within the data table placed inside a specific namespace. This topic is explored in more detail in part 5 of the book.
Prefix	The namespace prefix to use—usually the URI for the schema.

E.2 DATATABLE METHODS

You have already seen several DataTable methods—but on the DataSet. Many of the DataSet methods do little more than turn around and call the same method on each contained DataTable. For example, `AcceptChanges()` is present on the DataSet, but it can also be called on the DataTable directly; it does the same thing, but for one DataTable only.

The methods are split into three sets:

- *Primary methods*—These are methods that you will use commonly, or that are used automatically but are important enough to know about.

- *Data support methods*—These are methods used by the DataAdapter or by data-bound controls. You will almost never use them unless you are manually loading the DataTable.

- *Other methods*—These are other methods on the DataTable that you probably won't use often, but that are handy for specific tasks.

E.2.1 Primary DataTable methods

The methods in table E.4 are the ones you are most likely to use when working with a DataSet. A possible exception is `AcceptChanges`—although this method is important, it will frequently be called automatically for you by the DataAdapter. For that reason, it should really be in the next section, but it's important enough that it seemed more natural here.

Table E.4   Primary DataTable methods

Method	Purpose
AcceptChanges	Makes all changes within the DataTable official. All inserts, updates, and deletes become part of the standard data. This would normally be done after saving all the changes to a database.
RejectChanges	Rolls any changes to the DataTable back to the point when the DataTable was loaded, or to the last time AcceptChanges or RejectChanges was called.
NewRow	Creates a new row for the DataTable, structured to have the appropriate columns based on the DataTable. This is the primary method used to add rows to a DataTable: first a call to NewRow is made, then the new row is populated, and finally it's added to the Rows collection.
Clear	Removes all data from the DataTable. Note that the structure of the DataTable is not changed.
Copy	Makes an exact copy of the DataTable, including the structure and the data.
Clone	Makes an exact copy of the structure of the DataTable. The data is not copied.
GetChanges	Retrieves all the rows that have been changed since the DataTable was loaded or since AcceptChanges was last called. You can also specify that you want to retrieve only a certain type of change, such as deleted rows.
GetErrors	Retrieves all the rows in the DataTable that contain errors, such as constraint violations or illegal null fields.
Select	Allows a simple SQL statement to be executed against the DataTable and returns the result. This capability is one of the main topics of chapter 20.

E.2.2 DataTable data support methods

Because a DataTable is not tied to a database, it must have a number of support methods to allow data to be loaded and retrieved (table E.5). If you are working with a database, you will rarely use these methods yourself—rather, the DataAdapter will use them on your behalf. Likewise, methods are specifically provided for support of data-bound controls, such as the DataGrid.

Of course, if you are not using a DataAdapter to fill and save data from the DataTable, you will probably use some of these methods. Otherwise they are just of intellectual interest.

Table E.5 DataTable data support methods

Method	Purpose
BeginInit	When a DataTable is being used by a component, you might need to prevent access to data via that component until the DataTable is fully configured. This method is called when such initialization begins.
EndInit	After initialization is complete, stated by BeginInit, an EndInit call is made.
BeginLoadData	Normally, when data is added or changed within a DataTable, a number of things happen: the DataTable validates the data to make sure it does not violate any constraints, internal indexes are updated, and notifications are sent out. This behavior is generally desirable, but when you're loading the DataTable initially, it can cause a severe performance hit. Worse, a constraint might be violated because of the order in which data is loaded. To prevent such problems, a call to BeginLoadData shuts off all automatic behavior so that data can be loaded quickly and efficiently.
EndLoadData	After BeginLoadData has been called, all automatic behavior is turned off. Once the data is loaded, this behavior needs to be re-enabled by a call to EndLoadData. Not only does it re-enable automatic behavior from that point forward, it also brings indexes up to date and checks constraints.

E.2.3 Other DataTable methods

You may find a handful of other methods useful (table E.6). For example, Compute can be used to do calculations against the data.

Table E.6 Other DataTable methods

Method	Purpose
Compute	Does a computation against a particular set of rows in the DataTable. An example is shown next.
ImportRow	Imports a DataRow into the DataTable, with all its information (changes, errors, and so forth) maintained. This method is synonymous with doing an Add to the Rows property of the DataTable.
LoadDataRow	Updates an existing DataRow or adds a new DataRow from an array of data. The method does an Update if possible, by searching for a matching row based on primary key information. An example of this method is shown later.

Computing values against a DataTable

A number of capabilities within DataSets allow for calculations. For example, you can add a column to a DataTable whose value is calculated. Via the Compute method, you can do calculations against multiple rows, such as summing up the values within a column. This functionality is somewhat limited: for example, you cannot do calculations that involve more than one column. However, for certain types of operations, it can be quite useful.

The following example uses the Compute method to determine the last period for which there is a class from the Classes table:

```
public void TestDataSetCompute(SqlConnection conn)
{
    string strSQL = "SELECT * From Classes";

    // Create and fill the dataset
    SqlDataAdapter sda = new SqlDataAdapter(strSQL,conn);
    DataSet ds = new DataSet();
    sda.Fill(ds,"Classes");

    // Compute the last class
    DataTable dt = ds.Tables["Classes"];
    int iTotal = (int)dt.Compute("Max(Period)","");

    Console.WriteLine("Last class is {0}",iTotal);
}
```

Using the Compute method

You can pass two strings to the Compute method: the expression to evaluate and a filter that limits which rows will be included in the calculation. The format for both the expression and the filter is more or less SQL. However, there are some limitations. The expression is limited to a single column; and the filter can use multiple columns, but cannot use joins. The valid expressions that can be used are explained in more detail in chapter 20, which discusses querying the DataSet.

To be complete, figure E.3 shows the output from the listing.

Figure E.3
Output from the Compute
method example

E.3 DATATABLE EVENTS

To round out the conversation about DataTables, let's look at a number of events that the DataTable exposes to monitor changes. Most of these events will be used by data-bound controls to update the display, and so on. In some scenarios, using these events might be useful. For example, you might be using a DataGrid to display data, but also have a custom control that shows a graph of the data, in which case you will want to know when the data changes. Alternatively, you might want to change the value being put into a column before it goes into the data.

Table E.7 shows the events that are available on the DataTable. After the table is an example showing how to use one of the events.

Table E.7 DataTable events

Event	Purpose
ColumnChanging	A column in a particular row is about to be changed.
ColumnChanged	A column in a particular row just changed.
RowChanging	A row is about to be changed in some way.
RowChanged	A row was just changed.
RowDeleting	A row is about to be deleted.
RowDeleted	A row has been deleted.

Unfortunately, you cannot use the Changing methods to prevent the action from taking place. However, you can make changes to the data if you need to. The example in listing E.3 takes the data about to be changed in a column and uppercases it.

Listing E.3 Subscribing to a column-changing event

```
public void TestDataTableEvent(SqlConnection conn)
{
    // Create and fill the dataset
    string strSQL = "SELECT * From Classes";
    SqlDataAdapter sda = new SqlDataAdapter(strSQL,conn);
    DataSet ds = new DataSet();
    sda.Fill(ds,"Classes");
    DataTable dt = ds.Tables["Classes"];

    // Register for the column changing event        Subscribe to event ❶
    dt.ColumnChanging +=
            new DataColumnChangeEventHandler(OnColumnChanging);

    // Update a column in a row
    dt.Rows[2]["ClassName"] = "Astro-physics";     ❷  Change value

    PrintDataTable("Display the data",dt);
}

public void OnColumnChanging(object sender,DataColumnChangeEventArgs e)
{
    // Upper-case the value
    if(e.Column.ColumnName == "ClassName")                          ❸  Catch
        e.ProposedValue = e.ProposedValue.ToString().ToUpper();         event
}
```

1 As with any event, a new event handler is created and assigned to the event. The event handler takes as an argument the name of the method to handle the event. That method must match the expected signature, returning the appropriate data type (in this case `void`) and taking the appropriate arguments (the sender of the event—the DataTable—and an object that holds event-specific information).

2 This code is like any other to change the value of a column. However, because we have subscribed to the event, the `OnColumnChanging` method will be called automatically.

3 The `OnColumnChanging` method is called whenever any column is changed, and it's passed a `DataColumnChangeEventArgs` object that contains three important properties:

- `Column`—The column that is changing
- `Row`—The row that is changing
- `ProposedValue`—The value to which the column within the row will be changed

The `Column` property is used in this example to make sure the column we care about is the one changing. If this code didn't check, it would try to run against any column even if the data type was not `string`, which would cause problems.

The `ProposedValue` is the value that was set earlier. The example takes the value, uppercases it, and puts it back into the `ProposedValue`.

Example summary

As you can see in the example's output (figure E.4), the value is now capitalized.

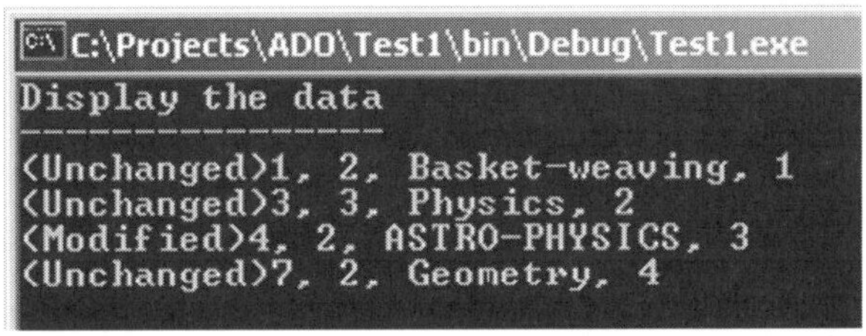

```
C:\Projects\ADO\Test1\bin\Debug\Test1.exe
Display the data

<Unchanged>1, 2, Basket-weaving, 1
<Unchanged>3, 3, Physics, 2
<Modified>4, 2, ASTRO-PHYSICS, 3
<Unchanged>7, 2, Geometry, 4
```

**Figure E.4
Output from listing E.3**

The other events work about the same way as this one. The only difference is that most of the other events take a `DataRowChangeEventArgs` parameter rather than the `DataColumnChangeEventArgs` parameter. This parameter is similar, but it has only two properties:

- `Row`—The row being changed or deleted
- `Action`—What is happening to the row (an enumerated value that can be equal to `Add`, `Change`, `Commit`, `Delete`, or `Rollback`)

E.4 SUMMARY

The DataTable is straightforward. Many of the more complex methods and properties are provided purely for tasks like data binding, which are of interest only to control builders. If you intend to build a data-bound control, the information in this appendix will provide some background, although creating new data-bound controls is beyond the scope of this book.

A P P E N D I X   F

The DataColumn

Although the DataColumn is an important and integral part of the DataTable, it is a much smaller class. Nonetheless, the DataColumn has some interesting properties that are worth exploring. For example, columns can autoincrement themselves and calculate their own values.

The DataColumn class has a fair number of properties, but all the public methods are derived from base classes and don't concern us, and there are no public events. If nothing else, this fact contributes to this appendix's being a little shorter than appendix E.

The DataColumn is one part of a tightly bound triad of classes: the DataTable, DataColumn, and DataRow. It is difficult to talk about any one of these classes without referencing the others, so you will see many examples showing all three classes.

The DataColumn represents a single field of data. Each row contains a value for that column. Frequently, the set of columns on a DataTable is determined when the data in a DataTable is loaded from a DataAdapter, but nothing prevents DataColumns from being arbitrarily added to a table. In fact, one of the nifty things a DataColumn can do is calculate its own value, so you can add a calculated column to a table that will then be displayed but not necessarily stored.

F.1   DATACOLUMN PROPERTIES

As you were probably expecting, I will show the DataColumn properties broken into several categories:

- *Basic properties*—These properties control basic behavior of the column and/or are frequently used.
- *Automatic values*—These properties allow for automatic determination of the value within a column.
- *Other properties*—These straggler properties are obscure or used only in special circumstances.

F.1.1   Basic DataColumn properties

The properties in table F.1 are important or commonly used.

Table F.1   Basic DataColumn properties

Property	Purpose
Table	The DataTable that contains the column.
Ordinal	The numerical position of the column within the table, starting with column 0.
ColumnName	The name of the column.
DataType	The data type of the column. This is not a database type, but is the .NET type. So, for instance, it might represent a `string` or a `double`. The `DataType` property returns a Type object that can be used to, for example, create instances of the type. You can also ask the Type for its name.
AllowDBNull	Whether a `null` value is allowed in the column. If this value is `false` and the code attempts to set the value to `null`, then an exception will be thrown.
MaxLength	The maximum length of the string the column can hold, if the column contains a string. Attempting to set a longer string will cause an exception to be thrown.
ReadOnly	Whether the column allows its data to be read. It might make sense to mark an automatically calculated column to be read-only.
Unique	If `true`, then putting a duplicate value in this column for multiple rows will not be allowed. Keep in mind that the unique check applies only to the data contained inside the DataTable. It doesn't matter if the database contains 1,000 duplicate values—if that data has not been put into the DataTable, then it will not be checked.
Caption	The pretty name for the column, which will be used by controls to label the column. If this value has not been set, then the column's name is used.

Breaking the rules

I covered this same material in chapter 17, but wanted to repeat it in context with the detailed discussion of DataColumn properties. Many of the properties listed in table F.1 let you specify rules about what data is or is not allowed in a column. Listing F.1 sets up a column with a number of these rules, and then demonstrates what happens when they are broken.

To save space, all of the errors are coded in a row—of course, once the first error has occurred, the next error will never take place. For the output, though, I commented out each error in turn to show the results.

Listing F.1   Violating rules on a DataColumn

```
public void DoTestDataColumnErrors()
{
    DataTable dt = new DataTable("Test");                  ❶ Manually
                                                             create table
    DataColumn dc =                                          and column
            new DataColumn("StringData",typeof(string));
    dt.Columns.Add(dc);

    try
    {
        DataRow dr = dt.NewRow();          ❷ Create and
        dt.Rows.Add(dr);                     add row

        // Exceed length                              ❸ Length
                                                        violation
        dc.MaxLength = 10;
        dr[dc] = "This value is longer than ten characters!";

        // Set value to null        ❹ Null value
        dr[dc] = "Test";              violation
        dc.AllowDBNull = false;
        dr[dc] = null;

        // Unique value        ❺ Unique
        dc.Unique = true;        violation
        dr[dc] = "Value1";
        dr = dt.NewRow();
        dt.Rows.Add(dr);
        dr[dc] = "Value1";

        // Read-only                  ❻ Read-only
        dc.ReadOnly = true;             violation
        dr[dc] = "Set a value";

        Console.WriteLine("Test completed");
    }
    catch(Exception ex)
    {
        Console.WriteLine(ex.ToString());
    }
}
```

❶ Up until now, we've created the DataTables and DataColumns using a DataAdapter. Nothing stops us from doing it directly, though. This code creates the table and the column and adds the column to the table.

❷ We can work with a row without adding it to a table. However, until a row is part of a table, none of the rules on any of the columns will be enforced. For the purpose of this example, the row is added up front so that each error is generated when its code is hit. If the row had not yet been added to the table, then there would have been no exceptions.

That is, there would have been no exceptions until the row was added to the table. At that point, the validity of each column would have been checked, and the add call would have thrown the exception. The exception, however, would have been the same as shown in the direct examples that follow.

❸ This piece of code sets the maximum length of the text in the column to 10, and then tries to put considerably more than 10 characters into the column. The result is an ArgumentException:

```
System.ArgumentException: Cannot set Column 'StringData' to
'This value is longer than ten characters!'. The value violates
MaxLength limit of this column.
```

❹ This violation presents a chicken-and-egg problem. Normally we would define the rules for a column up front, or have that information set based on the properties of the database table. Of course, the moment we create the row, the uninitialized row will have null for all the columns, including those that do not permit it.

This is usually not a problem because the row is often not added to the table until after the data has been set. That is one reason rows do not check their validity until after the row has been added to the table.

For the purposes of this example, though, we want to simulate a situation where the column is still null after the row has been added. To do so, we first put a value into the column, then set the rule, and then set the value to null.

If the value was not put in first, then setting the column to not allow nulls would have immediately thrown an exception. Instead, we don't get an exception until the value is set to null. The exception looks like this:

```
System.Data.NoNullAllowedException: Column 'StringData'
does not allow nulls.
```

In the example, the column was set to an explicit null. We could also have used the special database null object shown in part 2; it would have been useful if the value should have been null, but would also cause an exception when nulls are not allowed:

```
dr[dc] = DBNull.Value;
```

⑤ In order to test this rule, we need more than one row. This code sets the value in the row we have been using all along, and then creates a new row and attempts to set the value to be the same. As you probably expect by now, an exception is thrown:

```
System.Data.ConstraintException: Column 'StringData' is
constrained to be unique.  Value 'Value1' is already present.
```

⑥ It doesn't get more straightforward than this. The column is read-only, and the code attempts to set a value, with the expected result:

```
System.ArgumentException: Column 'StringData' is read only.
```

It isn't friendly to throw exceptions at your user all the time. However, this mechanism can allow for a fairly flexible interactive experience: the user edits the row, and then, when the row is added to the table, we catch the exception, give the user a formatted version of the exception to tell them the row is not legal, and let them try to fix the problem.

This is the default mechanism used by some of the GUI components, such as the DataGrid. Depending on your application and its audience, this default behavior may be perfectly acceptable. Of course, you might want to make the error messages more pleasant.

The point is that DataTables and their columns can take care of themselves—once you have set up the proper rules, the DataTable will prevent the data from becoming illegal.[1] In appendix G (and chapter 17, at a higher level), you will see how these rules can be applied when editing data rather than adding; chapter 18 shows how to set up even more complicated constraints based on multiple columns and other tables.

F.1.2 Automatic value properties

As well as being able to take care of its own legality, a column can, to some extent, be responsible for determining its own value. It can do this in several situations—if there is a default value for the column to set an initial value; if the value is incremented automatically, such as with a numeric identifier column; or if the column's value is calculated based on the values in other columns.

As you might expect, these automatically created values are mutually exclusive—you cannot have a default value and also autoincrement, and so on. Table F.2 shows the DataColumn properties associated with automatically determining a value.

Table F.2   DataColumn auto-value properties

Property	Purpose
DefaultValue	The value that should be put into a column when a new row is created. The value must be of the same data type as the column.
AutoIncrement	Whether the value in the column should be automatically incremented. This capability is supported only with numeric data types.

continued on next page

---

[1]   Although it can't control whether the data is sensible.

Table F.2   DataColumn auto-value properties *(continued)*

Property	Purpose
AutoIncrementSeed	The first value to use when automatically assigning values.
AutoIncrementStep	The amount to increase the value for each new row.
Expression	An expression used to calculate the value in the column based on, for example, the values in other columns.

Default values

The following code sets a default value for a column, and then creates a new row and displays the value in the column. It is not particularly complicated, but it shows that the property functions as advertised:

```
public void DoTestDefaultValue()
{
   DataTable dt = new DataTable("Test");
   DataColumn dc = new DataColumn("StringData",typeof(string));
   dc.DefaultValue = "A default!";
   dt.Columns.Add(dc);

   DataRow dr = dt.NewRow();
   Console.WriteLine("Value in column = {0}",dr[dc]);
}
```

I won't go into detail about this example. As you can see, the DefaultValue property for the column is set to A default!. When the new row is added, writing out the value should yield A default! even though it was not set directly, as you can see in the output (figure F.1)

Figure F.1
Output from the
default value test

Automatic increments

The next example uses the autoincrement properties to create an identifier value. Again, the code is self-explanatory.

```
public void DoTestAutoIncrement()
{
   DataTable dt = new DataTable("Test");
   DataColumn dc = new DataColumn("Counter",typeof(int));
   dc.AutoIncrement = true;
   dc.AutoIncrementSeed = 20;
   dc.AutoIncrementStep = 10;
   dt.Columns.Add(dc);

   DataRow dr = dt.NewRow();
   Console.WriteLine("Value in column = {0}",dr[dc]);
```

```
    dr = dt.NewRow();
    Console.WriteLine("Value in column = {0}",dr[dc]);

    dr = dt.NewRow();
    Console.WriteLine("Value in column = {0}",dr[dc]);
}
```

When the Counter column is created in this example, the `AutoIncrement` property is set to `true` and the value is seeded at `20`, with an incremental step of 10. The code then creates three rows and writes out the value in the column (figure F.2).

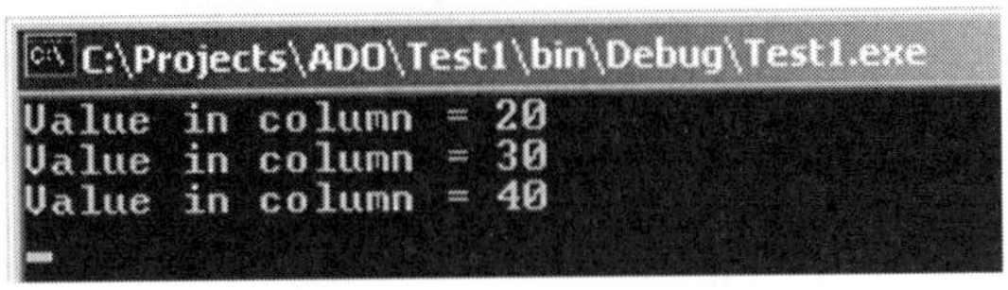

Figure F.2
Output from the
autoincrementing test

You must be careful when setting up an autoincrementing column in a table that already contains data. Just because the last value in a row in the table is already set doesn't mean the increment will take that fact into account. You must manually set the seed to match the last value plus the value of the increment. I understand that making assumptions about data can be a bad thing; but I think a method should exist to automatically determine the seed, even if the behavior isn't automatic.

Calculated columns

One of the cool features of a data column is its ability to calculate its value based on an expression. The details of what is legal in an expression were covered in chapter 20, but the example in listing F.2 shows how to set up a simple expression where the value in a column is the sum of two other columns.

Listing F.2   A calculated column

```
public void DoTestExpression()
{
    DataTable dt = new DataTable("Test");            ❶ Setup
    DataColumn dc = new DataColumn("Value1",typeof(int));
    dt.Columns.Add(dc);
    dc = new DataColumn("Value2",typeof(int));
    dt.Columns.Add(dc);
    dc = new DataColumn("Value3",typeof(int));
    dt.Columns.Add(dc);

    dc.Expression = "Value1 + Value2";     ❷ Set expression

    DataRow dr = dt.NewRow();
    dt.Rows.Add(dr);                ❸ Adding the row

    dr["Value1"] = 42;                              ❹ Get
    dr["Value2"] = 49;                                result

    Console.WriteLine("Value3 = {0}",dr["Value3"]);
```

```
        dr["Value2"] = 100;
        Console.WriteLine("Value3 = {0}",dr["Value3"]);
}
```

 ❺ Change
value

❶ This code sets up three columns named Value1, Value2, and Value3, all of type integer. There is no limitation on the data types that can be involved in expressions, but for this simple example, integers are convenient.

❷ This expression on the Value3 column adds the values in the Value1 and Value2 columns. Again, this expression can be more complicated, as you saw in chapter 20. The column names can be used to reference their contained value.

❸ Calculating the expression is another capability of a column that is not activated until the row has been added to the DataTable. Unlike with some of the validation rules listed earlier, if the value cannot be calculated yet, the DataTable will not throw an exception.

❹ This code puts a couple of values into the Value1 and Value2 columns. The code then writes out the value in the Value3 column, which should be the sum of the two values.

❺ To show that the expression is updated when the values change, the value in one of the columns is changed and the result is written out again.

Figure F.3 shows the output from the example.

```
C:\Projects\ADO\Test1\bin\Debug\Test1.exe
Value3 = 91
Value3 = 142
```

Figure F.3
Output from Listing F.2

As you can see, the initial value is 91, which is the sum of 42 and 49. The value then changes to 142, when the second value is changed from 49 to 100.

This is a painful way to do math, but it's handy if you are working with a whole table full of rows—especially if you are using a DataGrid that can show the calculated value for each row.

F.1.3   Other DataColumn properties

The last handful of properties on the DataColumn mostly are related to working with XML, which is covered in part 5 of the book. The other property, Extended-Properties, is a convenient place to add data that is attached to the DataColumn. Table F.3 provides a brief explanation of each of these properties.

Table F.3 DataColumn properties

Property	Purpose
ExtendedProperties	Sometimes it is convenient to store additional, application-specific information with a DataColumn. ExtendedProperties is a specialized hash table where you can place such information. You can add a property to this collection and reference it later, even if the DataSet has been remoted to another machine.
Namespace	DataSets and DataTables have a lot of support for working with XML. When you convert to XML, you can use this property to have the data within the data table placed in a specific namespace. This topic is explored in more detail in part 5 of the book.
Prefix	This property, which is also used when converting to XML, makes up part of the namespace.
ColumnMapping	This value is also used when converting to XML. It controls how the column is converted to XML—as an element or property, and so forth. It's covered in more detail in part 5.

F.2 SUMMARY

This appendix has highlighted the interesting things about the DataRow and also covered the "other stuff"—the information you have to know, and the information that might be of interest every now and then.

The DataRow

The DataRow is the third and final piece that directly makes up a DataTable—other pieces are associated, such as constraints and relationships, but they are not so integral. You can have a table without constraints, but it is not very useful to have one without columns or rows!

A DataRow is simply a single row of data contained within a table. A row has an entry for each column within the table—this is an important point, because for the row to be configured properly, it must be aware of the columns. This process is normally handled by having the DataTable create the new row directly, using the NewRow() method.

DataRows are not automatically part of a table—you must explicitly add them to the DataTable's Row collection for the table to know about them. In fact, much of the behavior of the row, such as determining if any columns contain invalid data, does not happen unless the DataRow has been added to a table. This was demonstrated in several examples from appendix F, because the rules for whether data is valid are generally set on a DataColumn.

This appendix goes into depth about the DataRow, covering all its public properties and methods. Unlike the DataColumn, which is heavy on properties, the DataRow has only a few properties, but a number of methods. As usual, I'll present examples where appropriate.

G.1 DATAROW PROPERTIES

The DataRow has only a handful of properties, so they are all shown in table G.1. Many of the properties are related to determining the state of the row and whether an error exists in the contained data.

Table G.1   DataRow properties

Property	Purpose
Table	This is the table with which the row is associated. Keep in mind, though, that the row can be associated with a table without being included in the table's Row collection—it means the structure of the row (the columns it contains) is based on the table.
Item	There is no property called Item. This is just the way the indexer on the row is described. The DataRow has three indexers:

Method	Syntax
by position (0-based)	row[3]
by name	row["TeacherName"]
by column	row[SomeColumn]

The positional indexer is slightly faster, but it is a small enough difference that it will only matter in performance-sensitive applications.

Any given column can have multiple versions of a value. For example, once a value has been changed, the DataRow holds onto the original value until changes are saved. You can use the indexer to access these other versions of the value. This topic is discussed in more detail later, with the HasVersion() method, and there is also an example.

Property	Purpose
RowState	The condition of the row based on when data was loaded or last saved. This value can be one of the following values from the DataRowState enum:

Value	Meaning
Unchanged	The row has not been changed since it was loaded, or since the last time AcceptChanges() was called.
Modified	The row has been changed in some manner, such as a change to one or more columns.
Added	This is a new row.
Deleted	The row has been marked for deletion. When the row is in this state, you cannot read the current value for the row.
Detached	The row is not associated with a DataTable. This is the case when a row has been created using the NewRow() method, but has not yet been added to the DataTable's Row collection.

Property	Purpose
HasErrors	This value indicates one or more errors within the row. It is caused either by a value's violating a rule on a column or a constraint or if an error has been explicitly set on a column. This value is passed up to the DataTable; so if the row has an error, the DataTable also has an error.
RowError	This value is a description of an error on a row. The error is a string and must be manually set to be present.
ItemArray	This property allows access to all the data within the row as an array. You can either retrieve all the data as an array or set all the values at one time as an array.

Working with errors will be demonstrated later in this appendix. The RowState property was shown in action in a number of examples, as was using the indexer for retrieving data.

G.1.1 Setting data as an array

This is a quick example to show how the data in a row can be set directly as a new array. This technique might be useful if, for example, you are retrieving data from a file or another source and want to put it into a DataTable for convenient manipulation. It is also handy to initialize a DataTable with hard-coded values without taking up much space.

The example in listing G.1 creates a new DataTable with three columns and then sets the data from an array.

Listing G.1   Setting data in a DataRow via the ItemArray method

```
public void DoTestAddRowFromArray()
{
    // The array of data (or the array of arrays of data!)      ❶ Create
    object[] aRows = {new object[] {"Hello",35,12.4},              array
                      new object[] {"Goodbye",42,123.45},
                      new object[] {"Back again",700,3.1415926}};

    // Create the DataTable with three columns
    DataTable dt = new DataTable();                              ❷ Build
    dt.Columns.Add(new DataColumn("String",typeof(string)));       DataTable
    dt.Columns.Add(new DataColumn("Integer",typeof(int)));
    dt.Columns.Add(new DataColumn("Float",typeof(float)));

    // Add a row for each row in the array, and set the data
    DataRow dr = null;
    foreach(object[] row in aRows)        ❸ Set data
    {
        dr = dt.NewRow();
        dr.ItemArray = row;
        dt.Rows.Add(dr);
    }

    // Print the results
    PrintDataTable(dt);            ❹ Display results
}
```

❶ This notation creates an array in which each element of the array is an array. Although we might get the array of data elsewhere, this is a useful way to initialize a hard-coded DataTable that might be used, for example, for a pick-list of legal values.

❷ Nothing is new here. I collapsed the code a little to save space, creating the new column and adding it to the table in one line.

❸ This code steps through each row of data within the array and assigns its value to the ItemArray property of the newly created DataRow. Note that it is a straight assign, which is a good indication that this is how the data in a DataRow is stored.

4 This code uses the `PrintDataTable` method that was written in chapter 16 to display results. Figure G.1 shows the output.

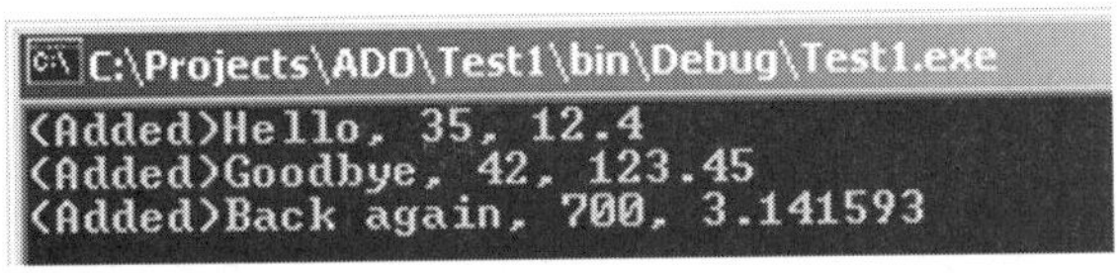

Figure G.1
Output from Listing G.1

G.2 DATAROW METHODS

The DataRow has more methods than properties, so I have broken them into several categories:

- *Basic methods*—These are the basic methods that you might use frequently.
- *Special "modes"*—These methods are related to the way changes on the row are handled because of a special mode or state.
- *Error methods*—These methods are used to work with errors within the row.
- *Other methods*—This category is a catch-all for methods that are either specialized or were the topic of another appendix or chapter.

G.2.1 Basic methods

The basic method are listed in table G.2.

Table G.2 Basic DataRow methods

Method	Purpose
Delete	Marks a row as deleted. Note that this method does not get rid of the row automatically—if it did, then when the DataAdapter wanted to save changes, it would not know about the row to delete. The row goes away when `AcceptChanges()` is called, which is done by the DataAdapter when saving back to the database.
	In one circumstance, the row will be removed from the DataTable when you call `Delete()`: if the row was added and never saved, then calling `Delete()` eliminates the row. This makes sense given that the DataTable is designed to work with the database. If the row has not yet been added to the real database, then there is no need for the DataAdapter to do any work to get rid of it.
HasVersion	Although it seems that, at any given time, only one value exists for each column in a row, in fact there may be as many as four. The following table shows the four versions of the data, represented by the DataRowVersion enum:

Value	Meaning
Default	This rather confusingly named value is the default value that will be returned when the column is normally accessed—if you ask for the data in the column.
Current	The official value for the column—that is, if some changes are in progress but have not been made permanent, then the `Current` value will not have that proposed value, but will have the official version of the data prior to the change taking place.

continued on next page

Table G.2 Basic DataRow methods *(continued)*

Method	Purpose
Original	If the value in a column has been changed but changes have not yet been accepted, the original value is within the column.
Proposed	When you're using the specialized edit mode, described in the next section, the value is not made permanent (set as the Current value) until the Edit mode is ended. In the meantime, the new value is stored as proposed.
	The HasVersion() method is used to determine if, at the current moment, the column within the row has a particular version of the data. Some of the values will not work as expected until the row has been added to the table.
IsNull	This method returns true if the column specified as an argument currently contains a null value. You can specify the column by passing the ordinal position, the name of the column, or the DataColumn object.

Column versions

As the description of the HasVersion() method explained, the same column within a row can have multiple different values. The example in listing G.2 demonstrates, and shows how to determine if a version is present and, if so, how to retrieve the value. This example also demonstrates the BeginEdit() and EndEdit() methods (described in the next section). These methods put the row into an edit mode during which changes are not made official until the EndEdit() method is called. You can also roll back changes by using the CancelEdit() method.

This example has some problems, which I will point out in the code explanation after the listing.

Listing G.2 Different versions of a value

```
public void DoTestVersions()
{
    // Create the table and the row                    ❶ Basic
    DataTable dt = new DataTable("Test");                 setup
    DataColumn dc = new DataColumn("Value1",typeof(string));
    dt.Columns.Add(dc);
    DataRow dr = dt.NewRow();
    dt.Rows.Add(dr);

    // Write out versions before making any changes    ❷ Initial
    Console.WriteLine("Initial values");                  values
    Console.WriteLine("--------------");
    WriteVersions(dr,dc);

    // Start an edit and make a change
                                                  Edit mode and ❸
    dr.BeginEdit();                                make change
    dr[dc] = "New value";
    Console.Write("\r\nValues after edit,");
    Console.WriteLine(" before ending the edit");
    Console.WriteLine("----------------------------------------");
    WriteVersions(dr,dc);
```

```
    // End editing
    dr.EndEdit();
    Console.WriteLine("\r\nAfter edit has been ended");
    Console.WriteLine("------------------------");
    WriteVersions(dr,dc);
}

public void WriteVersions(DataRow dr,DataColumn dc)
{
    Console.WriteLine("Value = {0}",dr[dc]);

    if(dr.HasVersion(DataRowVersion.Default))
        Console.WriteLine("Default value = {0}",
                    dr[dc,DataRowVersion.Default]);

    if(dr.HasVersion(DataRowVersion.Current))
        Console.WriteLine("Current value = {0}",
                    dr[dc,DataRowVersion.Current]);

    if(dr.HasVersion(DataRowVersion.Original))
        Console.WriteLine("Original value - {0}",
                    dr[dc,DataRowVersion.Original]);

    if(dr.HasVersion(DataRowVersion.Proposed))
        Console.WriteLine("Proposed value = {0}",
                    dr[dc,DataRowVersion.Proposed]);
}
```

4 Leave edit mode

5 Retrieve values

1 This code creates the DataTable with a single column and a single row.

2 Before any changes have been made, this code writes out the various "values of the values"—if any of the values have, well, values, then it writes them to the screen. It does so using the `WriteValues()` method which just prints out any values that are set.

The output from `WriteValues()` at this point looks like figure G.2.

Figure G.2
Values before any changes

As you might expect, all of the available values are blank. The first line `Value` = is the value retrieved if no special value is specified. Notice as the explanation continues that the value and the default value are always the same—the default value is the value you get by default when you don't specify any other value.

❸ This next section of code enters edit mode by calling the `BeginEdit()` method. Theoretically, the change will not become the current value until after we exit edit mode. After entering edit mode, we change the value to be equal to `New Value`. Figure G.3 shows the values as they now exist.

```
Values after edit, before ending the edit
------------------------------------------------
Value = New value
Default value = New value
Current value =
Proposed value = New value
```

Figure G.3
Values after entering edit mode

As before, the straight value is the same as the default value, which is the value we have set. So, for all intents and purposes, accessing the data will make it look as though the change has already taken place.

This is not really the case, though, as you can see; the current value is still blank, and the proposed value shows the new value. Not until we leave edit mode will the change become permanent.

❹ The call to `EndEdit()` makes our proposed change permanent. We could have also called `CancelEdit()` to throw away the proposed value. Figure G.4 shows the values after calling `EndEdit()`.

```
After edit has been ended
-----------------------------
Value = New value
Default value = New value
Current value = New value
```

Figure G.4
Values after leaving edit mode

As expected, the current value has now become the value that was previously proposed, and there is no longer a proposed value. The default value remains unchanged.

❺ This method writes out each value that is present. It first uses the `HasValue()` method to determine if the value is present, and then uses the special notation on the indexer to specify that a particular value is desired. The indexer takes a second argument, which is a value from the `DataRowVersion` enum. The first value could be any of the legal indexes. For example, it could have used the column's ordinal position:

```
dr[0,DataRowVersion.Current]
```

The original value

You may have noticed that there doesn't seem to be an original value at any point in the process. That is the case because the original value is set when `AcceptChanges()` is called. It will also be set if the data is retrieved via a DataAdapter. In my opinion, the creation of the row should count as a first call to `AcceptChanges()`, but it does not, which accounts for its absence from the example. The following code snippet shows the original value in use:

```
public void DoTestOriginalVersion()
{
    // Create the table and the row
    DataTable dt = new DataTable("Test");
    DataColumn dc = new DataColumn("Value1",typeof(string));
    dt.Columns.Add(dc);
    DataRow dr = dt.NewRow();
    dt.Rows.Add(dr);

    // A) AcceptChanges() called, but no data set
    dr.AcceptChanges();
    Console.WriteLine("Original value = {0}",
                    dr[dc,DataRowVersion.Original]);

    // B) Value changed, but AcceptChanges() not yet called
    dr[dc] = "A value";
    Console.WriteLine("Original value = {0}",
                    dr[dc,DataRowVersion.Original]);

    // C) AcceptChanges() called, then value changed
    dr.AcceptChanges();

    dr[dc] = "A different value";
    Console.WriteLine("Original value = {0}",
                    dr[dc,DataRowVersion.Original]);

    // D) After a final call to AcceptChanges()
    dr.AcceptChanges();
    Console.WriteLine("Original value = {0}",
                    dr[dc,DataRowVersion.Original]);
}
```

This code calls `AcceptChanges()`, sets the data, and writes out the original value each step of the way. Figure G.5 shows the output. Here are explanations for the lines:

Figure G.5
Output from the original value example

- *A*—The first line is after `AcceptChanges()` has been called, but no data has been set. The output shows that the original value is blank.

- *B*—The second line is after the value has been changed, but before `Accept-Changes()` is called again. Note that the original value is still blank. This makes sense because we are looking at the value from the last `Accept-Changes()`. The `A value` string has not yet been committed.

- *C*—The third line is called after the value has been changed to `A different value`. This happens after a call to `AcceptChanges()`, which commits the `A value`, making it original.

- *D*—The final line does not involve a change to the value, but one last call to AcceptChanges(). It commits the final value (A different value) so that it now becomes the original value.

G.2.2   Special modes

You have already seen many of these special modes demonstrated, both in the previous example and in previous chapters. Table G.3 shows more formal definitions.

Table G.3   DataRow mode methods

Method	Purpose
AcceptChanges	Makes all changes to the DataRow since the row was created, or since the last call to AcceptChanges(), permanent. This method is called for each row when AcceptChanges() is called on the DataTable, which is, in turn, called when AcceptChanges() is called on the DataSet.
RejectChanges	Throws away any changes made to the DataRow since the row was created, or since the last call to AcceptChanges(). As with AcceptChanges(), this call cascades from its parent.
BeginEdit	Puts the row into a special edit mode, where changes are pending but don't take place until the edit mode is left.
EndEdit	Exits the edit mode and makes the proposed changes permanent. This process is a little like committing the changes.
CancelEdit	Exits the edit mode and throws away the proposed changes. This process is somewhat like rolling back the changes.

Accepting or rejecting changes

The AcceptChanges/RejectChanges mechanism is critical to the use of a DataSet with a database. The DataAdapter uses these methods to keep the changes to the DataSet in sync with the changes to the database tables. When the DataAdapter writes changes to the database, it uses the original values to do updates and determines which rows need to be added or deleted.

After the DataAdapter has finished writing data, it calls AcceptChanges() on the DataSet, which in turn causes a call to the DataTable's version of Accept-Changes(). The DataTable throws away any rows that have been deleted, and then calls each remaining row's AcceptChanges() method.

The row then changes its state to be unchanged, and for each column, the current value becomes the original value.

Edit mode

Whereas accepting/rejecting changes is a global mode change, edit mode is a quick row-level operation. This mode is used extensively by data-bound controls, such as the DataGrid. As soon as a user begins to edit any data in a row, BeginEdit() is automatically called. Any changes made to that row are proposed until the user either moves off the row, which causes EndEdit() to be called, or presses Escape, which causes CancelEdit() to be called.

If `AcceptChanges()` is called while in edit mode, an automatic call to `End-Edit()` is made so that no changes are lost.

G.2.3   Error methods

The DataRow has several methods and properties for attaching error information to a row (via the `RowError` property) and for setting an error on a particular column within a row (table G.4). This capability is not automatic—you must set the errors and retrieve them yourself. An excellent use of this capability is in a three-tier environment, where the server determines problems, sets the errors on the row, and then returns the row to the client.

Table G.4   DataRow error methods

Method	Purpose
SetColumnError	Sets an error string on a particular column
GetColumnError	Retrieves an error from a particular column
GetColumnsInError	Returns a collection of all columns that have errors in the row
ClearErrors	Clears all the errors on the row, including the column errors and the row error

Using column error information

The example in listing G.3 sets errors on some columns and then retrieves those errors. Once again, a little imagination will come in handy to show how this might be useful in the real world.

Listing G.3   Column errors

```
public void TestRowErrors(SqlConnection conn)
{
    // Create and fill the dataset
    string strSQL = "SELECT * From Teachers";
    SqlDataAdapter sda = new SqlDataAdapter(strSQL,conn);
    DataSet ds = new DataSet();
    sda.Fill(ds,"Teachers");

    // Get a row and set some errors
    DataRow dr = ds.Tables["Teachers"].Rows[0];
    dr.SetColumnError("Classroom","This classroom is too cold");       ❶ Set
    dr.SetColumnError("Subject","Is this subject really useful?");         errors

    // Step through any columns with errors,              Retrieving
    // and display the error                              all columns
    ICollection coll = dr.GetColumnsInError();          ❷ with errors
    foreach(DataColumn dc in coll)
        Console.WriteLine("{0} ({1}): {2}",dc.ColumnName,
                                    dr[dc].ToString().Trim(),
                                    dr.GetColumnError(dc));

                                    Retrieve individual errors ❸
```

❶ This code is straightforward. The method specifies the column with the error and the string to set for the error. As with most column-access methods on the row, we can specify the column by name, ordinal, or column:

- *Name*—dr.SetColumnError("Classroom","Error");
- *Ordinal*—dr.SetColumnError(2,"Error");
- *Column*—dr.SetColumnError(dc,"Error");

Presumably some logic would be applied to determine an error. For example, the algorithm might check to determine if any classes existed in that classroom for that period before allowing a new classroom to be created.

❷ The GetColumnsInError() method simply returns a collection of DataColumns for each column in the row that has an error set on it. The code then steps through each column to display the error.

❸ The GetColumnError() method is the obvious inverse to SetColumnError(), retrieving the error that was set earlier on the column. The rest of the statement writes out the column name and the value within the column (figure G.6).

```
C:\Projects\ADO\Test1\bin\Debug\Test1.exe
Classroom (G9): This classroom is too cold
Subject (Math): Is this subject really useful?
```

Figure G.6
Output from Listing G.3

G.2.4   Other methods

Most of the time, the "other methods or properties" section on a class covers esoteric or little-used functionality. In this case, though, most of the methods are useful, but they are tied to the use of relationships (discussed in detail in chapter 18). For this reason they are mentioned here, but not explored in depth. The one exception is the SetUnspecified method, which is explained in table G.5.

Table G.5   Other DataRow methods

Method	Purpose
GetChildRows	Assuming a DataRelation is set up between this table and another, this method will return the set of rows in the other table that are children of the current row.
GetParentRow	If a relationship exists between this table and another, this method can return the parent of the current row from that other table.
GetParentRows	This method retrieves all rows that are parents of the current row via a particular relationship.
SetParentRow	This method specifies that a particular row in one table is the parent of the current table, via a particular relationship.
SetUnspecified	This method indicates that the value in the particular column for the row has no value, as though it had not been retrieved. It is not dissimilar to the concept of null for a database column, indicating that the value is not merely blank but has no value. This concept is one step further removed, however, because it implies that the column has not even been set to NULL—it has not been set.

G.3 SUMMARY

The DataRow is a straightforward class with an obvious purpose. Nonetheless, a few aspects of it can cause confusion, such as the way the different versions of the values are handled. This appendix has tried to clarify these concepts.

index